T0181906

Lecture Notes in Computer Science

Lecture Notes in Artificial Intelligence   14270

Founding Editor

Jörg Siekmann

The series Lecture Notes in Artificial Intelligence (LNAI) was established in 1988 as a topical subseries of LNCS devoted to artificial intelligence.

The series publishes state-of-the-art research results at a high level. As with the LNCS mother series, the mission of the series is to serve the international R & D community by providing an invaluable service, mainly focused on the publication of conference and workshop proceedings and postproceedings.

Huayong Yang · Honghai Liu · Jun Zou ·
Zhouping Yin · Lianqing Liu · Geng Yang ·
Xiaoping Ouyang · Zhiyong Wang
Editors

Intelligent Robotics and Applications

16th International Conference, ICIRA 2023
Hangzhou, China, July 5–7, 2023
Proceedings, Part IV

Springer

Editors
Huayong Yang
Zhejiang University
Hangzhou, China

Jun Zou ⓘ
Zhejiang University
Hangzhou, China

Lianqing Liu ⓘ
Shenyang Institute of Automation
Shenyang, Liaoning, China

Xiaoping Ouyang ⓘ
Zhejiang University
Hangzhou, China

Honghai Liu ⓘ
Harbin Institute of Technology
Shenzhen, China

Zhouping Yin
Huazhong University of Science
and Technology
Wuhan, China

Geng Yang ⓘ
Zhejiang University
Hangzhou, China

Zhiyong Wang
Harbin Institute of Technology
Shenzhen, China

ISSN 0302-9743   ISSN 1611-3349 (electronic)
Lecture Notes in Artificial Intelligence
ISBN 978-981-99-6491-8   ISBN 978-981-99-6492-5 (eBook)
https://doi.org/10.1007/978-981-99-6492-5

LNCS Sublibrary: SL7 – Artificial Intelligence

This Springer imprint is published by the registered company Springer Nature Singapore Pte Ltd.
The registered company address is: 152 Beach Road, #21-01/04 Gateway East, Singapore 189721, Singapore

Paper in this product is recyclable.

Preface

With the theme "Smart Robotics for Sustainable Society", the 16th International Conference on Intelligent Robotics and Applications (ICIRA 2023) was held in Hangzhou, China, July 5–7, 2023, and designed to encourage advancement in the field of robotics, automation, mechatronics, and applications. It aimed to promote top-level research and globalize quality research in general, making discussions and presentations more internationally competitive and focusing on the latest outstanding achievements, future trends, and demands.

ICIRA 2023 was organized and hosted by Zhejiang University, co-hosted by Harbin Institute of Technology, Huazhong University of Science and Technology, Chinese Academy of Sciences, and Shanghai Jiao Tong University, co-organized by State Key Laboratory of Fluid Power and Mechatronic Systems, State Key Laboratory of Robotics and System, State Key Laboratory of Digital Manufacturing Equipment and Technology, State Key Laboratory of Mechanical System and Vibration, State Key Laboratory of Robotics, and School of Mechanical Engineering of Zhejiang University. Also, ICIRA 2023 was technically co-sponsored by Springer. On this occasion, ICIRA 2023 was a successful event after the COVID-19 pandemic. It attracted more than 630 submissions, and the Program Committee undertook a rigorous review process for selecting the most deserving research for publication. The Advisory Committee gave advice for the conference program. Also, they help to organize special sections for ICIRA 2023. Finally, a total of 431 papers were selected for publication in 9 volumes of Springer's Lecture Note in Artificial Intelligence. For the review process, single-blind peer review was used. Each review took around 2–3 weeks, and each submission received at least 2 reviews and 1 meta-review.

In ICIRA 2023, 12 distinguished plenary speakers delivered their outstanding research works in various fields of robotics. Participants gave a total of 214 oral presentations and 197 poster presentations, enjoying this excellent opportunity to share their latest research findings. Here, we would like to express our sincere appreciation to all the authors, participants, and distinguished plenary and keynote speakers. Special thanks are also extended to all members of the Organizing Committee, all reviewers for peer-review, all staffs of the conference affairs group, and all volunteers for their diligent work.

July 2023

Huayong Yang
Honghai Liu
Jun Zou
Zhouping Yin
Lianqing Liu
Geng Yang
Xiaoping Ouyang
Zhiyong Wang

Publication Chairs

Xiaoping Ouyang	Zhejiang University, China
Zhiyong Wang	Harbin Institute of Technology, China

Regional Chairs

Zhiyong Chen	University of Newcastle, Australia
Naoyuki Kubota	Tokyo Metropolitan University, Japan
Zhaojie Ju	University of Portsmouth, UK
Eric Perreault	Northeastern University, USA
Peter Xu	University of Auckland, New Zealand
Simon Yang	University of Guelph, Canada
Houxiang Zhang	Norwegian University of Science and Technology, Norway
Duanling Li	Beijing University of Posts and Telecommunications, China

Advisory Committee

Jorge Angeles	McGill University, Canada
Tamio Arai	University of Tokyo, Japan
Hegao Cai	Harbin Institute of Technology, China
Tianyou Chai	Northeastern University, China
Jiansheng Dai	King's College London, UK
Zongquan Deng	Harbin Institute of Technology, China
Han Ding	Huazhong University of Science and Technology, China
Xilun Ding	Beihang University, China
Baoyan Duan	Xidian University, China
Xisheng Feng	Shenyang Institute of Automation, Chinese Academy of Sciences, China
Toshio Fukuda	Nagoya University, Japan
Jianda Han	Nankai University, China
Qiang Huang	Beijing Institute of Technology, China
Oussama Khatib	Stanford University, USA
Yinan Lai	National Natural Science Foundation of China, China
Jangmyung Lee	Pusan National University, Korea
Zhongqin Lin	Shanghai Jiao Tong University, China

Organization

Conference Chair

Huayong Yang   Zhejiang University, China

Honorary Chairs

Youlun Xiong   Huazhong University of Science and Technology, China

Han Ding   Huazhong University of Science and Technology, China

General Chairs

Honghai Liu   Harbin Institute of Technology, China

Jun Zou   Zhejiang University, China

Zhouping Yin   Huazhong University of Science and Technology, China

Lianqing Liu   Chinese Academy of Sciences, China

Program Chairs

Geng Yang   Zhejiang University, China

Li Jiang   Harbin Institute of Technology, China

Guoying Gu   Shanghai Jiao Tong University, China

Xinyu Wu   Chinese Academy of Sciences, China

Award Committee Chair

Yong Lei   Zhejiang University, China

Hong Liu	Harbin Institute of Technology, China
Honghai Liu	University of Portsmouth, UK
Shugen Ma	Ritsumeikan University, Japan
Daokui Qu	Siasun Robot and Automation Co., Ltd., China
Min Tan	Institute of Automation, Chinese Academy of Sciences, China
Kevin Warwick	Coventry University, UK
Guobiao Wang	National Natural Science Foundation of China, China
Tianmiao Wang	Beihang University, China
Tianran Wang	Shenyang Institute of Automation, Chinese Academy of Sciences, China
Yuechao Wang	Shenyang Institute of Automation, Chinese Academy of Sciences, China
Bogdan M. Wilamowski	Auburn University, USA
Ming Xie	Nanyang Technological University, Singapore
Yangsheng Xu	Chinese University of Hong Kong, China
Huayong Yang	Zhejiang University, China
Jie Zhao	Harbin Institute of Technology, China
Nanning Zheng	Xi'an Jiaotong University, China
Xiangyang Zhu	Shanghai Jiao Tong University, China

Contents – Part IV

3D Printing Soft Robots

Adaptive Fault Tolerant Controller for Nonlinear Active Suspension 3
  Weipeng Zhao and Liang Gu

Ultraviolet Curable Materials for 3D Printing Soft Robots: From
Hydrogels to Elastomers and Shape Memory Polymers 12
  Ruiqi Feng, Renwu Han, and Biao Zhang

Design and Grasping Experiments of a Three-Branch Dexterous Soft
Gripper 22
  Weihao Li, Yonghua Guo, Yu Han, and Jianqing Peng

Modelling Analysis of a Soft Robotic Arm Based on Pneumatic-Network
Structure 32
  Weizhuang Gong, Qin Bao, Kai Feng, and Yinlong Zhu

Integrated DLP and DIW 3D Printer for Flexible Electronics 45
  Qinghua Yu, Zixiao Zhu, Xiru Fan, and Dong Wang

Bi-Directional Deformation, Stiffness-Tunable, and Electrically
Controlled Soft Actuators Based on LCEs 4D Printing 53
  Wanglin Qiu, Yaohui Wang, Xiangnan He, Qi Ge, and Yi Xiong

Multi-material Integrated Printing of Reprogrammable Magnetically
Actuated Soft Structure 63
  Youchao Zhang, Huangyu Chen, Siqi Qiu, Yuan-Fang Zhang,
  and Xiaoyang Zhu

A Lightweight Jumping Robot with Untethered Actuation 71
  Jinqiang Wang and Dong Wang

Dielectric Elastomer Actuators for Soft Robotics

Landing Trajectory and Control Optimization for Helicopter in Tail Rotor
Pitch Lockup 85
  Xufei Yan, Renliang Chen, and Anhuan Xie

A Dual-Mode Micro Flapping Wing Robot with Water Gliding
and Taking-Off Motion 97
Fuguang Wang, Zhidong Xu, and Jihong Yan

A Self-loading Suction Cup Driven by Resonant-Impact Dielectric
Elastomer Artificial Muscles 113
Chuang Wu, Xing Gao, and Chongjing Cao

Model-free Adaptive Control of Dielectric Elastomer Actuator 125
Dun Mao, Yue Zhang, Jundong Wu, and Yawu Wang

Modeling and Design Optimization of a Pre-stretched Rolled Dielectric
Elastomer Actuator 138
Jaining Wu, Kai Luo, Peinan Yan, Xiazi Hu, Huangwei Ji, and Feifei Chen

Structural Dynamics Modeling with Modal Parameters
and Excitation Decoupling Method Based on Energy Distribution 150
Kun Chen, Jianfeng Gan, Xi Kang, and Peng Xu

Force Sensor-Based Linear Actuator Stiffness Rendering Control 162
Han Chen, Junjie Dai, Chin-Yin Chen, Yongfeng An, and Bing Huang

Design, Modeling and Control of a Dielectric Elastomer Actuated
Micro-positioning Stage 174
Peinan Yan, Guoying Gu, and Jiang Zou

Tension Distribution Algorithm of Flexible Cable Redundant Traction
for Stable Motion of Air-Bearing Platform 186
Jingchao Jia, Gang Wang, Honglei Che, and Jifu Wen

Research on High-Frequency Motion Control of Voice Coil Motors Based
on Fuzzy PID 197
Feng Huang, Chenxi Wang, Yang Fu, Lijun Wang, and Qipeng Li

Feedback Linearization with Improved ESO for Quadrotor Attitude Control ... 206
Yangyang Dong, Zequn Xia, Yongbin Wang, and Zijian Zhang

Design and Analysis of a High-performance Flexible Joint Actuator Based
on the Peano-HASEL Actuator 220
Wenjie Sun, Huwei Liang, Chenyang Wang, and Fei Zhang

Human-Like Locomotion and Manipulation

Walking Stability Analysis of Biped Robot Based on Actuator Response
Characteristics 235
  Pengyu Zhao, Yukang Mu, Siyuan Chen, Menglong Ding, Lan Zhang,
  Bingshan Jiang, Lingyu Kong, and Anhuan Xie

Design of an Actuator for Biped Robots Based on the Axial Flux Motor 247
  Qiang Hua, Weigang Zhou, Chao Cheng, Xiao Liu, Xingyu Chen,
  Lingyu Kong, Anhuan Xie, Shiqiang Zhu, and Jianjun Gu

Omnidirectional Walking Realization of a Biped Robot 258
  Jingge Tang, Peng Wang, Chao Liang, Xin Wang, Yun Liu, Jiawei Weng,
  Fan Wang, Dingkun Liang, Anhuan Xie, and Jianjun Gu

Reinforcement Learning and Sim-to-Real Method of Dual-Arm Robot
for Capturing Non-Cooperative Dynamic Targets 270
  Wenjuan Du, Nan Li, Yeheng Chen, and Jiangping Wang

Control of the Wheeled Bipedal Robot on Roads with Large and Unknown
Inclination 282
  Baining Tu, Biao Lu, and Minnan Piao

Nonsmooth Dynamic Modeling of a Humanoid Robot with Parallel
Mechanisms 294
  Jiaming Xiong, Dingkun Liang, Xin Wang, Yongshan Huang,
  Anhuan Xie, and Jason Gu

Human-Like Dexterous Manipulation for the Anthropomorphic Hand-Arm
Robotic System via Teleoperation 309
  Yayu Huang, Zhenghan Wang, Xiaofei Shen, Qian Liu, and Peng Wang

Design of a Compact Anthropomorphic Robotic Hand with Hybrid
Linkage and Direct Actuation 322
  Zechen Hu, Chunyang Zhou, Jinjian Li, and Quan Hu

Application of Compliant Control in Position-Based Humanoid Robot 333
  Chunyu Chen, Ligang Ge, and Jiangchen Zhou

Fast Walking of Position-Controlled Biped Robot Based on Whole-Body
Compliance Control 344
  Yiting Zhu, Ye Xie, Chengzhi Gao, Dingkun Liang, Lingyu Kong,
  Xin Wang, Anhuan Xie, and Jianjun Gu

Whole Body Balance Control for Bipedal Robots Based on Virtual Model
Control 355
    Chengzhi Gao, Ye Xie, Yiting Zhu, Dingkun Liang, Lingyu Kong,
    Xin Wang, Anhuan Xie, and Jianjun Gu

Design and Implementation of Lightweight Thigh Structures for Biped
Robots Based on Spatial Lattice Structure and Additive Manufacturing
Technology 368
    Hongjian Jiang, Lingyu Kong, Yu Zhang, Yuanjie Chen, Daming Nie,
    Anhuan Xie, Lintao Shao, and Shiqiang Zhu

A Humanoid Robot Foot with a Lattice Structure for Absorbing Ground
Impact Forces 380
    Lan Zhang, Lingyu Kong, Guanyu Huang, Weigang Zhou,
    Hongjian Jiang, Pengyu Zhao, Bingshan Jiang, Anhuan Xie,
    Shiqiang Zhu, and Yuanjie Chen

An Action Evaluation and Scaling Algorithm for Robot Motion Planning 392
    Ruiqi Wu, Chao Fan, Huifang Hou, Zihao Zhang, Longzhuo Wang,
    Xin Zhao, and Fei Chao

Design and Control of the Biped Robot HTY 404
    Yun Liu, Jiawei Weng, Fan Wang, Jingge Tang, Yunchang Yao,
    Xingyu Chen, Lingyu Kong, Dingkun Liang, Xin Wang, Shiqiang Zhu,
    Yuanjie Chen, Anhuan Xie, and Jason Gu

SPSOC: Staged Pseudo-Spectral Optimal Control Optimization Model
for Robotic Chinese Calligraphy 416
    Dongmei Guo, Huasong Min, and Guang Yan

Obstacle Avoidance Path Planning Method Based on DQN-HER 429
    Kailong Li, Fusheng Zha, Pengfei Wang, Wei Guo, Yajing Zang,
    and Lining Sun

Realizing Human-like Walking and Running with Feedforward Enhanced
Reinforcement Learning 439
    Linqi Ye, Xueqian Wang, and Bin Liang

Research on Target Trajectory Planning Method of Humanoid
Manipulators Based on Reinforcement Learning 452
    Keyao Liang, Fusheng Zha, Wentao Sheng, Wei Guo, Pengfei Wang,
    and Lining Sun

Study on the Impact Performance of the Joint Cycloid Reducer for Legged
Robots 464
    Shuting Ji, Tengyue Wei, and Jialin Li

An Optimal Configuration Solution of 8-DOF Redundant Manipulator
for Flying Ball 476
    Ziwu Ren, Zhongyuan Wang, Zibo Guo, and Licheng Fan

Smooth Composite-Space RRT: An Improved Motion Planner
for Manipulators Under Incomplete Orientation Constraint 488
    Jiangping Wang, Nan Li, Wei Song, Wenjuan Du, and Wenxuan Chen

Cooperative Control of Dual-Arm Robot of Adaptive Impedance
Controller Based on RBF Neural Network 499
    Tongyan Zhang, Ting Wang, Shiliang Shao, Zonghan Cao, Xinke Dou,
    and Hongwei Qin

Trajectory Tracking Control for Robot Manipulator Under Dynamic
Environment 513
    Yushi Wang, Yanbo Pang, Qingkai Li, Wenhan Cai, and Mingguo Zhao

Pattern Recognition and Machine Learning for Smart Robots

A High-Temperature Resistant Robot for Fixed-Point Firefighting 527
    Fang Li, Yujie Huang, Jiaqi Sun, Xiaodong Zhao, and Yingchao He

Multiscale Dual-Channel Attention Network for Point Cloud Analysis 537
    Wentao Li, Jian Cui, Haiqing Cao, Huixuan Zhu, Sen Lin,
    and Yandong Tang

Study on Quantitative Precipitation Estimation and Model's Transfer
Performance by Incorporating Dual Polarization Radar Variables 549
    Yanqin Wen, Jun Zhang, Zhe Liang, Di Wang, and Ping Wang

Research on Object Detection Methods in Low-Light Conditions 564
    Feifan Wang, Xi'ai Chen, Xudong Wang, Weihong Ren, and Yandong Tang

Image Recovery and Object Detection Integrated Algorithms for Robots
in Harsh Battlefield Environments 575
    Xudong Wang, Xi'ai Chen, Feifan Wang, Chonglong Xu,
    and Yandong Tang

A Fuzzy-Based Improved Dynamic Window Approach for Path Planning
of Mobile Robot 586
    Yue Zhu and Tongli Lu

Is the Encoder Necessary in DETR-Type Models?-Analysis of Encoder
Redundancy 598
    Liu Huan, Lin Sen, and Han Zhi

Image Enhancement Algorithm Based on Multi-scale Convolution Neural
Network 610
    Hu Luo, Jianye Liu, Xu Zhang, and Dawei Tu

Author Index 621

3D Printing Soft Robots

Adaptive Fault Tolerant Controller for Nonlinear Active Suspension

Weipeng Zhao$^{(\boxtimes)}$ and Liang Gu

Beijing Institute of Technology, Beijing 100081, China
zhaowpa@126.com

Abstract. In this paper, the fault tolerant control problem of nonlinear active suspension is concerned. A RBF-based SMC fault tolerant controller is developed to improve the ride comfort and handling stability under partial loss of actuator effectiveness fault. At first, a quarter car nonlinear active suspension model and fault model are established. Next a RBF-based SMC adaptive controller is conducted for the faulty suspension system. Simulation is provided and simulation results show that the proposed method can effectively compensate for faults and improve the ride comfort. Then the proposed controller is verified by the simulation.

Keywords: Fault tolerant · Nonlinear suspension · SMC · RBF

1 Introduction

Suspension systems are essential parts of modern vehicle, for that the suspension can increase the performance of safety, ride comfort and handling stability. According to the mold to of damper, suspension systems can be divided as three types: passive suspension systems, semi-active suspension systems and active suspension systems [1].

Compared with the passive suspension systems and semi-active suspension sys-tems, the active suspension systems make it possible to enhance the performance of the ride comfort and handling stability. As a result, active suspension system has been widely used in the vehicles in recent decades [2,3]. The difference between active suspension and the other two types of suspension systems is that active actuators are applied in active suspension systems to produce active force, which can replace the damper or both spring and damper [4]. On the other hand, many various sensors are used to monitor the road and vehicle conditions. On the basis of the above conditions, active suspension systems can produce active damping force to adapt to different road conditions in real time. And this feature make it possible to enable the vehicle to maintain optimal balance and control, thereby minimizing bumps and vibrations both passenger comfort and drive stability. Apart from that, active suspension can provide the benefit of increased suspension travel when required, which in turn improves the vehicle's off-road capabilities and ability to navigate rough terrain.

H. Yang et al. (Eds.): ICIRA 2023, LNAI 14270, pp. 3–11, 2023.
https://doi.org/10.1007/978-981-99-6492-5_1

Recently, many active control methods have been presented to vehicle suspnsion systems [5–9]. Such as output feedback method [5], adaptive fuzzy control method [6], H_∞ method [7], mixed H_2/H_∞ control algorithm [8], neural network control method [9], LQR control approaches [10] and so on.

However, the full reliability assumption, which states that every system's control component is operating optimally, underlies all of the aforementioned findings. As time progressed, numerous errors, particularly actuator and sensor faults, are anticipated to occur as automated control systems and actuators become more complicated. At the same time, because of their intricate construction and challenging working conditions, active suspension systems are sensitive and susceptible to errors, which may cause the system to function poorly or possibly fail entirely. A suspension system problem can have a big impact on the car's handling stability and ride comfort during the riding. In order to prevent faults in the control loop from leading to a system failure as a whole, it is crucial to design a fault-tolerant controller whose system stability and performance can tolerate both sensor and actuator faults. A technique known as fault tolerant control (FTC) allows a control system to function even when there is a fault. Therefore, fault tolerant control techniques are required to guarantee the suspension system's safe and dependable operation. The radial basis function (RBF) network-based fault tolerant control method for non-linear active suspension system is proposed in this research as a solution to this problem.

However, most researchers focus on the linear active suspension, and ignore the influence of the original nonlinear characteristics on the system. In fact, the springs and dampers of active suspension have certain nonlinear characteristics, and their specific manifestations are unpredictable, so the active suspension is a typical nonlinear system. When the model is simply linearized, the accuracy of the model will be greatly reduced and the control effect will be affected. Therefore, only a nonlinear model as the basis of research is of great significance in practical applications.

The rest of this paper is organized as follows: Sect. 2 gives the model of nonlinear of active suspension and fault system. In Sect. 3, a RBF-based SMC fault tolerant controller is presented. Section 4 provided the simulation results. Section 5 concludes the paper.

2   System Model

2.1   Nonlinear Active Suspension System Model

In this paper, a nonlinear quarter car active suspension systems with two degree of freedom is shown as Fig 1. A quarter nonlinear suspension system is used in this paper due to its simplicity and ability to accurately represent the key elements of an active suspension system, such as body acceleration, sprung mass displacement, tire and suspension deflections.

In this figure, m_s and m_u are the sprung mass and un-sprung mass; x_g refers to the road displacement; x_s and x_u stand for the displacement of the sprung mass and un-sprung mass; F_s denotes the nonlinear spring force; F_d denotes the

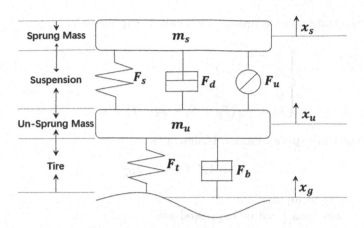

Fig. 1. Quarter Nonlinear Suspension Schematic Diagram.

nonlinear damping force; F_u denotes the main force of the actuator; F_t denotes the elastic force of the tire; F_b denotes the damping force of the tire.

The dynamic equation used to describe the quarter car nonlinear active suspension system can be established as follows:

$$\begin{cases} m_s \ddot{x}_s = F_u - F_s - F_d \\ m_u \ddot{x}_u = -F_u + F_s + F_d - F_t - F_b \end{cases} \tag{1}$$

The expressions for the linear tire elastic force and damping force of the tire in the suspension system are given by

$$\begin{cases} F_t = k_t (x_g - x_u) \\ F_b = c_t (\dot{x}_g - \dot{x}_u) \end{cases} \tag{2}$$

where k_t is is the elasticity stiffness of tire, c_t is the damping coefficient of tire.

The expressions for nonlinear spring and damper force [10] created by suspension are given by

$$F_s = k_s(x_s - x_u) + k_{sn}(x_s - x_u)^3$$
$$F_d = c_s(\dot{x}_s - \dot{x}_u) + c_{sn}(\dot{x}_s - \dot{x}_u)^3. \tag{3}$$

where k_s is the stiffness of spring, k_{sn} is the nonlinear stiffness of spring, c_t is the linear damping coefficient of damper, c_t is the nonlinear damping coefficient of damper.

In order to obtain the state space equation, defining the following state variables

$$X = \begin{bmatrix} x_s \ \dot{x}_s \ x_u \ \dot{x}_u \end{bmatrix}^T = \begin{bmatrix} x_1 \ x_2 \ x_3 \ x_4 \end{bmatrix}^T \tag{4}$$

Thus, the state space representation can be expressed by

$$
\begin{cases}
\dot{x_1} = x_2 \\
\dot{x_2} = \frac{1}{m_s}(-F_d - F_s + F_u) \\
\dot{x_3} = x_4 \\
\dot{x_4} = \frac{1}{m_u}(F_d + F_s - F_b - F_t - F_u)
\end{cases} \tag{5}
$$

Thus, the state space function is shown as

$$
\dot{X} = AX + BU + Hq \tag{6}
$$

where q is the road input.

Error system model can be expressed as

$$
\dot{E} = A_e E + B_e E + C_e X \tag{7}
$$

2.2   System Fault Description

Vehicle suspension systems are complex, which consists of mechanical components, electronic components and so on. Consequently, various kind of fault may occur. And in this paper, the actuator effectiveness loss namely the gain fault of actuator is concerned.

Think about a situation where an actuator operates as if it has a malfunction, losing some of its effectiveness and failing to deliver the necessary control force but continuing to operate the system.

F_u is considered as designed control input and F_{uf} is the actual control input what is produced or available from the actuator

When the actuator fault occurs, the F_{uf} can be expressed as

$$
F_{uf} = \delta F_u \tag{8}
$$

where δ is the effectiveness factor of the actuator, and $0 \leq \delta \leq 1$. The case $\delta = 0$ means that actuator is completely failed, the case $\delta = 1$ indicates that actuator is completely healthy, and the case $0 < \delta < 1$ means that the partial loss of effectiveness of the actuator.

3   Controller Design

3.1   RBF Neural Network

Radial based function (RBF) neural networks is a type of artificial method and has been widely used for system control. The RBF neural network algorithm consists of three layers: an input layer, a hidden layer, and an output layer. The schematic diagram for RBF neural network is shown as Fig 2.

RBF neural network possesses the capacity in mimicking the brain's way of thinking, and can approximate nonlinear functions well. Additionally, it has

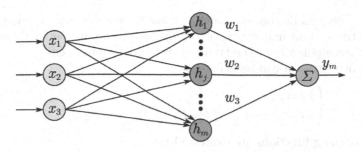

Fig. 2. Schematic Diagram for RBF Neural Network.

a straightforward structure, quick convergence, and good fault tolerance. The most significant benefit is that RBF neural networks can approximate unknown continuous functions with any level of accuracy.

The role of the input layer is to pass the external input into the neural network and to pass the signal to the hidden layer. The hidden layer consists of a radial nonlinear function at the centroid and transforms the input signal nonlinearly. The mapping relationship from the hidden layer to the output layer is linear. The working principle of the RBF neural network can be summarized as follows: after the external signal is input to the input layer, it undergoes a nonlinear change in the activation function of the implicit layer, and is finally given weights for linear superposition to the output layer.

The Gaussian function is chosen as the radial basis function. The RBF-based neural network algorithm can be expressed by

$$h_j = exp(-\frac{||x - c_j||^2}{b_j^2}) \tag{9}$$

where: x is the input of RBF neural network. j is the jth node of the hidden layer network. h is the output of the Gaussian function.

3.2 RBF-Based SMC Controller Design

A RBF-based SMC controller is proposed in this paper. The contorller structure schematic is shown as Fig 3. The control law consists of two parts: the nominal control law and the fault compensation law. The nominal control law is designed

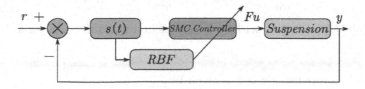

Fig. 3. Contorller Structure Schematic.

using the sliding mode control, which ensures the stability and tracking performance of the system under normal conditions, the fault compensation law is designed to compensate for the faults in the suspension system

The control system can be defined as

$$\begin{cases} \dot{x}_1 = x_2 \\ \dot{x}_2 = \frac{1}{m_s}(-F_d - F_s + F_u) = f(x) + bu + d(t) \end{cases} \tag{10}$$

The switching functions are expressed by

$$s(t) = ce(t) + \dot{e}(t) \tag{11}$$

where

$$\begin{cases} e(t) = r(t) - x_1 \\ \dot{e}(t) = \dot{r}(t) - x_2 \end{cases} \tag{12}$$

where $r(t)$ and $\dot{r}(t)$ are the observe signal suprung mass displacement and velocity.

The purpose of controller is to improve the performance of ride comfort under bumpy roads. So, the smaller the value of $r(t)$ or $\dot{r}(t)$, the better the ride comfort.

The radial basis vectors $H = [h_1, h_2, \cdots, h_n]^T$ of hidden layer are Gaussian functions. The output of RBF neural network is given as

$$y = \sum_{j=1}^{m} w_j exp(-\frac{||s - c_j||^2}{b_j^2}) \tag{13}$$

where w_j is weight factor. And the goal of RBF neural network is $s(t)\dot{s}(t) \to 0$. So adjustment indicators of RBF neural network is expressed as

$$E = s(t)\dot{s}(t) \tag{14}$$

The gradient descent method is used as learning algorithm.

$$dw_j = -\eta\frac{\partial E}{\partial w_j(t)} = \eta\frac{\partial(s\dot{s})}{\partial w_j(t)} = \eta\frac{\partial(s\dot{s})}{\partial u(t)} \cdot \frac{\partial u(t)}{\partial w_j(t)} \tag{15}$$

Let $\gamma = \frac{\partial(\dot{s})}{\partial u(t)}$, then

$$\frac{\partial(s\dot{s})}{\partial u(t)} = \frac{\partial(\dot{s})}{\partial u(t)} \cdot s(t) = \gamma s(t) \tag{16}$$

$$\frac{\partial u(t)}{\partial w_j(t)} = exp(-\frac{||s - c_j||^2}{b_j^2}) = h_j(s) \tag{17}$$

The weight learning algorithm of RBF neural network is shown as

$$dw_j = \gamma s(t)h_j(s) \tag{18}$$

The fault compensation law is given by

$$F_u = -(CB_e)^{-1}(CA_e E + CC_e X_e + y) \tag{19}$$

4   Results and Discussion

To assess the performance that the suggested strategy works. The simulation outcomes demonstrated the effectiveness of the RBF-based FTC method in correcting faults in nonlinear active suspension systems. In this part, extensive simulations are demonstrate the effectiveness of the proposed contoller. Passive and active control under healthy situation are compared to the performance of the designed control system. The parameters of suspension in this paper are given in Table 1. The continuous bump profile [11] is used as road input. The expression of time and displacement for continuous bump is expressed as

$$z = 0.08cos(2\pi t)sin(0.6\pi t) \tag{20}$$

The time response of continuous bump road profile is shown as Fig. 4.

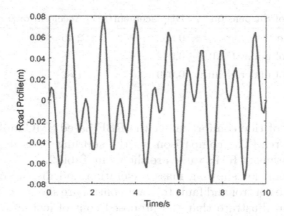

Fig. 4. Time Response of Continuous Bump Road Profile.

Table 1. Parameters of The Suspension.

Parameter	Value	Parameter	Value
m_s	290 kg	m_u	59 kg
k_s	14.5 kN/m	k_{sn}	160 kN/m
c_s	1385.4 Ns/m	c_{sn}	524.28 Ns/m
k_t	190 kN/m	c_t	170 Ns/m

The actuator effectiveness factor δ is considered as $\delta = 0.7$.

Comparisons of the proposed fault tolerant control method, the active control scheme, and the passive suspension for the suprung mass vertical displacement and acceleration are shown in Fig 5 and Fig 6, respectively.

The RMS value of the suprung mass acceleration and displacement are considerd to relate to the ride compfort. Hence, the RMS value are used to evaluate

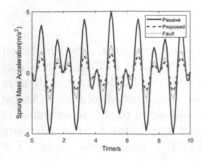

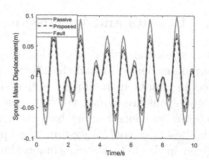

Fig. 5. Suprung Mass Acceleration   **Fig. 6.** Suprung Mass Displacement

Table 2. Performance comparison in terms of RMS value.

Type of Suspension	Displacement(m)	Acceleration(m/s^2)
Passive	0.058	2.46
Control under Fault	0.042	1.98
Control under Healthy	0.039	1.82

the performance of ride comfort under the RBF-based SMC fault tolerant control in this research. The comparison for the suprung mass displacement and acceleration in terms of RMS value are shown in Table 2.

The comparison for suprung mass accleration and displacement of passive suspension, active control and fault tolerant control are shown in Table 2. Table 2 and Fig. 5–Fig. 6 illustrate that the proposed control legislation works better than passive suspension response. Additionally, the controller provided in this paper significantly lessens the vibrations caused by road surface imperfections under the case of actuator faults, providing passengers with a comfortable ride.

5   Conclusion

In this paper, a actuator failure control problem is studied for a quarter car model, and a RBF-based SMC adaptive fault tolerant controller is presented to improve the vehicle dynamic performance under fault condition. The control strategy is created utilizing the RBF neural network sliding mode hybrid control methods and takes actuator failure into account. The suggested control law is set up so that the system are guaranteed performance in terms of ride quality and capacity to handle the road. The simulation results demonstrate the effectiveness of the devised controller.

References

1. Shen, Y., Chen, L., Yang, X.: Improved design of dynamic vibration absorber by using the inerter and its application in vehicle suspension. J. Sound Vibrat. **2**(5), 148–158 (2016)
2. Zapateiro, M.: Semiactive control methodologies for suspension control with magnetorheological dampers. IEEE/ASME Trans. Mechat. **17**(2), 370–380 (2012)
3. Sun, W., Gao, H.: Adaptive backstepping control for active suspension systems with hard constraints. IEEE/ASME Trans. Mechat. **18**(3), 1072–107 (2013)
4. Min, X., Li, Y., Tong, S.: Adaptive fuzzy optimal control for a class of active suspension systems with full-state constraints. IET Intell. Trans. Syst. **14**(5), 371–381 (2020)
5. He, Y., Wang, Q.G.: An Improved ILMI method for static output feedback control with application to multivariable PID control. IEEE Trans. Autom. Control **51**(10), 1678–1683 (2006)
6. Mailah, M.: Simulation of a suspension system with adaptive fuzzy active force control. Inter. J. Simulat. Modell. **6**(1), 25–36 (2007)
7. Gao, H., Sun, W., Peng, S.: Robust sampled-data control for vehicle active suspension systems. IEEE Trans. Control Syst. Technol **18**(1), 238–245 (2010)
8. Abdellari, E., Mehdi, D., M'Saad, M.: On the design of active suspension system by$H_\infty$and mixedH_2/H_infty: an LMI approach. In: American Control Conference 2000, Proceedings of the 2000 IEEE (2000). https://doi.org/10.1109/ACC.2000.876981
9. Tenchine, S., Gouze, P.: Design and simulation lqr control system for control bus suspension of half car model with passenger. Undergraduate Theses **28**(3), 273–289 (2005)
10. Kazemipour, A., Novinzadeh, A.B.: Adaptive fault-tolerant control for active suspension systems based on the terminal sliding mode approach. Proc. Instit. Mech. Eng. Part C: J. Mech. Eng. Sci. **234**(2), 501–511 (2020)
11. Liu, S., Zhou, H., Luo, X., et al.: Adaptive sliding fault tolerant control for nonlinear uncertain active suspen- sion systems. J. Franklin Inst. 253180–253199 (2016)

Ultraviolet Curable Materials for 3D Printing Soft Robots: From Hydrogels to Elastomers and Shape Memory Polymers

Ruiqi Feng[1,2], Renwu Han[1,2], and Biao Zhang[1(✉)]

[1] Frontiers Science Center for Flexible Electronics (FSCFE), Xi'an Institute of Flexible Electronics, Northwestern Polytechnical University, Xi'an 710072, People's Republic of China
iambzhang@nwpu.edu.cn

[2] Queen Mary University of London Engineering School, Northwestern Polytechnical University, Xi'an 710072, People's Republic of China

Abstract. Ultraviolet (UV) curing based 3D printing technologies have caught great attention by the designers of soft robots because of their advantages in combing printing accuracy and geometric complexity. To improve the design freedom and functionality of soft robots, the choice of suitable resins for 3D printing is of great importance. Here, we systematically summarized our recent developed photocurable soft materials (including hydrogels, elastomers, and shape memory polymers) that are suitable for 3D printing of soft robots. The functions and properties of these soft materials are discussed, of which the modulus varies from KPa to GPa, guaranteeing the controlled mechanical performance of formed robots. Besides, the large stretchability of these materials endows the fabricated robots with high deformation ability. Moreover, some other functionalities, such as self-healing, shape memory, recycling, provide promising ways for the design of intelligent soft robots.

Keywords: UV curable · digital light processing · 3D printing soft robots · Hydrogels · Elastomers · Shape memory polymers

1 Introduction

Soft robots have become an emerging topic because of their wide application and potential contribution to humanity in engineering construction, medical equipment, national defence science and technology and so on [1]. Unlike the rigid robots, soft robots can change the shape for safe and other geometries complexity which show the enormous potential ability in functionality and personalization [2, 3]. However, the typical manufacturing methods always generate objects with simple structures taking a lot of time, which not satisfy the need in intelligence and personalization in the future.

Additive manufacturing (AM), also known as 3D printing, typically builds 3D objects by adding layers of materials to form the desired shape. AM differs from traditional manufacturing techniques in that complex shapes can be created directly from digital models, which means the products from 3D printing have complex structures for functionality

H. Yang et al. (Eds.): ICIRA 2023, LNAI 14270, pp. 12–21, 2023.
https://doi.org/10.1007/978-981-99-6492-5_2

and personal customization. It can save much time for designers. 3D printing has developed rapidly, and has an extensive range of applications in soft robots [2], lightweight engineering [4], sensors [5], biomedical devices [6, 7], flexible electronics [8] and others. Among all the 3D printing technologies, UV curing based 3D printing has caught a lot of attention by the designers of soft robots because of its extreme advantages in printing speed and printing accuracy. It also has an extremely fast curing speed which can greatly save time for designers. Due to these advantages, the UV curing 3D printing shows its extreme potential value in soft robots.

Many kinds of soft robots have been produced by 3D printing, which demonstrate great deformation ability, shape memory effect, and recyclable performance [9]. Besides the structure design of soft robots, the materials also play a key role, which decide the threshold of the design of soft robots. In this short communication, we systemically summarized the development of materials used for soft robots based on our recent works. The developed photocurable soft materials, including hydrogels, elastomers, and shape memory polymers, are suitable for digital light processing (DLP) based 3D printing of soft robots. The functions and properties of these soft materials are discussed, of which the modulus varies from KPa to GPa [10], guaranteeing the controlled mechanical performance of formed robots. Moreover, the large stretchability of these materials endows the fabricated robots with high deformation ability. In addition, some other functionalities, such as self-healing, shape memory, recycling, provide promising ways for the design of intelligent soft robots. We hope the designers of soft robots can be inspired by this communication and promote further development in the field of soft robots by using the functional design and personalization.

2   UV Curable Materials for 3D Printing Soft Robots

2.1   Hydrogels

Hydrogels are special networks which contain a large amount of water [11]. Due to their porous and hydrated molecular structure, hydrogels are powerful candidates to mimic the native skin microenvironment and have been widely used in soft robots [12–14]. To achieve UV curing based 3D printing hydrogels, the high-efficient and water soluble photoinitiators are important. Irgacure 2959 (I2959) is a commercially available water soluble photoinitiator that has been used for the formation of hydrogels under UV irradiation [14]. However, due to its extremely low photo reactivity in the wavelength ranging from 385 nm ~ 405 nm which is the common range of UV source in DLP 3D printing, I2959 is not suitable for 3D printing hydrogels [15]. 2,4,6-trimethylbenzoyldiphenylphosphine oxide (TPO) is recognized as another highly efficient photoinitiator, but it is not soluble in water. To improve the solubility of TPO in water, amphiphilic sodium dodecyl Sulfate (SDS) was used to encapsulate TPO particles, resulting in water-dispersible nanoparticles that can initiate the photopolymerization in water (Fig. 1). In addition, a series of metal-phenyl(2,4,6-trimethylbenzoyl) phosphinates (M-TMPP)-based photoinitiators with excellent water solubility (up to ~50 g/L) were synthesized through a simple one-pot procedure (Fig. 1). By using M-TMPP as photoinitiator, 3D hydrogel based complex structures with high water content (80%), high resolution (~7 μm), high deformability (more than 80% compression), are fabricated according to DLP based

3D printing [16]. Moreover, by adjusting the ratio of monomers to crosslinkers, we can change the stretchability of hydrogels and regulate their mechanical properties. The photoinitiators and nanoparticles are shown in Fig. 1.

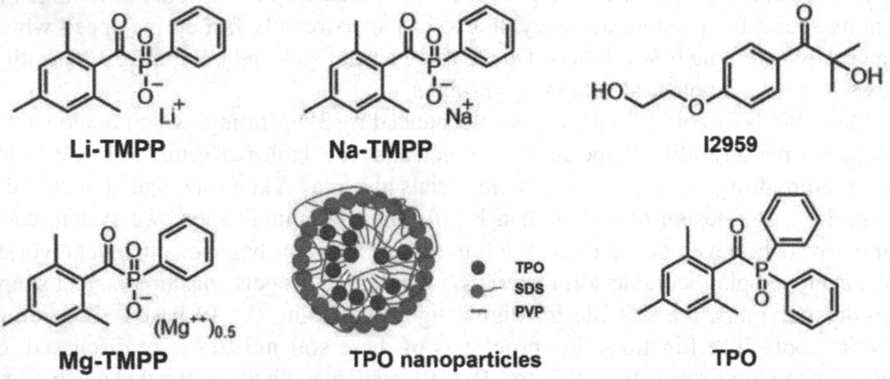

Fig. 1. The structures of photoinitiators: I2959, TPO, TPO nanoparticles and M-TMPPs.

Resolution is another particular key factor that can determine the quality of the fabricated structures. Because of the high transmission of light through hydrogels, it is necessary to add photoabsorbers to limit the expansion of the formed radicals to maintain the fidelity of formed hydrogel structures. To keep the high resolution and high-water content of the fabricated hydrogel structures, high-efficient and high water soluble photoabsorbers are needed. By the similar method that is used for preparation of TPO nanoparticles, a series of water-soluble photo-absorber have been successfully prepared via a volatile microemulsion method, which are suitable for 3D printing of high-resolution, high water content hydrogel structures [17].

The 3D printed hydrogels with high stretchability and high amount of water can also be used to bond covalently with several UV curable polymers [11]. At the same time, the cured hydrogels are conductive by simply adding the salt (i.e., LiCl) into hydrogel precursors which allows hydrogels to be used in flexible electronics. Moreover, the capability of 3D printing hydrogel with other materials (e.g., elastomer) promote us to fabricate more complex conductive hydrogel integrated devices and machines. As shown in Fig. 2 [18], a soft pneumatic actuator with a conductive hydrogel-based strain sensor was printed in one single step due to the strong interfacial bonding between the UV curable hydrogel and elastomer. The hydrogel sensing circuit was printed on an elastomer substrate to achieve the relation between resistance and deformation. When a negative pressure is applied to the soft pneumatic actuator (SPA), the bending angle is defined as negative, and the measured strain is positive since the layer where the hydrogel sensor locates is being stretched. The measured strain becomes negative when a positive pressure is applied, which leads to positive bending of the SPA where the hydrogel sensor is being compressed [18]. Under this way, we can measure the compressive strain on the SPA so that the strain sensor developed here can measure the actuations with both positive and negative bending. On the basis of this relation between bending angle and strain and the relation between resistance variation and strain, the SPA can sense its instantaneous bending during actuation.

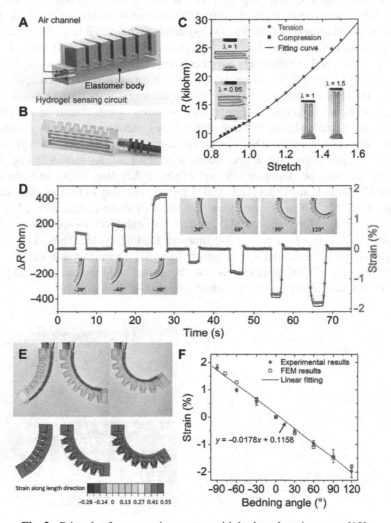

Fig. 2. Printed soft pneumatic actuator with hydrogel strain sensor [18].

2.2 Elastomers

Elastomers are a subclass within polymers that are widely used in manufacturing of automotive bumpers, rubber seals, flexible electronics, energy absorbers, and many others, due to their great stretchability, elasticity, and thermal insulation. They are also considered as the most potential materials in fabricating soft robots [20] The similar mechanical properties with human body leads to the well-established smooth interactions between elastomers and humans.

There are many widely used elastomers, such as Sylgard 184 and Ecoflex 0–30, but their thermal curing process constrains the manufacturing method to traditional ways, such as casting, cutting, moulding [21] and so on. Thus, the geometric complexity and function of soft robots from these traditional elastomers are limited [21]. In this situation, the development of new elastomer system which is suitable for 3D printing is of great importance to fabricate soft robots with geometric complexity and functions. Even though some UV curable elastomers have been developed, they have limited elongation at break (up to 170%–220%), which is not enough for certain advanced applications. To address these issues, a new highly stretchable elastomer system which is suitable for DLP 3D printing was reported and provided a solution of manufacturing complex 3D soft robots in simple and easy printing steps. This system contains highly stretchable elastomer which is UV curable (SUV) with some great properties, such as high printing resolution, fast processing speed and freedom design [20]. As shown in Fig. 3 [20], by varying the ratio of monomer (Epoxy Aliphatic Acrylate, EAA) and crosslinker (Aliphatic Urethane-based Diacrylate, AUD), the stretchability of formed elastomer can reach up to 1100%, which is more than five times of those commercial UV curable elastomers (Fig. 3). Moreover, the SUV system also exhibits an excellent mechanical repeatability which can bear over 1000 times of loading cycles. Thus, The DLP 3D printed pneumatically actuated soft actuators from SUV exhibit much larger bending deformation, and a 3D soft gripper was also fabricated using the one-step 3D printing method, demonstrating the ability to grab an object (Fig. 4a-h).

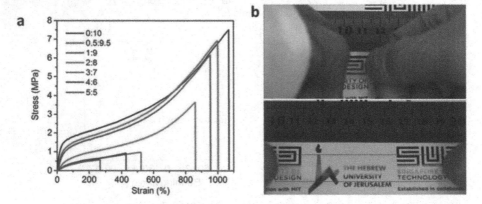

Fig. 3. The stress-strain behaviour of SUV elastomers [20].

In addition, the addition of EAA and AUD into TangoPlus, a commercial UV curable elastomer, can well tune the mechanical properties of resulting elastomeric materials. For example, the stretchability can be greatly enhanced from ~ 120% to 500%. The printed mini soft gripper can conform to the surfaces of different geometries (e.g., a strawberry) and lift them (Fig. 4i and j).

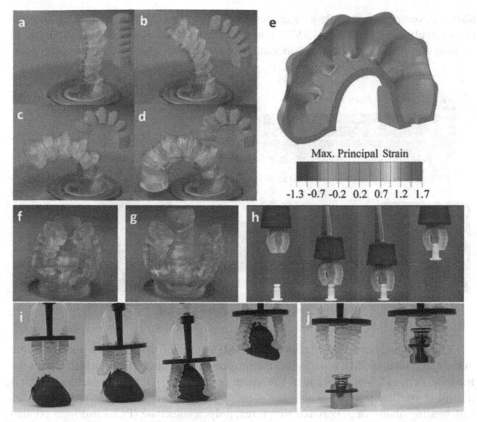

Fig. 4. 3D printed pneumatically actuated soft actuators and the demonstration of soft actuator [20, 21].

2.3 Shape Memory Polymers

Shape memory polymers (SMPs) are typical soft active materials that switch between a variable temporary shape and the original shape under external stimuli, such as light, heat, electricity, etc. Compared with other soft active materials, such as hydrogels, elastomers, SMPs have better stiffness [22]. Among them, the UV curable SMP are compatible with DLP 3D printing and able to achieve more complex geometries fabrication with high resolution [22]. However, the limited mechanical performance of UV curable SMPs constrains their further applications. To tackle these questions, a new SMP system with high deformation and anti-fatigue property and good compatibility with DLP 3D printing was reported. This SMP system is mainly consist of tert-butyl acrylate (tBA) as linear chain builder, aliphatic urethane diacrylate (AUD) as crosslinker, and diphenyl (2,4,6-trimethylbenzoly) phosphine oxide (TPO) is used as a photo initiator. In this system, the fabrication resolution is up to 2 μm and the stretchability during heating is very high, reaching about 1240% (Fig. 5) [22]. More importantly, this new system performs in anti-fatigue very well, which can be loaded more than 10000 times. Besides, this SMP can be fixed with a wonderful shape fixity about 100% at room temperature, but also recovered at an excellent shape-recovery ratio about 90% after heating. Due to these excellent properties, this SMP system can be regarded as a promising candidate in various engineering applications, including smart furniture, aerospace, and soft robots.

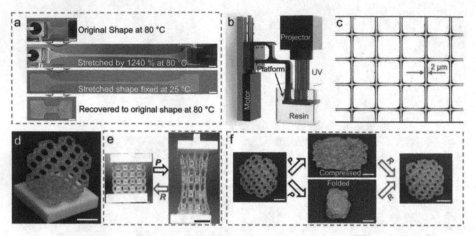

Fig. 5. Mechanically robust SMP system for DLP-based 4D printing [22].

The covalently crosslinked networks of SMP contribute the ability of "memory", but at the same time, if SMP is damaged, the broken part can not be fixed, which causes the increase in production costs and environment pollution [23]. Polycaprolactone (PCL) is a semi-crystalline polymer with a low melting point of around 60 °C. To improve the self-healing ability of 3D printed structures, polycaprolactone (PCL) was incorporated into a UV curable SMP network system as a self-healing agent to provide self-healing properties to the 4D-printed structures (Fig. 6a and b) [23]. This developed network is suitable for high resolution 4D printing that is enabled to fabricate complex 4D printing structures with high resolution [23]. The PCL linear polymers give 4D printed structures the ability of self-healing, and the mechanical properties of damaged structures can be restored to more than 90%. The development of self-healing SMP extends the life of high-resolution 4D printed structures and benefit various practical applications related to 4D printing soft robots (Fig. 6c) [23].

Moreover, the repeatedly recyclable 3D printing SMPs were also be realized based on catalyst-free dynamic thermosetting photopolymers (Fig. 7). By immobilizing the catalyst-free reversible bond into this new photopolymer, the resin forms a dynamic covalent crosslinked network structure on UV based 3D printing with controllable mechanical properties and elastic behaviour that can be used to thermally adapt SMPs. The development of covalent adaptive network (CAN) has facilitated the creation of recyclable

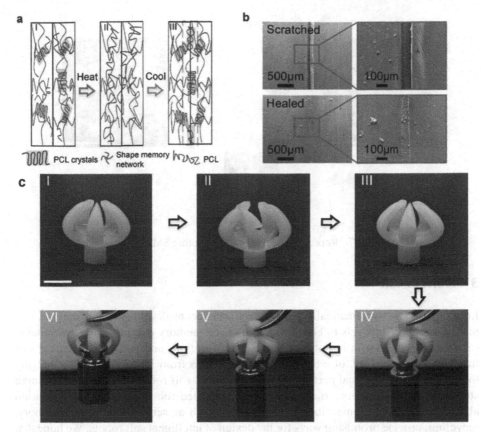

Fig. 6. Self-healing process and the demonstration of the repair process of a broken gripper [23].

photopolymers by incorporating dynamic covalent bonds (DCBs) into the structure [19, 24]. This CAN is not only compatible with DLP 3D printing but can also be reprocessed through a bond exchange reaction, which exhibits controllable mechanical properties with elastomeric behaviours to thermadapt shape memory effects. In addition, this network can be returned to acrylates functional photopolymers suitable for 3D printing, providing a recyclable thermosetting photopolymer platform for 3D printing [24]. The developed repeatedly recyclable 3D printing SMPs provides a potential possibility for fabricating sustainable soft robots.

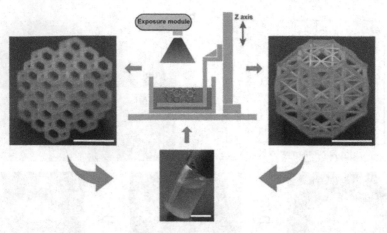

Fig. 7. Repeatedly recyclable 3D printing SMPs [24].

3   Conclusion

In summary, we systematically summarized our recent developed photocurable soft materials from hydrogels to elastomers and shape memory polymers that are suitable for DLP based 3D printing of soft robots. The functions and properties of these soft materials are discussed, of which the modulus varies from KPa to GPa, guaranteeing the controlled mechanical performance of fabricated soft robots. In addition, the large stretchability of these materials endows the fabricated robots with high deformation ability. Futhermore, some other functionalities, such as self-healing, shape memory, recycling, provide promising ways for the design of intelligent soft robots. We hope that researchers and engineers in the field of soft robots could get some inspiration from these materials and better promote the development of the field of soft robots.

Acknowledgments. B.Z. acknowledges the National Natural Science Foundation of China (No. 51903210), the Joint Research Funds of Department of Science & Technology of Shaanxi Province and Northwestern Polytechnical University (No. 2020GXLH-Z-021). This work was supported in part by the Education Department of Shaanxi Provincial Government with Project No. 20JK0931.

Competing Interests. The authors declare no competing interests.

References

1. Wang, H., Totaro, M., Beccai, L.: Toward perceptive soft robots: progress and challenges. Advanced Science **5**(9), 1800541 (2018)
2. Asbeck, A.T., De Rossi, S.M.M., Galiana, I., et al.: Stronger, Smarter, Softer: Next-Generation Wearable Robots. IEEE Robot. Autom. Mag. **21**(4), 22–33 (2014)
3. Rus, D., Tolley, M.T.: Design, fabrication and control of soft robots. Nature **521**, 467–475 (2015)

4. Compton, B.G., Lewis, J.A.: 3D-Printing of lightweight cellular composites. Adv. Mater. **26**(34), 5930–5935 (2014)
5. Zolfagharian, A., Kaynak, A., Bodaghi, M., et al.: Control-Based 4D Printing: Adaptive 4D-Printed Systems. Applied Science **10**(9), 3020 (2020)
6. Gonzalez-Henriquez, A.M., Sarabia-Vallejos, M.A., Rodriguez-Hernandez, J., et al.: Polymers for additive manufacturing and 4D-printing: Materials, methodologies, and biomedical applications. Prog. Polym. Sci. **94**, 57–116 (2019)
7. Langer, R.: New methods of drug delivery. Science **249**(4976), 1527–1533 (1990)
8. Gao, H., Li, J., Zhang, F., et al.: The research status and challenges of shape memory polymer-based flexible electronics. Materials Horizons **6**(5), 931 (2019)
9. Momeni, F., Hassani, S.M.M.N., Liu, X., et al.: A review of 4D printing. Materials & Design **112**, 42–79 (2017)
10. Yang, H., Li, C., Yang, M., et al.: Printing hydrogels and elastomers in arbitrary sequence with strong adhesion. Adv. Funct. Mat. **29**(27), 1901721 (2019)
11. Zhang, B., Li, S., Hingorani, H., et al.: Highly stretchable hydrogels for UV curing based high-resolution multimaterial 3D printing. J. Mat. Chemi. B **6**, 3246–3253 (2018)
12. Yuk, H., Lin, S., Ma, C., et al.: Hydraulic hydrogel actuators and robots optically and sonically camouflaged in water. Nature Communication **8**, 14230 (2017)
13. Warner, J., Soman, P., Zhu, W., et al.: Design and 3D printing of hydrogel scaffolds with fractal geometries. ACS Biomater. Sci. Eng. **2**(10), 1763–1770 (2016)
14. Wang, J., Stanic, S., Altun, A.A., et al.: A highly efficient waterborne photoinitiator for visible-light-induced threedimensional printing of hydrogels. Chem. Commun. **54**, 920–923 (2018)
15. Pawar, A.A., Saada, G., Cooperstein, I., et al.: High-performance 3D printing of hydrogels by water-dispersible photoinitiator nano particles. Science Advances **2**(4), 1501391 (2016)
16. Wang, H., Zhang, B., Zhang, J., et al.: General one-pot method for preparing highly water-soluble and biocompatible photoinitiators for digital light processing-based 3D printing of hydrogels. ACS Appl. Mater. Interfaces. **13**(46), 55507–55516 (2021)
17. He, X., Cheng, J., Sun, Z., et al.: A volatile microemulsion method of preparing water-soluble photo-absorbers for 3D printing of high-resolution, high-water-content hydrogel structures. Soft Matter (2023). https://doi.org/10.1039/D2SM01709A
18. Ge, Q., Chen, Z., Cheng, J., et al.: 3D printing of highly stretchable hydrogel with diverse UV curable polymers. Science Advances **7**(2), 4261 (2021)
19. Zhang, B., Kowsari, K., Serjouei, A., et al.: Reprocessable thermosets for sustainable three-dimensional printing. Nature Communication **9**, 1831 (2018)
20. Patel, D.K., Sakhaei, A.H., Layani, M., et al.: Highly stretchable and UV curable elastomers for digital light processing based 3D printing. Advanced Materials **29**(15), 1606000 (2017)
21. Hingorani, H., Zhang, Y.-F., Zhang, B., et al.: Modified commercial UV curable elastomers for passive 4D printing. Int. J. Smart Nano Mater. **10**(3), 225–236 (2019)
22. Zhang, B., Li, H., Cheng, J., et al.: Mechanically robust and UV curable shape memory polymers for digital light processing based 4D printing. Advanced Materials **33**(27), 2101298 (2021)
23. Zhang, B., Zhang, W., Zhang, Z., et al.: Self-healing four-dimensional printing with ultraviolet curable double network shape memory polymer system. ACS Appl. Mater. Interfaces. **11**(10), 10328–10336 (2019)
24. Cui, J., Liu, F., Lu, Z., et al.: Repeatedly recyclable 3D printing catalyst-free dynamic thermosetting photopolymers. Advanced Materials **35**(20), 2211417 (2023)

Design and Grasping Experiments of a Three-Branch Dexterous Soft Gripper

Weihao Li[1], Yonghua Guo[1], Yu Han[1,2], and Jianqing Peng[1,2(✉)]

[1] School of Intelligent Systems Engineering, Shenzhen Campus of Sun Yat-Sen University, Shenzhen 518107, China
pengjq7@mail.sysu.edu.cn
[2] Guangdong Provincial Key Laboratory of Fire Science and Technology, Guangzhou 510006, China

Abstract. Most existing soft grippers that rely on bending for grasping often need to squeeze objects to achieve a certain grasping force, which will potentially cause damage to objects especially those delicate and fragile. To solve this problem, a three-branch soft gripper design is proposed, which employs simple actuation but has excellent adaptive and dexterous grasping capabilities. In this paper, structure design will first be introduced in detail. Then, the force of the finger and the contact relationship with the object are analyzed by finite element modeling method. Finally, the pressure sensor is used to obtain the grasping force during grasping process. Furthermore, the grasping performance tests are conducted. Experiment results show that the proposed three-branch soft gripper shows remarkable ability on grasping objects of various shapes, sizes and delicacy.

Keywords: Soft Gripper · Dexterous Grasping · Finite Element Modeling · Grasping Performance

1 Introduction

Soft grippers provide significant solutions for grasping in unstructured environments [1], and have received more and more attention. One of the important advantages of soft grippers is the ability to achieve adaptive grasping [2], which means changing the shape or other characteristics according to different objects to achieve soft grasping [3]. Therefore, researchers are more concerned about how to achieve adaptive grasping when designing a soft gripper.

An important inspiration for designing a soft gripper with adaptive grasping ability comes from bionics [4]. When Leif Kniese, a German engineer, first discovered the Fin-Ray effect [5], many soft grippers based on this principle followed [6–9]. Utilizing the

This work was supported in part by the National Key R&D Program of China under Grant 2022YFB4703103, the National Natural Science Foundation of China under Grant 62103454, the Guangdong Basic and Applied Basic Research Foundation under Grant 2019A1515110680, the Shenzhen Municipal Basic Research Project for Natural Science Foundation under Grant JCYJ20190806143408992, and the Shenzhen Science and Technology Program under Grant JCYJ20220530150006014.

compliance of the Fin-Ray effect, this kind of soft gripper can bend and deform adaptively when grasping objects, thus forming an envelope to grasp. The German company Festo, long known for manufacturing pneumatic products, developed an octopus arm-inspired soft gripper [10, 11]. The gripper is made of silicone rubber and can bend inward by applying compressed air, thereby enveloping objects. Several suction cups are mounted on the surface to increase flexibility and stability. Inspired by chameleons, they also make a soft gripper based on cylinder push [12], which can realize the fitting grasp of objects of different shapes. Inspired by human fingers, there are also soft grippers that are tendon-driven to imitate the movement of finger joints [13, 14].

Of course, not all the inspiration comes from bionics. The development of technology has also given birth to some soft grippers. For example, using shape memory materials to make soft grippers [15, 16], which can be deformed or restored by applying different stimulus. Or the design of soft gripper can also be based on algorithms, such as topology optimization [17, 18].

For many of the soft grippers introduced above, an important way to achieve adaptive grasping is to form an envelope on the object, and a feasible and simple way to realize this is to bend the gripper inwards. Usually, this kind of envelope requires soft grippers to contact the object as much as possible, then squeeze with two or more fingers to complete the grasping. Essentially, it still needs to achieve a certain grasping force. However, for some delicate, fragile and deformable objects, excessive contact and extrusion caused by achieving the grasping force may result in deformation and damage to the objects. Therefore, it is necessary to design a dexterous soft gripper with special envelope that can reduce the burden of achieving the demanding force. Although there are indeed soft grippers that can ignore such contradiction, such as those grasping by adhesion [19, 20], granular jamming bags actuated by vacuuming [21, 22], etc., the research on compliant soft grippers based on their own structure is still lacking.

In this paper, we design an adaptive and dexterous soft gripper that takes advantage of embedded envelope to grasp. By embedding the object into the soft finger, it can realize soft and stable grasping without large deformation, so as to reduce the extrusion and force applied to the object. The second chapter will specifically introduce the structural design. The third chapter is the simulation and analysis of this soft gripper. The fourth chapter carries out experiments to measure the grasping force and verify the grasping ability. The fifth chapter is the summary of this paper.

2 Mechanical Design

2.1 Finger Design

We will first introduce the core of our soft gripper - the finger part, as shown in Fig. 1(a). Under specified constraints, this structure can achieve inward bending and form an embedded envelope while contacting objects, as shown in Fig. 1(b). The finger is made of thermoplastic polyurethane (TPU) and fabricated using injection molding, which contributes to be soft, elastic and have strong deformation recovery ability. Noting that there are three through-holes on finger, two at the top and one at the bottom. After fixing the three through-holes, the finger can bend inwards when the force is applied.

The grasping side of the finger is a continuous concave-convex design, which is formed by connecting vertical lines and curves from the view of profile. When grasping objects, the convex parts undertake the main force, prompting the fingers to bend inwards, and the concave part can play the role of cushioning and supporting. The continuous concave-convex design can form an embedded envelope one the object, that is, the object can be embedded in the concave parts. Collaborated with the contraction caused by the bending, the object can be grasped more firmly.

Making use of embedded envelope, such design is naturally superior for grasping objects of irregular shapes. For some objects it only has to embed it to those concave parts and just rely on the support to achieve grasping. Therefore, the proposed soft finger essentially converts a part of the traditional squeeze force into a support force that creates by the special structure. And the reduction of the squeeze force means reducing the risk of damage to the object.

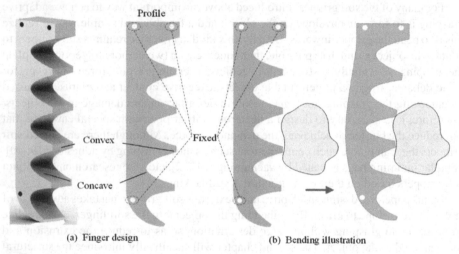

(a) Finger design   (b) Bending illustration

Fig. 1. The proposed finger design (a) and the bending illustration (b)

2.2 Overall Mechanical Design

Figure 2 shows the mechanical design of the overall three-branch soft gripper based on the finger mentioned above. Three fingers are distributed symmetrically. Each finger has a shell responsible for fixing its three through-holes, and the shell is fixed on the slider. We adopt 42 linear stepper motor as the driving source and use Arduino and A4988 stepper driver module to control the speed and steps of the stepper motor. When the stepper motor rotates, the screw nut slides vertically along the shaft. Under the traction of the connecting rod, the vertical movement of the screw nut on the shaft is converted into the horizontal movement of the slider on the rail. In short, the three-branch soft gripper implements a translational grasp.

The fixed connection frame plays the role of connecting and assembling different mechanisms of the soft gripper. And to facilitate the loading of the gripper on the manipulator, we horizontally place a flange connection on the top of the motor, and connect it to the frame with bolts to make it integrated.

It is worth mentioning that the designed three-branch center symmetrical mode is the best choice after fully considering the stability of grasping and reducing possible redundancy. Of course, two-branch or other multi-branch mode is also feasible to achieve the expected grasping effect.

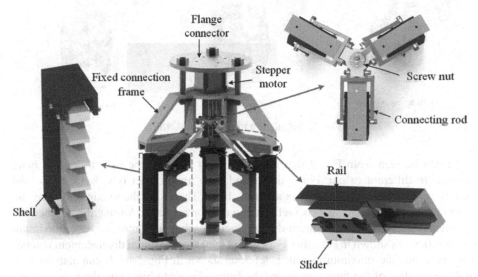

Fig. 2. The three-branch soft gripper design

3 Simulation

Due to the special structural design and restraint method of the finger, when it touches the object, its convex parts undertake the main force and thus bend inwards, while the concave parts can provide support for the part of the object embedded in it. In order to verify this kind of grasping effect, grasping simulations were carried out under ANSYS.

The mechanism of the proposed three-branch soft gripper is more complicated. But in essence, each finger is constrained in a predetermined way, and the three fingers are translated symmetrically at the same time for grasping. Therefore, we only extract the finger part for simulation. Then apply fixed constraints to the three through-holes on each finger, and made contact with the object in a three-finger symmetric manner. Here, we selected cube, cylinder and ellipsoid as the grasped objects for simulation respectively. In order to speed up the simulation without destroying the expected effect, we regarded the grasped object as rigid and fix it. Select frictional in the contact settings, and under the proper meshing and solving solution, the simulation results are shown in Fig. 3.

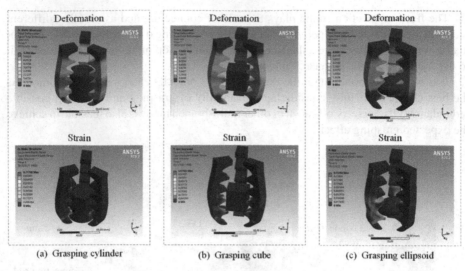

(a) Grasping cylinder   (b) Grasping cube   (c) Grasping ellipsoid

Fig. 3. Simulation results under ANSYS

It can be seen from Fig. 3 that for each object grasped, the soft finger will bend inwards to different extent. For cylinder and cube, the contact type is face-face and mainly reflects between the convex and the object. Therefore, the maximum force and deformation of the finger are also reflected in the convex parts. Among them, when the cylinder is grasped, the maximum displacement reaches 6.43 mm, and the maximum strain is 0.88, as shown in Fig. 3(a). For cube object, the maximum displacement reaches 7.92 mm, and the maximum strain is 0.57, as shown in Fig. 3(b). It can also be seen that the bending of the finger promotes the embeddings of object into the concave. For example, while grasping the cube in Fig. 3(b), the bottom of the cube embeds into the concave of the finger, realizing the function of supporting the object. Figure 3(a) shows a similar trend when grasps the cylinder. The ellipsoid object shown in Fig. 3(c) can be directly embedded in the concave of the finger to form a support for grasping. In this case, the maximum deformation is 4.96 mm and the maximum strain is 0.15.

Therefore, it can be seen from the above simulation analysis that the designed soft gripper can achieve the expected grasping effect.

4 Experiment

4.1 Grasping Force Measurement

As the rotation angle of stepper motor increases, the clamping degree between the soft gripper and the object also increases. To explore the grasping force variation during grasping process and the force relationship between three fingers, we installed pressure sensors on the convex of the fingers to capture the force values and applied force by running the motor at a constant speed. We built an experimental platform for grasping objects and measuring the grasping force, as shown in Fig. 4(a). The platform consists of the designed soft gripper, aluminum frame for holding, Arduino and A4988 stepper driver as controller and a laptop.

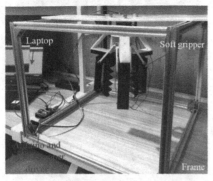

(a) Experimental platform

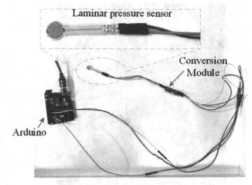

(b) Operation of the pressure sensor

Fig. 4. Experimental platform (a) and the operation of the pressure sensor (b)

In this experiment, we used the FSR laminar pressure sensor to measure the force, as shown in Fig. 4(b). We adopt the PR-C10-LT model with circular shape and its outer diameter is 10 mm. The sensor can measure pressure ranges from 20 g to 2 kg. The resistance of the sensor changes with the pressure. When using it to work, we first connected the sensor to a dedicated conversion module to convert the resistance signal into a voltage signal. The conversion relationship is:

$$U_0 = (1 + R_{AO-RES} \times \frac{1}{R_x}) \times 0.1 \tag{1}$$

where U_0 represents the output voltage value of the conversion module, R_{AO-RES} represents the module's feedback resistor value, R_x is the output resistance value of the pressure sensor.

The relationship between pressure and the resistance of the sensor is linear, that is:

$$\frac{1}{R_x} = aF + b \tag{2}$$

where F is the pressure, a and b are constant linear coefficients.

Substituting (2) into (1), it can be found that the relationship between the output voltage U_0 and pressure value F is also linear:

$$U_0 = \frac{aR_{AO-RES}}{10}F + \frac{1 + bR_{AO-RES}}{10} \tag{3}$$

Therefore, after Arduino receives the voltage signal output by the AO port of the conversion module, the voltage value can be mapped from 0.1 V–3.3 V to 20 g–2 kg through the proportional transformation, so as to realize the force measurement. In addition, to make the force measurement more accurate, we also calibrated the sensor before starting the experiment. Simply by placing an object of a given weight on the sensor, the sensor was calibrated after adjusting the parameters so that the measured weight is exactly the given weight.

 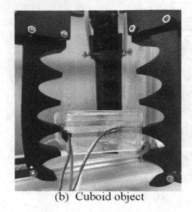

(a) Cylindrical object   (b) Cuboid object

Fig. 5. Measurement on cylindrical object (a) and cuboid object (b)

In this experiment, we performed force measurements on cuboid and cylindrical objects, as shown in Fig. 5. The grasping of these two shapes mainly utilizes the convex part of the finger, which facilitates the measurement of sensors installed on the convex. We first anti-rotated the motor to make the gripper just in contact with the object before grasping, then rotated the motor 108 degrees each time while recording the current measured value. The force change curve with motor angle as x axis and force value as y axis were drawn in MATLAB, as shown in Fig. 6.

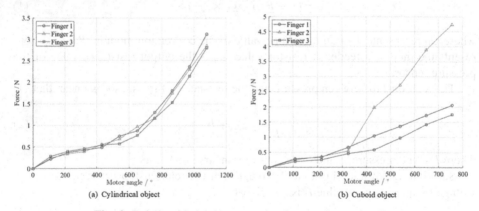

(a) Cylindrical object   (b) Cuboid object

Fig. 6. Relationship between grasping force and motor angle

It can be seen from Fig. 6 that while grasping the cylindrical object, the measured grasping forces of the three fingers are similar in both magnitude and variation trend, while they varies a lot when grasping the cuboid object. This is because the contact face of the cylinder is symmetrical to the three fingers, so the three fingers are consistent with their contact state. However, the contact face of the cuboid is asymmetrical for three fingers, resulting in different contact states for each finger, specifically reflected in whether the object is in full contact with the convex, and whether it is in parallel contact or oblique contact. It can also be seen that whether it is grasping a cylinder or a cuboid, the force increases slightly in small rotation angle, while the force increases rapidly in large rotation angle. This is because although the motor angle increases at a constant rate, under the proposed traction model, the distance that finger translates increases each time, resulting in an increasing degree of clamping to the object.

4.2 Grasping Performance Test

In order to test the grasping ability of the designed three-branch soft gripper, we selected several objects with different shapes, sizes and delicacy for grasping, as shown in Fig. 7. According to the results, the three-branch soft gripper has excellent adaptive and dexterous grasping capabilities. In some grasping cases, it only has to embed the object into the concave to achieve grasp. There is no need for large deformation to form a certain squeeze force which avoids excessive extrusion to the objects.

Fig. 7. Grasping performance test on different objects

5 Conclusion

In this paper, an adaptive and dexterous soft finger structure is designed and assembled into a three-branch soft gripper with translational grasping. Subsequently, the grasping simulation, grasping force test and the grasping ability test were carried out. The soft gripper and performing ANSYS grasping simulation are simplified, the force and deformation effect of the finger is obtained. The simulation results verified that the proposed design has the characteristics of adaptability and dexterity. The pressure sensors to the convex of the finger are attached, the grasping forces of the three fingers were measured and compared. The adaptive and dexterous grasping ability of the soft gripper was verified under the grasping experiment of various shapes, sizes, and delicacy. Further research will focus on how to realize the perception of grasping force without the pressure sensors, as well as the modeling of the embedded envelope and the evaluation of its contribution to grasping.

References

1. Hughes, J., Culha, U., Giardina, F., Guenther, F., Rosendo, A., Iida, F.: Soft manipulators and grippers: a review. Frontiers in Robotics and AI **3**, 69 (2016)
2. Manti, M., Hassan, T., Passetti, G., D'Elia, N., Laschi, C., Cianchetti, M.: A bioinspired soft robotic gripper for adaptable and effective grasping. Soft Rob. **2**(3), 107–116 (2015)
3. Shintake, J., Cacucciolo, V., Floreano, D., Shea, H.: Soft robotic grippers. Advanced materials **30**(29), 1707035 (2018)
4. Zhou, L., Ren, L., Chen, Y., Niu, S., Han, Z., Ren, L.: Bio-inspired soft grippers based on impactive gripping. Advanced Science **8**(9), 2002017 (2021)
5. Pfaff, O., Simeonov, S., Cirovic, I., Stano, P.: Application of fin ray effect approach for production process automation. Annals of DAAAM & Proceedings **22**(1), 1247–1249 (2011)
6. Ali, M.H., Zhanabayev, A., Khamzhin, S., Mussin, K.: Biologically inspired gripper based on the fin ray effect. In: 2019 5th International Conference on Control, Automation and Robotics (ICCAR), pp. 865–869. IEEE (2019)
7. Crooks, W., Rozen-Levy, S., Trimmer, B., Rogers, C., Messner, W.: Passive gripper inspired by Manduca sexta and the Fin Ray® Effect. Int. J. Adv. Rob. Syst. **14**(4), 1729881417721155 (2017)
8. Crooks, W., Vukasin, G., O'Sullivan, M., Messner, W., Rogers, C.: Fin ray® effect inspired soft robotic gripper: From the robosoft grand challenge toward optimization. Frontiers in Robotics and AI **3**, 70 (2016)
9. Xu, W., Zhang, H., Zheng, N., Yuan, H.: Design and experiments of a compliant adaptive grasper based on fish fin structure. In: 2018 IEEE International Conference on Robotics and Biomimetics (ROBIO), pp. 293–298. IEEE (2018)
10. Xie, Z., Domel, A.G., An, N., Green, C., Gong, Z., et al.: Octopus arm-inspired tapered soft actuators with suckers for improved grasping. Soft Rob. **7**(5), 639–648 (2020)
11. Festo Homepage: https://www.festo.com/PDF_Flip/corp/Festo_BionicCobot/en/, last accessed 17 April 2023
12. Festo Homepage, https://www.festo.com/us/en/a/8092533, last accessed 28 April 2022
13. Xu, Z., Todorov, E.: Design of a highly biomimetic anthropomorphic robotic hand towards artificial limb regeneration. In: 2016 IEEE International Conference on Robotics and Automation (ICRA), pp. 3485–3492. IEEE (2016)
14. Tavakoli, M., Lopes, P., Lourenco, J., Rocha, R.P., et al.: Autonomous selection of closing posture of a robotic hand through embodied soft matter capacitive sensors. IEEE Sens. J. **17**(17), 5669–5677 (2017)
15. Behl, M., Kratz, K., Zotzmann, J., Nöchel, U., Lendlein, A.: Reversible bidirectional shape-memory polymers. Advanced Materials **25**(32), 4466–4469 (2013)
16. Ge, Q., Sakhaei, A.H., Lee, H., et al.: Multimaterial 4D printing with tailorable shape memory polymers. Sci. Rep. **6**(1), 1–11 (2016)
17. Liu, C.H., Chen, T.L., et al.: Optimal design of a soft robotic gripper for grasping unknown objects. Soft Rob. **5**(4), 452–465 (2018)
18. Liu, C.H., Chung, F.M., Chen, Y., Chiu, C.H., Chen, T.L.: Optimal design of a motor-driven three-finger soft robotic gripper. IEEE/ASME Trans. Mechatron. **25**(4), 1830–1840 (2020)
19. Ruotolo, W., Brouwer, D., Cutkosky, M.R.: From grasping to manipulation with gecko-inspired adhesives on a multifinger gripper. Science Robotics **6**(61), eabi9773 (2021)
20. Shintake, J., Rosset, S., Schubert, B., Floreano, D., Shea, H.: Versatile soft grippers with intrinsic electroadhesion based on multifunctional polymer actuators. Adv. Mater. **28**(2), 231–238 (2016)

21. Amend, J., Cheng, N., Fakhouri, S., Culley, B.: Soft robotics commercialization: Jamming grippers from research to product. Soft Rob. **3**(4), 213–222 (2016)
22. Amend, J.R., Brown, E., Rodenberg, N., Jaeger, H.M., Lipson, H.: A positive pressure universal gripper based on the jamming of granular material. IEEE Trans. Rob. **28**(2), 341–350 (2012)

Modelling Analysis of a Soft Robotic Arm Based on Pneumatic-Network Structure

Weizhuang Gong, Qin Bao, Kai Feng, and Yinlong Zhu[✉]

College of Mechanical and Electronic Engineering, Nanjing Forestry University, Nanjing 210037, China
ylzhu@njfu.edu.cn

Abstract. As an important supplement of rigid robotic arms, soft robotic arms have infinite degrees of freedom theoretically and can realize more flexible movement. Soft robotic arms have a broad application prospect in the fields of man-machine cooperation, medical rehabilitation training, space and underwater exploration, etc. In this paper, a kind of soft robotic arm based on pneumatic-network structure was proposed. Each soft robotic arm module adopts three symmetrical and independent pneumatic-network cavity structures, and can realize axial extension and spatial bending motion after driving three cavities respectively. Based on the assumption of constant curvature and the theory of large deformation of beam, the bending model and elongation model of module motion were established. Moreover, considering the influence of its own gravity on bending performance, the bending models of single-module soft robotic arm were modified. Then, we built an experimental platform to test the bending and elongation motion of the soft robotic arm module, and compared the experimental results, simulation results and theoretical model results. It is shown from the experimental results that when the inflation pressure is in the range of $0 \sim 80$ kPa, the model results are close to the simulation results and experimental results. In this paper, the structural and theoretical basis for the follow-up research is laid, which shows that the soft robotic arm based on pneumatic-network structure has broad application prospects.

Keyword: Pneumatic-network · Soft robotic arm · Bending model · Elongation model

1 Introduction

Since the 20th century, the robot industry has been widely used in many fields such as industry, agriculture and medical treatment [1]. With the change of application environment, the traditional industrial robotic arm with rigid material as the main body has some problems, such as large mass, poor motion flexibility and limited motion range [2]. In the face of highly unstructured, narrow, irregular and other complex environments, the operation cannot be effectively completed. Therefore, it has become a hot research direction for the soft robotic arms that can be used in complex environment.

© The Author(s), under exclusive license to Springer Nature Singapore Pte Ltd. 2023
H. Yang et al. (Eds.): ICIRA 2023, LNAI 14270, pp. 32–44, 2023.
https://doi.org/10.1007/978-981-99-6492-5_4

The working principle of a pneumatic soft robotic arms is essentially a gas as the working medium and an elastic cavity that expands or contracts directionally in a certain spatial dimension under the action of the working air pressure and structural constraints [3]. The elastic cavity can be an elastic material with good tensile performance, or a thin shell or film structure that cannot be stretched but can be easily bent and folded, such as a soft pneumatic actuator based on a pleated film/origami thin shell structure [4]. The form of constraint structure determines the motion form and driving performance of pneumatic soft actuator. The constraint structure can be realized by fiber constraint structure [5], elastic air cell structure [6], corrugated structure [7], folding/folding structure [8] and so on. The structural design of pneumatic soft robotic arms plays a decisive role in its performance, so it is important to study its structural characteristics deeply for the development of pneumatic soft robots.

Different from rigid robots, the modeling method of soft robotic arms has infinite degrees of freedom in theory, and it is difficult to establish an accurate mathematical model to describe its motion because of the complexity of working environment and the nonlinear deformation of flexible materials [9]. Currently the constant curvature assumption is the most widely used method [10, 11], and Cosserat rod Theory is also one of the commonly used kinematics modeling theories, which is suitable for describing the motion of line-driven soft robotic arms [12, 13]. Neural network method, pseudo-rigid body model and Jacobian method [14–16] can also be used to model soft robots. However, due to the nonlinear deformation of hyperelastic materials, it is necessary to use the constitutive model of hyperelastic materials to describe the mechanical properties of silicone materials, so it is difficult to solve the model and its accuracy is poor. There are still many difficulties to be solved in establishing an applicable and relatively accurate model.

In this paper, a kind of soft robotic arm based on pneumatic-network structure was proposed. Each soft robotic arm module adopts three symmetrical and independent pneumatic-network cavity structures, and can realize axial extension and spatial bending motion after driving three cavities respectively. Based on the assumption of constant curvature and the theory of large deformation of beam, the bending model and elongation model of module motion were established. Moreover, considering the influence of its own gravity on bending performance, the bending models of single-module soft robotic arm were modified. Then, we built an experimental platform to test the bending and elongation motion of the soft robotic arm module, and compared the experimental results, simulation results and theoretical model results. It is shown from the experimental results that when the inflation pressure is in the range of 0 ~ 80 kPa, the model results are close to the simulation results and experimental results. In this paper, the structural and theoretical basis for the follow-up research is laid, which shows that the soft robotic arm based on pneumatic-network structure has broad application prospects.

2 Structure of The Soft Robotic Arm

The soft robotic arm designed in this paper is driven by air pressure, and it is made of super-elastic silicone material, which has large deformation capacity and is one of the commonly used materials for soft robot driven by air pressure. Pneumatic-driven soft robotic arm is usually composed of several same or different cavity structures, and the expected deformation can be produced by filling the cavities with gases with different pressures. As shown in Fig. 1, the stiffness of the confinement layer is much greater than that of the strain layer after the gas is introduced, so the strain layer is much more deformed than the confinement layer, and the whole body will bend to the confinement layer side, and the characteristics of the hyperelastic material make the actuator recover to its original state after the gas is exhausted. At the same time, single-chamber driving will produce bending motion in one direction, double-chamber driving will produce bending motion in two directions, and after three or more chambers are connected in parallel, they can produce spatial bending motion under different driving combinations and air pressures. Theoretically, the more chambers, the more degrees of freedom, but the system will be more complicated and difficult to control.

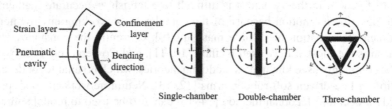

Single-chamber   Double-chamber   Three-chamber

Fig. 1. Deformation schematic diagram

When gas pressure is filled into the cavity, balloon effect will occur, which will lead to more energy used for expansion and deformation, and cannot achieve bending movement, and even damage the actuator, so it is necessary to improve the structure to limit its expansion. Winding fiber wires outside the chamber is one of the better solutions to the balloon effect, but it will increase the difficulty of manufacturing and modeling the soft robotic arm, and the pneumatic-network structure can limit the balloon effect under the condition of low air pressure, so that the actuator can achieve the expected movement.

The main working pressure of the soft robotic arm designed in this paper is $0 \sim 80$ kPa, so a relatively simple pneumatic-network structure is adopted, and the cavity structure is semi-circular. As shown in Fig. 2, the pneumatic-network structure in series enables the software driver to bend to the limiting layer side, and the space bending can be realized by connecting three or more cavities in parallel. As shown in Fig. 3, the structural parameters of the soft robotic arm are wall thickness $t_0 = 2.8$ mm, cavity interventricular space $b_0 = 3$ mm, chamber width $b_1 = 3$ mm, lumen radius $r_0 = 8$ mm and central empty triangle edge long $d_0 = 10$ mm.

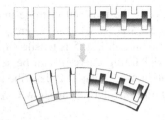

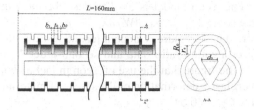

Fig. 2. Pneumatic-network structure   **Fig. 3.** Structural parameters of soft robotic arm

3 Soft Robotic Arm Modeling

3.1 Bending Model

We propose a simplified analysis model, in which the module bending is regarded as the central limiting layer subjected to bending moment, as shown in Fig. 4(a). Firstly, we analyze the force acting on the limiting layer of the single-cavity driving center, and then study the geometric model of multi-cavity deformation based on this.

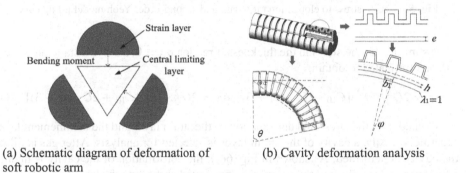

(a) Schematic diagram of deformation of soft robotic arm

(b) Cavity deformation analysis

Fig. 4. Deformation analysis of soft robotic arm module

3.1.1 Single-Cavity Driven Bending Model

Considering the driving air pressure P with only one cavity, the central limiting layer is assumed to be a beam with large deformation and the bending angle is θ. Select a chamber for analysis, and set the number of chambers as N, the gap as b_0, the width as b_1, the inner diameters as R_0 and r_0, the radius difference as h_0, the cavity thickness as t_0, the deformation as $t_0{}'$, the bending angle as φ, and the effective length of the software module as L, then the relationship between the bending angle θ and the bending angle φ of a single cavity is $\theta = L\varphi/b_1$. The cavity filled with gas will be deformed as shown in Fig. 4(b), where e is the distance between the joint surface of the confinement layer and the strain layer and neutral surface ($\lambda_1 = 1$). Assuming uniform deformation in the thickness direction of the cavity, $\lambda_1\lambda_2\lambda_3 = 1$ can be known from the incompressibility of the silicone material, then $\lambda_{3,h} = t_0{}'/t_0$, $\lambda_{2,h} = r_0{}'/r_0$.

The Yeoh model is used to describe the true stress of the material in three main directions: $\sigma_{i,h} = \lambda_{i,h} \partial W / \partial \lambda_{i,h} - p = 2\lambda_{i,h}^2 [C_{10} + 2C_{20}(I_1 - 3)] - p$, where p is hydrostatic pressure. Uniaxial tensile test on silica gel material, Fig. 5 is tensile stress and elongation ratio data and second-order Yeoh model fitting curve, it can be seen from the figure that the use of Yeoh model as constitutive model can well describe the superelastic deformation of the silica gel material used, the calculation can show $C_{10} = 0.11$, $C_{20} = 0.02$.

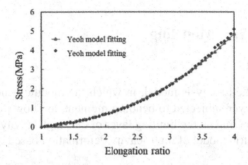

Fig. 5. Tensile stress to elongation ratio data and second-order Yeoh model fitting curve

Asuming that the stress in the thickness direction $\sigma_3 = 0$, the hydrostatic pressure p can be eliminated to obtain:

$$\sigma_1 = 2(\lambda_1^2 - \lambda_3^2)[C_{10} + 2C_{20}(I_1 - 3)], \sigma_2 = 2(\lambda_2^2 - \lambda_3^2)[C_{10} + 2C_{20}(I_1 - 3)] \quad (1)$$

Considering the stress and deformation of the strain layer and the confinement layer separately, firstly, a cavity of the strain layer is selected for analysis. After gas is filled, the cavity is deformed. As shown in Fig. 6(a), the deformation of the cavity is mainly geometric and tensile, and the stress σ_1 is generated at the stretched position. The axial main elongation ratio of the cavity at different heights h is:

$$\lambda_1 = (b_1 + \lambda_2 r_0 \varphi \sin \alpha + e\varphi)/b_1 \quad (2)$$

Since the cross section is symmetrical, the force in the horizontal direction is balanced, and the force balance equation in the vertical direction is $F_p = F_{\sigma 1} + F_{\sigma 2}$. The sum of the vertical components of the pressure acting on the interior of the chamber, and the vertical components of the axial principal stress σ_1 and the circumferential principal stress σ_1 are as follows:

$$F_p = \int_0^\pi \int_0^{b_1} PR_0' \sin \alpha \, dt d\alpha + 2 \int_0^\pi \int_0^{h_0} Pr_0' \cos \gamma \sin \alpha \, dt d\alpha \quad (3)$$

$$F_{\sigma 1} = 2 \int_0^\pi \int_0^{t_0'} \sigma_1 r_0' \sin\left(\frac{\varphi}{2}\right) dt d\alpha \quad (4)$$

$$F_{\sigma 2} = 2 \cdot 2 \int_0^\psi \int_0^{t_0'} \sigma_2\left(\frac{b_1}{\varphi} + e\right) \Big/ \cos \gamma \cos\left(\frac{\varphi}{2} - \beta\right) dt d\beta + 2 \cdot 2 \int_\psi^{\frac{\varphi}{2}} \int_0^{t_0'} \sigma_2\left(\frac{b_1}{\varphi} + e\right) \cos\left(\frac{\varphi}{2} - \beta\right) dt d\beta \quad (5)$$

where $\psi = h_0 \cos \gamma / b_1 + 2h_0 \cos \gamma \varphi$, $\cos \Upsilon$ and R_0' can be obtained from geometric relations.

For the limiting layer, the stress diagram is shown in Fig. 6(b). Considering the central stiffness layer as a large deformation beam, the contact surface between the stiffness layer and the strain layer is analyzed, and the plane constant curvature bending is formed under the joint action of air pressure P and stress σ_2. According to the large deformation equation of the beam:

$$M_{layer} = EI\theta/L = \varphi EI/b_1 \tag{6}$$

where E is the elastic modulus of the stiffness layer and I is the moment of inertia of the section.

$$M_P = \int_0^{L-t_0} 2Pr_0x\,dx + \sum_{n=1}^{N} \int_{(n-1)B}^{(n-1)B+b_1} 2Ph_0x\,dx \tag{7}$$

$$M_{\sigma 2} = \int_0^L 2\sigma_2 t_0 x\,dx + \int_{L-t_0}^L 2\sigma_2 R_0 x\,dx + \sum_{n=0}^{N-1} \left(\int_{nB+b_1}^{nB+b_1+t_0} 2\sigma_2 h_0 x\,dx + \int_{(n+1)B-t_0}^{(n+1)B} 2\sigma_2 h_0 x\,dx \right) \tag{8}$$

where $B = b_0 + b_1 + 2t_0$.

The moment balance equation acting on the end is $M_{layer} = M_P - M_{\sigma 2}$, and the moment balance equation of the limiting layer can be obtained simultaneously. The axial principal stress σ_1 and the circumferential principal stress σ_2 are expressed as follows, in which the axial principal elongation ratio λ_1 and σ_1 are related to α, while for σ_2, the axial principal elongation ratio is λ_1, $\sigma_2 = (b_1 + e\varphi)/b_1$.

$$\sigma_1 = 2(\lambda_{1,\sigma_1}^2 - \lambda_{3,\sigma_1}^2)[C_{10} + 2C_{20}(\lambda_{1,\sigma_1}^2 + \lambda_{2,\sigma_1}^2 + \lambda_{3,\sigma_1}^2 - 3)] \tag{9}$$

$$\sigma_2 = 2(\lambda_{2,\sigma_2}^2 - \lambda_{3,\sigma_2}^2)[C_{10} + 2C_{20}(\lambda_{1,\sigma_2}^2 + \lambda_{2,\sigma_2}^2 + \lambda_{3,\sigma_2}^2 - 3)] \tag{10}$$

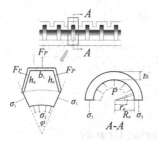

(a) Stress and deformation diagram of strain layer chamber

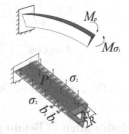

(b) Stress and deformation diagram of limiting layer

Fig. 6. Stress and deformation diagram

Assuming that the thickness direction of the cavity changes uniformly, that is, $\lambda_{3,\sigma 1} = \lambda_{3,\sigma 2} = \lambda_3$, it is solved by MATLAB numerical integration. For a given air pressure P, an initial value of φ is given, and the unknown quantity λ_3 can be solved by the moment balance equation of the limiting layer and related parameters. Then, the above results are taken into the force balance equation of the strain layer and verified. Figure 7 shows the relationship between the single-cavity pressurization bending angle θ and the air pressure P. When the single-cavity inflation air pressure increases gradually, the bending angle of the software module also increases gradually and changes approximately linearly.

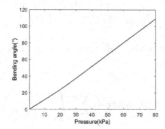

Fig. 7. Relationship between bending angle and air pressure driven by single cavity

3.1.2 Double-Cavity Driving Bending Model

According to the geometric model of single-cavity driving, the driving effect is considered separately, and then the results are coupled, that is, the limiting layer is affected by the resultant torque M_{layer}, resulting in the bending angle θ and the deflection angle φ with the Z_0 axis of the base coordinate system as the rotation axis.

According to the bending model, the relationship between the bending angle θ and the bending moment of the central limiting layer is $\theta = (L/EI)\, |M_{\text{layer}}|$. As shown in Fig. 8, when any two cavities are driven, the vector sum of bending moment acting on the central limiting layer is obtained from the geometric relationship, and the bending angle θ and deflection angle φ are as follows:

$$\theta = \frac{L}{EI} \left| M_{1,layer} + M_{2,layer} + M_{3,layer} \right|$$

$$\phi = \cos^{-1}\left(\frac{\left(M_{1,layer} + M_{2,layer} + M_{3,layer}\right) \cdot (-j)}{\left| M_{1,layer} + M_{2,layer} + M_{3,layer} \right|} \right) \tag{11}$$

where j is the unit vector in the positive direction of y_0.

3.2 Modification of Bending Model Considering Gravity

When the soft robotic arm is used for grasping tasks in the operating space, it is usually placed vertically, so the influence of its own gravity on deformation needs to be considered, so the established bending model needs to be revised.

As shown in Fig. 9, After considering the bending moment M_G acting on the bending motion by its own gravity, the bending angle changes from θ to θ'. The bending moment M_G under the action of gravity is considered after the driving bending deformation, and

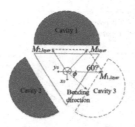

Fig. 8. Inflatable bending model of software module

the direction is opposite to that of M_{layer}, so the bending moment balance equation of the soft robotic arm module is shown in Eq. (12):

$$M'_{layer} = M_{layer} + M_G \tag{12}$$

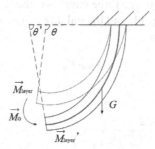

Fig. 9. Force analysis diagram of single module soft robotic arm for grasping

The gravity can be expressed as $G = mg = (mg/l)l$. The bending moment of gravity acting on the upper fixed surface of a single module soft robotic arm is as follows:

$$|M_G| = \int_0^{\theta'} \frac{l}{\theta'}(1 - \cos \beta)\frac{mg}{l}\frac{l}{\theta'}d\beta \tag{13}$$

The equilibrium equation after the bending moment M_G considering gravity is:

$$|M'_{layer}(\theta')| = |M_{layer}(\theta)| - |M_G(\theta')| \tag{14}$$

The relationship between the improved bending angle θ' and the original bending angle θ can be obtained as follows:

$$EI\theta'/l = EI\theta/l - mgl/\theta'\left(1 - \sin \theta'/\theta'\right) \tag{15}$$

According to the relationship between θ' and θ in Eq. (15), the numerical solution can be obtained. Figure 10 is a comparison diagram of the results of the single-cavity model considering gravity and the single-cavity model without considering gravity under the driving pressure of 0 ~ 80 kPa. It can be seen that the bending angle of the soft robotic arm module is reduced after considering gravity.

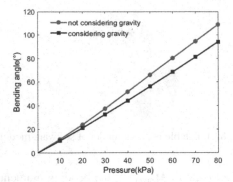

Fig. 10. Comparison diagram of single cavity bending model Considering gravity or not

3.3 Elongation Model

When the driving air pressure of the three cavities is the same, the module is elongated and deformed, as shown in Fig. 11, and the balance equation is established according to the section force balance method:

$$F_P = F_\sigma \tag{16}$$

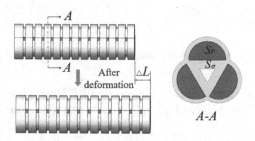

Fig. 11. Driving elongation deformation

It can be seen from the cross-section force action diagram that the air pressure action area is S_P and the axial principal stress action area is S_σ, then:

$$P \cdot 3S_P = s_1 \cdot S_\sigma = \sigma_1 / \lambda_1 \cdot S_\sigma \tag{17}$$

When driving elongation, the circumferential direction does not deform, that is, $\lambda_2 = 1$, and the corresponding circumferential principal stress $\sigma_2 = 0$, then the principal elongation ratio $\lambda_3 = 1/\lambda_1$ in the wall thickness direction, and the axial stress is $\sigma_1 = \partial W / \partial \lambda_1 - p/\lambda_1 = 2(\lambda_1 - 1/\lambda_1)$. The relationship between the air pressure P and the axial elongation ratio λ_1 can be obtained from Eq. (21) and (22) and related parameters, and the change of the length L with the air pressure P is shown in Fig. 12.

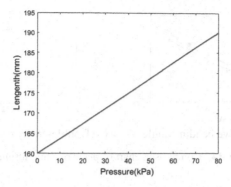

Fig. 12. Relationship between the length of soft robotic arm module and air pressure

4 Experimental Verification

4.1 Experimental Verification of Bending Model

As shown in Fig. 13, when the single-cavity or double-cavity is driven by the same air pressure, the soft robotic arm module will bend in plane. Fix it on a smooth horizontal plane with a fixture, and measure the bending angle of the single-cavity and double-cavity plane bending motion under different air pressures with a digital angle ruler.

Fig. 13. Experimental test chart of plane bending

Figure 14(a) and (b) show the comparison of experimental measurement results, simulation results and theoretical model results of bending angles driven by single cavity and double cavity with air pressure respectively. It can be seen that under the driving pressure of 0 ~ 80 kPa, the bending angles measured by single-cavity and double-cavity driving experiments are close to the theoretical model results and simulation results, and the errors are within the controllable range.

The soft robotic arm module is usually placed vertically when operating. From the simulation results and model results, it can be seen that gravity will have an impact on the bending deformation of the module at this time. On the test platform constructed as shown in Fig. 15, when the upper end face of the soft robotic arm module is fixed in the single-cavity drive or the double-cavity drive with the same air pressure, the soft robotic arm module will bend in a plane with the same deflection angle. The shown

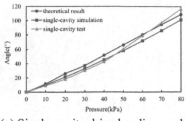
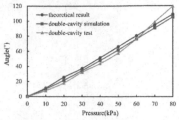

(a) Single-cavity drive bending angle   (b) Double-cavity drive bending angle

Fig. 14. Comparison chart of plane bending results

bending angle θ is measured with a digital display angle ruler, and the obtained results are averaged to reduce the error.

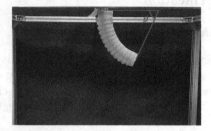

Fig. 15. Bending experiment test chart considering gravity

Figure 16(a) and (b) show the comparison between the measured experimental results, the simulation results and the theoretical model results. It can be seen from the figure that the bending angles of the plane bending motion of single-cavity and double-cavity driven by the same air pressure in the experiment are close to the theoretical model and the simulation results, but when the driving air pressure is greater than 60 kPa, the bending angles of the two modes all show a nonlinear increasing trend, which is slightly larger than the simulation and model results, and the errors are within the controllable range.

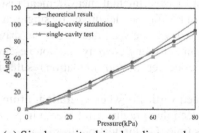
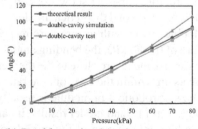

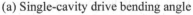

(a) Single-cavity drive bending angle   (b) Double-cavity drive bending angle

Fig. 16. Comparison diagram of plane bending results considering gravity

4.2 Experimental Verification of Elongation Model

As shown in Fig. 17, the length measurement experimental test platform uses the designed fixture to fix the upper end face, and the laser displacement sensor is placed under the soft robotic arm to measure the length change of the soft robotic arm module, and compares it with the simulation results and theoretical model results. As shown in Fig. 18, under the air pressure of 0 ~ 80 kPa, the experimental results show that the length of the soft robotic arm module varies between 0 ~ 35 mm. The greater the air pressure, the greater the length of the soft robotic arm module, and it is approximately linear, which is basically consistent with the results of simulation and model, and the error is within the controllable range.

Fig. 17. Elongation experimental test

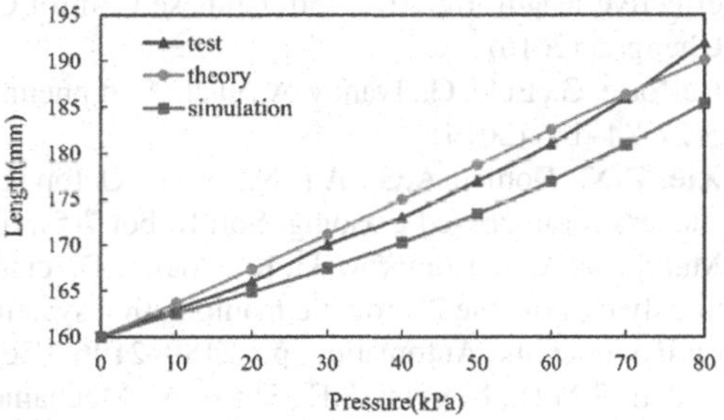

Fig. 18. Comparison of driving elongation results

5 Conclusion

In this paper, a pneumatic-driven soft robotic arm is designed, and the pneumatic-network structure is selected for the cavity. According to the assumption of constant curvature and the theory of large deformation beam, combined with the mechanical properties of materials described by Yeoh model, the bending model and elongation model of the soft robotic arm module are established. Aiming at the soft robotic arm used for grasping in gravity environment, the bending model is improved, and the bending model of single-module soft robotic arm considering gravity is obtained. An experimental platform is built to verify the accuracy of the bending model and elongation model of the software manipulator module, and the single-module of the soft robotic arm is analyzed experimentally. The experimental results show that when the inflation pressure is in the range of 0 ~ 80 kPa, the model results are close to the simulation results and experimental results. This paper lays the structural and theoretical foundation for the follow-up research, and shows that the soft robotic arm based on pneumatic-network structure has broad application prospects.

References

1. Tolley, M.T., Shepherd, R.F., Mosadegh, B., et al.: A resilient, untethered soft robot. Soft Rob. **1**(3), 213–223 (2014)

2. Gong, M., Li, X., Zhang, L.: Analytical inverse kinematics and self motion application for 7-DOF redundant manipulator. IEEE Access **7**, 18662–18674 (2019)
3. Marchese, A.D., Katzschmann, R.K., Rus, D.: A recipe for soft fluidic elastomer robots. Soft Robot **2**(1), 7–25 (2015)
4. Suulker, C., Slach, S., Althoefer, K.: Soft robotic fabric actuator with elastic bands for high force and bending performance in hand exoskeletons. IEEE Robo. Autom. Lett. **7**(4), 10621–10627 (2022)
5. Pillsbury, T.E., Guan, Q., Wereley, N.: Comparison of contractile and extensile pneumatic artificial muscles. In: 2016 IEEE International Conference on Advanced Intelligent Mechatronics (AIM), pp. 94–99. IEEE, Banff (2016)
6. Mosadegh, B., Polygerinos, P., Keplinger, C., et al.: Pneumatic networks for soft robotics that actuate rapidly. Adv. Funct. Mater. **24**(15), 2163–2170 (2014)
7. Hao, Y., Gong, Z., Xie, Z., et al.: Universal soft pneumatic robotic gripper with variable effective length. In: 2016 35th Chinese Control Conference (CCC), pp. 6109–6114. IEEE, Chengdu (2016)
8. Belforte, G., Eula, G., Ivanov, A., et al.: Soft pneumatic actuators for rehabilitation. Actuators **3**(2), 84–106 (2014)
9. Xie, Z.X., Domel, A.G., An, N., et al.: Octopus arm-inspired tapered soft actuators with suckers for improved grasping. Soft Robot **7**(5), 639 (2020)
10. Marchese, A.D., Komorowski, K., Onal, C.D., et al.: Design and control of a soft and continuously deformable 2D robotic manipulation system. In: 2014 IEEE International Conference on Robotics and Automation, pp. 2189–2196. IEEE, Hong Kong (2014)
11. Sadati, S.M.H., Naghibi, S.E., Shiva, A.: Mechanics of continuum manipulators, a comparative study of five methods with experiments. In: 2017 18th Annual Conference on Towards Autonomous Robotics (TAROS), pp. 686–702. TAROS, England (2017)
12. Renda, F., Giorelli, M., Calisti, M., et al.: Dynamic model of a multi-bending soft robot arm driven by cables. IEEE Trans. Rob. **30**(5), 1109–1122 (2014)
13. Fei, Y., Wang, J., Pang, W.: A novel fabric-based versatile and stiffness-tunable soft gripper integrating soft pneumatic fingers and wrist. Soft Rob. **6**(1), 1–20 (2019)
14. Giorelli, M., Renda, F., Ferri, G., et al.: A feed-forward neural network learning the inverse kinetics of a soft cable-driven manipulator moving in three-dimensional space. In: 2013 IEEE/RSJ International Conference on Intelligent Robots and Systems, pp. 5033–5039. IEEE, Tokyo (2013)
15. Tang, Y., Chi, Y., Sun, J., et al.: Leveraging elastic instabilities for amplified performance: Spine-inspired high-speed and high-force soft robots. Sci. Adv. **6**(19), 1–12 (2020)
16. Rus, D., Tolley, M.T.: Design, fabrication and control of soft robots. Nature **521**(7553), 467–475 (2015)

Integrated DLP and DIW 3D Printer for Flexible Electronics

Qinghua Yu⬥, Zixiao Zhu⬥, Xiru Fan⬥, and Dong Wang(✉)⬥

Institute of Robotics, School of Mechanical Engineering, Shanghai Jiao Tong University, Shanghai 200240, China
wang_dong@sjtu.edu.cn

Abstract. 3D printing is an efficient way to fabricate flexible electronics due to its ability to fabricate complex soft structures. However, the development of 3D printing flexible electronics is hindered by the development of multi-material 3D printing system that can integrate digital light processing and direct ink writing printing technologies. In this work, we develop an integrated DLP and DIW 3D printer that can fabricate multimaterial flexible electronics automatically. Complex matrix structures can be fabricated using bottom-up DLP printing, while the conductive electronics can be directly written on the matrix using DIW printing. Flexible electronics strain sensors and a multi-material soft pneumatic actuator are successfully printed. This work paves the way to fabricate flexible electronics automatically.

Keywords: Flexible Electronics · 3D Printing · Integrated Fabrication

1 Introduction

Flexible electronics [1, 2] consisting of soft matrix and conductive electronics show promising applications in areas such as stretchable electronics [3, 4], medical monitoring, diagnosis, and treatment [5–7], and soft robotics [8, 9] due to its great flexibility and ductility [3]. As traditional manufacturing methods cannot meet their manufacturing requirements [10, 11], 3D printing [12] have gained increasing attention due to its ability to fabricate complex soft structures [13] and print flexible circuit boards with special functions.

However, 3D printing flexible electronics often requires the combination of multiple additive manufacturing technologies [14], which significantly increases the complexity and costs. The development of 3D printing flexible electronics is hindered by the development of multi-material 3D printing system that can integrate digital light processing and direct ink writing printing technologies.

In this work, we develop an integrated DLP and DIW 3D printer that can fabricate multimaterial flexible electronics automatically. Complex matrix structures can be fabricated using bottom-up DLP printing, while the conductive electronics can be directly written on the matrix. A flexible electronics with embedded conductive wires and a multi-material soft pneumatic actuator is printed by the integrated printer, showing promising application in soft robotics. This work paves the way to fabricate flexible electronics automatically.

H. Yang et al. (Eds.): ICIRA 2023, LNAI 14270, pp. 45–52, 2023.
https://doi.org/10.1007/978-981-99-6492-5_5

2 Equipment Setup

2.1 DLP

Figure 1(a) shows the principle of bottom-up DLP 3D printing. We develop a DLP printing system composed of a UV projector (Wintech 4710, including a 405 nm UV-light source and a DMD module), a beam splitter, a resin tank with a transparent glass window coated with PDMS membrane, and a linear translation stage. The resolution of the projector is 1920 pixels × 1080 pixels. Compared to top-down DLP 3D printing, bottom-up DLP 3D printing has the advantage of printing more precise and complex models since it is not affected by liquid level fluctuations and splashes, thus the beam position is more stable, and is exempted from liquid level correction.

2.2 DIW

The setup of the DIW 3D printer is described below. We use three stepper motors and three screw slides to control the x, y and z direction motions, respectively. An Arduino microcontroller is used as an electronics platform and the upper computer interface was written in Python.

DIW's ink is transferred to a syringe barrel (Nordson EFD) and extruded by a precision fluid dispenser (Nordson EFD). The signal for extrusion is written in G-code to control the dispenser through an electromagnetic relay. Figure 1(b) shows the schematic of the developed DIW 3D printer.

2.3 Integrated DLP and DIW

Figure 1(c) shows the structure of the developed integrated printer, and Fig. 1(d) shows the process of integrated 3D printing. As shown in Fig. 1(d), the transition between the DLP and DIW 3D printing is operated by a rotation servo. As a bottom-up DLP 3D printing technology is used, after the DLP 3D printing the printing stage should rotate by 180° to facilitate the DIW 3D printing and vice versa. We add an air knife next to the DIW syringe barrel to blow away the residual resin before DIW printing.

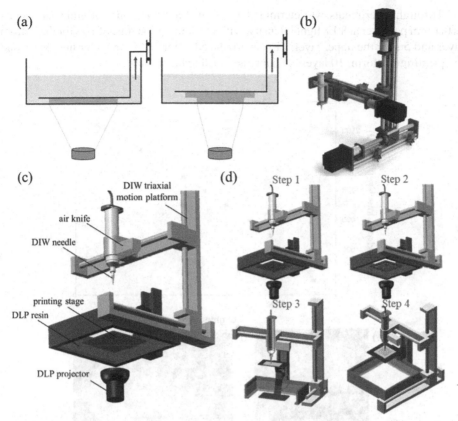

Fig. 1. Schematics of the integrated printer. (a) The principle of bottom-up DLP 3D printing. (b) The DIW system. (c) The integrated DLP and DIW 3D printing platform. (d) Printing process of the integrated printer.

3 Printing Parameters Characterization

3.1 DLP

The hybrid resin (hereinafter referred to as TEEA) is prepared by adding epoxy aliphatic acrylate (EAA) to the commercial UV-curable resin Tango. The weight ratio of Tango and EAA in the TEAA resin is 6:4. Before printing, the CAD model is sliced into images with desired layer thickness.

We measured the light intensity on the focal plane of the DLP projector under different led brightness levels by a UV light irradiation meter (Fig. 2(a)). The maximum irradiation intensity is around 2700 μW/cm^2.

The resin is cured under UV light irradiation. The accumulated light dose of the resin during a single exposure should be fine-tuned to avoid over-cure and under-cure [15]. If the light intensity is too strong, it will cause over-cure, resulting in warping or edge curling of the printed piece. When the light intensity is too weak, under-cure will occur and the printed part may fall into the tank causing printing failure.

Through experiments, we determined the optimal combination of printing parameters as 0.1 mm per layer at 80% light intensity, with an illumination time of 10 s for the bottom layer and 5 s for the upper layers. To ensure the adhesion between the printed piece and the printing platform, 10 layers of substrate need to be printed.

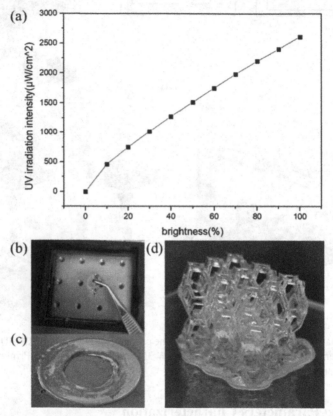

Fig. 2. (a) Dependence of the UV irradiation intensity on led brightness level. (b)The printed entity falls into the liquid tank when under-cure occurred. (c) Printing entity shape escapes when over-cure occurred. (d) Printed structure with high precision.

3.2 DIW

The key printing parameters in DIW 3D printing are the applied pressure and moving velocity [16]. First, we test a material which is a mixture of 24 wt.% Ecoflex 00–30 (Smooth-on inc.) part A/B, 12 wt.% SE1700 (Dow Corining Corp.), 1.2 wt.% SE1700 curing agent and 62.8 wt.% conductive Fe_3O_4 powder. The part A/B were prepared in equal mass. Straight lines are printed with different combinations of applied pressure and the moving velocities of the needle, as shown in Fig. 3(a). 300 and 250 kPa pressure is applied, while the moving velocities of the needle vary from 500 to 800 mm/min, with an interval of 100. We can observe that under higher pressure and lower moving velocity, the extruded ink is more curved, which validates that those two parameters have a vital influence on the fabrication quality.

The optimal combination of the applied pressure and the moving velocity of the needle is 160 kPa and 600 mm/min. Figure 3(b) shows that DIW ink is extruded into straight lines with the optimal combination of parameters, which facilitates as-design structures fabrication and is necessary for integrated printing.

Then we tested another material which is a mixture of 60 wt.% Ecoflex 00–30 part A/B, 30 wt.% SE1700 (Dow Corining Corp.), 3 wt.% SE1700 curing agent, 5 wt.% fumed silica nano and 2 wt.% red pigment. The optimal printing parameters combination, which is defined following the same procedure, is 120 kPa and 600 mm/min. Figure 3(c) shows the printed structures. An 'SJTU' pattern with 2 layers and geometric structures including a cube with 20 layers, a 4-layer square and a 4-layer circle were printed. These printed structures validate that DIW can print both flat and stereoscopic structures under appropriate parameters.

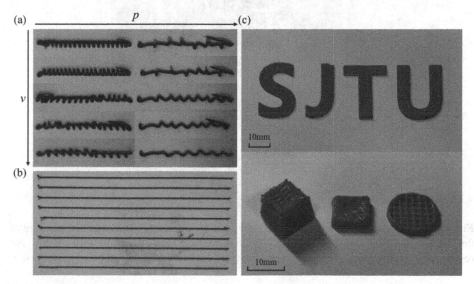

Fig. 3. Structures printed by DIW. (a) Straight lines printed with different pressure and velocity. (b) Straight lines printed with appropriate parameters. (c) A 2-layer 'SJTU' pattern and geometric structures including a 20-layer cube, a 4-layer square, and a 4-layer circle printed by DIW.

4 Flexible Electronics

We then use the DLP and DIW integrated 3D printer to fabricate flexible electronics. The objective structure of the flexible electronics is shown in Fig. 4(a). The conductive wires are embedded inside the soft matrix. Conventional 3D printing method requires the fabrication of half the soft matrix first. The matrix is then peeled away and the conductive wires are directly written on the matrix, followed by encapsulation using the matrix materials.

Using the DLP and DIW integrated 3D printer, the soft matrix is printed by DLP 3D printing and the conductive wires are written by DIW 3D printing using conductive ink. Thus, the flexible electronics can be fabricated automatically. Figure 4(b) shows the printed flexible electronics structures with various sizes. Energizing the printed flexible electronics validates the developed integrated 3D printer (Fig. 4(c)).

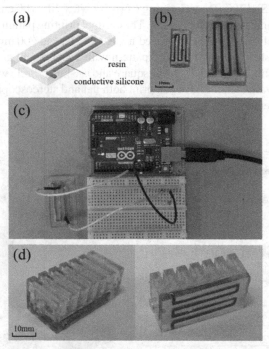

Fig. 4. Flexible electronics printed by the integrated 3D printer. (a) The objective structure of flexible electronic devices. (b) Two flexible electronic devices with a size of 10×20 and 20×40, respectively. (c) Energized flexible electronic devices. (d) Multimaterial soft pneumatic actuator.

Through testing with the LCR machine, we have validated the sensitivity and reliability of the strain resistance changes in multi-material flexible electronic devices which can serve as strain sensors. This provides strong support and evidence for their application. Further research and development will promote the application and innovation of multi-material flexible strain sensors, bringing more possibilities for future smart materials and flexible electronic devices.

Building on the foundation of multi-material flexible strain sensors, we have fabricated a multimaterial soft pneumatic actuator by incorporating a bendable structure with the multimaterial flexible strain sensor, as shown in Fig. 4(d). When the air chambers are inflated with a syringe, the actuator will bend and the sensor will conduct. Conversely, if the syringe is used to extract air from the air chambers, the actuator will bend in the opposite direction and the sensor will stretch. This bending and reverse bending mechanism controlled by the air chambers enables multi-material flexible actuators to have controllable deformation characteristics. The strain sensor is capable of measuring tensile strain and bending angle of the actuator by mapping the relation between strain/bending angle and resistance change. This provides broad prospects for their application in fields such as programmable robots, flexible manipulators, and artificial muscles.

5 Conclusions

In this work, we develop an integrated DLP and DIW 3D printer that can fabricate multi-material flexible electronics automatically. Complex matrix structures can be fabricated using bottom-up DLP printing, while the conductive electronics can be directly written on the matrix. Flexible electronics with embedded conductive wires are 3D printed, which show high conductivity, and changing resistance while stretching. The printed multimaterial flexible electronics devices show a promising application as a soft sensor. This work paves the way to fabricate flexible electronics automatically.

References

1. Peng, X., et al.: Integrating digital light processing with direct ink writing for hybrid 3D printing of functional structures and devices. Addit. Manuf. **40**, 101911 (2021). https://doi.org/10.1016/j.addma.2021.101911
2. Li, Z., et al.: Hydrogel-elastomer-based stretchable strain sensor fabricated by a simple projection lithography method. Int. J. Smart Nano Mater. **12**(3), 256–268 (2021)
3. Ge, Q., et al.: 3D printing of highly stretchable hydrogel with diverse UV curable polymers. Sci. Adv. **7**(2), eaba4261 (2021). https://doi.org/10.1126/sciadv.aba4261
4. González-Henríquez, C.M., Sarabia-Vallejos, M.A., Rodriguez-Hernandez, J.: Polymers for additive manufacturing and 4D-printing: materials, methodologies, and biomedical applications. Prog. Polym. Sci. **94**, 57–116 (2019)
5. Pettersson, A.B.V., et al.: Main clinical use of additive manufacturing (three-dimensional printing) in Finland restricted to the head and neck area in 2016–2017. Scand. J. Surg. **109**(2), 166–173 (2020)
6. Xu, Y., et al.: In-situ transfer vat photopolymerization for transparent microfluidic device fabrication. Nat. Commun. **13**(1), 918 (2022)
7. Zheng, B., et al.: Direct freeform laser fabrication of 3d conformable electronics. Adv. Funct. Materials **33**(1), 2210084 (2022). https://doi.org/10.1002/adfm.202210084
8. Mishra, A.K., et al.: Autonomic perspiration in 3D-printed hydrogel actuators. Sci. Robot. **5**(38), eaaz3918 (2020). https://doi.org/10.1126/scirobotics.aaz3918
9. Truby, R.L., et al.: Fluidic innervation sensorizes structures from a single build material. Sci. Adv. **8**(32), eabq4385 (2022). https://doi.org/10.1126/sciadv.abq4385
10. Yan, J., et al.: Direct-ink writing 3D printed energy storage devices: from material selectivity, design and optimization strategies to diverse applications. Mater. Today **54**, 110–152 (2022)
11. Cheng, M., Deivanayagam, R., Shahbazian-Yassar, R.: 3D printing of electrochemical energy storage devices: a review of printing techniques and electrode/electrolyte architectures. Batteries Supercaps **3**(2), 130–146 (2020)
12. Rayna, T., Striukova, L.: From rapid prototyping to home fabrication: how 3D printing is changing business model innovation. Technol. Forecast. Soc. Chang. **102**, 214–224 (2016)

13. Urrios, A., et al.: 3D-printing of transparent bio-microfluidic devices in PEG-DA. Lab Chip **16**(12), 2287–2294 (2016)
14. Zhang, Y.-F., et al.: Fractal-based stretchable circuits via electric-field-driven microscale 3D printing for localized heating of shape memory polymers in 4D printing. ACS Appl. Mater. Interfaces **13**(35), 41414–41423 (2021)
15. Choi, J.W., et al.: Sequential process optimization for a digital light processing system to minimize trial and error. Sci. Rep. **12**(1), 13553 (2022)
16. Hmeidat, N.S., et al.: Mechanical anisotropy in polymer composites produced by material extrusion additive manufacturing. Addit. Manuf. **34**, 101385 (2020). https://doi.org/10.1016/j.addma.2020.101385

Bi-Directional Deformation, Stiffness-Tunable, and Electrically Controlled Soft Actuators Based on LCEs 4D Printing

Wanglin Qiu[1], Yaohui Wang[1], Xiangnan He[2], Qi Ge[2], and Yi Xiong[1](✉)

[1] School of System Design and Intelligent Manufacturing, Southern University of Science and Technology, Shenzhen 518055, China
xiongy3@sustech.edu.cn

[2] Department of Mechanical and Energy Engineering, Southern University of Science and Technology, Shenzhen, People's Republic of China

Abstract. The integration of 3D printing with smart materials in 4D printing technology has attracted extensive research attention due to its capability of endowing static printed structures with dynamic behaviors and actions that evolve over time. One such promising smart material is liquid crystal elastomers (LCEs), which offer excellent reversible actuation performance and programmable anisotropy. However, the field of LCEs-based 4D printing faces challenges in achieving sufficient mechanical performance due to their low elastic modulus, which hinders their ability to handle tasks requiring relatively high load-bearing capacity. Moreover, there are also challenges related to their complex actuation environments, which further restrict the applications based on LCEs. In this work, we propose a paradigm for designing and manufacturing electrically-controlled soft actuators capable of reversible deformation and adjustable stiffness. Specifically, we integrate LCEs with continuous fiber-reinforced polymer composites (CFRP) and elastomeric materials into a multilayer sandwich structure. By combining CFRP, we significantly enhance the stiffness of the actuators without compromising their flexibility and adaptability. Furthermore, the inclusion of continuous carbon fibers (CCF) enables electrical control of the actuators. Finally, by incorporating pre-stretched elastomeric materials, we fabricate an electrically-controlled actuator with excellent mechanical performance and reversible actuation capabilities. As a demonstration, we create an intelligent soft gripper with outstanding mechanical performance and reversible actuation, exhibiting high load-bearing capacity and shape adaptability.

Keywords: 4D printing · Liquid crystal elastomers · Intelligent soft gripper

1 Introduction

In recent years, 4D printing has emerged as a cutting-edge manufacturing technology and has garnered significant research interest. This technology combines additive manufacturing (AM) techniques [1, 2] with smart materials, enabling printed structures

© The Author(s), under exclusive license to Springer Nature Singapore Pte Ltd. 2023
H. Yang et al. (Eds.): ICIRA 2023, LNAI 14270, pp. 53–62, 2023.
https://doi.org/10.1007/978-981-99-6492-5_6

to undergo specific morphological and property transformations in response to corresponding stimuli [3, 4]. This highly efficient design strategy offers immense design freedom and provides new avenues and means for the rapid fabrication of integrated smart devices. It has a wide range of applications, including active metamaterials, soft robotics, configurable optics, smart textiles, and bioengineering applications [5–8].

However, in the current stage, 4D printing typically requires manual programming of the printed structures, but excessive human intervention hinders the consistency of the driving process. Moreover, 4D printing usually achieves only one-way deformation, limiting its application prospects in scenarios that require repeated actions. To address these limitations, researchers have introduced a promising smart material, liquid crystal elastomers (LCEs), into the field of 4D printing [9–11]. This material exhibits significant actuation, reversible driving capabilities, and programmable anisotropic properties. However, challenges arise due to the low stiffness of LCEs and the complexity of the actuation environment, making it difficult for them to be applied in high-load conditions.

In this study, we propose a paradigm for designing and fabricating a reversible deformable and stiffness-tunable electronically controlled soft actuator. Specifically, we employ the direct ink writing (DIW) technique to fabricate layers of LCEs with uniaxial and uniformly reversible stretching capability. Additionally, we utilize the continuous fiber co-extrusion technique to fabricate a continuous fiber-reinforced polymer composite (CFRP) with a polylactic acid (PLA) matrix and continuous carbon fibers (CCF) reinforcement. The integration of CFRP not only significantly enhances the stiffness of the actuator but also provides an electrical pathway for actuation through CCF, which generates substantial Joule heating under voltage. Furthermore, we design the actuation forces of the pre-stretched LCEs layer and the pre-stretched elastomer layer to achieve the intended actuation within specific temperature ranges. When the temperature of the actuator rises above the glass transition temperature (T_g) of PLA, the overall stiffness of the actuator decreases. Moreover, the actuation force of LCEs is lower than that of the elastomer layer, resulting in bending towards the elastomer layer. Conversely, when the temperature exceeds the isotropic-to-anisotropic transition temperature (T_{NI}), the actuation force of LCEs surpasses that of the elastic layer, causing bending towards the LCEs layer. Ultimately, we utilize this actuator to fabricate an electronically controlled intelligent soft gripper with excellent load-bearing performance and high shape adaptability.

2 Methods and Materials

2.1 Materials

All chemicals and solvents were purchased from commercial supplies and used without further purification. The commercially available n-butylamine and the Irgacure 651 photoinitiator (Hewons Co Ltd., China) and photopolymerizable monomer 1,4-bis-[4-(6-acryloyloxhexyloxy)benzoyloxy]-2-methylbenzene (RM82, Hecheng Display Co Ltd., China) were used in the study.

2.2   Synthesis of LCE Ink

RM82 was heated and melted in a brown glass bottle and n-butylamine (1:1 mol ratio to RM82) mixed with 2 wt.% I-651 photoinitiator was added under vortex oscillation at 85 °C to obtain a uniform solution. The oligomer precursor was generated by performing the Michael addition reaction at 75 °C for 12 h.

2.3   Rheological Measurements

The rheological behavior of the polymer ink was analyzed using a rotational rheometer (HAAKE MARS 40, Germany) with a parallel plate geometry (diameter 25 mm, gap 1 mm) at temperatures of 25 °C, 45 °C, 65 °C, 85 °C, and 120 °C. Prior to testing, the LCE ink was thermally equilibrated at 120 °C for 5 min.

2.4   TGA Measurements

Thermal stability of the samples was evaluated through thermogravimetric analysis (TGA) using a thermal gravimetric analyzer (Netzsch TGA 209F1, Germany). The samples were subjected to heating from 30 to 600 °C at a heating rate of 10 °C/min under a nitrogen atmosphere.

2.5   Polarized Optical Microscope (POM) Photography

The alignment of the liquid crystal polymer was observed using polarized optical microscopy (POM) (Leica DM2700M, Germany) with crossed polarizers.

2.6   DSC Measurements

The differential scanning calorimetry (DSC) test was conducted on a differential scanning calorimeter (Netzsch DSC 214, Germany). Samples were heated from −60 to 150 °C to erase thermal history and then cycled between 150 and 60 °C at 10 °C/min.

2.7   DMA Measurements

Dynamic mechanical analysis (DMA) was conducted using a constant strain mode on a DMA tester (Netzsch DMA 242E, Germany). Elastomer samples (5 mm × 3 mm × 1 mm) were stretched to a length of 12 mm, and the actuation force was measured during the temperature ramp from 30 °C to 140 °C at a rate of 10 K/min. Similarly, LCEs samples (5 mm × 3 mm × 1 mm) were stretched to a length of 6 mm, and the actuation force was measured during the same temperature ramp.

3   Results and Discussion

3.1   Printing Process of LCEs Based on DIW Technique

In this study, we utilized an in-house developed direct ink writing (DIW) device for printing LCEs. As shown in Fig. 1a, the polymer ink was loaded into a steel barrel and the temperature was set to 100 °C. A stabilization period of 0.5 h was implemented to ensure a steady state before initiating the printing process. The LCE ink prepared from Fig. 1b was extruded through a 0.9 mm diameter nozzle under a pressure of 50 psi. The nozzle moved in a specific direction to deposit the LCE ink onto the printing platform. The printing system was controlled by a LabView program, and the printing path was generated using G-code produced by MATLAB software. Throughout the printing process, real-time crosslinking of the LCE ink was achieved by employing an ultraviolet light emitting diode (UV-LED) with an intensity of 0.8 mW/cm^2. The ink material was gradually layered following the printing path to complete the fabrication of the LCE samples. Subsequently, the samples were exposed to 365 nm UV light with an intensity of 20 mW/cm^2 for 0.5 h on each side to ensure uniform crosslinking.

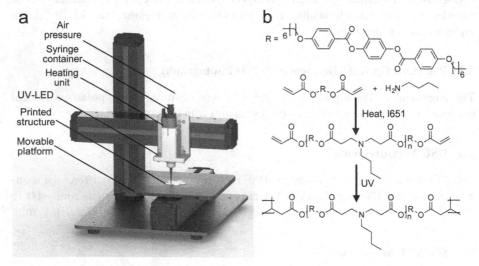

Fig. 1.   (a) The rendered image of the DIW printing equipment. (b) Synthesis of the LCEs.

3.2   Programming Mechanism of LCEs

LCEs possess remarkable programmable anisotropic properties, as depicted in Fig. 2a, illustrating the anisotropic programming mechanism. LCE ink has a high viscosity at room temperature (25 °C), so it requires preheating treatment. From Fig. 2b, it can be observed that the ink reaches a suitable viscosity for the DIW process and exhibits shear-thinning behavior at 45 °C. Additionally, to prevent material thermal decomposition, we experimentally determined the upper limit temperature for heating the ink to be

286 °C (Fig. 2c). The heated LCE ink is extruded onto the printing platform under the influence of air pressure. The shear force of the nozzle and the drawing force generated by the movement of the nozzle along the printing direction is utilized to control the orientation of the mesogens, achieving the anisotropy of the LCEs. Real-time UV light crosslinking helps to maintain the orientation of the mesogenic units. After printing, the LCEs structures are placed in a UV curing chamber for further crosslinking to ensure a complete ink reaction. The crosslinked LCEs samples can achieve reversible actuation under thermal stimulation, and T_{NI} is determined to be 102.5 °C from Fig. 2d.

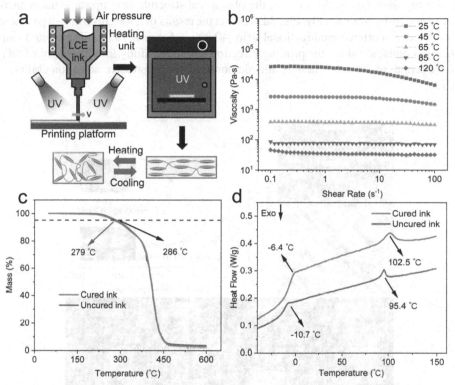

Fig. 2. (a) Schematic illustration of the printing process. (b) Log-log plots of the LC oligomer viscosity as a function of shear rate at different temperatures. (c) Thermogravimetric analysis of the LCE cured ink and the LCE uncured ink as a function of temperature, 5% weight loss at 279 °C and 286 °C, respectively. (d) DSC curve of the LCE cured ink and the LCE uncured ink.

3.3 Actuation Performance of LCEs

The actuation performance of LCEs is directly related to the orientation of their internal LCE mesogens. The alignment direction determines the direction of actuation and a higher degree of alignment results in a greater actuation capability. In this study, we fabricated a single-layer LCE film (20 mm × 15 mm × 0.1 mm) using a 0.9 mm nozzle diameter and a printing speed of 120 mm/min. The orientation of LCE mesogens was examined using a polarized optical microscope (POM). The obtained results, as shown in Fig. 3a-b, clearly demonstrated the molecular orientation-induced birefringence along the controlled printing paths. When observed parallel and at a 45° angle to the polarizer, the uniaxially printed LCE film exhibited dark and bright colors, respectively, indicating a satisfactory orientation of the LCE material.

Furthermore, as observed in Fig. 3c, it is evident that increasing the printing speed results in improved actuation performance. We designed a multilayered planar leaf structure with a printing speed of 60 mm/min for the bottom three layers and 120 mm/min for the top three layers. As a result, the planar leaf structure bent upwards under thermal stimulation. Additionally, Fig. 3d presents the results of a weight-lifting experiment conducted on a printed unidirectional strip (40 mm × 5 mm × 1 mm). The printed strip (0.27 g) contracted along the printing direction and successfully lifted a weight of 88 g over a length of 30 mm. These results demonstrate the impressive actuation ability of LCEs.

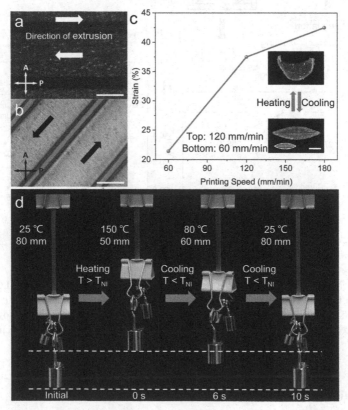

Fig. 3. (a) Polarized optical microscope images of the printed sample at 0° (dark) to the polarizer. Scale bar: 500 μm. (b) Polarized optical microscope images of the printed sample at 45° (bright) to the polarizer. Scale bar: 500 μm. (c) Reversible bending leaf structure and helical structure. Scale bar: 10 mm. (d) Photograph showing weight-lifting of a printed unidirectional strip.

3.4 Fabrication of LCEs-CFRP Actuators

CFRP is fabricated through a continuous fiber co-extrusion process, as depicted in Fig. 4a. Under the effect of a heater and motors, CCF and thermoplastic resin PLA are fed into the same melt pool and co-extruded onto the printing platform. As illustrated in Fig. 4b, CFRP is bonded to LCEs and pre-stretched elastic material using adhesive, enabling the fabrication of LCEs-CFRP actuators. It is worth noting that the electrical resistance of continuous carbon fibers, as shown in Fig. 4c, is directly proportional to their length, with a resistivity of 2.97×10^{-5} $\Omega \cdot m$. Therefore, by designing the length of the printing path, we can achieve the desired resistance value. The CFRP generates Joule heating under applied voltage, serving as an electrical heat source for the actuator. As indicated in Fig. 4d, the T_g temperature of the CFRP material is approximately 65 °C. When the temperature exceeds T_g, the storage modulus of CFRP significantly decreases. Hence, we can control the stiffness of the actuator by manipulating the temperature. Additionally, as depicted in Fig. 4e, we conducted tests to examine the relationship between the actuation force generated by LCEs and the elastomer under pre-stretched conditions with the temperature. From the results, it can be observed that as the temperature increases, the actuation force of LCEs gradually increases from 60 °C, while the actuation force of the elastic material remains largely unaffected by temperature. Notably, the actuation force of the pre-stretched elastic material is approximately 0.2 N, whereas the initial actuation force of LCEs is 0.43 N, reaching 1.1 N at 140 °C. Therefore, by designing the number of pre-stretched elastomer layers, we can determine the actuation direction of the LCEs-CFRP actuator. In this study, three pre-stretched elastic layers were used as the driving layer. Consequently, in the initial state, the actuation force of the elastomer layers exceeds that of the LCEs layer. However, as the temperature increases, the two forces gradually approach each other, with the actuation force of LCEs eventually surpassing that of the elastomer layers. As illustrated in Fig. 4f, CCF with a resistance value of 110 Ω was selected, and temperature regulation of the actuator was achieved by adjusting the applied voltage, thereby controlling the actuation direction of the actuator.

3.5 Electrically Controlled Intelligent Soft Gripper

Based on the developed actuator, we fabricated an electrically controlled intelligent gripper, as illustrated in Fig. 5a. In its initial state, no bending occurs. When a voltage of 14 V is applied, the temperature of the actuator exceeds T_g, causing a rapid decrease in the modulus of CFRP. At this point, the actuation force of LCEs is lower than that of the pre-stretched elastic material, causing the sample to bend toward the direction of the elastic material. Upon discontinuing the voltage input, the temperature quickly drops below T_g, and the increased stiffness of CFRP enables the structure to maintain its shape. The excellent mechanical performance of the actuator allows for effective grasping and load-bearing capabilities. When a voltage of 20 V is applied, the temperature rises above T_{NI}, and the actuation force of LCEs surpasses that of the elastic material, causing the sample to bend in the direction of LCEs. Upon power interruption, the sample slowly returns to a vertical state. However, as this process takes some time, by the time it reaches a near-vertical state, the temperature has already dropped below T_g, thus fixing its shape. The image in Fig. 5b verifies the feasibility of using this actuator to fabricate a

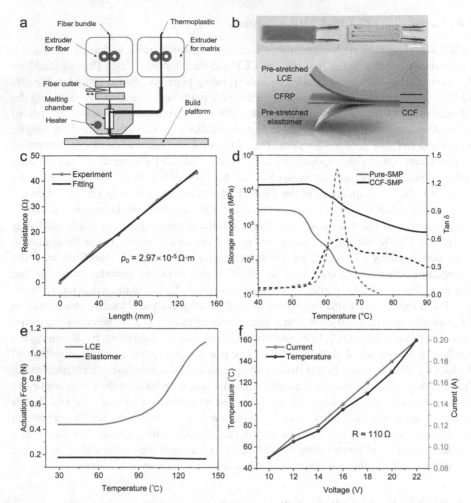

Fig. 4. (a) Schematic illustration of CFRP fabrication process. (b) Schematic illustration of LCE-CFRP actuator fabrication. Scale bar: 10 mm. (c) Correspondence between CCF length and resistance. (d) Storage modulus and loss tangent curves of pure SMP and CFRP with temperature variation. (e) Relationship between elastomer and LCEs actuation force with temperature variation. (f) Relationship between actuator temperature and applied voltage.

intelligent gripper. Figure 5c demonstrates the gripping process of the gripper, illustrating its ability to not only bear weight (more than 100 times) but also adapt to and lift objects with complex shapes.

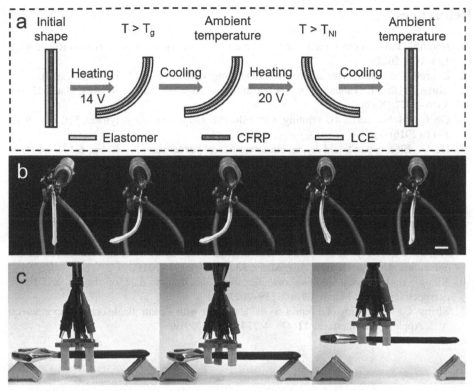

Fig. 5. (a) Schematic illustration of the actuator operation. (b) Photograph of the actuator in operation. Scale bar: 10 mm. (c) Photograph of the gripping process.

4 Conclusions

In this study, we successfully developed a highly load-bearing and shape-adaptive soft gripper with adjustable stiffness through electrical control. The incorporation of CFRP in the actuator provided the actuator with electrical control and tunable stiffness capabilities. The CCF in CFRP exhibited a linear relationship between length and resistance, enabling rapid heating under voltage application. This facilitated the heating of the PLA matrix, which is a typical thermoplastic material known for its adjustable stiffness under thermal influence. Moreover, the pre-stretched elastic material and LCEs enabled reversible bidirectional actuation of the gripper. The proposed approach opens up new avenues and prospects for the advancement of soft actuators based on LCEs.

Funding. This work is supported by the National Natural Science Foundation of China [No. 52105261], the Guangdong Basic and Applied Basic Research Foundation [No. 2022A1515010316], and the Shenzhen Science and Technology Program [No. JCYJ20210324104610028].

References

1. Boothby, J.M.: An untethered soft robot based on liquid crystal elastomers. Soft Robot. **9**(1), 154–162 (2022)
2. Bourell, D.: Materials for additive manufacturing. CIRP Ann. **66**(2), 659–681 (2017)
3. Christian Ohm, B.: Liquid crystalline elastomers as actuators and sensors. Adv. Mater. **22**(31), 3366–3387 (2010)
4. Ge, Q.: Multimaterial 4D printing with tailorable shape memory polymers. Sci. Rep. **6**(1), 1–11 (2016)
5. He, Q.: Electrospun liquid crystal elastomer microfiber actuator. Sci. Robot. **6**(57), eabi9704 (2021). https://doi.org/10.1126/scirobotics.abi9704
6. Li, Z.: Smart-fabric-based supercapacitor with long-term durability and waterproof properties toward wearable applications. ACS Appl. Mater. Interfaces. **13**(12), 14778–14785 (2021)
7. Sydney Gladman, A.: Biomimetic 4D printing. Nat. Mater. **15**(4), 413–418 (2016)
8. Thomsen, D.L.: Liquid crystal elastomers with mechanical properties of a muscle. Macromolecules **34**(17), 5868–5875 (2001)
9. Wu, J.: Liquid crystal elastomer metamaterials with giant biaxial thermal shrinkage for enhancing skin regeneration. Adv. Mater. **33**(45), 2106175 (2021)
10. Xiong, Y.: Intelligent additive manufacturing and design: state of the art and future perspectives. Addit. Manuf. **59**, 103139 (2022)
11. Zhang, C.: 4D printing of a liquid crystal elastomer with a controllable orientation gradient. ACS Appl. Mater. Interfaces **11**(47), 44774–44782 (2019)

Multi-material Integrated Printing of Reprogrammable Magnetically Actuated Soft Structure

Youchao Zhang[1], Huangyu Chen[1], Siqi Qiu[2], Yuan-Fang Zhang[2(✉)], and Xiaoyang Zhu[1(✉)]

[1] Shandong Engineering Research Center for Additive Manufacturing, Qingdao University of Technology, Qingdao, China
zhuxiaoyang@qtech.edu.cn
[2] Shien-Ming Wu School of Intelligent Engineering, South China University of Technology, Guangzhou, China
zhangyuanfang@scut.edu.cn

Abstract. The magnetically actuated soft structure has the unique advantages of remote actuation, free deformation, programmability, and high energy efficiency. The existing magnetically actuated soft structure has a single function, limited application scenarios, and poor flexibility. At the same time, the magnetically actuated performance is limited by the materials used during structure design and model preparation. In this paper, we propose an integrated process for manufacturing multi-material reconfigurable magnetically actuated soft structures that can program and reconfigure the model actuation mode by reversing the magnetic pole direction through the synergistic effect of an external heat source and magnetic field and can achieve hundreds of times faster and more accurate reconfiguration. By regulating, arranging, and designing the reprogramming units, the integrated printed model has a high magnetic particle mass ratio of 80%, the highest reported. This process expands the application scenario of reconfigurable magnetically actuated soft structures, which have a wide range of applications in soft robotics, aerospace, medical devices, flexible electronics, and other scenarios.

Keywords: 3D printing · Magnetic actuate · Soft structure · Multi − material

1 Introduction

The concept of reconfigurability is proposed to greatly improve the adaptability and flexibility of the actuatable soft structure. At the same time, it can realize different forms and functions in different working states. The actuatable soft structure can be intelligent enough to achieve autonomous judgment and control and be able to respond to external stimuli. And change its own morphology and structure to adapt to specific needs, providing more possibilities and opportunities for the application of actuatable soft structures.

H. Yang et al. (Eds.): ICIRA 2023, LNAI 14270, pp. 63–70, 2023.
https://doi.org/10.1007/978-981-99-6492-5_7

One of the main factors that determine the performance of reconfigurable soft body structures is reprogrammable materials, and commonly used reprogrammable materials include shape memory alloys [1], electrically variable materials [2], reprogrammable polymers [3], etc. Among them, magnetic reprogrammable materials directly regulate the morphology and motion of the model through magnetic action, eliminating the limitations of space and volume. They also avoid the potential leakage of electric fields, which other reprogrammable materials may face, and they achieve a more stable control effect. There are only two ways to achieve reprogramming from the magnetic material itself: the first is to apply a stronger alternating transient magnetic field to twist the magnetic domains. This method requires a demanding magnetic field, and as the number of reprograms increases, the magnetic field strength also increases, ultimately limiting the number of reprograms. The second method is to achieve magnetic steering by rotating the magnetic particles themselves. The transition between the free and locked states of the magnetic material can be achieved by using a phase change substrate to cover the magnetic material, with the locked state applying an external magnetic field to actuate the model and the free state applying an external magnetic field to redirect the magnetic particle. Based on the above principles, Kuang et al. [4] reported a magnetic dynamic polymer composite allowing laser heating with mask assistance to achieve reprogramming; Zhao et al. [5] mixed liquid metal with NdFeB powder to achieve model reconfiguration by simple heating and simple grasping and handling under magnetic field control; and Deng et al. [6] used a phase change polymer encapsulated with elastomer and magnetic particles. However, the concentration of magnetic particles in magnetic reprogrammable materials at this stage is limited to a certain extent because magnetic particles are attracted to each other and agglomerate when magnetic fields are applied. The magnetic particles need to be uniformly dispersed in the material to ensure the uniformity of the structure of magnetism.

The common preparation processes for reconfigurable soft structures are die-casting or 3D printing. Zhao et al. [5] realized the design of reconfigurable soft structures by encapsulating the reprogrammable magnetic materials through die-casting; Deng et al. [6] prepared reconfigurable magnetically actuated soft films through molds and cut them into the desired geometry using a CO2 laser. Although die-casting has the advantages of high product quality, high volume production capacity, and low manufacturing cost, its long production cycle, design limitations, and difficulty in manufacturing complex structures make it less flexible than 3D printing in the design of reconfigurable soft structures. To meet the expected deformation and actuation, the structural design needs to be flexible and constantly modified to meet the needs and applications. That is the advantage of 3D printing. 3D-printed reconfigurable soft structures, on the other hand, are highly restricted by materials and have high requirements for the rheology of the printed material. In order to realize 3D-printed reconfigurable magnetic structures, there is an urgent need for a preparation process to achieve complex structure design and adapt a high concentration of reprogrammable magnetic materials.

In this work, we propose a multi-material integrated process for printing reconfigurable magnetically actuated soft structures, which combines 3D printing technology to prepare a substrate-wireframe structure and configure a unique material system using magnetic materials and phase change materials. In order to verify the feasibility of the process, a set of reconfigurable magnetically actuated soft structures was printed in an integrated manner, and precise reconfiguration was achieved. The process solves the problem of the limited concentration of magnetic particles in reprogrammable magnetic materials, realizes the requirement of 3D printing reconfigurable soft body structures, adapts the corresponding high concentration of reprogrammable magnetic materials, and provides a new idea for the design and preparation of reconfigurable magneto-driven structures.

2 Results and Discussion

In this work, we first used a dispersion lubricant to encapsulate the NdFeB magnetic particles. Polyvinylpyrrolidone (PVP) was chosen here as the dispersion lubricant because of its excellent biocompatibility and desirable dispersion lubrication effect. By covering the surface of NdFeB magnetic particles with a uniform layer of dispersion lubricant, the magnetic particles are isolated from each other. This avoids the agglomeration of magnetic particles generated during the reprogramming process and also facilitates the reorientation of magnetic particles in the phase change material for rapid reprogramming. The produced NdFeB@PVP material was homogeneously mixed with paraffin wax (a liquid phase change-prone material) at a mass ratio of 7 to 1 to obtain a highly concentrated reprogrammable magnetic material. The low surface tension of paraffin wax makes it difficult to maintain the consistency of the molding under the conditions of melt deposition. The low surface tension of the material makes it difficult to maintain its original shape in the molten state. To solve these problems, a multi-jet printing system is introduced, as shown in Fig. 1 (a). By printing the wireframe structure, the reprogrammable magnetic units are divided to effectively ensure the molding consistency and printing stability of reprogrammable magnetic materials. The dual-jet printing system adopts direct ink-writing (DIW) molding technology and fused deposition molding (FDM) technology to print elastomeric materials and reprogrammable magnetic materials, respectively. The shape profile of the model is first designed, and the reprogrammable area is planned and designed on the substrate. The substrate is prepared by printing pre-configured elastomeric materials using DIW printing technology, and the temperature of the print substrate is regulated to achieve direct-write shaping of the wireframe area. By precisely regulating the parameters during wireframe printing, a high consistency of wireframe molding is achieved, which in turn improves the consistency of reprogrammable magnetic units. After the wireframe is printed, multiple reprogrammable cell areas are created. The printhead is switched, and the reprogrammable magnetic material is printed evenly into the wireframe by FDM. After completing the printing and filling of the reprogrammable magnetic material, the printhead is switched to continue printing the elastomeric material using DIW to realize the encapsulation of the reprogrammable unit area. The specific preparation flow is shown in Fig. 1 (b). Due to the high concentration of the prepared magnetic material, the magnetization strength of the model obtained in this work reaches about 15 mT compared with the reconfigurable magneto-actuated soft structure in previous studies. At the same unit mass, the magnetic field strength of the actuated model is correspondingly reduced by about 80%, and the energy required for actuation and reconfiguration is also reduced.

The reconfiguration principle of magnetic materials is mainly based on the phase transition controlled by an external thermal source, which reprograms the magnetic material to shift between the free state and the locked state. The model reconfiguration is achieved by an external magnetic field in the free state, and the model actuation is achieved by an external magnetic field in the locked state. To facilitate the preparation and improve the consistency of printing, the reprogrammable magnetic material is prepared without magnetic properties, and its magnetic domain distribution is disordered and undirected. The resulting soft structure is then magnetized with a high-frequency, high-intensity alternating magnetic field in a magnetizer to magnetize the magnetic particles in the model. At this time, the overall magnetic orientation of the reprogrammable magnetic material in the model remains uniform. The model is fixed on the experimental bench, and a certain temperature is applied to a certain area to melt the reprogrammable material in that area. At this time, the magnetic material is converted from the locked state to the free state, and the magnetic material is reoriented under the action of the applied magnetic field. When the magnetic field is maintained, the temperature is lowered, the magnetic material in the model is again changed from the free state to the locked state, and the orientation of the magnetic domains in this region of the model is changed. At this point, the magnetic field is applied, and the model is actuated. By repeating the above steps, the reprogramming of the magnetism is achieved.

As shown in Fig. 1 (c), the magnetization of the 2×1 cells is completed by applying a high-intensity alternating magnetic field perpendicular to the plane upward. A magnetic field perpendicular to the plane upward is applied again, and the model is not deformed or actuated. At this point, the model is completely fixed on the experimental bench, and an external heat source is used to apply a certain temperature to the right-hand unit. The reprogrammable magnetic material inside the model is transformed from a solid to a liquid state and from a locked to a free state. At this time, a magnetic field parallel to the plane and pointing to the right is applied, and the magnetic domains of the magnetic material in the material are transformed and the magnetism in this region is reoriented. The magnetic field is maintained, the external heat source is removed, and the temperature of the region is continuously reduced. As the temperature of the model decreases, the reprogrammable magnetic material again changes from the free state to the locked state, and the magnetism of the right cell of the model is reoriented. The model is bent by the magnetic field, which is applied perpendicular to the plane and upward again. With the magnetic field removed, the model returns to its initial form. The model is restrained again, and a certain temperature group is applied to the right-side unit using an external heat source, which causes the reprogrammable magnetic material inside the model to change from the locked state to the free state. By applying a magnetic field perpendicular to the plane and pointing downward, the magnetic domains of the magnetic material in the material are transformed, and the magnetic orientation of the region is again changed. With the removal of the external heat source, the temperature of the model is continuously reduced, and the magnetic material therein is again transformed from the free state to the locked state. When the constraint is removed and a magnetic field perpendicular to the plane is applied, the model is bent and deformed by the actuation of the unit under the action of the magnetic field. This time, the model is bent and folded until it overlaps completely on the left side. This demonstrates the excellent reconfigurability of the reprogrammable magnetic soft structures.

Based on the above principle and combined with the high degree of freedom obtained by 3D printing, a set of models was designed and prepared at the same time, as shown in Fig. 2. Firstly, a hollow cross structure, a hollow square lattice, and a simple lattice structure were designed as shown in Fig. 2 (a–c). Under the magnetic field of 100 mT, different spatial structural transformations were accomplished by continuously reconfiguring to achieve different magnetic arrangements. The hollow cross structure formed the spatial transformations of book pages (Fig. 2 a1), convex tables (Fig. 2 a2), and butterflies (Fig. 2 a3) under different magnetic arrangements, respectively. The hollow square lattice structure formed spatial transformations of beam type (Fig. 2 b1), fence type (Fig. 2 b2), and dish type (Fig. 2 b3) under different magnetic arrangements. The hollow grid structure formed wave-like (Fig. 2 c1), arch-bridge-like (Fig. 2 c2), and trench-like (Fig. 2 c3) spatial transformations under different magnetic arrangements, respectively. The above results demonstrate that the model prepared by this process has ideal reconfigurability and achieves equivalent actuation with a small field strength and a high magnetic particle mass ratio.

3   Material and Preparation

Reconfigurable magnetic soft structure preparation processes. We first spin-coat a layer of sacrificial substrate material on the surface of standard float glass and use it after curing to facilitate the subsequent demolding process after printing is completed. A multi-jet 3D printing device was developed and used to achieve integrated printing. Using DIW printing technology, the elastomer substrate and the elastomer wireframe are printed at a certain substrate temperature by adjusting the appropriate parameters to achieve the regionalization of the model. After the substrate model and wireframe are cured, the pre-configured reprogrammable magnetic material is filled into the wireframe reserved for each area of the model through FDM to realize the filling of the reprogrammable magnetic material. After the temperature drops below the melting point of paraffin wax, the model is encapsulated by adjusting the appropriate parameters and using direct write into type (DIW) 3D printing technology at a certain ambient temperature. After the encapsulation is completed, the model is kept at a certain ambient temperature for several hours to achieve complete curing and shaping, and the model is demolded and post-processed under the water stream.

Sacrificial substrate material configuration. Take hydroxypropyl methylcellulose and deionized water at a mass ratio of 1 to 20 at 85 °C and stir uniformly until the solution is viscous. Then lower the temperature, and as the temperature decreases, the viscosity of the solution further increases. When cooled to room temperature, the solution is a gray-white, turbid solution. Put it in the refrigerator to defoam for several hours, and then wait for use.

Disperse lubricating material configuration. Take polyvinylpyrrolidone, succinic acid, and ethanol in a ratio of 0.1:1:20 into the beaker and stir well to make PVP dispersion lubricant. Take NdFeB powder and mix PVP dispersion lubricant in a ratio of

1:10 by mass; stir evenly for 180 min under the speed of 600 rpm of a mechanical stirrer so that the surface of the NdFeB particles is evenly wrapped and coated with PVP dispersion.

Phase change material selection. Easy phase change material was taken, and paraffin wax was used as this phase change material in this paper. The reason for choosing paraffin wax is that the melting point of paraffin wax is more moderate than that of common phase change materials; too low a melting point results in slightly melting at a higher room temperature, which makes it difficult to keep the magnetic orientation of magnetic powder, while too high a melting point requires a higher temperature and at the same time requires high temperature stability of the model. Meanwhile, paraffin wax as a lubricant can effectively improve the lubrication between NdFeB powder, facilitate the NdFeB powder to turn in it, reduce the difficulty of reorientation, and improve the efficiency of reorientation.

Magnetic reprogrammable material configuration. The NdFeB powder coated with PVP solution is added to the molten paraffin wax at a ratio of 7 to 1 by mass, and the mixture of paraffin wax and NdFeB coated with PVP is obtained uniformly without precipitation or agglomeration after stirring well.

Polymer elastomer configuration. Polydimethylsiloxane (PDMS, DOWSIL 184) was taken and mixed well with the corresponding curing agent at a mass ratio of 10 to 1, and then acted under vacuum at -80 kPa for 20 min to draw off the air bubbles inside the material to realize the material and use it as a model overall framework in preparation and experiments.

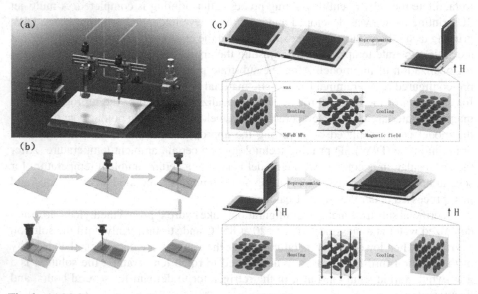

Fig. 1. (a) Multi-nozzle printing equipment used; (b)Model preparation flowchart; (c) Schematic diagram of the reconfiguration principle

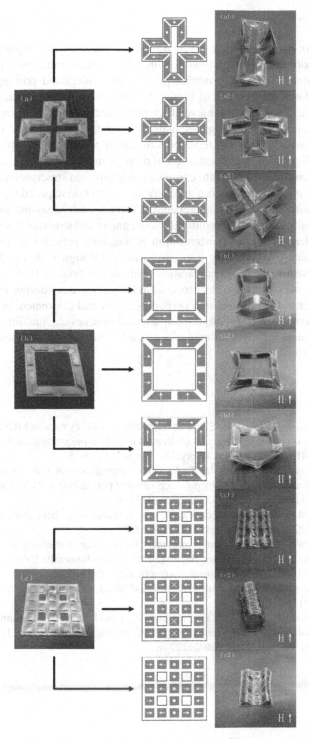

Fig. 2. Multiple reconfigurable drive models for design (a) hollow cross structure: book pages (a1) convex tables (a2) butterflies (a3); (b) hollow square lattice: beam (b1) fence (b2) dish (b3); (c) simple lattice structure: wave (c1) arch-bridge (c2) trench (c3)

4 Conclusion

In this paper, we propose an integrated printing process for reconfigurable, magnetically actuated soft structures configured with a high concentration of reprogrammable magnetic materials. The multi-material process with integrated printing by multiple printheads increases the freedom of model design. The configured material has a high magnetic particle mass ratio to achieve efficient and accurate reconfiguration and actuation. The phase change of the magnetic material is reversible and can be reprogrammed to different magnetic orientations repeatedly to achieve a variety of complex morphological changes. Also, the high concentration of reprogrammable magnetic material can be quickly and precisely deformed into complex predetermined structures under the action of external magnetic fields, reducing the energy consumption required for the reconfiguration and actuation processes. The prepared structural model demonstrates the fast and accurate reconfiguration of this reconfigurable magnetic soft structure. Overall, this work solves the problem of limited concentration of magnetic particles in reprogrammable magnetic materials by combining a unique structural design with a multi-jet printing process to achieve the integrated preparation of highly concentrated reconfigurable magnetically driven soft structures. The process has a high degree of design freedom, a high magnetic powder content, integrated preparation, fast and convenient reconfiguration, a precise and controllable reconfiguration area, and accurate actuation control, which have some prospects for application in magnetically actuated soft robotics, medical, and electronic industries.

References

1. Ivo, S., Eduardo, A., Miroslav, L.: Shape Memory alloys and polymers for MEMS/NEMS applications: review on recent findings and challenges in design, preparation, and characterization. Metals 11(3), 415 (2021). https://doi.org/10.3390/met11030415
2. Andrei, H., Ana-Maria, S., Mirela, T.: Flexible composites with variable conductivity and memory of deformation obtained by polymerization of polyaniline in PVA hydrogel. Polymers 14, 21 (2022). https://doi.org/10.3390/polym14214638
3. Zou, B., et al.: Magneto-thermomechanically reprogrammable mechanical metamaterials. Adv. Mater. 35, 8 (2023). https://doi.org/10.1002/adma.202207349
4. Kuang, X., et al.: Magnetic dynamic polymers for modular assembling and reconfigurable morphing architectures. Adv. Mater. 33, 30 (2021). https://doi.org/10.1002/adma.202102113
5. Zhao, R., Dai, H., Yao, H.: Liquid-metal magnetic soft robot with reprogrammable magnetization and stiffness. IEEE Robot. Autom. Lett. 7, 24535–24541 (2022). https://doi.org/10.1109/LRA.2022.3151164
6. Deng, H., Sattari, K., Xie, Y., Liao, P., Yan, Z., Lin, J.: Laser reprogramming magnetic anisotropy in soft composites for reconfigurable 3D shaping. Nat. Commun. 11(1), 6325 (2020). https://doi.org/10.1038/s41467-020-20229-6

A Lightweight Jumping Robot
with Untethered Actuation

Jinqiang Wang[1,2] and Dong Wang[1,2](✉) iD

[1] State Key Laboratory of Mechanical System and Vibration, School of Mechanical Engineering, Shanghai Jiao Tong University, Shanghai 200240, China
wang.dong@sjtu.edu.cn
[2] Meta Robotics Institute, Shanghai Jiao Tong University, Shanghai 200240, China

Abstract. Jumping motion is enlarging the robotic toolbox by providing agile and rapid locomotion functions that can overcome the limitations of environment and size. Although these jumping robots powered by novel mechanisms and functional materials have shown remarkable dexterity and adaptability, their intricate actuation mechanics make it challenging to realize the jumping robots lightweight and compact. To address this challenge and endow robots capable of untethered movements, we focused on ultralight magnetic carbon fiber beams that exhibit arch-like bending when triggered under magnetic field and induce a rapid release of stored strain energy after the magnetic field is removed. We evaluated their bending process under magnetic field and build untethered jumping robots with respect different geometries to help analyze their jumping performances. In our experiment, a single magnetic carbon fiber beam robot (0.8 g) with a height of 0.2 mm and a length of 80 mm is able to achieve a jumping height of 420 body heights and a jumping distance of 4.5 body length. By assembling two magnetic beams together, our robot can jump to more than 325 times of its body height carrying a payload of 3 times its body weight. These results demonstrate the developed jumping robot avails a new design strategy for lightweight and compact jumping robot to function in complicated conditions.

Keywords: Jumping robots · Lightweight · Untethered actuation · Carbon fiber · Hard magnetic soft material

1 Introduction

As an essential locomotion strategy with the reputation of high mobility, jumping motion is widely adopted by animals to escape predators, overcome obstacles,

Supported by the National Key Research and Development Program of China (No. 2022YFB4700900), the National Natural Science Foundation of China (Grant No. 52275025), the Interdisciplinary Program of Shanghai Jiao Tong University (Grant No. YG2021QN105) and the State Key Laboratory of Mechanical System and Vibration (Grant No. MSVZD202212).

H. Yang et al. (Eds.): ICIRA 2023, LNAI 14270, pp. 71–82, 2023.
https://doi.org/10.1007/978-981-99-6492-5_8

and gather foods. Inspired by the jumping mechanics in nature, researchers have developed effective jumping structures to enhance the maneuverability of smart robots when faced with challenging obstacles or complicated work environments [23]. Hawkes et al. used linear motors and hybrid springs to develop an engineered jumper that can jump over 30 m high [4]. Cho et al. used a cellular gear mechanism to develop the JumpRoACH jumper that can jump, crawl and self-right [7]. Zhao et al. used an active tail to control the MUS tailbot that can wheel on the ground, jump to overcome obstacles, and maneuver in midair [25]. Jiang et al. used the carbon fiber strip and motors to design a water surface jumping robot that has a jumping height of 9.5 cm [6]. Although these jumping robots have achieved excellent jumping performance and functions, but most of them required complicated structural design and sophisticated assembly to storage energy, which made the lightweight and miniaturization was extremely challenging.

In recent years, advances in functional materials have allowed researchers to develop some ultra-low (< 10 g) mass robots. Noh et al. created a flea-inspired catapult with 1.1 g weight and 30 cm jumping height via the usage of shape-memory alloy [12, 15]. Chen at al created a legless soft robot with 1.1 g weight and 8.45 mm jumping height using the dielectric liquid [2]. Liu et al. developed a 1 mm thick miniatured mobile soft robot with a jumping height of 0.8 body length through the pneumatic actuators [14]. However, the work range of these jumpers were limited by their tethered actuation, which made them inconvenient for the usage in cramped work environments. In addition, some researchers have developed some untethered jumping robots driven by chemical actuators [8, 22], light [1], heat [17, 19] and polyvinylidene difluoride [20]. However, their jumping heights were insufficient ($<$ its body height) to meet the requirements of crossing obstacles.

To address this challenge, in this work, we demonstrated an untethered jumping robot using the bending deformation of high-strength carbon fiber beam. Carbon fiber is a commercially available material with extremely stiff, light and strong mechanical property [13]. It can withstand large bending without breaking and instantly release the stored strain energy when unloaded. The usage of carbon fiber can effectively simplify the fabrication and reduce the weight. To realize untethered actuation, the magnetically response hard magnetic soft material (HMSM) was employed by embedding the hard-magnetic particles (e.g., neodymium-iron-boron alloy, NdFeB) into a soft polymeric matrix (e.g., silicone rubber, gels) [9, 10]. After magnetization, the HMSM has a strong tendency to align itself with the applied magnetic field. Hence, we bonded the tips of carbon fiber beams and the HMSM together using the chemical glue, forming a magnetic carbon fiber beam that can be shaped by a magnetic field. In this sense, an increasing magnetic field caused the beam to bend, while a decreasing magnetic field caused the bent beam to recover and leaded to a jumping displacement. Moreover, by assembly two magnetic beams together, the jumping height and load capacity of the jumper were significantly improved. In a typical robot, a jumper made of a single magnetic carbon fiber beam measured 0.8 g in mass,

80 mm in length and 0.2 mm in height can achieve a jumping height of 420 body heights.

Here, we presented the design, assembly and evaluation of the untethered jumping robot, which was divided into three sections. First, we presented the design and actuation principle of the robotic structures. The influence of the geometry on the bending of magnetic fiber beam was discussed. Next, we analyzed the energy conversion efficiency of a jumper through the analysis of experimental results. Last, we presented the jumping performance of the untethered jumper by measuring its jumping distance, jumping height and load capacity. The significance of this work can be concluded as three points. First, without additional power source, the developed jumping robot permits lightweight and compact structures. Compared with the works using servo motors [7,24,25], hybrid springs [4,15,18] and reduction gears [6,21], this work obviously reduces the manufacturing cost of jumping robot. Second, the untethered actuation allows the robot to get rid of the limitation of work environment, which ensures remote control and concealed motion for some special missions. Last, our jumping robot uses novel mechanisms to enhance its jumping performance as well as load capacity so as to overcome the obstacles with challenging height, length and weight. This work paves the way to design untethered, lightweight jumping robots with high jumping performance for future potential application in bionics, sensors, and robotics.

2   Design and Experimental Methods

2.1   Robot Design

To obtain a lightweight and compact jumper, high strength carbon fiber strip was chosen as the energy storage device. For untethered actuation, the magnetically response HMSM was introduced. As shown in Fig. 1(a), the commercially available 0.2 mm thick carbon fiber sheet (T300, Torayca, Japan) was cut into strips with the specific geometries (length (l), width (w) and thickness (t)). The HMSM was prepared by uniformly embedding the fine neodymium-iron-boron (NdFeB) particles with an average size of 5 μm (MQFP-B-2007609-089; Magnequench) into an uncured silicone-based rubber (Ecoflex 00-30; Smooth-On, Inc) at a volume ratio of 20%. After magnetization along the length direction of HMSM, we bonded it with the carbon fiber strip using a silicone glue (Sil-Poxy Silicone Adhesive-Smooth-On). The structure of jumping robot distributes symmetrically to ensure the stability of jumping process. Hence, each carbon fiber strip was assembled with the HMSM at both ends with a specific length of 5 mm, forming an untethered jumping robot prototype. It is noted that, the cross section of the HMSM is selected as 5 × 1.2 mm according to the curing process. The Young's modulus of carbon fiber and HMSM were respectively measured as 123 KPa and 15 GPa. The magnetization of the HMSM was tested as 115 KA/m.

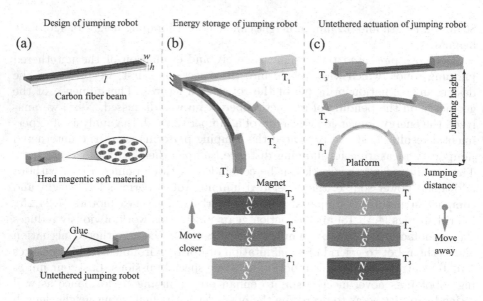

Fig. 1. Design and actuation mechanics of jumping robot. (a) Material and assembly of jumping robot. (b) Energy storage by the bending of carbon fiber beam. (c) Untethered actuation using a magnet.

The Untethered Actuation of Jumping Robot. Owing to the existence of HMSM, the application of magnetic field will produce magnetic torques and magnetic forces that drive the distal tip of magnetic fiber beam to bend toward the applied magnetic field. As shown in Fig. 1(b), we introduced a permanent magnet to form a spatial magnetic field beneath the jumper. We denoted the applied magnetic field as a vector $\mathbf{B}$ and the magnetization along the HMSM is denoted by a vector $\mathbf{M}$, the magnetic body torque density of HMSM can be expressed as [11]

$$\tau = \mathbf{M} \times \mathbf{B} \tag{1}$$

And the magnetic body force density is

$$\mathbf{b} = (\mathrm{grad}\mathbf{B})\,\mathbf{M} \tag{2}$$

When the magnet approached the jumper (from T_1 to T_3), the intensity of magnetic field increases and leaded to a larger magnetic torque and body force. Hence the magnetic carbon fiber bent to align its direction with the applied field. Due to the fixed boundary condition, the beam was axially compressed while it vertically bent, forming an arc shape. As long as the strength of the magnetic field was maintained, the bent beam retained its shape to storage the energy. In a jumping experiment, the centerline of jumping robot was fixed so that its two ends can bend simultaneously and form a semicircular shape. In this period, the energy was locked reliably. Once the magnet moved away from the jumping robot, the strength of magnetic field decreased rapidly and triggered the bent beam to recover its shape. As shown in Fig. 1c, when a jumping command arrived, the semicircular carbon fiber beam straightened out and took initiative to release the energy, thereby inducing a jumping locomotion.

In this work, we considered an axially magnetized cylinder NdFeB magnet (D80X40-N52, FOST Magnetic, Inc.) with a surface magnetic field of 550 mT. As shown in Fig. 3a, the magnet has a height (H) of 50 mm and a radium (R) of 25 mm. The magnetic field strength along the central axis of the magnet B_z can be expressed as a function of the distance (d) between the magnet surface and the HMSM as (17):

$$B_z(0,0,d) = \frac{B_0\sqrt{R^2+H^2}}{H}\left(\frac{d+H}{\sqrt{(d+H)^2}} - \frac{d}{\sqrt{d^2+R^2}}\right) \tag{3}$$

where B_0 demotes the surface magnetic field strength. We experimentally measured the magnetic field strength with a distance ranged from 0 to 200 mm. As shown in Fig. 3b, the magnetic field undergone a sharp decline in its initial phase ($d<25$ mm) and then remained almost constant. The field gradient along the central axis can be obtained as B_z. This gives the magnetic gradient ranging from -22.5 to -7.5 mT/mm over the range of actuation distance from 0 to 25 mm. It can be estimated from Eq. 2 that the magnetic body force per unit volume is on the order of 2587.5 to 862.5 KN/m^3. Hence, it is reasonable to use a permanent magnet to control the bending and releasing of magnetic fiber beam.

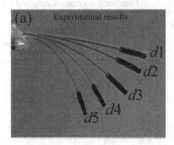 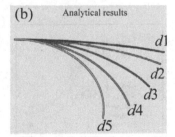

Fig. 2. Deflection of a cantilever magnetic carbon fiber beam under magnetic field. The experimental (a) and analytical (b) configurations of the magnetic beam as the intensity of magnetic field increases from d_1 to d_5.

The shear stress gave rise to magnetic moment across the HMSM can be equivalently considered to be a moment M_0 acting on the whole magnetic carbon fiber beam. With one end clamped and the other end free, the bending curvature of a cantilever beam as shown in Fig. 1b can be expressed as [3]:

$$\frac{d\kappa}{ds} = \frac{M_0}{EI} \tag{4}$$

where κ is the slope angle at point (x, y) along the beam, s is the distance from the fixed end to the free end, EI is the flexural rigidity of beam. Upon a magnetic field B, the applied moment M_0 should satisfy

$$M_0 = MB\sin(\varphi) \tag{5}$$

where M and B are the magnitude of magnetization and the applied magnetic field, φ is the angle between the vector $\mathbf{M}$ and $\mathbf{B}$. During bending, the beam was subjected to the following condition

$$\int_0^s \sin\kappa ds = 0, \ \kappa|_{s=0} = 0, \varphi = \frac{3\pi}{4} - \kappa|_{s=l} \tag{6}$$

By numerically integrating κ using the Eq. (4)–Eq. (5), we obtained the deformed configurations of a magnetic carbon fibers beam (l=80, w=4, h=0.2 mm) as shown in Fig. 2a, which shown an agreement with the experimental results (Fig. 2b). Therefore, the deformation process of the proposed jumping robot is predictable.

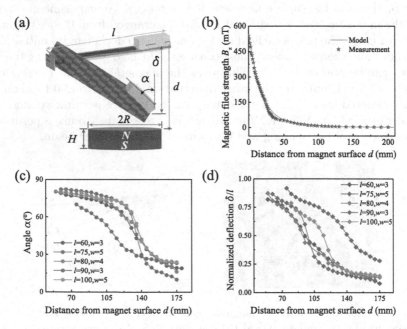

Fig. 3. Untethered actuation of jumping robot. (a) Schematic of magnetically driven bending of jumping robot. (b) The distribution of magnetic field intensity generated by a permanent magnet. (c) Bending angle and (d) normalized deflection of jumping robots increase with the decrease of distance from the magnet. Five groups of jumping robots were tested.

2.2   The Geometry Influence of Jumping Robot

Once the material is defined, the bending stiffness of a beam structure is related to its area moment of inertia and length. To investigate the geometry influence of jumping robot based on the magnetic carbon fiber beam, we experimentally measured the bending of jumping robots with different length (l) and width (w).

As denoted in Fig. 3a, the deflection of carbon fiber beam is shown as δ and the bending angle is expressed as α. To eliminate the effect of dimension units, we used the normalized deflection δ/l. As shown in Fig. 3c, we used a magnet to approach the magnetic carbon fiber beam from the distance $d = 175$ mm until they made contact. The bending angle at the tip shown an inversed S shape and approached to 90° as the decrease of the distance. Meanwhile, the normalized deflection was closed to 0.9 that indicates the axial strain of the beam. Both the bending angle and normalized deflection behaved a sharp increase when the distance d ranged from 120 mm to 90 mm that implies the instant and robust of the applied magnetic actuation. The geometries of jumping robots were selected as l=60, w=3; l==75, w=5; l=80, w=4; l=90, w=3; l=100, w=6. According to the results in Fig. 3c and 3d, the beam with a larger aspect ratio (l/w=30) shown a larger deflection but a smaller bending angle, which indicates a slender beam prefers overall bending not axial compression. To store more energy, the magnetic fiber beam should permit a larger axial compression, and lager bending angle and normalized deflection is in needed. Hence, the jumpers with the geometry l=80, w=4 and l=100, w=6 are more attractive.

3   Results and Discussion

3.1   Jumping Performance

Based on the design method is Sect. 2, the jumping robot prototype was built with five groups of geometries as shown in Fig. 3. Using the prototype and magnet, we conducted aerial maneuvering experiments to evaluate the jumping performance. The experiments were set up as follow. We first fixed the centerline of jumping robot and then used a magnet to approach the robot. When the robot achieved its maximum bending, we remained the distance of magnet and removed the limitation of robot. Owing to the strong magnetic moment and interaction, the robot was fixed on the platform with an arch-shape. A light cyan background and a vertically placed ruler were set to provide a reference to the jumping prototype. Once a jumping command arrived, the magnet was instantly removed away from the platform, and the prototype rapidly produced a jumping motion. The whole process was recorded by a camera (A7M3, SONY) with a frequency of 15 frame/s. The motion analysis of the jumping robot including jumping height, jumping velocity and jumping distance were implemented by an open motion analysis software Kinovea [16].

Each group of experiments were conducted four times with the same settings. In a typical experiment, as shown in Fig. 4a, the jumping height referred to the distance between the peak of robot and the platform. The jumping distance referred to the distance between the original position and the landing position. The jumping velocity referred to the take-off speed of the prototype. As shown in Fig. 4b–4d, the jumping height increased from zero to the peak and then decreased to zero. The jumping velocity decreased with time while the jumping distance increased with time. It can infer that the stored energy first converted into kinetic energy and transformed into the gravitational potential energy in the

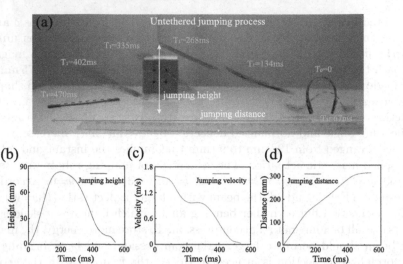

Fig. 4. Jumping process of the untethered jumping robot. (a) Aerial maneuvering results from video frames show the jumping trajectory in a single image. (b) The jumping height, (b) jumping velocity and (c) jumping distance are recorded with time. The dash lines represent the locations of robot body in the jumping process.

jumping process. To evaluate the energy conversion efficiency, we calculated the strain energy by approximately regarding the jumping prototype as an axially loaded beam and derived an equation in reference as [5]:

$$W = \frac{Ewt^3\pi^2\delta}{3l\,(4l - \delta)} \tag{7}$$

To simplify the calculation, we define the deflection δ of the robots if ($l<80$, $\delta=l/3$, if $l<80$, $\delta=l/2$). The energy conversion efficiency was defined as the ratio of the gravitational potential energy and the strain energy. The jumping performances of the five groups of jumping prototypes were concluded in Table 1. The results shown that the developed jumping robots have an average jumping height of 81.6 mm, an average jumping distance of 398.27 mm, and an average energy conversion efficiency of 29.13. Noted that, we excluded the result of group 60×3 because of the efficient biases.

3.2 Jumping Over Obstacle and Payload Capacity

As elaborated in the actuation part, the developed jumping robot can utilize the untethered actuation to trigger the jumping motion, and to produce the jumping height and jumping distance. To show the functionality of the developed untethered jumping robot, two groups of experiments were designed to jump over obstacles as shown in Fig. 5(a) and 5(g). The first case was to let the jumper cross over obstacle by high jump, where a jumper with a length of

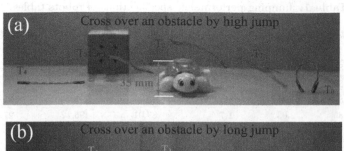

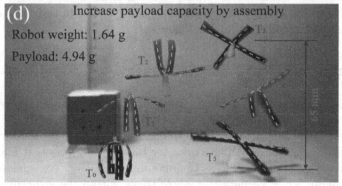

Fig. 5. Experimental test of jumping robot's ability to overcome obstacles and load. (a) Cross over an obstacle (175 times the thickness of robot) by high jump. (b) Cross over an obstacle (2.5 times the length of robot) by long jump. A four-leg jumping robot is created by cross-assembling two magnetic carbon fiber beams. The four-leg jumping robot can jumping over an obstacle with a height of 105 mm, and jump up to 65 mm with a payload that is three times its body weight. The dash lines represent the locations of robot body in the jumping process.

Table 1. Jumping performance specifications of robots tables.

Geometry	Weight (g)	Strain (mJ)	Velocity (m/s)	Height (mm)	Distance (mm)	Efficiency (%)
60 × 3	0.75	1.59	1.2	28.34	174.76	13.21
75 × 5	0.8	2.12	1.43	74.98	343.7	27.83
80 × 4	0.82	2.63	1.48	84.38	361.3	25.86
90 × 3	0.8	1.75	1.52	80.03	392.94	35.43
100 × 5	0.85	2.63	1.7	87.01	495.12	27.38

80 mm, a width of 5 mm and a height of 0.2 mm can easily jump over a turtle model (height 35 mm). In the second case, a jumper with a length of 100 mm, a width of 5 mm and a height of 0.2 mm can cross over a keyboard model with a length of 250 mm. The above experiments demonstrated the developed jumping robots have a satisfying obstacle crossing ability and improved adaptability to environment, which greatly increases their work ranges and freedom. In addition, we designed a four-leg untethered jumping robot by crossing the robot proto-type mentioned above, as shown in Fig. 5(c) and 5(d). The new four-leg jumper shown the similar bending and jumping process under the magnetic actuation. One intriguing consequence was that the four-leg jumpers permit enhance jump-ing performance. In Fig. 5(c), a four-leg jumper made of two carbon fiber beams with a length of 100 mm, a width of 5 mm and a height of 0.2 mm can jump over an obstacle with a height of 105 mm, that is over 500 times of its height. Meanwhile, the four-leg jumper shown a certain payload capacity. In Fig. 5(d), a 1.64 g four-leg jumper jumped over 65 mm carrying a 4.94 g payload. This means that although the developed robot is lightweight, it has a load capacity, which benefits the robot to implement transportation tasks. It also makes it possible to integrate sensing, monitoring and control on the basis of the current jumping robot prototype to realize robot intelligence.

4   Conclusions

In this work, we presented a lightweight and untethered jumping robot based on the high strength carbon fiber and magnetically driven soft material. To best our knowledge, it is the first attempt to combine the high strength carbon fiber and the magnetically activated soft material for the jumping robot. It allowed as to design the compact structures so as to maximum the energy conversion efficiency during the jump, while keeping the whole robot within the structural limit. To verify the feasibility of the proposed concept, a robotic prototype weighting 0.8 g and having a body length of 80 mm and a body height of 0.2 mm was fabricated. In experiment, the prototype was able to achieve a jumping height of 420 body heights and a jumping distance of 4.5 body length. Additionally, the proposed jumping mechanism permits scaling and assembling. When the scale of the jumping robots ranged from 60 mm to 100 mm, although they barely gained weight, their jumping height and jumping distance have significantly changed. Additionally, by assembling two robotic prototypes together, a new for-leg jumping robot can achieve an enhanced jumping performance as well as load capacity. It can jump up to 65 mm with a payload that is three times its body weight. With the lightweight structure and agile jumping locomotion ability, the proposed jumping robot can perform energy efficient jumping motion when faced with obstacle in the environment, which benefits many applications in sensors, monitors and robots. In the future, we would like to achieve the stable control, precise steering and continuous jump of the proposed jumping robot.

References

1. Ahn, C., Liang, X., Cai, S.: Bioinspired design of light-powered crawling, squeezing, and jumping untethered soft robot. Adv. Mater. Technol. 4(7), 1900185 (2019)
2. Chen, R., et al.: Legless soft robots capable of rapid, continuous, and steered jumping. Nat. Commun. 12(1), 7028 (2021)
3. Dong, L., Wang, J., Wang, D.: Modeling and design of three-dimensional voxel printed lattice metamaterials. Addit. Manuf. 69, 103532 (2023)
4. Hawkes, E.W., et al.: Engineered jumpers overcome biological limits via work multiplication. Nature 604(7907), 657–661 (2022)
5. Hird, J., Conn, A.T., Hauert, S.: Stochastic jumping robots for large-scale environmental sensing. Adv. Intell. Syst. 4(5), 2100219 (2022)
6. Jiang, F., Zhao, J., Kota, A.K., Xi, N., Mutka, M.W., Xiao, L.: A miniature water surface jumping robot. IEEE Rob. Autom. Lett. 2(3), 1272–1279 (2017)
7. Jung, G.P., et al.: Jumproach: a trajectory-adjustable integrated jumping-crawling robot. IEEE/ASME Trans. Mechatron. 24(3), 947–958 (2019)
8. Kim, Y., van den Berg, J., Crosby, A.J.: Autonomous snapping and jumping polymer gels. Nat. Mater. 20(12), 1695–1701 (2021)
9. Kim, Y., Parada, G.A., Liu, S., Zhao, X.: Ferromagnetic soft continuum robots. Sci. Robotics 4(33), eaax7329 (2019)
10. Kim, Y., Yuk, H., Zhao, R., Chester, S.A., Zhao, X.: Printing ferromagnetic domains for untethered fast-transforming soft materials. Nature 558(7709), 274–279 (2018)
11. Kim, Y., Zhao, X.: Magnetic soft materials and robots. Chem. Rev. 122(5), 5317–5364 (2022)
12. Koh, J.S., et al.: Jumping on water: surface tension-dominated jumping of water striders and robotic insects. Science 349(6247), 517–521 (2015)
13. Latifi, M.: Engineered Polymeric Fibrous Materials. Woodhead Publishing (2021)
14. Liu, Z., et al.: A 1 mm-thick miniatured mobile soft robot with mechanosensation and multimodal locomotion. IEEE Rob. Autom. Lett. 5(2), 3291–3298 (2020)
15. Noh, M., Kim, S.W., An, S., Koh, J.S., Cho, K.J.: Flea-inspired catapult mechanism for miniature jumping robots. IEEE Trans. Rob. 28(5), 1007–1018 (2012)
16. Nor Adnan, N.M., Ab Patar, M.N.A., Lee, H., Yamamoto, S.i., Jong-Young, L., Mahmud, J.: Biomechanical analysis using kinovea for sports application. In: IOP Conference Series: Materials Science and Engineering, vol. 342, p. 012097. IOP Publishing (2018)
17. Ta, T.D., Chang, Z., Narumi, K., Umedachi, T., Kawahara, Y.: Printable origami bistable structures for foldable jumpers. In: 2022 International Conference on Robotics and Automation (ICRA). pp. 7131–7137. IEEE (2022)

18. Tang, L., Wu, X., Liu, P., Li, Y., Li, B.: The feedback trajectory control of a sma-driven miniature jumping robot. In: 2022 International Conference on Robotics and Automation (ICRA), pp. 9769–9775. IEEE (2022)
19. Wang, Q., Tian, X., Li, D.: Multimodal soft jumping robot with self-decision ability. Smart Mater. Struct. **30**(8), 085038 (2021)
20. Wu, Y., et al.: Insect-scale fast moving and ultrarobust soft robot. Sci. Robot. **4**(32), eaax1594 (2019)
21. Yim, J.K., Wang, E.K., Fearing, R.S.: Drift-free roll and pitch estimation for high-acceleration hopping. In: 2019 International Conference on Robotics and Automation (ICRA), pp. 8986–8992. IEEE (2019)
22. Yu, K., et al.: Robust jumping actuator with a shrimp-shell architecture. Adv. Mater. **33**(44), 2104558 (2021)
23. Zhang, C., Zou, W., Ma, L., Wang, Z.: Biologically inspired jumping robots: a comprehensive review. Robot. Auton. Syst. **124**, 103362 (2020)
24. Zhao, J., Yan, W., Xi, N., Mutka, M.W., Xiao, L.: A miniature 25 grams running and jumping robot. In: 2014 IEEE International Conference on Robotics and Automation (ICRA), pp. 5115–5120. IEEE (2014)
25. Zhao, J., Zhao, T., Xi, N., Mutka, M.W., Xiao, L.: Msu tailbot: controlling aerial maneuver of a miniature-tailed jumping robot. IEEE/ASME Trans. Mechatron. **20**(6), 2903–2914 (2015)

Dielectric Elastomer Actuators for Soft Robotics

Landing Trajectory and Control Optimization for Helicopter in Tail Rotor Pitch Lockup

Xufei Yan[1] ⓘ, Renliang Chen[2], and Anhuan Xie[1](✉)

[1] Zhejiang Laboratory, Hangzhou 311100, Zhejiang Province, China
{yanxufei,xieanhuan}@zhejianglab.com
[2] Nanjing University of Aeronautics and Astronautics, Nanjing 210000, Jiangsu Province, China

Abstract. This paper studies the optimal landing trajectory and control strategy for helicopter in tail rotor pitch lockup. A flight dynamics model of a single rotor helicopter with a tail rotor is established. The optimal safe landing and control problem is formulated into a nonlinear optimal control problem, and solved numerically using direct multiple shooting and sequential quadratic programming algorithms. The optimal safe landing process and control strategies for the sample helicopter encountering high tail rotor pitch lockup and low tail rotor pitch lockup are investigated respectively. Simulation results show that when the tail rotor is stuck at high pitch, it provides a large lateral force, which is beneficial for a high-power state landing with low forward speed and descent rate. When the tail rotor is stuck at low pitch, it provides a small lateral force, which is beneficial for flying at an economic speed (low-power state), but is not conducive to a safe landing afterwards. If a conventional landing is attempted in this situation, the yaw rate at touchdown would be very high and could be dangerous. If an autorotation landing is applied, the landing will be safer with a much lower yaw rate at touchdown.

Keywords: Helicopter · Tail rotor pitch lockup · Flight dynamics model · Optimal control · Autorotation

1 Introduction

Conventional single rotor helicopter requires a tail rotor to balance the torque generated by the main rotor and to achieve heading control. In recent years, tail rotor failure has caused a considerable number of helicopter accidents (about 30% of all kinds of accidents) [1, 2]. Helicopter tail rotor failure can generally be classified into three categories: aerodynamic failure, complete failure of the tail rotor, and tail rotor pitch lockup [2–4]. Among them, tail rotor pitch lockup refers to the tail rotor pitch control mechanism being stuck at the current value and cannot be changed, which is known as frozen control state that any perturbation in power, speed, and sideslip angle will cause directional imbalance. Tail rotor pitch lockup accounts for the highest proportion in all tail rotor failures, close to 2/3 [4].

In recent years, some research has been done on the problem of helicopter tail rotor pitch lockup. Ref. [3] proposed a method of simulating various tail rotor malfunctions

© The Author(s), under exclusive license to Springer Nature Singapore Pte Ltd. 2023
H. Yang et al. (Eds.): ICIRA 2023, LNAI 14270, pp. 85–96, 2023.
https://doi.org/10.1007/978-981-99-6492-5_9

and flight test and handling methods. Ref. [4] mainly carried out landing flight tests for low pitch lockup, and gave basic operation suggestions for different tail rotor pitch lockups. Ref. [5] proposed an evaluation plan for tail rotor pitch lockup to ensure that flight test research can be carried out safely. Ref. [1] conducted numerical simulation on the safe flight of various tail rotor faults of helicopters, and proposed a control scheme to retrim it under specific flight conditions. Ref. [6] proposed a control method to ensure the safe flight of unmanned helicopters after tail rotor failure in hovering state. Ref. [7] discussed the different tail rotor pitch lockups, and conducted pilot-in-the-loop flight simulation to retrim it under specific flight conditions. Based on the above research, it seems necessary to further study the optimal safe landing procedure for helicopter in tail rotor pitch lockup.

This paper studies the optimal landing trajectories and control strategies for helicopter encountering different tail rotor pitch lockups. A flight dynamics model of a single rotor helicopter with a tail rotor was established. The optimal safe landing and control problem was formulated into a nonlinear optimal control problem, and solved numerically using direct multiple shooting and sequential quadratic programming algorithms. High tail rotor pitch lockup and low tail rotor pitch lockup were investigated respectively. When studying the low tail rotor pitch lockup, the article further discussed the safety of applying conventional landing and autorotation landing during the landing phase.

2   Flight Dynamics Modeling and Validation

2.1   Flight Dynamics Modeling

First, a rigid-body flight dynamics model of a conventional helicopter is presented. The model is composed of a main rotor, a tail rotor and an airframe with vertical tail and horizontal stabilizer. The aerodynamic forces and moments acting on the main rotor are calculated using the blade element method. The flapping motion of rotor is modeled using a second-order unsteady aerodynamic model, while the induced velocity is described using the first-order dynamic inflow model proposed by Pitt-Peters. The aerodynamic force and moment coefficients of the fuselage, horizontal tail, and vertical tail are obtained through interpolation of wind tunnel test data. The detailed modeling and validation process are described in Ref. [8] and will not be repeated here. The governing equation of the flight dynamics model is summarized below,

$$\dot{x}_b = f(x_b, u_b, t) \tag{1}$$

where $x_b = [x_B; x_F; x_I]$ is the state vector that contains fuselage motion state x_B, rotor flapping state x_F, and rotor inflow state x_I. $u_b = [\delta_{col}; \delta_{lat}; \delta_{lon}; \delta_{ped}]$ is the pilot control vector where δ_{col} is collective stick input, δ_{lat} is lateral stick input, δ_{lon} is longitudinal stick input, and δ_{ped} is pedal input, t is time.

It can be seen that when the helicopter encounters tail rotor pitch lockup, the tail rotor pitch will be fixed at the current value, and the pedal will be unable to function, the pilot can only control the main rotor collective pitch, lateral cyclic pitch and longitudinal cyclic pitch to perform a safe landing. In this paper, the first-order derivative of the control inputs with respect to time are used as the control variables, and the original control inputs are treated as part of the state variables to avoid discontinuities during numerical optimization [8].

$$
\begin{cases}
\dot{\delta}_{col} = u_{col} \\
\dot{\delta}_{lat} = u_{lat} \\
\dot{\delta}_{lon} = u_{lon}
\end{cases}
\tag{2}
$$

During the landing phase, the helicopter is affected by ground effect, which requires correction of the rotor-induced velocity using the ground effect factor f_G, expressed as follow [9],

$$
f_G = 1 - \frac{\sigma a \lambda}{4 C_T} \frac{(R/4z)^2}{1 + (\mu/\lambda)^2}
\tag{3}
$$

In this expression, σ represents rotor solidity, C_T represents rotor thrust coefficient, a represents the slope of the rotor blade lift curve, λ represents the inflow ratio of the rotor, R is the rotor radius, z is the height of the hub above the ground, and μ represents the advance ratio of the rotor.

In addition, the helicopter may encounter the vortex-ring state in the high oblique descent during landing procedure, which will cause unsteady aerodynamic behavior of rotor. To prevent entering the vortex ring state, it is necessary to keep the main rotor and tail rotor outside the vortex ring region, which can be expressed as a constraint condition [10].

$$
\begin{cases}
\dfrac{\mu^2 + \lambda^2 - \lambda \nu_0}{\sqrt{\mu^2 + \lambda^2}} \geq -0.28 \sqrt{\dfrac{C_T}{2}} \\
\dfrac{\mu_{TR}^2 + \lambda_{TR}^2 - \lambda_{TR} \nu_{0T}}{\sqrt{\mu_{TR}^2 + \lambda_{TR}^2}} \geq -0.28 \sqrt{\dfrac{C_{TR}}{2}}
\end{cases}
\tag{4}
$$

Here, μ_{TR} represents the advance ratio of the tail rotor, λ_{TR} is the inflow ratio of the tail rotor, ν_0 and ν_{0T} respectively denote the average non-dimensional induced velocities of the main rotor and tail rotor, and C_{TR} is the lift coefficient of the tail rotor.

During the safe landing procedure after low tail rotor pitch lockup, the pilot can choose to perform an autorotation landing in the final stage. In this case, the engine throttle is closed to idle mode, and the engine output power P_A and the rotor speed Ω can be described by the following differential equations [9, 11],

$$
\begin{cases}
\dot{P}_A = (0 - P_A)/t_p \\
\dot{\Omega} = \dfrac{P_A - (P_{MR} + P_{TR})/\eta}{(I_{MR} + k^2 I_{TR})\Omega}
\end{cases}
\tag{5}
$$

where t represents the engine response time, P_{MR} and P_{TR} denote the required power of the main rotor and tail rotor, respectively. η represents the transmission efficiency, I_{MR} and I_{TR} represent the rotational inertia moments of the main rotor and tail rotor, respectively. k is the proportionality factor between the main rotor speed and tail rotor speed.

Equations (1)–(5) form an augmented flight dynamics model for helicopter landing trajectory and control optimization during tail rotor pitch lockup. The differential equation form of the model is as follow,

$$\dot{x} = f(x, u, t) \tag{6}$$

where

$$\begin{cases} x = [x_F, x_R, x_I, \delta_{col}, \delta_{lat}, \delta_{lon}]^T \\ u = [u_{col}, u_{lat}, u_{lon}]^T \end{cases} \tag{7}$$

2.2 Model Validation

To verify the dynamic response accuracy of the proposed model, transient responses of the UH-60 helicopter AMES GEN HEL simulation in Ref. [12] were used for comparison, specifically for a one-inch right cyclic control input at hover. Figure 1 compares the calculated transient responses of translational velocities, angular velocities, and attitudes with those of the AMES GEN HEL simulation. The results demonstrate that the proposed model can capture the dynamic characteristics of the helicopter and has sufficient accuracy in dynamic responses.

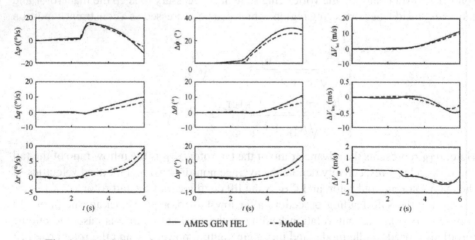

—— AMES GEN HEL   - - Model

Fig. 1. Model dynamic response validation with UH-60 AMES GEN HEL model

3   Formulation of Optimal Control Method

3.1   Problem Description

The optimal control problem corresponding to safe landing during tail rotor pitch lockup can be described as follow: In the event of tail rotor pitch lockup, find a control strategy from a class of strategies that meets the controllability and safety requirements, which can land the helicopter from the initial state to a specified target state, and optimize the performance index. The corresponding nonlinear optimal control problem (NOCP) can be expressed as follows.

(1) *Optimal variables*: Differential state vector x, the control vector u, and the free final time t_f (with the initial time set to 0).

(2) *Cost function*: The cost function of the NOCP is the performance index of the whole landing procedure, which is expected to reflect the safety and feasibility during the flight and touchdown process such as the variation of the flight states, time of flight, and the pilot control activity. Since the tail rotor pitch angle cannot be manipulated during the lockup condition, the performance index can be defined as follow,

$$\min J = w_t t_f + w_v \left(u_{e,f}^2 + v_{e,f}^2 + w_{e,f}^2 \right) + \frac{1}{t_f - t_0} \int_{t_0}^{t_f} L(u(t), \varphi(t), \theta(t), \psi(t)) \mathrm{d}t$$

(8)

$$L(u(t), \varphi(t), \theta(t), \psi(t)) =$$

$$w_u \cdot \left(u_{col}^2 / u_{col,\max}^2 + w_2 u_{lon}^2 / u_{lon,\max}^2 + w_3 u_{lat}^2 / u_{lat,\max}^2 \right) + $$

(9)

$$w_a \cdot \left(\phi^2 / \phi_{\max}^2 + w_5 \theta^2 / \theta_{\max}^2 + w_6 \psi^2 / \psi_{\max}^2 \right)$$

where the first and second terms of (8) represent the terminal state performance index, and the third term represents the state and control performance index of the whole optimal landing procedure. $u_{e,f}$, $v_{e,f}$, $w_{e,f}$ are the forward speed, lateral speed, and descent rate of the helicopter at t_f; $u_{col,\max}$, $u_{lon,\max}$, $u_{lat,\max}$ are the maximum values of the control variables; $\phi_{\max}$, $\theta_{\max}$, $\psi_{\max}$ are the maximum allowable roll, pitch, and yaw attitude angles respectively; w_t, w_v, w_u and w_a are the weighting factors of each item in the performance index. The specific values of the weight factors will be given in the case study in the next section.

(3) *Constraints*: The constraint equations consist of differential equations, initial boundary conditions, path constraints and terminal constraints.

The differential equations refer to the flight dynamics model (6). The initial boundary conditions are determined in the moment of initial pilot control actuation after tail rotor pitch lockup. This paper assumes that the helicopter is in a stable state when encountering tail rotor pitch lockup, and it takes a certain delay time (generally 1 s) for the pilot to start landing operation after discovering the tail rotor control failure. Therefore, the pilot response delay time t_d is considered, and the initial boundary conditions at time t_0 are the variables in the moment after t_d seconds delay.

$$x(t_0) = x_{\text{delay}}, \ u(t_0) = u_{\text{delay}}$$

(10)

The terminal constraints are determined by referring to the requirements for safe landing in the helicopter airworthiness regulations [13].

$$x_{f \min} \leq x(t_f) \leq x_{f \max}$$

(11)

where $x_{f \min}$, $x_{f \max}$ are the minimum and maximum values of the state variable at the final time, respectively, the specific values will be given in the case study.

The path constraints can be represented as:

$$\begin{cases} c_e(x(t), u(t), t) = 0 \\ c_i(x(t), u(t), t) \le 0 \end{cases}, t \in [t_0, t_f] \tag{12}$$

The path constraints of states are properly selected according to the vortex boundary (4) and specific requirements for rotorcraft of FAR (Federal Aviation Regulations). The constraints of the pilot control rates are selected according to the maximum physical rate limits of the servo booster. The specific values will also be given in the case study.

3.2 Numerical Solution Techniques

In this paper, direct multiple shooting collocation method [14] is applied by breaking the continuous autorotation procedure into discrete time nodes and segments. The discretizing process is shown in Fig. 2.

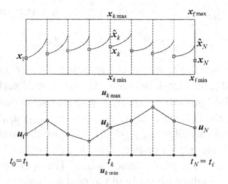

Fig. 2. Direct multiple shooting approach

According to Fig. 2, the solution time interval $[t_0, t_f]$ is discretized into N equally spaced nodes, the corresponding NLP (Nonlinear Programming) variables are

$$X = \left[(x, u)_1, (x, u)_2, ..., (x, u)_k, ..., (x, u)_N, t_f\right] \tag{13}$$

The shooting of discrete time segment k (denoted by x_{k+1}) can be described as

$$x_{k+1} - \hat{x}_{k+1} = 0, \quad k = 1, \cdots, N - 1 \tag{14}$$

where

$$\hat{x}_{k+1} = x_k + \int_{t_k}^{t_{k+1}} f(x, u, t)dt \tag{15}$$

During the integration process, the control variable $u(t)$ is obtained through linear interpolation with u_k and u_{k+1}.

The cost function of NOCP is also discretized as the sum of piecewise integrations,

$$\min J = w_t t_N + w_v \left(u_{d,N}^2 + v_{d,N}^2 + w_{d,N}^2 \right) + \frac{1}{t_f - t_0} \sum_{k=1}^{N-1} \int_{t_k}^{t_{k+1}} L(\boldsymbol{u}, \varphi, \theta, \psi) \mathrm{d}t \quad (16)$$

The constraints are enforced on the corresponding time nodes of X. The nonlinear programming problem can be effectively solved using SQP (Sequential Quadratic Programming) algorithm [15] to get the approximate solution of the original NOCP. To improve the convergence of numerical optimization, normalization and scaling of the optimal variables in NOCP are applied, the specific non-dimensional scaling process can be found in Ref. [9].

4   Landing Optimization in High Tail Rotor Pitch Lockup

This section provides a computational analysis of the optimal landing trajectory and control process for a helicopter encountering high tail rotor pitch lockup, which typically occurs during hovering, low-speed flight, and climbing. The UH-60A helicopter in Ref. [12] is used as the sample helicopter with gross weight of 7257 kg. In this case study, we assume that the helicopter is in a stable flight with at a low speed of 2 m/s at an altitude of 50 m with a heading angle of 0° in standard atmospheric condition. Then, the tail rotor is suddenly stuck at high pitch, rendering it uncontrollable. After a delay of 1 s, the pilot uses the remaining three controls to safely land the helicopter.

The initial boundary conditions are the state and control variables of the helicopter after experiencing high tail rotor pitch lockup for 1 s delay. Considering the specific requirements for a safe landing [13], Table 1 shows the terminal constraints.

Table 1. Terminal constraints in landing

Constraints	Min	Max	Constraints	Min	Max
$p(t_f)(°/s)$	−5	5	$\dot{x}(t_f)(\mathrm{m/s})$	0	12.2
$q(t_f)(°/s)$	−5	5	$\dot{y}(t_f)(\mathrm{m/s})$	−1.524	1.524
$r(t_f)(°/s)$	−5	5	$\dot{h}(t_f)(\mathrm{m/s})$	−1.524	0
$\phi(t_f)(°)$	−5	5	$h(t_f)(\mathrm{m})$	0	0
$\theta(t_f)(°)$	−5	10			

Considering the flight mission, safety and control system characteristics, the path constraints are proposed in Table 2.

In addition, the constraint Eq. (4) for vortex ring state boundary is also included to avoid entering the vortex ring state. Based on the analysis and conclusions in Subect. 3.1 of this paper, as well as previous simulation debugging, the weight factors for performance index (8) are selected as shown in Table 3. In this case study, when the number of discrete points N exceeds 30, the numerical simulation results basically no longer

Table 2. Path constraints in landing

Constraints	Min	Max	Constraints	Min	Max
$u(t)(\mathrm{m/s})$	0	20	$h(t)(\mathrm{m})$	0	60
$v(t), w(t)(\mathrm{m/s})$	−10	10	$y(t)(\mathrm{m})$	−50	50
$p(t), q(t), r(t)(°/\mathrm{s})$	−20	20	$x(t)(\mathrm{m})$	0	200
$\varphi(t), \theta(t)(°)$	−30	30	$\delta_{col,lon,lat}(t)(\%)$	0	100
$\psi(t)(°)$	−90	90	$u_{col,lon,lat}(t)(\%/\mathrm{s})$	0	25

Table 3. Weight factors selected

Weight factor	Description	Value
w_t	Weight factor for flight time	0.125
w_v	Weight factor for touchdown speed	0.125
w_u	Weight factor for pilot control activity	0.45
w_a	Weight factor for attitude changes	0.30

change, and the computational efficiency rapidly decreases. Therefore, this paper uses a value of 30 for the number of discrete points N in this study.

Figures 3 and 4 show the optimal landing process of the sample helicopter encountering high tail rotor pitch lockup. Where u_e, v_e, w_e denote the ground-axis forward velocity, lateral velocity, and descent rate, respectively; β refers to the helicopter's body slip angle; P_R represents the power required by the helicopter.

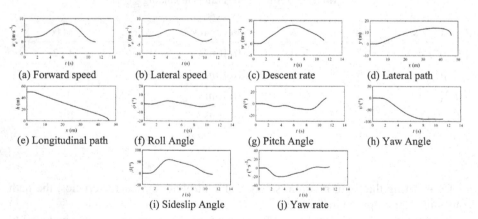

(a) Forward speed   (b) Lateral speed   (c) Descent rate   (d) Lateral path

(e) Longitudinal path   (f) Roll Angle   (g) Pitch Angle   (h) Yaw Angle

(i) Sideslip Angle   (j) Yaw rate

Fig. 3. State variables of optimal landing procedure in high tail rotor pitch lockup

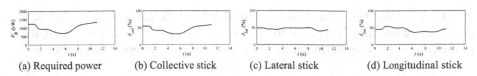

| (a) Required power | (b) Collective stick | (c) Lateral stick | (d) Longitudinal stick |

Fig. 4. Required power and controls of optimal landing procedure in high tail rotor pitch lockup

The following conclusions can be drawn from Figs. 3 and 4.

1. As the tail rotor thrust is relatively large, it is advantageous to use a high-power state to land with low forward speed and descent rate. During landing process, the large lateral force generated by the tail rotor will cause the helicopter to experience significant yaw motion, the pilot can compensate for some of the excess yaw moment through sideslip.

2. The optimal landing trajectory and control process obtained in this study are consistent with the suggestions for safe landing in high tail rotor pitch lockup, proposed in flight tests (Refs. [3, 4]). That is, when the tail rotor is stuck in a large pitch angle, using high power (low speed) can maintain directional balance. The main rotor collective pitch can be manipulated to maintain direction and sideslip angle until touchdown. This indicates that the numerical simulation results in this section are reasonable.

5   Landing Optimization in Low Tail Rotor Pitch Lockup

This section analyzes the optimal landing trajectory and control process for a helicopter experiencing low tail rotor pitch lockup. Low tail rotor pitch lockup generally corresponds to low power flight states such as descent or economical speed flight. The UH-60A helicopter in Ref. [12] is used as the sample helicopter with gross weight of 7257 kg. In this case study, it is assumed that the helicopter is in a stable flight at a height of 50 m and a track angle of 0° at an economic speed of 30 m/s in standard atmospheric conditions. Then, the tail rotor is suddenly stuck at low pitch and cannot be controlled. The pilot uses the remaining three control inputs to safely land the helicopter after a delay of 1 s.

When a low tail rotor pitch lockup occurs, the pilot can choose a conventional landing or an autorotation landing at a height of 2–3 m from the ground. Therefore, this paper discusses and analyzes these two methods respectively.

1) Conventional Landing
The initial boundary conditions are the state and control variables of the helicopter after experiencing low tail rotor pitch lockup for 1 s delay. During conventional landing, insufficient lateral force from the tail rotor can result in higher body angular velocities (especially yaw rate r) when touching down. Considering the requirements for safe landing, the terminal constraints are set in Table 4.

Considering the flight mission, safety and control system characteristics, the path constraints are proposed in Table 5. In addition, the constraint Eq. (4) for vortex ring state boundary is also included to avoid entering the vortex ring state.

The weighting factors are consistent with Table 3. Based on the analysis, in this case study, when the number of N for the multiple shooting method is set to 30, it can guarantee numerical optimization accuracy and good computational efficiency.

Table 4. Terminal constraints in conventional landing

Constraints	Min	Max	Constraints	Min	Max
$p(t_f)(°/s)$	−15	15	$\dot{x}(t_f)(m/s)$	0	12.2
$q(t_f)(°/s)$	−15	15	$\dot{y}(t_f)(m/s)$	−3.048	3.048
$r(t_f)(°/s)$	−40	40	$\dot{h}(t_f)(m/s)$	−1.524	0
$\phi(t_f)(°)$	−5	5	$h(t_f)(m)$	0	0
$\theta(t_f)(°)$	−5	10			

Table 5. Path constraints in conventional landing

Constraints	Min	Max	Constraints	Min	Max
$u(t)(m/s)$	0	50	$h(t)(m)$	0	60
$v(t), w(t)(m/s)$	−20	20	$y(t)(m)$	−50	50
$p(t), q(t)(°/s)$	−20	20	$x(t)(m)$	0	400
$r(t)(°/s)$	−60	60	$\delta_{col,lon,lat}(t)(\%)$	0	100
$\varphi(t), \theta(t)(°)$	−40	40	$u_{col,lon,lat}(t)(\%/s)$	0	25
$\psi(t)(°)$	−90	90			

2) Autorotation Landing at 3 m Above Ground

According to the description in Ref. [3], when a low tail rotor pitch lockup occurs, the pilot can choose an autorotation landing at a height of 2–3 m from the ground. Autorotation landing is a complex emergency maneuver. In order to reduce the difficulty of operation, this paper assumes that the helicopter is at a stable flight state and has a height of 3 m before performing autorotation landing. In addition, during autorotation landing, the engine is set in idle mode, so the corresponding differential Eq. (5) of engine output shaft power and rotor speed are included.

The constraint on rotor speed during the autorotation landing phase is incorporated into the path constraints as follow,

$$0.9 \leq \overline{\Omega}(t) \leq 1.1 \tag{17}$$

Figures 5 and 6 show the optimal landing process of the sample helicopter encountering low tail rotor pitch lockup.

The following conclusions can be drawn from Figs. 5 and 6.

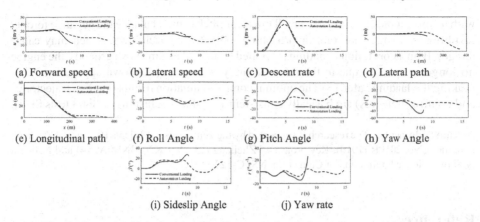

(a) Forward speed   (b) Lateral speed   (c) Descent rate   (d) Lateral path

(e) Longitudinal path   (f) Roll Angle   (g) Pitch Angle   (h) Yaw Angle

(i) Sideslip Angle   (j) Yaw rate

Fig. 5. State variables of optimal landing procedure in low tail rotor pitch lockup

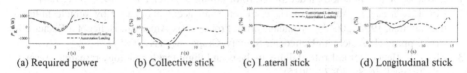

(a) Required power   (b) Collective stick   (c) Lateral stick   (d) Longitudinal stick

Fig. 6. Required power and controls of optimal landing procedure in low tail rotor pitch lockup

1. During landing, the pilot can reduce the main rotor collective pitch, thereby reducing the negative torque and balancing the heading. In this process, there will be a relatively large descent rate. For a conventional landing, the small tail rotor pitch cannot balance the negative torque, resulting in a large yaw rate (approaching -30 °/s) at touchdown, which may cause danger. If an autorotational landing is applied (executed at 3 m above ground), the engine no longer outputs torque to the rotor, so the yaw rate at touchdown approaches 0 °/s, making the landing safer.

2. The optimal landing trajectory and control process obtained in this section are consistent with the recommendations for safe landing after low tail rotor pitch lockup in helicopter flight tests (Refs. [3, 4]), that is, when the tail rotor is stuck at a small pitch, direction balance can be maintained with low power (near economic speed), but it is not conducive to landing maneuverability. When the height drops to about 2–3 m, the throttle should be closed to idle mode to perform autorotational landing. This case study shows that the numerical simulation results are reasonable.

6 Conclusion

This article studied the optimal landing trajectory and control process for helicopter encountering tail rotor pitch lockup using optimal control method, the results yielded the following conclusions. (1) For high tail rotor pitch lockup, as the tail rotor thrust is relatively large, it is advantageous to use a high-power state to land with low speed and descent rate. During landing process, the large lateral force generated by the tail rotor will cause the helicopter to experience significant yaw motion, the pilot can compensate for some of the excess yaw moment through sideslip. (2) For low tail rotor pitch lockup with a conventional landing, the small tail rotor pitch cannot balance the negative torque, resulting in a large yaw rate (approaching -30 °/s) at touchdown, which may cause danger. If an autorotational landing is applied (executed at 3 m above ground), the engine no longer outputs torque to the rotor, so the yaw rate at touchdown approaches 0 °/s, making the landing safer. (3) The optimal control simulation results (landing trajectories and control strategies) are basically consistent with the conclusions of flight tests [3, 4].

Acknowledgments. The research is supported by the Ten Thousand Talents Program of Zhejiang Province (No. 2019R51010), Key project of Zhejiang Lab (No. K2023NB0AC14) and National Natural Science Foundation of China (No. NSFC-12202406).

References

1. O'rourke, M.: Simulation model for tail rotor failure. J. Aircr. **31**(1), 197–205 (1994)
2. Liu, L., Pines, D.: Analysis of US civil rotorcraft accidents caused by vehicle failure or malfunction, 1998–2004. In: Annual Forum Proceedings-American Helicopter Society, vol. 61(2), pp. 1221. American Helicopter Society, Grapevine, TX (2005)
3. Zhao, J.: Helicopter tail rotor failure analysis and flight test technology research. Aeronaut. Sci. Technol. **26**(3), 70–73 (2015)
4. Arslan, Y.: Optimal trajectory generation and tracking for a helicopter in tail rotor failure. Middle East Technical University, dissertation (2022)
5. Frank, L., Thongsay, V.: US Army Airworthiness Approval for UH-60 Fly-By-Wire Aircraft Flight Testing. In: American Helicopter Society 66th Annual Forum. 64(1), pp. 438–453. American Helicopter Society, Phoenix, Arizona (2010)
6. Rajendran, S., Gu, D.: Fault tolerant control of a small helicopter with tail rotor failures in hovering mode. In: Control & Automation (ICCA), 11th IEEE International Conference, pp. 348–353. IEEE, Taichung, Taiwan (2014)
7. Andrea, R., Riccardo, B.M., Pietro, S., et al.: AW169 loss of tail rotor effectiveness simulation. In: 43rd European Rotorcraft Forum. ERF, Milano, Italy (2017)
8. Zhiming, Y., Xufei, Y., Renliang, C.: Prediction of pilot workload in helicopter landing after one engine failure. Chin. J. Aeronaut. **33**(12), 3112–3124 (2020)
9. Meng, W., Chen, R.: Study of helicopter autorotation landing following engine failure based on a six-degree-of-freedom rigid-body dynamic model. Chin. J. Aeronaut. **26**(6), 1380–1388 (2013)
10. Basset, P., Chen, C., Prasad, J., et al.: Prediction of vortex ring state boundary of a helicopter in descending flight by simulation. J. Am. Helicopter Soc. **53**(2), 39–151 (2008)
11. Yan, X., Chen, R., Zhu, S., et al.: Study of helicopter optimal autorotation landing procedure in tail rotor drive failure. In: 2022 IEEE International Conference on Robotics and Biomimetics (ROBIO), pp. 668–673. IEEE, Xishuangbanna, China (2022)
12. Mark, G.: Validation of a real-time engineering simulation of the UH-60A helicopter. Report No.: NASA TM-88360, NASA Ames Research Center, Washington, D.C. (1987)
13. KIM, S.: Certification of Transport Category Rotorcraft: 29–2C. Federal Aviation Administration, Department of Transportation, Washington (2014)
14. Betts, J.: Survey of numerical methods for trajectory optimization. J. Guid. Control. Dyn. **21**(2), 193–207 (1998)
15. Gill, P., Murray, W., Saunders, M.: User's guide for SNOPT version 7: Software for large-scale nonlinear programming. University of California, dissertation, pp. 4–29 (2007)

A Dual-Mode Micro Flapping Wing Robot with Water Gliding and Taking-Off Motion

Fuguang Wang[1], Zhidong Xu[1], and Jihong Yan[1,2](✉)

[1] State Key Laboratory of Robotics and System, Harbin Institute of Technology, Harbin 150001, Heilongjiang, China
jhyan@hit.edu.cn

[2] Laboratory for Space Environment and Physical Sciences, Harbin Institute of Technology, Harbin 150001, Heilongjiang, China

Abstract. Multi-mode motion equips robots with better flexibility and adaptation for dynamically complex environments as well as low energy consumption, becoming a hot spot of robot research. In this work, a dual-mode miniature flapping wing robot featuring gliding and take-off on the water surface is designed via string actuation and attitude adjustment mechanism. The string actuation composed of line and roller is lightweight and adjustable, providing the pneumatic power required for the robot. The posture-modulation mechanism of spatial six bar ensures non-interference of the two motion manners without increasing weight. The dynamic model is established to optimize water-surface glide performance, and lift-force experiments with different wings are carried out for better taking-off properties. The gliding speed and take-off height of the robot are 290.9 mm/s with body length ratio 2.64 and 105 mm with body height 2.1, respectively. This work can provide a reference for the research of the multi-mode flapping wing robot.

Keywords: Flapping wing robot · Dual-mode · Water surface gliding · Water surface take-off

1 Introduction

Flapping wing robots have broad application prospects in both air and water environments owing to their high flexibility and stealth, such as military reconnaissance, meteorological detection, disaster search and rescue [1–4]. However, most of them fail to achieve water-surface gliding and take-off at the same time, due to the unstructured and perturbable properties of water for providing stable support force. It is necessary to research a dual-mode flapping wing robot with water gliding and take-off capabilities.

The flapping wing robot does not need to consider the lack of support force when taking off on land, nor does it need to worry about the difference in drag force on both sides of the supporting feet after taking off, so the relevant technology is relatively mature. However, in the process of water surface take-off, the support force on the feet changes continuously with the instantaneous aerodynamic center position, the tilting moment interferes with the attitude of the body, and the dragging force requires higher

© The Author(s), under exclusive license to Springer Nature Singapore Pte Ltd. 2023
H. Yang et al. (Eds.): ICIRA 2023, LNAI 14270, pp. 97–112, 2023.
https://doi.org/10.1007/978-981-99-6492-5_10

lift, which makes the surface take-off very difficult, and the related technology is still in the initial stage. Our team has developed a string-driven flapping wing robot taking these factors into account [5]. The robot successfully achieved water surface take-off by experimentally optimizing the wings to increase lift force, and using passive air damping device to overcome the tipping moment. Zhang et al. developed a piezoelectric-driven flapping wing robot employing four thin titanium alloy hydrophobic support legs to glide on the water surface [6]. Qu et al. developed a flapping wing robot called Robomoth driven by piezoelectricity, can achieve water gliding and active yaw through two independent piezoelectric drivers. Yet, it cannot achieve water take-off limited by flapping mechanism [7].

It is more challenging to fulfil dual-mode motion of water gliding and take-off. It is necessary to ensure that the two modes of motion can be switched, but also to ensure that the two modes do not interfere with each other, while not gaining too much weight. Harvard University has achieved robot motion switching by generating hydrogen through the electrolysis of water and releasing energy using explosions [8]. However, this method is difficult to control and not easy to implement. Yogesh M et al. achieved dual-mode motion of flapping wing robot with water gliding and take-off by adjusting frequency [9]. However, the robot needs to install separate support feet when gliding on the water surface, and it uses piezoelectric-drive with high drive voltage, which is difficult to popularize. There are also studies using flapping wing robots combined with jumping motion to improve jumping performance [10], but then separately designed jumping mechanism to make the robot heavier. In a word, the dual-mode motion of water gliding and take-off still faces many challenges, such as motion switching, weight limitation, and attitude susceptibility to interference.

To solve the above problems, a dual-mode micro water gliding and take-off motion flapping wing robot is designed in this paper. The string actuation consists of rollers and lines, which are light and adjustable, and are used to generate aerodynamic forces for surface motion. The attitude adjustment mechanism is designed with a spatial six-bar composition, which can be used to switch between water gliding and take-off motions without increase weight. Water-surface gliding property of the robot is optimized by modeling dynamics. Systematic experiments are conducted to measure the lift of different wings for better take-off capability.

2   Robot Design

A. Prototype

The prototype of the water surface gliding and take-off dual-mode motion flapping wing robot is shown in Fig. 1. Robot parts are easily damaged under high-frequency flapping conditions. POM has good fatigue resistance, oxidation resistance, impact resistance, heat resistance and self-lubricating properties, which can better adapt to the working conditions of the flapping wing robot. The white parts in Fig. 1 are all 3D printed with POM material, and the printing accuracy is 0.02 mm. 0.7 mm and 1 mm carbon fiber bars are used for the leading edge bars and support legs, respectively. The robot has two motors, the flapping motor uses a 3.7 V /16000 kV micro hollow cup motor, the weight is 3.5 g, and the other attitude adjustment motor uses the ultra micro hollow cup motor, the rated voltage is 1.5 V, and the weight is only 0.5 g. The support feet are made of nickel foam and treated with a hydrophobic material. The total weight of the prototype is 10.7 g, the wingspan is 200 mm, the length and height are 110 mm and 50 mm respectively.

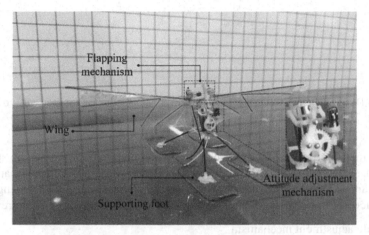

Fig. 1. Prototype of dual-mode mrico flapping wing robot

B. Flapping mechanism

The flapping mechanism is the power source of the robot, and its design requires lightweight, adjustable flapping amplitude and smooth flapping. Considering the above points, the string-driven flapping mechanism designed by our research group is adopted [5]. One end of the drive string is fixed on the end gear of the reducer, and the other end is fixed on the rollers on both sides of the frame with screws, when the end gear rotates, it will drive the rollers on both sides to rotate respectively, meanwhile, the rollers are designed with grooves, and the synchronous string is tied in the grooves to ensure the symmetry of the two rollers flapping, as shown in Fig. 2 (a).

The radius of the roller is r_2, the length of the crank is r_1, β is the Angle between the crank and the synchronization line, and the distance from the roller to the center of rotation of the crank is L_1. The mathematical equation is used to express the parameter relationship of the whole flapping mechanism:

$$\begin{cases} L = \sqrt{L_1^2 - r_2^2} \\ l_0 = L - r_1 \\ \psi = (\sqrt{L^2 + r_1^2 - 2Lr_1\cos\beta} - l_0)/r_2 \end{cases} \tag{1}$$

where L is the length from the tangent point of the roller and the synchronous string to O_2, l_0 is the length from the tangent point of the roller and the synchronous string to the crank in the initial state.

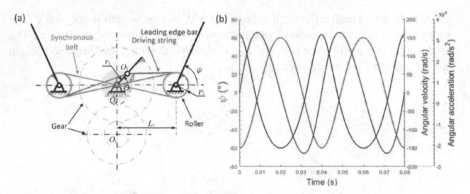

Fig. 2. (a) Design principle of flapping mechanism (b) kinematic performance curve of flapping mechanism

The kinematic performance curve of the whole flapping mechanism is shown in Fig. 2 (b), which shows that the flapping amplitude is 120°. The flapping amplitude can be changed by adjusting the screw tightness, and there is no sudden change in the flapping acceleration and the flapping is smooth, so it meets the design requirements.

C. Attitude adjustment mechanism

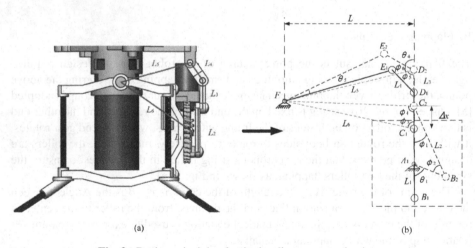

Fig. 3. Design principle of attitude adjustment mechanism

The direction of the aerodynamic force required for the flapping wing robot to glide and take off on the water surface is different, the forward force is needed for gliding on the water surface and the lift force is needed for take-off, therefore, the attitude adjustment mechanism is designed to change the direction of the aerodynamic force. The design was carried out using a spatial six-bar mechanism, as shown in Fig. 3, using a worm gear for deceleration, and can achieve self-locking, considering that the wing flapping is limited by the water surface, the design of its pitch angle amplitude is 20°

Specify that the original position of the rod is combined with letters and angle marker 1 and represented by a solid line, and the changing position of the rod is combined with letters and angle marker 2 and represented by a dashed line, and the motion relationship of each rod of the space six-bar mechanism:

$$\begin{cases} \Delta x = A_1 C_2 - A_1 C_1 \\ \phi_4 = \arccos\left(\dfrac{FC_2^2 + \Delta x^2 - FC_1^2}{2 \cdot FC_2 \cdot \Delta x}\right) \\ \phi_5 = \arccos\left(\dfrac{FD_2^2 + L_3^2 - FC_2^2}{2 \cdot FD_2 \cdot L_3}\right) \\ \phi_6 = \arccos\left(\dfrac{FD_2^2 + L_4^2 - L_5^2}{2 \cdot FD_2 \cdot L_4}\right) \\ \theta_4 = \pi - \phi_5 - \phi_6 \\ \theta_5 = \arccos\left(\dfrac{0.31 + \Delta x + L_4 \cdot \cos\theta_4}{L - L_4 \cdot \sin\theta_4}\right) \end{cases} \tag{2}$$

where $L_i(i = 1 \sim 5)$ is the length of the bar, Δx is the C_1 lifting height, ϕ_4 is the angle FC_2C_1, ϕ_5 is the angle FD_2C_2, ϕ_6 is the angle FD_2E_2, θ_4 is the angle between E_2D_2 and vertical direction, θ_5 is the pitch angle of attitude adjustment mechanism.

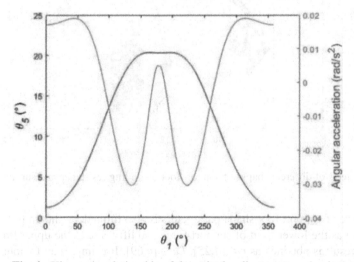

Fig. 4. Kinematic relationship of the attitude adjustment mechanism

According to the above kinematics of the six-bar mechanism, the relationship between the output angle of the attitude adjustment mechanism and the input angle of the motor is obtained, and the angular acceleration is obtained by deriving the time, as shown in Fig. 4. The maximum pitch angle of the six-bar mechanism is 20°, with no sudden change in acceleration and smooth motion, which meets the design requirements.

D. Support foot

The support foot should provide large support force and small gliding resistance when the flapping wing robot glides on the water, therefore, the shape of the support foot also needs to be designed. It is stipulated that the support foot area and thickness are the same, which means that the buoyancy term in the support force is the same, and only the surface tension term in the support force can be considered. Figure 5 shows the surface tension and sliding resistance corresponding to different shape support foot parameters, it can be seen that the triangular support foot corresponds to the largest surface tension, but not the smallest gliding resistance, oval support foot corresponds to the smallest gliding resistance, but not the largest surface tension, comprehensive consideration of gliding / take-off performance, take the smallest slope of the oval as the shape of the support foot.

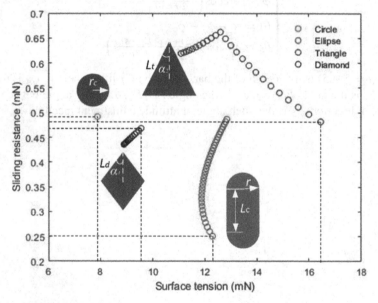

Fig. 5. Effects of different shapes of support foot on gliding resistance and surface tension

The range of support foot shape parameters is also limited, as shown in Fig. 6, with robot weight as the lower limit of support force and lift force as the upper limit of drag force, The result is obtained as $r \in [4,25]$, $Lc \in [6,69]$, It is important to note that there is a coupling between r and L_c.

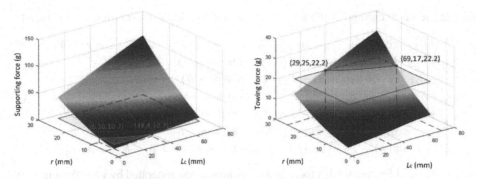

Fig. 6. Limitations on the range of support foot shape parameters

3 Performance Optimization

3.1 Water Surface Gliding Optimization

A. Dynamic model

The modeling of the aerodynamics of the flapping wing and the hydrodynamics of the support foot interface is the first step before the modeling of the water glide dynamics, which has been carried out by the group before [5, 11], As shown in Fig. 7, the force analysis diagram of the flapping wing robot gliding on the water surface is shown.

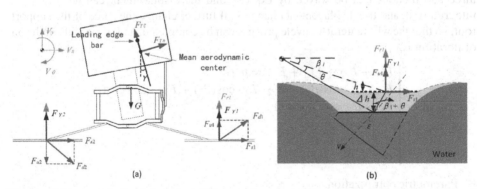

Fig. 7. (a) Force analysis of the robot gliding on the water surface (b) variation of the depth of the right support foot into the water.

The surface gliding of the robot is decomposed into three sub-motions, which are rotation around the center of mass, gliding motion in the horizontal direction and undulating motion in the vertical direction. Assuming that the robot has a small clockwise rotation and a motion to the right, for graphical clarity, Fig. 7.(b) shows the right support foot at the depth change of the water surface, and the three sub-motions are analyzed:

$$
\begin{cases}
((F_{T\zeta} \cdot \cos(\gamma) + F_{T\eta} \cdot \sin(\gamma)) \cdot X_1 - (F_{T\eta} \cdot \cos(\gamma) - F_{T\zeta} \cdot \sin(\gamma)) \cdot Y_1 \\
+ F_{\gamma 1} \cdot L_y \cdot \cos(\beta_1 + \theta) - F_{\gamma 2} \cdot L_z \cdot \cos(\beta_2 + \theta) \\
+ F_{r1} \cdot L_y \cdot \cos(\beta_1 + \theta) + F_{u1} \cdot L_y \cdot \cos(\beta_1 + \theta) \\
+ F_{s1} \cdot L_y \cdot \sin(\beta_1 + \theta) + F_{r2} \cdot L_z \cdot \cos(\beta_2 - \theta) \\
+ F_{u2} \cdot L_z \cdot \cos(\beta_2 + \theta) - F_{s2} \cdot L_z \cdot \sin(\beta_2 - \theta) = J \cdot \alpha \\
F_{T\eta} \cdot \cos(\gamma) - F_{T\zeta} \cdot \sin(\gamma) + F_{s1} + F_2 = m \cdot a_x \\
F_{T\eta} \cdot \sin(\gamma) - F_{T\zeta} \cdot \cos(\gamma) + F_{r1} + F_{r2} + F_{\gamma 2} + F_{u1} - F_{u2} = m \cdot a_y
\end{cases}
\tag{3}
$$

where $F_{T\zeta}$ and $F_{T\eta}$ are the lift force and horizontal force generated by wing flapping, γ is the attitude adjustment angle, X_1 and Y_1 are the force arms in the horizontal and vertical directions from the mean pneumatic center to the center of mass, $F_{\gamma 1}$ and $F_{\gamma 2}$ are the surface tension of the left and right support legs respectively, L_z and L_y are the distances from the left and right support legs to the center of mass, respectively, β_1 and β_2 are the angles between the left and right support legs to the center of mass and the horizontal direction, respectively, θ is the angle of rotation of the whole machine with respect to the center of mass, F_{r1} and F_{r2} are the buoyancy force of the left and right supporting feet respectively, F_{s1}, F_{s2}, F_{u1} and F_{u2} are the components of the left and right support foot dynamic pressure in the horizontal and vertical directions, respectively, J is the rotational inertia of the robot, α is the angular acceleration of the robot's rotation relative to the center of mass, m is the weight of the robot, g is the acceleration of gravity, a_x and a_y are the acceleration of the robot in the horizontal and vertical directions, respectively.

With the change of aerodynamic force, the acceleration change of the robot on the three sub-motions can be solved by Eq. (3), and the displacement can be solved by integrating it, and the displacement change will further change the force of the support foot, so that the whole iterative cycle process can be completed, and the initial condition of iteration is:

$$
\begin{cases}
F_{r1} + F_{r2} + F_{\gamma 1} + F_{\gamma 2} = mg \\
F_{r1} \cdot L_y \cdot \cos(\beta_1) - F_{r2} \cdot L_z \cdot \cos(\beta_2) + F_{\gamma 1} \cdot L_y \cdot \cos(\beta_1) \\
F_{\gamma 2} \cdot L_y \cdot \cos(\beta_2) = 0 \\
F_{T\zeta} = F_{T\eta} = 0 \\
F_{u1} = F_{u2} = 0 \\
F_{s1} = F_{s2} = 0
\end{cases}
\tag{4}
$$

B. Parametric optimization

The glide speed and glide stability are used as glide indicators, where the horizontal displacement represents the robot's glide speed and the rotation angle represents the robot's glide stability. Analyze the effects of flapping frequency, flapping amplitude, and pitch angle on glide indicators. The effect of frequency on the glide indicators is shown in Fig. 8. The analysis shows that frequency has a greater effect on gliding speed and gliding stability, the greater the flapping frequency the greater the gliding speed, but also the greater the rotation angle, indicating that the stability becomes worse with the increase of flapping frequency, taking into account, choose medium and high frequency as the conditions of gliding on the water surface of the flapping wing robot.

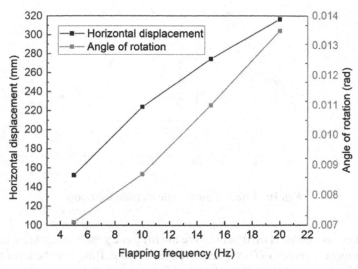

Fig. 8. Effect of frequency on glide indicators

The influence of flapping amplitude on gliding indicators is shown in Fig. 9. Analysis shows that flapping amplitude has little influence on gliding stability, but great influence on gliding speed, and the larger the flapping amplitude, the greater the gliding speed.

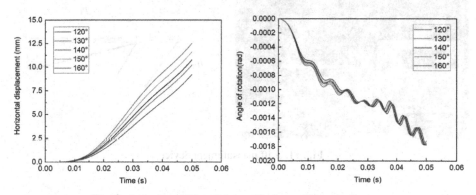

Fig. 9. Influence of flapping amplitude on sliding indicators

The effect of pitch angle on gliding indicators is shown in Fig. 10. The analysis shows that the pitch angle has little effect on the stability of the robot gliding on the water surface, but has a greater effect on the gliding speed, and the greater the pitch angle, the greater the gliding speed, therefore, the pitch angle of 20° is chosen as the condition for the robot gliding on the water surface.

3.2 Lift Force Optimization

A. Lift force measuring device

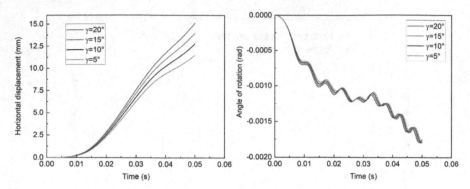

Fig. 10. Effect of pitch angle on glide indicators

A pressure sensor is used to measure the lift force generated by the wings with a measurement accuracy of 0.06 g and a range of 300 g. Based on the lever principle, the lift force generated by the robot flapping is converted to pressure, and the lift force measurement device is shown in Fig. 11(a).

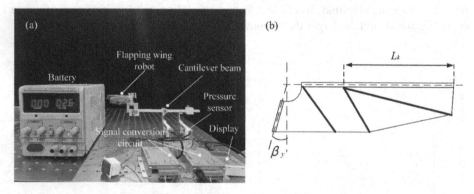

Fig. 11. Lift measurement device

B. Parametric optimization

In order to make the robot take-off smoothly from the water surface, the wing parameters are optimized to improve the lift. Here, three parameters that have a large impact on the lift are selected for optimization, namely, camber angle, wing rib layout and wing thickness. Camber angle is related to the Angle of attack of the wing during flapping. Figure 11(b) is the definition of camber angle, and Fig. 12 is the influence of the Angle of attack on lift. It can be seen that the Angle of attack has a great influence on the aerodynamic force, so it is necessary to optimize the camber angle.

The camber angle range is $10° \sim 30°$, with each wing at different voltages to do three experiments and take the average value, as shown in Fig. 13, for the effect of camber

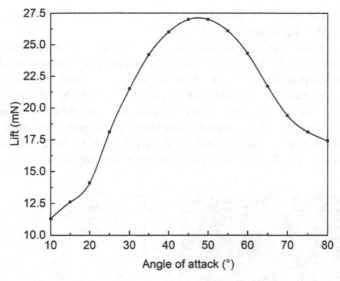

Fig. 12. Effect of angle of attack on lift

angle on the lifting force results, the experiment shows that the camber angle at 25°lifting force significantly increased, and when the voltage is 3.0 V, lifting force increased by 16.5% relative to the optimization before.

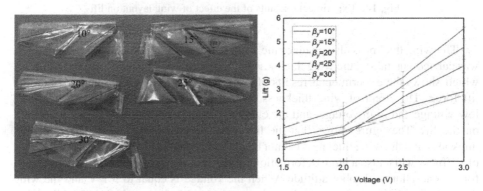

Fig. 13. Experimental results of the effect of camber angle on lift force

The wing rib layout and wing thickness together determine the wing stiffness, which not only affects the angle of attack, but also the deformation of the wing during flapping and thus the surrounding flow field, therefore, the wing rib layout and wing thickness need to be optimized. The wing rib layout includes the wing rib near the wing root and the wing rib near the wing tip, among which, the wing rib near the wing tip depends entirely on the wing stiffness when flapping because there is no constraint of the wing root bar, and it has more influence on the lift, therefore, the wing rib near the wing tip is chosen to be optimized for optimization. Define the distance of the end of the wing rib near the wing tip as L_k, as shown in Fig. 11(b).

The effect of different wing rib layout on the lift force is shown in Fig. 14. Experiments show that when the voltage is small, although the wing stiffness is different, but due to the low flapping frequency, the wing and air force is small, resulting in different stiffness wing deformation is not much difference, reflected to the lift force is not much difference, when the voltage is high, due to the different wing stiffness, the wing and air force increases, resulting in different stiffness wing deformation is different, the impact on the lift force is also highlighted, and when the voltage is 3.1 V, $L_k = 60$ mm, the lift force is maximum, which is 18.1% higher than before optimization.

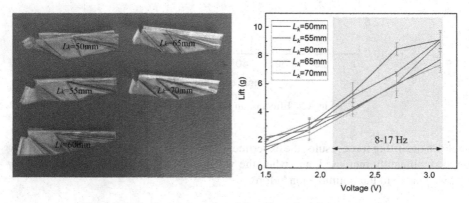

Fig. 14. Experimental results of the effect of wing layout on lift

The wing thickness also changes the wing stiffness, and the same experimental test was carried out, taking the wing thickness range from 13 to 25 μm, as shown in Fig. 15, which shows the experimental results of the effect of different wing thickness on the lift force. The effect of wing thickness on the lift is also divided into two intervals, low voltage and high voltage, and the effect is similar to the effect of wing rib layout on the lift. The figure shows that the lift force increases with the increase of wing thickness, but the wing thickness cannot be increased arbitrarily, otherwise, the increase of stiffness will cause a large deformation of the leading edge, which will affect the lift force generation and robot attitude. When the voltage is equal to 3.1 V and the wing thickness is 25 μm, it corresponds to the maximum lift force, which is 20.4% higher than that before optimization.

4 Experiment

The robot water surface motion experiment equipment is shown in Fig. 16. Including a transparent water tank, a high-speed camera, a spotlight, a fill lamp, a robot, a power source, a computer, a ruler cloth, etc. The length of a single cell of the ruler cloth is 32 mm, and the height of a single cell is 30 mm. In addition, the light position needs to be adjusted so that the robot is fully exposed to the exposure position during the motion.

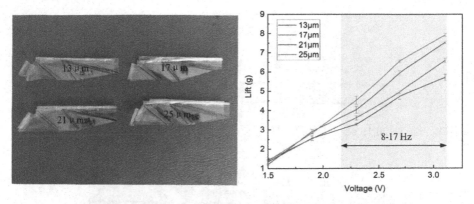

Fig. 15. Experimental results on the effect of wing thickness on lift force

Set the computer shooting speed to 2000 fps to capture the robot motion details. The relevant data are processed after the experiment.

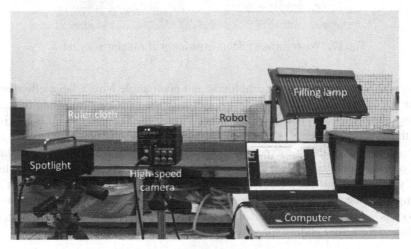

Fig. 16. Experimental equipment

4.1 Water Surface Gliding

This section uses the flapping wing robot to carry out water surface gliding experiments, the robot water surface gliding experiments are shown in Fig. 17, the robot can achieve water surface gliding, and the gliding attitude is stable, the gliding speed is 290.9 mm/s, the body length ratio is about 2.64.

High speed camera was used for simultaneous filming, and the process is not complete due to the limitation of saving video length. However, the experimental glide speeds was calculated by using high speed camera filming. The experimental results show that

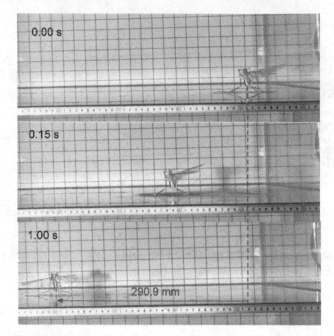

Fig. 17. Water surface gliding experiment of flapping wing robot

the flapping frequency, flapping amplitude and pitch angle have a large effect on the gliding speed, and the gliding speed increases with the increase of flapping frequency, flapping amplitude and pitch angle as shown in Fig. 18. The glide speed is maximum when the flapping frequency is 20Hz, the flapping amplitude is 160°, and the pitch angle is 20°. At the same time, the experimental results were compared with the calculation, and it can be found that the two trends are the same, but in the experimental results are small, which is because in the actual gliding, in order to prevent the support foot from piercing the water surface, the support foot profile was bent upward, so that the support foot is slightly larger, and the cable has a certain resistance to the robot, therefore, resulting in the actual gliding speed is small.

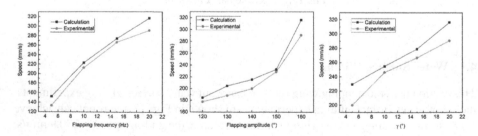

Fig. 18. Comparison of experimental and calculation speed

Table 1 demonstrates that our robot shows some superiority compared to other flapping wing robots in terms of water gliding speed.

Table 1. Comparison of water gliding speed of flapping wing robot

Units / Name	Drive way	Mass (g)	Gliding speed (mm/s)	Body length ratio	Ref
RoboFly	Piezoelectric	0.095	5	0.10	9
Shanghai Jiao Tong University	Piezoelectric	0.165	151	3.30	6
Robomoth	Piezoelectric	2.487	171	2.90	7
Proposed robot	**Motor**	**10.7**	**290.9**	**2.64**	—

4.2 Water Surface Take-Off

The flapping wing robot water surface take-off experiment is shown in Fig. 19. In Fig. 19 (d) the robot is shown achieving a water surface take-off. The height is 105 mm and the offset distance is 42.7 mm. However, the robot eventually overturns due to the accumulation of overturning moment with time. Experimental results can prove that the robot has the ability to take-off from the water surface.

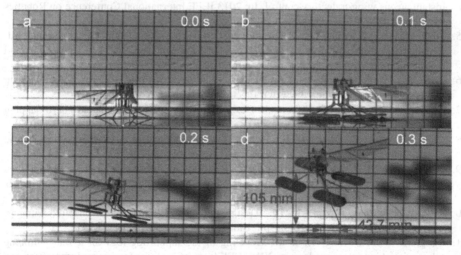

Fig. 19. Experiment on water surface take-off of flapping wing robot

5 Conclusion

A dual-mode micro flapping wing robot featuring fast surface gliding and take-off on the water surface is designed. A lightweight and adjustable string-driven flapping mechanism consisting of rollers and strings is adopted. A special six-bar attitude adjustment mechanism is designed to switch between two types of motion modes: water gliding and take-off. The robot's water gliding capability is improved by establishing the dynamics model. Systematic experiments are carried out to measure the lift of different wings for improving the water surface take-off property of robot. The gliding speed and take-off height of the robot are 290.9 mm/s with body length ratio 2.64 and 105 mm with body height 2.1, respectively. In further work, a control system will be introduced to enable the robot to water surface turn and control the take-off posture for enhancing the motion performance.

References

1. Keennon, M., Klingebiel, K., Won, H.: Development of the nano hummingbird: A tailless flapping wing micro air vehicle. 50th AIAA aerospace sciences meeting including the new horizons forum and aerospace exposition, p. 588 (2012)
2. Phan, H.V., Kang, T., Park, H.C.: Design and stable flight of a 21 g insect-like tailless flapping wing micro air vehicle with angular rates feedback control. Bioinspir. Biomim. 12(3), 036006 (2017)
3. Karásek, M., Muijres, F.T., De Wagter, C., et al.: A tailless aerial robotic flapper reveals that flies use torque coupling in rapid banked turns. Science 361(6407), 1089–1094 (2018)
4. Zhang, J., Cheng, B., Roll, J.A., et al.: Direct drive of flapping wings under resonance with instantaneous wing trajectory control. In: 2013 IEEE International Conference on Robotics and Automation. IEEE, pp. 4029–4034 (2013)
5. Ding, L., Wang, F., Yan, J., et al.: Experimental optimization of wing lift for a hummingbird-like micro flapping-wing robot. In: 2022 IEEE International Conference on Mechatronics and Automation (ICMA), pp. 1239–1244. IEEE (2022)
6. Zhou, S., Zhang, W., Zou, Y., et al.: Piezoelectric driven insect-inspired robot with flapping wings capable of skating on the water. Electron. Lett. 53(9), 579–580 (2017)
7. Chen, Y.H., Liu, Y.D., Liu, T.S., et al.: Design and analysis of an untethered micro flapping robot which can glide on the water. Science China Technol. Sci. 65(8), 1749–1759 (2022)
8. Chen, Y., Wang, H., Helbling, E.F., et al.: A biologically inspired, flapping-wing, hybrid aerial-aquatic microrobot. Science Robotics 2(11), eaao5619 (2017)
9. Chukewad, Y.M., James, J., Singh, A., et al.: RoboFly: An insect-sized robot with simplified fabrication that is capable of flight, ground, and water surface locomotion. IEEE Trans. Rob. 37(6), 2025–2040 (2021)
10. Truong, N.T., Phan, H.V., Park, H.C.: Design and demonstration of a bio-inspired flapping-wing-assisted jumping robot. Bioinspir. Biomim. 14(3), 036010 (2019)
11. Yang, K. Yan, J., Wang, T., et al.: Modeling of the supporting legs for a water-jumping robot mimicking water striders. In: 2016 IEEE International Conference on Information and Automation (ICIA), pp. 942–946. IEEE (2016)

A Self-loading Suction Cup Driven by Resonant-Impact Dielectric Elastomer Artificial Muscles

Chuang Wu[1,2], Xing Gao[1], and Chongjing Cao[1(✉)]

[1] Research Centre for Medical Robotics and Minimally Invasive Surgical Devices, Shenzhen Institute of Advanced Technology (SIAT), Chinese Academy of Sciences, Shenzhen 518055, China
cj.cao@siat.ac.cn

[2] School of Mechanical and Electrical Engineering, Xi'an University of Architecture and Technology, Xi'an 710055, China

Abstract. Suction cups are widely utilized in industries and robotics for object manipulation and robot locomotion. However, current suction cup designs typically rely on external forces to remove the enclosed fluid within the suction cups during their loading processes, which is impractical in some real-world applications due to the complicated force control or the absence of proper anchoring prior to the suction. Aiming to address this limitation, this paper presents a self-loading suction cup driven by a resonant-impact dielectric elastomer actuator (DEA). The resonant-impact mechanism developed in this work can achieve a continuous and efficient removal of the enclosed fluid in the suction cup without the need for an external normal force. First, the frequency responses of the proposed resonant-impact DEA are characterized in this paper via extensive experiments. Next, optimization of its impact performance is performed with respect to its key design parameter. Finally, the suction performances of the self-loading suction cup in both water and air environments are tested. This novel suction cup has potential applications in soft robotic locomotion, medical robotics, surveillance and environmental monitoring.

Keywords: Suction cup · Self-loading mechanism · Dielectric elastomer actuator

1 Introduction

Suction cups have been widely adopted in industries and robotics for manipulating a variety of objects and improving locomotion/anchoring performance [1–3]. In comparison to other switchable adhesion techniques such as the electro-adhesions (i.e. electrostatic forces) [4], dry adhesions (i.e. van der Waals forces) [5] and wet adhesions (i.e. capillary forces) [6], suction cups that are driven by pressure differentials have the advantages of a longer life cycle, wider adaptability and improved reliability [7–9].

Suction cups can be categorized by whether or not a continuous fluid removal device is utilized. Probably the most widely adopted suction cup systems in the industry are

© The Author(s), under exclusive license to Springer Nature Singapore Pte Ltd. 2023
H. Yang et al. (Eds.): ICIRA 2023, LNAI 14270, pp. 113–124, 2023.
https://doi.org/10.1007/978-981-99-6492-5_11

those that are connected to vacuum pumps and valves. Vacuum pumps can continuously remove air or fluid from the space enclosed by the suction cup and make contact with the substrate to achieve highly reliable attachments, even on porous substrates such as paper [10–13]. There are, however, some drawbacks to this approach. For example, bulky vacuum pumps and pressure-regulating valves may add substantial weight to the system, limiting their portability, particularly when a high degree of mobility or flexibility is required (e.g. in wall-climbing robots) [14]. The constant operation of vacuum systems also leads to poor energy efficiency and high noise levels.

Another type of suction cup does not rely on the continuously operating vacuum generator system to obtain a suction force. Rather, the suction force is achieved through these three crucial steps:

i. forming a seal between the suction cup rim and the contacting substrate;
ii. the removal of fluid enclosed between the suction cup and substrate;
iii. volume expansion of the enclosed space with a fixed mass of fluid to generate a pressure difference (i.e. suction force).

The seal formation prevents the fluid from flowing into the closed space, which is the key to generating a pressure difference between the inlet and outlet sides of the suction cup. In practice, it should be noted that fluid leakage of fluid will occur and that the leakage rate is typically positively correlated with the substrate roughness. Numerous novel bioinspired suction cups have been proposed to improve suction cup sealing, especially on rough substrates [15–18]. After the seal has formed and the fluid has been removed, the volume expansion of the enclosed space can simply be accomplished by the passive spring force of the deformed suction cup. In addition, many researchers are inspired by marine animals such as octopi to develop active closed-volume expansion mechanisms [19–24].

Despite the significant progresses in the sealing formation (step i) and active enclosed volume expansion (step iii), to the best of the authors' knowledge, the removal of the enclosed fluid (step ii), or the actual loading process during the suction, is less studied in the literature. Current studies mainly rely on the robotic arm or testing rig to apply a squeezing force to remove the enclosed fluid. However, this approach can be impractical in many real-world applications due to the complicated force control or the absence of proper anchoring prior to the suction. Aiming to address this limitation, this paper presents a self-loading suction cup driven by a resonant-impact dielectric elastomer actuator (DEA), as illustrated in Fig. 1. The DEA adopted in this design represents a novel soft actuation technology that features inherent compliances compared with conventional rigid actuators, high energy/power densities and efficiencies in its resonance [25–27]. Inspired by the impact mechanisms found in, e.g. pile driving and percussive drilling, we carefully design the DEA to actuate at its resonance and to achieve periodic impacts against the suction cup. This novel mechanism developed in this work can achieve a continuous and efficient removal of the enclosed fluid in the suction cup without the requirement of an external normal force.

The key contributes of this paper are:

i. To develop a novel resonant-impact DEA-driven suction cup that is capable of self-loading.

ii. To characterize the frequency responses of the resonant-impact DEA and to perform optimization in terms of its impact performance.
iii. To characterize the performance of the suction cup in both water and air environments via extensive experiments.

Fig. 1. The self-loading suction cup prototype developed in this work.

The rest of this paper is organized as follows. In Sect. 2, the resonant-impact DEA design is demonstrated, its fabrication process is introduced and its frequency responses are characterized. The impact performance of the DEA is then optimized with respect to its key design parameter. In Sect. 3, the working principle of the suction cup is introduced and its performance is characterized in both air and water conditions. Finally, the conclusion is drawn and future work is discussed in Sect. 4.

2   Actuator Characterization

2.1   Resonant-Impact DEA Design Overview

An ideal DEA consists of a piece of dielectric elastomer membrane sandwiched between two compliant electrodes. The membrane will exert thickness contraction and planar expansion if a voltage is applied across the electrodes. This work adopts a double cone DEA configuration due to its ease of fabrication and large stroke/force output [28–30]. The DEA consists of two identical circular DE membranes connected by a rigid rod in the center and fixed by ring-shaped support frames on the outer edges. A constraint is fixed to one side of the DEA with a gap G. The schematic illustration and the actuation principle of the resonant-impact DEA are shown in Fig. 2(a). When no voltage is applied, the two DE units have an identical out-of-plane deformation and the moving mass (i.e. the total mass of the central rod and disks) is in its rest position. When a voltage is applied to the bottom unit, the tension on its DE membrane reduces, thus causing the mass to move downwards and impact with the constraint if the stroke is sufficiently large (i.e. $\geq G$). When a voltage is applied to the top unit, the mass will move towards its upper end. By applying the actuation voltages alternatively with a suitable frequency close to its resonance, the periodic impact of the actuator will be realized, which will be characterized in the following subsection.

The fabrication process of the resonant-impact DEA is briefly introduced as follows. First, a piece of 100 μm thick silicone film with 1.1 × 1.1 pre-stretch ratio (ELASTOSIL 2030, Wacker Chemie AG) was bonded to a circular acrylic frame (20 mm ID) and a central disk (8 mm OD) to form a single unit. Second, custom carbon grease was hand-brushed on both sides of the membrane as the compliant electrodes. Third, a Nylon rod was connected to the central disks of the two units with the outer frames also connected to deform the membranes out-of-plane by 2.5 mm each. A domed steel cap was fastened to the bottom end of the rod to maximize the impact strength of the actuator. A piece of 2 mm thick acrylic beam with two ends clamped was used as the constraint.

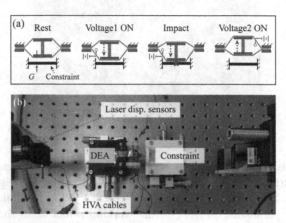

Fig. 2. (a) Schematic illustration of the resonant-impact DEA actuation principle. (b) Experimental setup of the frequency response characterization.

2.2 Frequency Response Characterization

The DEAs can demonstrate an optimal work/power output and electro-mechanical efficiency near the resonant frequency. Hence the aim of this subsection is to characterize the frequency responses of the resonant-impact DEAs and locate the frequency ranges where impacts can be triggered. The experimental setup is plotted in Fig. 2(b) and is described as follows. The DEA and the constraint were horizontally mounted to the testing rig. The two units of the DEA were actuated by two anti-phase sinusoidal frequency sweep (0 to 120 Hz in 240 s) voltage signals with the amplitude of 3.5 kV by two high voltage amplifiers (10/40A-HS, TREK). The gap G was varied from 0.2 to 1.6 mm with a step of 0.2 mm. Two laser displacement sensors (LK-G152 and LKGD500, Keyence) measured the deformation of the DEA and the center of the constraint respectively at a sampling rate of 40 kHz.

The frequency sweep results of the resonant-impact DEA with different G values are plotted in Fig. 3. It can be noted from the forward frequency sweep results that, at low frequencies, the oscillation amplitude of the DEA is lower than the gap G, hence no impact is triggered. As frequency increases, the oscillation amplitude also gradually increases and impact occurs when the amplitude $\geq G$. Further increase in the frequency will cause the oscillation amplitude to drop down sharply, which quickly terminates the impacts. Also note that the forward sweep and backward sweep results do not fully overlap, where a high-amplitude impact region in the forward sweep shows relatively low amplitudes with no impacts in the backward sweep. This is due to multiple stable solutions of the frequency responses, mainly caused by the constraint that introduced strong nonlinearity (discontinuity) of the system. By comparing the frequency sweep results with different G, it can be noted that the increase of G causes the reduction of frequency ranges where impacts can be triggered, which will have clear influences on the impact performance of the actuator. Due to this reason, we will attempt to optimize impact performance with respect to the gap G in the following subsection.

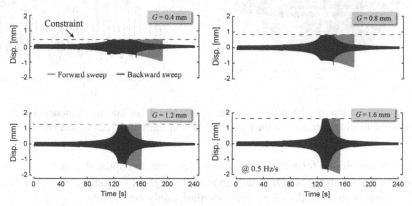

Fig. 3. Experimental results of the forward and backward frequency sweep with different constraint gaps $G = 0.4 - 1.6$ mm.

2.3 Impact Performance Optimization

For the application of suction cups proposed in this work, a higher impact frequency is preferable due to the greater number of impacts per unit time, which will lead to a shorter loading period and more rapid deployment of the suction cup. However, as demonstrated in the previous subsection, within the frequency band that impacts are triggered, at some frequencies there exist two stable solutions in the frequency responses of the actuator. This phenomenon is illustrated in Fig. 4 (a). In practical applications of the actuators, multiple stable solutions in the frequency responses are undesirable since unavoidable disturbances from the environments may cause sudden changes in the frequency responses of the actuator, leading to unpredictable and uncontrollable behaviors. Due to this reason, here we focus mainly on the frequency band that can realize the resonant-impact of the DEA and, at the same time, contains a single stable frequency response solution.

It can be noted from Fig. 4(b) that the constraint also deforms together with the moving mass during each impact. Also, note from Fig. 4(a) that the deformation amplitude of the constraint *Amp.* increases with the impact frequency. The deformation amplitude of the constraint can be a representation of the amount of force applied to the constraint during impacts. In our application, a larger impact force (i.e. a higher deformation amplitude *Amp.*) is advantageous since a larger impact force will lead to a greater deformation in the suction cup in each actuation cycle, thus resulting in a quicker and better loading of the suction cup.

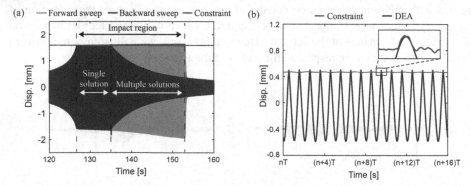

Fig. 4. (a) Illustration of the differences in forward and backward frequency sweeps. (b) Illustration of the displacements of the DEA and the constraint in 16 actuation cycles.

It can be concluded from the above discussions that, the optimal actuation frequency f_{max} for the resonant-impact DEA design is at the highest frequency which can realize periodic impacts and, at the same time, contains only one stable frequency response solution (i.e. the highest impact frequency in the backward sweep). At this frequency, the actuator can maintain its stability under environmental perturbations, maximizing both the number of impacts per unit of time and the loading force per impact.

As was demonstrated in the previous subsection, constraint gap G plays a crucial role in determining the impact characteristics of the actuator. As a result, here we experimentally investigate the effects of parameter G on the maximum impact frequency f_{max} and the maximum deformation amplitude of constraint *Amp.* (as a direct indication of the impact force) of the actuator. In this study, the gap G was varied from 0.2 to 1.6 mm with a step of 0.2 mm, f_{max} was recorded from the backward frequency sweep results and *Amp.* data was measured 5 times to eliminate random errors.

The experimental results are plotted in Fig. 5. It can be noted from Fig. 5(a) that f_{max} reduces gradually from 82.5 Hz to 68 Hz as G is increased from 0.2 mm to 1.6 mm. However, the constraint's deformation amplitude *Amp.* first shows a gradual increase with G, then peaks at $G = 0.8$ mm before decreasing as G increases further (Fig. 5(b)). Note from the above discussion that both f_{max} and *Amp.* play an important role in determining the impact performance of the actuator. As a result, an impact performance index is developed here to account for both factors by multiplying f_{max} & *Amp.* This index for each G value is then normalized with respect to the value for $G = 0.2$ mm and the results are shown in Fig. 5(c). It can be noted that the performance index decreases monotonically with the increasing G, which indicates that an actuator design with a minimum G value of 0.2 mm could yield the optimal impact performance. It is worth noting, however, a G value lower than 0.2 mm could lead to chaotic motions in the

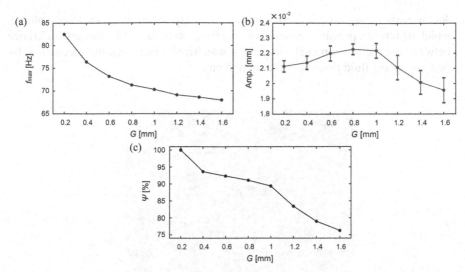

Fig. 5. (a) The maximum frequency for single frequency response solution of the resonant-impact DEA against the constraint gap G. (b) The deformation amplitude at the frequency f_{max} against G. (c) Impact performance index of the DEA against G.

actuator and dramatically increase the prototyping difficulties, hence a minimum G value of 0.2 mm is adopted for this study.

3   Suction Cup Characterization

3.1   Suction Cup Design Overview and Working Principle

The key components of the proposed suction cup are illustrated in Fig. 6, which mainly include a cylindrical shell, a DEA with a constraint for impact and a sucker. In this design, the acrylic support frames of the DEA were mounted to 3D-printed bases. A steel cap was fixed to the end-effector of the DEA to generate impacts with a 3D-printed constraint at the bottom. The gap between the steel cap and constraint was fixed at approximated 0.4 mm based on the optimization results in the previous subsection (G = 0.2 mm was not achieved here due to the fabrication tolerances in the 3D printing process). An off-the-shelf sucker with an OD of 50 mm was adopted in this prototype. The fabricated suction cup prototype has a total height of 50 mm and weighs 24.7 g.

The main working principle of the resonant-impact suction cup is illustrated in Fig. 7 and is described as follows:

i. In its initial step, the suction cup is stationary under its own gravitational force, no suction force is generated at this stage.
ii. As the actuation voltage is applied to the bottom unit of the DEA, the actuator drives the mass to move downwards.
iii. As the mass moves downwards, the front of the mass (steel cap) impacts with the constraint on the suction cup, where the resulting impact force squeezes some amount of fluid from the space enclosed by the suction cup and contacts the substrate.

iv. As the mass moves up, the inertia will cause an expansion in the enclosed volume, which results in a pressure reduction within the suction cup. This pressure difference between the suction cup enclosure and atmosphere helps to seal the suction cup by preventing any fluid flows into the suction cup.

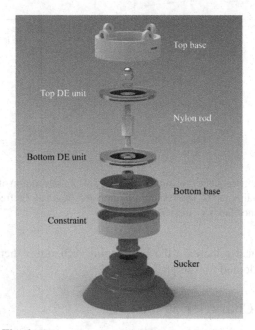

Fig. 6. Key components of the proposed suction cup.

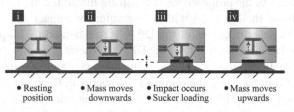

Fig. 7. Illustration of the working principle of the self-loading suction cup.

These steps are then repeated at the optimal frequency studied in the previous section for continuous loading of the suction cup until an equilibrium is reached. Once this loading process is done, the suction cup will be firmed and adhered to the substrate, where the elastic force in the suction cup (the force tries to recover the undeformed shape) will maintain the negative pressure within the suction cup. An external pulling force will also help to magnify the pressure difference by increasing the enclosed volume until the failure of the sealing.

3.2 Loading Performance Characterization

In this subsection, the loading performance of the proposed suction cup in both air and water environments are characterized experimentally. In this setup, the suction cup was placed vertically and the DEA was actuated by antiphase voltages at a fixed frequency. Two laser displacement sensors measured the displacement of the moving mass and the suction cup respectively. For experiments in air, a piece of smooth acrylic plate was adopted as the substrate. For experiments in water, a custom container with the same acrylic plate was adopted. Deionized water was filled into the container to submerge the sucker, but leaving the DEA part in air for simpler setup and better safety.

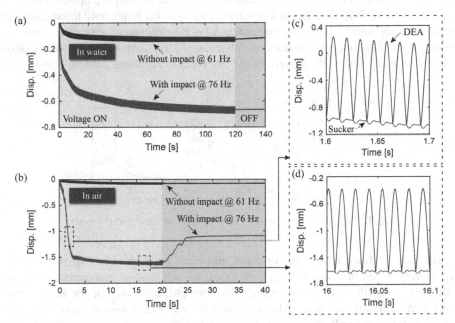

Fig. 8. (a) Comparison of the deformation of the suction cup in water with and without DEA-triggered impacts. (b) Comparison of the deformation of the suction cup in the air with and without DEA-triggered impacts, the zoomed-in boxes in (c) and (d) show the deformations of the suction cup and DEA during the loading stage and maintaining stage, respectively.

The measured deformations of the suction cup during the loading process in water and in air are plotted in Fig. 8(a) and (b) respectively. Note that, as a demonstration of the effectiveness of the resonant-impact mechanism, two actuation frequencies were tested, which are the frequency with no impacts triggered (61 Hz) and the optimal resonant-impact frequency f_{max} studied in the last Sect. (76 Hz). It can be noted that the resonant-impact suction cup demonstrates clear effectiveness in its loading capability both in water and air environments. It is also worth noting that the suction cup quickly finished loading in less than 5 s and turned into the maintaining stage after being in the air condition. However, the loading process is much slower in water, which could be due to the much higher viscosity and incompressibility of water. The detailed displacements of DEA's moving mass and the suction cup during the loading and maintaining stages in air condition are plotted in Fig. 8(c) and (d) respectively. It can be noted that the suction cup deforms further after the occurrence of each impact, which drives the suction cup to load and to maintain its deformation in the loading and maintaining stage respectively.

3.3 Suction Force Characterization

To directly demonstrate the effectiveness of active loading of the proposed suction cup, pull-off force experiments were also conducted. In these tests, the suction cup was placed on a piece of a smooth acrylic plate with no loading force applied to it apart from its own gravitational force. A linear rail was controlled to pull the suction cup upwards from its initial position via Nylon strings at a constant velocity of 0.1 mm/s until the suction cup was completely detached from the substrate. A laser displacement sensor measured the displacement of the linear rail and a load cell measured the suction force. Both actuation voltages OFF and ON at 76 Hz were tested five times to eliminate random errors.

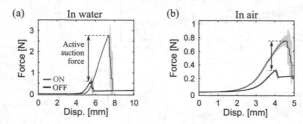

Fig. 9. Pull-off force experimental results (a) in water and (b) in air.

The pull-off force test results in water and in air are plotted in Fig. 9(a) and (b) respectively. It can be noted that, in both cases, the self-loading mechanism proposed in this paper significantly increases the maximum pull-off forces of the suction cup, which proves its effectiveness. Also note that the water case sees the most dramatic improvements in the pull-off force by over 4 times compared with its passive state. The improvement in the pull-off force is over 1.5 times in air, which could be due to the higher leakage rate of the off-the-shelf sucker in air.

4 Conclusion

In this work, a novel self-loading suction cup driven by a resonant-impact DEA was developed, which attempted to address the limitation of external loading force demands in conventional suction cup designs. The key findings of this paper are summarized as follows:

i. The impact performance of the resonant-impact DEA is determined by both the impact frequency and the amplitude of the impact force.
ii. The constraint gap G shows crucial effects on the impact performance of the resonant-impact DEA. It is demonstrated in experiments that a smaller G value will lead to improved impact performance.

iii. The self-loading suction cup demonstrates clear effectiveness in both water and air environments, where the maximum pull-off forces of the suction cup are increased by over 4 times and 1.5 times in water and in air, respectively.

This novel suction cup design proposed in this paper can have potential applications in enhanced soft robotic locomotion (e.g. wall-climbing), medical robotics, surveillance and environment monitoring (e.g. unmanned underwater robots). Future work shall investigate more compact DEA configurations and develop multi-layer fabrication techniques to further improve the loading performance of the suction cup.

This work was supported in part by the National Natural Science Foundation of China under Grant 52105038, in part by the Guangdong Basic and Applied Basic Research Foundation under Grant 2020A1515110175, in part by the Shenzhen Fundamental Research Project under Grant JSGG20201103094400002.

References

1. Shintake, J., Cacucciolo, V., Floreano, D., Shea, H.: Soft Robotic Grippers. Adv. Mater. **30**(29), 170735 (2018)
2. Zhang, Y., Yang, D., Yan, P., Zhou, P., Zou, J., Gu, G.: Inchworm Inspired Multimodal Soft Robots With Crawling, Climbing, and Transitioning Locomotion. IEEE Trans. Robot. **38**(3), 1806–1819 (2021)
3. Tiwari, A., Persson, B.N.J.: Physics of suction cups. Soft Matter **15**(46), 9482–9499 (2019)
4. Graule, M.A., et al.: Perching and takeoff of a robotic insect on overhangs using switchable electrostatic adhesion. Science **352**(6288), 978–981 (2016)
5. Hawkes, E.W., Eason, E.V., Christensen, D.L., Cutkosky, M.R.: Human climbing with efficiently scaled gecko-inspired dry adhesives. J. R. Soc. Interface **12**(102), 20140675 (2015)
6. Vogel, M.J., Steen, P.H.: Capillarity-based switchable adhesion. Proc. Natl. Acad. Sci. **107**(8), 3377–3381 (2010)
7. Baik, S., Kim, D.W., Park, Y., Lee, T.J., Ho Bhang, S., Pang, C.: A wet-tolerant adhesive patch inspired by protuberances in suction cups of octopi. Nature **546**(7658), 396–400 (2017)
8. Wang, W., Wang, K., Zong, G.H., Li, D.Z.: Principle and experiment of vibrating suction method for wall-climbing robot. Vacuum **85**(1), 107–112 (2010)
9. Lee, H., Um, D.S., Lee, Y., Lim, S., Jun Kim, H., Ko, H.: Octopus-inspired smart adhesive pads for transfer printing of semiconducting nanomembranes. Adv. Mater **28**(34), 7457–7465 (2016)
10. Koivikko, A., Drotlef, D., Dayan, C.B., Sariola, V., Sitti, M.: 3D-printed pneumatically controlled soft suction cups for gripping fragile, small, and rough objects. Adv. Intell. Syst. 2100034 (2021)
11. Koivikko, A., Drotlef, D.M., Sitti, M., Sariola, V.: Magnetically switchable soft suction grippers. Extrem. Mech. Lett. **44**, 101263 (2021)
12. Song, S., Drotlef, D.M., Son, D., Koivikko, A., Sitti, M.: Adaptive self-sealing suction-based soft robotic gripper. Adv. Sci. **8**(17), 1–11 (2021)
13. Cao, C., Gao, X., Conn, A.T.: A magnetically coupled dielectric elastomer pump for soft robotics. Adv. Mater. Technol. **4**(8), 1900128 (2019)
14. Wang, K., Wang, W., Zhang, H., Fang, J.: Suction force of vibrating suction method based on pi theorem: Analysis and experiment. Vacuum **86**(12), 1783–1788 (2012)
15. Sandoval, J.A., Jadhav, S., Quan, H., Deheyn, D.D., Tolley, M.T.: Reversible adhesion to rough surfaces both in and out of water, inspired by the clingfish suction disc. Bioinspiration and Biomimetics **14**(6), 066016 (2019)

16. Xu, H., Yang, F., Zhang, Y., Jiang, X., Wen, L.: A biomimetic suction cup with a v-notch structure inspired by the net-winged midge larvae. IEEE Robot. Autom. Lett. **7**(2), 3547–3554 (2022)
17. Sareh, S., et al.: Anchoring like octopus: Biologically inspired soft artificial sucker. J. R. Soc. Interfac **14**(135), 20170395 (2017)
18. Okuno, Y., Shigemune, H., Kuwajima, Y., Maeda, S.: Stretchable Suction Cup with Electroadhesion. Adv. Mater. Technol. **4**(1), 1–6 (2019)
19. Bing-Shan, H., Li-Wen, W., Zhuang, F., Yan-Zheng, Z.: Bio-inspired miniature suction cups actuated by shape memory alloy. Int. J. Adv. Robot. Syst. **6**(3), 151–160 (2009)
20. Cao, C., Wang, L., Gao, X.: A monolithic electrostatic–hydraulic coupled suction pad. Advanced Intelligent Systems, 2200425 (2023)
21. Sholl, N., Moss, A., Kier, W.M., Mohseni, K.: A soft end effector inspired by cephalopod suckers and augmented by a dielectric elastomer actuator. Soft Robot. **6**(3), 356–367 (2019)
22. Wang, S., Luo, H., Linghu, C., Song, J.: Elastic energy storage enabled magnetically actuated, octopus-inspired smart adhesive. Adv. Funct. Mater. **31**(9), 1–9 (2021)
23. Hu, X., Fu, Y., Liu, Y., Liu, B., Qu, S.: Acarid suctioncup-inspired rapid and tunable magnetic adhesion. Adv. Mater. Technol. **2100004**, 1–9 (2021)
24. Zhang, C., et al.: Hydraulically coupled dielectric elastomer actuators for a bioinspired suction cup. Polymers (Basel) **13**(20), 3481 (2021)
25. Shi, Y., et al.: A processable, high-performance dielectric elastomer and multilayering process. Science **377**, 228–232 (2022)
26. Chen, Y., et al.: Controlled flight of a microrobot powered by soft artificial muscles. Nature. **575** (2019)
27. Cao, C., et al.: On the mechanical power output comparisons of cone dielectric elastomer actuators. IEEE/ASME Trans. Mechatronics **26**(6), 3151–3162 (2021)
28. Hau, S., Rizzello, G., Seelecke, S.: A novel dielectric elastomer membrane actuator concept for high-force applications. Extrem. Mech. Lett. **23**, 24–28 (2018)
29. Cao, C., Chen, L., Hill, T.L., Wang, L., Gao, X.: Exploiting bistability for high-performance dielectric elastomer resonators. IEEE/ASME Trans. Mechatronics 1–12 (2022)
30. Cao, C., et al.: Toward broad optimal output bandwidth dielectric elastomer actuators. Sci. China Technol. Sci. **65**(5), 1137–1148 (2022)

Model-free Adaptive Control of Dielectric Elastomer Actuator

Dun Mao[1,2,3], Yue Zhang[1,2,3], Jundong Wu[1,2,3], and Yawu Wang[1,2,3](✉) iD

[1] School of Automation, China University of Geosciences, Wuhan 430074, China
wangyawu@cug.edu.cn
[2] Hubei Key Laboratory of Advanced Control and Intelligent Automation for Complex Systems, Wuhan 430074, China
[3] Engineering Research Center of Intelligent Technology for Geo-Exploration, Ministry of Education, Wuhan 430074, China

Abstract. Soft robots are usually driven by soft actuators, and the dielectric elastomer actuator (DEA) is recognized as one of the most promising soft actuators. However, the DEA has complex nonlinear char- acteristics, which brings great challenges to its control. So, how to use the appropriate method to control the DEA has become a problem worth pondering. This paper proposes three model-free adaptive control (MFAC) methods to realize the tacking control of the DEA. These meth- ods avoid the complex process of establishing the dynamic model of the DEA, and only need the input and output data to control. Thus, these methods have a strong adaptability and generalization ability. To verify the effectiveness of the proposed methods, some simulations are imple- mented. More importantly, some actual experiments are implemented to further demonstrate the validity of the methods. The root-mean-square errors (RMSEs) of the simulation results are less than 0.35%, and the RMSEs of the actual experimental results can be maintained at about 6.5%, which fully reflects the excellence of the proposed methods.

Keywords: Dielectric elastomer actuator · Model-free adaptive control · Tracking control · Simulation · Experiment

1 Introduction

Rigid robots used in the traditional assembly and transportation industry are gradually unable to meet the complex and changeable working environment of human beings. Thus, various soft robots have attracted the extensive discussion and research. In the past few decades, soft robotics have become a new field of continuous development. Among them, the dielectric electro active polymer (DEAP) is one of the most promising materials for soft actuators.

The DEAP material [1, 2] is widely concerned because of its unique mechanical properties [3]. Compared with traditional piezoelectric materials, the DEAP material has obvious advantages such as the greater strain capacity, light weight, high driving efficiency and good seismic performance. So, it is one of the most po- tential bionic materials. According to the different mechanism of the action, the DEAP material is

H. Yang et al. (Eds.): ICIRA 2023, LNAI 14270, pp. 125–137, 2023.
https://doi.org/10.1007/978-981-99-6492-5_12

divided into the electronic type and ionization type. The ionic DEAP often requires the relative solution environment. It needs the continuous energy supply to maintain the shape and its energy efficiency is relatively low. Compared with the ionic DEAP, the electronic DEAP has obvious advantages of large deformation ($>100\%$), high energy density ($>3.4\text{MJ}\cdot\text{m}^{-3}$), fast reaction speed (on the order of millisecond), light weight and low cost. Thus, based on the electronic DEAP material, the dielectric elastomer actuator (DEA) has a wide range of applications in the field of soft robots [4], such as DEA wearable humanoid robot, climbing robot, swimming robot and flying robot, etc.

The quality of the control method of the DEA is related to whether the soft robot can be put into the application. The DEA has complex nonlinear char- acteristics(such as asymmetric hysteresis property and creep property), which brings a big challenge to its control. The asymmetric hysteresis property of the DEA refers that there is no straight line that can divide the hysteresis loops of the displacement versus driving voltage curve into two symmetric parts. The creep property of the DEA refers that its displacement slowly shifts upward under the actuation of the periodic driving voltage.

Until now, some control methods have been proposed to realize the control of the DEA. According to whether the controller design is based on the mathemat- ical model, the controllers for controlling the DEA are mainly divided into two categories: the model-based controller (MBC) and model-free controller (MFC).

In [5], a diaphragm actuator of the dielectric elastomer was designed and fabricated for the human pulse signal tracking. A physical model was developed to capture the dynamic of the actuator, and then an H-infinity controller was designed for the actuator based on the physical model to achieve the robust control. In [6], a dynamic model of the DEA composed of asymmetric hysteresis model and creep model was established. Then, the hysteresis and creep non- linearity of the DEA were compensated by designing an inverse compensation feedforward controller. Finally, the tracking control of the DEA was realized by a compound controller. However, MBCs have very complicated mathematical expressions, which makes them difficult to be implemented in engineering.

Different from the MBC, the design of the MFC does not depend on the mathematical model of the DEA. So, the MFC is more suitable for practical en- gineering. To realize the control of the DEA, a PID controller was used in the [7]. However, the PID controller cannot deal with complex nonlinear characteristics of the DEA well. In [8], the iterative learning control method was employed to control the crawling robot based on the DEA, but the anti-interference ability of the iterative learning control is poor. So, it is not able to control the behavior of the DEA well. Thus, it is necessary to design a better MFC.

The model-free adaptive control (MFAC) method proposes a concept called pseudo-partial derivative (PPD) and a new dynamic linearization method [9, 10]. This method gets rid of many basic problems such as the precise modeling and model reduction. The MFAC may be effective in overcoming the hysteresis and creep nonlinearities of the system, and using the MFAC method can realize good control effect with millimeter-level errors for tracking a wide range of trajectories. Moreover, the MFAC excels in practical engineering.

Inspired by the above considerations, this paper presents three MFAC meth- ods for the DEA with complex nonlinear characteristics. Firstly, the basic prin- ciples of these three MFAC methods are briefly introduced. Then, by using the Hammerstein-Wiener model to describe the dynamic characteristic of the DEA, the effectiveness of the proposed methods is preliminarily verified in simula- tions. Finally, several actual experiments are implemented to further verify the effectiveness and universality of the presented methods.

2 Model-free Adaptive Control Method

In many previous references, the control of the DEA is based on its dynamic model. However, due to the obvious nonlinear characteristics of the DEA (such as asymmetric, rate dependent, stress dependent, temperature dependent hys- teresis nonlinearity and creep nonlinearity), its dynamic modeling is very com- plicated and difficult. The model-free adaptive control (MFAC) method has been developed to solve the control problem of nonlinear systems[11, 12]. The MFAC method has the advantage of simplicity that can be used to directly design the controller without establishing the system model.

Thus, three MFAC methods are presented to realize the tracking control of the DEA. The key of the MFAC method is the dynamic linearization technology. In general, there are three types of the dynamic linearization technology, which are the compact form dynamic linearization (CFDL), the partial form dynamic linearization (PFDL) and the full form dynamic linearization (FFDL). Here, we take the FFDL as an example to give a detailed description of the MFAC method.

The DEA system can be represented by the following general single-input- single-output discrete-time nonlinear system:

$$y(k + 1) = f(y(k), \cdots, y(k - ny), u(k), \cdots, u(k - nu)) \quad (1)$$

where $y(k) \in R$ and $u(k) \in R$ are the input and output of the system at k -th sampling time, $f(\cdot)$ is a nonlinear function, ny and nu are the orders of system output and input.

The following assumptions are made for nonlinear systems (1).

Assumption 1: *The partial derivative of the nonlinear function $f(\cdot)$ with respect to the control input signal $u(k)$ is continuous.*

Assumption 2: *The nonlinear system (1) satisfies the generalized Lipschitz condition. That is, for any time $k_1 \neq k_2$, $k1 \geq 0$, $k2 \geq 0$ and $u(k_1) \neq u(k_2)$, one can obtain:*

$$|y(k_1 + 1) - y(k_2 + 1)| \leq b|u(k_1) - u(k_2)| \quad (2)$$

where b > 0 is a constant.

Assumption 1 is a typical constraint condition for general nonlinear systems in control system design. Assumption 2 is a restriction on the upper bound of the rate of change of system output. From the energy point of view, the bounded input energy changes should produce the bounded output energy changes in the system. In this paper, we are going to use the MFAC method to achieve the tracking control of the DEA.

Thus, we will not establish the dynamic model of the DEA like (1). In this way, we cannot strictly verify whether the DEA meets Assumption 1 and Assumption 2 from the theoretical perspective. However, many practical systems satisfy these two assumptions, such as temperature con- trol system, pressure control system, liquid level control system, etc. So, we also assume that the DEA satisfies these two assumptions, whose reasonability will be verified through actual experiments in the following developments.

If the nonlinear system (1) satisfies the Assumption 1 and Assumption 2, $\|\Delta H_{Ly,Lu}(k)\| \neq 0$ and $\Delta u(k) = u(k) - u(k-1) \neq 0$ for all time k, then (1) can be equivalently expressed as:

$$\Delta y(k+1) = \varphi_{Ly,Lu}^T(k)\Delta H_{Ly,Lu}(k) \tag{3}$$

where $\Delta y(k+1) = y(k+1) - y(k)$, $\varphi_{Ly,Lu}^T(k) = [\varphi_1(k), \cdots, \varphi_{Ly}, \varphi_{Ly+1}, \cdots, \varphi_{Ly+Lu}]^T \in R^{Ly+Lu}$ is an unknown but bounded pseudo-gradient, $\Delta H_{Ly,Lu} = [\Delta y(k), \cdots, \Delta y(k - Ly + 1), \Delta u(k), \cdots, \Delta u(k - Lu + 1)]^T$, Ly Lu are pseudo-orders.

Based on (3), (1) can be rewritten as

$$y(k+1) = y(k) + \varphi_{Ly,Lu}^T(k)\Delta H_{Ly,Lu}(k) \tag{4}$$

The control performance index function is chosen as follow.

$$J(u(k)) = [yr(k+1) - y(k+1)]^2 + \lambda[u(k) - u(k-1)]^2 \tag{5}$$

where $yr(k+1)$ is the desired input signal and $\lambda > 0$ is the weighting factor.

By substituting (4) into (5), and solving the extreme value of $J(u(k))$ corre- sponding to $u(k)$, the following control rate can be obtained.

$$
\begin{aligned}
u(k) = u(k-1) &+ \frac{\rho_{Ly+1}\varphi_{Ly+1}(k)}{\lambda + \varphi_{Ly+1}(k)^2}[y_r(k+1) - y(k)] \\
&- \frac{\varphi_{Ly+1}\sum_i^{Ly}\rho_i\varphi_i(k)\Delta y(k-i+1)}{\lambda + \varphi_{Ly+1}(k)^2} \\
&- \frac{\varphi_{Ly+1Lu}\sum_{i=Ly+2}^{Ly+Lu}\rho_i\varphi_i(k)\Delta u(k+Ly-i+1)}{\lambda + \varphi_{Ly+1}(k)^2}
\end{aligned}
\tag{6}
$$

where $\rho_i \in (0, 1]$, $i = 1, 2, \cdots, Ly + Lu$ is an additional step size factor that makes the control rate (6) more general.

For general nonlinear systems, the pseudo-gradient PG $\varphi_{Ly,Lu}(k)$ is time- varying and unknown. So, the control rate (6) cannot be directly applied. Thus,

it is necessary to use the parameter estimation method to estimate the $\varphi_{Ly,Lu}(k)$ online. The estimation criterion function of PPD $\varphi_{Ly,Lu}(k)$ is selected as

$$J(\hat{\varphi}_{L_y,L_u}(k)) = [\Delta y(k) - \hat{\varphi}_{L_y,L_u}^T(k)\Delta H(k-1)]^2$$
$$+\mu[\hat{\varphi}_{L_y,L_u}(k) - \hat{\varphi}_{L_y,L_u}(k-1)]^2 \qquad (7)$$

where $\hat{\varphi}_{L_y,L_u}(k)$ is the estimated value of PG $\varphi_{L_y,L_u}^T(k)$, $\mu > 0$ is the weighting factor.

By calculating the extremum of (7) with respect to $\hat{\varphi}_{L_y,L_u}(k)$, the estimated algorithm of $\hat{\varphi}_{L_y,L_u}(k)$ can be obtained.

$$\hat{\varphi}_{L_y,L_u}(k) = \hat{\varphi}_{L_y,L_u}(k-1) + \frac{\eta\Delta H(k-1)}{\mu + \|\Delta H(k-1)\|^2}[\Delta y(k)$$
$$-\hat{\varphi}_{L_y,L_u}(k-1)\Delta H(k-1)] \qquad (8)$$

where $\eta \in (0, 2]$ is an additional step size factor, which is used to make the parameter estimation algorithm (8) more flexible and general.

The principle of the MFAC based on the other two dynamic linearization technologies is similar. When Ly is 0 and Lu is 1, the FFDL-based MFAC method can be transformed into the CFDL-based MFAC method. When Ly is 0 and Lu is i (i is a positive integer), the FFDL-based MFAC method can be transformed into the PFDL-based MFAC method.

Theoretically, the smaller the PG order is, the less the computational burden will be. However, the dynamic behavior of $\varphi_{L_y,L_u}(k)$ will be more complicated, which makes the controller design difficult. The performance of the controller will improve with the increase of the gradient order. Relatively speaking, the FFDL-based MFAC method has more adjustable degrees of freedom and greater design flexibility than the CFDL-based MFAC method and the PFDL-based MFAC method.

3 Simulations

In this part, the effectiveness of three MFAC methods are preliminarily verified through simulations. The controller parameters can also be optimized, which facilitates the following actual experiments.

We employ the Hammerstein-Wiener model to describe the dynamic char- acteristic of the DEA, and take it as the controlled object in simulations. The specific modeling process can be found in our previous work [13]. In addition, to evaluate the accuracy of the tracking control, we define the root-mean-square error as the index, which is

$$e = \sqrt{\frac{1}{N}\sum_{j=1}^{N}(D_{Ej} - D_{Mj})^2} \times 100\% \qquad (9)$$

where N is the number of sampling points D_{Ej} is the measured displacement of the DEA at the j-th sampling point. D_{Mj} is the output of the Hammerstein- Wiener model at the j-th sampling point.

Firstly, we use the following sine-like wave with multi-amplitude and multi- frequency as the desired trajectory to perform the simulations by employing three MFAC methods, respectively.

$$
\begin{cases}
t \leq 1 : \\
D(t) = \sin(\pi f_1 t) + 0.02 \\
t > 1 : \\
t_m = rem(t - 1, 0.6/f_1 + 1.7/f_2) \\
t_m < 0.6/f_1 : \\
D(t) = \sin(\pi f_1 (t_m + 1)) \\
0.6/f_1 \leq t_m < 0.6/f_1 + 1.7/f_2 : \\
D(t) = 0.25 \sin(2\pi f_2 (t_m - 2)) + 0.75 \sin(2\pi f_2)
\end{cases}
\tag{10}
$$

in which $f1 = 1/5$ (Hz), $f2 = 2/5$ (Hz), rem(a,c) is the remainder of a divided by c.

We use the trial-and-error method to adjust the controller parameters. The specific adjustment principle is given below. (1) Considering that λ is a constraint factor that represents the change rate in the output of the constraint system, it has the most obvious influence on the dynamic performance of the whole control system, and should be adjusted first. (2) Other parameters, such as ρ and μ, are adjusted. Following the above principles, we try our best to tune the controller parameter when employing these three MFAC methods. The adjusted controller parameters are shown in Table 1.

Table 1. Controller parameters when employing three MFAC methods in simulations

Symbol	CFDL-based MFAC method	PFDL-based MFAC method	FFDL-based MFAC method
Ly	0	0	2
Lu	1	2	2
λ	0.013	0.02	0.11
η	6	10	0.23
μ	13	0.1	23
$\rho 1$	0.4	0.8	0.98
$\rho 2$	0	0.5	0.98
$\rho 3$	0	0	1.95
$\rho 4$	0	0	0.98
$u(0)$	0	0	0
$y(0)$	0	0	0

The comparisons of the desired trajectory and the output of the dynamic model when employing three MFAC methods are shown in Fig. 1. In addition, the corresponding control errors are also drawn in Fig. 1. Moreover, the corre- sponding root-mean-square errors are shown in Table 2. From Table 2, we can find that the control performance when employing the FFDL-based MFAC method is the best, which conforms to the theory. This is because a longer pseudo-gradient can take into account more input and output changes in a slid- ing time window of a certain length, thereby making the trajectory tracking effect better.

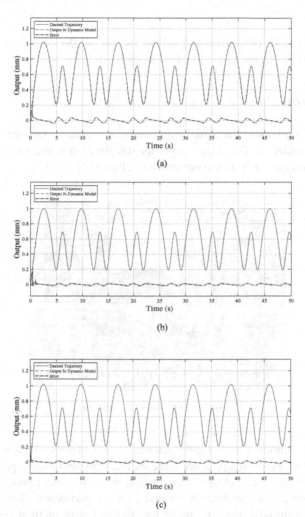

Fig. 1. Comparisons of sine-like desired trajectory and output of dynamic model, as well as corresponding control errors when using three MFAC methods. (a) CFDL-based MFAC method (b) PFDL-based MFAC method (c) FFDL-based MFAC method

It should be noted that the simulations are carried out in an ideal envi- ronment. However, there are many uncertain disturbances in practice. Thus, in order to further explore the feasibility of three MFAC methods in engineering application, practical experiments are needed. In addition, to ensure the high performance of DEA, as well

Table 2. The root-mean-square errors of simulations when employing three MFAC methods

Type of wave	CFDL-based	PFDL-based	FFDL-based
	MFAC method MFAC method MFAC method		
Sine-like	2.1977%	1.4748%	1.1235%

as to avoid negative displacement and severe vi- bration, the frequency of the desired trajectory should be limited to the low frequency band.

4 Experiments

In this part, we implement the actual experiments to further verify the effective- ness of three MFAC methods. The whole experimental platform is shown in Fig. 2, and its detail descriptions can be found in our previous study [14].

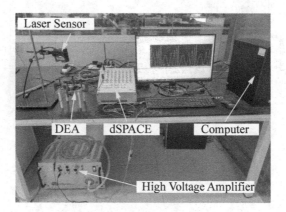

Fig. 2. Experimental platform

Firstly, we still choose (10) as the desired trajectory, and respectively use three MFAC methods to conduct experiments. Since there are uncertainties (such as parameter pertur- bation, external disturbance, etc.) in experiments, the con- troller parameters optimized in the simulations cannot be directly applied on the experiments. Thus, the controller parameters are optimized again by using the trial-and-error method according to the principles mentioned in the previous section, and the results are shown in Table 3.

The comparisons of desired trajectory and the measured displacement of the DEA are shown in Fig. 3. In addition, the corresponding control errors are added in Fig. 3. Meanwhile, the corresponding root-mean-square errors are shown in Table 4. It can be seen from this table that the CFDL-based MFAC method works best in the experiment, which is inconsistent with the conclusion in the simulation. There are two main reasons: (1) The experiment environment is different with the simulation environment. (2) The

Table 3. Controller parameters when employing three MFAC methods in experiments

Symbol	CFDL-based	PFDL-based	FFDL-based
	MFAC method	MFAC method	MFAC method
Ly	0	0	2
Lu	1	2	2
λ	0.05	0.025	0.2
η	1	15	0.23
μ	10	0.1	20
$\rho 1$	0.4	0.25	0.1
$\rho 2$	0	0.25	0.98
$\rho 3$	0	0	2.5
$\rho 4$	0	0	0.98
$u(0)$	0	0	0
$y(0)$	0	0	0

Table 4. The root-mean-square errors of experiments when employing three MFAC methods

Waves\Methods	Sine-like	Tanglesome	Square
CFDL	3.4186%	4.9775%	3.2948%
PFDL	3.6151%	6.4871%	3.1296%
FFDL	4.6570%	5.9633%	2.8355%

controller parameters may not be adjusted to the optima by employing the trial-and-error method.

In order to further verify the effectiveness of these three MFAC methods in practical experiments, we chose two additional waves as the desired trajec- tories for experiments. The controller parameters are consistent with that in the previous experiments. Experimental results and control errors are shown in Fig. 4 and Fig. 5. In addition, the corresponding root-mean-square-errors are added to Table 4 to facilitate the comparison. As can be seen from Table 4, the CFDL-based MFAC method in the tanglesome wave experiment has the best performance. However, the FFDL-based MFAC method works best in the square wave experiment. This is due to the fact that more PG components share the dynamic performance of the system and can better suppress overshoot.

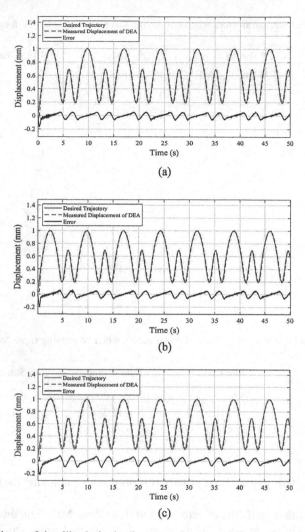

Fig. 3. Comparisons of sine-like desired trajectory and measured displacement of DEA, as well as corresponding control errors when using three MFAC methods. (a) CFDL- based MFAC method (b) PFDL-based MFAC method (c) FFDL-based MFAC method

All in all, even though some complex trajectories with multifrequency are adopted and the dynamic model of the DEA is not established, the root-mean- square errors of all experiment results are below 6.5%, indicating that three MFAC methods are effective and have certain universality for the tracking con- trol of the DEA. In addition, the experimental results demonstrate that the assumption in the section II is reasonable.

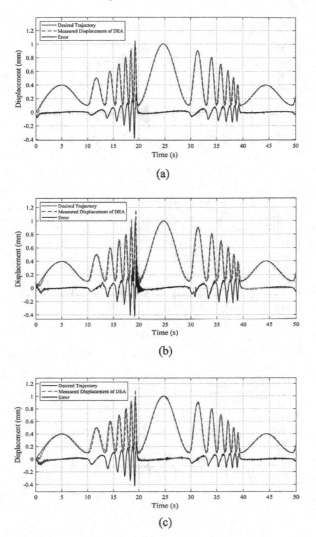

Fig. 4. Comparisons of tanglesome desired trajectory and measured displacement of DEA, as well as corresponding control errors when using three MFAC methods. (a) CFDL-based MFAC method (b) PFDL-based MFAC method (c) FFDL-based MFAC method

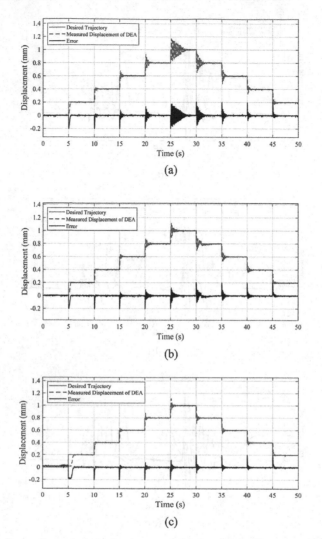

Fig. 5. Comparisons of square desired trajectory and measured displacement of DEA, as well as corresponding control errors when using three MFAC methods. (a) CFDL- based MFAC method (b) PFDL-based MFAC method (c) FFDL-based MFAC method

5 Conclusion

In order to realize the tracking control of the DEA, this paper adopts three MFAC methods. By using these methods, the complex process of building the dynamic model of the DEA can be avoided. To preliminarily verify the effec- tiveness of three MFAC methods, the simulations are implemented. Then, some actual experiments are further implemented to demonstrate the performance of the proposed methods in practice application. Since the root-mean-square er- rors of all experiment results are below 6.5%, the proposed methods are more remarkable from the perspective of the practice application.

References

1. Tryson, M., Kiil, H.E.: Dielectric electro active polymers: Development of an industry. Electroactive Polymer Actuators and Devices. San Diego, CA **7642**, 555–563 (2010)
2. Mockensturm, E.M., Goulbourne, N.: Dynamic response of dielectric elastomers. Int. J. Non-Linear Mech. **41**(3), 388–395 (2006)
3. Romasanta, L.J., L´opez-Manchado, M.A., Verdejo, R.: Increasing the performance of dielectric elastomer actuators: a review from the materials perspective. Progress in Polymer Science **51**, 188–211 (2015)
4. Guoying, G., Jian, Z., Limin, Z., et al.: A survey on dielectric elastomer actuators for soft robots. Bioinspiration & Biomimetics **12**(1), 011003 (2017)
5. Zhihang, Y., Zheng, C., Asmatulu, R., et al.: Robust control of dielectric elastomer di- aphragm actuator for human pulse signal tracking. Smart Materials and Structures **26**(8), 085043 (2017)
6. Yawu, W., Peng, H., Jundong, W., et al.: Modelling and compound control of intelligently dielectric elastomer actuator. Control. Eng. Pract. **126**, 105261 (2022)
7. Ramson, S.Q.X.P.F., Graaf, D.D., et al.: An adaptive control system for dielectric elastomers. In: IEEE International Conference on Industrial Technology, pp. 335–340. Hong Kong, China (2005)
8. Haochen, C., Xuefeng, L., Wenyu, L., et al.: Iterative learning control for motion trajectory tracking of a circular soft crawling robot. Frontiers in Robotics and AI **6**, 113 (2019)
9. Hou, Z., Jin, S.: Model free adaptive control. CRC Press, Boca Raton, FL, USA (2013)
10. Zhongsheng, H., Shuangshuang, X.: On model-free adaptive control and its stability analysis. IEEE Trans. Autom. Control **64**(11), 4555–4569 (2019)
11. Shuangshuang, X., Zhongsheng, H.: Model-free adaptive control for unknown MIMO non-affine nonlinear discrete-time systems with experimental validation. IEEE Trans. Neur. Netw. Learn. Sys. **33**(4), 1727–1739 (2020)
12. Dong, L., Guanghong, Y.: Event-based model-free adaptive control for discrete-time nonlinear processes. IET Control Theory Appl. **11**(15), 2531–2538 (2017)
13. Peng, H., Wenjun, Y., Yawu, W.: Dynamic modeling of dielectric elastomer actuator with conical shape. Plos One **15**(8), e0235229 (2020)
14. Peng, H., Jundong, W., Chunyi, S., Wang, Y.: Tracking control of soft dielectric elastomer actuator based on nonlinear PID controller. International Journal of Control (2022). https://doi.org/10.1080/00207179.2022.2112088

Modeling and Design Optimization of a Pre-stretched Rolled Dielectric Elastomer Actuator

Jaining Wu[1,2], Kai Luo[1,2], Peinan Yan[1,2], Xiazi Hu[1,2], Huangwei Ji[1,2], and Feifei Chen[1,2(✉)]

[1] State Key Laboratory of Mechanical System and Vibration, Shanghai Jiao Tong University, Shanghai 200240, China
ffchen@sjtu.edu.cn
[2] School of Mechanical Engineering, Shanghai Jiao Tong University, Shanghai 200240, China

Abstract. Dielectric elastomer actuators (DEAs) possess characteristics closest to human muscles and have been rapidly developed. The rolled DEA is considered more suitable as a driving module due to its ability to output unidirectional deformation. This paper proposes a high-performance actuator, which is connected in series by a spring and a DEA, wherein the spring realizes the pre-stretching of the DEA. To predict the mechanical behavior of the structure, the rolled DEA is simplified into a single-layer tubular DEA, and a static model is established to predict the free displacement and blocking force under different input voltages, spring stiffness coefficients, and geometric parameters of the structure. The optimal pre-stretch effect was tailored by finding the optimal combination of spring stiffness and pre-stretch through a two-dimensional search, thereby maximizing the free displacement, blocking force, or equivalent work. Under the optimal parameter combination aimed at maximizing the equivalent work, the system achieves a free displacement of 0.43 mm and a blocking force of 0.57 N. These values are 3.6 times higher for free displacement and 1.54 times higher for blocking force compared to the springless structure. The effectiveness of the theoretical analysis model is verified by experiments, and relevant manufacturing processes are introduced. This study offers a promising approach to analyzing the effect of pre-stretch on the performance of rolled DEAs, opening up new possibilities for soft robotics applications.

Keywords: Soft robotics · Dielectric elastomer actuator · Pre-stretch

1 Introduction

Soft robotics has emerged as a prominent field of research in recent years, garnering significant attention from the scientific community and the general public alike. Soft robots have a broad range of applications, including wearable

Supported by the National Natural Science Fo6undation of China (Grants No. 52275026 and 51905340).

H. Yang et al. (Eds.): ICIRA 2023, LNAI 14270, pp. 138–149, 2023.
https://doi.org/10.1007/978-981-99-6492-5_13

devices [1], artificial muscles [2], and minimally invasive surgical robots [3]. A crucial challenge in developing these robots is designing effective actuators that can actuate a soft body and enable locomotion, manipulation, and other tasks [2]. Human muscles, which have high energy density (0.4–40 J/kg), wide frequency response (1–200 Hz), and large strain (5–30%), serve as the inspiration for the design of actuators. Among various actuator technologies, dielectric elastomer actuators (DEAs) possess characteristics that are closest to human muscles and have been rapidly developed. However, the actuation forces generated by these thin-film actuators are relatively limited, typically falling within the millinewton range for an electric field of approximately 10 MV/m. Therefore, researchers have proposed various techniques for increasing the output force of DEAs, including stacking multiple layers [4] or rolling [5].

The rolled DEA is considered more suitable as a driving module due to its ability to convert biaxial expansion into linear motion along the roll axis. For example, Chen et al. proposed a miniature flying robot that is driven by a multi-layered DEA rolled into a cylindrical shell to generate linear actuation [6]. This robot is capable of producing approximately 1.8mN of lift. Tang et al. utilized rolled DEAs as the elongation unit in the development of a pipeline inspection robot [7]. Sholl et al. utilized a rolled DEA to generate adhesive forces and developed a soft suction cup end effector resembling an octopus suction cup [8]. Nagai et al. developed underwater robots using rolled DEAs. The angle and torque of their tail fin at 1200 V were measured as 2.2° and 11.3 mN·mm, respectively [9]. However, the rolled DEAs still face the challenge of limited output force and displacement, which hinders their practical application in certain fields.

Applying pre-stretch to dielectric elastomers is an effective approach to improve their performance by increasing breakdown fields and suppressing electromechanical instability. Lau et al. developed a lightweight shell using crossply laminate of carbon fiber reinforced polymer to pre-stretch a rolled DEA [10]. They equivalently model the rolled DEA as a spring and analyze the influence of the frame stiffness and the equivalent stiffness of the rolled DEA on the actuator displacement. However, their theoretical analysis is not applicable to large deformation scenarios. Pei et al. studied a type of spring rolled DEA that can achieve multi-degree-of-freedom motion, and ultimately demonstrated a small walking robot, MERbot, with one 2-DOF spring roll as each of its six legs [11]. However, they did not discuss the effect of the pre-stretch amount on the performance of the actuator. Lau et al. achieved a large hoop pre-stretch in the rolled DEA by adding two rigid rings at both ends to realize fuller actuation potential of the tubular dielectric elastomer [12]. Although these methods can improve the performance of rolled DEA by increasing pre-stretch, they mostly rely on this characteristic without in-depth investigation on the impact of different levels of pre-stretch on the performance of rolled DEA. Therefore, the potential of pre-stretch cannot be fully exploited.

This paper proposes a serial structure that combines a spring with a rolled DEA to achieve axial pre-stretch of the DEA through the tensile force of the spring. To predict the free displacement and blocking force under different input voltages, spring stiffness coefficients, and geometric parameters of the structure, the rolled DEA is simplified into a single-layer tubular DEA, and a static model of the simplified rolled DEA and the spring combination is established. Based on the theoretical analysis model, we analyzed the influence of pre-stretch on the free displacement and blocking force. The optimal pre-stretch effect was tailored by finding the optimal combination of spring stiffness and pre-stretch through a two-dimensional search, thereby maximizing the free displacement, blocking force, or equivalent work. Under the optimal parameter combination aimed at maximizing the equivalent work, the system achieves a free displacement of 0.43 mm and a blocking force of 0.57 N. These values are 3.6 times higher for free displacement and 1.54 times higher for blocking force compared to the springless structure. Finally, the effectiveness of the theoretical analysis model is verified by experiments, and relevant manufacturing processes are introduced.

2   Modeling

Rolled DEA refers to the configuration obtained by rolling thin sheets into a helical shape along the axial direction, as illustrated in Fig. 1 for its axial cross-sectional schematic diagram. In this figure, the red lines depict the positive electrode, the black lines represent the negative electrode, and the gray area denotes the elastic material. The positive and negative electrodes are arranged alternately, ensuring that each layer of the elastic material is subjected to an electric field. In order to simplify the model, the multi-layer rolled DEA is simplified into a single-layer tubular DEA, with the principle of ensuring that the electric field inside the elastic material remains constant. If the number of layers of rolled DEA is n and the voltage of a single layer is U_r, the equivalent number of layers of the tubular DEA is 1, and the equivalent voltage is U_t. Neglecting the electrode thickness, the relationship between U_r and U_t is as follows:

$$U_t = nU_r. \tag{1}$$

Zhu *et al.* proposed an analytical method for tubular DEAs pre-stretched by a load [13]. Figure 2 illustrates the three states of the equivalent tubular DEA spring structure. L_D represents the total length of the tubular DEA spring structure, and it will be treated as a design variable in next section. First, the

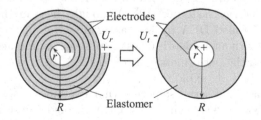

Fig. 1. Axial cross-section schematic diagram of rolled DEA and tubular DEA.

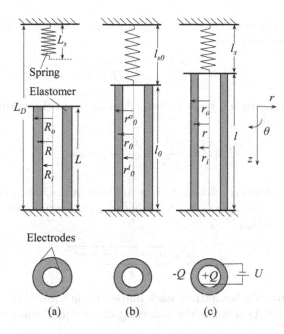

Fig. 2. Schematic of the tubular DEA spring structure in (a) an undeformed state, (b) a pre-stretched state and (c) an actuated state.

DEA is in its undeformed state, with a length of the original length L, inner radius R_i, outer radius R_o, and a radius of R at any internal point. The spring is undeformed and its length is L_s. Then, the spring is connected to the DEA to bring it into a pre-stretched state with a length of l_0, an inner radius of r_0^i, an outer radius of r_0^o, and a radius of r_0 at any internal point. The length of the spring is l_{s0}. Finally, in the electro-actuated state, the DEA is subject to a voltage difference U between the two inner and outer surfaces, causing a charge Q on the inner surface, which is balanced by a charge on the outer surface, and the tube deforms into a state of generalized plane strain, so that the axial strain takes the same value everywhere in the tube. In this state, the DEA has a length of l, inner radius of r_i, outer radius of r_o, and a radius of r at any internal point. The length of the spring is l_s.

The deformation state of DEA can be described by the axial stretch ratio λ_z and the radius $r(R)$ at any point inside the tube. In this paper, the dielectric elastomer is considered to be incompressible. Therefore, the volume of the tubular structure enclosed by radii R_i and R before deformation is equal to that enclosed by radii r_i and r after deformation,

$$\left(R^2 - R_i^2\right) = \lambda_z \left(r^2 - r_i^2\right). \tag{2}$$

Since R_i is determined by the manufacturing process, any point's radius $r(R)$ can be described by the parameters λ_z and r_i. Therefore, the deformation of the entire DEA can be regarded as a two-degree-of-freedom system, with these degrees of freedom being λ_z and r_i. Thus, the outer radius after deformation can be readily obtained as follows:

$$r_o = \sqrt{r_i^2 + (R_o^2 - R_i^2)\lambda_z^{-1}}. \tag{3}$$

The circumferential stretch ratio is defined as $\lambda_\theta = \frac{r}{R}$. Substituting Eq. 2 into this expression yields:

$$\lambda_\theta(r) = \frac{r}{\sqrt{R_i^2 + \lambda_z(r^2 - r_i^2)}}. \tag{4}$$

As seen from the above equation, λ_θ is a function of r. Due to the incompressibility assumption, the radial stretch is related to the axial and circumferential stretches as $\lambda_r = (\lambda_z\lambda_\theta)^{-1}$. Thus,

$$\lambda_r(r) = \frac{\sqrt{R_i^2 + \lambda_z(r^2 - r_i^2)}}{r\lambda_z}. \tag{5}$$

Under the state of deformation, each material point inside the dielectric elastomer actuator (DEA) satisfies the following stress equilibrium equation:

$$\frac{d\sigma_r}{dr} + \frac{\sigma_r - \sigma_\theta}{r} = 0. \tag{6}$$

where σ_r represents the radial stress and σ_θ represents the circumferential stress.

If the potential at any point with a radius of r inside the DEA is represented by $V(r)$, then the potential difference between the inner and outer surfaces is $U = V(r_o) - V(r_i)$. The radial electric field strength within the DEA can be expressed as:

$$E = -\frac{dV}{dr}. \tag{7}$$

Gauss's law requires that the electric displacement is divergence free, so that

$$D = \frac{Q}{2\pi r\lambda_z L}. \tag{8}$$

We incorporated the Gent model into the material model proposed in Zhu's paper [13]. Thus, the material model can be formulated as follows:

$$\sigma_\theta - \sigma_r = \frac{\mu J_{lim}}{J_{lim} - I_1 + 3}\left(\lambda_\theta^2 - \lambda_\theta^{-2}\lambda_z^{-2}\right) - \varepsilon E^2, \tag{9}$$

$$\sigma_z - \sigma_r = \frac{\mu J_{lim}}{J_{lim} - I_1 + 3}\left(\lambda_z^2 - \lambda_\theta^{-2}\lambda_z^{-2}\right) - \varepsilon E^2, \tag{10}$$

$$D = \varepsilon E, \tag{11}$$

where $\mu, J_{lim}, \varepsilon$ denote the initial shear modulus, stretch limit, and permittivity respectively. $I_1 = \lambda_r^2 + \lambda_\theta^2 + \lambda_z^2$ denotes the first invariant of left Cauchy-Green deformation tensor.

A combination of Eqs. 7, 8, and 11 gives

$$U = \frac{Q}{2\pi\varepsilon\lambda_z L} \log\frac{r_o}{r_i}.$$ (12)

By substituting Eqs. 8, 9, and 11 into Eq. 6 and integrating r from r_i to r_o, we can obtain the expression for Q. This is done using the boundary condition that both the inner and outer surfaces of the tube are traction-free, i.e., $\sigma_r(r_i) = \sigma_r(r_o) = 0$. Since the analytical form is rather lengthy, we briefly state that it is a function of several parameters, including λ_z, r_i, r_o, as well as other geometric and material parameters,

$$Q\left(\lambda_z, r_i, r_o, R_i, R_o, L, \mu, \varepsilon, J_{lim}\right),$$ (13)

where λ_z, r_i and r_o are the only variables, other material parameters are determined by the material, and geometric parameters are determined during the manufacturing process. By substituting Eqs. 3 and 13 into Eq. 12 and eliminating the variable r_o, we can obtain the expression for U:

$$U\left(\lambda_z, r_i, R_i, R_o, \mu, \varepsilon, J_{lim}\right).$$ (14)

Inserting Eqs. 8, 9, and 11 again into Eq. 6, but now integrating Eq. 6 from r_i to r, we obtain the distribution of the radial stress:

$$\sigma_r\left(\lambda_z, r, r_i, R_i, R_o, \mu, J_{lim}\right).$$ (15)

Inserting Eq. 15 into Eqs. 9 and 10, we obtain:

$$\sigma_\theta\left(\lambda_z, r, r_i, R_i, R_o, \mu, J_{lim}\right),$$ (16)

$$\sigma_z\left(\lambda_z, r, r_i, R_i, R_o, \mu, J_{lim}\right).$$ (17)

Therefore, the axial force generated by the DEA can be expressed as follows:

$$F_{\mathrm{DEA}}\left(\lambda_z, r_i\right) = \int_a^b 2\pi r \sigma_z dr,$$ (18)

where F_{DEA} is a function of λ_z and r_i, while other parameters are determined by the material property or manufacturing process.

In the actuated state, the spring force is expressed as

$$F_k = K\left(l_s - L_s\right).$$ (19)

where K represents the spring stiffness coefficient. By geometric relationships, we can obtain:

$$l_s = L_D - l,$$ (20)

$$l = \lambda_z L.$$ (21)

Inserting Eqs. 20 and 21 into Eq. 19, we obtain an expression for F_k as a function of the variable λ_z:

$$F_k\left(\lambda_z\right) = K\left(L_D - \lambda_z L - L_s\right).$$ (22)

In conclusion, the equation for force balance can be expressed as follows:

$$F_k(\lambda_z) = F_{\text{DEA}}(\lambda_z, r_i). \tag{23}$$

The solution yields the values of λ_z and r_i, which serve as descriptors for the comprehensive state of the DEA.

3   Design Exploration

In the following, we aim to optimize the spring stiffness coefficient K and the total length L_D of the spring-rolled DEA structure by considering the objectives of free displacement, blocking force, and their product, known as the equivalent work, respectively.

First, we consider the calculation of free displacement. In the initial state shown in Fig. 2(b), setting Eq. 14 to zero and combining it with Eq. 23, we solve for λ_z, denoted as λ_{z0}, which represents the axial stretch ratio in the unactuated equilibrium state. In the equilibrium state after applying voltage (as shown in Fig. 2(c)), we set Eq. 14 to the input voltage U_{in} and combine it with Eq. 23 to solve for λ_z. The expression for free displacement is given as follows:

$$U_{\text{end}} = L(\lambda_z - \lambda_{z0}). \tag{24}$$

Next, we discuss the calculation of blocking force. By fixing λ_z to λ_{z0}, we introduce the blocking force F_b and modify Eq. 23 as follows:

$$F_b + F_k(\lambda_{z0}) = F_{\text{DEA}}(\lambda_{z0}, r_i). \tag{25}$$

By incorporating Eq. 14 and assigning it to U_{in}, the blocking force F_b can be determined through subsequent calculations.

The calculations for free displacement and blocking force mentioned above are performed using Newton's method to solve a system of two equations. Finally, a two-dimensional search is conducted for the L_D and K, and the results are presented in Sect. 4.3, as shown in the surface plot in Fig. 4. In the aforementioned calculation process, the material and geometric parameters are listed in the following Table 1.

4   Experiment

4.1   Fabrication

The spring-rolled DEAs were fabricated using the following procedures: (1) A single-layer dielectric elastomer membrane(ELASTOSIL® Film 2030, 100 μm) was coated with carbon grease on a 10 mm × 70 mm region. (2) Another layer of dielectric elastomer membrane was overlaid onto the previously electrode-coated dielectric elastomer film, and any trapped air bubbles were expelled.

Table 1. Material and geometric parameters

Parameter	Value
Shear modulus (μ)	0.32 MPa
Tensile strength (J_{lim})	10
Relative permittivity (ε_r)	1.47
Initial inner radius (R_i)	3.6 mm
Initial outer diameter (R_o)	4.2 mm
Effective length of DEA in axial direction (L)	10 mm

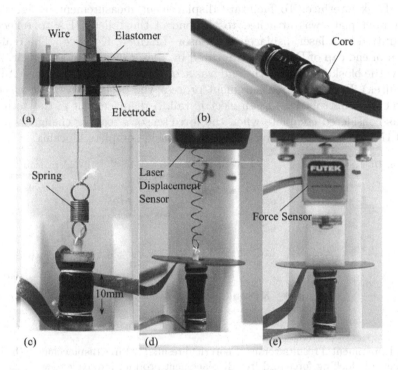

Fig. 3. Experiment of spring-rolled DEA structure: (a) manufacturing process; (b) rolled DEA without spring; (c) spring-rolled DEA without pre-stretch; (d) free displacement measurement; (e) blocking force measurement.

(3) The same-sized electrode was coated on the upper layer of the film. (4) The conductive tape was attached to the excess portion of the pre-prepared electrode. As shown in Fig. 3(a) and (b), two cores with a diameter of 7 mm and grooves were used as supports to roll up the DEA, and the grooved positions were tightened with ropes.(5) As shown in Figs. 3(c), the cores were equipped with holes at their ends, allowing them to be connected to the spring using ropes. The assembled components were then positioned on a dedicated supporting structure.

The rolled DEA had an inner diameter of 7.2 mm, an outer diameter of 8.4 mm, an effective length of 10 mm, and consisted of 6 layers.

4.2 Setup

The fabricated spring-rolled DEA was connected to the high-voltage amplifier (10/10B-HS, Trek, Inc.) with a fixed output-input gain of 1000 and was controlled by a dSPACE-DS1103 control board equipped with digital-to-analog converters. The voltage signal could be conveniently modulated in MAT-LABE/Simulink software and it was directly downloaded to control broad via ControlDesk interface. To facilitate displacement measurement, a lightweight carbon fiber plate was attached to the end of the rolled DEA to reflect the laser emitted by a laser displacement sensor (LKH085, Keyence). The real-time location of end cap of DEAs was captured by a laser displacement sensor. Additionally, the blocking force at the end was acquired using a force sensor (LSB210-25lb, Futek). During the measurement process, the position of the force sensor was precisely controlled using an electric rail. A displacement of the actuator's end was considered complete when the force sensor's reading changed by more than 0.1N for every 0.1 mm movement, indicating complete blocking.

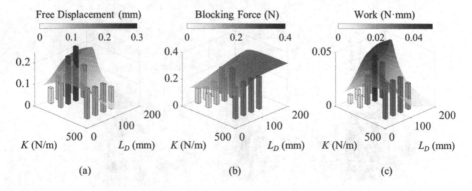

Fig. 4. Experimental results versus theoretical results: (a) free displacement; (b) blocking force; (c) blocking force and free displacement product (equivalent work).

4.3 Experimental Results

Figure 4 illustrates the comparison between theoretical and experimental values of free displacement, blocking force, and the product of blocking force and free displacement, referred to as the equivalent work. Theoretical predictions are depicted by surfaces, while experimental measurements are represented by bar charts. The experiments were conducted for three sets of spring stiffness values ($K = 35, 132, 387$ N/m) and four sets of total length values ($L_D = 46, 76, 106, 136$ mm). Additionally, the blocking force and free displacement of the springless rolled DEA were measured separately, as shown in Table 2. The experimental results for the optimal $K = 132$ N/m and $L_D = 106$ mm combinations, which

Table 2. Performance comparison between springless and optimal structures

Structure	Free displacement (mm)	Blocking force (N)	Work (10^{-3} J)
Springless	0.07	0.11	0.0077
Optimal	0.25	0.17	0.0425

are determined based on work consideration, are also recorded in the Table 2. All the data mentioned above were measured at a voltage of 4000 V.

Figure 5 presents the voltage sweep curve of the optimized actuator structure($K = 132$ N/m and $L_D = 106$ mm) in both experimental and theoretical analyses. The blue curve represents the experimental values obtained through the voltage quasi-static loading with a slope of 100 V/s. The black curve, represents the theoretical values calculated at that specific voltage. At its breakdown voltage of 5500 V, the free displacement is 0.43 mm, and the blocking force is 0.57 N.

4.4   Discussion

So far, we have validated this type of spring-rolled DEA through theoretical analysis and experimental investigations. From the perspective of free displacement, the relationship between elongation (L_D) and spring stiffness coefficient (K) plays a crucial role. When the spring stiffness is relatively low, increasing the elongation can result in an increase in free displacement. This allows the dielectric elastomer actuator (DEA) to maintain a favorable pre-stretched state with minimal variation in spring force during deformation. However, in the case of higher spring stiffness, an increase in the elongation range leads to a decrease in free displacement. This is attributed to the significant variation in spring force, causing the DEA to experience substantial changes in its pre-stretched state, ultimately resulting in a less favorable pre-stretched condition. From the standpoint of blocking force, both increasing the spring stiffness and elongation can contribute to an increase in blocking force. When the spring stiffness is increased, it effectively enhances the overall stiffness of the system. As a result, a higher

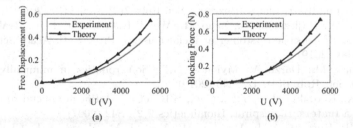

Fig. 5. The displacement-voltage relationship curve of the optimized actuator structure.

spring stiffness leads to a greater overall system stiffness, resulting in a larger output force. The equivalent work represents the combined effect of these two factors.

The selected material, ELASTOSIL® Film 2030, has a relatively high Young's modulus of approximate 1 MPa, making it relatively stiff and resulting in a smaller free displacement. However, it offers the advantage of a higher blocking force per cross-sectional area.

This work exhibits certain areas where further improvements and refinements can be made. The average error between experimental and theoretical values is 30%. Below, we will focus on analyzing the reasons for the presence of this error. In terms of theoretical modeling, firstly, we simplified the rolled DEA to an equivalent tubular DEA, neglecting the electrode portions sandwiched between layers and the relative sliding between layers. Secondly, at larger elongations, the DEA gradually exhibits a waist-like shape (i.e., waist constriction), while the theoretical model assumes a uniformly cylindrical shape along the axial direction, which introduces geometric error under large deformations. In terms of manufacturing processes, it is inevitable that some air bubbles remain between layers, which cannot be completely eliminated, ultimately affecting the performance of the actuator.

5   Conclusion

This paper proposes a serial structure that combines a spring with a rolled DEA to achieve axial pre-stretch, resulting in improved performance(i.e., free displacement and blocking force). The theoretical analysis and experimental verification demonstrate that the optimal parameter combination leads to a significant increase in free displacement and blocking force compared to the springless structure. This approach offers a promising method to enhance the capabilities of DEA actuators, opening up new possibilities for their application in various fields.

References

1. Quinlivan, B.T., et al.: Assistance magnitude versus metabolic cost reductions for a tethered multiarticular soft exosuit. Sci. Rob. **2**(2), eaah4416 (2017)
2. Duduta, M., Hajiesmaili, E., Zhao, H., Wood, R.J., Clarke, D.R.: Realizing the potential of dielectric elastomer artificial muscles. Proc. Natl. Acad. Sci. **116**(7), 2476–2481 (2019)
3. Runciman, M., Darzi, A., Mylonas, G.P.: Soft robotics in minimally invasive surgery. Soft Rob. **6**(4), 423–443 (2019)
4. Jung, K., Koo, J.C., Lee, Y.K., Choi, H.R., et al.: Artificial annelid robot driven by soft actuators. Bioinspirat. Biomimetics **2**(2), S42 (2007)
5. Zhao, H., Hussain, A.M., Duduta, M., Vogt, D.M., Wood, R.J., Clarke, D.R.: Compact dielectric elastomer linear actuators. Adv. Func. Mater. **28**(42), 1804328 (2018)

6. Chen, Y., et al.: Controlled flight of a microrobot powered by soft artificial muscles. Nature **575**(7782), 324–329 (2019)
7. Tang, C., et al.: A pipeline inspection robot for navigating tubular environments in the sub-centimeter scale. Sci. Rob. **7**(66), eabm8597 (2022)
8. Sholl, N., Moss, A., Kier, W.M., Mohseni, K.: A soft end effector inspired by cephalopod suckers and augmented by a dielectric elastomer actuator. Soft Rob. **6**(3), 356–367 (2019)
9. Nagai, T., Shintake, J.: Rolled dielectric elastomer antagonistic actuators for biomimetic underwater robots. Polymers **14**(21), 4549 (2022)
10. Lau, G.K., Lim, H.T., Teo, J.Y., Chin, Y.W.: Lightweight mechanical amplifiers for rolled dielectric elastomer actuators and their integration with bio-inspired wing flappers. Smart Mater. Struct. **23**(2), 025021 (2014)
11. Pei, Q., Rosenthal, M., Stanford, S., Prahlad, H., Pelrine, R.: Multiple-degrees-of-freedom electroelastomer roll actuators. Smart Mater. Struct. **13**(5), N86 (2004)
12. Lau, G.K., Tan, D.D.T., La, T.G.: Large axial actuation of pre-stretched tubular dielectric elastomer and use of oil encapsulation to enhance dielectric breakdown strength. Smart Mater. Struct. **24**(4), 045025 (2015)
13. Zhu, J., Stoyanov, H., Kofod, G., Suo, Z.: Large deformation and electromechanical instability of a dielectric elastomer tube actuator. J. Appl. Phys. **108**(7), 074113 (2010)

Structural Dynamics Modeling with Modal Parameters and Excitation Decoupling Method Based on Energy Distribution

Kun Chen[1], Jianfeng Gan[2], Xi Kang[1], and Peng Xu[1(✉)]

[1] School of Mechanical Engineering and Automation, Harbin Institute of Technology (Shenzhen), Shenzhen 518055, China
xupeng919@hit.edu.cn

[2] Shenzhen Institute of Artificial Intelligence and Robotics for Society, The Chinese University of Hong Kong (Shenzhen), Shenzhen 518172, China

Abstract. Modal parameter is powerful for studying the dynamical characteristics of mechanical systems. For dynamics characteristics observation of chatter suppression of machine tool, dynamics model establishment using modal parameters is essential. To increase the accuracy of the model, its dimension should be increased so that is greater than the number of excitations that can be actually measured. This drawback restricts the development of the structural dynamics model. This paper establishes a modal parameters structural dynamics model of a 3-axis high-precision machine tool and proposes an excitation decoupling method to address this issue. Firstly, a 3-direction 3-order modal structural dynamics model is designed. Based on the proportion of vibration energy, a decoupling method is invented to expand the dimension of external excitation. Secondly, experimental modal analysis is performed on the tool center point of the machine tool, its first 3-order natural frequencies, damping ratios, and dynamic stiffness in spatial orthogonal directions are measured and extracted. Finally, the dynamic responses of the machine tool under free vibration, forced vibration, and mixed vibration are simulated. Their conclusions are verified by vibration theory to ensure the quality of the raised algorithm. This model can balance the modeling quality and solvability of the dynamic equations, leading to brilliant simulation conclusion.

Keywords: Structural dynamics · Excitation decoupling · Experimental modal analysis · Vibration simulation

1 Introduction

Advanced manufacturing technology with machine tool is promising to process the parts with high precision, low surface roughness values and complex contour shapes. However, its machining quality and efficiency are restricted by random vibration. To suppress this destructive phenomenon, studies regarding its dynamic properties are necessary. Modal parameter is a classical tool to express the dynamical characteristics of mechanical systems [1], they are composed of natural frequency, damping ratio, mode shape, modal mass, and dynamic stiffness. By identifying, analyzing, and processing these parameters [2–5], a structural dynamic model can be established to observe the dynamic characteristics, achieve vibration prediction, and realize chatter suppression.

Many scholars have explored this field and achieved plentiful results. Modal parameters can be employed to research the dynamic characteristics of the system. Huynh et al. [6] identified the flexible parameters of the system by matching the measured frequency response function (FRF) curves obtained from experimental modal analysis (EMA) with those obtained from virtual experimental modal analysis (VEMA). Yang et al. [7] used the Gaussian process regression algorithm and modal parameters from multiple systems to predict the dynamic characteristics of the system under any configuration in the workspace. This algorithm could achieve a good prediction results. Modal parameters and their structural dynamics are profitable for stability prediction. Ding et al. [8] proposed a fully-discretized method (FDM) to predict stability in the milling process based on modal parameters and structural dynamics, which had high computational efficiency without losing any numerical accuracy. Ji et al. [9] and Zhou et al. [10] have also proposed similar algorithms using modal parameters and structural dynamics. In addition, modal parameters and their structural dynamics can realize chatter suppression. Guo et al. [11] designed an active-contact robot milling system and used FDM to predict its milling stability. By selecting appropriate operation parameters, chatter could be effectively suppressed. Chen et al. [12] used the FDM combined with the Bayesian principle to optimize modal parameters referring to experimental results. A stability diagram lobe with high quality was generated to ensure and enhance the chatter suppression effect.

In existing studies, scholars prefer to simplify the structural dynamics model in the frequency domain or extract the characteristic properties in the time domain. It is rare to directly apply the modal parameter structural dynamics to vibration simulation due to a fatal flaw. The accuracy of modal parameter structural dynamics model can be improved by expanding its dimension. When its number is bigger than the external excitations that can be measured, this system of equations does not satisfy the solvable condition. To tackle this problem, decoupling of the existing excitations is feasible. In this paper, the structural dynamics model of a 3-axis high-precision machine tool is established by its modal parameters, and a matching excitation decoupling method is developed. This innovation can decouple the external excitations in each direction based on the energy distribution of the vibrations, ensuring that the dimension of the dynamics model matches the number of external excitations. The following advantages are demonstrated in this method.

1. The modal parameter structural dynamics model has a high modeling quality. It contains dynamic properties from 3 spatial orthogonal directions and the first 3-order modes of the system, integrating 9 DOF and involving 27 modal parameters.
2. After decoupling the excitations by energy proportions of vibrations, only 3 external excitations in the spatial orthogonal directions are required to satisfy the 9-dimension structural dynamics modeling, which is more in line with the actual situation.

In Sect. 2, the modal parameter structural dynamics model and its associated excitation decoupling method are introduced. Section 3 provides the process, principles, and conclusions of system modal parameters measurement through EMA. Simulation conclusions of machine tool response in different situations are described in Sect. 4.

2 Structural Dynamics Modeling and External Excitation Decoupling Method

Dynamic characteristics of a 3-axis high-precision machine tool are investigated in this article. The structural dynamics model includes 3-directions and 3-orders modal parameters. It contains a total of 9 DOF to restore the dynamic characteristics of the machine tool's TCP as much as possible. At the same time, to expand the dimension of external excitation, this article proposes an excitation decoupling method based on the distribution of vibration energy of each order. The 3-dimension measured external excitation can be expanded to 9-dimension to meet the needs of dynamics modeling.

2.1 Structural Dynamics Modeling

First, the modeling method of the structural dynamics is proposed. Considering the first 3-order dynamic characteristics of the machine tool's TCP, the obtained modal parameter structural dynamics equation is shown below

$$
\begin{bmatrix} m_{x,1} & & & & & & \\ & \ddots & & & & & \\ & & m_{x,n} & & & & \\ & & & m_{y,1} & & & \\ & & & & \ddots & & \\ & & & & & m_{y,n} & \\ & & & & & & m_{z,1} & \\ & & & & & & & \ddots \\ & & & & & & & & m_{z,n} \end{bmatrix}
\begin{bmatrix} \ddot{x}_1(t) \\ \vdots \\ \ddot{x}_n(t) \\ \ddot{y}_1(t) \\ \vdots \\ \ddot{y}_n(t) \\ \ddot{z}_1(t) \\ \vdots \\ \ddot{z}_n(t) \end{bmatrix} +
$$

$$
\begin{bmatrix} C_x & & \\ & C_y & \\ & & C_z \end{bmatrix}
\begin{bmatrix} \dot{X}(t) \\ \dot{Y}(t) \\ \dot{Z}(t) \end{bmatrix} +
\begin{bmatrix} K_x & & \\ & K_y & \\ & & K_z \end{bmatrix}
\begin{bmatrix} X(t) \\ Y(t) \\ Z(t) \end{bmatrix} =
\begin{bmatrix} F_x \\ F_y \\ F_z \end{bmatrix} = F
\tag{1}
$$

On the left side of Eq. (1), $X(t)$, $Y(t)$, and $Z(t)$ are the n-dimension vectors representing the first n-order vibration in the XYZ directions of the robot's inertia coordinate system, where the elements $x_j(t)$, $y_j(t)$ and $z_j(t)$ represent the vibration amplitudes of the jth-order mode, with units of meter, and $j = 1, 2,\ldots, n$, where $n = 3$. $m_{x|y|z,j}$ is the modal mass in different directions and modes, with units of kg. It cannot be directly measured. Usually, it needs to be calculated using Eq. (2), where k and ω are the stiffness and natural frequency of each mode, with units of N/m and rad/s, respectively. They can be obtained through EMA. $C_{x|y|z}$ and $K_{x|y|z}$ are the n-order diagonal matrices, representing the modal damping and modal stiffness of the system, with units of N/m and N·s/m, respectively, as shown in Eq. (3). Parameters in these matrices are modal parameters at different directions and modes, with ω still the natural frequency, and ξ the damping ratio of each mode.

$$
m = k / \omega^2
\tag{2}
$$

$$C_x = \begin{bmatrix} 2m_{x,1}\xi_{x,1}\omega_{x,1} & & \\ & \ddots & \\ & & 2m_{x,n}\xi_{x,n}\omega_{x,n} \end{bmatrix}$$

$$K_x = \begin{bmatrix} m_{x,1}\omega_{x,1}^2 & & \\ & \ddots & \\ & & m_{x,n}\omega_{x,n}^2 \end{bmatrix} \tag{3}$$

At the right side of Eq. (1), $F_{x|y|z}$ includes 3 excitations at XYZ directions, the exciting vector F constructed by them has 9 dimensions, which corresponds to 9 DOF of the model. Considering that only 3 excitations on XYZ directions can be measured in reality, an excitation decoupling method is necessary to expand the excitation vector from 3-dimension to 9-dimension.

2.2 Excitation Decoupling Method

An excitation decoupling method based on vibration energy distribution is proposed in this part. The application of this algorithm depends on the following assumptions:

Vibration Energy Comes from External Excitation. The motion of the machine tool's TCP can be regarded as a superposition of macro-motion and micro-vibration, which are caused by the motor and external excitation, respectively, and can be considered decoupled from each other. If the vibration is entirely caused by external excitation, the energy of the vibration comes entirely from external excitation.

Vibration Energy has Three Forms. The three forms of vibration energy are kinetic energy, potential energy, and energy loss. Among them, the kinetic energy of the system is the energy exhibited by the system's vibration motion, and the potential energy of the system is the energy accumulated due to the deformation of the system. Due to the damping ratio, energy loss also occurs in the system.

In summary, during the vibration, external excitation provides kinetic energy, potential energy, and energy loss for the first 3-order modes of vibration. By calculating the energy of each mode of vibration in a certain direction and determining their ratios, the excitation in that direction can be decoupled.

On the one hand, the calculation of kinetic and potential energy of vibration is straightforward. Assuming the mass of a certain mode is m in kg, the stiffness is k in N/m, the vibration amplitude is x in meter, and the vibration velocity is dx in m/s, then the kinetic energy E_k and potential energy E_p of vibration are given by Eqs. (4) and (5), respectively.

$$E_k = \frac{1}{2}m dx^2 \tag{4}$$

$$E_p = \frac{1}{2}kx^2 \tag{5}$$

On the other hand, to quantitatively evaluate the energy loss caused by damping, the concept of loss factor is needed. The loss factor η is defined as the ratio of the energy dissipated in one cycle of the system to 2π times the maximum elastic potential energy of the system. To calculate it, the relationship between the loss factor η and the damping ratio ξ is shown in Eq. (7)

$$\eta = \frac{\text{energy loss in one period}}{2\pi \times \text{the biggest elastic potential energy}} \tag{6}$$

$$\eta = 2\xi \tag{7}$$

In the simulation, the loss factor can be used to calculate the energy loss. Let dt be the simulated time step with the unit of seconds. Set the natural frequency of the vibration as f with the unit in Hz, so its corresponding vibration period is $T = 1/f$ with the unit in also seconds. Assume that the maximum elastic potential energy of the system during vibration is equal to the total energy E at the current time, which is shown in Eq. (8). Then, the energy loss E_{loss} during a simulation time step can be calculated using Eq. (9)

$$E = E_k + E_p \tag{8}$$

$$E_{loss} = 2\pi \eta E \frac{dt}{T} = 4\pi \zeta \left(E_k + E_p\right) \frac{dt}{T} \tag{9}$$

After obtaining the kinetic energy, potential energy, and energy loss of the vibration, the total vibration energy can be calculated. If the energy loss in each simulation time step is concentrated at the beginning of the step, the total vibration energy E_a of the system at that time can be calculated using Eq. (10), which includes the kinetic energy, potential energy, and energy loss of the vibration.

$$E_a = E_k + E_p + E_{loss} \tag{10}$$

Based on the obtained energy values of each order vibration, their energy proportions can be calculated to decouple the external excitation. Let the energy of the first 3-order vibrations in a certain direction at any time be E_{a1}, E_{a2}, and E_{a3}, with the sum of E_A. The ratios of these 3 energies to the total energy are denoted as r_1, r_2, and r_3, as shown in Eq. (11). These 3 elements jointly form an energy ratio vector $R = [r_1, r_2, r_3]$. Let the current external excitation value in this direction be F. It can be divided into 3 parts corresponding to the first 3-order vibrations, namely F_1, F_2, and F_3. Their decoupling conclusions based on the vibration energy distribution are shown in Eq. (12)

$$r_1 = \frac{E_{a1}}{E_A}, r_2 = \frac{E_{a2}}{E_A}, r_3 = \frac{E_{a3}}{E_A} \tag{11}$$

$$F_1 = Fr_1, F_2 = Fr_2, F_3 = Fr_3 \tag{12}$$

At the first instant in dynamic simulation, an initial energy ratio vector R should be provided artificially to implement the first external excitation decoupling. To prevent influences of artificially proposed R on simulation conclusion, a dynamic-matching method is used to initialize it. Firstly, the initial excitation is decoupled by the initial R to calculate decoupled excitation and the corresponding energy ratios. Using the new energy ratio to calculate a new R, the above process can be repeated. When the neighboring calculated results of vector R are similar enough, the R vector in the last time will be taken as the real initial energy ratio.

3   Experimental Modal Analysis of Machine Tool

By installing sensors at the TCP of the machine tool, EMA can be performed for the machine tool structure, which enables the acquisition of the system FRF and the extraction of the system modal parameters. These parameters are used to establish a modal parameter structural dynamics model to reflect the vibration characteristics of the machine tool's TCP. This section will introduce the specific operation of EMA, the principle of parameter identification, and the extraction conclusions.

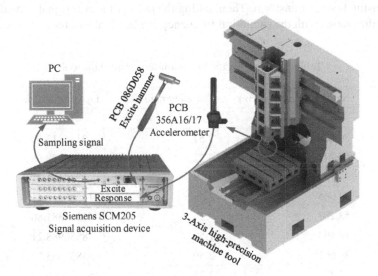

Fig. 1. Experiment set-up

Before EMA conduction, it is necessary to set up the experimental environment according to Fig. 1. In this project, the PCB 086D058 impact hammer and PCB 356A16/17 accelerometers are used to measure the excitation and response signals, respectively. The accelerometer is fixed at the TCP of the machine tool using adhesive wax. Data collection is performed by the Siemens SCM205 signal acquisition device.

During the experiment, the tester holds the impact hammer and excites the TCP of the machine tool in a specified direction. The signals from the force sensor in the impact hammer and the accelerometer at the machine tool end are collected by the data acquisition card and processed in a PC, the resulting curve is the FRF of the machine tool system. By analyzing the FRF curve, dynamic stiffness curves, and vibration signals, the natural frequencies, damping ratios, and dynamic stiffness parameters of the machine tool can be obtained. The identification methods for these parameters are given below.

Natural Frequency Identification Method. When the excitation frequency is close to a certain natural frequency of the system, the resonance will occur and the response signal will show a significant peak called "formant". Look for the formants in the FRF, their frequencies are exactly the natural frequencies, and their unit is Hz.

Damping Ratio Identification Method. The damping ratio ζ of a formant can be calculated by FRF in dB form. Given the center frequency of the formant as f_0 and the frequencies at which the curve is 3 dB below the peak value as f_1 and f_2, the damping ratio ζ can be calculated by Eq. (13). The damping ratio is a scalar without unit

$$\zeta = f_0/(f_2 - f_1) \tag{13}$$

The Method for Identifying Dynamic Stiffness. After measuring the excitation and response signals, both signals are transformed from the time domain to the frequency domain using Fourier transform. Then, taking the ratio of the two signals, the dynamic stiffness that varies with the excitation frequency can be obtained. Its unit is N/m.

Table 1. Measured modal parameters of machine tool

Direction	Natural frequency (Hz)	Damping ratio (%)	Dynamic stiffness (N/m)
X	14.144	1.48	413783.92
	39.668	2.57	2146213.69
	53.246	3.22	9223438.66
Y	14.150	1.49	1730181.21
	39.665	2.58	11225253.51
	53.282	3.26	46584381.86
Z	14.193	1.50	8536988.21
	39.661	2.59	33854655.22
	53.275	3.25	163620000.00

In this study, the identification targets are the first 3-order natural frequencies, damping ratios, and dynamic stiffness of the machine tool's TCP. The resulting 27 identified parameters are shown in Table 1, where the direction refers to the *XYZ* directions of the sensors attached to TCP. To eliminate the influence of spindle vibration and focus on the low-frequency dynamic characteristics of the machine tool structure, the sampling cut-off frequency was set to 200 Hz.

4   Vibration Simulation and Analysis

After completing the extraction of modal parameters, a complete dynamic model of the machine tool structure can be obtained, which can be used for system dynamic characteristic simulation. By using vibration theory to analyze the simulation results, the correctness of the conclusions can be verified. Simulating the machine tool under free vibration can verify the effect of the structural dynamics modeling. Simulation under forced vibration can confirm the effectiveness of the external excitation decoupling method. Simulation under mixed vibration conditions can comprehensively demonstrate the quality of the simulation model in this paper.

4.1   Simulation and Analysis of the System's Free Vibration

Without external loads, let the initial position of the machine tool's TCP deviate from its stable position, the free vibration occurs. Before simulation, the displacement distribution between different modes should be determined. Assuming the end of the machine tool deviates from the initial position by a distance of a mm in the X direction of the sensor coordinate system, and the stiffness of the first 3-order mode in X direction is K_1, K_2, and K_3, respectively, which are inversely proportional to the deformation of each DOF. Then the displacement distribution of the first 3-order modes, namely x_1, x_2, and x_3, can be obtained by

$$
\begin{aligned}
x_1 &= \frac{K_2 K_3 a}{K_1 K_2 + K_2 K_3 + K_3 K_1} \\
x_2 &= \frac{K_1 K_3 a}{K_1 K_2 + K_2 K_3 + K_3 K_1} \\
x_3 &= \frac{K_1 K_2 a}{K_1 K_2 + K_2 K_3 + K_3 K_1}
\end{aligned}
\tag{14}
$$

Assuming the initial displacement is 1 mm, the short-time Fourier transform results of the simulation are shown in Fig. 2. The three bands in the figure correspond to the natural frequencies of the first three modes, which are 14 Hz, 40 Hz, and 53 Hz, respectively. The image shows that the free vibration is dominated by the first mode. The second and third modes are not significant. Mode 1 has the lowest natural frequency, the lowest difficulty of excitation, the smallest damping ratio, the slowest energy dissipation rate, the longest duration, the lowest dynamic stiffness, and the largest initial energy. Mode 2 has a higher natural frequency, greater excitation difficulty, larger damping ratio, faster energy dissipation rate, shorter duration, higher dynamic stiffness, and smaller initial energy. Mode 3 has a high natural frequency and extremely high stiffness, which is not obvious in the processing results. These simulation results are consistent with the vibration theory.

Free vibration simulation does not involve excitation decoupling. The results depend entirely on the structural dynamics model. Simulation results in this section proved the effectiveness of the structural dynamics model.

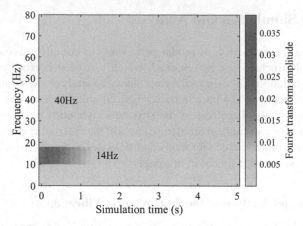

Fig. 2. Short-time Fourier transform conclusion of free vibration

4.2 Simulation and Analysis of the System's Forced Vibration

Applying external loads at the machine tool's TCP in its stable state can cause forced vibration. Sine waves with amplitudes of 50 N and frequencies of 3.2 Hz and 32 Hz are applied at the TCP, and the short-time Fourier transform results of the simulation signals are shown in Fig. 3.

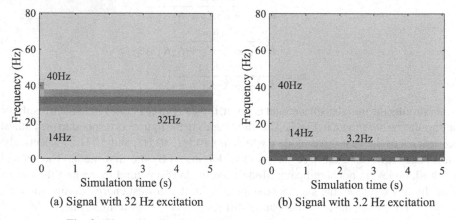

(a) Signal with 32 Hz excitation   (b) Signal with 3.2 Hz excitation

Fig. 3. Short-time Fourier transform conclusion of forced vibration

When the external excitation is first applied, the system undergoes a sudden state change, and both free and forced vibrations occur at TCP. Bands in the time-frequency spectrum appear at the natural frequencies of the machine tool at 14 Hz and 40 Hz, as well as at the excitation frequencies of 3.2 Hz and 32 Hz, but no corresponding vibration is observed at the natural frequency of 53 Hz. As the simulation progresses, the natural frequency bands disappear quickly, while the forced vibration bands remain unchanged. The above results indicate that sudden external loads can trigger both free and forced vibrations, with the free vibration decaying rapidly over time and the forced vibration remaining exist throughout the simulation, the conclusion is consistent with the vibration theory.

Forced vibration is not only influenced by the structural dynamics model but also involves external excitation decoupling. The simulation results demonstrate the effect of the excitation decoupling algorithm in this paper.

4.3 Simulation and Analysis of the System's Mixed Vibration

Applying external loads to a machine tool's TCP in an unstable initial state will result in both free and forced vibration. On the one hand, assuming an initial displacement of 1 mm occurs in the X direction of the sensor coordinate system, which is also decoupled by the method in Subsect. 4.1. On the other hand, continuous sine waves with a duration of 2 s, amplitude of 500 N, and frequencies of 3.2 Hz and 32 Hz are applied to the unstable system. After 2 s, the external force is stopped. Short-time Fourier transform results of the signal simulated in conditions above are shown in Fig. 4.

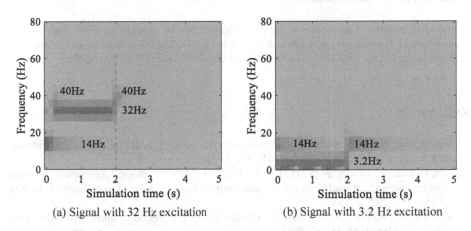

(a) Signal with 32 Hz excitation   (b) Signal with 3.2 Hz excitation

Fig. 4. Short time Fourier transform conclusion of mixed vibration

At the beginning of the simulation, there are 3 components in the vibration, namely free vibration due to the unstable initial position, free vibration due to the sudden mutation of excitation, and forced vibration due to continuous excitation. The 14 Hz and 40 Hz natural frequency components are visible, as well as the 3.2 Hz and 32 Hz excitation frequencies. This is consistent with the conclusion of free and forced vibrations in previous contents. After the 2 s excitation, the machine tool's TCP, which did not return to its stable state, continues to experience free vibration. The bands at 14 Hz and 40 Hz natural frequencies, which have not completely decayed, are illuminated again, while the bands at 3.2 Hz and 32 Hz, corresponding to external excitation, begin to decay. The simulation results show that mixed vibration involves both free and forced vibrations, its the simulation results can simultaneously reflect the performance of structural dynamic modeling and external excitation decoupling algorithms. The above simulation phenomenon is consistent with the conclusions of Subsects. 4.1 and 4.2, which once again proves the quality of the modal parameter structural dynamics model and the excitation decoupling method presented in this paper.

5 Conclusion

This paper develops a 3-direction 3-order modal parameter structural dynamics model for a high-precision machine tool and designs a matching external excitation decoupling algorithm. The rich dynamic characteristics of the machine tool are ensured by the modal parameters involved in its structural dynamics model. The external force decoupling algorithm solves the problem of the mismatch between the number of external excitations and the dimension of the dynamics equation. The model and the algorithm can jointly ensure high-quality and efficient simulation. Their effect is verified through vibration simulation and theoretical analysis. Dynamic characteristics of the machine tool's TCP exhibits in the simulation are consistent with the analysis results referring to vibration theory. In the future, the influence of system vibration mode shapes on the simulation results can be further considered.

Acknowledgements. This work was supported in part by the Guangdong Basic and Applied Basic Research Foundation under Grant 2021A1515110043, Shenzhen Science and Technology Program under Grants JSGG20210420091602007 and GXWD20220811151912002.

References

1. Xu, P., et al.: Stiffness modeling of an industrial robot with a gravity compensator considering link weights. Mech. Mach. Theory **161**, 104331 (2021)
2. Xu, P., Gao, Y., Yao, X., Ng, Y.H., Liu, K., Bi, G.: Influence of process parameters and robot postures on surface quality in robotic machining. Inter. J. Adv. Manuf. Technol. **124**(7), 2545–2561 (2023)
3. Cordes, M., Hintze, W., Altintas, Y.: Chatter stability in robotic milling. Rob. Comput.-Integrated Manuf. **55**, 11–18 (2019)
4. Mohammadi, Y., Ahmadi. K.: In-process frequency response function measurement for robotic milling. In: Experimental Techniques, pp. 1–20 (2022)
5. Wu, J., Peng, F., Tang, X., Yan, R., Xin, S., Mao, X.: Characterization of milling robot mode shape and analysis of the weak parts causing end vibration. Measurement **203** (2022)
6. Fei, C., Liu, H., Li, S., Li, H., An, L., Lu, C.: Dynamic parametric modeling-based model updating strategy of aeroengine casings. Chin. J. Aeronaut. **34**(12), 145–157 (2021)
7. Dong, C.Z., Ye, X.W., Jin, T.: Identification of structural dynamic characteristics based on machine vision technology. Measurement **126**, 405–416 (2018)
8. Huynh, H.N., Assadi, H., Dambly, V., Rivière-Lorphèvre, E., Verlinden, O.: Direct method for updating flexible multibody systems applied to a milling robot. Rob. Comput.-Integrated Manuf. **68**, 102049 (2021)
9. Lei, Y., Hou, T., Ding, Y.: Prediction of the posture-dependent tool tip dynamics in robotic milling based on multi-task gaussian process regressions. Rob. Comput.-Integrated Manuf. **81**, 102508 (2023)
10. Ding, Y., Zhu, L., Zhang, X., Ding, H.: A full-discretization method for prediction of milling stability. Int. J. Mach. Tools Manuf **50**(5), 502–509 (2010)

11. Ji, Y., Wang, L., Song, Y., Wang, H., Liu, Z.: Investigation of robotic milling chatter stability prediction under different cutter orientations by an updated full-discretization method. J. Sound Vibration **536** (2022)
12. Zhou, K., Feng, P., Xu, C., Zhang, J., Wu, Z.: High-order full-discretization methods for milling stability prediction by interpolating the delay term of time-delayed differential equations. Inter. J. Adv. Manuf. Technol. **93**(5–8), 2201–2214 (2017)
13. Guo, K., Zhang, Y., Sun, J.: Towards stable milling: Principle and application of active contact robotic milling. Int. J. Mach. Tools Manuf **182**, 103952 (2022)
14. Chen, G., Li, Y., Liu, X., Yang, B.: Physics-informed Bayesian inference for milling stability analysis. Int. J. Mach. Tools Manuf **167**, 103767 (2021)

Force Sensor-Based Linear Actuator Stiffness Rendering Control

Han Chen[1,2], Junjie Dai[2], Chin-Yin Chen[2(✉)], Yongfeng An[2], and Bing Huang[3]

[1] College of Mechanical Engineering, Zhejiang University of Technology, Hangzhou 310023, China

[2] Zhejiang Key Laboratory of Robotics and Intelligent Manufacturing Equipment Technology, Ningbo Institute of Materials Technology and Engineering, CAS, Ningbo 315201, China
chenchinyin@nimte.ac.cn

[3] Ningbo Zhongda Leader Intelligent Transmission Co., Ltd., Ningbo, China

Abstract. Different stiffness on the actuator can broaden its range of applications and improve its motion control performance. Precise stiffness rendering is advantageous for improving collision safety. However, there are mechanical impedance and friction, which will affect system stiffness. This study applies a force sensor to measure them directly and compensate them by the motor. To make the actuator exhibit ideal stiffness, a PD controller is introduced for stiffness rendering. Simulation and experimental results verify that this method can accurately render stiffness less than the mechanical stiffness for parallel-structured linear actuators.

Keywords: Actuators · Stiffness Rendering · Force Sensor

1 Introduction

Industrial robots are widely used in various industrial fields such as automobile, shipbuilding, and aerospace due to their high efficiency and low-cost advantages compared to manual grinding and polishing [1–3]. The polishing process directly affects the quality of workpieces. Having smooth contact and stable force tracking is crucial for polishing. Installing an actuator at the robot's end is common practice to achieve stable force tracking [4,5]. The actuator can achieve good results in force tracking [6]. However, force control will result in a high-impact force during contact, which is detrimental to stability. The solution is to make the actuator more "soft," so the actuator's stiffness must vary in different environments. For example, the actuator should exhibit low stiffness in high-stiffness

This work was supported by the Key Research and Development Program of Zhejiang Province (2022C01096, 2022C01101), and in part by the Ningbo Key Project of Scientific and Technological Innovation 2025 (2022Z067, 2021Z068, 2021Z128).

environments such as grinding and polishing to prevent assertive collision behavior and avoid damaging equipment and workpieces.

Rendering stiffness on actuators is commonly achieved through the design of passivity-based controllers [7]. Nevertheless, there are limitations to using passivity-based controllers in the impedance-controlled series elastic actuators (SEA), primarily due to the concatenation of virtual and mechanical stiffness, resulting in a stiffness rendering limited by the lower of the two [8]. In impedance control, the required stiffness often needs to exceed the actuator's inherent stiffness to improve motion control performance [9]. Calanca [10] proposed an acceleration-based controller to overcome the inherent stiffness limitation, but this method is also limited by the performance of force controllers. Lee [11] designed a passive control framework using energy monitoring at the load port, combining time-domain passive observers and controllers, and proposed the passivity observer and passivity controller to achieve a maximum stiffness rendering of up to five times the mechanical stiffness in SEA impedance control. However, this method depends on linear models, and its effectiveness is unknown in non-linear models. Abner [12] applied a noise-reducing disturbance observer to the inner-loop velocity control of SEA, achieving a safe stiffness rendering of three times the mechanical stiffness. However, its effectiveness varies in different actuators due to structural factors.

This paper aims to address the problem of small range and high modeling influence in stiffness rendering. To solve these issues, this paper analyzes the differences in force signals obtained from installing force sensors at different locations and identifies the installation position. Then, a direct measurement decoupling method using a force sensor is proposed to achieve accurate and wide-ranging stiffness rendering. Section 2 introduces the parallel structure linear actuator used. Section 3 discusses the force signals obtained from different positions of force sensors and the decoupling of mechanical impedance and friction using a force sensor, describing the process of stiffness rendering. Finally, in Sect. 4, simulation and experiments are conducted on the proposed force sensor decoupling and stiffness rendering method. The results show that this method achieves decoupling of mechanical impedance and friction and realizes stiffness rendering lower than the mechanical stiffness.

2 System Dynamics Modeling

2.1 The Structure of Linear Actuator

The designed linear actuator, as shown in Fig. 1, is primarily composed of a voice coil motor, tension springs, and a nitrogen spring. Other components of the linear actuator include a moving platform, a fixed platform, a fixed outer sleeve, a movable inner sleeve, a guiding device, and a position encoder. The fixed outer sleeve, fixed inner sleeve, voice coil motor, and nitrogen spring are concentrically mounted from the inside out. The fixed outer sleeve, stator, and nitrogen spring rigid body are fixed and connected to the fixed platform by screws. The mover is respectively connecting with a nitrogen spring push rod, a movable sleeve, and a movable platform through a flange. The tension springs directly connect the moving platform and the fixed platform. Fixed and movable parts are guided by three rails, and limit blocks are set at the rails to restrict travel.

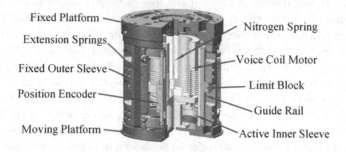

Fig. 1. The structure of the linear actuator.

The voice coil motor is the force source of the linear actuator's mechanical system, the nitrogen gas spring provides passive damping, and the tension springs increase the mechanical stiffness of the system while balancing the initial tension of the nitrogen gas spring. The position encoder measures the relative position between the moving and fixed platforms. The main mechanical specifications of the actuator are shown in Table 1. More specific details are given in [13].

Table 1. Main mechanical performance indicators of the actuator.

Features	Indicators
Mass	5.5 KG
Minimum profile size	$\phi 145\,mm*150\,mm$
Stiffness	$2\,N/mm$
Range of motion	$20\,mm$
Continuous output force	$125\,N$

2.2   Actuator Dynamics Analysis

The actuator differs from SEA in that the force applied by the voice coil motor and mechanical impedance are parallel. The actuator can be modeled as two rigid parts connected by spring and damping, the fixed and moving platforms, as shown in Fig. 2. M_m and M_f are the inertia of the fixed platform and moving platform, respectively; K_m and B_m represent the mechanical stiffness and damping of the actuator, which includes friction between the fixed platform and the moving platform. X represents the relative displacement between the moving platform and the fixed platform; F represents the output force of the voice coil motor, which acts directly on the moving platform and the fixed platform, assuming that the motion direction in Fig. 2 is positive.

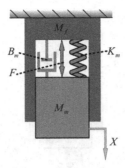

Fig. 2. The dynamics modeling of the actuator.

The dynamic of the actuator moving platform can be easily given as:

$$M_m \ddot{x} + B_m \dot{x} + K_m x = F \tag{1}$$

The transfer function of the actuator position and force can be easily obtained as follows:

$$\frac{X(s)}{F(s)} = \frac{1}{M_m s^2 + B_m s + K_m} \tag{2}$$

We aim to control the system described by Eq. 2 to exhibit the desired stiffness and damping, but the inherent properties of the mechanical system prevent the change of K_m and B_m. Moreover, the presence of friction affects the actual performance of the actuator, resulting in a fixed stiffness and damping when it comes into contact with the environment. Although this fixed passive compliance can provide some compliance during contact with the environment, it could not be conducive to achieving compliant contact in environments with different stiffness and limiting the system's response speed.

3   Force Sensor-Based Mechanical Impedance Decoupling and Stiffness Rendering

After the dynamic analysis of the actuator in the previous section, due to the presence of fixed mechanical impedance and difficult-to-model friction, this paper proposes to directly measure the mechanical impedance and friction of the actuator through a force sensor and use it to decouple the system. We achieve stiffness rendering of the actuator by controlling the voice coil motor.

3.1   Force Measured in Different Positions

Modeling is commonly used to describe the actuator's friction and mechanical impedance. However, the model's accuracy is affected due to the nonlinear characteristics of mechanical friction and nitrogen gas spring. Therefore, this paper proposes directly measuring these nonlinear forces using a force sensor, without

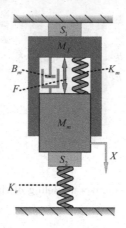

Fig. 3. The different locations of the force sensors.

the need for accurate model establishment, to obtain online nonlinear force. In the actuator of this paper, the force sensor can be installed at different positions to measure force information in different environments, as shown in Fig. 3.

K_e is the equivalent stiffness of the environment. The contact force with the environment F_{ext} is:

$$F_{ext} = K_e x \tag{3}$$

The force sensor locations can measure different force information, and the force that can be measured at S_1 and S_2 are:

$$\begin{cases} F_{S1} = F - K_m x - B_m \dot{x} \\ F_{S2} = F_{ext} = F - K_m x - B_m \dot{x} - M_m \ddot{x} \end{cases} \tag{4}$$

The force measured at S_2 includes the inertial force of the moving platform. Unavoidable vibrations occur when the actuator comes into contact with the environment, and this causes the inertial force of the moving platform to vary continuously. Therefore, the force sensor at S_2 is only suitable for providing feedback on contact force. On the other hand, since the fixed platform is connected to the sensor S_1 through a flange, the fixed platform does not move, so M_f has no effect on the dynamic performance of the system. So the force measured at S_1, including the force of the voice coil motor, mechanical stiffness, mechanical damping, and friction, can be directly obtained. The force constant of the voice coil motor and the current sent by the controller can determine the force of the voice coil motor. Hence, the force sensor at S_1 can dynamically measure the mechanical impedance and friction.

3.2   Force Sensor-Based Decoupling of Mechanical Impedance and Friction

As shown in Fig. 3, the measured force at location S_1 includes the voice coil motor's output force, mechanical impedance, and friction. The force measured

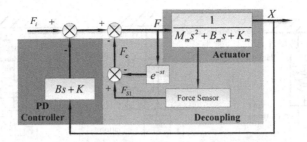

Fig. 4. Force sensor-based stiffness rendering control loop.

by the force sensor at S_1 is:

$$F_{S1} = F - K_m x - B_m \dot{x} \tag{5}$$

The moving platform dynamics is:

$$F - K_m x - B_m \dot{x} = M_m \ddot{x} \tag{6}$$

The mechanical and frictional coupling force F_c is:

$$\begin{aligned} F_c &= K_m x + B_m \dot{x} \\ &= F - F_{S1} \end{aligned} \tag{7}$$

According to Eq. 7, the force sensor can measure the mechanical impedance, the friction between the moving platform and the fixed platform, and the output force of the voice coil motor. By real-time measurement of the dynamically coupled forces using the force sensor, the voice coil motor can accurately compensate for this non-linear force component.

3.3   Force Sensor-Based Stiffness Rendering Control

The decoupling control loop based on the force sensor is illustrated in Fig. 4. To eliminate the force controller's influence on the stiffness rendering of the system, the force controller is removed from the control loop, resulting in the proposed control loop. The controller's output in the previous control cycle caused the actuator's behavior at the current time, and the force sensor measures the force at the current time instant. So the decoupling part of the force sensor is shown in Fig. 4. The PD controller (with P and D representing the desired stiffness (K) and damping (B), respectively) is introduced into the system, with the measured position from the position encoder denoted as X and the input force F_i as the input to the entire system. The transfer function of the coupling system can be expressed as:

$$\frac{X(s)}{F_i(s)} = \frac{1}{M_m s^2 + (B + B_m)s + (K + K_m)} \tag{8}$$

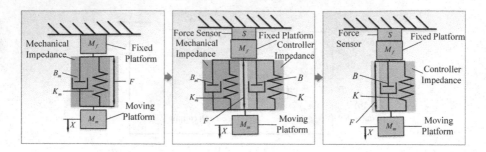

Fig. 5. The process of force sensor-based decoupling and stiffness rendering.

Based on Eq. 8, the stiffness corresponding to this transfer function is the sum of the mechanical and desired stiffness. Therefore, after compensating for the dynamically measured coupled force using the voice coil motor, the ideal transfer function can be expressed as:

$$\frac{X(s)}{F_i(s)} = \frac{1}{M_m s^2 + Bs + K} \tag{9}$$

Compared to the unchangeable mechanical stiffness in Eq. 2, the method of force sensor decoupling has resulted in the ideal stiffness expressed in Eq. 9. The complete decoupling and rendering process is shown in Fig. 5.

4 Simulation and Experiment

4.1 Simulation

To simulate the proposed method in this paper using MATLAB Simulink, set the mechanical stiffness of the actuator to 2 N/mm and the damping to 0.4 N/(mm/s). Set the stiffness of the PD controller to 1 N/mm, 2 N/mm, and 7 N/mm for different simulations. To avoid the influence of inertia on stiffness testing, use a sinusoidal input force with a frequency of 0.1 Hz and amplitudes of 5 N, 10 N, and 35 N. Compare the decoupling controller's effect on the mechanical impedance of the actuator.

The simulation results, as shown in Fig. 6, demonstrate that the decoupling controller successfully achieves decoupling of the mechanical impedance of the actuator, and it exhibits the desired stiffness characteristics. The stiffness is the sum of the PD controller's set stiffness and the actuator's inherent mechanical stiffness without the coupling controller. Additionally, the displacement response amplitude is reduced because the input force amplitude remains the same as when the decoupling controller is activated.

4.2 Experiment Setup

In order to verify the proposed method, we conducted related experiments on the actuator. As shown in Fig. 7, for the measurement and decoupling of mechanical impedance and friction, a force sensor (model: ATI Gamma) is installed

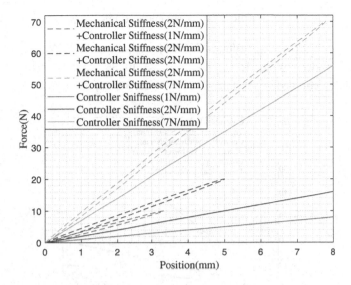

Fig. 6. Simulations comparing decoupling and coupled stiffness renderings.

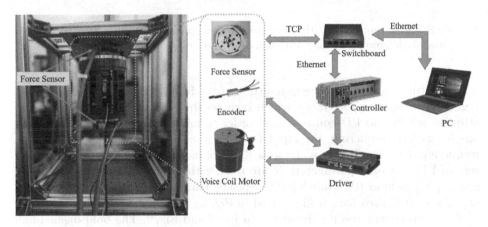

Fig. 7. The experiment platform for stiffness rendering.

between the experiment platform frame and the fixed platform of the actuator. The actuator's driver (model: Copley ADP-09036) is configured as a current loop. The position encoder (model: Fagor L2SY) measures the displacement, and the real-time controller(model: NI CompactRIO-9042) with a control frequency of 500 Hz.

4.3 Friction and Mechanical Impedance Compensation Experiments

To evaluate the decoupling controller's performance, we design a comparative experiment. The experiment set the stroke to 10mm due to the limited stroke

Table 2. Experiment settings.

Features	Stiffness(N/mm)	Amplitude of $F_i(N)$
decoupling	1, 2, 7	5, 10, 35
coupled	0, 1, 2, 7	30, 35, 40, 65

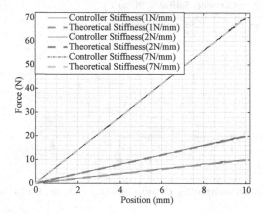

Fig. 8. Stiffness rendering with force sensor decoupling, controller damping set to $0\,\text{N}/(\text{mm/s})$, different controller stiffness: : $0\,\text{N/mm}$, $1\,\text{N/mm}$, $2\,\text{N/mm}$, and $7\,\text{N/mm}$.

of the actuator (20 mm). The magnitude of the input force F_i was determined based on the system's stiffness, which includes the mechanical stiffness and the stiffness set by the PD controller. In order to minimize the effect of damping on the stiffness rendering, the input force F_i is set as a sinusoidal signal with a frequency of 0.1 Hz. Because of the stiffness of mechanical is $2\,\text{N/mm}$, multiple sets of PD controller parameters K are used, with all the PD controllers having a damping ratio of $0\,\text{N}/(\text{mm/s})$. The specific parameters are shown in Table 2, and the control structure is illustrated in Fig. 4.

The experiment results are shown in Fig. 8 and Fig. 9. The bold dashed line represents the ideal stiffness, while the thin solid line represents the stiffness during the experiment. The mechanical system stiffness is $2\,\text{N/mm}$. In the coupled experiment, the actuator requires higher forces to move at extreme positions (0 mm and 10 mm) because of friction. Due to the nonlinearity of the mechanical system and the sliding friction, there are instances of stick-slip during motion. Additionally, at lower virtual stiffness values, the stiffness slightly deviates from the actual stiffness due to nonlinear factors such as friction. However, when the virtual controller stiffness is set to $7\,\text{N/mm}$, the total stiffness approaches the ideal stiffness (sum of mechanical and virtual controller stiffness). When using the force sensor decoupling method, the stiffness aligns with the theoretically set virtual controller stiffness and matches the virtual PD controller stiffness.

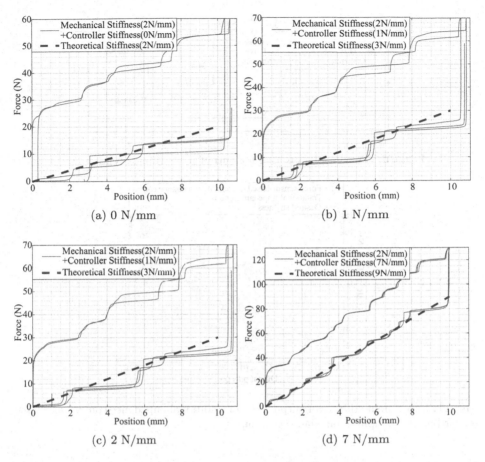

(a) 0 N/mm

(b) 1 N/mm

(c) 2 N/mm

(d) 7 N/mm

Fig. 9. Stiffness rendering without force sensor decoupling, controller damping set to $0\,\mathrm{N}/(\mathrm{mm/s})$, different controller stiffness.

4.4 Output Port Stiffness Rendering

A further experiment is conducted on the experiment platform to verify the stiffness rendering at the output port. The PD controller's stiffness is $1\,\mathrm{N/mm}$, and the damping is $0.2\,\mathrm{N}/(\mathrm{mm/s})$. The control loop is shown in Fig. 10. The force controller utilized a PID controller(The proportional gain is 0.55, the integral time is set to 0.00055, and the derivative time is set to 0), and the moving platform is manually pushed.

The experiment results, as shown in Fig. 11, the desired position is used as the desired force after the PD controller, because the environmental force is used as the desired force error, the actual position deviates from the desired position, so the system exhibits impedance characteristics. While traditional impedance control can achieve the desired stiffness at the actuator's output port, but in two near-extreme positions are not the ideal stiffness, this is because of the static

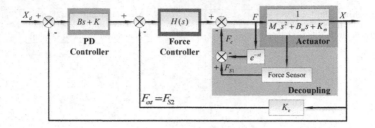

Fig. 10. The control loop used for output port stiffness rendering.

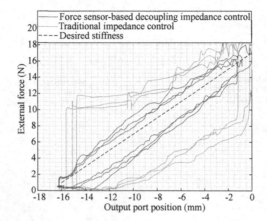

Fig. 11. Experiment stiffness of output port in traditional impedance control, and force sensor-based decoupling impedance control.

friction. In contrast, the method proposed in this paper decouples friction and mechanical impedance, allowing the output port to maintain the desired stiffness even near extreme positions.

5   Conclusion and Future Work

This paper introduces the structure of the employed actuator and conducts a dynamic analysis of its characteristics. The dynamic properties of the actuator's moving platform are analyzed, and the differences in the measured forces at different sensor positions are discussed. By dynamically measuring the impedance and friction information of the mechanical system using a force sensor and implementing decoupling, the presentation of the desired stiffness is achieved. Through simulation and experiment on the designed actuator using force sensor decoupling, the results demonstrate that decoupling with force sensors can achieve the desired stiffness and render a stiffness lower than mechanical stiffness. In the future, we will analyze the accuracy level and error of the control method and explore adaptive adjustment of the stiffness and damping of the impedance controller to achieve stable force tracking and improve the accuracy, stability, and performance of force control.

References

1. GE, J., Deng, Z., Li, W., Li, C., Chen, X., Peng, D.: Research progresses of robot grinding and polishing force compliance controls. China Mech. Eng. **32**(18), 2217 (2021)
2. Jing-Zheng, L., Jia, L., Sheng-Qiang, Y., Jing-Jing, Z., Zhi-Jie, Q.: Fuzzy impedance control for robot impact force. In: 2021 33rd Chinese Control and Decision Conference (CCDC), pp. 340–344. IEEE (2021)
3. Zhu, D., Feng, X., Xu, X., Yang, Z., Ding, H.: Robotic grinding of complex components: a step towards efficient and intelligent machining - challenges, solutions, and applications. Rob. Comput.-Integrated Manuf. **65**, 101908 (2020)
4. Zeng, X., Zhu, G., Gao, Z., Ji, R., Ansari, J., Lu, C.: Surface polishing by industrial robots: a review. Inter. J. Adv. Manufa. Technol. **125**(9–10), 3981–4012 (2023)
5. Dai, J., Chen, C.Y., Zhu, R., Yang, G., Wang, C., Bai, S.: Suppress vibration on robotic polishing with impedance matching. In: Actuators, vol. 10, p. 59. MDPI (2021)
6. Li, Z., Wang, H., Zhao, H., Ding, H.: Force impact suppression of contact transition state in robot grinding and polishing of industrial blades. Proc. Inst. Mech. Eng. C J. Mech. Eng. Sci. **236**(13), 7387–7397 (2022)
7. Ott, C., Albu-Schaffer, A., Kugi, A., Hirzinger, G.: On the passivity-based impedance control of flexible joint robots. IEEE Trans. Rob. **24**(2), 416–429 (2008)
8. Mehling, J.S., O'Malley, M.K.: A model matching framework for the synthesis of series elastic actuator impedance control. In: 22nd Mediterranean Conference on Control and Automation, pp. 249–254. IEEE (2014)
9. Sariyildiz, E., Ohnishi, K.: On the explicit robust force control via disturbance observer. IEEE Trans. Industr. Electron. **62**(3), 1581–1589 (2014)
10. Calanca, A., Muradore, R., Fiorini, P.: Impedance control of series elastic actuators: passivity and acceleration-based control. Mechatronics **47**, 37–48 (2017)
11. Lee, H., Ryu, J.H., Lee, J., Oh, S.: Passivity controller based on load-side damping assignment for high stiffness controlled series elastic actuators. IEEE Trans. Industr. Electron. **68**(1), 871–881 (2020)
12. Asignacion, A., Haninger, K., Oh, S., Lee, H.: High-stiffness control of series elastic actuators using a noise reduction disturbance observer. IEEE Trans. Industr. Electron. **69**(8), 8212–8219 (2021)
13. Xiong, C., Yang, G., Liu, L., Feng, K., Chen, C.Y., Zhang, G.: Design and analysis of a high-precision force control device for grinding robots. Modular Mach. Tool Autom. Manuf. Tech. **2022**(004), 157–161 (2022)

Design, Modeling and Control of a Dielectric Elastomer Actuated Micro-positioning Stage

Peinan Yan[1,2], Guoying Gu[1,2], and Jiang Zou[1,2(✉)]

[1] Robotics Institute, School of Mechanical Engineering, Shanghai Jiao Tong University, Shanghai 200240, China
[2] State Key Laboratory of Mechanical System and Vibration, School of Mechanical Engineering, Shanghai Jiao Tong University, Shanghai 200240, China
zoujiang@sjtu.edu.cn

Abstract. In this paper, we propose one kind of a dielectric elastomer actuated micro-positioning stage (DEAMS) that can achieve both large stroke and high resolution. To this end, a customized multilayer dielectric elastomer actuator (DEA), made of silicone, is designed and fabricated, which can generate a linear movement. Then based on the DEA, a DEAMS is designed with a stroke of nearly 1 mm and resolution of 480 nm. Next, several dynamic tests are conducted to reveal its dynamic responses: i) the natural frequency of the DEAMS can reach 80 Hz; ii) its output displacement shows both slow-time creep and rate-dependent hysteresis because of the inherent viscoelasticity. Lastly, a direct inverse hysteresis compensation (DIHC) controller based on a phenomenological hysteresis model and a closed-loop controller are adopted to remove hysteresis and creep, respectively. Experimental results demonstrate that with our control method, the DEAMS can achieve high-precision tracking control, which may pave the way for its applications in the field of micro/nano manipulations.

Keywords: dielectric elastomer actuators · micro-positioning stage · dynamic modeling · high-precision real-time tracking control

1 Introduction

Micromanipulation technologies play an increasing role in exploring microcosms. During the past decade, various remarkable achievements have been reported in the fields of micro-electromechanical systems (MEMS) [1], biomedical engineering [2] and atomic force microscope [3]. The key of the micromanipulation technologies depends on the micro/nano-positioning stages [4]. In general, existing

This work was supported in part by the National Natural Science Foundation of China under Grant 52275024, and in part by Natural Science Foundation of Shanghai under Grant 23ZR1435500.

micro/nano-positioning stages are actuated by rigid actuators such as piezoelectric actuators [5,6]. However, to achieve larger displacement, piezoelectric actuators usually need to combine with flexible hinges and transmission mechanisms, resulting in structure complexity and high costs [7,8].

Different from piezoelectric actuators, dielectric elastomer actuators (DEAs) show the advantage of large strain, actuating-transmitting-integrated characteristic and high energy density, which provides a new solution for actuating micro/nano-positioning stages [9,10]. A DEA usually consists of a dielectric elastomer membrane sandwiched by two compliant electrodes. When a voltage is applied, the Maxwell stress between the electrodes squeezes the dielectric elastomer membrane, resulting in thickness decrease and area expansion [11]. Based on this working principle, different configurations (such as stack [12], helix [13] and cylinder [14,15]) have been proposed to generate different actuation modes, which have shown emerging applications in soft robotics [16,17]. In our previous work, we have developed a dielectric elastomer actuated stage (made of acrylic elastomer, VHB 4910) that can generate a two-DOF motion with sub-micrometer resolution [18]. However, due to the serious viscoelasticity of VHB 4910, its natural frequency is very low (<1 Hz), limiting its applications.

In this work, we present design, modeling and control of a dielectric elastomer actuated micro-positioning stage (DEAMS) which can achieve large stroke, high natural frequency and sub-micrometer resolution. To this end, we firstly adopt silicone and carbon nanotube (CNT) as dielectric elastomer membrane and electrode, respectively, to design and fabricate one kind of multilayer DEA that can generate linear movement. Then based on the multilayer DEA, a DEAMS is designed with a stroke of nearly 1 mm and resolution of 480 nm and its dynamic responses are systematically investigated. The experimental results demonstrate that its natural frequency can reach 80 Hz. Due to the inherent viscoelasticity, the dynamic responses of the DEAMS show complex nonlinearity, including slow-time creep and rate-dependent hysteresis. Lastly, a phenomenological hysteresis model is established to describe the hysteresis nonlinearity and a DIHC controller is further established to eliminate it. To further remove the creep and model uncertainty, a closed-loop controller is adopted to form a two-level controller. Different periodical trajectories tracking experimental results demonstrate that with the two-level controller, the DEAMS can achieve high-precision tracking control when the frequency is in a range of 0.5 Hz to 5.0 Hz. The maximum error and the root-mean-square error can be reduced from 33.22% to 6.60% and 15.68% to 3.33%, respectively, verifying the effectiveness of our controller.

2   Design and Fabrication of the DEAMS

Since the platform performance highly depends on the actuator, the DEA is firstly designed. The dielectric elastomer materials include silicones, acrylics and others. Silicone-based DEAs exhibit less viscoelasticity loss hence higher natural frequency. Therefore, we design a multilayer DEA made of silicone and CNT as described in [14].

The dielectric elastomers are composed of Ecoflex 0030 and Dow Corning Sylgard 184 at a mixture ratio of 1:1. The ratio of Ecoflex 0030 Part A and Part B is 1:1. The ratio of Dow Corning Sylgard 184 Base and Agent is 40:1.

The single-walled CNTs from Nanjing XFNANO Materials Tech are chosen as compliant electrodes. The original ultrapure CNT solution is diluted and then filtered through a filter to gain a layer of CNT electrode. Based on the model in [14], overlarge resistance deriving from less CNT leads to slow charging and discharging, which has negative influence on natural frequency. Prior research has also shown that excess CNT will lead to low breakdown voltage [19]. The sheet resistance is consequently chosen as 5 $k\Omega^{-1}$ to balance the breakdown voltage and the natural frequency, which is measured by four-probe resistance measurements.

Step 1: All the aforementioned silicone components are mixed by Thinky Mixer (MZ-8).

Step 2: The thin films are blade cast onto a PET film substrate by the Zehntner ZAA 2300 film applicator. After casting, the silicone films are cured at 110° in vacuum for 1 h. The cured films are measured to be 40 ± 3 μm per layer.

Step 3: Compliant electrodes are applied onto the thin films utilizing a specific mask.

Step 4: Repeat Step 2–3 to fabricate 8 layers of silicones and electrodes alternately.

Step 5: The stacked structure is cut by laser into strips. As shown in Fig. 1(a), the strip is rolled for a cylinder shape. Silver paste is applied on both sides for mechanical connection with the end cap and electrical connection with the wire. Then the whole structure is cured at 80° for over 8 h.

Therefore, the cylinder DEA will generate axial strain with exciting voltages as shown in Fig. 1(b). The DEA is shown in Fig. 1(c) while the whole length is 14 mm and the active length is 10 mm.

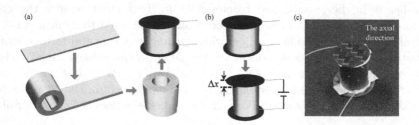

Fig. 1. The structure of the multilayer DEA: (a) The rolling process; (b) The initial state and activated state; (c) The photograph of the multilayer DEA.

Then based on the linear movement generated by the DEA, we establish the DEAMS. Here one end of the cylinder DEA is fixed on a customized frame. Another end is connected with a 3D-printed terminal.

3 Experimental Setup

To evaluate the performance of the DEAMS and achieve real-time tracking control, we establish an experimental setup as shown in Fig. 2, which mainly consists of a displacement sensor (D4/F17, resolution of 50 nm, attocube, Germany), a sensor controller (IDS3010, attocube, Germany), a high voltage amplifier (Trek 10/10B-HS, fixed gain of 1000, TREK, USA), a control module (MicroLabBox, dSPACE, Germany) and the DEAMS. The high voltage amplifier is utilized to provide controllable voltages to the multilayer DEA. The displacement sensor is employed to measure the output displacement of the DEAMS. In order to reflect the output measuring laser of the sensor, a silicon wafer is added to the terminal. The sensor controller processes the displacement signals and then sends them to the control module. The control module is employed to generate control signals to the high voltage amplifier and capture the real-time signals from the sensor controller. The DEAMS and the displacement sensor are respectively mounted on two manual lift platforms for convenient adjustment. All the components are mounted on a high-precision optical board. The sample rate is set as 10000 Hz.

It should be noted that many sparks combined with displacement decrease can be observed when the voltage amplitude exceeds 1500 V, standing for severe local breakdown and electrode degradation as described in [20]. As a result, the maximum applied voltage is set to be 1300 V in the following experiments.

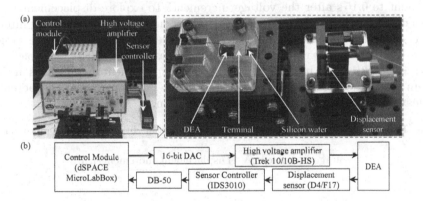

Fig. 2. The experimental setup. (a) Experimental platform; (b) Block diagram.

4 Experimental Results

4.1 Stroke and Resolution Characterization

Based on the experimental setup, a stroke test is conducted by applying a sinusoidal voltage of 1 Hz, which can be written as:

$$V_{sin}(t) = \frac{A}{2}\sin(2\pi t - \frac{\pi}{2}) + \frac{A}{2} \tag{1}$$

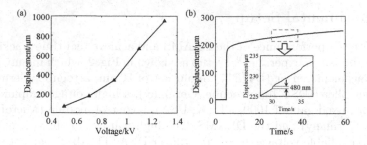

Fig. 3. Characterization of (a) Stroke; (b) Resolution.

where A represents amplitude of the input voltage. The amplitude is set from 500 V to 1300 V stepped by 200 V while the duration time of each test is set as 60 s. The results demonstrate that stroke can exceed 900 μm as shown in Fig. 3(a). Then a stair voltage is applied for resolution characterization, which can be written as:

$$V_{stair}(t) = 0.7 + iV_{inc} \ (kV) \quad i = 1, 2...10 \tag{2}$$

where V_{inc} is the voltage increment, i is the sequence number of the voltage increment. The voltage keeps constant for 5 s after each voltage increment. The displacement increment is defined as the displacement from 0.05 s before the voltage increment to 0.15 s after the voltage increment. To explore displacement increments corresponding to different voltage increments, an average moving filter of 0.1 s is applied to reduce signal noise. Ten displacement increments are averaged as the final result in each test. Experimental results are listed in Table 1. As shown in Fig. 3(b), the minimum recognizable displacement increment is around 480 nm when the voltage increment equals 0.5 V, demonstrating the potential applications of the DEAMS in micromanipulation.

Table 1. Corresponding displacement increments under different voltage increments.

Voltage increment/V	Displacement increment/μm
50	55.50
10	7.44
5	3.87
1	0.88
0.5	0.48

4.2 Dynamic Response Analysis

For exploring amplitude-frequency characteristic of the DEAMS, a sweeping frequency test is conducted. Here the input voltage can be written as:

$$V_{sweep}(t) = 0.55 \sin[\pi \frac{(400 - 1)t + 1}{99.75} - \frac{\pi}{2}] + 0.55 \ (kV) \tag{3}$$

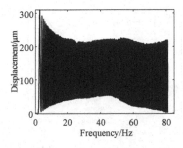

Fig. 4. The sweep frequency response of the DEAMS.

The frequency is in the range of 1 Hz to 400 Hz while the duration time is 99.75 s. Due to the severe vibration of the platform terminal near the natural frequency, displacement over 80 Hz including the displacement peak can not be measured accurately. Figure 4 shows the amplitude-frequency characteristic of the DEAMS. It can be seen that: i) the natural frequency of the DEAMS exceeds 80 Hz; ii) in the lower frequency range, the DEAMS show larger displacement. Hence, we choose 0.5 Hz to 5.0 Hz as the frequency range for the control experiment in the following section. In order to reveal the viscoelasticity of the DEAMS, we conduct a series of dynamic tests under sinusoidal exciting voltages with the same amplitude but different frequencies. Here the input voltage can be written as:

$$V_{in}(t) = 0.4\sin(2\pi f t - \frac{\pi}{2}) + 0.7 \ (kV) \tag{4}$$

where f is the input frequency. The frequency is set from 0.5 Hz to 5.0 Hz stepped by 0.5 Hz while the duration time of each test is set as 60 s. The intrinsic viscoelasticity of the DEA can be divided into creep and hysteresis. In the whole test, the output displacement can be divided into the transition region and the stable region owing to the creep effect, which is shown in Fig. 5(a). In each test, the displacement first drifts in the transition region due to the slow-time creep. Then in the stable region where the drift trend is negligible, there is a phase lag between the output displacement and the input voltage. Figure 5(b) shows the hysteresis loops under different frequencies, which exhibits rate-dependent and asymmetric hysteresis characteristic within the frequency range of 0.5 Hz to 5.0 Hz. Coupling of the creep viscoelasticity and the hysteresis viscoelasticity results in severe nonlinearity between the input voltage and the output displacement as shown in Fig. 5(c).

4.3 Hysteresis Description

For high-precision real-time movement control, we first adopt the modified rate-dependent Prandtl-Ishlinskii model (MRPIM) in our previous work to describe the hysteresis viscoelasticity quantificationally [21]. Based on the discrete form of the MRPIM, the relationship between the reference displacement and the input voltage can be written as:

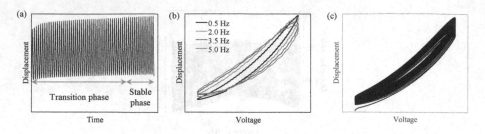

Fig. 5. The response of the stage under a sinusoidal voltage. (a) Creep effect; (b) Hysteresis effect; (c) The nonlinearity between input voltage and output displacement.

$$V(t) = g_1 y_d^5(t) + g_2 y_d^4(t) + g_3 y_d^3(t) + g_4 y_d^2(t) + g_5 y_d(t) + \sum_{i=1}^{5} a_i F_{r_i}[y_d](t) \quad (5)$$

where g_1, g_2, g_3, g_4, g_5 are five constants, $V(t)$ is the input voltage and $y_d(t)$ is the reference output displacement, $F_r[y](t)$ is a rate-dependent play operator, N is the number of rate-dependent play operators, a_i is the weight factor of the i th rate-dependent play operator. Here the rate-dependent play operator can be expressed as:

$$W(0) = F_r^h[y_d](0) = f_r^h[y_d(0), V(0)] \quad (6)$$

$$W(t) = F_r^h[y_d](t) = f_r^h[y_d(t), F_r^h[y_d](t - \tau)] \quad (7)$$

$$f_r^h[y_d(t), W(t)] = \max\{h_l[y_d(t), \dot{y}_d(t)] - r, \min[h_r[y_d(t), \dot{y}_d(t)], W(t)]\} \quad (8)$$

where $\dot{y}_d(t)$ represents the derivation of the reference displacement, r is the constant threshold of corresponding rate-dependent play operator and τ represents the sampling time. $h_l[y_d(t), \dot{y}_d(t)]$ and $h_r[y_d(t), \dot{y}_d(t)]$ are two dynamic envelope functions depending on $y_d(t)$ and $\dot{y}_d(t)$, which can be expressed as:

$$h_l[y_d(t), \dot{y}_d(t)] = y_d(t) - \alpha \, |\dot{y}_d(t)| \quad (9)$$

$$h_r[y_d(t), \dot{y}_d(t)] = y_d(t) + \beta \, |\dot{y}_d(t)| \quad (10)$$

$$\dot{y}_d(t) = \frac{y_d(t) - y_d(t - \tau)}{\tau} \quad (11)$$

where α, β are two constants. In this work, five rate-dependent play operators are chosen and corresponding thresholds are respectively set as 0, 0.2, 0.4, 0.6 and 0.8. The parameter identification method is the same as that in [21]. The lower and upper limit values are set as -4 and 4, respectively. Here hysteresis loops under 0.5, 2.0, 3.5, 5.0 Hz are applied for parameter identification. Table 2 lists the parameters of the identified MRPIM. Figure 6 shows the comparison between experimental data and identified model.

Table 2. Parameters of the identified MRPIM.

i	r_i	a_i	g_i	α	β
1	0	−0.3018	−1.3466	0.0254	0.0861
2	0.2	−0.0002	2.0060		
3	0.4	−0.0240	1.0318		
4	0.6	−0.1311	−3.3740		
5	0.8	−0.0851	3.0945		

Then to evaluate the model accuracy, the root-mean-square error and maximum error are respectively defined as follows:

$$e_{rms} = \frac{\sqrt{\frac{1}{N}\sum_{i=1}^{N}(V_{mi} - V_i)^2}}{\max(V_i) - \min(V_i)} \times 100\% \tag{12}$$

$$e_m = \frac{\max(|V_{mi} - V_i|)}{\max(V_i) - \min(V_i)} \times 100\% \tag{13}$$

where V_{mi} and V_i represent the output voltage of the identified model and the actual voltage, respectively, N is the sampling quantity within one cycle. Based on the identified parameters, the model errors are listed in Table 3. It can be seen that: i) the model error is relatively small at low frequencies, ii) the root-mean-square error is lower than 5%, proving the effectiveness of the MRPIM.

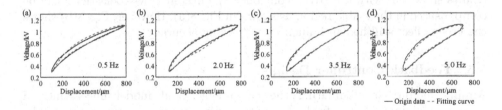

Fig. 6. The comparison between experimental data and identified model.

4.4 Inverse Hysteresis Compensation

Based on the identified MRPIM, a DIHC controller is designed to compensate for the hysteresis effect as shown in Fig. 7. To verify the effectiveness of the DIHC controller, different sinusoidal trajectory tracking experiments are conducted, which can be written as:

$$V_{in}(t) = 250\sin(2\pi f t - \frac{\pi}{2}) + 400 \ (\mu m) \tag{14}$$

Table 3. Model errors of the identified MRPIM under different frequencies.

Frequency/Hz	$e_{rms}/\%$	$e_m/\%$	Frequency/Hz	$e_{rms}/\%$	$e_m/\%$
0.5	2.90	6.67	3.0	2.54	10.00
1.0	2.16	5.33	3.5	2.94	12.27
1.5	2.26	6.26	4.0	3.26	13.75
2.0	2.35	6.02	4.5	3.64	14.66
2.5	2.39	8.22	5.0	4.16	16.21

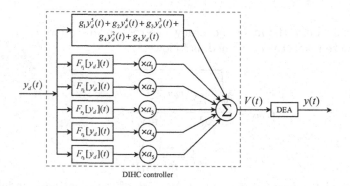

Fig. 7. Block diagram of the DIHC controller.

where f is the frequency. The frequency is set from 0.5 Hz to 5.0 Hz stepped by 0.5 Hz while the duration time of each test is set as 60 s. The experimental results show that with the DIHC controller, the hysteresis viscoelasticity can be compensated in the stable region as shown in Fig. 8(a). However, Fig. 8(b) shows the creep effect still has an influence on tracking accuracy.

4.5   Feedback Controller Design

Aiming at further eliminating the creep effect and model uncertainty, a proportional-integral (PI) feedback controller is introduced. Parameters in the PI controller are adjusted by a trial-and-error method. Then its transfer function can be expressed as:

$$PI = 0.03 + \frac{0.12}{s} \tag{15}$$

The block diagram is shown in Fig. 9. In order to verify the effectiveness of the two-level tracking control approach, the same reference trajectory tracking experiments are conducted as described in the previous section. We should mention that since the displacement data from the sensor all initiates from zero in each test, in order to ensure the same workspace, the reference point of the PI controller is set as 3 μm then the constant in the reference trajectory is set as 397 μm. Figure 9 shows the tracking results with both DIHC controller and PI controller. It can be seen that compared to the single DIHC controller, the two-level

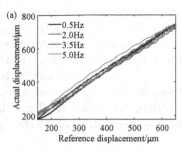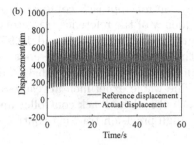

Fig. 8. The experimental results with the DIHC controller: (a) comparison between actual displacement and reference displacement with the DIHC controller under different frequencies; (b) comparison between the real time output displacement and reference displacement.

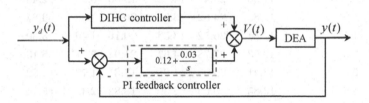

Fig. 9. Block diagram of the two-level tracking control approach.

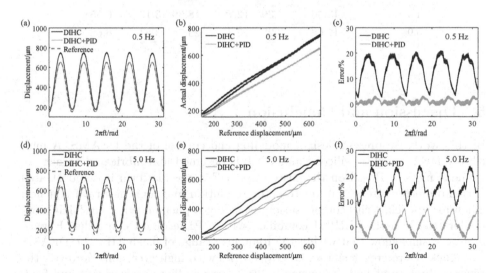

Fig. 10. Experimental results with both DIHC and PI controllers under different frequencies. When the frequency of the input voltage is 0.5 Hz: (a) the real-time output displacements; (b) the relationship between reference displacement and actual displacement; (c) the comparison of tracking errors. When the frequency of the input voltage is 5.0 Hz: (a) the real time output displacements; (b) the relationship between reference displacement and actual displacement; (c) the comparison of tracking errors.

tracking control approach compensates for the creep effect effectively: i) when the frequency of the reference trajectory equals 0.5 Hz (Fig. 10(a)–(c)), e_{rms} and e_m are reduced from 14.14% and 19.95% to 0.95% and 2.48%, respectively; ii) when the frequency of the reference trajectory equals 5.0 Hz (Fig. 10(d)–(f)), e_{rms} and e_m are reduced from 16.41% and 23.74% to 3.33% and 6.60%, respectively. The whole experimental results are listed in Table 4, demonstrating that with both the PI feedback controller and the DIHC controller, the DEAMS can achieve high-precision tracking control in the frequency range of 0.5 Hz–5.0 Hz.

Table 4. Tracking errors under different frequencies.

Controller	Without		DIHC		DIHC+PI	
Frequency/Hz	e_{rms}/%	e_m/%	e_{rms}/%	e_m/%	e_{rms}/%	e_m/%
0.5	11.53	23.42	14.14	19.95	0.95	2.48
1.0	11.83	24.82	13.96	20.90	1.89	3.84
1.5	12.34	26.52	13.53	20.16	1.46	3.30
2.0	12.93	27.78	14.67	21.92	2.31	5.13
2.5	13.41	29.08	11.08	17.31	1.77	4.32
3.0	13.85	30.03	12.39	18.82	2.48	5.14
3.5	14.56	31.42	14.01	20.53	2.74	5.54
4.0	14.94	32.06	15.56	22.70	2.10	5.00
4.5	15.36	32.39	12.70	18.39	3.10	6.55
5.0	15.68	33.22	16.41	23.74	3.33	6.60

5   Discussion and Conclusion

In this work, we present design, modeling and control of the DEAMS. A multilayer DEA based on silicone and CNT is designed and fabricated to achieve a linear motion. Based on the customized DEA, the platform is demonstrated with millimeter stroke, sub-micrometer resolution and high natural frequency. Then for viscoelasticity compensation, we adopt a phenomenological DIHC controller based on the MRPIM combined with a PI feedback controller. Experimental results show that within the frequency range of 0.5–5.0 Hz, the DEAMS can track the reference sinusoidal trajectories with high precision. However, the severe vibration at high frequency limits corresponding measurement and feedback control, demonstrating the necessity of platform design iteration. Further work can also focus on two-DOF platform designs for workspace expansion and high-precision models to facilitate applications of the micro-displacement platform actuated by DEA.

References

1. Pan, P., et al.: MEMS-based platforms for mechanical manipulation and characterization of cells. J. Micromech. Microeng. **27**(12), 123003 (2017)
2. Liu, J., et al.: Robotic adherent cell injection for characterizing cell-cell communication. IEEE Trans. Biomed. Eng. **62**(1), 119–125 (2015)
3. Garcia, R.: Nanomechanical mapping of soft materials with the atomic force microscope: methods, theory and applications. Chem. Soc. Rev. **49**(16), 5850–5884 (2020)
4. Wu, Z., et al.: Survey on recent designs of compliant micro-/nano-positioning stages. Actuators **7**(1), 5 (2018)
5. Bhagat, U., et al.: Design and analysis of a novel flexure-based 3-DOF mechanism. Mech. Mach. Theory **74**, 173–187 (2014)
6. Wang, D.H., et al.: A monolithic compliant piezoelectric-driven microgripper: design, modeling, and testing. IEEE/ASME Trans. Mechatron. **18**(1), 138–147 (2013)
7. Li, Y., et al.: Design and analysis of a totally decoupled flexure-based XY parallel micromanipulator. IEEE Trans. Rob. **25**(3), 645–657 (2009)
8. Lyu, Z., et al.: Design of a new bio-inspired dual-axis compliant micromanipulator with millimeter strokes. IEEE Trans. Rob. **39**(1), 470–484 (2023)
9. Pelrine, R., et al.: High-speed electrically actuated elastomers with strain greater than 100%. Science **287**(5454), 836–839 (2000)
10. Jordan, G., et al.: Actuated micro-optical submount using a dielectric elastomer actuator. IEEE/ASME Trans. Mechatron. **16**(1), 98–102 (2011)
11. Guo, Y., et al.: Review of dielectric elastomer actuators and their applications in soft robots. Adv. Intell. Syst. **3**(10), 2000282 (2021)
12. Kovacs, G., et al.: Stacked dielectric elastomer actuator for tensile force transmission. Sens. Actuat. A **155**(2), 299–307 (2009)
13. Carpi, F., et al.: Helical dielectric elastomer actuators. Smart Mater. Struct. **14**(6), 1210 (2005)
14. Zhao, H., et al.: Compact dielectric elastomer linear actuators. Adv. Func. Mater. **28**(42), 1804328 (2018)
15. Huang, J., et al.: Large, uni-directional actuation in dielectric elastomers achieved by fiber stiffening. Appl. Phys. Lett. **100**(21), 211901 (2012)
16. Gu, G., et al.: Soft wall-climbing robots. Sci. Robot. **3**(25), eaat2874 (2018)
17. Tang, C., et al.: A pipeline inspection robot for navigating tubular environments in the sub-centimeter scale. Sci. Robot. **7**(66), eabm8597 (2022)
18. Ding, N., et al.: Design of dielectric-elastomer actuated XY stages with millimeter range and submicrometer resolution. In: 2020 International Conference on Manipulation, Automation and Robotics at Small Scales (MARSS), pp. 1-6. IEEE, Toronto (2020)
19. Kim, S., et al.: Laser-assisted failure recovery for dielectric elastomer actuators in aerial robots. Sci. Robot. **8**(76), eadf4278 (2023)
20. Ren, Z., et al.: A high-lift micro-aerial-robot powered by low-voltage and long-endurance dielectric elastomer actuators. Adv. Mater. **34**(7), 2106757 (2022)
21. Zou, J., et al.: Feedforward control of the rate-dependent viscoelastic hysteresis nonlinearity in dielectric elastomer actuators. IEEE Robot. Automat. Lett. **4**(3), 2340–2347 (2019)

Tension Distribution Algorithm of Flexible Cable Redundant Traction for Stable Motion of Air-Bearing Platform

Jingchao Jia[1], Gang Wang[1], Honglei Che[2(✉)], and Jifu Wen[1]

[1] School of Modern Posts, Beijing University of Posts and Telecommunication, Beijing 100876, China
[2] Beijing Key Laboratory of Metro Fire and Passenger Transportation Safety, China Academy of Safety Science and Technology, Beijing 100012, China
`Honglei_C1983@163.com`

Abstract. A novel air-bearing platform driven by flexible cables is proposed, which is mainly used for full-physics simulation of the satellite docking experiments. However, the redundant driven of the flexible cables may lead to non-unique distribution of tension, thus affecting stable motion of the air-bearing platform. To tackle with this problem, a tension distribution algorithm with the minimum 2-norm of the average tension as the optimization goal is proposed in the article. Specifically, the kinematics model of the air-bearing platform driven by the flexible cables is established, and the mapping relationship between the cable length and the velocity of the air-bearing platform is obtained. The static equilibrium equation of the cable driven air-bearing platform is analyzed and a mathematical optimization model of the flexible cable tension distribution problem is established. The tension of each flexible cable is decomposed using the force-closed method, and the multi-objective optimization problem of the mathematical optimization model is converted into a signal-objective optimization problem. Numerical simulation and experimental work is carried out to evaluate the tension distribution algorithm on the stable motion of the driven system under the specific trajectory of the air-bearing platform. The results show that the tension distribution algorithm has an important impact on improving the stability of the air-bearing platform.

Keywords: Air-bearing Platform · Cable Driven · Tension Distribution Algorithm

1 Introduction

The air-bearing platform is a kind of simulation device for simulating the operation of tiny satellites on the ground. It is widely used in the full physical simulation experiments of precision instruments and spacecraft [1]. It provides a ground experiment method for satellite attitude control and orbit change flight, and meets the demand of aerospace

Beijing Chaoyang District Collaborative Innovation Project Under Grant No. CYXC2208.

technology. The control method of the existing air-bearing platform mainly apply the pneumatic servo drive, but the pneumatic servo drive has the disadvantages of low control accuracy and difficult direction control, etc. [2]. Based on this, the flexible cable parallel mechanism can be used as the position servo drive of the air-bearing platform.

Rigid parallel mechanisms have the advantages of high stiffness, high accuracy, and stability, making them widely used in fields such as precision machining, assembly, and motional. Examples of their application include over constrained mechanical arms [3, 4] and RPR equivalent parallel mechanism series design and applications [5]. Compared with the traditional rigid mechanism, it has the advantages of simple structure, rapid deployment, provides a large workspace, high load capacity, good dynamic performance, and structure and high reliability. Due to these advantages, cable-driven robots are well-suited for use in a wide variety of applications, including crane-like applications, e.g. [6], rehabilitation [7], and camera system [8]. Therefore, it can be applied for the position servo drive control of the air-bearing platform. But at the same time, the following challenges are faced: 1) The flexible cable driven can only be pulled but not compressed, and redundant drives must be used to make the air-bearing platform fully controllable; 2) The flexible cable parallel mechanism driven by the plane is affected by the terminal attitude. It must be properly distributed for stable operation.

Consequently, approaches to the cable driven tension distribution algorithm has been received increased attention. For example, the objective function can be the 1-norm [9] of t but these choices are prone to cable tension discontinuities along a trajectory. In order to solve the problems of computation speed and continuous solution, Pott et al. presented a closed-form method in [10], and then improved the method in [11]. Gouttefarde et al. [12] proposed a tension distribution algorithm that considers the centroid of the tension solution space of a convex polyhedron as the solution index. This algorithm is only applicable to n-DOF parallel mechanisms with n + 2 ropes. Gui et al.[13] proposed a non-iterative tension distribution algorithm based on geometric analysis method for a 6 DOF cable driven parallel robot with 2 redundant cables. Lim et al.[14] utilized a modified gradient projection method to obtain an adjustable tension solution for a planar cable driven parallel robot with 2 redundant cables. Vincenze et al.[15] proposed the use of the analytic Centre to solve the tension distribution problem.

Therefore, the objective of this study is to propose a tension distribution algorithm with the minimum 2-norm of the average tension as the optimization goal, which enhances the stability of the air-bearing platform during the docking process. This paper is structured as follows. In Sect. 2, the kinematics and statics of cable redundant driven system is established. The tension distribution algorithm with the minimum 2-norm of the average tension are proposed in Sect. 3. Following that, in Sect. 4, numerical simulation is conducted to validate the rationality of the proposed algorithm under different indicators. Then, Sect. 5 presents the developed research prototype of the cable redundant driven system. The cable redundant driven system of tension distribution experiments is carried out and the results are employed to validate the analytical the impact of tension distribution algorithms on stability. Finally, in Sect. 6, the conclusion is given.

2 Kinematic Modeling and Analysis of Cable Driven Air-Bearing Platform System

2.1 System Description

As shown in Fig. 1, the institutional model studied in this paper is as follows. The planar cable driven system is mainly composed of three parts, i.e., static platform, air-bearing platform, and cable. Affected by the unidirectional force characteristics, a redundant driven must be used to ensure that the air-bearing platform is fully controllable. Therefore, the number of degrees of freedom m of the air-bearing platform and the number n of driven units must satisfy the relationship $n \geq m+1$. It can be seen that the 3-DOF planar flexible cable driven realizes the retraction and release of the flexible cable through 4 motors through coordinated control, and pulls the air-bearing platform to move to the desired position.

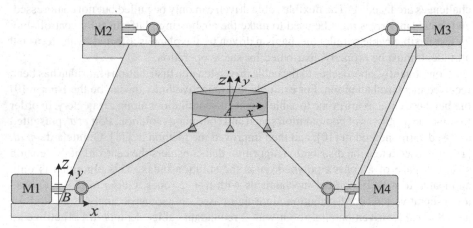

Fig. 1. Schematic diagram of the planar flexible cable driven system

2.2 Kinematic Modeling of Cable Driven System

In order to facilitate the description of the system, the kinematics model of the cable-driven robot shown in Fig. 2 is established. In Fig. 2, the base coordinate system $B - xy$ fixed to the glass platform and the reference coordinate system $A - x'y'$ fixed to the air-bearing platform are respectively established. Among them, $B_i(x_{bi}, y_{bi})$ represent the coordinates of the rope exit point on the static platform, and $A_i(x_{ai}, y_{ai})$ represent the coordinates of the rope hinge point on the moving platform. Since the air-bearing platform moves in a plane on the glass platform, the pose of the air-bearing platform can be represented by $P = [x, y, \theta]$, where the position given by $p = [x, y]^T$ and the rotation angle given by θ.

From the size closed connection in Fig. 2, combined with the principle of vector closure, it can be seen that the vector of the ith flexible cable vector is

$$d_i = (b_i - p - {}^B r_A a_i)/l_i \tag{1}$$

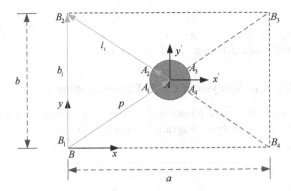

Fig. 2. Geometric model for the planar flexible cable driven system

where $d_i = \frac{b_i - p - {}^B r_A a_i}{\|b_i - p - {}^B r_A a_i\|}$ $(i = 1, 2, 3, 4)$ is the unit vector directed from the air-bearing platform A to B; b_i is the position vector of the exit point on the static platform in the global coordinate system; p is the local coordinate is the position vector in the global coordinate system; a_i is the position vector of the hinge point of the rope on the moving platform in the local coordinate system; ${}^B r_A$ is the rotation transformation matrix from the local coordinate system to the global coordinate system.

$$ {}^B r_A = \begin{bmatrix} c\theta & -s\theta \\ s\theta & c\theta \end{bmatrix} \tag{2} $$

where θ is the rotation angle of the local coordinate system relative to the global coordinate system, $c\theta = \cos\theta$, $s\theta = \sin\theta$. The length of the ith flexible cable can be obtained as

$$ l_i = (l_i^T \cdot l_i)^{1/2} \tag{3} $$

Differentiate the two sides of Eq. (1) with respect to time, we can obtain

$$ \dot{l_i} d_i + l_i \dot{d_i} = -\dot{p} - {}^B \dot{r}_A u_i \tag{4} $$

Multiplying both sides of Eq. (4) by d_i^T and rearranging, we can get

$$ \dot{l_i} = d_i^T (-\dot{p} - w \times {}^B r_A a_i) \tag{5} $$

According to the property of the vector triple mixed product, we can get

$$ \dot{l_i} = -\left[d_i^T \ ({}^B r_A a_i \times d_i)^T \right] \begin{bmatrix} \dot{p} \\ w \end{bmatrix} \tag{6} $$

Equation (6) can be simplified as

$$ \dot{L} = -J^T \dot{P} \tag{7} $$

where $\dot{P} = [\dot{x}, \dot{y}, w]^T$ represents the velocity and angular velocity of the end-effector, $\dot{L} = [\dot{l}_1, \dot{l}_2, \dot{l}_3, \dot{l}_4]$ represents the change rate of the rope length with time, $J =$

$$\left[\begin{array}{cccc} d_1 & d_2 & d_3 & d_4 \\ {}^B r_A \cdot a_1 \times d_1 & {}^B r_A \cdot a_2 \times d_2 & {}^B r_A \cdot a_3 \times d_3 & {}^B r_A \cdot a_4 \times d_4 \end{array}\right], J \in R^{3 \times 4}$$ is the structure matrix of the 3-DOF cable driven parallel mechanism.

2.3 Static Equilibrium Analysis of Cable Driven System

The force analysis of the above-mentioned planar four cables parallel mechanism is carried out, and the force analysis diagram is shown in Fig. 3.

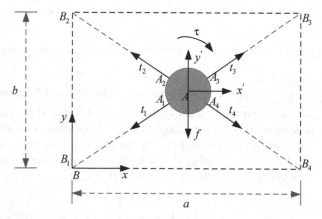

Fig. 3. Static equilibrium model for the planar flexible cable driven system

From the static equilibrium of the system, we have

$$\begin{cases} \sum_{i=1}^{m} t_i + f = 0 \\ \sum_{i=1}^{n} {}^B r_A a_i \times t_i + \tau = 0 \end{cases} \tag{8}$$

Equation (8) can be simplified as

$$Jt + W = 0 \tag{9}$$

where $t = \begin{bmatrix} t_1 & t_2 & t_3 & t_4 \end{bmatrix}^T$ is the set of cable tensions; $W = -\begin{bmatrix} f & \tau \end{bmatrix}$ is the external force and external moment received by the air-bearing platform.

3 Optimal Solution of Cable Tension of Cable Driven Air-Bearing Platform System

3.1 Tension Optimization Model of Cable Driven System

For a fully constrained cable driven robot $m > n$, J is a 3×4 matrix, Eq. (9) is underdetermined, the solution to the cable tension is an overdetermined problem, i.e., when the air-bearing platform is located in the feasible workspace, the tension solution obtained by Eq. (9) is not necessarily a feasible solution. It is necessary to optimize the design of the cable tension according to the control requirements. In the actual control process, the tension distribution of the flexible cable is required to satisfy the linear inequality: $0 \leq t_{min} \leq t_i \leq t_{max}\ i = 1, \cdots, m$. Therefore, in the real-time control of the fully constrained cable parallel robot, for a certain pose of the air-bearing platform, it is necessary to calculate the unique solution of the corresponding cable tension distribution in real time through the cable tension distribution algorithm.

According to the research results of Verhoeven [16], it can be known that taking $p = 2$, combined with Eq. (9) and constraint conditions, the optimal tension distribution can be expressed as follows

$$
\begin{aligned}
\text{minimize} \qquad & g(t) = \|t\|_2 = \sqrt{\sum_{i=1}^{m} t_i^2} \\
\text{subject to} \qquad & t_{min} \leq t_i \leq t_{max} \\
\text{linear constraints } & W_i = -\sum_{i=1}^{m} J t_i
\end{aligned} \tag{10}
$$

3.2 Optimal Solution of Cable Tension in Cable Driven System

When the air-bearing platform runs to the edge of the parallel robot's workspace, in order to ensure that the tension distribution value is within a feasible range, the algorithm shown in Eq. (10) is improved. First, combine the idea of force closure to split each cable force

$$
t = t_s + t_h \tag{11}
$$

where t_s is the specific solution term, and t_h is the general solution term of the cable tension. Affected by the one-way force of the cable, the cable parallel robot with 3-DOF in the plane is usually arranged redundantly, resulting in the structure matrix J is not a square matrix, so the pseudo-inverse J^+ of the structure matrix is defined. Equation (9) can be rewritten as

$$
t = J^+(-W) + Null(J)\lambda \tag{12}
$$

where $J^+ = J^T(JJ^T)^{-1}$, $Null(J) = \begin{bmatrix} n_1 & n_2 & n_3 & n_4 \end{bmatrix}^T$ is the one-dimensional null-space basis of the structure matrix J, and λ is an arbitrary scalar.

Substitute Eq. (12) into $0 \leq t_{min} \leq t_i \leq t_{max}\ i = 1, \cdots, m$ to get

$$
\max_{1 \leq i \leq m} \frac{t_{i,min} + (J^+W)_i}{Null(J)_i} \leq \lambda \leq \min_{1 \leq i \leq m} \frac{t_{i,max} + (J^+W)_i}{Null(J)_i} \tag{13}
$$

Equation (13) forms a single-objective linear constraint on λ, and for different objective functions, an optimization model of the cable tension on λ can be constructed. In order to ensure that the cable tension is far from the upper and lower limits and to maintain the continuity of the tension during the motion process, the t will be first decomposed.

$$
t = t_m + t_v \tag{14}
$$

where $t_m = \frac{1}{2}(t_{min} + t_{max})$ is the average value of the maximum and minimum tension of the cable; t_v is an arbitrary force vector satisfying certain conditions.

Therefore, Eq. (9) can be rewritten as

$$Jt_v = -W - Jt_m \qquad (15)$$

Multiply J^{+T} on both sides of Eq. (12) yields

$$t_v = -J^{+T}(W + J^T t_m) \qquad (16)$$

Taking the minimum 2-norm of the difference between the cable force t and t_m is taken as the tension optimization goal, and the improved flexible cable tension distribution optimization model is

$$\begin{cases} \text{minimize} & g(t_v) = \|t_v\|_2 \\ \text{subject to} & \underline{\lambda} \leq \lambda \leq \overline{\lambda} \\ \text{linear constraints} & W_i = -\sum_{j=1}^{m} J_j t_j \end{cases} \qquad (17)$$

In Eq. (17), assuming that $g(t_v) = A\lambda^2 + B\lambda + C$ we can obtain $\frac{\partial F}{\partial \lambda} = 2A\lambda + B = 0$: (1)$\underline{\lambda} \leq \lambda \leq \overline{\lambda}$, at this time $\lambda = 0$; (2) $\lambda \leq \underline{\lambda}$, at this time $\lambda = \underline{\lambda}$; (3) $\lambda \geq \overline{\lambda}$, at this time $\lambda = \overline{\lambda}$.

The specific process of the solution of tension optimal model is as follows.

(1) Input the real-time position coordinates X_i and structural parameters of the air-bearing platform.
(2) Obtain the structure matrix $J(X_i)$ and generalized external force vector $W(X_i)$ corresponding to X_i.
(3) Solve the generalized inverse matrix of J: $J^+ = J^T(JJ^T)^{-1}$.
(4) By $J^+ J = I$, multiply $Jt_v = -W - Jt_m$ by left with the generalized inverse matrix J^+.
(5) Obtain the cable force optimization result: $t = t_m - J^+(W + Jt_m)$, check t whether the obtain cable force satisfies $0 \leq t_{min} \leq t_i \leq t_{max}(i = 1, 2, 3, 4)$.
(6) Judging whether this solution is the last pose, if not, return to (1) to solve the cable pull force of the next pose; otherwise, stop.

4 Simulation Work

4.1 Simulation Parameters and Trajectory Planning

Simulation works are conducted to evaluate the performance of the optimal algorithm for cable tension distribution mentioned above. The structural parameters of the cable driven system are listed in Table 1.

To illustrate the validity and feasibility of the tension distribution algorithm when the air-bearing platform run on a specific track. First, set the air-bearing platform to move in a straight line, given two point $P_1(x_1, y_1)$, $P_2(x_2, y_2)$ in the space, the expression of each interpolation point is

$$s = \sqrt{(x_2 - x_1)^2 + (y_2 - y_1)^2} \qquad (18)$$

Table 1. Parameter of cable driven system

System parameters	value
Quality of the platform m_p	30 kg
Lower limit of cable tension t_{min}	100 N
Upper limit of cable tension t_{max}	2000 N
Pulley 1 position B_1	(0, 0)
Pulley 2 position B_2	(0, 4)
Pulley 3 position B_3	(6, 4)
Pulley 4 position B_4	(6, 0)

$$\begin{cases} x(k) = x_1 + \delta_k(x_2 - x_1) \\ y(k) = y_2 + \delta_k(y_2 - y_1) \end{cases} \tag{19}$$

where δ_k is the normalization factor, $\delta_k \in [0, 1]$, S is the distance between the straight line ends.

Select the allowable maximum speed, maximum acceleration, and maximum jerk of the cable traction system as 2 m/s, 3 m/s^2, and, respectively, and the total interpolation time is 10s. The coordinates of the starting point and the ending point are selected as $P_1(1, 1), P_2(4, 3)$, and the feed speed of the air-bearing platform is 0.02 m/s. The resulting straight-line trajectory is shown in Fig. 4.

The length $l_1 \sim l_4$ of the flexible cable presents periodic changes due to the symmetrical distribution of the driving mechanism, as shown in Fig. 5 and Fig. 6 shows the variation of the ideal cable force when the air-bearing platform is running along the desired trajectory. The cable force $t_1 \sim t_4$ changes continuously, and the cable force of each flexible cable is within the constraint range.

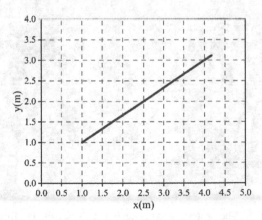

Fig. 4. The linear motion trajectory of the air-bearing platform

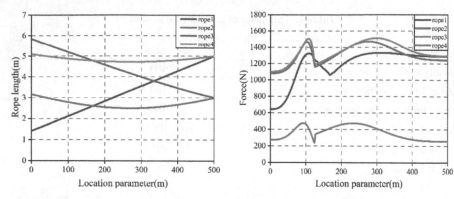

Fig. 5. Change of cable length   **Fig. 6.** Change of cable force

5   Experiment

As displayed in Fig. 7, the test platform is established and it is mainly formed with an end-effector, driven system, measuring equipment, i.e., air-bearing platform, tension sensor, position camera and data acquisition computer. The tension sensor is installed at the bottom of the air-bearing platform to measure the magnitude of the cable tension during move. The position sensor is installed on the air-bearing platform and it is utilized for measuring the position. The data acquisition computer is used to simultaneously record the changes in cable length and air-bearing platform position. The data acquisition program is written using the ROS framework with the C++ language.

Fig. 7. The prototype of the designed air-bearing platform

To verify the influence of the tension distribution algorithm on the stability of the air-bearing platform, we conducted a series of experiments and analysis. Firstly, specific values $t_{min} = 100\,N$, $t_{max} = 2000\,N$ are set to ensure that all cable tensions are feasible and non-negative. Secondly, when the air-bearing platform moved along the straight line trajectory shown in Fig. 4, the attitude angle of the air-bearing platform is always set to a specific value $\begin{bmatrix} 0, & 0, & 0 \end{bmatrix}^T$, and the above tension distribution algorithm is used to obtain the actual trajectory of the air-bearing platform. Finally, 500 trajectory points are taken, and the trajectory error of the air-bearing platform in the x, y directions are obtained, respectively, as shown in Fig. 8 and Fig. 9. It can be seen from the figures that errors in the x, y directions vary between 0–0.006, which is in the millimeter range. The position change is small, indicating high stability. Therefore, it can be considered that this tension distribution algorithm has a good impact on the stability of the air-baring platform.

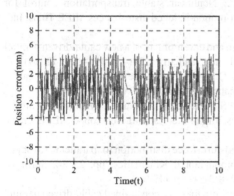

Fig. 8. Tracking error in the x direction

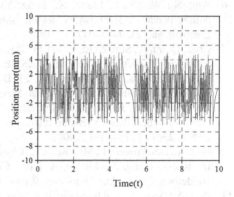

Fig. 9. Tracking error in the y direction

From the above analysis, it can be seen that when the air-bearing platform is performing linear motion. The cable length and cable tension are continuously changing, and the changes are all within the given constraint range, and the error change is small, which shows that the rationality of the algorithm for solving the cable tension distribution problem in a fully constrained cable-driven system.

6 Conclusion

In this paper, a tension allocation algorithm is proposed based on the 2-norm of cable tension as an optimization objective, to realize the stable motion of a planar cable driven air-bearing platform system. The algorithm can ensure the continuity and real-time dynamics of cable tension allocation during the docking process by the closed-form solution in the 2-norm. By transforming the multi-objective optimization function into a single objective optimization function for the optimization model, the difficulty of solving the tension allocation is reduced greatly. Finally, the simulation and experimental studies are conducted and the results indicate that the air-bearing platform can move smoothly to the desired location during the docking process.

References

1. Banerjee, A., et al.: On the design, modeling and experimental verification of a floating satellite platform. IEEE Robot. Automat. Lett. **7**(2), 1364–1371 (2022)
2. Santaguida, L., Zhu, Z.H.: Development of air-bearing microgravity testbed for autonomous spacecraft rendezvous and robotic capture control of a free-floating target. Acta Astronaut. **203**, 319–328 (2023)
3. Shen, X., Xu, L., Li, Q.: Motion/force constraint indices of redundantly actuated parallel manipulators with over constraints. Mech. Mach. Theory **165**, 104427 (2021)
4. Zhang, N., Huang, P., Li, Q.: Modeling, design and experiment of a remote-center-of-motion parallel manipulator for needle insertion. Robot. Comput. Integrat. Manufact. **50**, 192–202 (2018)
5. Li, Q., et al.: New family of RPR-equivalent parallel mechanisms: design and application. Chin. J. Mech. Eng. **30**(2), 217–221 (2017)
6. Sun, N., Wu, Y.M., Liang, X., Fang, Y.C.: Nonlinear stable transportation control for double-pendulum shipboard cranes with ship-motion-induced disturbances. IEEE Trans. Ind. Electron. **66**(12), 9467–9479 (2019)
7. Chen, Q., Zi, B., Sun, Z., Li, Y., Xu, Q.: Design and development of a new cable-driven parallel robot for waist rehabilitation. IEEE/ASME Trans. Mechatron. **24**(4), 1497–1507 (2019)
8. Duan, B.Y., Qiu, Y.Y., Zhang, F.S., Zi, B.: On design and experiment of the feed cable-suspended structure for super antenna. Mechatronics **19**, 503–509 (2009)
9. Borgstrom, P.H., Jordan, B.L., Sukhatme, G.S., Batalin, M.A., Kaiser, W.J.: Rapid computation of optimally safe tension distributions for parallel cable-driven robots. IEEE Trans. Robot. **25**(6), 1271–1281 (2009)
10. Pott, A., Bruckmann, T., Mikelsons, L.: Closed-form force distribution for parallel wire robots. In: Kecskeméthy, A., Müller, A. (eds.) Computational Kinematics, pp. 25–34. Springer, Heidelberg (2009). https://doi.org/10.1007/978-3-642-01947-0_4
11. Pott, A.: An improved force distribution algorithm for over-constrained cable-driven parallel robots. In: Thomas, F., Gracia, A.P. (eds.) Computational Kinematics. MMS, vol. 15, pp. 139–146. Springer, Dordrecht (2014). https://doi.org/10.1007/978-94-007-7214-4_16
12. Gouttefarede, M., Lamaury, J., Reichert, C., Bruchmann, T.: A versatile tension distribution algorithm for n-DOF parallel robots driven by n+2 cables. IEEE Trans. Robot. **31**(6), 1444–1457 (2015)
13. Gui, Z., Tang, X., Hou, S., Sun, H.: Non-iterative geometric method for cable-tension optimization of cable-driven parallel robots with 2 redundant cables. Mechatronics **59**, 49–60 (2019)
14. Lim, W.B., Yeo, S.H., Yang, G.: Optimization of tension distribution for cable-driven manipulators using tension-level index. IEEE/ASME Trans. Mechatron. **19**(2), 676–683 (2014)
15. Di Paola, V., Goldsztejn, A., Zoppi, M., et al.: Analytic Center Based Tension Distribution for Cable-Driven Platforms (CDPs) (2023)
16. Verhoeven, R.: Analysis of the Workspace of Tendon-Based Stewart Platforms. University of Duisburg-Essen, Duisburg (2006)

Research on High-Frequency Motion Control of Voice Coil Motors Based on Fuzzy PID

Feng Huang[1,2(✉)], Chenxi Wang[2], Yang Fu[1], Lijun Wang[3], and Qipeng Li[1]

[1] School of Mechanical and Energy Engineering, Zhejiang University of Science and Technology, Hangzhou, China
hf@zust.edu.cn
[2] Zhejiang Lianyi Motor Co., Ltd., Hangzhou, China
[3] School of Automation and Electrical Engineering, Zhejiang University of Science and Technology, Hangzhou, China

Abstract. Voice coil motors are widely used in high-precision manufacturing and processing fields because of their simple mechanical structure, fast dynamic response, and high linearity. The motion control algorithms and control accuracy of voice coil motors have become the focus of industry research. In this paper, the mechanical structure and electrical system of a voice coil motor are modeled, and a cascade fuzzy PID controller is designed for the motor. Then the control simulation is carried out in Simulink to verify the control method. The simulation results show that the performance of the designed fuzzy PID controller is superior to the classical PID controller in terms of adapting load change.

Keywords: Linear voice coil motor · System modeling · Fuzzy PID algorithm · High-frequency motion control

1 Introduction

A linear voice coil motor is an actuator that relies on the driver to receive electrical impulses and convert them into linear displacements. It has the advantages of small size, simple mechanical structure and fast dynamic response, high motion accuracy, etc. It is also widely used in precision positioning systems and high-frequency motion occasions [1, 2], such as positioning operations in the production of disks and laser discs, lens positioning in optical systems, precision electron tube and vacuum tube control in medical devices and so forth. In the process of actually controlling the voice coil motor for high-frequency movement, due to the existence of nonlinear factors such as inertia and load change, the control algorithms must have stronger adaptability and anti-interference to ensure the high motion accuracy of the motor.

At present, many researchers have carried out a lot of researches on the control algorithm of voice coil motors, mainly including PID control, automatic disturbance rejection control, neural network control, sliding mode control and other algorithms. Based on the classical PID, the fuzzy PID can adjust PID parameters to achieve better control effects [3–5] according to certain fuzzy logic rules. Compared with the classical PID algorithm, the fuzzy PID has stronger robustness and reliability [6].

In this paper, the fuzzy PID control algorithm of the linear voice coil motor is designed. The function of automatic adjustment of controller parameters is realized by the fuzzy method to adapt the load changes of the motor system. The error curve is used as the evaluation standard, and the better reliability and stability of the algorithm are verified by comparing the control effect with the classical PID algorithm.

2   Working Principle of the Linear Voice Coil Motor

Like many commonly used motors, the working principle of voice coil motors can be summarized simply as the movement of energized conductors under the action of amperage forces in a magnetic field. The operating principle is shown in Fig. 1. Permanent magnets and rigid flux loops provide a magnetic field of constant magnetic strength, and the outside of the kinematic part is wrapped with tubular coils. The amperage F of the kinematic part is defined as follows:

$$F = BIL \cdot sin\alpha \tag{1}$$

where B is the magnetic field strength, I is the current flowing through the wire, L is the length of the wire, α is the angle between the current direction and the magnetic field direction. If the magnetic field is constant, the movement of the kinematic part depends on the magnitude and direction of the current flowing into the coil [7]. Introducing the desired current to the tubular coil, the voice coil motor will move under the action of ampere force, which is the working principle of the linear voice coil motor.

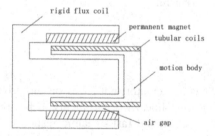

Fig. 1. Cross-sectional view of the motor

3   Voice Coil Motor Modeling

In the ideal case of no load, the voice coil motor mechanical displacement system can be abstracted into the simple model, as shown in Fig. 2.

$x(t)$ is the linear displacement of the motion part of the voice coil motor, m is the mass of the motion part, and $F(t)$ is the ampere force. The dynamic equation of the system is as follows:

$$F(t) = m \cdot \ddot{x}(t) \tag{2}$$

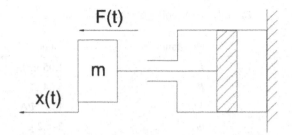

Fig. 2. Mechanical model of the voice coil motor

Knowing that the ampere force $F(t)$ of formula (1) is proportional to the current i_e, and the force constant is K_m, and then:

$$F(t) = K_m \cdot i_e \tag{3}$$

Combining Eqs. (2) and (3) and performing the Laplace Transform:

$$\frac{X(s)}{I_e(s)} = \frac{K_m}{m \cdot s^2} \tag{4}$$

The mathematical model of the voice coil motor electrical system is as follows:

$$u = i_e R + L\frac{di_e}{dt} + e_b \tag{5}$$

where u is the armature voltage across the motor, R is the coil resistance, L is the inductance constant and e_b is the back EMF, where the definition of e_b is:

$$e_b = nBlv \tag{6}$$

where n is the number of the coil turns in the magnetic field, l is the coil constant, and v is the speed of the kinematic part.

Combining (5) and (6) and performing the Laplace Transform yields:

$$I_e(s) = \frac{U(s) - nBlsX(s)}{Ls + R} \tag{7}$$

Synthesis of (4) and (7) yields:

$$\frac{X(s)}{U(s)} = \frac{K_m}{s(mLs^2 + mRs + K_m nBl)} \tag{8}$$

(8) is the system transfer function of the voice coil motor. That is, the expression of the corresponding displacement amount is obtained through the given armature voltage.

The actual reference values of the relevant parameters of the voice coil motor are shown in Table 1.

Table 1. Voice coil motor parameter values

Parameters	Constants	Values
Coil inductance	L	1.05 mH
Coil resistance	R	5.04 Ω
Force constant	Km	12.7 N/A
Kinematic mass	m	245.2 g
Back EMF	Kb	12.7 V/M/S

4   Control System Design

This system adopts position control. The total input of the system is the position, forming a position-closed loop with the position feedback. The output of the position controller is given to the speed loop, forming a speed-closed loop with the velocity feedback. The speed loop controller calculates the set-point of the current loop. The current loop controller calculates the voltage between the motor terminals. The load change of the motor is equivalent to the external force directly acting on the motor, and the speed loop is required to dynamically adjust the control output according to the external force to ensure the stability of the system. Therefore, the adaptive fuzzy control is considered to be applied to the speed loop. The overall block diagram of the control system is shown in Fig. 3.

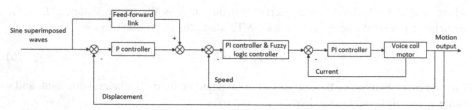

Fig. 3. The overall structure of the control system

The fuzzy controller has a dual-input and dual-output structure. With the speed error and its differentiation as inputs, the outputs are the correction amount of the proportional and integral parameters. The domains of velocity error E and error rate EC are $X = [-1000,1000]$, $Y = [-1000,1000]$, respectively, and the output domains are $Z1 = [4, 7]$, $Z2 = [-3,3]$. The input and output use the same fuzzy set [NB, NM, NS, O, PS, PM, PB]. Except for the subsets NB and PB which use the Gaussian membership function, the rest of the subsets use the triangle membership function [8–10]. The fuzzy rules designed according to the division of fuzzy language variables on the input and output domains are shown in Table 2 and Table 3.

Table 2. Fuzzy rules of Kp

E	EC						
	NB	NM	NS	O	PS	PM	PB
NB	PB	PB	PB	PB	PM	PS	O
NM	PB	PB	PB	PB	PM	O	O
NS	PM	PM	PM	PM	O	PS	NS
O	PM	PM	PS	O	NS	NS	NM
PS	PS	PS	O	NS	NM	NM	NM
PM	PS	O	NS	NM	NM	NM	NB
PB	O	O	NM	NM	NM	NB	NB

Table 3. Fuzzy rules of Ki

E	EC						
	NB	NM	NS	O	PS	PM	PB
NB	NB	NB	NM	NM	NS	O	O
NM	NB	NB	NM	NS	NS	O	O
NS	NB	NM	NS	NS	O	PS	PS
O	NM	NM	NS	O	PS	PM	PM
PS	NM	NS	O	PS	PS	PM	PB
PM	O	O	PS	NM	PM	PB	PB
PB	O	O	PS	PM	PM	PB	PB

5 Simulation Setup

The voice coil motor model and controller are implemented in Matlab/Simulink (Math-Works), as shown in Fig. 4. During the simulation process, the values of the controller parameters are shown in Table 4. The system uses a high-frequency sinusoidal super-imposed wave as the input, whose mathematical expression is as follows. The variable parameters are the amplitude, frequency of the two sine waves.

$$f(t) = A_1\sin(2\pi f_1 t) + A_2\sin(2\pi f_2 t) \tag{9}$$

The system without fuzzy control is simulated first to determine the PID parameters that make the output displacement curve of the system optimal. After repeated parameter adjustment, the classical PID parameters that make the output effect the best are taken according to Table 4. On this basis, while the determined PID parameters are kept unchanged, the fuzzy controller is added to the system. After adjusting the quantification factors of the input and output of the fuzzy logic control module, the output curve is the best when the quantification factors' values are taken from Table 4.

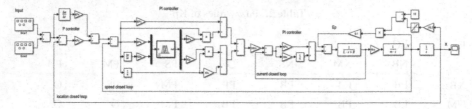

Fig. 4. The Simulink implementation of the voice coil motor model and controllers

Table 4. The values of the controller parameters

Parameters	Variables	Values	Parameters	Variables	Values
Location scale factor	KPx	45	Current integration factor	KIu	1
Feed-forward factor	KFx	1	Speed deviation quantification factor	KPe	0.3
Speed scale factor	KPv	2000	Velocity deviation differential quantification factor	KDe	1×10^{-5}
Speed integration factor	KIv	1000	The adjusting factor of the scale factor	KPa	1000
Current scale factor	KPu	20	The adjusting factor of the integration factor	KIa	0.2

There are two modes adopted to verify the effectiveness of fuzzy PID algorithm. The values of the movement amplitude and frequency are shown in Table 5. In the meanwhile, based on whether or not the motor has a load on it, the simulation is divided into two groups—Group 1 & Group 2. In Group 1, the simulations are run under the no-load condition, while in Group 2 the situation is under the load of 600 g.

Table 5. The values of the movement amplitude and frequency

Simulation type	Values of input-parameter
Simulation mode 1	$A1 = A2 = 1$ mm, $f1 = 50$ Hz, $f2 = 100$ Hz
Simulation mode 2	$A1 = A2 = 0.5$ mm, $f1 = 100$ Hz, $f2 = 200$ Hz

6 Results and Analysis

Simulation results are described through system's output displacement curves and error curves, which will display the different control effects of two algorithms. The simulation results of Group1 are shown as follows in Fig. 5 and Fig. 6.

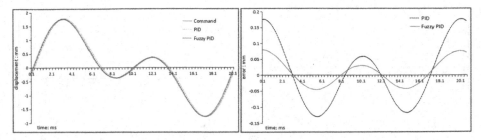

Fig. 5. The displacement curves and error curves of simulation mode 1 without load

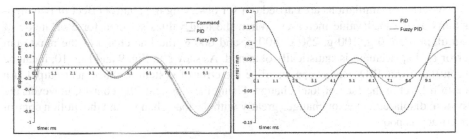

Fig. 6. The displacement curves and error curves of simulation mode 2 without load

It can be seen that the actual displacement curve of the system is more in line with the command curve after adding fuzzy control. The error under fuzzy PID control is significantly smaller than the error under PID control. It can be concluded that the effect of fuzzy control is better.

Now, a load of 600 g is added to the voice coil motor. Keeping the previously adjusted parameters unchanged, the Group2 simulation is carried out, and the simulation results are shown as follows in Fig. 7 and Fig. 8.

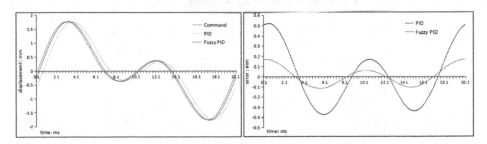

Fig. 7. The displacement curves and error curves of simulation mode 1 with a load of 600 g

According to the comparison of error curves, with a load on the motion part, the error range of the system displacement output under fuzzy control is still smaller. The advantages of the adaptive adjustment ability of fuzzy control are more obvious.

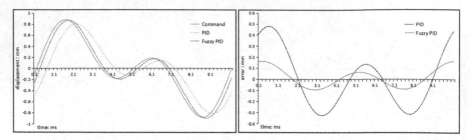

Fig. 8. The displacement curves and error curves of simulation mode 2 with a load of 600 g

A series of simulations are carried out for observing the control effect of two algorithms as the load value increases. When the load values selected for each mode of simulation are 0 g, 100 g, 250 g, 400 g, and 600 g, the line charts of the maximum error of displacement is statistically obtained. As shown in Fig. 9 and Fig. 10, it can be seen that fuzzy PID control can stabilize the error of system displacement output at a certain level in the face of load change. Using the classical PID control, however, the system displacement error changes greatly with the load change, and the motion control accuracy is poor.

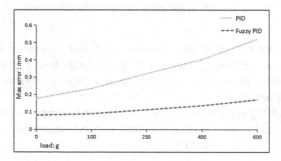

Fig. 9. Max error curves of simulation mode 1

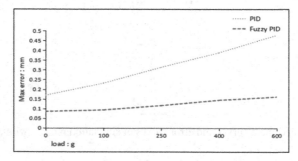

Fig. 10. Max error curves of simulation mode 2

Based on all comparisons above, it's easy to see that the control effect of fuzzy PID is well beyond that of PID under conditions of different values of load.

7 Conclusions

In this paper, the effectiveness and reliability of the fuzzy PID control algorithm designed for the high-frequency motion of a voice coil motor are verified by the comparative simulations with the systemic mathematical modeling. This algorithm design can provide an effective scheme for the motion control of voice coil motors so that they can be better applied to the field with extremely high requirements for motion accuracy and motion frequency, especially the fast tool servo systems in CNC machining, and physical or material experiments that require high-frequency precise vibration sources.

Acknowledgments. This work is supported by the "Pioneer" and "Leading Goose" R&D Program of Zhejiang (Grant No. 2023C01056) and the Zhejiang Provincial Key R&D projects (Grant No. 2022C04022).

References

1. Wang, L., Wang, Z., Wang, F, Shi, G., Xu, R.: Robust finite-time adaptive control for high performance voice coil motor-actuated fast steering mirror. Rev. Sci. Instrument. **93**(12) (2022)
2. Ning, Z., Mao, Y., Huang, Y., Gao, C.: Robust current control of voice coil motor in tip-tilt mirror based on disturbance observer framework. IEEE Access **9**, 96814–96822 (2021)
3. Li, R., Gong, P.: Fuzzy PID speed controller of DC motor based on MATLAB. J. Phys. Conf. Ser. **2417**(1), 012037 (2022)
4. Zhang, D., Wang, J.: Fuzzy PID speed control of BLDC motor based on model design. J. Phys. Conf. Ser. **1303**, 012124 (2019)
5. Zhang, W., Zhang, F., Zhang, J., Zhang, J., Zhang, J.: Based on brushless DC motor of fuzzy and PID control system. IOP Conf. Ser.: Mater. Sci. Eng. **452**(4), 042075 (2018)
6. Gao, X., Wang, S., Cui, Y., Wu, Z., Yong, Y.: Anti-interference control of servo motor system based on intelligent fuzzy PID. Southwest Inst. Tech. Phys. (China) (2021)
7. Zhao, B., et al.: Application of fuzzy sliding mode control in voice coil motor control system. J. Phys. Conf. Ser. **2281**(1), 012009 (2022)
8. Kaloi, M.K.: Fuzzy-PID based control scheme for PMDC series motor speed control. Ind. J. Sci. Technol. **13**(28), 2911–2923 (2020)
9. Shi, G.S., Huang, L., Hu, W.: The brushless DC motor adaptive fuzzy PID servo controller design. Appl. Mech. Mater. **246–247**, 838-841 (2012)
10. Liu, H., Liu, Y., Xue, G., Chen, Z., Zhang, Y.: Stability of the cone probe driven by hydraulic motor based on fuzzy PID. J. Phys. Conf. Ser. **1549**(4), 042081 (2020)

Feedback Linearization with Improved ESO for Quadrotor Attitude Control

Yangyang Dong[1], Zequn Xia[2], Yongbin Wang[1,3], and Zijian Zhang[1(✉)]

[1] College of Astronautics, Nanjing University of Aeronautics and Astronautics, Nanjing 210016, China
zhangzijian999@163.com
[2] System Design Institute of Hubei Aerospace Technology Academy, Wuhan 430040, China
[3] Beijing Institute of Space Mechanics and Electricity, Beijing 100094, China

Abstract. Aiming at the nonlinear and strong coupling characteristics of quadrotor aircraft, as well as the attitude control problems with modeling errors and unknown disturbances, an improved active disturbance rejection control scheme is proposed in this paper. The feedback linearization method is used to convert the attitude dynamics model of unmanned aerial vehicles into a linear model, reducing the system error caused by small disturbance assumptions. The structure of the extended state observer (ESO) is improved so that it can simultaneously use the measurement information of angle and angular velocity to improve its estimation accuracy for time-varying disturbances; Based on the improved ESO, the design of an active disturbance rejection controller was completed and the stability of the control system was demonstrated. The simulation experimental results show that the self disturbance rejection controller based on improved ESO has strong anti-jamming and robustness.

Keywords: Quadrotor UAV · Active disturbance rejection control (ADRC) · Attitude control · Extended state observer (ESO)

1 Introduction

In recent years, quadrotor UAV has been widely used in surveillance, search, reconnaissance and other social and military applications due to its simple structure, convenient operation, free hover, vertical take off and landing and other advantages [1].

Due to the underactuated characteristic of quadrotor UAV, its position control is realized by controlling the attitude angle. Therefore, attitude stability is the first problem to be solved in the design of quadrotor. For the attitude control problem of quadrotor, scholars have proposed many effective control methods,Such as PID control [2], Sliding mode control [3], geometric control [4], backstepping control [5], etc. The above control methods are difficult to deal with large disturbances and modeling errors. In the presence of unknown disturbances and modeling errors, the control performance of the above methods may significantly deteriorate, sometimes leading to instability of the closed-loop system.

© The Author(s), under exclusive license to Springer Nature Singapore Pte Ltd. 2023
H. Yang et al. (Eds.): ICIRA 2023, LNAI 14270, pp. 206–219, 2023.
https://doi.org/10.1007/978-981-99-6492-5_19

The active disturbance rejection control (ADRC) is a modelless control method [6–9] proposed by Professor Han Jingqing. Its core idea is to combine the internal uncertainties and external disturbances of the system into a "total disturbance", take it as an extended state of the system, construct an extended state observer (ESO) to estimate it and cancel it in the control path, which has been widely used in UAV flight control [10–12].

The core of Active disturbance rejection control is the estimation and compensation of total disturbance by ESO. ESO can only achieve convergence of the estimation error to 0 for constant disturbances, and for time-varying disturbances, ESO usually requires high gain to ensure that the disturbance estimation error is small enough. However, Increasing the gain of the observer in the presence of high-frequency measurement noise will incredibly degrade estimation performance. There is a tradeoff between the state estimation speed and the robustness to measurement noise [14]. Some scholars improve control performance by combining ADRC with other control methods. Such as Embedded Model Control (EMC) [14], Global Fast Terminal Sliding Mode (GFTSM) [15], low-frequency disturbance compensator (LFDC) [16] etc.

Other scholars have improved the control effect of ADRC by improving ESO. At present, the main improvement directions are as follows: 1.Improving the fal function in nonlinear ESO [17]; 2. Combining multiple observers, including cascading multiple ESOs to achieve high estimation performance at low gain [18], and cascading ESOs with KF to reduce their sensitivity to measurement noise [19]; 3. Improve the ESO parameter tuning method, such as using AESO with adaptive observer gain [20] and ESKF with disturbance as an extended state variable added to KF for estimation [21]; 4. Incorporate known model information [22] or disturbance information [23] into ESO design to improve disturbance estimation efficiency.

The sensors of quadrotor are usually able to obtain measurement information of angle and angular velocity. However, traditional ESO can only utilize angle or angular velocity information, and the utilization rate of measurement information is insufficient. Reference [24] proposes a compensation function observer (CFO) that adopts the idea of pure integration, compensation, and transfer function types, changing the structure of ESO. It can simultaneously utilize the measurement information of angular velocity and angle, making CFO two types higher than ESO, with high accuracy and strong convergence. Reference [25] uses radial basis function (RBF) neural networks instead of linear filters on its basis, further improving estimation accuracy. However, both CFO structures are sensitive to measurement noise. At the same time, reference [25] adopts the small disturbance assumption and directly replaces Euler's angular velocity with attitude angular velocity, which brings additional system errors.

This article proposes an improved ESO based autonomous disturbance rejection controller for unmanned aerial vehicle attitude. The feedback linearization technique is used to linearize the nonlinear model of the unmanned aerial vehicle, avoiding system errors caused by small disturbance assumptions. An improved ESO is proposed, which can simultaneously utilize measurement information of angle and angular velocity, and has higher disturbance estimation accuracy. Unlike the CFO in reference [24], the improved ESO in this paper only has an integration link between the disturbance estimation value and measurement information, which has a strong filtering effect on measurement noise and higher engineering application value. Finally, the design and stability proof of the self disturbance rejection controller were completed based on the improved ESO. Through numerical simulation, it has been proven that the anti-interference ability and robustness of the controller proposed in this paper are stronger than those of traditional ADRC.

2 Problem Description

Attitude angle of unmanned aerial vehicles $\chi = [\varphi, \theta, \psi]^{\perp}$ to describe φ, θ, ψ respectively represent the pitch angle, roll angle, and yaw angle of the quadrotor. The inertial coordinate system is selected as the NED coordinate system, and according to the rotation order of "ZYX", Let R_b^W denote the transformation matrix between body frame $\{B\}$ and world frame $\{w\}$ that using Euler–Lagrange formulation, which can be expressed as can be expressed as:

$$R_b^W = R(\psi)R(\theta)R(\varphi)$$

$$= \begin{bmatrix} c_\psi c_\theta & c_\psi s_\theta s_\varphi - s_\psi c_\varphi & c_\psi s_\theta c_\varphi + s_\psi s_\varphi \\ s_\psi c_\theta & s_\psi s_\theta s_\varphi + c_\psi c_\varphi & s_\psi s_\theta c_\varphi - c_\psi s_\varphi \\ -s_\theta & c_\theta s_\varphi & c_\theta c_\varphi \end{bmatrix} \tag{1}$$

where c_α, s_α represent $cos\alpha$ and $sin\alpha$. According to formula (1), the attitude kinematics model of UAV is as follows:

$$\dot{\chi} = A(\chi)\omega_b = \begin{bmatrix} 1 & s_\varphi t_\theta & c_\varphi t_\theta \\ 0 & c_\varphi & -s_\varphi \\ 0 & s_\varphi/c_\theta & c_\varphi/c_\theta \end{bmatrix} \omega_b \tag{2}$$

where: ω_b is the angular velocity of the drone system, and by taking the derivative of Eq. (2), we can obtain

$$\ddot{\chi} = \dot{A}(\chi)\omega_b + A(\chi)\dot{\omega}_b \tag{3}$$

According to the Euler equation, it can be obtained that:

$$\dot{\omega}_b = J^{-1}\left(\tau - \omega_b^\wedge J\omega_b + d_0\right) \tag{4}$$

where d_0 is an unknown external disturbance, τ is the control torque in the three coordinate axes of the drone, and J is the drone inertia matrix. By combining Eqs. (2), (3), and (4), we can obtain the UAV attitude dynamics model as follows:

$$\ddot{\chi} = A(\chi)J^{-1}\tau + C(\chi, \dot{\chi}) + A(\chi)J^{-1}d_0 \tag{5}$$

where:

$$C(\chi, \dot{\chi}) = \dot{A}(\chi)\omega - A(\chi)J^{-1}\omega^\wedge J\omega$$
$$\omega = A^{-1}(\chi)\dot{\chi} \tag{6}$$

In order to ensure the validity of the model, the amplitude of the roll angle in this paper is limited to 60° (60° is considered as a large angle in this study, and the roll angle of the UAV is far less than 60° when the quadrotor is operated normally), $A(\chi)$ is always reversible.

3 Control Scheme

3.1 Improving ESO

For second-order systems:

$$\begin{cases} \dot{x}_1 = x_2 \\ \dot{x}_2 = \overline{f}(x_1, x_2, w) + b_0 u_0 \end{cases} \tag{7}$$

where x_1, x_2 are the state variables of the system; W represents external disturbance; $\overline{f}(x_1, x_2, w)$ is the sum of internal and external disturbances in the system; The parameter b_0 represents the high-frequency gain of the system, which cannot be accurately obtained. Its estimated value b is used instead; u_0 is the system control input quantity. Equation (7) can be written in the following form:

$$\begin{cases} \dot{x}_1 = x_2 \\ \dot{x}_2 = f + b u_0 \end{cases} \tag{8}$$

where $f = \overline{f}(x_1, x_2, w) + (b_0 - b)u_0$ represents the total disturbance. Define y_1 and y_2 as the measured values of state variables x_1 and x_2, respectively. The current improved ESO design is as follows:

$$\begin{cases} \dot{\overline{z}}_1 = \overline{z}_2 \\ \dot{\overline{z}}_2 = bu + \beta_1(y_1 - \overline{z}_1) + \overline{z}_3 \\ \dot{\overline{z}}_3 = \beta_3(y_1 - \overline{z}_1) + \beta_2(y_2 - \overline{z}_2) \end{cases} \tag{9}$$

where, $\overline{z}_1, \overline{z}_2, \overline{z}_3$ are estimates of state variables x_1, x_2, and total disturbance f, $\beta_1, \beta_2, \beta_3$ is to improve the ESO gain coefficient. Define error variables:

$$\overline{e} = \begin{bmatrix} \overline{e}_1 \\ \overline{e}_2 \\ \overline{e}_3 \end{bmatrix} = \begin{bmatrix} x_1 \\ x_2 \\ f \end{bmatrix} - \begin{bmatrix} \overline{z}_1 \\ \overline{z}_2 \\ \overline{z}_3 \end{bmatrix} \tag{10}$$

By taking the derivative of time and substituting Eq. (8) into Eq. (10), we can obtain:

$$\dot{\overline{e}} = \begin{bmatrix} 0 & 1 & 0 \\ 0 & -\beta_1 & 1 \\ -\beta_3 & -\beta_2 & 0 \end{bmatrix} \overline{e} + \begin{bmatrix} 0 \\ 0 \\ \dot{f} \end{bmatrix} \tag{11}$$

The characteristic equation of Eq. (11) is:

$$\lambda^3 + \beta_1 \lambda^2 + \beta_2 \lambda + \beta_3 = 0 \tag{12}$$

From Eq. (11), The improved ESO proposed in this article has the same characteristic equation as the third-order LESO, so the conclusion of parameter tuning and stability proof of the third-order LESO can be directly applied to the improved ESO. By performing a Laplace transform on Eq. (11), we can obtain:

$$\overline{e}_3(s) = \frac{s^2(s + \beta_1)f(s)}{s^3 + \beta_1 s^2 + \beta_2 s + \beta_3} \tag{13}$$

From Eq. (13), it can be seen that the improved ESO asymptotically converges for constant and slope perturbations, while LSO only asymptotically converges for constant perturbations. Therefore, this article designs an improved ESO with higher disturbance estimation accuracy than LESO.

3.2 Controller Design

Define virtual control quantity $u = A(\chi)B^{-1}\tau = [u_\varphi, u_\theta, u_\psi]^T$ where $B = diag([b_x, b_y, b_z])$ is the estimated value of the drone inertia matrix J. Total disturbance $d = C(\chi, \dot{\chi}) + A(\chi)^{-1}d_0 + A(\chi)(J^{-1} - B^{-1})\tau = [d_\varphi, d_\theta, d_\psi]^T$. The attitude dynamics model of unmanned aerial vehicles can be written in the following series integration form:

$$\begin{cases} \ddot{\varphi} = u_\varphi + d_\varphi \\ \ddot{\theta} = u_\theta + d_\theta \\ \ddot{\psi} = u_\psi + d_\psi \end{cases} \tag{14}$$

Measurement information is attitude angle χ And body angular velocity ω_b. Let $\eta = \dot{\chi} = A(\chi)\omega = [\eta_\varphi, \eta_\theta, \eta_\psi]^T$ is the attitude angular velocity. Taking the pitch channel as an example, an improved ESO is used to estimate the total disturbance of the pitch channel d_φ, the mathematical expression is as follows:

$$\begin{cases} \dot{z}_{\varphi 1} = z_{\varphi 2} \\ \dot{z}_{\varphi 2} = u_x + \beta_{\varphi 1}(\varphi - z_{\varphi 2}) + z_{\varphi 3} \\ \dot{z}_{\varphi 3} = \beta_{\varphi 3}(\varphi - z_{\varphi 1}) + \beta_{\varphi 2}(\eta_x - z_{\varphi 2}) \end{cases} \tag{15}$$

where $z_{\varphi 1}, z_{\varphi 2}, z_{\varphi 3}$ is observed values of the pitch angle φ, Pitch angular velocity η_φ and Total disturbance of pitch channel $d_\varphi, \beta_{\varphi 1}, \beta_{\varphi 2}, \beta_{\varphi 3}$ are observer gains, take $\beta_{\varphi 1} = 3\omega_{\varphi 0}, \beta_{\varphi 2} = 3\omega_{\varphi 0}^2, \beta_{\varphi 3} = \omega_{\varphi 0}^3$. $\omega_{\varphi 0}$ is the normal number to be designed. Based on the estimated value $z_{\varphi 3}$. The total disturbance can be actively compensated in the forward path of feedback control, and the control law is designed as follows:

$$u_\varphi = k_{p\varphi}(\varphi_d - z_{\varphi 1}) + k_{d\varphi}(\dot{\varphi}_d - z_{\varphi 2}) - z_{\varphi 3} \tag{16}$$

where, $k_{p\varphi}, k_{d\varphi}$ to provide feedback gain, a pole assignment based method is used for parameter tuning. Let $k_{p\varphi} = \omega_{\varphi 1}^2, k_{d\varphi} = 2\omega_{\varphi 1}, \omega_{\varphi 1}$ is the normal number to be designed, φ_d is the expected pitch angle, $\dot{\varphi}_d$ is the expected pitch angular velocity. Similar to the pitch channel, the controller design for the roll channel is as follows:

$$\begin{cases} \dot{z}_{\theta 1} = z_{\theta 2} \\ \dot{z}_{\theta 2} = u_y + \beta_{\theta 1}(\theta - z_{\theta 2}) + z_{\theta 3} \\ \dot{z}_{\theta 3} = \beta_{\theta 3}(\theta - z_{\theta 1}) + \beta_{\theta 2}(x_2 - z_{\theta 2}) \\ u_\theta = k_{p\varphi}(\theta_d - z_{\theta 1}) + k_{d\varphi}(\dot{\theta}_d - z_{\theta 2}) - z_{\theta 3} \end{cases} \tag{17}$$

The controller design for the yaw channel is as follows:

$$\begin{cases} \dot{z}_{\psi 1} = z_{\psi 2} \\ \dot{z}_{\psi 2} = u_\psi + \beta_{\psi 1}(\psi - z_{\psi 2}) + z_{\psi 3} \\ \dot{z}_{\psi 3} = \beta_{\psi 3}(\psi - z_{\psi 1}) + \beta_{\psi 2}(\eta_\psi - z_{\psi 2}) \\ u_\psi = k_{p\psi}(\psi_d - z_{\psi 1}) + k_{d\psi}(\dot{\psi}_d - z_{\psi 2}) - z_{\psi 3} \end{cases} \tag{18}$$

Actual control quantity τ Calculate as follows:

$$\tau = BA^{-1}(\chi)u$$
$$= BA^{-1}(\chi) \begin{bmatrix} k_{p\varphi}(\varphi_d - z_{\varphi 1}) + k_{d\varphi}(\dot{\varphi}_d - z_{\varphi 2}) - z_{\varphi 3} \\ k_{p\theta}(\theta_d - z_{\theta 1}) + k_{d\theta}(\dot{\theta}_d - z_{\theta 2}) - z_{\theta 3} \\ k_{p\psi}(\psi_d - z_{\theta 1}) + k_{d\psi}(\dot{\psi}_d - z_{\psi 2}) - z_{\psi 3} \end{bmatrix} \tag{19}$$

3.3 System Stability Analysis

Lemma 1 [26]. The nonlinear system

$$\dot{x} = f(t, x, u) \tag{20}$$

Let $V : [0, \infty) \times R^n \to R$ be a continuously differentiable function such that

$$\alpha_1(\|x\|) \le V \le \alpha_2(\|x\|) \tag{21}$$

$$\frac{\partial V}{\partial t} + \frac{\partial V}{\partial x} f(t, x, u) \le -W_3(x), \forall \|x\| \ge \rho(\|u\|) > 0 \tag{22}$$

$\forall f(t, x, u) \in [0, \infty) \times R^n \times R^m$, where α_1, α_2 are class κ_∞ functions, ρ is a class κ function, and $W_3(x)$ is a continuous positive definite function on R^n. Then the system (20) is input to state stable.

Proposition 1. The attitude dynamics (14) driven by control law (16), (19) with the disturbance estimates given by (15), (17), (18) renders the closed loop attitude error dynamics locally input to state stable (ISS) with respect to derivative of the disturbance, if the derivative that satisfies $|d|$ is bounded.

Proof: Substitute the definitions of Eqs. (15), (16), (17), (18), and total disturbance d into Eq. (14) to obtain:

$$\begin{cases} \ddot{\varphi} - k_{p\varphi}(\varphi_d - z_{\varphi 1}) + k_{d\varphi}(\dot{\psi}_d - z_{\varphi 2}) + d_\varphi - z_{\varphi 3} \\ \ddot{\theta} = k_{p\varphi}(\theta_d - z_{\theta 1}) + k_{d\varphi}(\dot{\theta}_d - z_{\theta 2}) + d_\theta - z_{\theta 3} \\ \ddot{\psi} = k_{p\psi}(\psi_d - z_{\psi 1}) + k_{d\psi}(\dot{\psi}_d - z_{\psi 2}) + d_\psi - z_{\psi 3} \end{cases} \tag{23}$$

Taking the pitch angle channel as an example, define the pitch angle tracking error and pitch angle velocity tracking error as follows:

$$e_{c\varphi} = \begin{bmatrix} e_{p\varphi} \\ e_{d\varphi} \end{bmatrix} = \begin{bmatrix} \varphi_d \\ \dot{\varphi}_d \end{bmatrix} - \begin{bmatrix} \varphi \\ \dot{\varphi} \end{bmatrix} \tag{24}$$

Define the pitch angle channel to improve ESO estimation error as follows:

$$e_{z\varphi} = \begin{bmatrix} e_{z\varphi 1} \\ e_{z\varphi 2} \\ e_{z\varphi 3} \end{bmatrix} = \begin{bmatrix} \varphi \\ \dot{\varphi} \\ d_\varphi \end{bmatrix} - \begin{bmatrix} z_{\varphi 1} \\ z_{\varphi 2} \\ z_{\varphi 3} \end{bmatrix} \tag{25}$$

Let $e_\varphi = [e_{c\varphi}, e_{z\varphi}]^T$. Its derivative of time is:

$$\dot{e}_\varphi = A_\varphi e_\varphi + D \tag{26}$$

where

$$A_\varphi = \begin{bmatrix} A_{c\varphi} & C \\ 0_{3\times 2} & A_{z\varphi} \end{bmatrix}, A_{z\varphi} = \begin{bmatrix} 0 & 1 & 0 \\ 0 & -\beta_{\varphi 1} & 1 \\ -\beta_{\varphi 3} & -\beta_{\varphi 2} & 0 \end{bmatrix}$$

$$A_{c\varphi} = \begin{bmatrix} 0 & 1 \\ -k_{p\varphi} & -k_{d\varphi} \end{bmatrix}, C = \begin{bmatrix} 0 & 0 & 0 \\ -k_{p\varphi} & -k_{d\varphi} & 1 \end{bmatrix}, D = \begin{bmatrix} 0_{5\times 1} \\ \dot{d}_\varphi \end{bmatrix}$$

Coefficient matrix A_φ The characteristic equation of is:

$$\left| \lambda I_{5\times 5} - \begin{bmatrix} A_{c\varphi} & C \\ 0_{3\times 2} & A_{z\varphi} \end{bmatrix} \right| = 0 \tag{27}$$

where, $I_{n\times n}$ represents an n-order identity matrix. Simplify Eq. (27) to obtain:

$$(\lambda + \omega_{\varphi 1})^2 (\lambda + \omega_{\varphi 0})^3 = 0 \tag{28}$$

where $\omega_{\varphi 1}, \omega_{\varphi 0}$ is a normal number, as can be seen from the above equation, The eigenvalues of A_φ are all negative real numbers, A_φ is a Hurwitz matrix, that is, there exists a positive definite matrix P_1, such that $A_\varphi^T P_1 + P_\varphi A_1 = -I$. Construct Lyapunov function candidates:

$$V = \frac{1}{2} e_\varphi^T P_1 e_\varphi \tag{29}$$

where:

$$\frac{\lambda_{\min}(P_1)}{2} \|e_\varphi\|^2 \leq V \leq \frac{\lambda_{\max}(P_1)}{2} \|e_\varphi\|^2 \tag{30}$$

The Lyapunov function candidate has a derivative over time:

$$\dot{V} = -e_\varphi^T e_\varphi + 2e_\varphi^T P_1 D$$
$$\leq -\|e_\varphi\|^2 + 2\lambda_{\max}(P_1)\|e_\varphi\|\dot{d}_\varphi \tag{31}$$

The norm of the derivative of the total disturbance d is bounded, without loss of generality. Assuming its upper bound is q, choose an appropriate optimization constant $\gamma \in (0, 1)$, Eq. (31) can be transformed into:

$$\dot{V}_1 \leq -(1 - \gamma)\|e_\varphi\|^2, \forall \|e_\varphi\| \geq \frac{2\lambda_{\max}(P_1)q}{\gamma} \tag{32}$$

Therefore, the dynamics of pitch angle error is a local ISS. Proof of roll angle channel and yaw angle channel as above.

4   Simulation

4.1   Testing of the Error Analysis

This section conducts performance comparison simulation tests for improved ESO, ESO, and CFO in different environments. The simulation model adopts a simple 2-way integral series model, as shown in Eq. (8). Among them, the value of parameter b is taken as 1, f is the disturbance of the simulation input, u_0 is the control variable (mainly used for performance comparison and simulation of the observer, not focusing on the controller, the control variable can be taken arbitrarily), and the state variables x_1 and x_2 can be measured.

Both ESO and improved ESO use the bandwidth method for parameter tuning, with a bandwidth of 20 and corresponding parameters $\beta_1 = 60$, $\beta_{\varphi2} = 1200$, $\beta_{\varphi3} = 8000$. CFO parameter adjustment method refers to [25], and the constant term in the Characteristic polynomial selected is consistent with the improved ESO, corresponding parameters $l_1 = 71.43$, $l_2 = 755.92$, $\lambda = 10.58$. The result of applying disturbance $f = \sin(2t)$ without measurement noise is shown in Fig. 1:

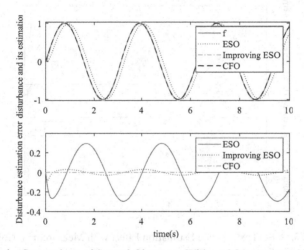

Fig. 1. Comparison of Several Observers Without Measurement Noise

Apply white noise with a sampling frequency of 0.01 s and a power spectral density of 10-9 to the feedback value, and the results are shown in Fig. 2 and Fig. 3.

When there is no measurement noise, the average absolute error of ESO is 0.1881, and the amplitude is 0.296; The average absolute error of improved ESO is 0.0202, with an amplitude of 0.0296; The average absolute error of CFO is 0.0003, with an amplitude of 0.0005. When there is measurement noise, the average absolute error of ESO is 0.1894, and the amplitude is 0.4012; The average absolute error of improved ESO is 0.0627, with an amplitude of 0.2704; The average absolute error of CFO is 0.1696, with an amplitude of 2.1886. In the absence of measurement noise, the improved ESO disturbance estimation accuracy proposed in this paper is 9.31 times that of ESO. In the presence of measurement noise, the improved ESO disturbance estimation accuracy is

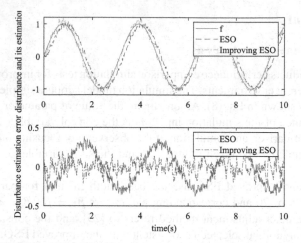

Fig. 2. ESO and Improved ESO Disturbance Estimation Performance with Measurement Noise

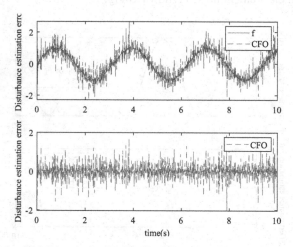

Fig. 3. CFO Disturbance Estimation Effect with Measurement Noise

3.02 times that of ESO and 2.7 times that of CFO. Considering the widespread presence of measurement noise in engineering applications, the improved ESO proposed in this article has more engineering application value.

4.2 Test of the Control System Robustness

Compare the improved ADRC proposed in this article with the traditional ADRC simulation, The unmanned maneuvering mechanical model used in the simulation is described by Eqs. (2) and (4), and the inertia matrix J is

$$J = \begin{bmatrix} 0.00533 & 0 & 0 \\ 0 & 0.00354 & 0 \\ 0 & 0 & 0.00664 \end{bmatrix} \text{kg} \cdot \text{m}^2$$

The parameters of the controller and observer designed for simulation are shown in Table 1.

Table 1. ADRC parameters

Type	Value
$\begin{bmatrix} \omega_{\varphi 1} & \omega_{\theta 1} & \omega_{\psi 1} \end{bmatrix}$	[10,10,10]
$\begin{bmatrix} \omega_{\varphi 0} & \omega_{\theta 0} & \omega_{\psi 0} \end{bmatrix}$	[50,50,50]
B	$diag$ ([0.00533,0.00354, 0.00664])

Set the pitch angle of the drone and the expected roll angle as a square wave signal with an amplitude of 45° and a frequency of 0.1 Hz. The expected yaw angle is set to a square wave signal with an amplitude of 45° and a period of 10 s. Starting from the pitch channel $t = 2$ s, a rectangular wave signal with an amplitude of 0.1N and a duty cycle of 40% is added to simulate constant disturbance. At $t = 5$ s, a sine signal of 0.1sin (2t) is added to simulate time-varying disturbances in the roll channel, and at $t = 10$ s, a sine signal of 0.1sin (2t) is also added to simulate time-varying disturbances in the yaw channel.

The tracking effects of pitch, roll, and yaw angles under disturbance are shown in Figs. 4, 5, and 6, respectively. From the figure, it can be seen that under the same parameters, the control effect of ADRC based on improved ESO is almost identical to that of traditional ADRC in the absence of disturbances. Under constant perturbation, both controllers can converge to zero in tracking error, but the convergence speed of ADRC based on improved ESO is significantly faster than that of traditional ADRC. Under time-varying disturbances, the tracking error of ADRC based on improved ESO is significantly smaller than that of traditional ADRC.

The estimated inertia matrix B used in the above simulation is the same as the inertia matrix J of the drone model, but in engineering applications, we may not be able to obtain accurate model parameters. In order to verify the performance of the controller proposed in this article under model parameter uncertainty, the inertial matrix J of the unmanned aerial vehicle is proportionally amplified, and ADRC and improved ADRC are used for simulation verification under different amplification factors. Taking the pitch channel as an example, the remaining parameters and input conditions of the simulation are the

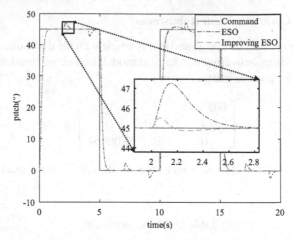

Fig. 4. Comparison of Tracking Effects of Downward Pitch Angle under Disturbance Action

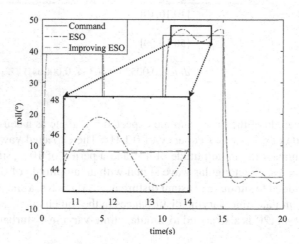

Fig. 5. Comparison of Tracking Effects of Downward Roll Angle under Disturbance Action

same as before, without additional disturbance. The tracking effect of the controller using traditional ESO is shown in Fig. 7, the tracking effect of the improved ESO controller is shown in Fig. 8:

Comparing Figs. 7 and 8, it can be concluded that the ADRC controller based on improved ESO has stronger robustness.

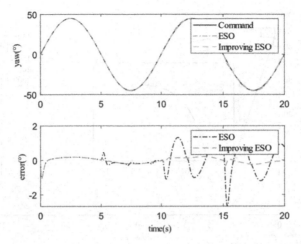

Fig. 6. Comparison of Tracking Effects of Yaw Angle under Disturbance Action

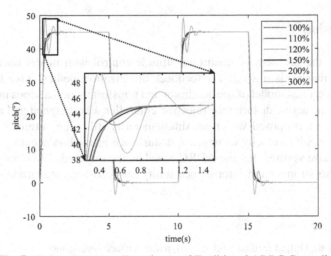

Fig. 7. Robust Response Experiment of Traditional ADRC Controller

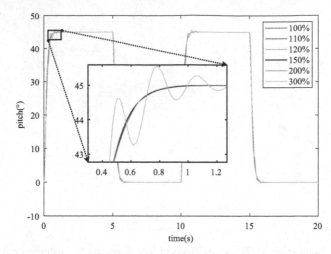

Fig. 8. Robust Response Experiment of ADRC Controller Based on Improved ESO

5 Conclusion

In this paper, the problem of quadrotor attitude control with model uncertainty and external disturbances is studied. The feedback linearization method is used to linearize the attitude dynamics model of the quadrotor and transform it into a series integral form. On this basis, an active disturbance rejection controller was designed and an improved ESO structure was proposed, which can simultaneously utilize measurement information of angle and angular velocity to improve disturbance estimation accuracy. Simulation experiments have verified that the ADRC based on the improved ESO design proposed in this paper has stronger anti-interference ability and robustness than traditional ADRC.

References

1. Zhu, G., et al.: Output feedback adaptive dynamic surface sliding-mode control for quadrotor UAVs with tracking error constraints. Complexity **2020**, 1–23 (2020)
2. Tayebi, A., Mcgilvray, S.: Attitude stabilization of a VTOL quadrotor aircraft. IEEE Trans. Control Syst. Technol. **14**(3), 562–571 (2006)
3. Runcharoon, K., Srichatrapimuk, V.: Sliding mode control of quadrotor. In: International Conference on Technological Advances in Electrical. IEEE (2013)
4. Lee, T.: Exponential stability of an attitude tracking control system on SO (3) for large-angle rotational maneuvers. Syst. Control Lett. **61**(1), 231–237 (2012)
5. Raffo, G.V., Ortega, M.G., Rubio, F.R.: Backstepping/nonlinear H∞ control for path tracking of a quadrotor unmanned aerial vehicle. In: American Control Conference. IEEE (2008)
6. Han, J.: The "extended state observer" of a class of uncertain systems (Chinese). Control Decis. (1995)
7. Gao, Z., Huang, Y., Han, J.: An alternative paradigm for control system design. In: Proceedings of the 40th Conf. Decision Control, Orlando, pp. 4578–4585 (2001)
8. Han, J.: From PID to active disturbance rejection control. IEEE Trans. Ind. Electron. **56**(3), 900–906 (2009)

9. Han, J.: Active Disturbance Rejection Control Technique—The Technique for Estimating and Compensating the Uncertainties. Nat. Def. Ind. Press, Beijing, China (2009)
10. Zhang, Y., et al.: A novel control scheme for quadrotor UAV based upon active disturbance rejection control. Aerosp. Sci. Technol. **79**, 601–609 (2018)
11. Niu, T., Xiong, H., Zhao, S.: Based on ADRC UAV longitudinal pitching Angle control research. In: 2016 IEEE Information Technology, Networking, Electronic and Automation Control Conference, pp. 21–25. IEEE, Chongqing (2016)
12. Yuan, Y., Cheng, L., Wang, Z., Sun, C.: Position tracking and attitude control for quadrotors via active disturbance rejection control method. Sci. China Inf. Sci. **62**(1) (2019)
13. Ahrens, J.H., Khalil, H.K.: High-gain observers in the presence of measurement noise: a switched-gain approach. Automatica **45**, 936–943 (2009)
14. Lotufo, M.A., et al.: UAV quadrotor attitude control: an ADRC-EMC combined approach. Control. Eng. Pract. **84**, 13–22 (2019)
15. Yu, X., et al.: Anti-interference design of UAV's attitude control system based on improved ADRC (Chinese). Electron. Opt. Control (12),027 (2020).
16. Xiong, J., et al.: Sliding mode dual-channel disturbance rejection attitude control for a quadrotor. IEEE Trans. Industr. Electron. **69**(10), 10489–10499 (2021)
17. Yang, W., Lu, J., Jiang, X., Wang, Y.: Design of quadrotor attitude active disturbance rejection controller based on improved ESO (Chinese). Syst. Eng. Electron. **44**(12), 3792–3799 (2022)
18. Łakomy, K., Madonski, R.: Cascade extended state observer for active disturbance rejection control applications under measurement noise. ISA Trans. **109**, 1 (2021). https://doi.org/10.1016/j.isatra.2020.09.007
19. Sun, H., et al.: Composite control design for systems with uncertainties and noise using combined extended state observer and Kalman filter. IEEE Trans. Industr. Electron. **69**(4), 4119–4128 (2022). https://doi.org/10.1109/TIE.2021.3075838
20. Wang, S., Chen, J., He, X.: An adaptive composite disturbance rejection for attitude control of the agricultural quadrotor UAV. ISA Trans. **129**, 564–579 (2022). https://doi.org/10.1016/j.isatra.2022.01.012
21. Xue, W., et al.: Extended state filter based disturbance and uncertainty mitigation for nonlinear uncertain systems with application to fuel cell temperature control. IEEE Trans. Industr. Electron. **67**(12), 10682–10692 (2020). https://doi.org/10.1109/TIE.2019.2962426
22. Zhang, H., Zhao, S., Gao, Z.: An active disturbance rejection control solution for the two-mass-spring benchmark problem. In: 2016 American Control Conference (ACC), pp. 1566–1571. IEEE, Boston (2016). https://doi.org/10.1109/ACC.2016.7525139. http://ieeexplore.ieee.org/document/7525139/
23. Stanković, M.R., et al.: Optimised active disturbance rejection motion control with resonant extended state observer. Int. J. Control **92**(8), 1815–1826 (2019). https://doi.org/10.1080/00207179.2017.1414308
24. Qi, G., Li, X., Chen, Z.: Problems of extended state observer and proposal of compensation function observer for unknown model and application in UAV. IEEE Trans. Syst. Man Cybernet. Syst. **52**(5), 2899–2910 (2022). https://doi.org/10.1109/TSMC.2021.3054790
25. X, C., et al.: Compensation function observer and its application in UAV attitude control (Chinese). Acta Aeronaut. Astronaut. Sin. 1–17 (2023)
26. Sharma, M., Kar, I.: Nonlinear disturbance observer based geometric control of quadrotors. Asian J. Control **23**(4), 1936–1951 (2021)

Design and Analysis of a High-performance Flexible Joint Actuator Based on the Peano-HASEL Actuator

Wenjie Sun[1(⊠)], Huwei Liang[1], Chenyang Wang[1], and Fei Zhang[2]

[1] School of Mechanical and Precision Instrument Engineering, Xi'an University of Technology, Xi'an 710048, China
sunwenjie2017@xaut.edu.cn

[2] CAS Center for Excellence in Nanoscience, Beijing Key Laboratory of Micro-Nano Energy and Sensor, Beijing Institute of Nanoenergy and Nanosystems, Chinese Academy of Sciences, Beijing 101400, China

Abstract. The Peano-HASEL actuator, which relies on the fluidic conductivity and hydraulic amplification of a liquid dielectric, not only fundamentally addresses the issue of electrical breakdown failure in electrically driven soft actuators but can also generate significant contraction forces. As a result, this type of actuator holds tremendous potential for use in a wide range of applications in fields such as flexible robotic grippers, biomimetic actuators, and artificial muscles. However, using inextensible flexible shells limits the strain that can be generated by the Peano-HASEL actuator to around 30%. To overcome this shortcoming, this paper introduces a flexible bistable beam and combines it with the operating principle of the Peano-HASEL actuator to realize a flexible joint actuator with superior performance characteristics to standard Peano-HASEL actuators. The experimental work undertaken here analyzes the influence of the volume of the liquid dielectric on the performance of the Peano-HASEL actuator unit. It also investigates the effects of different electrode materials, the position of the actuator unit, and the spacing between rigid element on either side of the hinge on the performance of the actuator. Furthermore, this work explores the correlation between the size of the flexible bistable beam and the improvement in the performance of the flexible joint actuator. The developments presented in this study provide a practical method to improve the design of Peano-HASEL actuators as well as essential insights for further research into related actuator design and applications.

Keywords: Peano-HASEL Actuator · Bistable Beam · Snap-through Instability · Performance Enhancement

1 Introduction

Robots play essential roles in both everyday human life and industry. Traditional robots comprise rigid materials, such as metal, plastic, and ceramics. Although they possess many positive characteristics, such as fast response speeds, high output performance, and precise control, they often lack adaptability and even pose safety risks when they are used in unstructured environments or to handle fragile or delicate objects. However, developing soft robots using materials such as polymeric polymers permit the creation of machines with unprecedented deformability and adaptability, as well as great potential for use in human-machine interaction. This evolution away from rigid materials has given rise to a broader concept of robotics and has created a new frontier in academic research termed "soft robotics" [1–3].

As an essential component in soft robots, soft actuators can be classified into different types based on their actuation methods; these actuation methods include fluid-driven [4, 5], thermally-driven [6], light-driven [7, 8], magnetically driven [9], and electrically driven [10–13] designs. Electrically driven actuators, which are typically based on dielectric elastomers, have become a research hotspot due to their advantages over the competing actuation methods; these advantageous properties include large deformations, fast response, high energy density, and ease of control. However, the continuous application of high voltages often leads to the electrical breakdown failure of the dielectric elastomers [14]. While it is possible to reduce the risk of electrical breakdown via the preparation of high-performance dielectric materials and the design of actuation mechanisms that exhibit bistability [15, 16], the fundamental issue of electrical breakdown was not fully resolved prior to the introduction of hydraulically amplified self-healing electrostatic (HASEL) actuation in 2018 [17]. HASEL fully addresses the issue related to the electrical breakdown failure of electrically driven actuators.

In HASEL actuators, the traditional solid-state dielectric is replaced with a hybrid-state dielectric that encapsulates a liquid. By utilizing the flow of a liquid dielectric, the HASEL actuation structure is endowed with self-healing capabilities that are of extreme importance when the structure undergoes electrical breakdown. Additionally, the hydraulic amplification effect induced by the liquid dielectric means this actuation structure has superior actuation performance compared with traditional dielectric elastomers [18–20]. In order to simplify the fabrication process of HASEL actuators, Kellaris et al. proposed a structure called the Peano-HASEL actuator [21], which can generate deformations including contractions. This design uses a typical flexible inextensible film, such as PET or BOPP film, as the solid dielectric that encapsulates the liquid dielectric; this effectively eliminates the need for the pre-stretching of the traditional elastomeric film and compliant electrodes, significantly simplifying the design and fabrication process of the actuator. Via the careful selection of the geometric dimensions and materials utilized to construct the flexible encapsulation shell in the Peano-HASEL actuator, this actuator holds vast potential for applications in areas including flexible robotic arms, biomimetic actuators, and artificial muscles [22–24].

Due to the limitations of the flexible inextensible liquid-encapsulation shell in the Peano-HASEL actuator, it can only generate a strain of up to 27%, which is significantly less than conventional HASEL and dielectric elastomer actuators. Bistable structures utilize instability to achieve a rapid snap-through transition between two stable states. Such transitions have been widely used in fluid-driven and dielectric elastomer actuators [25–28]. It is well established that the response of an actuator can be amplified via the use of bistable structures [29]. Driven by the possibility of achieving considerable improvements in actuation performances, this paper combines the characteristics of bistable actuation with the principles of the Peano-HASEL actuators to achieve a flexible joint structure with significantly enhanced performance. In this work, the effectiveness and feasibility of this design are demonstrated via experimental work; this work establishes a practical method for the improvement of the design of Peano-HASEL actuators and provides important insights for the widespread application of such actuators.

2 Design of Flexible Joint Actuators Based on the Peano-HASEL Actuator

Figure 1(a) illustrates the fabrication process of the Peano-HASEL-based actuator unit considered here. The process begins with the preparation of a precut rectangular polyethylene (PE) film with a thickness of 0.05 mm. Electrodes (in this experiment, the electrodes used are composed of cured graphene ink or aluminum foil) are then attached to the film. To avoid short circuits caused by edge electric fields, the size of the electrode is smaller than the dimensions of the rectangular PE film. Two identical PE-electrode composite films are then thermally bonded to each other while ensuring the presence of a filling port for the injection of liquid. A syringe is then used to inject a given volume of Dow Corning silicone oil into the cavity between the two layers of the composite films. The silicone fluid used in this study is PMX-200, which has a viscosity of 100 cSt. This paper focuses on the static performance of the hinge and therefore does not consider dynamic effects, such as the viscosity of the silicone fluid or the inertia of the actuator. In previous studies [29], the effects of the viscosity of liquid dielectrics on the dynamic performance of actuators have been investigated. After degassing and confirming a good seal has been created, the filling port is closed, and the fabrication of the Peano-HASEL actuator unit is complete.

The Peano-HASEL actuator unit, rigid elements, flexible units, and bistable beams are combined to form the flexible joint actuator, as shown in Fig. 1(b). In contrast with existing designs [30], this study includes flexible units linking the two rigid elements shown in Fig. 1(b) providing the required support framework for the hinge design. This design also facilitates the installation of the bistable beam components. When the Peano-HASEL actuator unit is subjected to an electrical excitation, the rigid framework constrains the actuator unit to generate a circumferential bulging deformation, resulting in the rotational displacement of the hinge-driven structure. As the excitation voltage increases, the actuator unit triggers the snap-through deformation of the bistable beams, which leads to an amplification of the deformation of the flexible joint structure.

Figure 1(c) presents a schematic showing the configurations of the flexible joint structure in different states. Without liquid in the designed cavity, the joint structure is flattened, and the support framework consists of the rigid and flexible rotating elements. One side of the PE film cavity, which is of length L, is attached to the support framework; the upper and lower sides of the shell are covered with electrodes of a length L_E, where $L_E = L/2$. When the cavity is filled with liquid dielectric (PMX silicone oil), the configuration of the bistable beam becomes upwardly convex, and the initial angle of the hinge structure is found to be θ_0. When a voltage Φ is applied to the actuation unit, the Maxwell stress between the electrodes compresses the flow of the liquid and simultaneously compresses the bistable beam. When the voltage reaches a critical value, the bistable beam undergoes a snap-through deformation, causing the hinge to rotate to an angle of θ.

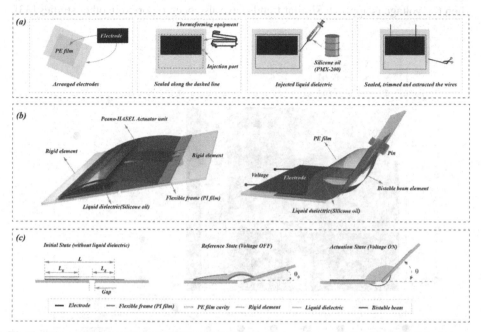

Fig. 1. Diagram of the Peano-HASEL-based flexible joint actuator: (a) Fabrication of the Peano-HASEL actuator unit. (b) Three-dimensional model of the flexible joint actuator. (c) Schematic of the deformation of the flexible joint actuator.

In this experiment, the rigid elements consist of a 0.6mm-thick PET sheet. A 75-um-thick polyimide (PI) flexible frame is used to connect the two rigid elements with a minimum spacing of 2 mm to prevent interference. The length of the Peano-HASEL actuator unit is 28 mm, and its width is 44 mm. The electrode length used here is half the length of the actuator, and the electrode width is 40 mm; the composite film has 2-mm-wide boarders on both sides of the electrode to avoid short circuits induced by edge electric fields. The bistable beam is made from a PI film and has a length of 34 mm and a width of 8 mm.

Considerable experimental research has been conducted on the actuation performance of Peano-HASEL actuation units, and their key design parameters have been optimized [31, 32]. In this paper, we analyze the influence of the volume of the liquid dielectric on the actuation performance of the actuator. Figure 2 shows the performance of the Peano-HASEL actuator containing different volumes of the liquid dielectric. The figure shows that when the volume of the liquid dielectric (V_L) is 6 mL, the maximum actuation displacement for a fixed actuation voltage is achieved; this volume of liquid occupies 50% of the cavity. The mechanism that explains this observation is as follows: When the volume of liquid in the cavity is greater than 6 mL, the liquid inside the electrode region cannot be completely compressed under the action of the applied voltage, which results in a decrease in the electrostatic force for a given voltage. On the other hand, when the volume of the liquid is less than 6 mL, the liquid inside the electrode region does not fill the non-electrode region, leading to the presence of gaps in the cavity when the voltage is applied. Similar trends have also been reported in other studies [33].

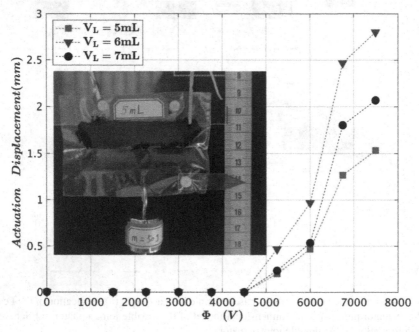

Fig. 2. The influence of the volume of the liquid dielectric on the performance of the Peano-HASEL actuator.

3 Performance of the Flexible Joint Actuator Without the Bistable Beam

Figure 3 depicts the experimental setup used for the performance testing of the flexible joint actuator. In Fig. 3(a), the method used to establish the blocking force of the actuator is shown, while Fig. 3(b) illustrates the measurement of the actuation angle. During the blocking force tests, a virtual platform was created in LabVIEW, and a high-voltage amplifier (AMPS series, Matsusada, Japan) was employed to generate the actuation voltage. The test data from the force sensor (ZNLBS-II type, Zhongnuo, China) are sampled and collected using a data acquisition card (National Instruments USB-6341, National Instruments, America). For the actuation angle measurements, the bending angle of the actuator at a given voltage is directly recorded using a high-definition camera. All experimental data processing is performed in MATLAB.

Figure 4 depicts the influence of various electrode materials on the blocking force of the actuator. The electrodes considered here are a flexible electrode that is primarily

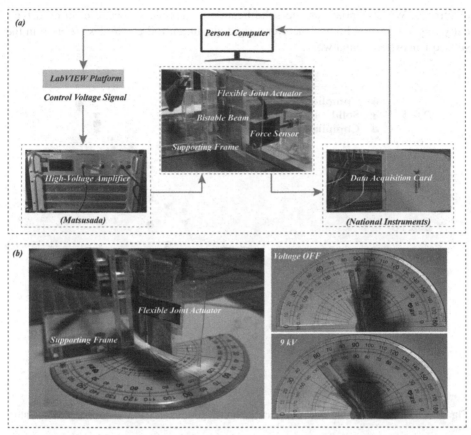

Fig. 3. Experimental setup and methodology for the testing of the flexible joint actuator: (a) Blocking force testing of the flexible joint actuator. (b) Actuation angle measurements of the flexible joint actuator.

constructed from a curable graphene ink and a rigid electrode made primarily of aluminum foil. Three joint actuators are investigated here; the specification of the actuators is identical apart from the electrodes: One actuator has graphene flexible electrodes on both sides, the second actuator has rigid aluminum foil electrodes on both sides, and the third actuator has a graphene electrode on one side and a rigid aluminum foil electrodes on the other. The experimental results show that the blocking force of the joint actuators is largely independent of the type of electrodes used. It can be seen, however, that the actuator with the graphene electrodes on both sides exhibits slightly enhanced actuation responses at certain voltages compared with the other two electrode designs; the difference between the actuators considered here gradually diminishes with increasing actuation voltage. At an actuation voltage of 9 kV, the actuation responses of the three designs are very similar.

Furthermore, it was observed that the flexible graphene electrodes are adversely affected by environmental factors, which can cause cracking and detachment of the electrodes. We also note that the solidification of flexible graphene electrodes typically requires several hours. Therefore, rigid aluminum foil electrodes are used in the subsequent experimental work.

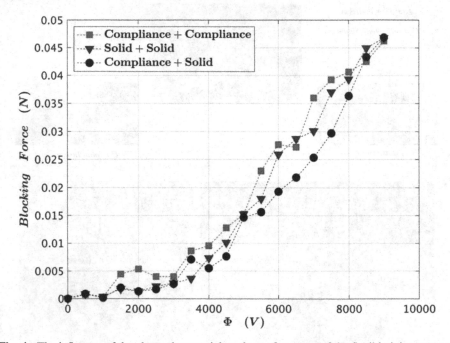

Fig. 4. The influence of the electrode material on the performance of the flexible joint actuator.

It was found experimentally that the positioning of the Peano-HASEL actuation unit on the flexible PI frame significantly impacts the performance of the joint actuator. Figure 5 shows the dependence of the joint actuator force response on the positioning (L_Z) of the Peano-HASEL actuation unit. As shown in the inset of Fig. 5, three specific positions were selected for the experiment: $L_Z = 0$, where the end of the actuation unit coincides with the center of the hinge; $L_Z = L_E/2$, where the distance from the end of the actuation unit to the hinge center is half the length of the electrode; and $L_Z = L_E$, where the distance from the end of the actuation unit to the hinge center is equal to the length of the electrode. It was found that the joint actuator exhibits significant actuation performance when $L_Z = L_E/2$. This is because when the liquid in the cavity of the electrode area is squeezed, in the configuration $L_Z = L_E/2$, a near-perfect cylindrical deformation occurs at the hinge position, which results in a large output response than that observed in the other two configurations.

In addition to the positioning of the actuation unit, the distance between the two rigid elements on either side of the flexible hinge is a critical design parameter that affects the performance of the joint actuator. Figure 6 shows the effect of this gap on the actuation angle and blocking force of the actuator. The results show that a smaller gap results in a larger actuation deformation response from the actuator. The gap significantly impacts

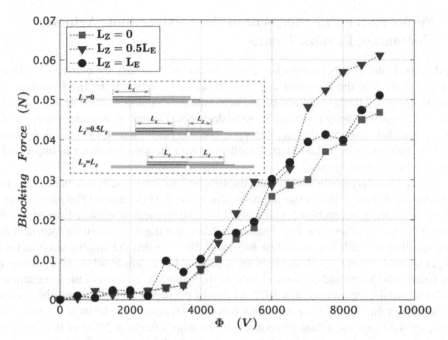

Fig. 5. The effect of the positioning of the Peano-HASEL actuator on the performance of the joint actuator.

the actuation angle, whereas the effect of the size of the gap on the measured blocking force is relatively small. However, it was noted during the experiment that if the gap is too small, interference between the rigid elements can hinder the actuation performance. Thus, a gap of 2 mm is considered as the optimal distance between the rigid elements on either side of the flexible hinges in this joint actuator.

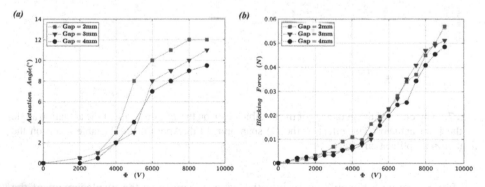

Fig. 6. The influence of the gap between the rigid elements on either side of the hinge on the performance of the joint actuator: The effect of the gap size on (a) the actuation angle and (b) the blocking force.

4   Performance Enhancement of the Flexible Joint Actuator Containing Bistable Beams

In this work, the effects of three key design parameters, namely the electrode material, the positioning of the actuation unit, and the distance between the rigid elements on either side of the flexible hinges, on the performance of the joint actuator were investigated. The optimal design parameters were determined based on the experimental work. Here, it is demonstrated that combining a bistable beam, which exhibits large snap-through deformations under external excitation, with the joint actuator can improve the performance of the actuator.

When considering a bistable beam, the span and thickness are two critical geometric parameters. Figure 7 shows the improvement in the performance of the joint actuator when the actuator is combined with a bistable beam element of various dimensions. As shown in Fig. 7(a), there is a significant amplification in the response of the joint actuator as a result of the addition of the bistable beam. We note that the amplification factor is larger when the span of the bistable beam is smaller. For example, when the thickness of the beam is 0.15 mm and the span is 30 mm, the actuation response of the joint actuator with the bistable beam design is 167% of that of the joint actuator without the bistable beam design. In Fig. 7(b), we see that when the thickness of the beam is 0.20 mm and the span is 32 mm, the actuation response of the joint actuator is 250% of that observed in the actuator without the bistable beam. Additionally, it is seen that a thicker beam results in a higher amplification factor. These findings are because a thicker beam with a smaller span can store more energy, triggering a larger actuation response in the joint actuator.

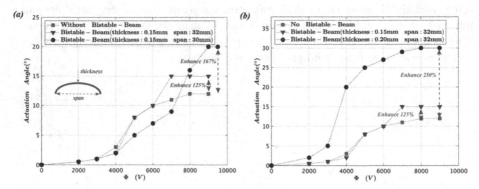

Fig. 7. The effect of the geometry of the bistable beam on the amplification of the actuation angle of the joint actuator: The effect of the (a) span and (b) thickness of the bistable beam on the actuation amplification effect.

Incorporating a bistable beam into the actuator amplifies the displacement of the actuator and increases the blocking force. Figure 8 shows the blocking force of the joint actuator with the bistable beam. The experimental results obtained here demonstrate that the blocking force of the actuator with the bistable beam is 202% of that of the actuator without the bistable beam. To induce the transition in the bistable beam structure, the

Peano-HASEL actuator must be driven by a sufficiently high voltage. Prior to the snap-through transition of the bistable beam being triggered, the beam prevents the actuation of the Peano-HASEL actuator, so, for small voltage, the blocking force is higher in actuators without the bistable beam. From the result shown in Figs. 7 and 8, it can be concluded that utilizing the snap-through instability of a bistable beam effectively addresses the limitation of the original Peano-HASEL actuators. This discovery opens new design possibilities and broadens the potential range of applications of the Peano-HASEL actuation technology.

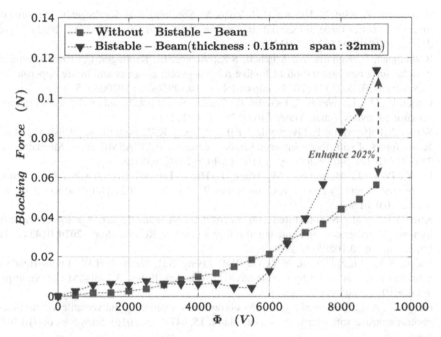

Fig. 8. The amplification of the blocking force induced by the introduction of a bistable beam into the flexible joint actuator.

5 Conclusion

In order to increase the range of deformation that are possible in Peano-HASEL actuators and thus address one of the primary limitations of such designs, this study utilizes the snap-through deformation of a bistable beam in a Peano-HASEL-based actuator to create a flexible joint actuator with superior actuation performance. The experimental analysis presented in this work investigates the effect of the electrode materials, the positioning of the actuator on the hinge, and the distance between the rigid elements in the actuator on the performance of the proposed actuator. Through experimental work, it is found here that the flexible joint actuator incorporating the bistable beam exhibits a significantly increased displacement and blocking force; the increase in the displacement and blocking force are found to be up to 2.5 times and close to 2 times, respectively, those of the design without a bistable beam. The findings of this research provide new insights into the possible developments and the subsequent utilization of the Peano-HASEL technology.

Funding. This work was supported by the Natural Science Foundation of China (Grant No. 11902248).

References

1. Rothemund, P., Kim, Y., Heisser, R.H., Zhao, X., Shepherd, R.F., Keplinger, C.: Shaping the future of robotics through materials innovation. Nat. Mater. **20**, 1582–1587 (2021). https://doi.org/10.1038/s41563-021-01158-1
2. Rothemund, P., Kellaris, N., Mitchell, S.K., Acome, E., Keplinger, C.: HASEL artificial muscles for a new generation of lifelike robots—recent progress and future opportunities. Adv. Mater. **33**, 2003375 (2021). https://doi.org/10.1002/adma.202003375
3. Gupta, U., Qin, L., Wang, Y., Godaba, H., Zhu, J.: Soft robots based on dielectric elastomer actuators: a review. Smart Mater. Struct. **28**, 103002 (2019)
4. Wang, Z., Polygerinos, P., Overvelde, J.T.B., Galloway, K.C., Bertoldi, K., Walsh, C.J.: Interaction forces of soft fiber reinforced bending actuators. IEEE/ASME Trans. Mechatron. **22**, 717–727 (2017). https://doi.org/10.1109/TMECH.2016.2638468
5. Li, Y., Peine, J., Mencattelli, M., Wang, J., Ha, J., Dupont, P.E.: A soft robotic balloon endoscope for airway procedures. Soft Robot. **9**, 1014–1029 (2022). https://doi.org/10.1089/soro.2020.0161
6. Kim, Y.I., et al.: Nanotextured soft electrothermo-pneumatic actuator for constructing lightweight, integrated, and untethered soft robotics. Soft Robotics Soro. **2020**, 0142 (2021). https://doi.org/10.1089/soro.2020.0142
7. Kwan, K.W., Li, S.J., Hau, N.Y., Li, W.-D., Feng, S.P., Ngan, A.H.W.: Light-stimulated actuators based on nickel hydroxide-oxyhydroxide. Sci. Robot. **3**, eaat4051 (2018). https://doi.org/10.1126/scirobotics.aat4051
8. Palagi, S., et al.: Structured light enables biomimetic swimming and versatile locomotion of photoresponsive soft microrobots. Nat. Mater. **15**, 647–653 (2016). https://doi.org/10.1038/nmat4569
9. Mao, G., et al.: Soft electromagnetic actuators. Sci. Adv. **6**, eabc0251 (2020). https://doi.org/10.1126/sciadv.abc0251
10. Yin, L.-J., et al.: Soft, tough, and fast polyacrylate dielectric elastomer for non-magnetic motor. Nat. Commun. **12**, 4517 (2021). https://doi.org/10.1038/s41467-021-24851-w
11. Tang, C., et al.: A pipeline inspection robot for navigating tubular environments in the sub-centimeter scale. Sci. Robot. **7**, eabm8597 (2022). https://doi.org/10.1126/scirobotics.abm8597
12. Li, G., et al.: Self-powered soft robot in the mariana trench. Nature **591**, 66–71 (2021). https://doi.org/10.1038/s41586-020-03153-z
13. Chen, Y., et al.: Controlled flight of a microrobot powered by soft artificial muscles. Nature **575**, 324–329 (2019)
14. Diaham, S., Zelmat, S., Locatelli, M.-L., Dinculescu, S., Decup, M., Lebey, T.: Dielectric breakdown of polyimide films: area, thickness and temperature dependence. IEEE Trans. Dielect. Electr. Insul. **17**, 18–27 (2010). https://doi.org/10.1109/TDEI.2010.5411997
15. Hu, W., Zhang, S.N., Niu, X., Liu, C., Pei, Q.: An aluminum nanoparticle–acrylate copolymer nanocomposite as a dielectric elastomer with a high dielectric constant. J. Mater. Chem. C **2**, 1658 (2014). https://doi.org/10.1039/c3tc31929f

16. Sun, W., Liang, H., Zhang, F., Li, B.: Theoretical study of the electroactive bistable actuator and regulation methods. Int. J. Smart Nano Mater. **14**, 36–56 (2023). https://doi.org/10.1080/19475411.2022.2152128

17. Acome, E., et al.: Hydraulically amplified self-healing electrostatic actuators with muscle-like performance. Science **359**, 61–65 (2018). https://doi.org/10.1126/science.aao6139

18. O'Neill, M.R., et al.: Rapid 3D printing of electrohydraulic (HASEL) tentacle actuators. Adv. Funct. Mater. **30**, 2005244 (2020). https://doi.org/10.1002/adfm.202005244

19. Mitchell, S.K., et al.: An easy-to-implement toolkit to create versatile and high-performance HASEL actuators for untethered soft robots. Adv. Sci. **6**, 1900178 (2019). https://doi.org/10.1002/advs.201900178

20. Ly, K., Mayekar, J.V., Aguasvivas, S., Keplinger, C., Rentschler, M.E., Correll, N.: Electro-hydraulic rolling soft wheel: design, hybrid dynamic modeling, and model predictive control. IEEE Trans Robot **38**, 3044–3063 (2022). https://doi.org/10.1109/TRO.2022.3167438

21. Kellaris, N., Gopaluni Venkata, V., Smith, G.M., Mitchell, S.K., Keplinger, C.: Peano-HASEL actuators: muscle-mimetic, electrohydraulic transducers that linearly contract on activation. Sci. Robot. **3**, eaar3276 (2018). https://doi.org/10.1126/scirobotics.aar3276

22. Kim, S., Cha, Y.: Rotary motion and manipulation using electro-hydraulic actuator with asymmetric electrodes. IEEE Robot. Autom. Lett. **5**, 3945–3951 (2020). https://doi.org/10.1109/LRA.2020.2983693

23. Kellaris, N., Venkata, V.G., Rothemund, P., Keplinger, C.: An analytical model for the design of Peano-HASEL actuators with drastically improved performance. Extreme Mech. Lett. **29**, 100449 (2019). https://doi.org/10.1016/j.eml.2019.100449

24. Yoder, Z., et al.: Design of a high-speed prosthetic finger driven by Peano-HASEL actuators. Front. Robot. AI **7**, 586216 (2020). https://doi.org/10.3389/frobt.2020.586216

25. Rothemund, P., et al.: A soft, bistable valve for autonomous control of soft actuators. Sci. Robot. **3**, eaar7986 (2018). https://doi.org/10.1126/scirobotics.aar7986

26. Leveraging elastic instabilities for amplified performance: spine-inspired high-speed and high-force soft robots. Sci. Adv. **13** (2020)

27. Wang, Y., Gupta, U., Parulekar, N., Zhu, J.: A soft gripper of fast speed and low energy consumption. Sci. China Technol. Sci. **62**(1), 31–38 (2018). https://doi.org/10.1007/s11431-018-9358-2

28. Liu, Y., Liu, B., Yin, T., Xiang, Y., Zhou, H., Qu, S.: Bistable rotating mechanism based on dielectric elastomer actuator. Smart Mater. Struct. **29**, 015008 (2020). https://doi.org/10.1088/1361-665X/ab51d7

29. Overvelde, J.T.B., Kloek, T., D'haen, J.J.A., Bertoldi, K.: Amplifying the response of soft actuators by harnessing snap-through instabilities. Proc. Natl. Acad. Sci. USA **112**, 10863–10868 (2015). https://doi.org/10.1073/pnas.1504947112

30. Kellaris, N., et al.: Spider-inspired electrohydraulic actuators for fast, soft-actuated joints. Adv. Sci. **8**, 2100916 (2021). https://doi.org/10.1002/advs.202100916

31. Rothemund, P., Kellaris, N., Keplinger, C.: How inhomogeneous zipping increases the force output of Peano-HASEL actuators. Extreme Mech. Lett. **31**, 100542 (2019). https://doi.org/10.1016/j.eml.2019.100542

32. Kirkman, S., Rothemund, P., Acome, E., Keplinger, C.: Electromechanics of planar HASEL actuators. Extreme Mech. Lett. **48**, 101408 (2021). https://doi.org/10.1016/j.eml.2021.101408

33. Park, T., Kim, K., Oh, S.-R., Cha, Y.: Electrohydraulic actuator for a soft gripper. Soft Rob. **7**, 68–75 (2020). https://doi.org/10.1089/soro.2019.0009

Human-Like Locomotion
and Manipulation

Walking Stability Analysis of Biped Robot Based on Actuator Response Characteristics

Pengyu Zhao[1], Yukang Mu[1], Siyuan Chen[1], Menglong Ding[1], Lan Zhang[1],
Bingshan Jiang[1], Lingyu Kong[1], and Anhuan Xie[1,2(✉)]

[1] Zhejiang Lab, Hangzhou 311100, China
xieanhuan@zhejianglab.com
[2] Zhejiang University, Hangzhou 310058, China

Abstract. The walking stability of a biped robot is affected by variable factors. A stable walking pattern for an electric-driven robot may not be stable for a hydraulic-electric hybrid robot due to the difference in the actuator's control performance. Aiming at this issue, the influence of the actuator response characteristic on the biped robot walking stability was studied. The control error of the foot swing angle due to the different actuator response characteristics was analyzed. The walking stability criterion to determine the foot swing angle based on the ZMP method was proposed. Then, the maximum allowable control error was calculated. According to the calculation results, the optimization of the control loop to reduce the difference in response characteristics was introduced. The optimization performance was validated in simulation. The simulation results show that the method can improve the stability of the hybrid biped robot. This work provides an optimization basis for the robot drive control from the perspective of actuator response characteristics.

Keywords: Biped Robot · Actuator Response · Walking Stability · Stable Criterion

1 Introduction

Biped robot has flexible movement mode and humanoid structure, which can replace human to complete a variety of complex tasks. So, it has always been a research hotspot in the field of robotics. The walking stability of biped robots is one of the key points and difficulties in the research of biped robots.

In recent years, there has been a lot of research on the stable walking of biped robots. The definition of stability varies depending on the interpretation of the state of equilibrium [1]. Based on the different definitions of stability, some scholars have proposed a variety of stable walking gaits. Some of the important methods include the zero-moment point (ZMP) [2–4], the capture point (CP) [5–7], the foot rotation indicator (FRI) [8, 9], and the centroidal moment pivot (CMP) [10–12].

The ZMP is the most widely used criterion for measuring the system's stability [13]. The equivalent resultant force of a load distributed along the sole, which results from

© The Author(s), under exclusive license to Springer Nature Singapore Pte Ltd. 2023
H. Yang et al. (Eds.): ICIRA 2023, LNAI 14270, pp. 235–246, 2023.
https://doi.org/10.1007/978-981-99-6492-5_21

gravitation and inertial effects, is defined as the ZMP [14]. And the minimum polygon region of all contact points between the sole and the ground is defined as the supporting polygon. Then, the core idea of the ZMP criterion is to make the ZMP located in the support polygon [15].

The general biped walking pattern generation algorithm based on the ZMP simplifies the robot into a linear inverted pendulum model (LIPM). The LIPM provides analytical solutions and reduces the difficulties of biped robot locomotion planning [16]. The traditional LIPM considers the robot as a mass point. It is usually used to estimate the robot's center of mass (COM) position and velocity [17]. The pelvis is expected to maintain vertical and the feet are expected to parallel to the ground during walking [18]. In the case that the response characteristics of the actuator are not considered, that is, the robot joint actuator is assumed to be an ideal actuator and the response speed is fast enough, then the LIPM can achieve good results. However, in a practical robot considering the response characteristics of the actuators, the actual joint angles always deviate from the reference angles. It is difficult to strictly maintain the pelvis and foot angle.

In our recent work, we generate a walking pattern that can ensure the biped robot walks stably with all joints driven by electrical motors. However, when we change some of the actuators into hydraulic cylinders, the stability of walking is broken. The robot's feet swing at an increased angle to the ground, resulting in a gradual tilt of the pelvis and eventual toppling. Further analysis shows that this phenomenon is mainly caused by the different response characteristics of the electrical motors and the hydraulic cylinders.

Aiming at this problem, the influence of actuator response characteristics on biped robot walking stability is studied. The tracking error of the angle between the foot and the pelvis, which leads to the swing of the foot, was obtained. The range of the foot swing angle to keep the robot stable was calculated. Finally, a method to increase walking stability was proposed.

2 System Configuration

The construction of the biped robot studied in this work is shown in Fig. 1a). The robot consists of 1 pelvis and 2 legs. Each leg consists of a thigh, a calf, and a foot, and is formed in series by the hip, knee, and ankle joints. There are 6 degrees of freedom (DOFs) within each leg. The DOFs of hip roll, hip pitch, and knee pitch are driven by hydraulic cylinders, due to the large required drive torque. While other DOFs, including hip yaw, ankle pitch, and ankle roll, are driven by electric motors. Since the efficiency of hydraulic drive is low especially when the driving force is low, this setting can improve the overall energy efficiency of the drive system. So, it is an electric-hydraulic hybrid robot.

The topology structure and parameter definitions are shown in Fig. 1b)–d). Where l_{Fh} and l_{Fv} are the length of the foot in the horizontal and vertical direction; q_{Hp}, q_{Kp} and q_{Ap} are the angle of hip pitch, knee pitch, and ankle pitch, respectively; q_P is the inclination angle of the pelvis in the sagittal plane; x and z are the position of the COM in the horizontal direction (forward and backward directions) and vertical direction, respectively.

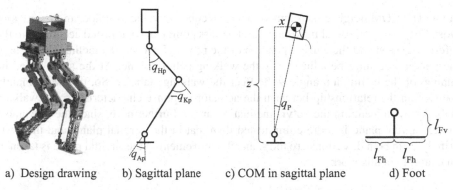

a) Design drawing   b) Sagittal plane   c) COM in sagittal plane   d) Foot

Fig. 1. Structure and parameter definitions of robot

The hydraulic drive system includes 1 hydraulic pump unit (HPU) and 6 integrated hydraulic cylinder units (IHCUs). The HPU supplies constant pressure oil to the hydraulic system. Each IHCU includes a hydraulic cylinder, a servo valve, and two pressure sensors. Both ends of an IHCU are hinged to limb structures on either side of a hydraulic-driven joint. The servo valve controls the hydraulic cylinder to extend or retract, driving the corresponding joint to move. The pressure sensors measure the pressure of each chamber. The electric-driven joints are driven by direct current (DC) motors. The hip yaw motor is coaxial with the joint and drives the DOF directly. The ankle pitch and ankle roll motors are mounted in the calf and drive the ankle joint through four-bar linkages. This layout has the advantage of rising the motor's center of mass (COM) position while saving ankle joint mounting space. The structure of the IHCU and DC motor are shown in Fig. 2.

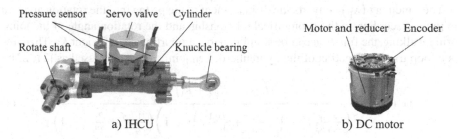

a) IHCU   b) DC motor

Fig. 2. Structure of IHCU and DC motor

3   Mathematical Model

To analyze the influence of the response characteristics of joint actuators on the walking stability of the biped robot, the mathematical model of the hydraulic-driven joint, the electric-driven joint, and the kinematics model of the robot is established.

In this work, preview control of ZMP [19] is used to generate the walking pattern. The algorithm simplifies the robot as a LIPM, where the robot is considered as a mass point. The COM height z is assumed to have a constant value as it does in the previous work [20]. The horizontal movement of the mass point can be adjusted according to the reference speed and the current position of the robot. However, the inclination angle of the pelvis q_P cannot be adjusted by the walking pattern alone. At the same time, the change of the inclination angle will affect the walking stability. So, this work mainly focuses on the relationship between the actuator response characteristics and walking stability by influencing the pelvis inclination angle. Furthermore, since the movement in the sagittal plane is more complicated than that in the coronal plane, and the basic principles in both directions are the same, the movement in the sagittal plane is taken as an example in this work.

Hydraulic Driven Joint

For the convenience of calculation, it is assumed that the actuators have the same load characteristics under various robot positions. This means that the inertia mass, moment of inertia, and damping are the same. The block diagram of a hydraulic-driven joint is shown in Fig. 3.

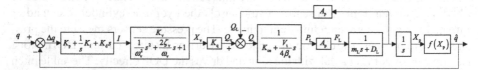

Fig. 3. Block diagram of hydraulic-driven joint

The controllers of the actuators are proportion-integration-differentiation (PID) controllers. The coefficients of each item are K_p, K_i and K_d.

The function $f(X_p)$ converts the displacement of the piston into the rotation angle of the joint. According to the geometrical relationship and the rotation angle of the joints during walking, the function can be simplified to a proportional coefficient K_r. Then, the open loop transfer function of the hydraulic-driven joint can be expressed as [21, 22]:

$$G_h(s) = \frac{(K_d s^2 + K_p s + K_i)\frac{K_v K_q K_r}{A_p}}{s^2\left(\frac{V_t m_L}{4\beta_e A_p^2}s^2 + \left(\frac{m_L K_{ce}}{A_p^2} + \frac{D_L V_t}{4\beta_e A_p^2}\right)s + 1\right)\left(\frac{1}{\omega_v^2}s^2 + \frac{2\zeta_v}{\omega_v}s + 1\right)} \tag{1}$$

where X_p is the piston position; K_q is the flow gain of the valve; A_p is the effective area of the hydraulic cylinder piston; V_t is the sum of two chambers of the hydraulic cylinder; m_L is the sum of the converted mass of the piston end load and the piston mass; β_e is the oil volume modulus of elasticity; K_{ce} is the total flow pressure coefficient; D_L is the damping factor corresponding to the piston and the load; X_v is the displacement of valve core; I is the input current of the valve; K_v, ω_v, and ζ_v are the gain, natural frequency and damping ratio of the servo valve, respectively.

Electric Driven Joint

The block diagram of an electric-driven joint is shown in Fig. 4.

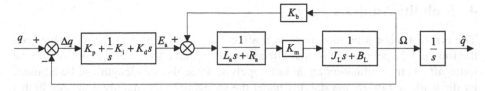

Fig. 4. Block diagram of electric-driven joint

Then, the open loop transfer function of the electric-driven joint can be expressed as [23]:

$$G_e(s) = \frac{(K_d s^2 + K_p s + K_i) K_m}{s^2((L_a s + R_a)(J_L s + B_L) + K_b K_m)} \tag{2}$$

where K_m is the motor torque constant; K_b is the electromotive force constant; L_a is the armature inductance; R_a is the armature resistance; J_L is the equivalent rotational inertia acting on the motor; B_L is the motor friction constant.

Foot Posture

In this work, q is the reference angle of a joint, $\hat{q}$ is defined as the actual joint angle; $\tilde{q}$ indicates the error of the joint angle. According to the geometric relationship, the angle between the pelvis and the foot q_{FP} can be calculated as:

$$q_{FP} = q_{Hp} + q_{Kp} + q_{Ap} \tag{3}$$

The response characteristic of $\tilde{q}_{FP}$ is:

$$\tilde{q}_{FP}(s) = \left(q_{Hp}(s) + q_{Kp}(s) + q_{Ap}(s)\right) - \left(G_{Hp}q_{Hp}(s) + G_{Kp}q_{Kp}(s) + G_{Ap}q_{Ap}(s)\right) \tag{4}$$

where G_{Hp}, G_{Kp} and G_{Ap} are the close loop transfer functions of the hip pitch joint, knee pitch joint, and ankle pitch joint, respectively. The specific form of the transfer functions can be derived from Eqs. (3) and (5) according to the joint drive mode.

The response characteristics of the hydraulic-driven joints are similar, but different from those of the electric-driven joints. Approximately, we assume that $G_{Hp} \approx G_{Kp}$. Combine the Eqs. (6) and (9), we have:

$$\tilde{q}_{FP}(s) = \left(1 - G_{Hp}\right)q_{FP}(s) + \left(G_{Ap} - G_{Hp}\right)q_{Ap}(s) \tag{5}$$

For the given walking pattern,

$$q_{FP} \equiv 0 \tag{6}$$

Then

$$\tilde{q}_{FP}(s) = \left(G_{Ap} - G_{Hp}\right)q_{Ap}(s) \tag{7}$$

Therefore, to reduce the swing angle of the foot, (i.e. $\tilde{q}_{FP}$), the response characteristics of the ankle pitch joint should be similar to those of the hip and knee pitch joints.

4 Stability Analysis

The error of robot joint motion control affects the step length and the angle between the foot and the pelvis. The former affects the horizontal position of the foot. While the latter affects the inclination angle of the pelvis. Since the step length can be adjusted by the walking pattern, the stability under the swinging foot is mainly discussed in this section.

In order to simplify the complexity of the analysis, the following assumptions are made:

(1) The feet of the robot are ideal rigid bodies. No deformation occurs during the movement;
(2) The swing angles of the feet and the pelvis are small. The swing angle of the feet varies from $\tilde{q}_{FP}$ to $-\tilde{q}_{FP}$ in a constant speed within each step.

For assumption (1), the actual deformation of the feet is much smaller than the distance between the feet and the ground which is caused by the swing angle. For assumption (2), the COM translational error caused by the swing angle is much smaller than the translational motion. Thus, the simplification does not make a significant impact.

The movement of the robot consists of two parts: COM translational motion and rotation around the contact point of the foot contact with the ground. The COM translational motion is ideal, independent of the swing of the pelvis and the feet.

The influence of the foot swing on the inclination angle of the pelvis is divided into two parts. The first part is the inclination caused by the change of the contact point on the ground, and the second part is the rotation caused by the deviation of the support force from the central position.

For the inclination caused by the change of the contact point on the ground, the inclination angle is calculated as:

$$q_{Pp} = \arctan\left(\frac{1}{z}\left(\begin{array}{l} l_{Fh}(1 - \cos(\tilde{q}_{FP} + \hat{q}_P)) + l_{Fv}\sin(\tilde{q}_{FP} + \hat{q}_P) \\ +l_{Fh}(1 - \cos(\tilde{q}_{FP} - \hat{q}_P)) + l_{Fv}\sin(\tilde{q}_{FP} - \hat{q}_P) \end{array}\right)\right) \quad (8)$$

For the rotation caused by the deviation of the support force from the central position, the total contact time of a foot within one step is:

$$t_F = \frac{1}{2}\sqrt{\frac{z}{g}} \quad (9)$$

Due to the swing of the foot, the contact point is either on the front or back of the foot. The contact time of the foot front with the ground t_{Ff} and the contact time of the foot back with the ground t_{Fb} are:

$$\begin{cases} t_{Ff} = \frac{\tilde{q}_{FP} + \hat{q}_P}{2\tilde{q}_{FP}}t_F \\ t_{Fb} = \frac{\tilde{q}_{FP} - \hat{q}_P}{2\tilde{q}_{FP}}t_F \end{cases} \quad (10)$$

The angular accelerations when the foot's front and back contact with the ground are expressed as $\ddot{q}_{Pff}$ and $\ddot{q}_{Pfb}$. Then

$$\begin{cases} \ddot{q}_{Pff} = \frac{g(-l_{Fh}\cos(\tilde{q}_{FP} + \hat{q}_P) + z\sin\hat{q}_P)}{z^2} \\ \ddot{q}_{Pfb} = \frac{g(l_{Fh}\cos(\tilde{q}_{FP} - \hat{q}_P) + z\sin\hat{q}_P)}{z^2} \end{cases} \quad (11)$$

Under zero initial conditions, the rotation angle is

$$q_{Pf} = \int \int_0^{t_{Ff}} \ddot{q}_{Pff} dt + \int \int_{t_{Ff}}^{t_F} \ddot{q}_{Pfb} dt \tag{12}$$

If the robot can reach a stable state, at the beginning and end of the walking cycle, there should be:

$$\Delta \hat{q}_p = q_{Pp} + q_{Pf} = 0 \tag{13}$$

At the same time, the projection of the robot's COM on the ground should be located in the foot support area:

$$l_{Fh} > z \tan \hat{q}_P \tag{14}$$

By solving Eq. (13) and inequation (14), we can figure out the range of $\tilde{q}_{FP}$. The results obtained are necessary and insufficient conditions to keep the robot stable. We only consider the situation in the stable state, without considering the rotational angular velocity, angular acceleration, and the state in the adjustment process.

5 Simulation Verification

In order to verify the analysis results, simulations are carried out. The simulation models are built in MATLAB/Simulink. Firstly, the mathematical models of hydraulic-driven joints and electric-driven joints are built to obtain the response characteristics of different actuators. Secondly, the simulation model of the robot, which contains the mechanical system, drive system, and control system, is built. The walking pattern generated based on the ZMP method is utilized to obtain the walking characteristics. At last, the optimization of the actuator response is carried out to increase the stability of the biped robot.

5.1 Actuator Response

Since the response characteristics of the joints driven by the same type of drive systems are similar, the left hip pitch and left ankle pitch joints are taken as examples. The parameters of the actuators are listed in Table 1. According to the transfer functions of the joints and the parameters of the hydraulic components and electric components, the closed loop pole-zeros can be obtained, which is shown in Fig. 5.

Since the response characteristics of the joints are different, the control error of the angle between the foot and the pelvis is large. In order to make the response characteristics similar, the closed-loop main poles of the two systems should be brought close to each other. The simplest way is to add a first-order inertial element into the electric-driven point control loop. According to the then the parameters of the system, the first-order inertial element is set as $\frac{1}{5.88 \times 10^{-3} s + 1}$. Then, the pole-zeros of the system are shown in Fig. 6.

Table 1. Parameters of hydraulic and electric components

Hydraulic System Parameter	Value	Electric System Parameter	Value
$K_v \cdot K_q \cdot K_r$ (m$^2 \cdot$ rad/s $\cdot$ A)	5.75×10^{-6}	K_m (N $\cdot$ m/A)	11
K_{ce} (m^3/s $\cdot$ Pa)	6.35×10^{-12}	K_b (V $\cdot$ s/rad)	4.73
A_p (m^2)	4.1233×10^{-4}	L_a (H)	9.1×10^{-4}
m_L (kg)	5	R_a (Ω)	0.47
D_L (Ns/m)	421	J_L (kg $\cdot$ m^2)	4×10^{-3}
β_e (Pa)	8×10^8	B_L (N $\cdot$ m $\cdot$ s/rad)	1×10^{-3}
ω_v (Hz)	200		
ζ_v	0.5		

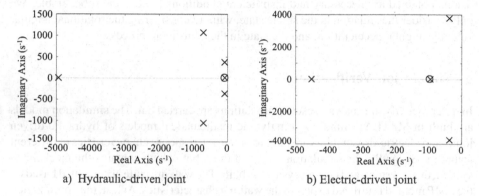

a) Hydraulic-driven joint   b) Electric-driven joint

Fig. 5. Closed loop pole-zero map of joints

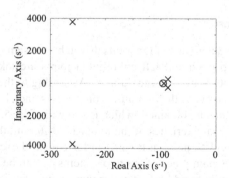

Fig. 6. Optimized electric-driven joint pole-zero map

5.2 Walking Simulation

In order to validate the influence of the actuator response characteristics on the stability of the biped robot, a simulation of biped walking is carried out. During walking, the height of COM is set as $z = 1000$ mm. The walking is divided into four parts. During 1–3 s, the robot remains standing and motionless. During 3–4 s, the robot adjusts its posture preparing to walk. During the 4–10 s, the robot accelerates uniformly in a straight line. During 10–20 s, the robot walks at a constant speed of 1 m/s. The parameters of the robot geometry are $l_{Fh} = 135$ mm and $l_{Fv} = 49$ mm. According to the analysis in Chapter 4, to ensure the robot walking stability, the swing angle of the foot should satisfy $\tilde{q}_{FP} < 2.7975$ deg.

The simulation without electric-driven joint optimization is obtained. The simulation result is shown in Fig. 7.

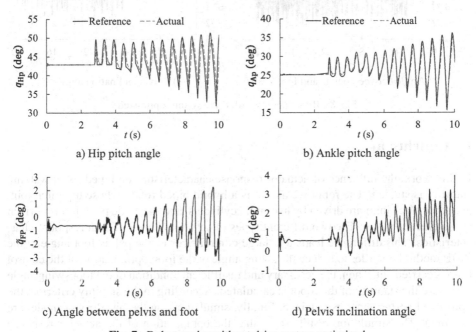

a) Hip pitch angle

b) Ankle pitch angle

c) Angle between pelvis and foot

d) Pelvis inclination angle

Fig. 7. Robot angles without drive system optimized

In this simulation, the maximum value of the angle between the pelvis and the foot is 3.21 deg. The pelvis inclination angle is generally increasing during the simulation. At $t = 10.5$ s, the robot falls due to the large inclination angle of the pelvis.

In contrast, the simulation after the optimization of the electric-driven joint is obtained. The simulation result is shown in Fig. 8. In this simulation, the maximum value of the angle between the pelvis and the foot is 1.73 deg. During the simulation, the biped robot is stable.

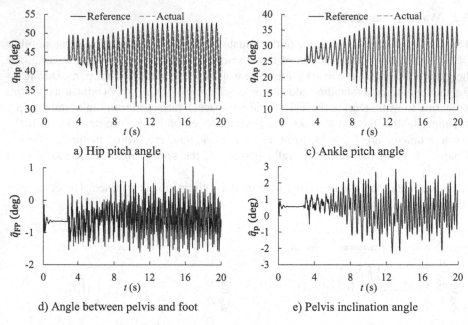

a) Hip pitch angle

c) Ankle pitch angle

d) Angle between pelvis and foot

e) Pelvis inclination angle

Fig. 8. Robot angles with drive system optimized

6 Conclusion

In this work, the influence of actuator response characteristics on biped robot walking stability is studied. The robot we aim at is a hybrid biped robot, whose hip pitch joint and knee pitch joint are driven by hydraulic cylinders, and the ankle pitch joint is driven by an electric motor. The two different types of actuators have different response characteristics. This difference leads to a large control error of the pelvis-foot angle in the ZMP method. In order to reduce the swing angle of the foot, optimization of the control loop is carried out. Then, the necessary and insufficient condition of the foot swing angle to ensure the stability of the robot is calculated. According to the stability criterion, the optimized performance is obtained. Finally, simulations on the biped robot model are obtained. The simulation results show that the optimization of the actuator response characteristics can improve the stability of the biped robot.

This work is not limited to hybrid robots. Since the actuator's response characteristic varies with different parameters or loads, the conclusion can also guide the design of the parameter matching of the actuators and the design of the biped robot mechanical structure. Future work includes further precision of the stability criteria and experimental validation.

Acknowledgment. The work presented in this paper is supported by the National Natural Science Foundation of China (Grant No. 52205076), the Key Research Project of Zhejiang Lab (No. G2021NB0AL03), China Postdoctoral Science Foundation (Grant No. 2022M712926), and the Youth Foundation Project of Zhejiang Lab (No. K2023NB0AA01).

References

1. Ilewicz, G., et al.: Biomechanical criterion of dynamic stability based on ZMP formula and Flash-Hogan principle of minimum jerk. J. Theor. Appl. Mech. 3–9 (2023)
2. Joe, H.M., Oh, J.H.: A robust balance-control framework for the terrain-blind bipedal walking of a humanoid robot on unknown and uneven terrain. Sensors **19**(19), 4194 (2019)
3. Elhosseini, M.A., et al.: Biped robot stability based on an A-C parametric whale optimization algorithm. J. Comput. Sci. **31**, 17–32 (2019)
4. Ando, T., Watari, T., Kikuuwe, R.: Reference ZMP generation for teleoperated bipedal robots walking on non-flat terrains. In: 2021 IEEE/SICE International Symposium on System Integration (SII), pp. 794–800. IEEE (2021)
5. Joe, H.M., Oh, J.H.: Balance recovery through model predictive control based on capture point dynamics for biped walking robot. Robot. Auton. Syst. **105**, 1–10 (2018)
6. Kim, I.S., Han, Y.J., Hong, Y.D.: Stability control for dynamic walking of bipedal robot with real-time capture point trajectory optimization. J. Intell. Rob. Syst. **96**, 345–361 (2019)
7. Kim, S.H., Hong, Y.D.: Dynamic bipedal walking using real-time optimization of center of mass motion and capture point-based stability controller. J. Intell. Rob. Syst. **103**(4), 58 (2021)
8. He, B., et al.: Hybrid CPG–FRI dynamic walking algorithm balancing agility and stability control of biped robot. Auton. Robot. **43**, 1855–1865 (2019)
9. Xie, S., et al.: Compliant bipedal walking based on variable spring-loaded inverted pendulum model with finite-sized foot. In: 2021 6th IEEE International Conference on Advanced Robotics and Mechatronics (ICARM), pp. 667–672. IEEE (2021)
10. Raza, F., Zhu, W., Hayashibe, M.: Balance stability augmentation for wheel-legged biped robot through arm acceleration control. IEEE Access **9**, 54022–54031 (2021)
11. Hsu, H.K., et al.: Whole-body momentum control with linear quadratic state incremental walking pattern generation and a centroidal moment pivot balancing strategy for humanoid robots. Adv. Robot. **36**(14), 679–699 (2022)
12. Xu, H., et al.: Disturbance rejection for biped robots during walking and running using control moment gyroscopes. IET Cyber-Syst. Robot. **4**(4), 268–282 (2022)
13. Haldar, A.I., Pagar, N.D.: Predictive control of zero moment point (ZMP) for terrain robot kinematics. Mater. Today: Proc. (2022)
14. Farid, Y., Siciliano, B., Ruggiero, F.: Review and descriptive investigation of the connection between bipedal locomotion and non-prehensile manipulation. Annu. Rev. Control (2022)
15. Kim, J.H.: Multi-axis force torque sensors for measuring zero-moment point in humanoid robots: a review. IEEE Sens. J. **20**(3), 1126–1141 (2019)
16. Xie, Z., Li, L., Luo, X.: Three-dimensional aperiodic biped walking including the double support phase using LIPM and LPM. Robot. Auton. Syst. **143**, 103831 (2021)
17. Paredes, V.C., Hereid, A.: Resolved motion control for 3d underactuated bipedal walking using linear inverted pendulum dynamics and neural adaptation. In: 2022 IEEE/RSJ International Conference on Intelligent Robots and Systems (IROS), pp. 6761–6767. IEEE (2022)
18. Han, L., et al.: A heuristic gait template planning and dynamic motion control for biped robots. Robotica 1–17 (2023)
19. Kajita, S., et al.: Biped walking pattern generation by using preview control of zero-moment point. In: 2003 IEEE International Conference on Robotics and Automation (Cat. No. 03CH37422), vol. 2, pp. 1620–1626. IEEE (2003)
20. Park, H.Y., et al.: A new stability framework for trajectory tracking control of biped walking robots. IEEE Trans. Industr. Inf. **18**(10), 6767–6777 (2022)
21. Guo, Y.Q., Zha, X.M., Shen, Y.Y., et al.: Research on PID position control of a hydraulic servo system based on Kalman genetic optimization. Actuators **11**(6), 162 (2022). MDPI

22. Qi, W., Yang, B., Chao, Y.: Research on hydraulic servo valve control based on fuzzy RBF. J. Phys. Conf. Ser. **2417**(1), 012029 (2022). IOP Publishing
23. Ekinci, S., Hekimoğlu, B., Izci, D.: Opposition based henry gas solubility optimization as a novel algorithm for PID control of DC motor. Eng. Sci. Technol. Int. J. **24**(2), 331–342 (2021)

Design of an Actuator for Biped Robots Based on the Axial Flux Motor

Qiang Hua[1], Weigang Zhou[1], Chao Cheng[1], Xiao Liu[2], Xingyu Chen[1],
Lingyu Kong[1], Anhuan Xie[1(✉)], Shiqiang Zhu[1], and Jianjun Gu[1]

[1] Zhejiang Lab, Hangzhou 310000, Zhejiang, China
xieanhuan@zhejianglab.com
[2] Shenzhen Xiaoxiang Electric Technology Co., Ltd., Shenzhen, China

Abstract. High-performance actuators are critical to the biped robot, which are required to be high torque output, high dynamic response, and lightweight. The quasi-direct drive (QDD) actuation has the advantages of fast response and simple structure and has been widely used in quadruped robots, but its output torque and torque density are relatively low. Based on the scheme of QDD, a high torque and high torque density actuator is proposed for biped robots. It adopts an axial flux motor with a peak torque of 12.5 Nm and a two-stage planetary reducer with a reduction ratio of about 16. For the axial flux motor current is very large, we also design the driver with high current output capacity and introduce the air cooling method based on small fans. As a result, the proposed actuator has a maximum torque of 206 Nm, a maximum speed of 120 rpm, and weighs only 2 kg. Lots of experiments have been carried out to measure the characteristics of the actuator, and it has been successfully applied to our biped robot, which can meet the requirements of walking at a speed of 6 km/h.

Keywords: biped robot · quasi-direct drive (QDD) actuation · the axial flux motor · high torque density

1 Introduction

Wheeled or tracked machines make our lives very convenient, but unfortunately, nearly half of the land on Earth is inaccessible to these machines [1]. The wheeled robots were utilized in the rescue of the Fukushima nuclear accident in Japan in 2011, but the results were not ideal because these robots could not overcome the complexity of the environment. Bipedal robots, which mimic the way humans move, are considered the most promising type of robot for assisting people in both human and natural environments. At present, significant progress has been made in the development of biped robots, but there are still many challenges to realizing real applications. As with other dynamic legged robots, one of the challenges is the design of the actuators [2].

Compared to gas drive and hydraulic drive, electric actuators have many advantages such as high precision and simplified control. Generally speaking, there are three main forms of electric drive actuator: conventional actuation, series elastic actuation (SEA),

H. Yang et al. (Eds.): ICIRA 2023, LNAI 14270, pp. 247–257, 2023.
https://doi.org/10.1007/978-981-99-6492-5_22

and quasi-direct drive [3] actuation. Conventional actuation adopts a high-speed and low torque motor with a large reduction ratio reducer (usually harmonic reducer). As a result, it can output high torque and has good control bandwidth. However, these conventional actuators also have some limitations due to their high deceleration ratio, such as mechanical impedance, inertia, and friction. On the other hand, SEAs have an elastomer between the reducer and the output end. By measuring the deformation of the elastomer, the output torque can be obtained to facilitate the realization of high-precision force control. Due to the existence of elastomers, SEAs have some disadvantages such as complex and expensive hardware structure, low stiffness, and poor dynamic performance. The QDD actuation consists of a high-torque motor and a low-reduction ratio reducer (usually < 10:1). It has the advantages of precise torque control, fast high-frequency response, and strong impact resistance. However, the output torque and torque density of traditional QDD actuation are relatively low in comparison to other electric actuators. In bipedal robots, conventional actuators [4, 5] or series elastic actuators (SEAs) [6, 7] are commonly used. However, with the development of technology, QDD actuation is also being applied to bipedal robots, such as MIT Humanoid Robot [8].

The motor is a very important component in actuators. Currently, there are two commonly used motor structures in robots: frameless motors and outer rotor motors. The frameless motor has the advantages of a simple structure, convenient integrated design, and the outer rotor torque density is higher, and the cost is low. To further improve the torque density of the motor, the axial flux motors have been applied to the robots [9].

This paper focuses on the design of a high-torque actuation with a simple structure just like QDD. The axial flux motor with high torque density and the planetary reducer with two stages of reduction are adopted to improve the actuator's torque density. Section II introduces the design of the actuator. The performance of the proposed actuator is verified by experiments in Section III. In Section IV, the proposed actuators are applied to the biped robot. The work is concluded in the end.

2 Actuator Design

To meet the motion requirements of the biped robot, the actuator is required to have the characteristics of high torque, high speed, and lightweight. The maximum torque required is more than 200Nm, the max speed required is 100rpm or greater, and the weight and size required are the less the better. Based on the scheme of QDD, the designed actuator uses a motor with higher torque density, and increases the deceleration ratio, to meet the torque demand.

2.1 High Torque Density Motor

Because of the small deceleration ratio of the actuation, the required torque capacity of the motor is very high. Compared with the radial flux permanent magnet motor, the axial flux motor has a shorter flux path, which can make more effective use of magnetic materials, and has the advantages of compact structure, high torque density, and high power density [10].

Axial flux motors can be divided into a variety of topological structures according to the number of rotors and matching mode. Under the double-stator single-rotor structure, the axial magnetic tension of the motor rotor from the upper and lower stators will cancel each other, which can reduce the bearing force, further reduce the mechanical loss of the motor, and effectively improve the power density and efficiency of the motor. Therefore, in this design, the axial flux motor adopts the form of a double-stator single-rotor, and the motor is shown in Fig. 1(a). The magnetic field of the motor is simulated by finite element analysis. At the rated current, the magnetic field intensity of the motor can reach up to 2.1T, as shown in Fig. 2(a). The characteristic diagram of the designed motor is shown in Fig. 1(c). The maximum torque of the motor can reach 12.5Nm and the maximum power can reach 1.05kW.

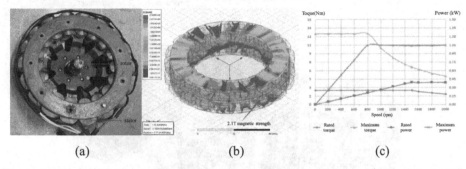

(a)   (b)   (c)

Fig. 1. (a) The axial flux motor. (b) Magnetic density simulation diagram. (c) The characteristic diagram of the proposed motor.

The comparison of parameters between the designed axial flux motor and commercial motors is shown in Table 1. The proposed axial flux motor has a compact structure and a high peak torque density of 16.0 Nm/kg, which is bigger than other motors.

Table 1. Comparison of motor parameters.

Motor	TQ ILM 115x25 [11]	Allied Motion KMF109 03 [12]	This work
Types	frameless	outer rotor	axial flux
Rated voltage	48 V	42-72 V	48 V
Peak torque	12.7 Nm	13.6 Nm	12.5 Nm
Weight	1.07 kg	1.27 kg	0.78 kg
Peak torque density	11.9 Nm/kg	10.7 Nm/kg	16.0 Nm/kg
Size (diameter * length)	115*39 mm	109.7*54 mm	110*25 mm

2.2 Actuators Structure Design

To meet the high torque and lightweight design requirements of the biped robot, we developed a compact actuator, whose structural composition is shown in Fig. 2. It includes the designed motor, a two-stage planetary gear reducer, and a multi-turn absolute value high precision magnetic encoder. To reduce the overall size, the first stage reducer is embedded into the hollow inside of the stator of the motor. The total deceleration ratio of the two-stage planetary gear reducers is 16.227. The encoder single-turn resolution is 17 bits, and the multi-turn resolution is 16 bits. The expected maximum output torque of the actuator is 203 Nm, which can meet the torque requirements of the biped robot.

Encoder   shell   Motor stator   Motor rotor   Motor stator   First stage reducer   shell   Second stage reducer   shell

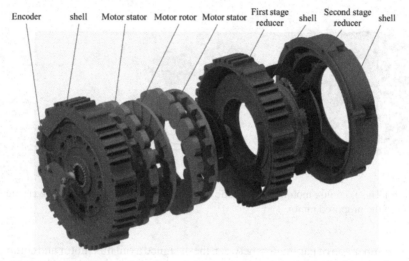

Fig. 2. The structure diagram of the proposed actuator. It weighs 2.0 kg and has a diameter of 130 mm and a length of 90 mm.

Overheat is one of the main problems of actuators, especially for high current actuators. The peak current of the designed motor is very large, and its amplitude can reach up to 70A, which can generate lots of heat.

To avoid this problem, it is necessary to design the heat dissipation of the actuator. There are three common cooling methods, such as natural cooling, air cooling, and liquid cooling. The forced air cooling is applied to increase the heat dissipation effect of actuators. Specifically, slots are cut in the actuator's shell, where two fans are added on. One fan is for air suction and the other is for air blowing, so as to form air convection. A simulation diagram of airflow in the case of forced air cooling by fans is shown in Fig. 3.

The fan weighs only 12.7 g but has a maximum speed of 23000 rpm, which can generate effective cooling airflow. At the same time, a temperature sensor is embedded in the axial flux motor to detect the motor temperature. When the temperature reaches the set threshold, the fans are turned on for heat dissipation.

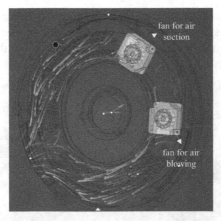

Fig. 3. Simulation diagram of airflow.

2.3 Actuator's Drivers with High Current Output

The peak current of the proposed motor is very large, which puts forward high require-ments for driver design. The designed driver includes the driver board and the control board, which are shown in Fig. 4(a) and Fig. 4(b). The driver board is mainly equipped with MOSFETs, current sampling resistors, and other power devices. The control board mainly realizes signal sampling processing and runs the motor control algorithm. To improve the output current capacity, the power circuit of the driver board uses multiple high-power and low-resistance MOSFETs in parallel, and the parallel circuit need to be the same to prevent the parallel current unbalance.

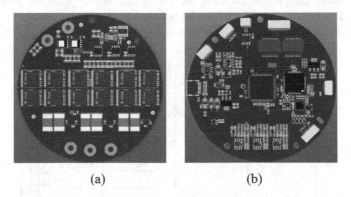

(a)   (b)

Fig. 4. (a) The driver board. (b) The control board.

The power components of the driver board will heat up seriously when a large current flows through. Therefore, the driver board is tightly fixed with the rear cover of the actuator through the heat conduction pad. To achieve good heat dissipation, lots of grooves are designed on the structure of the rear cover to increase the area of contact with the air. The picture of the actuator's rear cover is shown in Fig. 5(a). Under the rated working condition of the motor, the thermal simulation of the drive board with the rear cover is carried out. As shown in Fig. 5(b), the maximum temperature of the MOSFETs is less than 70 °C, which indicates the good heat dissipation of the driver board.

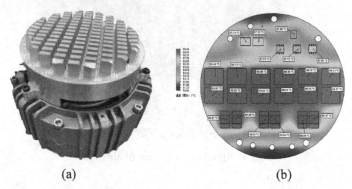

(a)   (b)

Fig. 5. (a) The picture of the actuator's rear cover. (b) The thermal simulation results of the drive board with the rear cover.

2.4 Actuators Control Method

The control structure of the drive controller is shown in Fig. 6. It is based on the vector control method, and supports the traditional three-closed-loop control structure and the compliant control. The traditional control is generally suitable for target tracking and locations, such as position servo control. For the application of biped robots, compliant control is mainly adopted to improve the interaction ability with the ground during walking, and its control parameters can be adjusted by the PD regulator.

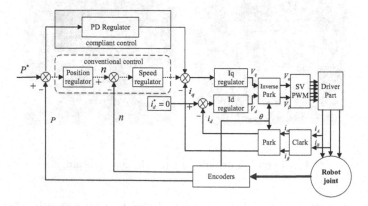

Fig. 6. The block diagram of the actuator's control.

In the process of dynamic walking or running, the biped robot has a high requirement for driver explosion, and the actuator motor may be damaged in the state of continuous high current output. Therefore, a peak current control method based on a low-pass filter is adopted. The peak current output time can be controlled by the inertia hysteresis response characteristics of the low-pass filter [13].

At the same time, the duration of the peak current is adjusted in real-time by collecting the motor temperature. When the motor temperature is low, a larger duration is used to improve the driving capacity. When the system temperature is high, a smaller duration is used to ensure that the motor is not damaged. The control block diagram is shown in Fig. 7.

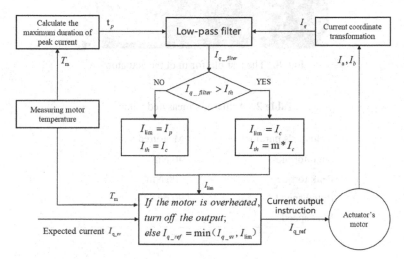

Fig. 7. The principle of peak current control.

3 Experiment and Analysis

3.1 Performance Test

To verify the actual performance of the designed actuator, a test platform is set up, including a loading system with a maximum load capacity of 500Nm, a torque and speed sensor, a power supply, and power analyzer, and so on, as shown in Fig. 8.

Based on the above equipment platform, a series of experiments were carried out, among which some test data were shown in Table 2, and the maximum torque reached 206 Nm, which verified the effectiveness of the design.

At the same time, the relationship between the actuator speed and torque under continuous and discontinuous working areas is tested, as shown in Fig. 9(a). In addition, the torque-current curve of the actuator is tested, as shown in Fig. 9(b). Due to the low deceleration ratio of the actuator, the output torque-current has a good linearity, so that the torque control can be controlled through the current loop.

The proposed actuator in this paper with other actuators is shown in Table 3. Compared with the conventional actuator, the driver has similar torque density but higher speed. Compared with a QDD, this actuator has higher torque output and torque density. It shows that the proposed joint has good performance.

Fig. 8. The test platfor m of the actuator.

Table 2. Actuator's measured value.

Actuator's parameters	Measured value
rated torque	40 Nm
Peak torque	206 Nm
Rated speed	90 rpm
Max speed	120 rpm

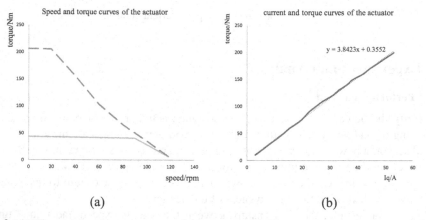

(a)   (b)

Fig. 9. (a) The speed and torque curves of the actuator. (b) The current and torque curves of the actuator.

3.2 Temperature Test

The current of the proposed actuator's motor is very large, and it is easy to overheat if the heat dissipation is not handled well. In the case of no external heat dissipation, the actuator works at rated conditions and the actuator's shell temperature can reach 100 °C

Table 3. The specifications of the proposed actuator compared with other actuators

Actuators	Conventional [14]	MIT QDD [8]	This work
Reducer ratio	101	6	16.227
Weight	1.8 kg	1.174 kg	2 kg
Dimensions	90*100 mm	120*44 mm	130*75 mm
Peak torque	182 Nm	68 Nm	206 Nm
Max speed	60 rpm	430 rpm	120 rpm
Peak torque density	101 Nm/kg	58 Nm/kg	103 Nm/kg

after 20 min. After the two fans are added to enhance heat dissipation, the actuator's shell temperature can run stably for a long time under the same working condition, and the temperature is stable at 65 °C. The actuator's shell temperature curve with time under different heat dissipation conditions is shown in Fig. 10. It can be seen that the heat dissipation of the fans significantly improves the heat dissipation of the actuator.

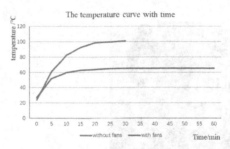

Fig. 10. The actuator's shell temperature curve with time under different heat dissipation conditions.

3.3 Actuator's Driver Test

Because the driver uses two MOSFETs in parallel, it may face the problem of uneven flow and unbalanced power dissipation between MOSFETs in parallel. Therefore, temperature changes of the parallel MOSFETs were recorded under rated operating conditions of the actuator, as shown in Fig. 11(a). The temperature difference between the two parallel MOSFETs is small, indicating that the current of the parallel MOSFETs is balanced. As shown in Fig. 11(b), the maximum output current amplitude can reach 127A, which is larger than the requirements of the actuator's motor.

To test the peak current control method mentioned above, the maximum current is set to 70A and the maximum duration to 3s. The input current instruction is a pulse with 5s duration and 100A amplitude, the actual output current of the driver is shown in Fig. 11(c). In the beginning, the current is limited to the maximum current of 70A. After 3s, the current drops to 35A to protect the system, which verifies the effectiveness of the method.

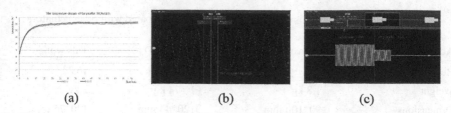

(a)   (b)   (c)

Fig. 11. (a) The temperature changes of the parallel MOSFETs. (b) The maximum output current amplitude can reach 127A. (c) The actual output current after processing by the peak current control method.

3.4 Application

The proposed actuators are applied to our biped robot, as shown in Fig. 12(a) and Fig. 12(b). The height of the biped robot is 1.4 m, and its weight is about 60 kg. The robot legs have 12 joints, among which the knee pitch and hip pitch adopt the proposed actuators. At present, the maximum walking speed of our biped robot can reach 6 km/h. When the robot accelerates to the speed of 6 km/h, the torque and speed of the knee and hip pitch actuators are shown in Fig. 12(c).

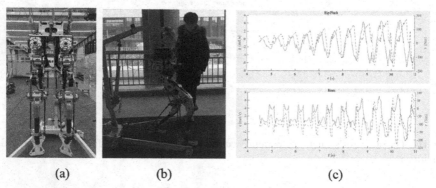

(a)   (b)   (c)

Fig. 12. (a) The picture of the biped robot. (b) The picture of the biped robot walking. (c) The torque and speed of the knee and hip pitch actuators.

4 Conclusion

This paper introduces a design of an actuator for the biped robot. To improve torque output and torque density, the actuator uses a high-torque density axial flux motor and a two-stage planetary deceleration. To solve the problem of overheating, two fans are used for air cooling to strengthen actuator's heat dissipation. At the same time, an actuator driver with a large current output capacity is designed based on the parallel MOSFETs. A series of experiments were carried out to test the performance of the actuator. The maximum torque of the proposed actuator can reach 206Nm and the mass is only 2.0 kg. Compared with other actuators, it has good advantages. Finally, it is applied to a biped robot, which can meet the requirements of 6 km/h walking.

Acknowledgment. This work is supported by National Natural Science Foundation of China (Grants 52205034), "Pioneer" and "Leading Goose" R&D Program of Zhejiang (No. 2023C01177), Key Research Project of Zhejiang Lab (No. G2021NB0AL03), the National Natural Science Foundation of China (Grant No. 52205076).

References

1. Raibert, M.H.: Legged robots that balance. MIT press (1986)
2. Wensing, P.M., Wang, A., Seok, S., et al.: Proprioceptive actuator design in the mit cheetah: Impact mitigation and high-bandwidth physical interaction for dynamic legged robots. IEEE Trans. Rob. **33**(3), 509–522 (2017)
3. Yu, S., Huang, T.H., Yang, X., et al.: Quasi-direct drive actuation for a lightweight hip exoskeleton with high backdrivability and high bandwidth. IEEE/ASME Trans. Mechatron. **25**(4), 1794–1802 (2020)
4. Englsberger, J., Werner, A., Ott, C., et al.: Overview of the torque-controlled humanoid robot TORO. In: 2014 IEEE-RAS International Conference on Humanoid Robots, pp. 916–923. IEEE (2014)
5. Kaneko, K., Kaminaga, H., Sakaguchi, T., et al.: Humanoid robot HRP-5P: an electrically actuated humanoid robot with high-power and wide-range joints. IEEE Rob. Autom. Lett. **4**(2), 1431–1438 (2019)
6. Tsagarakis, N.G., Caldwell, D.G., Negrello, F., et al.: Walk-man: a high-performance humanoid platform for realistic environments. J. Field Rob. **34**(7), 1225–1259 (2017)
7. Radford, N.A., Strawser, P., Hambuchen, K., et al.: Valkyrie: Nasa's first bipedal humanoid robot. J. Field Rob. **32**(3), 397–419 (2015)
8. Chignoli, M., Kim, D., Stanger-Jones, E., et al.: The MIT humanoid robot: Design, motion planning, and control for acrobatic behaviors. In: 2020 IEEE-RAS 20th International Conference on Humanoid Robots (Humanoids), pp. 1–8. IEEE (2021)
9. Huang, R., Song, Z., Dong, Z., et al.: Design of a new double side axial-flux actuator for robot dog. In: 2022 International Conference on Electrical Machines (ICEM), pp. 900–906. IEEE (2022)
10. Amin, S., Khan, S., Bukhari, S.S.H.: A comprehensive review on axial flux machines and its applications. In: 2019 2nd International Conference on Computing, Mathematics and Engineering Technologies (iCoMET), pp. 1–7. IEEE (2019)
11. TQ-Group Homepage. https://www.tq-group.com
12. Allied Motion Homepage. https://www.alliedmotion.nl/
13. Meng, F., Huang, Q., Yu, Z., et al.: Explosive electric actuator and control for legged robots. Engineering **12**, 39–47 (2022)
14. Hua, Q., Zhou, W., Zhu, S., et al.: Design of a high-torque robot joint and its control system. J. Phys. Conf. Series **2281**(1), 012007 (2022)

Omnidirectional Walking Realization of a Biped Robot

Jingge Tang[1,2], Peng Wang[1,2], Chao Liang[1,2], Xin Wang[1,2(✉)], Yun Liu[1,2],
Jiawei Weng[1,2], Fan Wang[1,2], Dingkun Liang[1,2], Anhuan Xie[1,2],
and Jianjun Gu[1,2,3]

[1] Research Center for Intelligent Robotics, Research Institute of Interdisciplinary
Innovation, Zhejiang Lab, Hangzhou 311100, China
xin.wang@zhejianglab.com
[2] Zhejiang Engineering Research Center for Intelligent Robotics,
Hangzhou 311100, China
[3] Department of Electrical Engineering, Dalhousie University,
Halifax, NS B3H 4R2, Canada

Abstract. The purpose of this paper is to discuss the omnidirectional
realization of a walking gait for the biped robot, HTY. Firstly, the paper
introduces the structure and kinematics of the robot. Subsequently, a
modular gait generation system is proposed, comprising a ZMP generator, swing leg generator, center of mass (CoM) generator, foot placement
generator, and inverse kinematics (IK) module. These modules are used
to obtain the trajectory of joint angles required for humanoid walking,
based on the desired motion. Finally, the proposed gait generation system
is validated through simulations and experiments on the HTY prototype.
The results confirm the effectiveness of the gait generation system and
demonstrate the omnidirectional walking ability of the HTY.

Keywords: Biped robot · Humanoid walking · Walk gait generation

1 Introduction

The development of biped robots, intelligent bionic robots that mimic human
walking, began in the 1970 s. After years of research and technology advancement, these robots have achieved impressive capabilities, such as walking, climbing stairs, jumping, and running. Biped robots offer better terrain adaptability
compared to wheeled or crawler robots, and have a wide range of potential applications in fields such as exploration, disaster response, industrial inspections,
education, and scientific research. [1].

The field of biped robots has seen many notable achievements, including the
HRP family [2–5] Honda's ASIMO [6,7], Atlas [8], Cassie [9], COMAN [10],

Supported by Key Research Project of Zhejiang Lab (No. G2021NB0AL03) and Zhejiang Provincial Natural Science Foundation of China (No. LQ23F030010).

and HUBO [11]. HRP4 aims to cooperate with humans and can perform various manipulations like humans. The HRP4 robot is designed to cooperate with humans and can perform various manipulations like a human. ASIMO, on the other hand, can interact with humans and provide services in working and living environments. Atlas is highly agile and can complete challenging movements such as running, jumping, and backflips. Cassie is a dynamic bipedal robot capable of walking and running for search, rescue, and package delivery. COMAN focuses on a compliant approach that allows for safe cooperation with people. This paper will specifically address the research and development of biped robots for navigating stairs, slopes, uneven ground, and hazardous environments.

Developing a stable walking gait is critical for biped robots. Currently, There are several methods used for generating walking gait, including model-based gait [12,13], bionics-based gait [14,15], and natural dynamics-based gait [16]. The model-based gait is a mathematical representation of human walking, which employs the concepts of ZMP and periodicity to ensure dynamic stability, and is widely used in practice [17–19].

For free walking mission, Zhejiang Lab has developed a biped robot named HTY. The biped robot HTY consists of waist, left leg, and right leg, as depicted in Fig. 1. Each leg adopts a series structure, which has six Degrees of Freedoms (DOFs) connected through rotational joints. The hip joint features 3 DOFs: hip yaw, hip roll, and hip pitch, with the axes intersecting at a single point. The knee joint has 1 DOF, while the ankle joint has 2 DOFs, ankle pitch and ankle roll. Additionally, the prototype is equipped with encoder, IMU, and force/torque sensor to gather real-time information. The innovation of this paper is to propose the gait generation system that can implement omnidirectional walking of HTY on flat ground, consisting of the ZMP generator, CoM generator, foot placement generator, swing foot generator, and IK.

The structure of this paper is as follows: In Sect. 2, the HTY's kinematics is briefly introduced. Section 3 presents the details of each module of the gait generation system. In Sect. 4, simulation and experimental verification are carried out based on the simulation environment and the prototype platform. Finally, this paper is summarized.

2 Kinematics

In Fig. 2, the coordinate systems which is always taken in a right-handed orientation and the structural parameters of HTY are indicated. The world coordinate system, denoted as $\{O\}$, is positioned at the midpoint of the line connecting the two feet in the initial standing state. The y-axis points to the left leg, and the z-axis extends vertically upward. For instance, considering the left leg, we define the local coordinate system $\{i\}(i = 1, ..., 6)$ for each link, where each axis aligns with $\{O\}$. $\{0\}$ represents the base coordinate system, which is fixed on the robot body and situated at the midpoint of the line formed by the intersection of the three axes of the two hips.

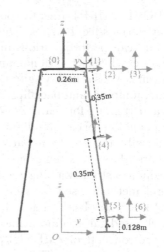

Fig. 1. The biped robot HTY.

Fig. 2. Description of the coordinate systems.

The position and attitude of frame $\{i\}$ with respect to frame $\{O\}$ are described by d_i and R_i, respectively, This leads to the formation of the homogeneous transformation matrix as follows:

$$T_i = \begin{bmatrix} R_i & d_i \\ 0_{1\times 3} & 1 \end{bmatrix}$$

The homogeneous transformation matrix, denoted as T_i^{i-1}, represents the transformation from $\{i\}$ to $\{i-1\}$. Consequently, the forward kinematic expression can be defined as:

$$T_i = T_{i-1}T_i^{i-1} \tag{1}$$

3   Motion Generation System

In order to achieve omnidirectional and stable walking of the biped robot, a modular approach is employed to develop the gait generation system. This system comprises several modules, as depicted in Fig. 3 shows.

By defining the desired gait pattern, a set of foot placement positions are planned as input to the system, denoted as $p = [p_0, p_1, \cdots, p_{n-1}]$. The corresponding attitude is $r = [r_0, r_1, \cdots, r_{n-1}]$. Each $p_i(i = 0, \cdots, n-1)$ is a 3D vector indicating the position with respect to frame $\{O\}$. The walking cycle corresponding to each step is $T_{s,i}(i = 0, \cdots, n-1)$.

The ZMP module takes discrete foot placements as input and generates a continuous ZMP trajectory as output. The purpose of foot placement module is to obtain the discrete foot placements and attitudes of the left foot and right foot according to the foot placements of system input and the ZMP generator. Then,

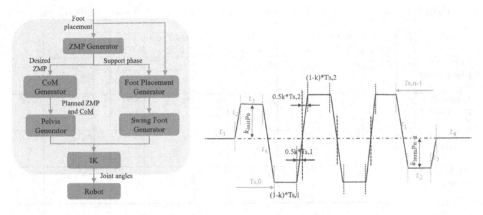

Fig. 3. The composition of gait generation system.

Fig. 4. Planning strategy diagram of ZMP.

the CoM trajectory is planned by the CoM generator. However, the CoM is not equal to the pelvis, so it's essential to convert the movement of the CoM into the movement of the pelvis according to the kinematics. When the biped robot walks, the left and right feet alternate in swinging motion. Polynomial curves are utilized to generate a continuous trajectory for the swinging foot with lift height h, ensuring smooth and coordinated movements. After obtaining the position of the pelvis and the two feet, the joint angles are solved according to IK module to control the movement of the robot.

3.1 ZMP Trajectory Generator

During walking, there are single support phases (SSP) and double support phases (DSP). In SSP, the ZMP remains on the support foot, while in DSP, it transitions from the previous support foot to the next support foot. The generation of the ZMP trajectory is divided into three steps: the beginning, the dynamic cycles, and the end. The ZMP planning algorithm can be observed in Fig. 4.

The initial step, from p_0 to p_1, requires the robot to enter the gait cycle with sufficient initial velocity. Therefore, the first step's walk time is divided into four stages: t1 for initial still time, t2 from the resting position to $k_{init}p_0$, and $t3$ for the SSP time. The fourth stage, t4, represents the DSP time, during which the ZMP transitions from $k_{init}p_0$ to p_1. During the dynamic cycles, the foot placement moves from p_i to p_{i+1}, The walking period $T_{s,i}$ is equal to the sum of the SSP and DSP times, with the proportion of DSP time expressed as k. In the last step, from p_{n-2} to p_{n-1}, the robot transitions smoothly from periodic motion to the still state. The time of the last step also consists of four parts: t_1 for the DSP time, when the ZMP moves to the desired position $k_{term}p_{n-1}$, t_2 for holding time, and t_3 for returning to the stationary state.

Table 1. Foot placement generation strategy when the left foot lands on p_0.

Time	$T_{s,0}$	$(1-k)T_{s,1}$	$0.5kT_{s,1}+0.5kT_{s,2}$	$(1-k)T_{s,2}$	$0.5kT_{s,2}+0.5kT_{s,3}$	$(1-k)T_{s,3}$	$0.5kT_{s,3}+0.5kT_{s,4}$	$(1-k)T_{s,4}$	$\cdots$	$(1-k)T_{s,n-2}$	$T_{s,n-1}$
Left foot placement d_{lf}	p_0	255	p_2	p_2	p_2	255	p_4	p_4	$\cdots$	p_{n-2}	p_{n-2}
Right foot placement d_{rf}	p_1	p_1	p_1	255	p_3	p_3	p_3	255	$\cdots$	255	p_{n-1}
Left foot attitude r_{lf}	0	255	r_2	r_2	r_2	255	r_4	r_4	$\cdots$	r_{n-2}	r_{n-2}
Right foot attitude r_{rf}	0	0	0	255	r_3	r_3	r_3	255	$\cdots$	255	r_{n-1}

Table 2. Foot placement generation strategy when the right foot lands on p_0.

Time	$T_{s,0}$	$(1-k)T_{s,1}$	$0.5kT_{s,1}+0.5kT_{s,2}$	$(1-k)T_{s,2}$	$0.5kT_{s,2}+0.5kT_{s,3}$	$(1-k)T_{s,3}$	$0.5kT_{s,3}+0.5kT_{s,4}$	$(1-k)T_{s,4}$	$\cdots$	$(1-k)T_{s,n-2}$	$T_{s,n-1}$
Left foot placement d_{lf}	p_1	p_1	p_1	255	p_3	p_3	p_3	255	$\cdots$	255	p_{n-1}
Right foot placement d_{rf}	p_0	255	p_2	p_2	p_2	255	p_4	p_4	$\cdots$	p_{n-2}	p_{n-2}
Left foot attitude r_{lf}	0	0	0	255	r_3	r_3	r_3	255	$\cdots$	255	r_{n-1}
Right foot attitude r_{rf}	0	255	r_2	r_2	r_2	255	r_4	r_4	$\cdots$	r_{n-2}	r_{n-2}

3.2 Foot Placement Trajectory Generator

Firstly, it is necessary to identify whether the initial placement corresponds to the left or right foot. Then, the positions of the left and right feet are assigned based on the current support phase and the alternating pattern of left and right legs. During turning, the coordinate system transformation matrix is utilized to adjust and update the foot placements, ensuring the desired motion is achieved.

Assuming that the first foothold p_0 is the left foot, the position and posture of two feet are planned in Table 1, which 255 indicates that foot is in the swing stage. If the first placement p_0 is the right foot, the position and posture of two feet are designed in Table 2.

3.3 CoM Trajectory Generator

In this section, the CoM trajectory is obtained by optimizing the ZMP tracking error, as discussed in [18].

The expected ZMP $\mathbf{zmp}_{ref}$ is gained according to the ZMP generator, while the actual ZMP satisfies the equation

$$\mathrm{zmp} = x - \frac{z_c}{g}\ddot{x} \tag{2}$$

in which, x is the CoM position, g is the acceleration of gravity, z_c is the height of CoM, and $u = \ddot{x}$ stands for the system input. Hence, the tracking error can be written as:

$$\mathrm{zmp}_e = \mathrm{zmp}_{ref} - \mathrm{zmp}$$

In order to realize the tracking of the expected ZMP trajectory, the feedback controller is designed by using the information of m steps in the future

$$u = -\boldsymbol{K}\boldsymbol{X} + \boldsymbol{f}\mathbf{zmp}_{\mathrm{pre}} \tag{3}$$

in which, $\boldsymbol{K}$ is the controller gain, $\boldsymbol{X} = [\mathrm{zmp}_e, x, \dot{x}, \ddot{x}]$ is the system state, $\mathbf{zmp}_{\mathrm{pre}}$ is the reference value of m steps in the future, and $\boldsymbol{f}$ is the weighting factor of the reference value.

The CoM trajectory that ensures system stability is obtained by minimizing the optimization function and calculating the feedback gain using the LQR theory.

To maintain normal walking during turns, the attitude of the CoM needs to be updated. The posture of the CoM is calculated by:

$$\boldsymbol{R}_{CoM} = \frac{1}{2}(\boldsymbol{r}_{lf} + \boldsymbol{r}_{rf}) \tag{4}$$

3.4   Pelvis Trajectory Generator

The motion of the pelvis is kinematically related to the motion of CoM, which will be solved using the three-point mass method described in [20].

The mass of the upper torso is m_{upper}, the mass of the left foot is m_{lf}, and the mass of the right foot is m_{rf}. According to the structural parameters, 25% of mass of the left leg is distributed to m_{upper}, and 75% is distributed to the left foot. The same goes for the right leg.

To maintain an upright posture while walking, the attitude of the pelvis $\boldsymbol{R}_0$ is aligned with that of CoM $\boldsymbol{R}_{CoM}$. The positions of the CoM and the relative position from the pelvis to the CoM are denoted as $\boldsymbol{d}_{CoM}$, $\boldsymbol{d}_{pelvis}^{CoM}$, respectively. As a result, the pelvis position $\boldsymbol{d}_{pelvis}$ can be expressed as follows:

$$m_{upper}(\boldsymbol{d}_{pelvis} + \boldsymbol{R}_0\boldsymbol{d}_{pelvis}^{CoM}) + m_{lf}\boldsymbol{d}_{lf} + m_{rf}\boldsymbol{d}_{rf} = m_{total}\boldsymbol{d}_{CoM} \tag{5}$$

4   Simulation and Experiment

Simulation analysis and experimental verification of the proposed biped gait generation system were conducted based on the Gazebo environment and the physical prototype. The system schematic diagram can be seen in Fig. 5. The implementation of the motion algorithm and the coding of each module were completed using the software framework, primarily in C++.

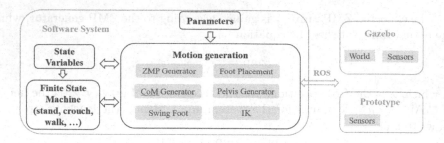

Fig. 5. Schematic diagram of software system.

4.1 Walking

In terms of the structural parameters and limits of the robot, the expected forward foot placements are given:

$$p = \begin{bmatrix} 0.0 & 0.0 & 0.1 & 0.2 & 0.3 & 0.4 & 0.5 & 0.5 \\ 0.13 & -0.13 & 0.13 & -0.13 & 0.13 & -0.13 & 0.13 & -0.13 \\ 0.0 & 0.0 & 0.0 & 0.0 & 0.0 & 0.0 & 0.0 & 0.0 \end{bmatrix}, \quad r = 0$$

Set $z_c = 0.51$ m, $T_{s,i} = 1$ s, $h = 0.08$ m, $k = 20\%$, $k_{init} = 0.7$, and $k_{term} = 0.3$. According to the discrete footholds corresponding to the expected walking, the ZMP, CoM, and swing foot trajectories are obtained, as shown in Fig. 6, in which the real ZMP is calculated by the force/torque sensor in Gazebo simulation, seen in Fig. 7.

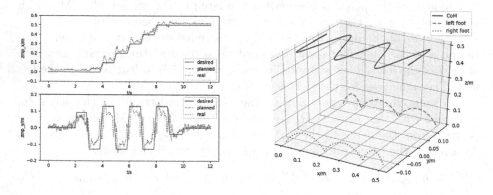

Fig. 6. ZMP, CoM, and feet trajectories.

Considering the difference between the robot model and prototype, tuning coefficients, named as $k_{y,left}$ and $k_{y,right}$, are introduced to the CoM trajectory in y direction during the experiment, for the purpose of controlling the amplitude of left and right swings respectively. Let $k_{y,left} = 1.18$ and $k_{y,right} = 1.25$,

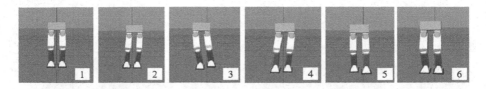

Fig. 7. Walking simulation with forward step length of 0.1m.

Fig. 8. Walking experiment with forward step length of 0.1 m.

and other parameters are consistent with those in the above simulation. The experiment result is shown in Fig. 8. The robot is initially in crouch state. At the first step, the body swings to the left, then swings to the right, and walks with lifted left foot. During the final step, the body's swinging motion reduces, allowing for a quicker transition to a stationary state.

4.2 Turning

In the simulation conducted in Gazebo, a left turn angle of 5° was desired. Input of the system is:

$$p = \begin{bmatrix} 0.0 & 0.0 & 0.1 & 0.2 & 0.3 & 0.4 & 0.5 & 0.5 \\ 0.13 & -0.13 & 0.13 & -0.13 & 0.13 & -0.13 & 0.13 & -0.13 \\ 0.0 & 0.0 & 0.0 & 0.0 & 0.0 & 0.0 & 0.0 & 0.0 \end{bmatrix},$$

$$r = \begin{bmatrix} 0 & 0 & 0 & 0 & 0 & 0 & 0 & 0 \\ 0 & 0 & 0 & 0 & 0 & 0 & 0 & 0 \\ 0 & 0 & 5 & 10 & 15 & 20 & 25 & 25 \end{bmatrix}$$

The results of the ZMP and CoM analysis indicate that the robot moves to the left while advancing, as depicted in Fig. 9. Furthermore, the left turn motion is clearly evident in the trajectories of the left and right feet. Screenshots captured during the motion process in both the simulation (Fig. 10) and the physical experiment (Fig. 11) illustrate the rotation of the body towards the left from its initial position.

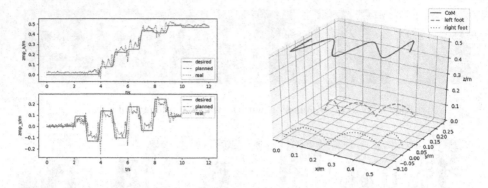

Fig. 9. ZMP, CoM, and feet trajectories.

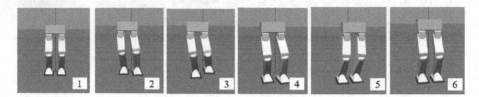

Fig. 10. Left turning simulation with degree of 5°

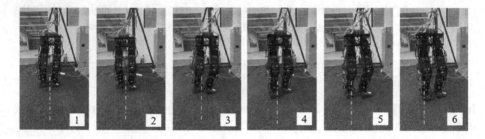

Fig. 11. Left turning experiment with degree of 5°

4.3 Walking Freely

In addition to walking forward and turning, the position and attitude of each foot placement can be designed to achieve optional walking within the reachable range of the structure. Define the expected foot placements as:

$$
p = \begin{bmatrix} 0.0 & 0.0 & 0.1 & 0.1 & 0.1 & 0.1 & 0.0 & 0.0 & 0.1 & 0.1 & 0.2 & 0.2 \\ 0.13 & -0.13 & 0.13 & -0.13 & 0.18 & -0.08 & 0.18 & -0.08 & 0.18 & -0.08 & 0.18 & 0.08 \\ 0.0 & 0.0 & 0.0 & 0.0 & 0.0 & 0.0 & 0.0 & 0.0 & 0.0 & 0.0 & 0.0 & 0.0 \end{bmatrix}
$$

$$
r = \begin{bmatrix} 0 & 0 & 0 & 0 & 0 & 0 & 0 & 0 & 0 & 0 & 0 & 0 \\ 0 & 0 & 0 & 0 & 0 & 0 & 0 & 0 & 0 & 0 & 0 & 0 \\ 0 & 0 & 0 & 0 & 0 & 0 & 0 & 0 & 0 & 0 & 5 & 5 \end{bmatrix}
$$

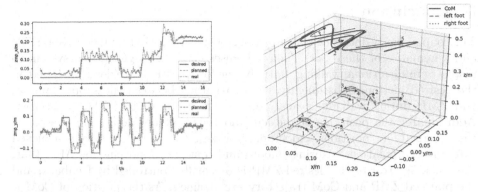

Fig. 12. ZMP, CoM, and feet trajectories.

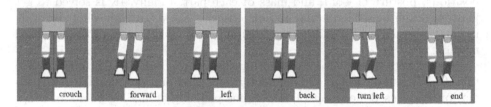

Fig. 13. Free walking simulation in Gazebo.

Fig. 14. Free walking experiment of the HTY.

The simulation and experiment were conducted. The trajectories of the ZMP, CoM, and two feet align with the expected movement, and numbers $1 \sim 5$ in Fig. 12 indicate the sequence in which the trajectories are executed. Figure 13 illustrates the simulation result, while Fig. 14 displays a screenshot from the physical experiment, capturing the moment when the HTY's motion transitions. These results confirm that the robot successfully performs forward, left, backward, and turning movements as intended.

5 Conclusion

This paper firstly introduces the prototype structure of the biped robot HTY and kinematics of the robot. Then it focuses on the gait generation system to realize omnidirectional walking. Initially, the foot positions are designed based on the desired motion. Subsequently, the relationship between the support phases and ZMP during walking is analyzed to obtain the desired ZMP trajectory. Additionally, the positions of the left and right feet are determined based on the designed foot positions and support phases. The foot trajectory is achieved through interpolation, ensuring smooth and continuous movements. After that, the tracking error of the desired ZMP is optimally controlled by feedback, and the planned ZMP and CoM trajectory are attained. As the position of CoM is different from that of pelvis, the motion of the pelvis is calculated based on feet positions, posture of CoM, and mass of each part. Finally, IK is solved to get joint angles of legs. Simulation and experiments show that the robot can walk in various forms, which verifies the feasibility and effectiveness of the proposed method.

Future work will involve investigating the control of thse CoM to avoid torso tilt, studying stable walking in different ground environments through state estimation and closed-loop control, and online planning of landing points to adapt to the environments.

References

1. Al-Shuka, H.F.N., Allmendinger, F., Corves, B., et al.: Modeling, stability and walking pattern generators of biped robots: a review. Robotica **32**, 907–934 (2013)
2. Hirukawa, H., Kanehiro, F., Kaneko, K., et al.: Humanoid robotics platforms developed in HRP. Rob. Auton. Syst. (2004)
3. Kaneko, K., Kanehiro, F., Morisawa, M., et al.: Humanoid robot hrp-4-humanoid robotics platform with lightweight and slim body. In: 2011 IEEE/RSJ International Conference on Intelligent Robots and Systems, San Francisco, pp. 4400–4407 (2011)
4. Kaneko, K., Kaminaga, H., Sakaguchi, T., et al.: Humanoid robot HRP-5P: an electrically actuated humanoid robot with high-power and wide-range joints. IEEE Rob. Autom. Lett. **4**(2), 1431–1438 (2019)
5. Caron, S., Kheddar, A., Tempier, O.: Stair climbing stabilization of the HRP-4 humanoid robot using whole-body admittance control. In: IEEE International Conference on Robotics and Automation (2019)
6. Hirai, K., Hirose, M., Haikawa, Y., et al.: The development of humanoid Honda robot. In: IEEE International Conference on Robotics and Automation, Leuven, vol. 2, pp.1321–1326 (1998)
7. Shigemi, S., Goswami, A., Vadakkepat, P.: ASIMO and humanoid robot research at Honda, pp. 55–90. A Reference, Humanoid Robotics (2018)
8. Atmeh, G.M., Ranatunga, I., Popa, D.O., et al.: Implementation of an adaptive, model free, learning controller on the Atlas robot. In: 2014 American Control Conference, Portland, pp. 2887-2892 (2014)
9. Reher, J., Ma, W.L., Ames, A.D.: Dynamic walking with compliance on a cassie bipedal robot. In: 2019 18th European Control Conference (ECC), pp. 2589–2595 (2019)

10. Zhou, C., Wang, X., Li, Z., et al.: Overview of gait synthesis for the humanoid COMAN. J. Bionic Eng. **14**(1), 15–25 (2017)
11. Park, I.W., Kim, J.Y., Lee, J., Oh, J.H.: Mechanical design of the humanoid robot platform. HUBO. Adv. Rob. **21**(11), 1305–1322 (2007)
12. Zhang, Z., Zhang, L., Xin, S., et al.: Robust walking for humanoid robot based on divergent component of motion. Micromachines **13**(7), 1095 (2022). https://doi.org/10.3390/mi13071095
13. Sugihara, T.: Standing stabilizability and stepping maneuver in planar bipedalism based on the best COM-ZMP regulator. In: IEEE International Conference on Robotics and Automation, Kobe, pp. 1966–1971 (2009)
14. Fukuoka, Y., Kimura, H., Cohen, A.H.: Adaptive dynamic walking of a quadruped robot on irregular terrain based on biological concepts. Inter. J. Rob. Res. **22**(3–4), 187–202 (2003)
15. Shi, Y., Wang, P., Li, M., et al.: Bio-inspired equilibrium point control scheme for quadrupedal locomotion. IEEE Trans. Cognitive Developm. Syst. **11**(2), 200–209 (2018)
16. Garcia, M., Chatterjee, A., Ruina, A., et al.: The simplest walking model: stability, complexity, and scaling. J. Biomech. Eng. **120**(2), 281–288 (1998)
17. Gabriel, T., Han, M.W.: Control of a humanoid robot based on the ZMP method. IFAC Proceed. Volumes **41**(2), 3065–3069 (2008)
18. Kajita, S., Kanehiro, F., Kaneko, K., et al.: Biped walking pattern generation by using preview control of zero-moment point. In: 2003 IEEE International Conference on Robotics and Automation (Cat. No. 03CH37422)
19. Pratt, J., Carff, J., Drakunov, S., et al.: Capture point: a step toward humanoid push recovery. In: 2006 6th IEEE-RAS International Conference on Humanoid Robots, Italy, pp. 200–207 (2006)
20. Takenaka, T., Matsumoto, T., Yoshiike, T.: Real time motion generation and control for biped robot-1st report: Walking gait pattern generation. In: IEEE/RSJ International Conference on Intelligent Robots and Systems, St. Louis, USA, pp. 1084–1091 (2009)

Reinforcement Learning and Sim-to-Real Method of Dual-Arm Robot for Capturing Non-Cooperative Dynamic Targets

Wenjuan Du[✉], Nan Li, Yeheng Chen, and Jiangping Wang

Zhejiang Lab, Hangzhou 311121, Zhejiang, China
dwj_sia_china@163.com

Abstract. The gradual increase of space debris such as invalid satellites poses a great threat to human space exploration activities. Dual-arm robots are increasingly being used in on-orbit capture tasks due to their flexible and stable characteristics. Modeling and controlling a high-dimension dual-arm robot are difficult, and planning a collision-free path for it takes a long time, hence, it's difficult to capture a dynamic non-cooperative target with a dual-arm robot. To address these problems, this paper proposes an intelligent capture algorithm based on the PPO algorithm with the A2C framework, as the reinforcement learning algorithm requires no model of the robot. Collision detection is introduced into the training so that the strategy network obtained from the training does not need real-time collision detection when it's applied to a real robot, namely, it can output relevant control commands in real-time without path planning time. Furthermore, the randomization method improves the generalization ability of the model. The Actor-Networks have been tested in both simulations and on a real robot. The average capture rate is 96.8% in the simulation and a target with rotation speed in the range $[-3.0, 3.0]°/s$ can be caught in the real world, which proves the effectiveness of the intelligent capture algorithm proposed.

Keywords: On orbit capture · Reinforcement learning algorithm · Dynamic non-cooperative target

1 Introduction

With the increasing frequency of human activities in outer space, space launch missions are increasing year by year. However, the invalid rocket terminal stage, failed satellites, and spacecraft debris disintegrated due to the failure of launch missions are still left in space, forming a large number of space debris. This has posed a huge threat to the continued exploration of space. Therefore, the on-orbit

This Research Supported by Center-initiated Research Project of Zhejiang Lab (No. 2021NB0AL01); Science and Technology on Space Intelligent Control Laboratory (No. K2022EA2KE01).

capture task of non-cooperative targets in space has become a research hotspot in the aerospace field [3, 11]. Researchers have proposed of nets [4], flying claws [7], robotic arms, and other methods for free rolling non-cooperative targets' on-orbit capture. Among them, nets, flying claws, and other methods cannot be reused on other tasks. The robotic arms have greater flexibility and can be used for on-orbit maintenance and other tasks in addition to capture. The dual-arm robots have a larger operating space compared to the single-arm robots and form a closed chain structure with a docking ring after capture, resulting in better capture stability.

The acquisition and control algorithms for dual-arm robots aiming at non-cooperative targets can be divided into two categories: traditional methods [2, 8, 10] and reinforcement learning methods [1, 5, 12]. The steps of traditional algorithms include modeling, parameter identification, collision-free path planning, and robot end trajectory tracking. In this process, dynamic modeling is complex, parameter identification has significant errors, and collision-free path planning takes a lot of time in dynamic target acquisition.

The reinforcement learning algorithm is a model-free control algorithm. By selecting an appropriate reward function, the trained strategy function can select the optimal action of the robot based on real-time state feedback of the environment, ultimately completing the capture of dynamic targets. It avoids the establishment of complex dynamic models, does not require parameter identification, and can avoid collisions with the environment by introducing collision models during the training process. Compared to traditional algorithms, the controller has high computational efficiency and good real-time performance and has greater advantages when facing dynamic target acquisition tasks.

Most existing capture tasks for non-cooperative targets have simplified the task scenarios, such as considering that non-cooperative targets only have relative linear velocity without self-rotation or are simply set as relatively stationary targets, without considering collision detection with non-cooperative targets. The robotic arms executing the tasks are mostly low degree of freedom single arm structures, which are relatively small in search space and easy to achieve. Researchers often use simulation environments based on CPU for reinforcement learning training, such as MATLAB, Pybullet, VREP, etc. The training efficiency is extremely low, and as the number of robot degrees of freedom and environmental state observations increases, the training time further increases. This results in training convergence time exceeding the tolerable range and even being unable to converge, making adjustment and optimization more difficult. This makes it difficult for reinforcement learning algorithms to achieve good results and put them into practical use.

This paper focuses on a non-cooperative dynamic target capture mission and studies a reinforcement learning algorithm for dual-arm robots based on PPO [9], aiming to solve key problems such as difficulty in dynamic modeling and long collision detection time in traditional algorithms. This article uses the IsaacGym simulation platform [6] that supports GPU computing to build a training environment, greatly reducing training time. Introducing collision detection during the training process avoids the problem of capture failure caused by collisions

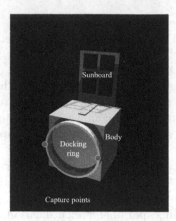

Fig. 1. The components of the non-cooperate target.

with the target during the capture process. The random target speed is introduced into the training to increase the strategy model's generalization ability and avoid its poor robustness due to overfitting.

This paper is organized as follows: Sect. 1 introduces the problem to be solved in the capture of the dynamic non-cooperate targets. Section 2 introduces the capture scenario and the simulation environment in detail. Section 3 proposes the capture method based on the PPO reinforcement learning algorithm. Section 4 shows the results of simulations and experiments. Lastly, a conclusion is made in Sect. 5.

2   Task Scenario and Simulation Environment

2.1   Task Scenario

The capture mission scenario consists of two targets: a non-cooperative target and a service spacecraft. The non-cooperative target is a failed satellite that is in a free-floating state and rotates around its own Z-axis (up-axis). After derotation, the rotation speed will be decreased to $[-1, 1]°/s$. The servicing spacecraft is equipped with a dual-arm robot system that receives control commands from a ground measurement and control center to capture the non-cooperative target.

The non-cooperative target model is shown in Fig. 1, including (1) a docking ring; (2) a body; (3) a sunboard. The docking ring is a 2 cm thick circular ring protruding from the body. The farthest points on the left and right sides of the docking ring (as shown by the red dot in Fig. 1) are taken as the capture points - the points that dual-arm robot should reach to complete the capture mission.

The service spacecraft model is shown in Fig. 2. The loads carried on the service spacecraft include (1) A 14 DOFs dual-arm robot and two 2-finger grippers that each have one DOF. The dual-arm robot consists of two 7 DOFs Rokae robotic arms, which are symmetrically installed on the service spacecraft. The

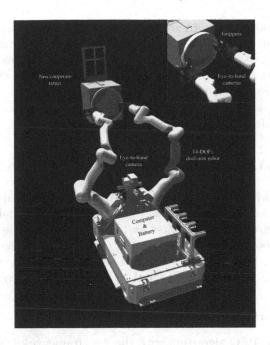

Fig. 2. The components of the service spacecraft.

Z-axes of the robots' bases are at a 45 angle to the Z-axis of the spacecraft. (2) A eye-to-hand RGBD camera and two eye-in-hand cameras are visual detection devices used to discover non-cooperative targets, rebuild their models, and perform semantic analysis. The cameras work together to provide real-time states of the non-cooperate target, such as positions and orientations of the two capture points, to our reinforcement learning control algorithms. Yet this article focuses on reinforcement learning algorithms and the visual implementation part will not be mentioned in detail here. (3) A computer equipped with the visual and control system. (4) A battery system to supply power for the whole system.

The process of capturing a non-cooperative target is as follows: discovering a target → approaching the target → derotating the target → modeling and tracking → semantic analysis → capturing.

Firstly, the eye-to-hand camera is used to detect a non-cooperative target.

Secondly, the service spacecraft is controlled to approach the non-cooperative target, and its attitude is adjusted to make sure the non-cooperative target is within the reachable area.

Thirdly, a contact/non-contact method is used to eliminate the rotation of the non-cooperative target and reduce its rotation speed to within $[-1, 1]°/s$.

Fourthly, the eye-to-hand camera and the eye-in-hand cameras are used together to model, track and semantically analyze the non-cooperative target for obtaining the necessary information about the non-cooperate target, like the capture points' positions and orientations, etc.

Fifthly, the real-time information of the non-cooperate target and the dual-arm system is sent to the controller. Then, the controller runs a reinforcement learning (RL) algorithm and sends the computed joint angles to the dual-arm system in real time. When the end of the robotic arm reaches the capture point, the gripper closure command is sent to complete the capture.

In this paper, we mainly focus on the fifth step, which is training and sim-to-real of the reinforcement learning algorithm.

3 Capture Algorithm Based on PPO

The capture algorithm aims to capture a dynamic derotated non-cooperative target with a dual-arm robot that has 14 DOFs. The traditional way is to model and recognize the robot system first and then find a suitable control strategy to control the robot. However, a 14 DOFs robot is very difficult to model and control due to its high dimensionality. In this paper, we try to use a method based on the PPO algorithm with the A2C framework to solve the problem.

3.1 PPO Algorithm Process

The process of the PPO algorithm with the A2C framework is shown as follows:

(1) Set a certain capacity for an experience pool. Input the current state s into the Actor-New network and output action a through sampling. Execute a in the environment and receive rewards r and the next state s_-. Store $[s, a, r, s_-]$ in the experience pool and continue cycling (1) until the experience pool is full. Then go to (2).

(2) Input the last "next state" last s_- in the experience pool into the Critic-Network, output v_-, use v_- and r in the experience pool to calculate $R[t] = r[t] + \gamma * v_-$, and obtain the set R.

(3) Combine all s in the experience pool into a state set, input it into the Critical network, and output the value set v. Calculate the dominance function based on the set R and the set v, i.e. $adv = Q - v$;

(4) Use the mean square error of the dominance function as the loss function of the Critical network, that is, $c\_loss = MSE(adv)$, then backpropagation and updates network parameters;

(5) Importance sampling: input the state set s into Actor-New and Actor-Old networks respectively, get the probability of each action $prob1$ and $prob2$ by combining action set a, and calculate the importance weight, that is, $ratio = prob2/prob1$;

(6) Calculate the objective function of the Actor-network (1) by combining $ratio$, adv, and clipping method.

$$a\_loss = \sum min\{ratio * adv, clip(ratio, 1 - \epsilon, 1 + \epsilon)adv\}(st, at) \quad (1)$$

Maximizing the objective function and updating Actor-New network parameters through backpropagation;

(7) Cycle (5)–(6) with a certain number of steps $UPDATE\_STEPS$: After the loop ends, assign the Actor-New network parameters to the Actor-Old network, and at this point, both Actor-Networks are updated;

(8) Cycle (1) to (7).

3.2 Actor and Critic Network Structure

The PPO algorithm with the A2C framework contains two networks: an Actor-Network and a Critic-Network. The actor-network takes the observation states of the dual-arm robot and the non-cooperate target as inputs and computes the dual-arm robot's joint angles as outputs. The observation states contain 36 elements as follows:

1. obs[0:14] — Dual-arm DOF positions: joint angles.
2. obs[14:20] — Left & right hands' positions: the left/right hand refers to the mid-point between the two fingers of the left/right gripper.
3. obs[20:26] — Left & right markers' positions, the markers are the capture points shown in Fig. 1.
4. obs[26:32] — Left & right error vector: the left/right error vector is pointing from the left/right hand to the left/right marker.
5. obs[32:33] — Distance between the left hand and the left marker.
6. obs[33:34] — Distance between the right hand and the right marker.
7. obs[34:35] — Altitude error between the left hand and the left marker.
8. obs[35:36] — Altitude error between the right hand and the right marker.

The Actor-Network and the Critic-Network have the same network architecture. They both have 3 hidden layers each with 265, 265, and 128 neurons.

The Actor-Network's output layer has 14 neurons, each of which represents a DOF position variation of the dual-arm robot. The value of each neuron is between -1 and 1 and will be scaled and clamped to satisfy the max speed constraint of each robot joint. As communication delay cannot be eliminated in the real-world system, the real robot cannot run at its maximum joint velocities. Hence, the maximum joint velocities in the simulation are set to 0.3 times the maximum joint velocities in the real world. The difference in velocities between the simulation and the real world can cause a diffusion of the RL algorithm so we should not make the velocities of the robot as inputs.

The Critic-Network's output layer has only 1 neuron, which represents the value v.

3.3 Reward Function

A reward function determines the instant reward r_t that the agent received after each action a_t is applied to the environment, and the learning purpose of an agent is to learn a strategy or policy that maximizes the accumulated discount reward $G_t = \sum_{i=t}^{T} \gamma^{i-t} r_i$, where γ is the discount factor and T is the end time step.

During the process of a non-cooperative target capture mission, the distances and attitude errors between the left/right arm and the left/right capture point are the most concerned indicators in the task.

The distance between hands and capture points can be computed by (2), where p_{hand} indicates the position of the center of two fingers of the gripper, and p_{marker} indicates the position of the left or right capture point. They should be in the same coordinate system. In this paper, vectors are indicated in the world coordinate system unless they are specified.

$$d_{error} = \|p_{hand} - p_{marker}\| \tag{2}$$

The altitude error between a hand and its corresponding capture point is computed by their quaternions. Firstly, the quaternion error q_{error} is computed by (3), where q^* indicates the conjugate of q. Then, let $q_{error} = [x, y, z, w]$ and translate it to the corresponding axis and angle of rotation $[\hat{v}, \Omega]$ by (4). As the 2-norm of the axis $\hat{v}$ is always 1, the angle Ω is taken to represent the difference between the hand and the marker.

$$q_{error} = \frac{q_{hand} * q_{marker}^*}{\|q_{hand} * q_{marker}^*\|} \tag{3}$$

$$\Omega = 2acos(w)$$
$$\hat{v} = \frac{[x, y, z]}{\sqrt{1 - w^2}} \tag{4}$$

A reward function is designed as shown in (5), where dl/dr is the distance between the left/right hand and the left/right capture point, and dql/dqr is the altitude error between the left/right hand and the left/right capture point. The smaller the error e is, the greater the reward r will be.

In the simulation, the error e varies approximately between 0 to 8.5, and most of the time, it varies between 0 to 1.5. The reward function is plotted in Fig. 3, and it shows that the steepest section of the reward function curve is between $[0.5, 1.5]$. When the variable falls within this range, the reward function changes significantly, and each small decrease in the variable brings significant benefits. Therefore, in the early stages of training, the agent will actively reduce the error for obtaining a greater reward. This design can effectively accelerate the convergence speed of training. But when the error decreases to between $[0, 0.5]$, the curve becomes flat. At this point, the reduction of variables cannot bring about a significant increase in reward, making it difficult for training to achieve higher accuracy. Therefore, segmented rewards were given to the error of $[0, 0.5]$, as shown in the Eq. (6). The following conditions are executed in sequence, that is, if the error is less than 0.005 and all conditions are met, the reward obtained will be multiplied by $2^5 = 32$ times.

$$e = dl + dr + \frac{dql}{5.0} + \frac{dqr}{5.0}$$
$$r = \frac{1.0}{1.0 + e^4} \tag{5}$$

$$\begin{aligned}
&\text{if} \quad e < 0.4 \qquad \text{then} \quad r = 2r \\
&\text{if} \quad e < 0.2 \qquad \text{then} \quad r = 2r \\
&\text{if} \quad e < 0.05 \qquad \text{then} \quad r = 2r \\
&\text{if} \quad e < 0.02 \qquad \text{then} \quad r = 2r \\
&\text{if} \quad e < 0.005 \qquad \text{then} \quad r = 2r
\end{aligned} \qquad (6)$$

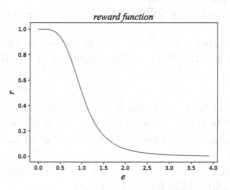

Fig. 3. The reward function curve.

3.4 Terminate Conditions

In addition, if a collision happens between the non-cooperate target and the dual-arm robot or in between the dual-arm robot system, the current episode will be force ended. Obviously, the accumulated discount reward G_t, in this case, will be smaller than in the non-collision case.

The divergence cases should be taken into consideration also. If a divergence case happens, the robot will not approach but rather escape from the target and stay there to avoid any collision, but this is not what we want either. Lastly, the torques of the robot joints should not be larger than the max torques they can bear.

Based on the above analysis, the termination conditions of the episode are listed as follows:

If the target is hit by the robot:

(1) The sum of the velocities of the non-cooperate target is larger than 15.
(2) The displacement of the target is larger than 0.4 m.
    If the target is hit by the robot or a divergence happens:
(3) The distance dl or dr is larger than 4.0 m.
    If the joint torques are out of limits:
(4) Any joint's torque is larger than its max value.
    Naturally terminated:
(5) Current step is larger than the max episode step.

3.5   Randomization

The most powerful simulation tools cannot even fully simulate the real world. Hence, how to transplant the model obtained in the simulation to the real world is a very difficult problem. Randomization is an important tool for generating a model with strong adaptability, and it has been proved that with proper randomization the model obtained in the simulation can be transplanted to a real robot system without further training.

In the capture mission, the following states are randomized:

(1) The initial joint angles of the dual-arm robot are randomized to between -10 and $10°$, while the initial joint angles of the real robot are all set to zero.

   The targets are divided into two classes depending on their rotation directions, forward $[0.0, 5.0]°/s$ and reverse $[-5.0, 0.0]°/s$.
(2) The initial Z-axis speed of the target is randomized to $[0.0, 5.0]°/s$ or $[-5.0, 0.0]°/s$.
(3) The initial position of the target locates within a square area with a center of $[1.3, 0.0, 1.3]$ and a side length of $0.2\,m$.

3.6   Design of the Pre-capture Points

In the experiment, it was found that directly approaching the capture points on the satellite docking ring would make the RL algorithm difficult to converge. Therefore, two pre-capture points were introduced. They have the same altitude as the capture points but are $0.14\,m$ away from them along the direction of the X-axis of the satellite. With the pre-capture points, the grippers will not directly approach the capture points but first adjust the attitudes to be perpendicular to the satellite at a certain distance before capturing the satellite. By artificially designing pre-capture points, the RL algorithm avoids collisions with satellites caused by grippers when they are approaching the docking ring from unreasonable directions, reducing the search space and enabling faster convergence.

4   Simulation and Experiment Results

4.1   Simulation Results

We trained two models for forward and reverse rotation cases separately, and obtained two Actor-Networks, called π_f and π_r. The machine we used for training has an RTX3080Ti GPU with 12G VRAM.

Capture Rate. The two Networks are tested separately in the simulation. Take π_f as an example, we set the Z-axis speed of the target in between $[0.9, 1.1]$, $[1.9, 2.1]$, $[2.9, 3.1]$, $[3.9, 4.1]$, $[4.8, 5.0]$ separately, run 1000 times, and record the capture rate in Table 1. If the distances dl and dr are both less than $0.04\,m$, the capture will be successful. The test result of the π_r is shown in Table 2. The position of the target is randomized.

We can see that, the capture rate of the actor-network with forward-rotating targets performs better in different speed ranges, with the median range performing best, reaching a success rate of 99.3%, and it performs worst in the [4.8, 5.0]°/s range, but also achieves a success rate of 92.5%.

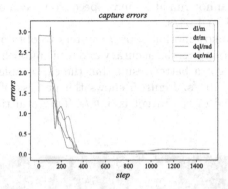

Fig. 4. The error curves.

The capture rate of the actor-network for reverse rotation targets is excellent in the speed range of $[-1.9, -2.1]$, $[-2.9, -3.1]$, $[-3.9, -4.1]$, $[-4.8, -5.0]°/s$, but it performs poorly in the range of $[-0.9, -1.1]°/s$, achieving only 86.1% success rate.

Table 1. Capture rate of π_f.

Average Z-axis speed of target	1.002	2.001	3.000	4.001	4.902
Capture rate	98.0%	99.1%	99.3%	99.1%	92.5%

Table 2. Capture rate of π_r.

Average Z-axis speed of target	-1.003	-1.999	-2.996	-4.000	-4.903
Capture rate	86.1%	99.8%	99.6%	99.0%	96.2%

Capture Error. The capture error e is the sum of the distances dl, dr, and the altitude errors dql, dqr. The error curves during one capture mission are shown in Fig. 4. In the simulation, one step is 0.01 s, and during the first 100 steps, namely 1 s, the robot does not move. The distance errors decrease lower than 0.02 m and the altitude errors decrease lower than 0.11 rad after 4 s.

4.2   Experiments

In our experiments, we used an RGB-D camera to rebuild and track the target and obtain the positions and orientations of the two capture points, together with the states of the dual-arm robot, they are sent to the Actor-Network and get the robot's joint angles of the next step. As the communication delay always exists between the robot controller and the RGB-D camera and the RL Actor-Network, the robot cannot run at its max speed, so we can only capture a target with a speed lower than $1.0°/s$.

We also used a Nokov motion capture system to obtain the capture points' positions and orientations, as the accuracy and topic publish rate are both higher than the camera, we got a better result that the capturable speed of the target can be increased to $3.0°/s$. Figure 5 shows the process of a capture mission, and the rotation speed of the target is $3.0°/s$. The total time of the process is approximately 10 s.

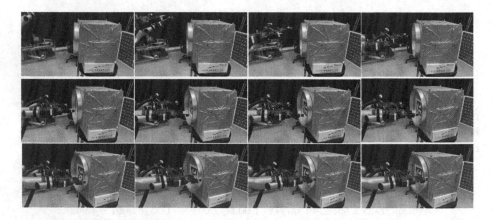

Fig. 5. The capture process with Nokov.

5   Conclusion

This article trains non-cooperative target capture tasks based on the reinforcement learning algorithm PPO with A2C framework, obtains capture strategy networks for non-cooperative targets rotating at different speeds, and tests their capture rates and errors at different speed ranges of $[-5, 5]°/s$. The average capture rate reaches 96.88%, with distance errors of less than 2 cm and altitude errors of less than 0.11 rad.

The main innovations of this article are as follows: (1) A model-free method based on PPO with A2C framework is proposed for capturing a dynamic non-cooperative target. This method avoids modeling a high-dimension model for the dual-arm robot and saves a lot of time in planning a collision-free path during capture, which increases the dual-arm robot's ability to capture a dynamic non-cooperate target. (2) A randomization method is applied in training to increase the generalization ability of the model and make sure the model that is trained in the simulations can be used on a real robot without further training.

References

1. Ai, H., Zhu, A., Wang, J., Yu, X., Chen, L.: Buffer compliance control of space robots capturing a non-cooperative spacecraft based on reinforcement learning. Appl. Sci. **11**(13), 5783 (2021)
2. Bylard, A., MacPherson, R., Hockman, B., Cutkosky, M.R., Pavone, M.: Robust capture and deorbit of rocket body debris using controllable dry adhesion. In: 2017 IEEE Aerospace Conference, pp. 1–9 (2017). https://doi.org/10.1109/AERO.2017.7943844
3. Dong, H., Gangqi, D., Huang, P., Zhiqing, M.: Capture and detumbling control for active debris removal by a dual-arm space robot. Chin. J. Aeronaut. **35**(9), 342–353 (2022)
4. Guang, Z., Jing-rui, Z.: Space tether net system for debris capture and removal. In: 2012 4th International Conference on Intelligent Human-Machine Systems and Cybernetics, vol. 1, pp. 257–261 (2012). https://doi.org/10.1109/IHMSC.2012.71
5. Ma, Z., Wang, Y., Yang, Y., Wang, Z., Tang, L., Ackland, S.: Reinforcement learning-based satellite attitude stabilization method for non-cooperative target capturing. Sensors **18**(12), 4331 (2018)
6. Makoviychuk, V., et al.: Isaac Gym: high performance GPU-based physics simulation for robot learning. arXiv preprint arXiv:2108.10470 (2021)
7. Man, W., Li, X., Zhang, Z., An, J., Zhang, G., Yu, D.: Research on space target on-orbit capturing methods. In: Tan, J. (ed.) ICMD 2021. MMS, vol. 111, pp. 321–343. Springer, Singapore (2022). https://doi.org/10.1007/978-981-16-7381-8_22
8. Nishida, S.I., Kawamoto, S.: Strategy for capturing of a tumbling space debris. Acta Astronautica **68**(1), 113–120 (2011). https://doi.org/10.1016/j.actaastro.2010.06.045. https://www.sciencedirect.com/science/article/pii/S0094576510002365
9. Schulman, J., Wolski, F., Dhariwal, P., Radford, A., Klimov, O.: Proximal policy optimization algorithms. arXiv preprint arXiv:1707.06347 (2017)
10. Xueyan, A., Zhang, R., Wei, L.: Terminal sliding mode control of attitude synchronization for autonomous docking to a tumbling satellite. In: Proceedings 2013 International Conference on Mechatronic Sciences, Electric Engineering and Computer (MEC), pp. 2760–2763. IEEE (2013)
11. Yoshida, K., Dimitrov, D., Nakanishi, H.: On the capture of tumbling satellite by a space robot. In: 2006 IEEE/RSJ International Conference on Intelligent Robots and Systems, pp. 4127–4132 (2006). https://doi.org/10.1109/IROS.2006.281900
12. Zhu, A., Ai, H., Chen, L.: A fuzzy logic reinforcement learning control with spring-damper device for space robot capturing satellite. Appl. Sci. **12**(5), 2662 (2022)

Control of the Wheeled Bipedal Robot on Roads with Large and Unknown Inclination

Baining Tu[1], Biao Lu[1,2], and Minnan Piao[3(✉)]

[1] Institute of Robotics and Automatic Information Systems, College of Artificial Intelligence, Nankai University, Tianjin 300350, People's Republic of China
{2013552,lubiao}@mail.nankai.edu.cn
[2] Institute of Intelligence Technology and Robotic Systems, Shenzhen Research Institute of Nankai University, Shenzhen 518083, People's Republic of China
[3] College of Computer Science and Technology, Civil Aviation University of China, Tianjin 300300, People's Republic of China
mnpiao@cauc.edu.cn

Abstract. To keep the balance and the stable movement of a wheeled bipedal robot (WBR) on a road with large, unknown and continuously variable inclination, a control strategy based on nonlinear sliding mode controller (SMC) and unscented kalman filter (UKF) is proposed in this study. This strategy can directly identify the angle of the slope in real-time based on the nonlinear model, which helps to cope with various unknown road conditions. Simulations have shown that the proposed control architecture can tackle with gentle, sharp and sinusoidal terrains in both small and large scale with the extreme inclination of $47.5°$. Besides, the WBR can start at a slope even exceed $20°$ without any prior information about the surroundings, which demonstrates its robustness to the initial terrain condition. Results also show that the proposed strategy works more swift and stable, compared to three other control architectures: single LQR, single SMC and SMC combined with extended kalman filter (EKF).

Keywords: Nonlinear sliding mode control (SMC) · Unscented kalman filter (UKF) · Real-time inclination identification

1 Introduction

Nowadays, WBR has been one representative member of the mobile robots for its simple structure, flexible motion and energy efficiency [1]. Particularly, it has been applied to security patrol, assisting human work, etc. [2–5]. An important difference between WBR and other mobile robots is that the former one is an underactuated system and extra balance control method need to be considered.

This work is supported by the National Natural Science Foundation of China under Grant 62203450.

Most existing researches on WBR are carried out on a horizontal road, or a slope with an inclination below 15°. There are plenty of remarkable methods to handle these situations. Specifically, linear controllers such as PID [6] and LQR [7] can achieve self-balance with the approximate linearized system model. Many nonlinear controllers are also applied to balance control. Specifically, in [8], SMC and back-stepping controller are designed for balancing as well as trajectory tracking. MPC in [9], fuzzy logic controller in [6,10] and integral SMC in [11] are adopted to effectively overcome uncertainties on a slope with a small inclination. However, in practical working situations, the WBR will face more different road conditions, especially a slope with large, unknown and continuously changing inclination. Recently, Zhou *et al.* [12] propose a control architecture based on SMC combined with EKF [13]. Their method can guarantee the stable movement of the robot on continuous uneven ground. However, the extreme inclination in their experiments only reaches to 16.7°, which seems not enough to handle more complex situations.

To further improve the ability to cope with large inclinations, we design our architecture directly on the nonlinear model of WBR. For the controller, nonlinear SMC is adopted for its insensitivity to uncertainties and disturbances. The specific structure of the controller is inspired by Liu's researches on two-joint arm robots [14]. In order to match with the nonlinear model, UKF [15] is adopted as the observer. The main idea of UKF is unscented transform (UT), a method to calculate the statistical characteristics of the random variables after nonlinear transmission [16]. This transform takes multi-information of the state space as the initial sample points, which helps UKF to estimate the real state or the unknown parameters of the system. Compared to EKF, UKF is more accurate because it directly uses the real system model without any approximation or linearization. In the proposed strategy, UKF is used to identify the inclination in real-time, and the estimated angle is used to calculate the expected equilibrium point of the pendulum for assisting SMC on unknown terrains. Simulations are carried out to verify the robustness and adaptability of the proposed strategy.

The rest of this paper is arranged as follows. In Sect. 2, the WBR model is introduced. Control architecture based on SMC and UKF is designed in Sect. 3. Section 4 provides confirmatory and comparative experiments. Finally, some conclusions are drawn in Sect. 5.

2   System Model

Figure 1 shows the simplified WBR model used in this study. m is the quality of the body. m_w and I_w are the quality and the rotation inertia of each wheel, respectively. R is the radius of the wheel, and L is the distance between the centroid of the body and the axial center of the wheel. α denotes the inclination of the pendulum with the vertical position as zero point. φ represents the inclination of the slope with the horizontal position as zero point. τ stands for the torque provided by the motor. x represents the position of the wheels and f_r represents the friction between the wheels and the ground. The positive directions

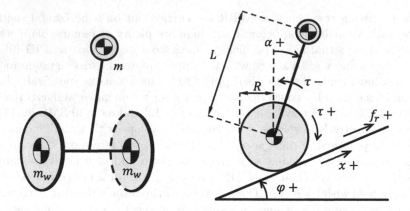

Fig. 1. The simplified model of WBR.

of these vectors are indicated in Fig. 1. The WBR can usually be represented by [17]:

$$a\ddot{x} + b\ddot{\alpha} - mL\sin(\alpha + \varphi)\dot{\alpha}^2 + (m + 2m_w)g\sin\varphi = \tau/R - f_r \qquad (1)$$

$$b\ddot{x} + mL^2\ddot{\alpha} - mgL\sin\alpha = -\tau \qquad (2)$$

where $a = m + 2m_w + 2\frac{I_w}{R^2}$, $b = mL\cos(\alpha + \varphi)$. Define $\boldsymbol{q} = [x, \alpha]^T$ as the state vector. To make controller design more concise, the dynamic equation can be rewritten to the following form:

$$\boldsymbol{M}(\boldsymbol{q})\ddot{\boldsymbol{q}} + \boldsymbol{C}(\boldsymbol{q}, \dot{\boldsymbol{q}})\dot{\boldsymbol{q}} + \boldsymbol{G}(\boldsymbol{q}) = \boldsymbol{u} + \boldsymbol{d}(t) \qquad (3)$$

where $\boldsymbol{d}(t)$ denotes the lumped disturbances. $\boldsymbol{M}, \boldsymbol{C}, \boldsymbol{G}, \boldsymbol{u}$ are given as:

$$\boldsymbol{M} = \begin{bmatrix} a & b \\ b & mL^2 \end{bmatrix} \quad \boldsymbol{C} = \begin{bmatrix} 0 & -mL\sin(\alpha + \varphi)\dot{\alpha} \\ 0 & 0 \end{bmatrix}$$

$$\boldsymbol{G} = \begin{bmatrix} (m + 2m_w)g\sin\varphi \\ -mgL\sin\alpha \end{bmatrix} \quad \boldsymbol{u} = \begin{bmatrix} \frac{\tau}{R} \\ -\tau \end{bmatrix}. \qquad (4)$$

Assumption

To make the analysis more complete, we adopt a reasonable assumption. The lumped disturbances $\boldsymbol{d}(t)$ has the following property:

$$|\boldsymbol{d}(t)| \le [\bar{d}_1, \bar{d}_2]^T \qquad (5)$$

where $\bar{d}_1$ and $\bar{d}_2$ represent the upper bound of the disturbances.

3   Control Architecture

3.1   Controller Design

In order to keep the balance of the robot, the equilibrium point should be calculated firstly. When the system state reaches the desired equilibrium point, one has $\ddot{x} = \ddot{\alpha} = \dot{\alpha} = 0$. Substituting these variables into (1) and (2), we can get α_d as the equilibrium angle of the pendulum:

$$\alpha_d = \sin^{-1}\left[\frac{(m + 2m_w)\sin\hat{\varphi}}{mL/R}\right] \tag{6}$$

where $\hat{\varphi}$ represents the estimation of the slope, and its specific estimation method will be proposed in next subsection.

The reference signal for q is defined as $q_d = [x_d, \alpha_d]^T$. Hence, the error states can be obtained as:

$$e = [e_1, e_2]^T = [x_d - x, \alpha_d - \alpha]^T \tag{7}$$

and the derivative of the error can be obtained as:

$$\dot{e} = [\dot{e}_1, \dot{e}_2]^T = [\dot{x}_d - \dot{x}, \dot{\alpha}_d - \dot{\alpha}]^T = [v_d - \dot{x}, -\dot{\alpha}]^T . \tag{8}$$

To make the derivation more concise, we define:

$$H(q, \dot{q}) = C(q, \dot{q})\dot{q} + G(q). \tag{9}$$

Therefore, the dynamic Eq. (3) can be rewritten as:

$$M\ddot{q} + H = u + d(t). \tag{10}$$

Design the manifold as follows:

$$s = \begin{bmatrix} \dot{e}_1 + c_1 e_1 \\ \dot{e}_2 + c_2 e_2 \end{bmatrix} \tag{11}$$

where the coefficients $c_1, c_2 \in \mathbb{R}$. The derivative of the manifold is obtained as:

$$\dot{s} = \begin{bmatrix} c_1\dot{e}_1 \\ c_2\dot{e}_2 \end{bmatrix} + \begin{bmatrix} \ddot{q}_{1d} \\ \ddot{q}_{2d} \end{bmatrix} - M^{-1}(u + d - H). \tag{12}$$

To ensure the states converge to desired values quasi-exponentially fast, $\dot{s}$ can be designed as follows:

$$\dot{s} = -\varepsilon\,\mathrm{sgn}(s) - ks + M^{-1}(d_c - d) \tag{13}$$

where the coefficients $\varepsilon, k \in \mathbb{R}^+$, and d_c refers to:

$$d_c = \begin{bmatrix} -\bar{d}_1\mathrm{sgn}(s_1) \\ -\bar{d}_2\mathrm{sgn}(s_2) \end{bmatrix}. \tag{14}$$

Choose the Lyapunov function as:

$$V = \frac{1}{2}s^T s \geq 0. \tag{15}$$

Combining (5) (13) (14), one can derive:

$$\dot{V} = s^T \dot{s} \leq 0. \tag{16}$$

Substituting (13) into (12), the control input is obtained:

$$u = M(q, \hat{\varphi})\left(\begin{bmatrix} c_1\dot{e}_1 \\ c_2\dot{e}_2 \end{bmatrix} + \begin{bmatrix} \ddot{q}_{1d} \\ \ddot{q}_{2d} \end{bmatrix} + \varepsilon\,\mathrm{sgn}(s) + ks\right) + H - d_c \tag{17}$$

where $\ddot{q}_d = [a_d, 0]^T$, a_d represents the reference of the acceleration of the robot.

3.2 Filter Design

Without extra sensors nor prior information about the ground conditions, we need to design an observer to estimate the inclination ($\hat{\varphi}$) in real-time. Since the model is supposed to cope with large slope changes, the values of both α and φ are actually large, which leads to the fact that the equations cannot be simply linearized. Therefore, we consider designing the unscented kalman filter directly on the nonlinear model.

The filter model is constructed as:

$$\begin{cases} \varphi_{k+1} = f(\boldsymbol{x}_k, \varphi_k, \tau_k) + w_k \\ \tau_k = h(\boldsymbol{x}_k, \varphi_k) + v_k \end{cases}$$

$$w_k \sim N(0, Q_k), v_k \sim N(0, R_k) \tag{18}$$

where $\boldsymbol{x}_k = [\boldsymbol{q}, \dot{\boldsymbol{q}}]^T$ is the real-time state observed by IMU and encoder. w_k and v_k represent zero-mean Gaussian white noise with variances Q_k and R_k, respectively. The state transition equation $f(\cdot)$ can be obtained through (1):

$$f_k = \sin^{-1}\left[\frac{-a\ddot{x} - b(\varphi_k)\ddot{\alpha} + mL\sin(\alpha + \varphi_k)\dot{\alpha}^2 + \tau_k/R}{(m + 2m_w)g}\right]. \tag{19}$$

The observer equation $h(\cdot)$ can be obtained through (2):

$$h_k = -b(\varphi_k)\ddot{x} - mL^2\ddot{\alpha} + mgL\sin\alpha. \tag{20}$$

UKF Algorithm
In this algorithm, we define variables as follows: P is the variance matrix. $\hat{\varphi}$ and $\hat{\tau}$ are the estimation of the slope angle and the motor torque, respectively. Φ and T are the collection of sample points based on $\hat{\varphi}$ and $\hat{\tau}$, respectively. $(\sqrt{P})_i$ represents the i_{th} column of the square root of the matrix. λ is used to control the distance between the sample points and the average value $\hat{\varphi}$. η is the decay factor. ω denotes the weight of each sample point. n represents the dimension of the state space of the filter, and $n = 1$ in this case.

Step 1: Initialization:

$$\hat{\varphi}_0 = E[\varphi_0] = 0, \tag{21}$$

$$P_0 = E[(\varphi_0 - \hat{\varphi}_0)(\varphi_0 - \hat{\varphi}_0)^T] = 1. \tag{22}$$

Step 2: Sample points calculation:

$$\begin{cases} \Phi_{0,k} = \hat{\varphi}_k \\ \Phi_{i,k} = \hat{\varphi}_k + (\sqrt{(n+\lambda)P_k})_i, (i = 1, 2, \ldots, n) \\ \Phi_{i+n,k} = \hat{\varphi}_k - (\sqrt{(n+\lambda)P_k})_i, (i = 1, 2, \ldots, n), \end{cases} \tag{23}$$

$$\begin{cases} \omega_0^{(m)} = \frac{\lambda}{n+\lambda} \\ \omega_0^{(c)} = \frac{\lambda}{n+\lambda} + \eta, (0 < \eta < 1) \\ \omega_i^{(m)} = \omega_i^{(c)} = \frac{0.5}{n+\lambda}, (i = 1, 2, \ldots, 2n). \end{cases} \tag{24}$$

Step 3: Time updating:

$$\Phi_{i,k+1|k} = f(\boldsymbol{x}_k, \Phi_{i,k}, \hat{\tau}_k), \tag{25}$$

$$\hat{\varphi}_{k+1|k} = \sum_{i=0}^{2L} \omega_i^{(m)} \Phi_{i,k+1|k}, \tag{26}$$

$$P_{k+1|k} = Q_k + \sum_{i=0}^{2n} \omega_i^{(c)} [\Phi_{i,k+1|k} - \hat{\varphi}_{k+1|k}][\Phi_{i,k+1|k} - \hat{\varphi}_{k+1|k}]^T, \tag{27}$$

$$T_{i,k+1|k} = h(\boldsymbol{x}_k, \Phi_{i,k+1|k}), \tag{28}$$

$$\hat{\tau}_{k+1|k} = \sum_{i=0}^{2n} \omega_i^{(m)} T_{i,k+1|k}. \tag{29}$$

Step 4: Measurement updating:

$$P_{\tau\tau} = R_k + \sum_{i=0}^{2n} \omega_i^{(c)} [T_{i,k+1|k} - \hat{\tau}_{k+1|k}][T_{i,k+1|k} - \hat{\tau}_{k+1|k}]^T, \tag{30}$$

$$P_{\varphi\tau} = \sum_{i=0}^{2n} \omega_i^{(c)} [\Phi_{i,k+1|k} - \hat{\varphi}_{k+1|k}][T_{i,k+1|k} - \hat{\tau}_{k+1|k}]^T, \tag{31}$$

$$K_{k+1} = P_{\varphi\tau} P_{\tau\tau}^{-1}, \tag{32}$$

$$\hat{\varphi}_{k+1} = \hat{\varphi}_{k+1|k} + K_{k+1}(\tau_k - \hat{\tau}_{k+1|k}), \tag{33}$$

$$P_{k+1} = P_{k+1|k} - K_{k+1} P_{\tau\tau} K_{k+1}^T, \tag{34}$$

where in (33), the inclination is estimated as $\hat{\varphi}_{k+1}$, and then, it is transmitted to SMC for calculating the equilibrium angle α_d in (6).

4   Simulation

The parameters of the WBR in this research are choosen as:

$$m = 6\,\mathrm{kg}, \ m_w = 1.5\,\mathrm{kg}, \ L = 0.2\,\mathrm{m}, \ R = 0.052\,\mathrm{m}, \\ I_w = 0.002\,\mathrm{kg}\cdot\mathrm{m}^2, \ g = 9.8\,\mathrm{m/s}^2. \tag{35}$$

We assume that the disturbance has the following form:

$$\boldsymbol{d}(t) = 0.01 \cdot [\sin(t), \sin(t)]^T. \tag{36}$$

The initial states of the system are decided as:

$$x(0) = 0, \ \alpha(0) = 0, \ \dot{x}(0) = 0, \ \dot{\alpha}(0) = 0. \tag{37}$$

The parameters of SMC are chosen as:

$$c_1 = 5, \quad c_2 = 5, \quad k = 15, \quad \varepsilon = 1, \quad \bar{d}_1 = 0.01, \quad \bar{d}_2 = 0.01. \tag{38}$$

To deal with the chattering problem, we replace the term $\mathrm{sgn}(s)$ in (14) and (17) with $\tanh(10s)$. The parameters of UKF are chosen as:

$$\lambda = 0.01, \quad \eta = 0.5, \quad Q_k = 1, \quad R_k = 1. \tag{39}$$

For the entire system, the control period is set to $T_s = 0.01$ s. A process noise is added to τ as the disturbance from the motor, and a measurement noise is added to the system state x as the disturbance from IMU and encoder. Both noises are white noises with their power at 1×10^{-4}. Besides, the driving matrix of the measurement noise is set to $I_{4\times4}$. Notably, we set $a_d = 0\,\mathrm{m/s^2}, v_d = 0.25\,\mathrm{m/s}, x_d = 0.25t\,\mathrm{m}$ as the references. Besides, all of the simulations carried out in this research have a common precondition: the prior terrain information is unknown.

4.1   Moving on Different Terrains

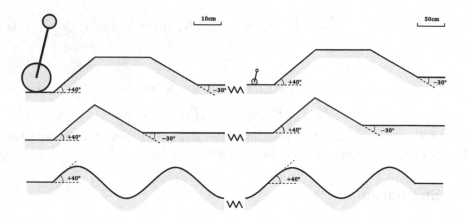

Fig. 2. Left: Small scale terrains. Right: Large scale terrains. Top: Gentle turning points. Middle: Sharp turning points. Bottom: Sinusoidal slopes.

Figure 2 shows some probable situations a WBR will face. Moving from small scale terrains to large scale terrains, three types of simulations are carried out. The results are shown in Fig. 3, 4 and 5, where the solid lines represent the angle observed by the robot and the dashed lines represent the expected angle in the physical world. As one can see, the controlled α only has acceptable delay and small overshoot, which indicates the proposed architecture can estimate the inclination in time and cope with different terrains.

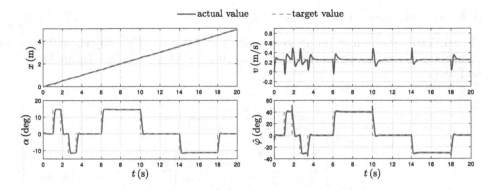

Fig. 3. Results of Gentle Terrains.

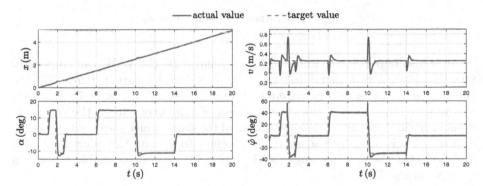

Fig. 4. Results of Sharp Terrains.

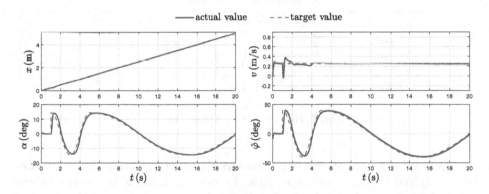

Fig. 5. Results of Sinusoidal Terrains.

4.2   Robustness Verification

A real WBR system may not start at a horizontal terrain. To verify the influence of initial inclination, we let the robot start at a 20° slope. The results are shown in Fig. 6.

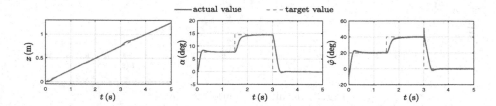

Fig. 6. Robustness to Initial Terrain.

It is also important to find out the extreme angle the WBR can cope with. One can learn a fact that $-90° < \alpha + \varphi < 90°$. Substituting it into (6), the theoretical feasible set of our system is obtained as $-68.7° < \varphi < 68.7°$. However, the value of the inner algebraic expression of (19) may exceed the definition domain of $\sin^{-1}$ due to the large variation of the slope, which means the practical domain of φ is actually narrower. We attempt to add up the angle gradually, and find that the extreme angle is 47.5° (Fig. 7), with a reasonable τ between $-7.0\,\mathrm{N} \cdot \mathrm{m}$ and $5.1\,\mathrm{N} \cdot \mathrm{m}$.

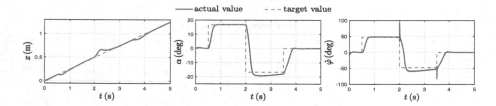

Fig. 7. Robustness to Angle Range.

Finally, the change of system parameters also need to be considered. According to (6) and (19), one can learn that the value of L has a big impact on the estimation. We set $L = 0.2 + 0.03\sin(0.5\pi t)\,(\mathrm{m})$ to verify the robustness, and the results are shown in Fig. 8.

These three simulations demonstrate the robustness of the proposed strategy to certain initial terrain, angle range, and parameter changes.

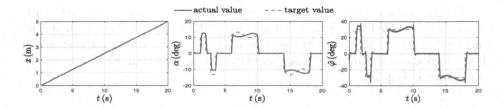

Fig. 8. Robustness to Parameter Changes.

4.3 Comparison with Other Control Architectures

For comparative analysis, three other control architectures are carried out. The first one is SMC alone. The second one is SMC combined with EKF. To derive the linearized approximation for EKF to use, (19) and (20) are first-order Taylor expanded on φ_k, then the state matrix and the observe matrix are derivated as:

$$A_{k+1} = \frac{\partial f}{\partial \varphi} = \frac{mL\dot{\alpha}^2}{(m + 2m_w)g}, \quad H_{k+1} = \frac{\partial h}{\partial \varphi} = mL(\alpha + \varphi)\ddot{x}. \tag{40}$$

Besides, Q_k is set to 0.1 in EKF for better performance. The third one is LQR alone. In LQR approach, the cost function is set as:

$$J = \int_0^\infty [\boldsymbol{x}^T \boldsymbol{Q} \boldsymbol{x} + \tau^T \boldsymbol{R} \tau] \mathrm{dt} \tag{41}$$

where $\boldsymbol{Q} = \mathrm{diag}[10, 10, 1, 1]$, $\boldsymbol{R} = 1$. The feedback gain is obtained as $k = [-2.8013, -15.9269, -2.9980, -2.8762]$. Besides, to find out how UKF performs with a linear controller, we let UKF work with LQR simultaneously but separately.

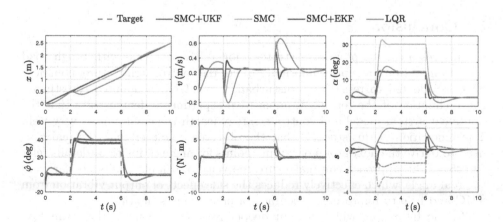

Fig. 9. Comparison with Other Control Architectures.

Figure 9 shows the results of these control architectures tackling with a 40°
slope. It is observed that, SMC combined with UKF can accurately estimate the
inclination and rapidly track the reference signals, and it works the best of the
four. To find out the ability of EKF and UKF, Q_k is set to 1 in EFK, and results
are shown in Fig. 10.

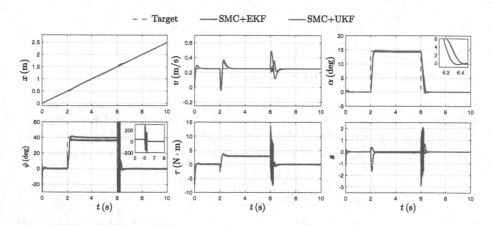

Fig. 10. Comparison between UKF and EKF with the same Q_k.

Apparently, in the same situation, UKF works better than EKF when they
are combined with SMC. Besides, Q_k evaluates the acceptable intensity of the
system noise transmitting to the observer. Hence, the results also indicate that
UKF is more robust to noise than EKF in this case.

It also worth noticing that, for the third control architecture, although LQR
and UKF seems to work right separately, they can not work well together for
oscillation and divergence.

5   Conclusion

In this research, we propose a strategy for WBR to tackle with tough road
conditions without any prior information. For the control architecture, nonlinear
SMC is adopted to resist large disturbance, and UKF is adopted to estimate
the inclination of the terrain. Comparative experiments demonstrate that the
nonlinear system model and control strategy match the environment very well.
The innovation of this study is that the observed $\hat{\tau}$, rather than the real τ, is
used to derive the next group of sample points for angle estimation (details refer
to (25)). This approach can make sure the value of sample points not far from
the real angle, which effectively reduces the side effects of output vibration from
SMC and help to improve the accuracy of parameter estimation.

In the future, we will carry out deeper researches to make the estimation
more precise. We will also try to expand the usage of UKF in related work such
as estimating the centroid of humanoid robots.

References

1. Bjelonic M., Klemm V., Lee J., Hutter M.: A survey of wheeled-legged robots. In: Cascalho J.M., Tokhi M.O., Silva M.F., Mendes A., Goher K., Funk M. (eds) Robotics in Natural Settings. CLAWAR 2022. Lecture Notes in Networks and Systems, vol. 530. Springer, Cham (2023). https://doi.org/10.1007/978-3-031-15226-9_11

2. Klemm V. et al.: Ascento: a two-wheeled jumping robot. In: International Conference on Robotics and Automation (ICRA), pp. 7515–7521 (2019)

3. ETH Zürich: This robot is a security guard - Ascento. https://www.youtube.com/watch?v=VWfBvq4QfEY. Accessed 20 May 2023

4. Boston Dynamics: Introducing handle.https://youtu.be/-7xvqQeoA8c. Accessed 20 May 2023

5. Jung, T., et al.: Development of the humanoid disaster response platform DRC-HUBO+. IEEE Trans. Rob. **34**(1), 1–17 (2018)

6. Goher, K.M., Fadlallah, S.O.: Control of a two-wheeled machine with two-directions handling mechanism using PID and PD-FLC algorithms. Int. J. Autom. Comput. **16**, 511–533 (2019)

7. Johnson, T., et al.: Implementation of a perceptual controller for an inverted pendulum robot. J. Intell. Rob. Syst. **99**, 683–692 (2020)

8. Esmaeili, N., Alfi, A., Khosravi, H.: Balancing and trajectory tracking of two-wheeled mobile robot using backstepping sliding mode control: design and experiments. J. Intell. Rob. Syst. **87**, 601–613 (2017)

9. Cao, H., Lu, B., Liu, H., Liu, R., Guo, X.: Modeling and MPC-based balance control for a wheeled bipedal robot. In: 41st Chinese Control Conference (CCC), pp. 420–425. IEEE, Hefei (2022)

10. Huang, J., Ri, M., Wu, D., Ri, S.: Interval type-2 fuzzy logic modeling and control of a mobile two-wheeled inverted pendulum. IEEE Trans. Fuzzy Syst. **26**(4), 2030–2038 (2018)

11. Xu, J.-X., Guo, Z.-Q., Lee, T.H.: Design and implementation of integral sliding-mode control on an underactuated two-wheeled mobile robot. IEEE Trans. Ind. Electron. **61**(7), 3671–3681 (2013)

12. Zhou, H., et al.: Control of the two-wheeled inverted pendulum (TWIP) robot moving on the continuous uneven ground. In: International Conference on Robotics and Biomimetics (ROBIO), pp. 1588–1594. IEEE, Dali (2019)

13. Welch, G., Bishop, G.: An introduction to the kalman filter. In: 28th International Conference on Computer Graphics and Interactive Techniques (SIGGRAPH), Course 8, pp. 27599–23175. Association for Computing Machinery, Los Angeles (2001)

14. Liu, J.: Sliding Mode Control and Matlab Simulation: The Design Method of Advanced Control System, 4th edn., pp. 172–173. Tsinghua University Press, Beijing (2021)

15. Wan, E.A., Van Der Merwe, R.: The unscented kalman filter for nonlinear estimation. In: IEEE Adaptive Systems for Signal Processing. Communications, and Control Symposium (AS-SPCC), pp. 153–158. IEEE, Lake Louise (2000)

16. Julier, S.J.: The scaled unscented transformation. In: American Control Conference (ACC), pp. 4555–4559. IEEE, Anchorage (2002)

17. Xu, J., Guo, Z., Lee, T.: Synthesized design of a fuzzy logic controller for an underactuated unicycle. Fuzzy Sets Syst. **207**, 77–93 (2012)

Nonsmooth Dynamic Modeling of a Humanoid Robot with Parallel Mechanisms

Jiaming Xiong[1,2], Dingkun Liang[1,2], Xin Wang[1,2(✉)], Yongshan Huang[1,2], Anhuan Xie[1,2], and Jason Gu[3]

[1] Research Center for Intelligent Robotics, Research Institute of Interdisciplinary Innovation, Zhejiang Lab, Hangzhou 311100, China
{xiongjm,liangdk,xin.wang,huangys,xieanhuan}@zhejianglab.com
[2] Zhejiang Engineering Research Center for Intelligent Robotics, Hangzhou 311100, China
[3] Department of Electrical and Computer Engineering, Dalhousie University, Halifax, NS B3H 4R2, Canada
jason.gu@dal.ca

Abstract. This paper establishes a nonsmooth dynamic model for a humanoid robot with parallel mechanisms. Firstly, the constraint equations of the parallel mechanism are derived through kinematic analysis. By combining the links involved in closed-loop constraints into aggregate nodes, the topology of the robot can be equivalent to a tree structure. Equivalent physical quantities for the aggregate nodes are defined to unify their treatment with individual nodes during dynamic modeling. Subsequently, the contact and impact dynamics of the robot are modeled using constraint-based methods, with a frictional multiple impacts model employed for impacts. Due to the high degree of freedom of the robot, recursive methods are adopted to calculate the corresponding dynamic matrices. Finally, numerical examples are provided to illustrate the dynamic model of the robot. A comparison with the compliance-based methods of Simscape Multibody demonstrates that our dynamic model can reflect more realistic physical processes, providing a more accurate simulation environment for the motion control of the robot. The simulation of standing balance control is also performed based on our dynamic model.

Keywords: Humanoid robot · Nonsmooth dynamics model · Constraint-based methods · Simulation

1 Introduction

A humanoid robot is a robot designed to resemble the human body, enabling it to interact with tools and environments intended for humans. The concept of humanoid robots can be traced back to the late 15th century, marked by Leonardo da Vinci's initial sketch [1]. However, systematic research and development of humanoid robots have gained prominence only in recent decades. Notably, the first real-world humanoid robot,

Supported by Key Research Project of Zhejiang Lab (No. G2021NB0AL03) and Zhejiang Provincial Natural Science Foundation of China under Grant No. LQ23F030010.

H. Yang et al. (Eds.): ICIRA 2023, LNAI 14270, pp. 294–308, 2023.
https://doi.org/10.1007/978-981-99-6492-5_26

WABOT-1, was developed by researchers from Waseda University in 1973 [2]. The field of humanoid robots encompasses various disciplines, with dynamics and control playing a crucial role in ensuring the robot's stable movements. A comprehensive overview of research in these areas can be found in [3–5], which provides relevant papers along with insightful comments.

From a dynamics perspective, humanoid robots are typical multibody systems with degrees of freedom that can exceed 30. This poses significant challenges for dynamic modeling. As a result, simplified dynamic models are widely employed in the literature, such as the linear inverted pendulum model and COM-ZMP model [6]. These models are used for generating walking patterns and designing walking stabilizers for robots [7]. However, they deviate significantly from the robot's actual motion, especially for high-dynamic behaviors such as fast walking or running. Consequently, their applicability is limited in such scenarios.

Some researchers also established the robot's complete dynamic model using open-source dynamics libraries, such as RBDL and Pinocchio [8,9]. These libraries employ recursive algorithms [10], including Articulated-Body Algorithm, Composite-Rigid-Body Algorithm and Newton-Euler Inverse Dynamics Algorithm, to efficiently solve the robot's dynamics. However, they typically rely on URDF files to acquire the robot's configuration description, which poses difficulties in directly applying them to robots with parallel mechanisms. The recursive solution of dynamics for parallel mechanisms remains a challenging problem.

Modeling the foot-ground interaction of the robot presents its own set of challenges due to the presence of nonsmooth factors, including contact separation transitions under unilateral constraints, transitions between sticking and sliding caused by friction effects, and abrupt state changes resulting from impacts. Generally, there are two approaches to express contact interface interactions: compliance-based methods and constraint-based methods [11]. In compliance-based methods, contact forces are represented as functions of local deformations within the contact region using contact constitutive relations. The mathematical structure of the dynamic equation remains unchanged under non-contact and contact states, and thus these methods are widely applied in dynamic simulation software such as Simscape Multibody. However, they often assume zero friction coefficients when the relative velocity is zero, which contradicts physical laws. Additionally, when computing impacts between rigid bodies, the dynamic differential equations can exhibit stiffness issues, requiring a reduction in integration step to ensure computational stability. Constraint-based methods can address the aforementioned problems, but they involve complex modeling processes due to the structural changes in dynamic equations. Moreover, when solving for contact forces using constraint equations, singularities may arise, such as hyperstatic problems and Painlevé paradox [12].

This paper utilizes constraint-based methods to develop an accurate nonsmooth dynamic model for a humanoid robot with parallel mechanisms. The main contributions of the paper are as follows: (1) We creatively combine nonsmooth dynamic modeling methods with numerical recursive algorithms of dynamic matrices, which requires transforming the robot's topology into an equivalent tree structure by aggregating the links involved in closed-loop constraints into aggregate nodes. (2) We solve the contact dynamics by using linear complementarity conditions [11], and employ the multiple

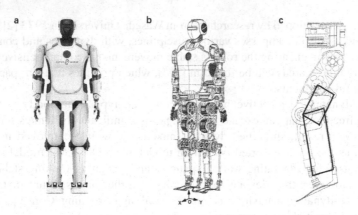

Fig. 1. Schematic diagrams of the humanoid robot: a. the appearance; b. the CAD model; c. parallel mechanisms

impacts model proposed by Liu et al. [13, 14] to transform the impact dynamics from second-order differential equations to a first-order impulse level, facilitating efficient solution. (3) We provide numerical examples to demonstrate the effectiveness of the dynamics model, specifically exhibiting simulation results of the robot's standing balance control.

The rest of this paper is organized as follows. Section 2 provides a description of the robot's model and addresses the kinematics of the parallel mechanisms. Section 3 establishes a nonsmooth dynamic model for the robot. In Sect. 4, numerical examples are presented. Finally, Sect. 5 concludes our study.

2   Robot Model and Kinematics Analysis

In this section, we begin with a detailed description of the configuration of the humanoid robot, and then analyze the kinematics of the parallel mechanisms contained in the two legs. To deal with the dynamic modeling of these parallel mechanisms, we introduce a set of equivalent physical quantities, which allows us to treat the robot as an equivalent tree structure.

2.1   Configuration Description

As shown in Figs. 1a-b, the humanoid robot consists of 39 rigid bodies: the base link, the left (right) hip yaw link, the left (right) hip roll link, the left (right) hip pitch link, the left (right) knee pitch link, the left (right) ankle pitch link, the left (right) ankle roll link, the left (right) knee motor, the left (right) knee rod, the left (right) ankle outer motor, the left (right) ankle inner motor, the left (right) ankle outer rod, the left (right) ankle inner rod, the left (right) shoulder pitch link, the left (right) shoulder roll link, the left (right) shoulder yaw link, the left (right) elbow pitch link, the left (right) wrist yaw link, the left (right) wrist roll link, the neck yaw link and the neck pitch link.

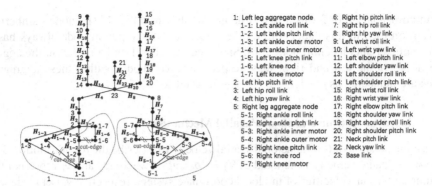

The following labels appear in the figure:

1: Left leg aggregate node
1-1: Left ankle roll link
1-2: Left ankle pitch link
1-3: Left ankle outer motor
1-4: Left ankle inner motor
1-5: Left knee pitch link
1-6: Left knee rod
1-7: Left knee motor
2: Left hip pitch link
3: Left hip roll link
4: Left hip yaw link
5: Right leg aggregate node
5-1: Right ankle roll link
5-2: Right ankle pitch link
5-3: Right ankle inner motor
5-4: Right ankle outer motor
5-5: Right knee pitch link
5-6: Right knee rod
5-7: Right knee motor

6: Right hip pitch link
7: Right hip roll link
8: Right hip yaw link
9: Left wrist roll link
10: Left wrist yaw link
11: Left elbow pitch link
12: Left shoulder yaw link
13: Left shoulder roll link
14: Left shoulder pitch link
15: Right wrist roll link
16: Right wrist yaw link
17: Right elbow pitch link
18: Right shoulder yaw link
19: Right shoulder roll link
20: Right shoulder pitch link
21: Neck pitch link
22: Neck yaw link
23: Base link

Fig. 2. Topology of the humanoid robot

The robot kinematics in this study employ the following coordinate systems: the world coordinate system $\mathscr{F}_w = \{O; XYZ\}$ and local coordinate systems for each link. These coordinate systems are defined based on the initial state of the humanoid robot, where its legs and arms are hanging vertically down, and its feet are parallel to the horizontal ground. The origin O of $\mathscr{F}_w$ is positioned on the horizontal ground, with X and Z axes pointing forward and upward, respectively, while the Y axis is determined by the right-hand rule. The local coordinate systems for each link are established parallel to $\mathscr{F}_w$. The base link's origin is set as the midpoint between the intersection points of the left hip yaw and hip roll joint axes, as well as the right hip yaw and hip roll joint axes. The origins of other links are situated along the joint axes connected to their parent links. In principle, the origin can be selected arbitrarily along the joint axis.

From a robot topology perspective, each link can be regarded as a node, with the base link acting as the root node from which the two legs, two arms, and head branch out. The arms and head have open-loop structures, while each leg incorporates closed-loop structures. This is due to the presence of a four-bar linkage used for knee pitch transmission and two four-bar linkages used for ankle pitch and ankle roll transmissions. In Fig. 1c, it can be observed that the four-bar linkage for the knee joint remains in the same plane throughout the robot's motion, forming a parallelogram shape. Consequently, the corresponding constraint relationships are relatively straightforward. The four-bar linkages for the ankle joints also form parallelograms when the ankle roll angle is zero. However, if this angle deviates from zero, they will no longer be confined to the same plane but instead form spatial quadrilaterals, resulting in more complex constraint equations. Considering that the ankle outer and inner rods have significantly smaller masses compared to other links, they can be neglected in the dynamic modeling, and only the corresponding constraints, specifically the constant length of the linkages, need to be retained.

According to recursive algorithms for handling closed-loop structures [10], after equivalent processing of physical quantities such as spatial inertia (see Sect. 2.3 for details), the knee pitch link, ankle pitch link, ankle roll link, knee motor, knee rod, ankle outer motor and ankle inner motor in each leg can be combined into an aggregate node, while the corresponding constraints are cut off. In this way, the overall topology of the humanoid robot forms a tree structure, as shown in Fig. 2. The node numbering convention used in this paper follows the principle that the parent node always has a larger number than its child node [10]. Specifically, nodes 1 and 5 represent the aggregate nodes in the left and right legs, respectively. The nodes within these aggregate nodes are numbered as $k-1, k-2, \cdots, k-7$, where $k = 1, 5$.

2.2   Closed-Loop Constraints of Parallel Mechanisms

We use the notation of 6-dimensional spatial velocity to describe the robot's motion. For node k, its spatial velocity is denoted as $V_k = [\omega_k^T, v_k^T]^T$, where ω_k and v_k represent the angular and linear velocities of the local coordinate system, respectively. Let us denote the rotation angle of node k with respect to its parent node $\varphi(k)$ as θ_k, and we have the following kinematic relationship:

$$V_k = \phi_{\varphi(k),k}^T V_{\varphi(k)} + H_k^T \dot{\theta}_k, \tag{1}$$

where $H_k \in \mathbb{R}^{1 \times 6}$ is the hinge map matrix that maps θ_k to the relative spatial velocity between nodes k and $\varphi(k)$, $\phi_{\varphi(k),k} \in \mathbb{R}^{6 \times 6}$ is the rigid body transformation matrix defined as follows:

$$\phi_{\varphi(k),k} = \begin{bmatrix} I_3 & \hat{l}_{\varphi(k),k} \\ 0_{3 \times 3} & I_3 \end{bmatrix}, \tag{2}$$

where I_3 represents the 3×3 identity matrix, $0_{3 \times 3}$ denotes a 3×3 zero matrix, $l_{\varphi(k),k} \in \mathbb{R}^3$ represents the position vector from the origin of the local coordinate system of node $\varphi(k)$ to that of node k, and $\hat{}: \mathbb{R}^3 \to \mathfrak{so}(3)$ denotes the hat map, which maps a 3-dimensional vector to the corresponding skew-symmetric matrix in the special orthogonal Lie algebra $\mathfrak{so}(3)$.

For the knee joint transmission, as it always forms a planar quadrilateral, the geometric constraints can be simply expressed as $\theta_{k-5} = \theta_{k-7}, \theta_{k-6} = -\theta_{k-7} (k = 1, 5)$. For the ankle joint transmissions, based on the condition that the lengths of the ankle rods are constant, we can obtain geometric constraint equations for both two legs: $g_{k,i}(\theta_{k-1}, \theta_{k-2}, \theta_{k-3}, \theta_{k-4}) = 0 (k = 1, 5, i = 1, 2)$. The expressions of $g_{k,i}$ are highly nonlinear and complex, and thus they do not have analytical solutions for the forward kinematics problem. However, through differentiation, we can derive linear relationships between $\dot{\theta}_{k-1}, \dot{\theta}_{k-2}$ and $\dot{\theta}_{k-3}, \dot{\theta}_{k-4}$. By combining the differential forms of the knee and ankle joint transmissions, we have the following velocity relationships:

$$\dot{q}_k = X_k \dot{\theta}_k, \quad k = 1, 5, \tag{3}$$

where $q_k = [\theta_{k-1}, \theta_{k-2}, \cdots, \theta_{k-7}]^T$ and $\theta_k = [\theta_{k-3}, \theta_{k-4}, \theta_{k-7}]^T$ represent the rotation angles and independent rotation angles of aggregate node k, respectively, and the coefficient matrix $X_k \in \mathbb{R}^{7 \times 3}$ is the function of q_k.

Therefore, the configuration space of the humanoid robot is 32-dimensional, whose coordinates are selected as $q = [q_j^T, \theta_{23}^T]^T$, where $q_j = [\theta_1^T, \theta_2, \theta_3, \theta_4, \theta_5^T, \theta_6, \cdots, \theta_{22}]^T$ represents the independent joint angles of the robot, $\theta_{23} = [\gamma_1, \gamma_2, \gamma_3, x, y, z]^T$ is a set of coordinates for the floating base link, with $\gamma = [\gamma_1, \gamma_2, \gamma_3]^T$ representing three Euler angles that define the orientation of the local coordinate system relative to the world coordinate system $\mathscr{F}_w$ in a 3-1-2 sequence, and (x, y, z) denoting the coordinates of the origin of the local coordinate system in $\mathscr{F}_w$. Accordingly, the velocity of the robot is defined as $v = [\dot{q}_j^\mathrm{T}, V_{23}^\mathrm{T}]^\mathrm{T}$.

2.3 Equivalent Physical Quantities of Aggregated Nodes

Corresponding to the spatial velocity description, the spatial inertia of node k is defined as follows:

$$M_k = \begin{bmatrix} J_k & m_k \hat{p}_k \\ -m_k \hat{p}_k & m_k I_3 \end{bmatrix} \in \mathbb{R}^{6\times6}, \tag{4}$$

where m_k, $p_k \in \mathbb{R}^3$ and $J_k \in \mathbb{R}^{3\times3}$ represent the mass, the position vector of the center of mass (COM) in the local coordinate system, and the inertia tensor with respect to the local coordinate system, respectively. The spatial acceleration $\alpha_k \in \mathbb{R}^6$ is defined as the time derivative of V_k in the local coordinate system. Based on Eq. (1), we have the following equation: $\alpha_k = \phi_{\varphi(k),k}^\mathrm{T} \alpha_{\varphi(k)} + H_k^\mathrm{T} \ddot{\theta}_k + a_k$, where $a_k \in \mathbb{R}^6$ is the Coriolis spatial acceleration, and for a rotary pin hinge, its expression is given by $a_k = [(\hat{\omega}_k \triangle \omega_k)^\mathrm{T}, (\hat{v}_k \triangle \omega_k)^\mathrm{T}]^\mathrm{T}$, where $\triangle \omega_k = \omega_k - \omega_{\varphi(k)}$. In addition, the gyroscopic force vector $b_k \in \mathbb{R}^6$ is defined as $b_k = \bar{V}_k M_k V_k$, where

$$\bar{V}_k = \begin{bmatrix} \hat{\omega}_k & \hat{v}_k \\ 0_{3\times3} & \hat{\omega}_k \end{bmatrix} \in \mathbb{R}^{6\times6}.$$

For the two aggregated nodes in two legs, we need to define equivalent physical quantities so that they can be uniformly processed with other individual nodes in dynamic modeling. The equivalent spatial inertia, spatial acceleration and gyroscopic force vector are defined as $M_k = \mathrm{diag}(M_{k-1}, M_{k-2}, \cdots, M_{k-7}) \in \mathbb{R}^{42\times42}$, $\alpha_k = [\alpha_{k-1}^\mathrm{T}, \alpha_{k-2}^\mathrm{T}, \cdots, \alpha_{k-7}^\mathrm{T}]^\mathrm{T} \in \mathbb{R}^{42}$, $b_k = [b_{k-1}^\mathrm{T}, b_{k-2}^\mathrm{T}, \cdots, b_{k-7}^\mathrm{T}]^\mathrm{T} \in \mathbb{R}^{42}$, respectively, where $k = 1, 5$. The definition of the equivalent rigid body transformation matrices $\phi_{2,1} \in \mathbb{R}^{6\times42}$ for the connection between nodes 2 and 1, and $\phi_{6,5} \in \mathbb{R}^{6\times42}$ for the connection between nodes 6 and 5, are as follows: $\phi_{\varphi(k),k} = E_k A_k (k = 1, 5)$, where $\varphi(1) = 2$, $\varphi(5) = 6$, $E_k = [0_{6\times6}, 0_{6\times6}, 0_{6\times6}, 0_{6\times6}, \phi_{\varphi(k),k-5}, 0_{6\times6}, \phi_{\varphi(k),k-7}] \in \mathbb{R}^{6\times42}$, and

$$A_k = \begin{bmatrix} I_6 & 0_{6\times6} & 0_{6\times6} & 0_{6\times6} & 0_{6\times6} & 0_{6\times6} & 0_{6\times6} \\ \phi_{k-2,k-1} & I_6 & 0_{6\times6} & 0_{6\times6} & 0_{6\times6} & 0_{6\times6} & 0_{6\times6} \\ 0_{6\times6} & 0_{6\times6} & I_6 & 0_{6\times6} & 0_{6\times6} & 0_{6\times6} & 0_{6\times6} \\ 0_{6\times6} & 0_{6\times6} & 0_{6\times6} & I_6 & 0_{6\times6} & 0_{6\times6} & 0_{6\times6} \\ \phi_{k-5,k-2} & \phi_{k-2,k-1} & \phi_{k-5,k-2} & \phi_{k-5,k-3} & \phi_{k-5,k-4} & I_6 & 0_{6\times6} & 0_{6\times6} \\ 0_{6\times6} & 0_{6\times6} & 0_{6\times6} & 0_{6\times6} & 0_{6\times6} & I_6 & 0_{6\times6} \\ 0_{6\times6} & 0_{6\times6} & 0_{6\times6} & 0_{6\times6} & 0_{6\times6} & \phi_{k-7,k-6} & I_6 \end{bmatrix} \in \mathbb{R}^{42\times42}.$$

The equivalent hinge map matrices for the two aggregated nodes are defined as $H_k = X_k^\mathrm{T} \underline{H}_k A_k \in \mathbb{R}^{3\times42} (k = 1, 5)$, where $\underline{H}_k = \mathrm{diag}(H_{k-1}, H_{k-2}, \cdots, H_{k-7})$. Finally, the definition of the equivalent Coriolis space acceleration is as follows: $a_k = \underline{a}_k + A_k^\mathrm{T} \underline{H}_k^\mathrm{T} \dot{X}_k \dot{\theta}_k \in \mathbb{R}^{42} (k = 1, 5)$, where $\underline{a}_k = A_k^\mathrm{T} a_k'$ and $a_k' = [a_{k-1}^\mathrm{T}, a_{k-2}^\mathrm{T}, \cdots, a_{k-7}^\mathrm{T}]^\mathrm{T}$.

3   Nonsmooth Dynamic Modeling

In this section, we establish a nonsmooth dynamic model for the humanoid robot. Considering the high degree of freedom of the robot, we first provide recursive algorithms for solving the dynamic matrices included in the dynamic equation. Then, we deal with the contact dynamics and impact dynamics sequentially.

3.1   Dynamic Equation and Recursive Algorithms

In this paper, we model foot-ground contact by considering four contact points on each foot, which are positioned at the four vertices of a rectangle. This results in a total of 8 possible contact points, denoted as $c_1, c_2, \cdots, c_8$. In the local coordinate system of node $1-1$ (node $5-1$), the coordinates of $c_1(c_5)$, $c_2(c_6)$, $c_3(c_7)$ and $c_4(c_8)$ are (x_{f1}, y_f, z_f), $(x_{f1}, -y_f, z_f)$, (x_{f2}, y_f, z_f), $(x_{f2}, -y_f, z_f)$, respectively, where $x_{f1} > 0, x_{f2} < 0, y_f > 0, z_f < 0$ are four contact parameters. The spatial velocity $\boldsymbol{V}_{c_i} = [\boldsymbol{\omega}_{c_i}^T, \boldsymbol{v}_{c_i}^T]^T$ of c_i can be obtained through a forward kinematic recursive relationship starting from the base link. We decompose the velocity of the contact points into two parts: $\boldsymbol{v}_{c_i} = [\boldsymbol{v}_{\tau c_i}^T, \dot{\delta}_{c_i}]^T$, where $\boldsymbol{v}_{\tau c_i}$ and $\dot{\delta}_{c_i}$ represent the tangential and normal velocities, respectively. Let $\dot{\boldsymbol{\delta}}_c = [\dot{\delta}_{c_1}, \dot{\delta}_{c_2}, \cdots, \dot{\delta}_{c_8}]^T$, $\boldsymbol{v}_c^\tau = [\boldsymbol{v}_{\tau c_1}^T, \boldsymbol{v}_{\tau c_2}^T, \cdots, \boldsymbol{v}_{\tau c_8}^T]^T$, and we can obtain the equations: $\dot{\boldsymbol{\delta}}_c = \boldsymbol{W}^T(\boldsymbol{q})\boldsymbol{v}$, $\boldsymbol{v}_c^\tau = \boldsymbol{N}^T(\boldsymbol{q})\boldsymbol{v}$, where $\boldsymbol{W} \in \mathbb{R}^{32 \times 8}, \boldsymbol{N} \in \mathbb{R}^{32 \times 16}$. Taking time derivatives of them, and letting $\boldsymbol{S}^n = \dot{\boldsymbol{W}}^T \boldsymbol{v}$, $\boldsymbol{S}^\tau = \dot{\boldsymbol{N}}^T \boldsymbol{v}$, we have

$$\ddot{\boldsymbol{\delta}}_c = \boldsymbol{W}^T(\boldsymbol{q})\dot{\boldsymbol{v}} + \boldsymbol{S}^n, \quad \dot{\boldsymbol{v}}_c^\tau = \boldsymbol{N}^T(\boldsymbol{q})\dot{\boldsymbol{v}} + \boldsymbol{S}^\tau. \tag{5}$$

Based on the above notations, the dynamic equation of the robot can be written as follows:

$$\boldsymbol{M}(\boldsymbol{q})\dot{\boldsymbol{v}} + \boldsymbol{C}(\boldsymbol{q}, \boldsymbol{v}) = \boldsymbol{W}(\boldsymbol{q})\boldsymbol{F}^n + \boldsymbol{N}(\boldsymbol{q})\boldsymbol{F}^\tau + \boldsymbol{B}\boldsymbol{u}, \tag{6}$$

where $\boldsymbol{M} \in \mathbb{R}^{32 \times 32}$ is the mass matrix of the robot system, $\boldsymbol{C} \in \mathbb{R}^{32}$ represents the Coriolis and gravitational force term, $\boldsymbol{B} = [\boldsymbol{I}_{26}, \boldsymbol{0}_{26 \times 6}]^T \in \mathbb{R}^{32 \times 26}$ is the joint selection matrix, $\boldsymbol{u} \in \mathbb{R}^{26}$ is the vector of joint torques, $\boldsymbol{F}^n = [f_{nc_1}, f_{nc_2}, \cdots, f_{nc_8}]^T$, $\boldsymbol{F}^\tau = [\boldsymbol{f}_{\tau c_1}^T, \boldsymbol{f}_{\tau c_2}^T, \cdots, \boldsymbol{f}_{\tau c_8}^T]^T$, and where f_{nc_i} and $\boldsymbol{f}_{\tau c_i}$ are the normal and tangential contact forces of c_i, respectively.

As shown in Algorithm 1 and Algorithm 2, we utilize the recursive Composite-Rigid-Body Algorithm and Newton-Euler Inverse Dynamics Algorithm to compute $\boldsymbol{M}$ and $\boldsymbol{C}$, respectively. Due to the presence of aggregate nodes and the floating root node, the degrees of freedom differ for each node. Therefore, the assignments of $\boldsymbol{M}$ and $\boldsymbol{C}$ in these algorithms should be understood as block matrices. Among them, $\boldsymbol{M}$ is divided into a block matrix of size 23×23, with the dimensions of the diagonal blocks as follows: the $(1,1)$ and $(5,5)$ blocks are 3×3 matrices; the $(23,23)$ block is a 6×6 matrix; and for $k \neq 1, 5, 23$, the (k,k) block is a 1×1 matrix. The blocking of $\boldsymbol{C}$ is consistent with that of $\boldsymbol{M}$. Additionally, we explain some symbols in the algorithms: (1) For node k, $\mathscr{C}(k)$ represents the set of all its child nodes, where $\mathscr{C}(2) = 1$ and $\mathscr{C}(6) = 5$. (2) For the root node, $\dot{\theta}_{23}$ means $\boldsymbol{V}_{23}$ (rather than the time derivative of $\boldsymbol{\theta}_{23}$), and $\boldsymbol{H}_{23} = \boldsymbol{I}_6$. (3) The term $\boldsymbol{M}_k \boldsymbol{g}_k$ represents the gravity term, where for an individual node $k \neq 1, 5$, we have $\boldsymbol{g}_k = \boldsymbol{g} = [0, 0, 0, 0, 0, -9.81\text{m/s}^2]^T$. However, for the two aggregate nodes, we have $\boldsymbol{g}_k = [\boldsymbol{g}^T, \boldsymbol{g}^T, \cdots, \boldsymbol{g}^T]^T \in \mathbb{R}^{42}$ $(k = 1, 5)$.

Algorithm 1. Recursive computation of mass matrix

for all nodes k (tips-to-base gather) **do**

  $R_k = \sum_{\forall j \in \mathscr{C}(k)} \phi_{k,j} R_j \phi_{k,j}^{\mathrm{T}} + M_k$

  $j = k, \quad X_k = R_k H_k^{\mathrm{T}}, \quad M(k,k) = H_k X_k$

  while $j < 23$ **do**

    $l = \varphi(j)$

    $X_l = \phi_{l,j} X_j$

    $M(l,k) = M^{\mathrm{T}}(k,l) = H_l X_l$

    $j = l$

  end while

end for

Algorithm 2. Recursive computation of Coriolis and gravitational force term

$V_{\varphi(23)} = 0, \quad \alpha_{\varphi(23)} = 0$

for all nodes k (base-to-tips scatter) **do**

  $V_k = \phi_{\varphi(k),k}^{\mathrm{T}} V_{\varphi(k)} + H_k^{\mathrm{T}} \dot{\theta}_k$

  $\alpha_k = \phi_{\varphi(k),k}^{\mathrm{T}} \alpha_{\varphi(k)} + a_k$

end for

for all nodes k (tips-to-base gather) **do**

  $f_k = \sum_{\forall j \in \mathscr{C}(k)} \phi_{k,j} f_j + M_k \alpha_k + b_k - M_k g_k$

  $C(k) = H_k f_k$

end for

3.2 Contact Dynamics

To solve Eq. (6), the contact forces F^n and F^τ should be determined. We utilize the linear complementarity conditions to detect the contact state and calculate the normal contact force at each possible contact point [11]. At the displacement and velocity levels, these conditions can be written as follows:

$$\begin{cases} \delta_{c_i} f_{nc_i} = 0, & \delta_{c_i} \geq 0, \quad f_{nc_i} \geq 0, \\ \dot{\delta}_{c_i} f_{nc_i} = 0, & \dot{\delta}_{c_i} \geq 0, \quad f_{nc_i} \geq 0, \end{cases} \quad i = 1, \cdots, 8. \tag{7}$$

When $\delta_{c_i} > 0$ or $\delta_{c_i} = 0$ together with $\dot{\delta}_{c_i} > 0$, we know from Eq. 7 that $f_{nc_i} = 0$, corresponding to a free state. When $\delta_{c_i} = 0$ and $\dot{\delta}_{c_i} < 0$, c_i is in an impact state, which will be discussed in Sect. 3.3. The contact at point c_i is established only when both conditions $\delta_{c_i} = 0$ and $\dot{\delta}_{c_i} = 0$ are satisfied simultaneously. In this case, f_{nc_i} should be determined according to the linear complementary at the acceleration level:

$$\ddot{\delta}_{c_i} f_{nc_i} = 0, \quad \ddot{\delta}_{c_i} \geq 0, \quad f_{nc_i} \geq 0, \quad i = 1, \cdots, 8. \tag{8}$$

On the other hand, we use the Coulomb friction law to determine tangential contact forces [15]:

$$
\begin{cases}
\boldsymbol{f}_{\tau c_i} = -\mu_d f_{nc_i} \dfrac{\boldsymbol{v}_{\tau c_i}}{\|\boldsymbol{v}_{\tau c_i}\|}, & \text{if } \boldsymbol{v}_{\tau c_i} \neq \boldsymbol{0}, \\[2mm]
\boldsymbol{f}_{\tau c_i} = -\mu_s f_{nc_i} \dfrac{\dot{\boldsymbol{v}}_{\tau c_i}}{\|\dot{\boldsymbol{v}}_{\tau c_i}\|}, & \text{if } \boldsymbol{v}_{\tau c_i} = \boldsymbol{0}, \dot{\boldsymbol{v}}_{\tau c_i} \neq \boldsymbol{0}, \quad i = 1, \cdots, 8, \\[2mm]
\|\boldsymbol{f}_{\tau c_i}\| \leq \mu_s f_{nc_i}, & \text{if } \boldsymbol{v}_{\tau c_i} = \boldsymbol{0}, \dot{\boldsymbol{v}}_{\tau c_i} = \boldsymbol{0},
\end{cases}
\tag{9}
$$

where μ_d and μ_s are the slip and stick friction coefficients. Combining the dynamic Eq. (6) with Eqs. (5), (8) and (9), we can solve the contact forces f_{nc_i} and $\boldsymbol{f}_{\tau c_i}$ under the constraint conditions $\ddot{\delta}_{c_i} = 0$ or $\dot{\boldsymbol{v}}_{\tau c_i} = \boldsymbol{0}$.

However, singularities can arise when multiple potential contact pairs close simultaneously, leading to a mismatch between the number of independent constraints and the equilibrium equations derived from fundamental mechanics principles. Additionally, when the system is in contact, ignoring small-scale deformations on the contact interface can result in normal singularity. Furthermore, the discontinuity of Coulomb friction makes it challenging to determine the static friction force when the tangential velocity at the contact point is zero. This issue is particularly pronounced when multiple closed contact pairs have zero tangential velocities, as the lack of tangential compliance in Coulomb's friction law can lead to tangential singularities.

Noting that the position vectors $\boldsymbol{r}_{c_i}$ $(i = 1, \cdots, 8)$ of c_i in the world coordinate system $\mathscr{F}_w$ always satisfy the relationships: $\boldsymbol{r}_{c_1} + \boldsymbol{r}_{c_4} = \boldsymbol{r}_{c_2} + \boldsymbol{r}_{c_3}$ and $\boldsymbol{r}_{c_5} + \boldsymbol{r}_{c_8} = \boldsymbol{r}_{c_6} + \boldsymbol{r}_{c_7}$. When all four contact points of a foot are in contact with the ground, solving the normal contact forces f_{nc_i} $(i = 1, 2, 3, 4$ or $i = 5, 6, 7, 8)$ using the constraint equations $\ddot{\delta}_{c_i} = 0$ $(i = 1, 2, 3, 4$ or $i = 5, 6, 7, 8)$ results in only three independent equations, forming a hyperstatic problem. It is necessary to introduce small-scale normal displacements on the contact interface. Additionally, although small displacements exist, the tangential plane of the contact layer is still assumed to be rigid. Based on this, deformation compatibility conditions between small displacements at each contact point are established, which further lead to additional constraint conditions for the normal contact forces. Assuming that the contact parameters are the same for all contact points, the additional constraint conditions are

$$
f_{nc_1} + f_{nc_4} = f_{nc_2} + f_{nc_3}, \quad f_{nc_5} + f_{nc_8} = f_{nc_6} + f_{nc_7}.
\tag{10}
$$

On the other hand, we denote the horizontal position vector of c_i as $\boldsymbol{r}_{\tau c_i}$, i.e., $\boldsymbol{r}_{c_i} = [\boldsymbol{r}_{\tau c_i}^{\mathrm{T}}, \delta_{c_i}]^{\mathrm{T}}$. When two contact points c_k and c_l on the same foot are simultaneously in tangential sticking state, it can be proven that the following relationship holds: $(\dot{\boldsymbol{v}}_{\tau c_k} - \dot{\boldsymbol{v}}_{\tau c_l}) \cdot (\boldsymbol{r}_{\tau c_k} - \boldsymbol{r}_{\tau c_l}) = 0$. This means that the tangential constraint equations $\dot{\boldsymbol{v}}_{\tau c_k} = \boldsymbol{0}$ and $\dot{\boldsymbol{v}}_{\tau c_l} = \boldsymbol{0}$ are not independent, and an additional constraint condition need to be added:

$$
(\boldsymbol{f}_{\tau c_k} - \boldsymbol{f}_{\tau c_l}) \cdot (\boldsymbol{r}_{\tau c_k} - \boldsymbol{r}_{\tau c_l}) = 0.
\tag{11}
$$

If there are more than two contact points on the same foot simultaneously in tangential sticking state, Eq. (11) need to be added pairwise as additional conditions.

3.3 Impact Dynamics

In this section, we utilize the multiple impacts model proposed by Liu et al. [13, 14] to handle the foot-ground impact problem, where the frictional effect is also considered.

Based on the characteristics of extremely short duration and significant impulsive forces observed in rigid body collisions, the following two assumptions are introduced: (1) the robot's configuration during impact is invariant; (2) the non-impulsive forces during impact can be neglected. Therefore, multiplying both sides of Eq. (6) by the infinitesimal time element dt, we obtain the dynamic equation at the impulsive level:

$$M(q)dv = W(q)dP^n + N(q)dP^{\tau}, \tag{12}$$

where $dP^{\tau} = F^{\tau}dt$ and $dP^n = F^n dt$ represent the tangential and normal infinitesimal impulses, respectively. Similarly, multiplying both sides of Eq. (5) by dt yields the following equations:

$$d\dot{\delta}_c = W^T(q)dv, \quad dv_c^{\tau} = N^T(q)dv. \tag{13}$$

Obtaining the distribution of infinitesimal impulse at different impact points is crucial for solving Eq. (12). According to the multiple impacts model proposed in [13], the distribution of normal infinitesimal impulse is related to the potential energy E_{c_i} at different impact points c_i, whose infinitesimal variation can be calculated as $dE_{c_i} = -f_{nc_i}d\delta_{c_i} = -f_{nc_i}\dot{\delta}_{c_i}dt = -\dot{\delta}_{c_i}dP_{c_i}^n$, where $dP_{c_i}^n = f_{nc_i}dt$. If energy dissipation is taken into account during the impact process, a coefficient of restitution $e_{c_i} \in [0,1]$ should be introduced to represent the different work paths during compression and restitution, and then the variation of E_{c_i} is revised as follows:

$$dE_{c_i} = \begin{cases} -\dot{\delta}_{c_i}dP_{c_i}^n, & \text{if } \dot{\delta}_{c_i} \leq 0, \\ -\dfrac{1}{e_{c_i}^2}\dot{\delta}_{c_i}dP_{c_i}^n, & \text{if } \dot{\delta}_{c_i} > 0. \end{cases} \tag{14}$$

On the other hand, we can utilize the constitutive relationship of the contact point to get a relationship between f_{nc_i} and E_{c_i}. For the constitutive relationship in a power form: $f_{nc_i} = k_i(-\delta_{c_i})^{\eta_i}$, it can be proved that $f_{nc_i} = (\eta_i + 1)^{\eta_i/(\eta_i+1)}k_i^{1/(\eta_i+1)}E_{c_i}^{\eta_i/(\eta_i+1)}$ [11]. Therefore, the ratio of the normal infinitesimal impulses between different impact points can be written as follows:

$$R_{ij}^n = \frac{dP_{c_i}^n}{dP_{c_j}^n} = \frac{f_{nc_i}}{f_{nc_j}} = \frac{(\eta_i+1)^{\frac{\eta_i}{\eta_i+1}}k_i^{\frac{1}{\eta_i+1}}E_{c_i}^{\frac{\eta_i}{\eta_i+1}}}{(\eta_j+1)^{\frac{\eta_j}{\eta_j+1}}k_j^{\frac{1}{\eta_j+1}}E_{c_j}^{\frac{\eta_j}{\eta_j+1}}}. \tag{15}$$

We always choose the impact point c_l with the maximum potential energy as the primary impact point, and define $dP_{c_l}^n$ as the primary differential impulse. Based on Eq. (15), we obtain the normal impulse distribution law: $dP^n = R^n dP_{c_l}^n$, where $R^n = [R_{1l}^n, R_{2l}^n, \cdots, R_{8l}^n]^T$. We note that for the point c_i that is not in the impact state, its potential energy E_{c_i} is always zero, and thus we have $R_{il}^n = 0$ and $dP_{c_i}^n = 0$.

To account for the frictional effect, it is generally assumed that Coulomb's friction law still applies during the impact process. Letting $dP_{c_i}^{\tau} = f_{\tau c_i}dt$, and denoting μ_{id} and μ_{is} as the slip and stick friction coefficients in the impact process, we have the following equations:

$$\begin{cases} \mathrm{d}\boldsymbol{P}_{c_i}^\tau = -\mu_{id}\mathrm{d}P_{c_i}^n \dfrac{\boldsymbol{v}_{\tau c_i}}{\|\boldsymbol{v}_{\tau c_i}\|}, & \text{if } \boldsymbol{v}_{\tau c_i} \neq \boldsymbol{0}, \\[2mm] \mathrm{d}\boldsymbol{P}_{c_i}^\tau = -\mu_{is}\mathrm{d}P_{c_i}^n \dfrac{\dot{\boldsymbol{v}}_{\tau c_i}}{\|\dot{\boldsymbol{v}}_{\tau c_i}\|}, & \text{if } \boldsymbol{v}_{\tau c_i} = \boldsymbol{0},\, \dot{\boldsymbol{v}}_{\tau c_i} \neq \boldsymbol{0}, \quad i = 1,\cdots,8. \\[2mm] \|\mathrm{d}\boldsymbol{P}_{c_i}^\tau\| \leq \mu_{is}\mathrm{d}P_{c_i}^n, & \text{if } \boldsymbol{v}_{\tau c_i} = \boldsymbol{0},\, \dot{\boldsymbol{v}}_{\tau c_i} = \boldsymbol{0}, \end{cases} \quad (16)$$

Therefore, we can derive the tangential impulse distribution law: $\mathrm{d}\boldsymbol{P}^\tau = \boldsymbol{R}^\tau \mathrm{d}P_{c_l}^n$, where for the case $\boldsymbol{v}_{\tau c_i} = \boldsymbol{0}$ and $\dot{\boldsymbol{v}}_{\tau c_i} = \boldsymbol{0}$, $\mathrm{d}\boldsymbol{P}_{c_i}^\tau$ should be determined according to Eqs. (12) and (13) under the constraint $\mathrm{d}\boldsymbol{v}_{\tau c_i} = \boldsymbol{0}$. As a result, we obtain a first-order differential impulse impact model where $\mathrm{d}P_{c_l}^n$ is used as the integration step:

$$\boldsymbol{M}(\boldsymbol{q})\mathrm{d}\boldsymbol{v} = (\boldsymbol{W}(\boldsymbol{q})\boldsymbol{R}^n + \boldsymbol{N}(\boldsymbol{q})\boldsymbol{R}^\tau)\,\mathrm{d}P_{c_l}^n. \quad (17)$$

By selecting the principal impact point, we can achieve a variable-step computational scheme based on physical significance, thereby improving computational speed and stability. The impact process finishes once the potential energy of all impact points has been released, i.e., $E_{c_i} = 0\,(i = 1,\cdots,8)$. As a result, $\boldsymbol{v}$ is updated after each computation, while $\boldsymbol{q}$ and t remain unchanged.

Singularities can also arise in impact dynamics. Since the normal impulse distribution law has resolved the problem of normal singularity in multiple impacts, we only need to consider the tangential singularity caused by multi-point adhesion. When two impact points, c_k and c_l, on the same foot are simultaneously in the state of tangential adhesion, an additional constraint condition need to be added:

$$(\mathrm{d}\boldsymbol{P}_{c_k}^\tau - \mathrm{d}\boldsymbol{P}_{c_l}^\tau) \cdot (\boldsymbol{r}_{\tau c_k} - \boldsymbol{r}_{\tau c_l}) = 0. \quad (18)$$

4   Simulations

In this section, we illustrate the nonsmooth dynamic model of the robot through two numerical examples. The first one considers the fixed base link and studies the contact and impact behavior between the legs and ground under the influence of gravity. The second one presents a simulation of standing balance control for the robot based on the Dynamic Balance Force Control (DBFC) method [16].

The two examples use the same geometric parameters, mass and inertia parameters, and contact parameters for the robot. Due to space limitations, we do not list the parameters of each link in this paper. Without loss of generality, we assume that each contact point has the same material properties, and we use the Hertz contact theory to describe the contact properties on the elastic boundary layer near the contact point, i.e., $\eta_i = 3/2$. As a result, Eq. (15) can be simplified as $R_{ij}^n = (E_{c_i}/E_{c_j})^{3/5}$. In addition, the coefficient of restitution is set as $e_{c_i} = 0$, and the friction coefficients are set as $\mu_d = \mu_{id} = 0.8$ and $\mu_s = \mu_{is} = 0.9$, respectively.

4.1   Dynamic Response Under Gravity with a Fixed Base Link

To fix the base link, we set $\boldsymbol{\theta}_{23} \equiv [0,0,0,0,0,z_0]^\mathrm{T}$ and $\boldsymbol{V}_{23} \equiv \boldsymbol{0}$, where $z_0 = 1\,\mathrm{m}$ is the hight of base link. Additionally, we assume a damping coefficient of $0.5\,\mathrm{N} \cdot \mathrm{m} \cdot \mathrm{s}/\mathrm{rad}$

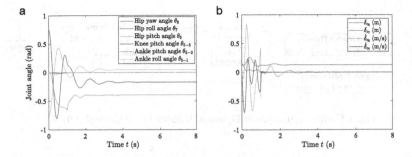

Fig. 3. Simulation results in the case of a fixed base link

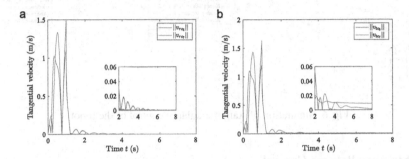

Fig. 4. Tangential velocities of c_5, c_7 in a. our model; b. compliance-based methods of Simscape Multibody

for each joint of the robot. The initial state of the robot is set as $\theta_{1-7}(0) = -0.8\,\text{rad}$, $\theta_2(0) = 0.8\,\text{rad}$, $\theta_{5-7}(0) = 0.8\,\text{rad}$, $\theta_6(0) = -0.8\,\text{rad}$, while all other components of $q(0)$ and $v(0)$ are set to 0. In this initial state, the robot is not in contact with the ground.

We obtain the simulation results using MATLAB. Figure 3a presents the evolution curves of the joint angles of the right leg over time, which quickly converge to constant values under the foot-ground interaction. Figure 3b shows the evolution curves of the normal displacements and velocities for two representative points c_5 and c_7. We can see that δ_{c_7} and δ_{c_5} converge to 0 and a non-zero value, respectively, meaning that c_7 is a contact point, but c_5 is not. We further compare our contact/impact model with the compliance-based methods used in Simscape Multibody of MATLAB, using the same friction coefficients. Figures 4a and 4b present the evolution curves of $\|v_{c_5}\|$ and $\|v_{c_7}\|$ in both models. While the overall trends are similar, tangential velocities in our model quickly tend to 0, whereas in the other model, they deviate from 0 even at the end of the simulation. This discrepancy arises because Simscape Multibody assumes zero friction force when the velocity is zero, which contradicts physical phenomena. In contrast, our model employs constraint-based methods to solve contact forces and can give an accurate prediction of the robot's motion.

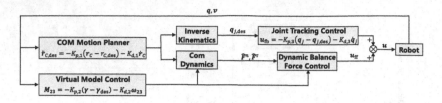

Fig. 5. Control algorithm of Dynamic Balance Force Control (DBFC)

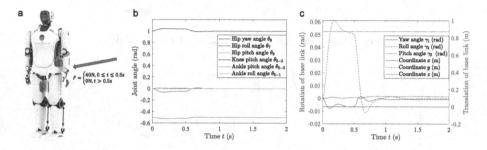

Fig. 6. Simulation of standing balance control of the robot

4.2 Standing Balance Control

In this section, we consider a floating base link and give a simulation of standing balance control for the robot using the DBFC method. The control algorithm is shown in Fig. 5, where r_C is the position vector of the robot's COM in the world coordinate system $\mathscr{F}_w$, M_{23} is the virtual moment exerted on the base link, $\hat{F}^n$ and $\hat{F}^\tau$ are the contact forces solved from the COM dynamics responsible for maintaining the momentum balance and angular momentum balance during the contact, u_{fb} and u_{ff} represents the feedback and feedforward components of joint torque, which are obtained through a PD controller and the DBFC method, respectively. Here, the main idea of DBFC is to combine the dynamic equation (6) with the constraints $\ddot{\delta}_c = 0$ and $\dot{v}_c^\tau = 0$ to determine the joint torque u_{ff}. By summing u_{fb} and u_{ff}, we obtain the total joint torque u for the robot, which is then input into Eq. (6). A detailed explanation of the control law can be found in reference [16]. However, a difference exists between this paper and reference [16] regarding the modeling of contact forces. In reference [16], a point-foot model is used, where the contact force for each foot is represented as a concentrated force and moment. In contrast, this paper considers that each foot consists of four contact points, with each point subjected to a concentrated force. While this treatment increases the dimensionality of the contact forces, it provides a more accurate representation of the actual contact states of the robot.

We set the robot's desired configuration as: $\theta_{1-3,des} = \theta_{1-4,des} = \theta_{2,des} = -0.5\,\text{rad}$, $\theta_{1-7,des} = 1\,\text{rad}$, $\theta_{5-3,des} = \theta_{5-4,des} = \theta_{6,des} = -0.5\,\text{rad}$, $\theta_{5-7,des} = 1\,\text{rad}$, $\theta_{23,rad} = [\gamma_{des}^T, x_{des}, y_{des}, z_{des}]^T = [0,0,0,0,0,0.8733\,\text{m}]$, and the all other components of $q_{j,des}$ are 0. Here, the value of z_{des} satisfies the condition that the robot is precisely standing on the ground. The desired position vector of the robot's COM in this configuration is then calculated as $r_{C,\text{des}} = [-0.0178, -0.0011, 0.7735]^\text{T}$. As shown in Fig. 6a, we assume that the robot is subjected to a thrust force of 40 N during the initial 0.5 s. This force is applied at the origin of the base link's local coordinate system, and its direction remains aligned with the X axis of the local coordinate system throughout this period. We set the PD coefficients as $K_{p,1} = 120$, $K_{d,1} = 10$, $K_{p,2} = 120$, $K_{d,2} = 10$, $K_{p,3} = 250$ and $K_{d,3} = 10$, respectively, and then perform the simulation for the robot's standing balance control. Figures 6b–c show the numerical results, where the evolution curves of the right leg's joint angles as well as the base link's rotation and translation coordinates are presented. We can see that under the action of the control law shown in Fig. 5, the robot can maintain a stable standing balance even in the presence of thrust disturbances.

5   Conclusion and Discussion

This paper presents a novel approach for modeling the nonsmooth dynamics of humanoid robots with parallel mechanisms. By combining the links involved in closed-loop constraints into aggregate nodes, the robot's topology is equivalent to a tree structure, and recursive methods are used to compute dynamic matrices. Both the contact and impact dynamics are modeled using constraint-based methods, and simulation results show that our model can reflect more realistic physical processes than the compliance-based methods of Simscape Multibody. Additionally, we use the nonsmooth dynamic model to carry out a simulation for the standing balance control of the robot. In summary, this paper establishes an accurate dynamic simulation environment for motion control of humanoid robots. The methods presented in this paper can also be applied to nonsmooth dynamic modeling of other robots with parallel mechanisms.

References

1. Moran, M.E.: The da Vinci robot. J. Endourol. **20**(12), 986–990 (2007)
2. Kajita, S., Hirukawa, H., Harada, K., et al.: Introduction to Humanoid Robotics. Springer, Heidelberg (2014). https://doi.org/10.1007/978-3-642-54536-8
3. Al-Shuka, H.F.N., Allmendinger, F., Corves, B., et al.: Modeling, stability and walking pattern generators of biped robots: a review. Robotica **32**(6), 907–934 (2014)
4. Gienger, M., Steil, J.J.: Humanoid kinematics and dynamics: open questions and future directions. In: Goswami, A., Vadakkepat, P. (eds.) Humanoid Robotics: A Reference, pp. 893–902. Springer, Dordrecht (2019). https://doi.org/10.1007/978-94-007-7194-9_8-1
5. Moro, F.L., Sentis, L.: Whole-Body Control of Humanoid Robots. In: Goswami, A., Vadakkepat, P. (eds.) Humanoid Robotics: A Reference, pp. 1161–1183. Springer, Dordrecht (2019)
6. Sugihara, T., Yamane, K.: Reduced-order models. In: Goswami, A., Vadakkepat, P. (eds.) Humanoid Robotics: A Reference, pp. 811–848. Springer, Dordrecht (2019). https://doi.org/10.1007/978-94-007-6046-2_56
7. Kajita, S., Morisawa, M., Miura, K., et al.: Biped walking stabilization based on linear inverted pendulum tracking. In: 2010 IEEE/RSJ International Conference on Intelligent Robots and Systems, 4489–4496. IEEE, New York (2010)
8. Neuman, S.M., Koolen, T., Drean, J., et al.: Benchmarking and workload analysis of robot dynamics algorithms. In: 2019 IEEE/RSJ International Conference on Intelligent Robots and Systems (IROS), 5235–5242. IEEE, New York (2019)

9. Singh, S., Russell, R.P., Wensing, P.M.: Efficient analytical derivatives of rigid-body dynamics using spatial vector algebra. IEEE Rob. Autom. Lett. **7**(2), 1776–1783 (2022)
10. Jain, A.: Robot and Multibody Dynamics: Analysis and Algorithms. Springer, New York (2010). https://doi.org/10.1007/978-1-4419-7267-5
11. Wang, J., Liu, C., Zhao, Z.: Nonsmooth dynamics of a 3d rigid body on a vibrating plate. Multibody Syst. Dyn. **32**(2), 217–239 (2014)
12. Ivanov, A.P.: Singularities in the rolling motion of a spherical robot. Int. J. Non-Linear Mech. **145**, 104061 (2022)
13. Liu, C., Zhao, Z., Brogliato, B.: Frictionless multiple impacts in multibody systems. I. Theoretical framework. Proc. Royal Soc. Lond. A: Math. Phys. Eng. Sci. **464**(2100), 3193–3211 (2008)
14. Liu, C., Zhao, Z., Brogliato, B.: Frictionless multiple impacts in multibody systems. II. Numerical algorithm and simulation results. Proc. Royal Soc. Lond. A: Math. Phys. Eng. Sci. **465**(2101), 1–23 (2009)
15. Shi, T., Liu, Y., Wang, N., et al.: Toppling dynamics of regularly spaced dominoes in an array. J. Appl. Mech. **85**(4), 041008 (2018)
16. Stephens, B.J., Atkeson, C.G.: Dynamic balance force control for compliant humanoid robots. In: 2010 IEEE/RSJ International Conference on Intelligent Robots and Systems, pp. 1248–1255. IEEE, New York (2010)

Human-Like Dexterous Manipulation for the Anthropomorphic Hand-Arm Robotic System via Teleoperation

Yayu Huang[1,2], Zhenghan Wang[1,2], Xiaofei Shen[1], Qian Liu[1], and Peng Wang[1,2,3(✉)]

[1] Institute of Automation, Chinese Academy of Sciences, Beijing 100190, China
peng_wang@ia.ac.cn
[2] School of Artificial Intelligence, University of Chinese Academy of Sciences, Beijing 100049, China
[3] Centre for Artificial Intelligence and Robotics, Hong Kong Institute of Science and Innovation, Chinese Academy of Sciences, Hong Kong 999077, China

Abstract. Teleoperation has the potential to enable robots to replace humans in high-risk scenarios and catastrophic events, performing manipulation tasks efficiently and securely under human guidance. However, achieving human-like dexterous manipulation remains challenging, particularly for anthropomorphic hand-arm robotic systems with high degrees of freedom. Accurately capturing the operator's motion and providing real-time intuitive feedback to enhance the sense of telepresence place substantial demands on human-robot perception and interaction. Moreover, the inherent physical and functional differences between anthropomorphic hand-arm robots and humans pose challenges in ensuring the accuracy and reliability of dexterous teleoperation. To overcome these challenges, we present an integrated approach involving an anthropomorphic hand-arm robot system, a wearable motion capture and force feedback system, and a set of motion mapping and force mapping methods. We conducted experiments on both simulation and real-world platforms to evaluate the usability and effectiveness of our proposed approach, with the results demonstrating significant advancements in achieving human-like dexterity via teleoperation.

Keywords: Dexterous Manipulation · Teleoperation · Anthropomorphic hand-arm robots · Motion mapping · Force mapping

1 Introduction

Advances in robotics manufacturing and artificial intelligence technologies have enabled researchers to achieve autonomous dexterous manipulation in anthropomorphic robots [1–6]. While offering great potential for solving complex and dexterous manipulation tasks, the unreliability and instability of autonomous learning pose challenges for its application in sophisticated scenarios. To address

© The Author(s), under exclusive license to Springer Nature Singapore Pte Ltd. 2023
H. Yang et al. (Eds.): ICIRA 2023, LNAI 14270, pp. 309–321, 2023.
https://doi.org/10.1007/978-981-99-6492-5_27

this, human-like dexterous manipulation via teleoperation has emerged as a viable solution, serving as a bridge between humans and robots. By combining the decision-making experience of human intelligence with the powerful manipulation capabilities of robots, teleoperation allows robots to effectively replace humans and perform intricate manipulations in environments that are either inaccessible or hazardous to human operators. This approach has found widespread use in various real-world domains, including industrial production, medical treatment, mining, and explosive ordnance disposal. Nevertheless, achieving human-like dexterous teleoperation in anthropomorphic robots presents a complex and multifaceted challenge. Precisely capturing human motion and providing real-time force feedback prove to be demanding tasks. Moreover, the disparities between anthropomorphic robots and humans in physical aspects such as size, weight, and kinematics, as well as functional aspects such as sensing, actuation, force, and velocity, further complicate the realization of seamless teleoperation. Consequently, a comprehensive dexterous teleoperation system necessitates the careful consideration of three fundamental sub-problems: how to capture human motion, how to map human motion to the robot effectively, and how to give feedback to the human on the forces perceived by the robot.

In this paper, we present a comprehensive framework that addresses the challenges of achieving human-like dexterous manipulation in anthropomorphic hand-arm robot systems through teleoperation, focusing on the three subproblems mentioned earlier. Firstly, we develop a wearable system utilizing a data glove and three IMUs (Inertial Measurement Units) to accurately capture human hand-arm motion. Next, we propose two distinct mapping methods: a hybrid mapping approach for hand motion mapping and a motion modification approach for arm motion mapping. These methods are effective in accurately translating human motions to the robot. Finally, we introduce a force-feedback system based on a hand exoskeleton, which utilizes a nonlinear mapping method to enhance the operator's sense of immersion by mapping the perceived force from the robot to the operator.

The subsequent sections of this paper are organized as follows. Section 2 provides a comprehensive overview of related work on motion capture of human hands, human motion mapping, and feedback in teleoperation. In Sect. 3, we present the proposed framework for achieving human-like dexterous manipulation via teleoperation. The specific methods utilized, including the hand motion mapping method, the arm motion mapping method, and the force mapping law, are detailed in Sect. 4. To validate the effectiveness of the framework, experimental results obtained from both simulation and real-world platforms are presented in Sect. 5. Finally, we give a conclusion in Sect. 6.

2 Related Work

2.1 Motion Capture of Human Hands

Capturing human motion, especially human hand motion can be achieved in a visual way or a haptic way [7].

Vision-based methods typically rely on camera input to capture motion. Some works extract motion information, such as wrist pose, hand pose parameters, hand shape parameters, and keypoint positions, from the visual data [8,9]. Still, other works do not focus on specific motion Information but directly predict the pose of the robot hand that is visually similar to the human hand pose [10]. Vision-based approaches offer advantages in terms of cost-effectiveness and ease of deployment but are limited by camera capabilities and algorithms. Furthermore, the absence of haptic feedback represents a significant drawback.

Haptic-based approaches, on the other hand, rely heavily on wearable devices to estimate human posture and obtain feedback. Data gloves are the most common type of wearable device, providing information such as the position and motion of the fingers and the whole hand, as well as haptic feedback information. Exoskeletons are typically worn on the dorsum and involve rigid links for providing kinesthetic feedback to the hand. Haptic-based approaches, although more complex and costly to implement, offer the significant advantage of providing controllable motion and feedback.

In this work, we target to design a haptic-based system that captures human hand-arm motion, making teleoperation controllable and realistic.

2.2   Human Motion Mapping

Mapping human motion onto a hand-arm robot is another key problem in teleoperation, where the difficulty comes from the mismatch between human and robot including workspace, configuration, and manipulation resolution [11]. The problem is commonly decomposed into two parts to be considered: hand-motion mapping and arm-motion mapping.

The most frequently used methods for hand motion mapping are direct Cartesian mapping and direct joint mapping. Direct Cartesian mapping involves scaling, optimizing, or transforming the fingertip positions of the human hand and leading the robot fingertip to that specified position. This method is applicable to various robotic hands but is limited to precision grasps. Direct joint mapping directly employs the corresponding joint values of the human hand to control the robot hand. This method is intuitive and straightforward but only suitable for robots with similar kinematics to the human hand. In this work, we aim to design a hybrid mapping algorithm that combines the advantages of both methods. This hybrid mapping algorithm is intended to be simpler, more intuitive, easier to implement, and collision-free compared to previous algorithms [12,13].

In the context of arm motion mapping, two categories can be distinguished: direct mapping and motion modification [14]. The former directly utilizes the original human demonstration data (joint angles, positions, trajectories) without modification, which is simple and intuitive but does not consider the differences in body structure and size. The latter addresses the variations in body structure and size by scaling the obtained human position data, resulting in a more reasonable mapping. Therefore, in this work, we employ the motion modification method to the changes in the human hand position, thus achieving more natural teleoperation of the robotic arm.

2.3   Feedback in Teleoperation

Feedback is crucial in teleoperation, and while visual feedback is essential for providing information about the position and objects in the remote environment, haptic feedback becomes paramount as the robot approaches objects and vision becomes occluded. Realistic, accurate, and low-delay haptic feedback serves as a vital source of human-robot interaction information, greatly enhancing the operator's sense of immersion. Haptic feedback can be categorized into tactile feedback, which enables the perception of object texture and shape, and kinesthetic feedback, which allows for the perception of force and contact. In this work, we investigate the force-feedback system, where the hand exoskeleton serves as an interface between the human and the robot.

3   Framework

Our objective is to develop a framework for human-like dexterous manipulation via teleoperation for the anthropomorphic hand-arm robotic system. This framework empowers operators to perform natural motions, guiding the robot to execute various intricate manipulations. An overview of the framework is depicted in Fig. 1.

The **interaction system** serves as the interface between the operator and the robot, capturing human motions and providing feedback. Human finger motions and arm motions are measured by a data glove and three IMUs attached to the upper arm, forearm, and hand, respectively. The estimated angle information is converted into position information through forward kinematics. The hand motion mapping method and the arm motion mapping method are then employed to determine the hand and arm joint angles of the robot, respectively.

The **hand-arm robotic system** consists of a robotic arm and a CASIA Hand, which features 25 joint degrees of freedom and 21 degrees of actuation, with a force sensor attached to each fingertip. The desired joint angles are executed by the robot controller. During interactions with the environment, force

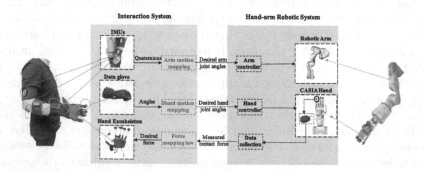

Fig. 1. The framework of human-like dexterous manipulation for the anthropomorphic hand-arm robotic system via teleoperation.

information is generated and processed according to a specific force mapping law. This force feedback is naturally conveyed to the operator through the wearable hand exoskeleton, enhancing their perception of the robot's contact forces.

4   Methods

4.1   Hand Motion Mapping

Our objective is to develop a hybrid mapping method that leverages the advantages of both direct Cartesian mapping and direct joint mapping approaches. For this purpose, we utilize MANO [15], which represents the human hand with 15 ball joints and 15*3 degrees of freedom. To align it with the structure of the actual human hand, we simplify the model to have 20 degrees of freedom, with 4 degrees of freedom assigned to each finger. Fig. 2(a) shows the differences in kinematic structure between the simplified MANO model and the CASIA Hand.

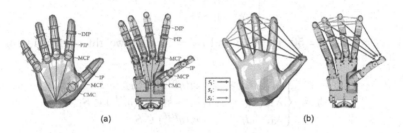

(a)   (b)

Fig. 2. MANO and CASIA Hand.(a)Kinematic structure. (b)Vector group.

Considering the factors of fingertip orientation and distance, joint angle, and self-collision, we follow DexPilot [16] to formulate the hand motion mapping problem as a non-linear optimization problem, with the specific objective function:

$$\min \sum_{i=1}^{n} w_1(d_i)||v_i(q_t^{RH}) - s(d_i)\hat{v}_i(q_t^{MH})||^2 + w_2(d_i)||q_t'^{RH} - q_t'^{MH}|| + w_3||q_t^{RH} - q_{t-1}^{RH}||^2 \tag{1}$$

Where q_t^{MH}, q_t^{RH} respectively represent the joint angles of MANO and CAISA Hand at time t, $v_i(q_t^{MH}) \in \mathbb{R}^3$, $v_i(q_t^{RH}) \in \mathbb{R}^3$ respectively represent the vectors obtained by forward kinematics of MANO and CAISA Hand in the world coordinate system, pointing from one key point to another, as shown in Fig. 2(b). n represents the total number of vectors. Furthermore, $d_i = ||v_i(q_t^{MH})||$ and $\hat{v}_i(q_t^{MH}) = \frac{v_i(q_t^{MH})}{||v_i(q_t^{MH})||}$. $q_t'^{RH}$ and $q_t'^{MH}$ are the structurally corresponding joints in the MANO and CASIA Hand, including the DIP, PIP, and MCP joints of the index, middle, ring, and little fingers.

The distance coefficient function $s(d_i)$ is defined as:

$$s(d_i) = \begin{cases} \eta_1, & d_i \leq \varepsilon \wedge v_i(q_t^{RH}) \in S_1 \\ \eta_2, & d_i \leq \varepsilon \wedge v_i(q_t^{RH}) \in S_2 \\ \eta_3, & d_i \leq \varepsilon \wedge v_i(q_t^{RH}) \in S_3 \\ \alpha d_i, & d_i > \varepsilon \end{cases} \qquad (2)$$

Where ε is the distance threshold parameter, the scaling factor $\alpha = 1.5$ represents the difference in size between CASIA hands and MANO, $\eta_1 = 1 \times 10^{-4}$ m keeps the thumb fingertip close to the other fingertip during precision grasp, $\eta_2 = 0.025$ m and $\eta_3 = 0.03$ m force a safe distance between fingertips and between the neighboring joints to avoid collisions. The weight coefficient function $w_1(d_i)$ is defined as:

$$w_1(d_i) = \begin{cases} \mu_1, & d_i \leq \varepsilon \wedge v_i(q_t^{RH}) \in S_1 \\ \mu_2, & d_i \leq \varepsilon \wedge v_i(q_t^{RH}) \in S_2 \\ \mu_3, & d_i \leq \varepsilon \wedge v_i(q_t^{RH}) \in S_3 \\ \mu_4, & d_i > \varepsilon \end{cases} \qquad (3)$$

Where $\mu_1 = 45$, $\mu_2 = 50$, $\mu_3 = 25$ and $\mu_4 = 10$. The weight coefficient function $w_2(d_i)$ is defined as:

$$w_2(d_i) = \begin{cases} \lambda_1, & d_i > \varepsilon_2 \wedge v_i(q_t^{RH}) \in S_1 \\ \lambda_2, & d_i \leq \varepsilon_2 \wedge d_i > \varepsilon_1 \wedge v_i(q_t^{RH}) \in S_1 \\ \lambda_3, & d_i \leq \varepsilon_1 \wedge v_i(q_t^{RH}) \in S_1 \end{cases} \qquad (4)$$

Where $\lambda_1 = 0.1$, $\lambda_2 = 0.05$, $\lambda_3 = 0.01$, $\varepsilon_1 = 0.02$ and $\varepsilon_2 = 0.04$. These values are chosen to ensure reasonableness, considering that precision grasp is more likely than power grasp when the thumb is too close to the other fingers, and thus the attention to joint similarity should be reduced. Additionally, we added an L2 normalization term with $w_3 = 1 \times 10^{-3}$ to improve smoothness and temporal consistency.

For implementation, we use Sequential Least-Squares Quadratic Programming (SLSQP) algorithm in NLopt [17] to optimize the above objectives in real-time.

4.2   Arm Motion Mapping

The arm motion mapping algorithm aims to enable the dexterous robot hand to replicate the motion of the operator's hand in Cartesian space, ensuring controllability during operation. To simplify the process, we focus only on the hand's position and orientation, disregarding the arm shape that aims to maintain similarity between the human and the robot. Consequently, it becomes essential to calculate the relative position and orientation of the human hand based on the data obtained from the three IMUs. We model the human arm as a 7-degree-of-freedom system, with 3 degrees of freedom for the shoulder joint, 1 degree

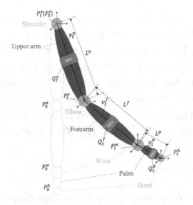

Fig. 3. Diagram of the human arm model.

of freedom for the elbow joint, and 3 degrees of freedom for the wrist joint. Three IMUs are attached to the upper arm, forearm, and hand, respectively, and they are calibrated to the initial state where the arm naturally hangs down and the palm faces toward the body. As shown in Fig. 3, the following variables are defined:

- The length of each link: upper arm L^u, forearm L^f, hand L^p.
- The quaternion of each link at time t: upper arm Q_t^u, forearm Q_t^f, palm Q_t^p.
- The position of each joint at time t: shoulder joint P_t^s, elbow joint P_t^e, wrist joint P_t^w.
- The vector of each link at time t: upper arm v_t^u, forearm v_t^f, hand v_t^p.

The position of the hand P_t^h at time t is:

$$P_t^h = P_0^s + Q_t^u * v_0^u + Q_t^f * v_0^f + Q_t^p * v_0^p \tag{5}$$

Where the operation rule for multiplying a quaternion by a vector is defined as:

$$Q * v = Im(Q \otimes v \otimes Q^{-1}) \tag{6}$$

In order to cope with the difference in structure and size between the human arm and the robotic arm, the changes in the position of the human hand are modified to yield the target position of the robotic hand.

$$pos_t^{TA} = [\rho_1 \ \rho_2 \ \rho_3] \cdot (P_t^h - P_0^h) + pos_0^{RA} \tag{7}$$

where pos_t^{TA} is the target position of the robotic hand at time t, ρ_1, ρ_2, ρ_3 are scaling factors, and pos_0^{RA} is the initial position of the robot hand.

It is worth noting that the slave arm includes all degrees of freedom of the robotic arm and two degrees of freedom of the CASIA wrist. We formulate the arm motion mapping as an optimization problem, the optimization objective is:

$$\min w_{pos}||pos(q_t^{RA}) - pos_t^{TA}||^2 + w_{quat}(1 - \left\langle quat(q_t^{RA}), quat_t^{TA}\right\rangle^2) + \beta||q_t^{RA} - q_{t-1}^{RA}||^2 \tag{8}$$

Where q_t^{RA} represents the joint angles of the robotic arm at time t, while $pos(q_t^{RA})$ and $quat(q_t^{RA})$ respectively indicate the position and rotation of the CASIA Hand at time t. It is worth noting that $quat_t^{TA}$ is equivalent to the previously mentioned Q_t^p. $\langle q_1, q_2 \rangle$ denotes the inner product of the corresponding quaternions. As with the hand motion mapping, the objective function includes an L2 normalization term to improve smoothness and temporal consistency and likewise optimizes the above objective in real-time using Sequential Least-Squares Quadratic Programming (SLSQP) algorithms in NLopt [17].

4.3   Force Mapping Law

Force mapping involves transferring the force experienced by the robot's fingertips to the operator's hands. The level of realism in force transfer directly influences the operator's immersion in the task. Although linear mapping is widely used, it falls short in providing a truly realistic experience to the operator due to variations in human sensitivity to different forces (Fig. 4).

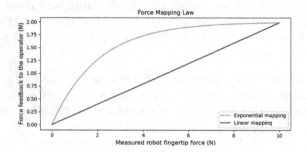

Fig. 4. Diagram of the force mapping law.

Inspired by [18], we formulate the force feedback model as an exponential function as follows, making it more sensitive to small forces and less sensitive to large forces.

$$F^H = \sigma(-e^{\tau F^R} + \xi) \tag{9}$$

Where F^H denotes the force fed back to the human and F^R denotes the force perceived by the robot, $\sigma = 2, \tau = -0.5, \xi = 1$. Notably, we have limited the range of force feedback to ensure comfortable operation.

5   Experiment

5.1   Experimental Setup

The overall experimental setup consisted of :

- The data glove is equipped with 19 optical fibers, 15 of which are attached to the DIP, PIP, and MCP joints of the index, middle, ring, and little finger, as well as the IP, MCP, and CMC joint of the thumb, with which the flexion/extension angles are measured. Additionally, 4 fibers are attached between each of the five fingers, with which the abduction/adduction angles are measured.

- A hand exoskeleton is positioned on the dorsum of the hand and is capable of providing a maximum force feedback of 6.5N at each of the five fingertips.
- Three IMUs are affixed to the upper arm, forearm, and hand. These IMUs provide orientation information relative to the global coordinate system. The orientation is represented by quaternions and is based on the three-dimensional angular velocity, acceleration, and magnetic field.
- A CASIA Hand, with 21 degrees of actuation and 25 human-like degrees of freedom, including 16 on the fingers, 5 on the thumb, 2 on the palm, and 2 on the wrist. At each fingertip, a Contactile Force Sensor is attached to provide 3D force information from the slave side.
- A KUKA LBR iiwa with 7 degrees of freedom.

5.2 Simulation Experiments

To empirically validate the effectiveness of the hand motion mapping method, we present several mappings from MANO to CASIA Hand in Fig. 5. The experimental results demonstrate that the method adequately considers factors such as fingertip position, joint angle, and self-collision, resulting in visually plausible outcomes.

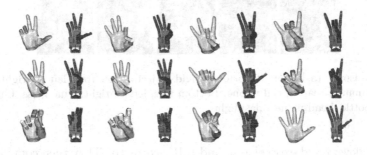

Fig. 5. Hand motion mapping results between the MANO and the CASIA Hand.

For further validation, we conducted a comparative evaluation with direct Cartesian mapping and direct joint mapping in the MuJoCo [19]. This evaluation is illustrated in Fig. 6, where we selected two objects for precision grasp and power grasp scenarios. The results demonstrate that our method outperforms both direct Cartesian mapping and direct joint mapping approaches, achieving successful outcomes in both precision grasp and power grasp tasks.

5.3 Real-World Experiments

To further verify the system's reliability, we conducted three physical experiments in the real world. Two operators participated and were instructed to wear

Fig. 6. Methods compared on the precision grasp task (left) and power grasp task (right).

Fig. 7. Grasping tasks for 3D printed rigid objects. Top row, left to right: bottle, glasses, hammer, teapot, cell phone. Bottom row, left to right: wine glass, binoculars, cleanser bottle, headphones, flashlight.

the data glove, hand exoskeleton, and IMUs correctly. They then completed the necessary calibration steps and warm-up exercises before engaging in teleoperation tests.

1) Grasping tasks for 3D printed rigid objects: In this experiment, the robot grasps the object standing upright on the table, lifts it to at least 5 cm above the table, and holds it for at least 5 s, as shown in Fig. 7.
2) Stacking blocks task: In this experiment, the robot first picks up the red block and places it in the given position, then returns to the initial pose, picks up the green block and stacks it on top of the red block, and finally repeats the above process to stack the yellow block on top of the green block. This teleoperation process is illustrated in Fig. 8.
3) Grasping tasks for non-rigid objects: In this experiment, the robot delicately grasps the flexible and deformable object from the table, lifting it to a minimum height of 5 cm above the surface. Throughout the process, the robot

Fig. 8. Stacking blocks task. The teleoperation process is shown from left to right.

Fig. 9. Grasping tasks for non-rigid objects. Left to right: toy candle, dixie cup, yogurt box, tissue, doll.

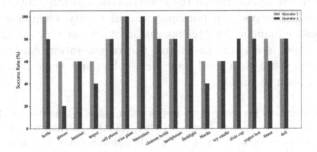

Fig. 10. Success rate of teleoperation tasks.

ensures that the object remains relatively free from significant deformation, as demonstrated in Fig. 9.

Figure 10 displays the average success rates for each task, with each operator performing the tasks five times within a three-minute time limit. Grasping rigid 3D printed objects requires precise control of the robot hand to achieve a reasonable grasp posture, posing significant challenges. Failures in this task often occur due to object pose changes resulting from collisions between the object and the fingers. Notably, this phenomenon is more pronounced when grasping objects such as glasses, hammers, and teapots. The stacking blocks task demands accurate control of the robot arm to precisely stack blocks on top of each other, given the small surface area of the blocks. Challenges in this task include inaccurate stacking positions, arm shaking, and premature or delayed release of objects, resulting in block slippage and task failure. When grasping non-rigid objects, operators adjust their hand poses based on force feedback from the hand exoskeleton to minimize object deformation during the process. However, we observed that the effectiveness of the hand exoskeleton varied depending on the operator. When operators exhibited excessive resistance or were unprepared for the force feedback, the hand exoskeleton proved ineffective or even counterproductive.

6   Conclusion

This paper presents a framework for human-like dexterous manipulation via teleoperation for the anthropomorphic hand-arm robotic system. Our framework incorporates a wearable system comprising a data glove, three IMUs, and a hand exoskeleton to capture human hand-arm motion and provide force feedback. Additionally, we have developed an anthropomorphic robotic system consisting of a robotic arm and a CASIA Hand equipped with force sensors at the fingertips for executing operations. To enable seamless interaction, we have designed a set of mapping algorithms for translating human motion to robot motion and robot forces to human forces. Experiments conducted on the simulation platform and real-world platform demonstrated the effectiveness and reliability of the system.

Future work involves incorporating virtual reality technology to provide visual feedback, enhancing the teleoperation experience for smoother control. Additionally, there are plans to extend the teleoperation capabilities from a single hand-arm robot to a dual hand-arm robot and delve into the realm of human-robot fusion technology.

Acknowledgement. This work was supported in part by the National Natural Science Foundation of China under Grants (91748131, 62006229, and 61771471), in part by the Strategic Priority Research Program of Chinese Academy of Science under Grant XDB32050106, and in part by the InnoHK Project.

References

1. Duan, H., Wang, P., Li, Y., Li, D., Wei, W.: Learning human-to-robot dexterous handovers for anthropomorphic hand. IEEE Trans. Cogn. Dev. Syst. **15**, 1224–1238 (2022). https://doi.org/10.1109/TCDS.2022.3203025
2. Li, Y., Wei, W., Li, D., Wang, P., Li, W., Zhong, J.: Hgc-net: deep anthropomorphic hand grasping in clutter. In: 2022 International Conference on Robotics and Automation (ICRA), pp. 714–720 (2022). https://doi.org/10.1109/ICRA46639.2022.9811756
3. Wei, W., et al.: Dvgg: deep variational grasp generation for dextrous manipulation. IEEE Rob. Autom. Lett. **7**(2), 1659–1666 (2022). https://doi.org/10.1109/LRA.2022.3140424
4. Wei, W., Wang, P., Wang, S.A.: Generalized anthropomorphic functional grasping with minimal demonstrations. arXiv:2303.17808 (2023)
5. Li, W., Wei, W., Wang, P.: Continual learning for anthropomorphic hand grasping. IEEE Trans. Cogn. Dev. Syst. (2023)
6. Li, W., Wei, W., Wang, P.: Neuro-inspired continual anthropomorphic grasping. Iscience **26**, 1–17 (2023)
7. Li, R., Wang, H., Liu, Z.: Survey on mapping human hand motion to robotic hands for teleoperation. IEEE Trans. Circ. Syst. Video Technol. **32**(5), 2647–2665 (2021)

8. Qin, Y., Su, H., Wang, X.: From one hand to multiple hands: imitation learning for dexterous manipulation from single-camera teleoperation. IEEE Rob. Autom. Lett. **7**(4), 10873–10881 (2022)

9. Zahlner, S., Hirschmanner, M., Patten, T., Vincze, M.: Teleoperation system for teaching dexterous manipulation. Google Scholar (2020)

10. Li, S., et al.: Vision-based teleoperation of shadow dexterous hand using end-to-end deep neural network. In: 2019 International Conference on Robotics and Automation (ICRA), pp. 416–422. IEEE (2019)

11. Liu, G., Geng, X., Liu, L., Wang, Y.: Haptic based teleoperation with master-slave motion mapping and haptic rendering for space exploration. Chin. J. Aeronaut. **32**(3), 723–736 (2019). https://doi.org/10.1016/j.cja.2018.07.009

12. Chattaraj, R., Bepari, B., Bhaumik, S.: Grasp mapping for dexterous robot hand: a hybrid approach. In: 2014 Seventh International Conference on Contemporary Computing (IC3), pp. 242–247. IEEE (2014)

13. Meattini, R., Chiaravalli, D., Biagiotti, L., Palli, G., Melchiorri, C.: Combined joint-cartesian mapping for simultaneous shape and precision teleoperation of anthropomorphic robotic hands. IFAC-PapersOnLine **53**(2), 10052–10057 (2020)

14. Liang, Y., Li, W., Wang, Y., Xiong, R., Mao, Y., Zhang, J.: Dynamic movement primitive based motion retargeting for dual-arm sign language motions. In: 2021 IEEE International Conference on Robotics and Automation (ICRA), pp. 8195–8201. IEEE (2021)

15. Romero, J., Tzionas, D., Black, M.J.: Embodied hands: modeling and capturing hands and bodies together. arXiv preprint arXiv:2201.02610 (2022)

16. Handa, A., et al.: Dexpilot: vision-based teleoperation of dexterous robotic hand-arm system. In: 2020 IEEE International Conference on Robotics and Automation (ICRA), pp. 9164–9170. IEEE (2020)

17. Johnson, S.G.: The nlopt nonlinear-optimization package. https://github.com/stevengj/nlopt

18. Park, S., Park, Y., Bae, J.: Performance evaluation of a tactile and kinesthetic finger feedback system for teleoperation. Mechatronics **87**, 102898 (2022)

19. Todorov, E., Erez, T., Tassa, Y.: Mujoco: a physics engine for model-based control. In: 2012 IEEE/RSJ International Conference on Intelligent Robots and Systems, pp. 5026–5033. IEEE (2012)

Design of a Compact Anthropomorphic Robotic Hand with Hybrid Linkage and Direct Actuation

Zechen Hu, Chunyang Zhou, Jinjian Li, and Quan Hu[✉]

Beijing Institute of Technology, Beijing 100083, China
huquan@bit.edu.cn

Abstract. This paper presents a newly developed small-sized, dexterous hand with multiple degrees of freedom (DOFs). With five fingers and a total of thirteen active degrees of freedom, this hand is comparable in size to an adult male's hand. High-performance motors are installed in each finger, along with a combination of linkages and bevel gear mechanisms to ensure flexibility and high load capacity. The design of flexible linkages enhances the adaptive capability during grasping processes. The transmission mechanisms were analyzed to derive the inverse kinematic relationship between motor motion and finger joint motion. In addition, the DH parameters and four-bar linkage kinematics were utilized to calculate the workspace of the dexterous hand. Based on theoretical analysis of the workspace, it has been demonstrated that the dexterous hand has the ability to perform diverse tasks including object grasping and manipulation.

Keywords: Robotic hand · Multiple degrees of freedom · Compact transmission

1 Introduction

The human hand is incredibly versatile and can perform complex grasping and manipulation tasks. It plays an integral role in daily life and human productivity. Thus, anthropomorphic robotic hand become the one of the most essential components of humanoid robots. Developing a robotic hand comparable in size, flexibility, and load capacity has proven to be a daunting challenge. As a result, it remains one of the most difficult tasks in the field of robotics and has received a lot of attention. [1].

The existing multi-finger anthropomorphic robotic hands can be categorized based on their driving mechanisms: direct-driven, tendon-driven, and linkage-driven. Direct-driven robotic hands utilize miniature motors combined with gearboxes to drive finger joint rotations. For instance, the DLR-HIT II robotic hand

Supported by National Science Foundation of China, 12272039.

developed by Deutsches Zentrum für Luft- und Raumfahrt (DLR) employs harmonic drives as a form of gear reduction [2]. The SSSA-MyHand has 3 degrees
of freedom and utilizes spur gears for power transmission [3]. The Six Degree-
of-Freedom Open Source Hand employs a system of bevel gears for power transmission [4]. In tendon-driven robotic hands, the actuators and controllers are
contained in the forearm and connected to the finger joints through tendons
such as the Shadow Dexterous Hand from the Shadow Robot, the Robonaut
2 hand developed by NASA [5], and the DLR Hand Arm System [6]. Linkage-
driven robotic hands use motors enclosed within the hand to control rigid linkages for transmitting motion to the finger joints. Examples of such robotic hands
include the Schunk SVH robotic hand and the ILDA robotic hand from Ajou
University [7].

Different driving mechanisms have their own advantages and disadvantages.
Direct-driven robotic hands, despite their compact nature, have limited payload
capacity. Tendon-driven robotic hands can meet the need for full degrees of
freedom (DOFs) and compact size. However, they rely on winches that are bulky
and enclosed within the forearm, ultimate the versatility of the robotic hand
and leads to increased maintenance costs. In comparison, linkage-driven robotic
hands have a greater payload capacity, but with fewer DOFs.

To address these challenges, we propose a hybrid transmission approach that
combines linkage mechanisms with direct drive using bevel gears, creating a
multi-DOFs dexterous hand configuration. With compact size, high integration,
and quick installation ability, the proposed robotic hand can be easily integrated
into a humanoid robot or other collaborative devices.

2   Mechanical Design of the Hand

2.1   Mechanical Description

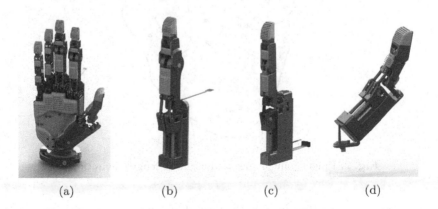

(a)   (b)   (c)   (d)

Fig. 1. Overall design of the proposed anthropomorphic robotic hand.

The overall structure of the proposed anthropomorphic robotic hand is shown in Fig. 1a. The size and shape of the hand are roughly similar to that of an adult male hand. The hand is designed with modularity and consists of five fingers. The index and middle fingers use Module 1 (3 DOFs, Fig. 1b), while the ring and little fingers use Module 2 (2 DOFs, Fig. 1c), and the thumb uses Module 3 (3 DOFs, Fig. 1d). It results a total of 13 active DOFs. This configuration allows for stable grasping and manipulation of objects with various shapes.

The proposed anthropomorphic robotic hand design stands out from others due to its emphasis on flexibility and precision. By utilizing linkage mechanisms and bevel gears for direct drive, the hand has more DOFs in a smaller volume, ensuring its versatility in diverse human working environments. Additionally, elastic linkages instead of rigid ones were employed, providing passive compliance to the fingers and enhancing their ability to adapt to grasping objects and withstand impacts.

The palm of the hand is fabricated using aluminum alloy 3D printing, which has multiple locating holes and threaded holes to create secure connections with finger modules, circuit boards, quick-release devices, and other components. The dexterous hand can be easily installed on a robotic arm or any fixed position using the quick-release device located at the wrist.

2.2   Finger Linkage Design

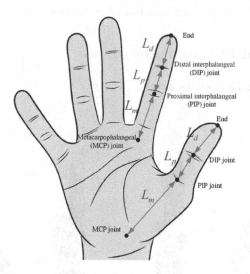

Fig. 2. Finger joint names and segment length definitions

The primary objective during the initial design concept was to create a robotic hand that could mimic the movements of a human hand as accurately as possible. To achieve this, the lengths of the finger segments in our dexterous hand were made closely matched those of a human hand. The references for the design are the measured lengths of finger segments from adult male hands. However, it had to consider various constraints such as transmission structure, range of motion, and modular components, which led us to round the values and obtain specific parameters for the finger segments. The defined lengths of the finger segments are presented in Fig. 2, and more details on the specific parameters can be found in the accompanying Table 1.

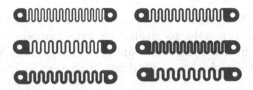

Fig. 3. Different flexible linkages.

The human hand exhibits excellent adaptability to the shape of objects during grasping and manipulation, thanks to the flexibility provided by biological tendons and skin tissues. It is aimed to achieve similar adaptive capabilities in our robotic hand for manipulation. Therefore, passive compliance was introduced by replacing some rigid linkages with flexible linkages. Various tests were conducted using various specifications of flexible linkages, as shown in Fig. 3, and ultimately achieved passive compliance in the joints.

Table 1. Finger Segment Lengths (Measured Values are marked with *).

Length (mm)	L_m	L_p	L_d
index finger	46.72*/52	24.63*/29	26.16*/26
middle finger	50.39*/52	27.29*/29	29.09*/26
ring finger	47.05*/45	25.23*/25	25.52*/25
little finger	35.94*/36	18.22*/25	25.55*/25
thumb	76.32*/79	37.21*/36	27.53*/28

2.3 Finger Joint/Transmission Structure Design

The design of the transmission structure is greatly constrained by the shape of the robotic hand and the dimensions of off-the-shelf components. Generally, larger loads and more DOFs result in larger volumes. The human hand is a great source of inspiration for designing functional systems. Among the fingers, the index and middle ones are the most flexible, while the thumb is primarily responsible for grasping tasks. Thus they are given the highest priority for active

DOFs, typically three DOFs, within the given volume constraints. On the other hand, the ring and little fingers play a supporting role in grasping and manipulation tasks, and thus, they are assigned two active DOFs while meeting the volume constraints.

Considering that humans are usually unable to independently control the DIP joint for motion, all DIP joints in the dexterous hand are designed as coupled joints, moving in conjunction with the PIP joint. Specifically, due to the lack of one DOFs in the ring finger and little finger, their PIP joints are coupled with the MCP joint.

The four-bar linkage mechanism is used to achieve coupled joints, with carefully designed linkage lengths to ensure accurate mapping of joint angles. As shown in Fig. 4, by utilizing the constraint conditions in SolidWorks, the lengths of the linkages that satisfy the specified conditions can be quickly calculated.

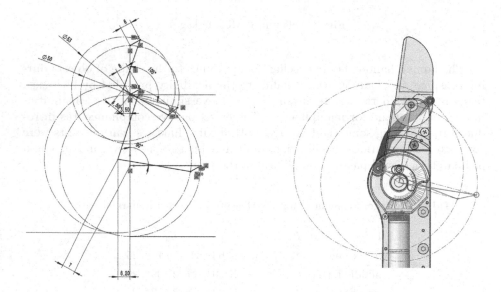

Fig. 4. Planning linkage parameters for motion range.

A dual PSS chain is employed at the MCP joint of the index finger and middle finger for bending and rolling motions. The dual PSS chain is a set of differential mechanisms where the MCP joint bends when the sliders move in the same direction and rolls when the sliders move in opposite directions (Fig. 5). Its advantages lie in the ability to use ball screws to convert the rotational motion into linear motion, providing a large transmission ratio and enhancing the load capacity of the dexterous hand [7]. Additionally, adopting the dual PSS chain allows the integration of the motor and ball screws in the palm area, reducing the inertia of the finger.

In confined spaces where complex transmission structures are challenging to implement, two precision-machined bevel gears are used for transmission at a

2:1 transmission ratio. The shape of the bevel gears is optimized based on the motion range to prevent collisions with other components during motion.

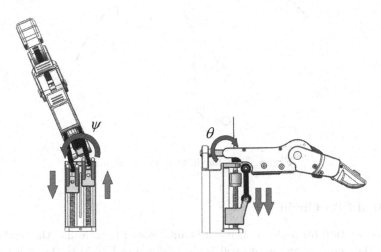

Fig. 5. Motion of dual PSS chain.

3   Modeling and Analysis

3.1   Four-Bar Linkage Mechanism

In the proposed robotic hand, each finger contains a four-bar linkage mechanism. Therefore, solving the angular relationship of the four-bar linkage mechanism is crucial for workspace analysis. The simplified linkage and parameter definitions are shown in Fig. 6.

We would like to obtain the rotation angle of link D after the rotation of link B by θ_1, which is the relationship between θ_1 and $\theta_2 - \theta_3$. Through geometric calculations, the following relationship can be obtained,

$$\begin{cases} L_E = \sqrt{L_A{}^2 + L_C{}^2 - 2L_A L_C \cos\left(\theta_1 + \theta_5\right)} \\ \theta_4 = \arccos\left(\frac{L_C - L_A \cos(\theta_1 + \theta_5)}{L_E}\right) \\ \theta_3 = \arccos\left(\frac{\left(L_E{}^2 + L_D{}^2 - L_B{}^2\right)}{2L_E L_D}\right) - \theta_4 \end{cases} \quad (1)$$

In the Eq. (1), the lengths of the links L_A, L_B, L_C, L_D are provided by the structural design. θ_2 and θ_5 are determined through initial position measurements.

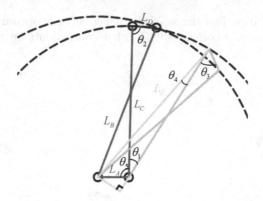

Fig. 6. Four-bar linkage mechanism.

3.2   Dual PSS Chain

As the foundation for motor control, it is anticipated to establish the relationship between the bending angle and roll angle (defined in Fig. 5) of the index finger's MCP joint and the displacement of the lead screw nut. The model and parameter definitions of the dual PSS chain are depicted in Fig. 7.

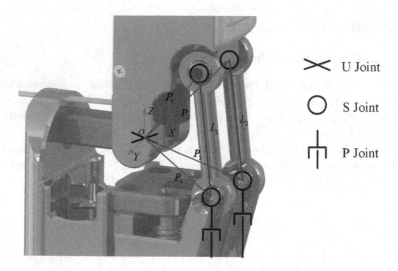

Fig. 7. Model of dual PSS chain.

In the description, the origin of the inertial coordinate system $OXYZ$ is located at the intersection of the rotation axis of universal joint in MCP joint. The X-axis and Y-axis coincide with the rotation axis at the initial position. $\mathbf{P}_1, \mathbf{P}_2, \mathbf{P}_3, \mathbf{P}_4$ represents the position vector of the center of the spherical joint at the initial position, and L_1, L_2 represents the distance between the centers of the spherical joint. The parameters in Fig. 7 can all be measured and obtained. Construct the rotation matrix by bending angle θ and roll angle ψ:

$$\mathbf{R}_Y = \begin{bmatrix} \cos\theta & 0 & \sin\theta \\ 0 & 1 & 0 \\ -\sin\theta & 0 & \cos\theta \end{bmatrix}, \mathbf{R}_X = \begin{bmatrix} 1 & 0 & 0 \\ 0 & \cos\psi & -\sin\psi \\ 0 & \sin\psi & \cos\psi \end{bmatrix}, \mathbf{R} = \mathbf{R}_X\mathbf{R}_Y. \quad (2)$$

After rotation, $\mathbf{P}_1$ and $\mathbf{P}_2$ can be written as:

$$\mathbf{P}_1^r = \mathbf{R}\mathbf{P}_1, \mathbf{P}_2^r = \mathbf{R}\mathbf{P}_2. \quad (3)$$

Denote $\mathbf{P}_3, \mathbf{P}_4$ after the displacement as $\mathbf{P}_3^t, \mathbf{P}_4^t$, since the center distance of the spherical joint is always constant

$$\left\|\mathbf{P}_1^r - \mathbf{P}_4^t\right\| = L_1, \left\|\mathbf{P}_2^r - \mathbf{P}_3^t\right\| = L_2. \quad (4)$$

By simultaneously solving Eqs. (2), (3), and (4), an analytical expression of $\mathbf{P}_3^t, \mathbf{P}_4^t$ in terms of θ and ψ can be obtained. Then, by subtracting $\mathbf{P}_3^t, \mathbf{P}_4^t$ from $\mathbf{P}_3, \mathbf{P}_4$, we have the displacement of the lead screw nut.

3.3 PSU Chain

Similarly, it is also necessary to establish the relationship between the bending angle θ, roll angle ψ of the ring finger's MCP joint, and the displacement of the lead screw nut in the PSU motion chain. The model and parameter definitions of the PSU motion chain are depicted in Fig. 8.

In the description, the origin of the inertial coordinate system $OXYZ$ is located at the intersection of the rotation axis of universal joint in MCP joint. The X-axis and Y-axis coincide with the rotation axis at the initial position. $\mathbf{P}_1$ represents the position vector of the center of the cylindrical hinge at the initial position, $\mathbf{P}_2$ represents the direction vector of the cylindrical hinge at the initial position. It is evident that $\mathbf{P}_2 = \begin{bmatrix} 0 & 1 & 0 \end{bmatrix}^T$. $\mathbf{P}_3$ represents the position vector of the center of the spherical joint at the initial position, and $\mathbf{P}_4$ represents the position vector of the center of the cylindrical hinge. It can be observed that the rotation axes of the brass universal joint do not intersect. L_1 represents the distance between the two axes, and L_2 represents the distance from the center of the spherical joint to the closer center of the cylindrical hinge.

The rotation matrix constructed from the bending angle θ and roll angle ψ is consistent with Eq. (2). The rotated $\mathbf{P}_1, \mathbf{P}_2$ is consistent with Eq. (3). A clear geometric relationship is that $\mathbf{P}_2$ is always perpendicular to the direction of L_1, and the sizes of L_1 and L_2 remain constant. By representing the displaced $\mathbf{P}_3$ as $\mathbf{P}_3^t$, we have

$$\begin{cases} (\mathbf{P}_4 - \mathbf{P}_1^r)\,\mathbf{P}_2^r = 0 \\ \|\mathbf{P}_4 - \mathbf{P}_1^r\| = L_1 \\ \|\mathbf{P}_4 - \mathbf{P}_3^t\| = L_2 \end{cases}. \quad (5)$$

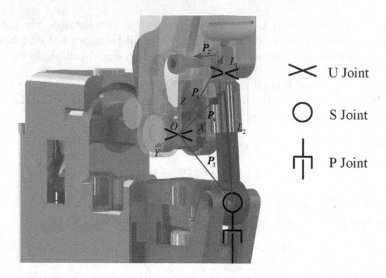

Fig. 8. Model of PSU chain.

$\mathbf{P}_3^t$ contains 1 unknown variable, and $\mathbf{P}_4$ contains 3 unknown variables. The above 3 geometric constraints are not sufficient to solve for $\mathbf{P}_3^t$. An additional less obvious geometric constraint is that the centers of the spherical joint, the two cylindrical hinges, and the $\mathbf{P}_2^r$ vector always lie in the same plane, which can be expressed as follows

$$\mathbf{P}_4 - \mathbf{P}_3^t = k\mathbf{P}_2^r + q\left(\mathbf{P}_4 - \mathbf{P}_1^r\right), \tag{6}$$

where k and q are real numbers, by simultaneously solving Eqs. (2), (3) and (5), an analytical expression of $\mathbf{P}_3^t$ in terms of θ and ψ can be obtained. Then, by subtracting $\mathbf{P}_3^t$ from $\mathbf{P}_3$, we have the displacement of the lead screw nut.

3.4 Workspace Analysis

The fingers of the robotic hand were modeled using the Denavit-Hartenberg (DH) parameters for forward kinematics. The coupling motion of the four-bar linkage mechanism was taken into account. The workspace of each finger's fingertip (indicated by yellow triangles) was computed, as shown in Fig. 9.

From Fig. 9f, it can be observed that the workspace of the thumb's fingertip overlaps significantly with the workspace of multiple fingers. This indicates that the thumb is capable of coordinating with other fingers to perform grasping, manipulation, and other tasks similar to the human hand.

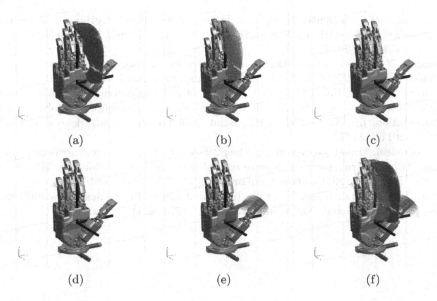

(a)   (b)   (c)

(d)   (e)   (f)

Fig. 9. Workspace for dexterous hands. a) to e) represent the individual workspace of each finger. f) the workspaces of all fingers are superimposed.

4   Conclusion

In this paper, a new compact and versatile anthropomorphic robotic hand with multiple DOFs is introduced. The proposed hand consists of five fingers, providing a total of 13 active DOFs. It has a comparable volume to that of an adult male hand. Each finger is equipped with high-performance motors and features a transmission structure that combines linkages and bevel gears, which offers both compact size and high load capacity. To improve adaptability during grasping, the hand also includes flexible linkages. Kinematic analysis of the selected transmission mechanisms is conducted. The inverse kinematic relationship between motor motion and finger joint motion was obtained. Additionally, the operational space of the dexterous hand is calculated using DH parameters combined with the kinematics of the four-bar linkage. Theoretical analysis of the motion space demonstrates the robotic hand's capabilities for object grasping and manipulation. Future work will focus on implementing tactile sensing and addressing motion control of the entire dexterous hand.

References

1. Piazza, C., Grioli, G., Catalano, M.G., et al.: A century of robotic hands. Ann. Rev. Control Rob. Auton. Syst. **2**, 1–32 (2019)
2. Chen, Z., Lii, N. Y., Wimboeck, T., et al.: Experimental study on impedance control for the five-finger dexterous robot hand DLR-HIT II. In: 2010 IEEE/RSJ International Conference on Intelligent Robots and Systems, pp. 5867–5874. IEEE, Taipei (2010)

3. Controzzi, M., Clemente, F., Barone, D., et al.: The SSSA-MyHand: a dexterous lightweight myoelectric hand prosthesis. IEEE Trans. Neural Syst. Rehabil. Eng. **25**(5), 459–468 (2016)
4. Krausz, N.E., Rorrer, R.A.: Design and fabrication of a six degree-of-freedom open source hand. IEEE Trans. Neural Syst. Rehabil. Eng. **24**(5), 562–572 (2015)
5. Bridgwater, L.B., Ihrke, C.A., Diftler, M.A., et al.: The robonaut 2 hand-designed to do work with tools. In: 2012 IEEE International Conference on Robotics and Automation, pp. 3425–3430. IEEE, Saint Paul (2012). https://doi.org/10.1109/ICRA.2012.6224772
6. Grebenstein, M., Albu-Schäffer, A., Bahls, T., et al.: The DLR hand arm system. In: 2011 IEEE International Conference on Robotics and Automation, pp. 3175–3182. IEEE, Shanghai (2011). https://doi.org/10.1109/ICRA.2011.5980371
7. Kim, U., Jung, D., Jeong, H., et al.: Integrated linkage-driven dexterous anthropomorphic robotic hand. Nat. Commun. **12**(1), 7177 (2021)

Application of Compliant Control in Position-Based Humanoid Robot

Chunyu Chen[✉], Ligang Ge, and Jiangchen Zhou

Ubtech Robotics Corp. Ltd., Shenzhen, China
{chunyu.chen,greg.ge,jiangchen.zhou}@ubtrobot.com

Abstract. In this paper, we study the comprehensive application of compliant control in position-based humanoid robot. In order to enhance the external disturbance resistance and terrain adaptability of humanoid robot, we propose three compliant controller which apply to the control system. Firstly, we propose the body compliant controller based on linear inverted pendulum and spring-damping model (LIP-SDM) which can achieve the compliant response of the body. Secondly, we design an compliant controller based on single-link spring-damping model, which can achieve compliant response when the swing leg collides with an obstacle. Finally, an compliant controller of ankle joint is proposed which is based on the compliant inverted pendulum (CIP) model for terrain adaptation. The application of three compliant controllers effectively enhances the adaptability of humanoid robots to external disturbances and uneven terrain. The proposed methods are implemented on our humanoid robot, UBTECH Walker, and its performance are demonstrated through improved stability and adaptability during standing and walking.

Keywords: Compliant Control · Humanoid Robot · Linear Inverted Pendulum

1 Introduction

In recent years, there has been a growing enthusiasm for researching humanoid robots, which not only resemble humans in appearance but are also expected to perform many of the tasks that humans do. However, there is still a long way to go for humanoid robots to move from theoretical environments to real-life situations, especially in terms of how to achieve stable walking on uneven surfaces and maintain the robot's stability when subjected to external forces. These will be the key issues that need to be addressed for humanoid robots to be successfully implemented in practical applications.

When humanoid robots are disturbed by external forces or walking on uneven surfaces, how to maintain stability is a hot and critical issue in research. Researchers try to solve this problem from different dimensions, including plan layer and control layer.

From the perspective of gait planning, Kajita proposed a method using the zero-moment point (ZMP) as a stability criterion [1]. They simplified the humanoid robot to a linear inverted pendulum model of a point mass, and based on this model, they proposed a stable gait generation method combined with ZMP [2, 3]. However, this method still has certain limitations. This method cannot handle uneven terrain and resist external disturbances very well. Similarly, to address the above issues, Jerry Pratt proposed the concept of Capture Point (CP) [4]. The CP concept takes into account the robot's future motion and predicts the point where the robot will come to a stop, allowing the robot to adjust its motion accordingly. To achieve online gait planning for humanoid robots, Jerry Pratt used a combination of the linear inverted pendulum model and the concept of Capture Point [5, 6]. Several studies have been made to adjust the robot's foothold based on CP and divergent component of motion (DCM) [7, 8]. Based on the two online gait planning methods of ZMP and CP, it is possible to adjust the foot placement to achieve walking on restricted uneven terrain or resist external disturbances.

Although footstep adjustment can be used in the planning layer to adapt to terrain, the application of compliant control in the control layer can significantly enhance the humanoid robot's adaptability to terrain and resistance to impacts. Impedance control and damping control have been proposed to adjust the position of a foot based on measured contact force for stable contact [9, 10]. Mingon Kim proposed a hybrid model of the linear inverted pendulum model and spring-damped model (LIP-SDM), where compliant control is used in gait planning to improve the humanoid robot's adaptability to terrain [11]. Hyoin Kae proposed a compliant inverted pendulum (CIP) model, which effectively enhances the humanoid robot's adaptability to terrain and resistance to external disturbances [12, 13]. Yuta Kojio proposed a method of compliant control based on angular momentum [14].

However, the use of compliant control may lead to poorer position tracking performance, but it can improve the stability and terrain adaptability of humanoid robots for position control. Therefore, we focus on studying the comprehensive application of compliant control in the control layer to improve stability and robustness. In this paper, we propose a comprehensive approach of compliant control applied to position-controlled humanoid robots.

The remainder of the paper is organized as follows. Section 2 introduces the system architecture of the proposed method. Section 3 proposes the comprehensive application of compliant control to position-controlled humanoid robots. Section 4 describes our experiments of the proposed method. Finally, conclusions are provided in Sect. 5.

2 System Overview

Figure 1 shows the system architecture of the proposed method applied to humanoid robot Walker. The system is mainly divided into modules such as gait generator, state estimator, compliant controller, kinematics calculator and humanoid robot. The gait generator is mainly used to generate the motions of foot and waist of the humanoid robot, and this part will not be highlighted in this paper. The state estimator is mainly used to estimate the state of the humanoid robot, including the pose, velocity, angular velocity, force, and ZMP of the body and foot. The kinematics module mainly calculates the joint angles and angular velocities of the humanoid robot based on the poses of the body and feet. The compliant controller is the core module of this article, which is mainly divided into body compliant controller, joint compliant controller and foot compliant controller. The specific details and application of the compliant controller will be described in Sect. 3. In this paper, we uses UBTECH humanoid robot Walker as an experiment platform.

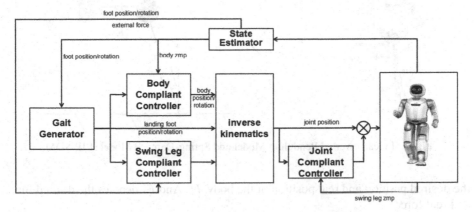

Fig. 1. System Architecture of the Proposed Method

3 Proposed Method

This section is devoted to describing the proposed compliant control method, applying to humanoid robot. In order to improve the adaptability and anti-interference ability of humanoid robot to the environment, we propose a comprehensive application scheme of the body compliant control of humanoid robot, the foot compliant control of swing leg and the joint compliant control of ankle.

3.1 The Body Compliant Controller Based on LIP-SPM

To enhance walking stability and anti-disturbance ability, we need a model with gait planning and compliant control to design controllers. For humanoid robot with compliant motion control, Mingon Kim proposed LIP-SPM. Firstly, the body compliant controller of the humanoid robot can be realized based on the LIP-SPM model. Secondly, the preview controller based on this model is realized to realize the gait planning of humanoid robot.

When designing the controller, we divide the LIP-SDM into LIPM and spring-damped model. The spring-damped model assumes that there is a spring and dumper between the desired COM and real COM. In Fig. 2, we describe the spring-damped model as a second-order system.

$$M_b \ddot{x}_c^d + B_b(\dot{x}_c^d - \dot{x}_c^r) + K_b(x_c^d - x_c^r) = F^d - F^r \tag{1}$$

where M_b, B_b and K_b denotes the mass of the LIP, the damping coefficient and stiffness coefficient for the spring-damped model. $\ddot{x}_c^d$ Denotes the desired acceleration of the body. $\dot{x}_c^d$ And $\dot{x}_c^r$ denotes the desired velocity and real velocity of the body. x_c^d And x_c^r denotes

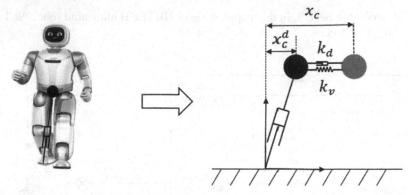

Fig. 2. Linear Inverted Pendulum Model and Spring-Damped Model (LIP-SDM)

the desired position and real position of the body. F^d And F^r denotes the desired force and real force.

As we all know, we usually use ZMP to describe the stability in humanoid robot gait generation. In the horizontal plane, we can get the ZMP of the humanoid robot and as follow:

$$p = \frac{\sum_{i=1}^{N} p_i f_i}{\sum_{i=1}^{N} f_i} \tag{2}$$

where p, p_i and f_i denote the total ZMP, the position and value of force i. In the support domain of the humanoid robot, we assume that the ZMP calculated by detection has an equivalent relationship with the force in LIP-SDM.

Based on the above assumption and Eq. (1), we can get

$$\ddot{x}_c^d = k_b^d (\dot{x}_c^d - \dot{x}_c^r) + k_b^p (x_c^d - x_c^r) - k_b^z (p_b^d - p_b^r) \tag{3}$$

where p_b^d and p_b^r denote the desire ZMP and real ZMP. k_b^p, k_b^d and k_b^z denote the gains, damping and external force coefficients for spring-damping model.

The assumptions of the LIPM are that the total mass is concentrated at on point at the COM and that the height from ground is constant. The equation of the LIPM is

$$p = x_c - \frac{z_c}{g} \ddot{x}_c \tag{4}$$

where z_c is the height of the COM, g is the gravitational acceleration and p denotes the ZMP.

Based on the analytical solution of Eq. (4), we can get the equation

$$\delta x(t) = \frac{z_c}{g} \ddot{x}_c cosh(\omega T) + \frac{\dot{x}}{\omega} sinh(\omega T) - \frac{z_c}{g} \ddot{x}_c \tag{5}$$

where $\delta x(t)$ denotes the error of the position, ω is the frequency of the LIPM and T denotes the step time.

Therefore based on the Eq. (3) and (5), we can get the desire x for the next step

$$x(t) = \sum_{\tau=0}^{\tau=nT} \delta x(T) + x(0) \tag{6}$$

where $x(t)$ denotes the desire position of the next step, n is the time and $x(0)$ the initial position at initial state.

3.2 The Compliant Controller of Swing Leg Based on Single Link Model

In order to better deal with collision situation when robot kicking obstacles during walking or colliding with stairs, we propose a simplified model which is a single-link spring-damping model based on the floating base. The application of this model can effectively deal with the impact force when it collides with an object. Combined with the gait generator and planning, it can re-plan the trajectory of the body and effectively improve the humanoid robot's ability to handle collisions.

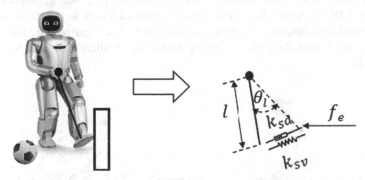

Fig. 3. A Single-Link Spring-Damping Model Based on the Floating Base

Based on the spring-link model, we can get the dynamic equation of the system as follow

$$\tau = (M_l l^2 + I)\ddot{\theta}_l - M_l g l sin\theta_l \tag{7}$$

where τ denotes the torque of the joint, θ_l is the position of joint and $\ddot{\theta}_l$ is the acceleration of joint. M_l, l and I denotes the mass, length and inertia of the leg.

During the practical application, we simplify the model and ignore the friction of joint. Referring to the law of the Eq. (1), we design the control law of the single-link spring-damping model, in Fig. 3 and as follow,

$$\ddot{\theta}_l = k_l^d (\dot{\theta}_l^d - \theta_l^r) + k_l^P (\theta_l^d - \theta_l^r) - k_b^z (\tau_d - f_e l cos\theta_l) + \frac{M_l g l sin\theta_l}{M_l l^2 + I} \tag{8}$$

where k_l^P, k_l^d and k_b^z are the coefficients of the single-link spring-damping model. θ_l^d, θ_l^r, $\dot{\theta}_l^d$ and θ_l^r denotes the desire and real position and velocity of the joint. τ_d is the desire torque and f_e is the external force.

Based on the Eq. (8), we can get the joint position by integrating $\ddot{\theta}_l$ twice. During the practical application, we assume that the compliant controller only acts in the forward direction of the swing leg, while other position and orientation maintain the planned motion. When the external force exceeds a certain threshold, the controller is triggered to keep the swing leg planning in its current state.

$$x_l^d(t) = x_l^d(t_{tri}) + l\sin\theta_l(t) \tag{9}$$

where $x_l^d(t)$ is the desired position of the swing leg, $x_l^d(t_{tri})$ is the position at the time of t_{tri}, and t is the now time.

By correcting the position of the swing leg, the body of humanoid robot is re-planned, thereby maintaining its stability when the swing leg of humanoid robot hits an obstacle.

3.3 The Compliant Controller of Ankle Based on CIP

Humanoid robots based on position control rely on external force or torque sensors to achieve flexible contact with the ground when walking on uneven terrain. In order to make humanoid robots better adapt to terrain, Hyoin Bae proposed a compliant inverted pendulum (CIP) model for state estimation of humanoid robots. In this paper, we propose a model based on a compliant inverted pendulum model to design the compliant controller of ankle which can make the swinging leg posture automatically adapt to terrain during landing phase.

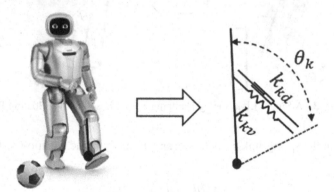

Fig. 4. The Compliant Inverted Pendulum (CIP) Model

As shown in Fig. 4, the CIP model is made by adding a virtual spring and a damper to the conventional inverted pendulum model. Based on the Sect. 3.1 and 3.2, we design the control law of the ankle for humanoid robot.

In order to design the compliant controller, we make two assumptions. Firstly, we assume that the humanoid robot is equivalent to an inverted pendulum based on the landing position of the swing leg. Secondly, we assume that the ZMP of the swing leg has an equivalent effect on the force and torque, which is the same as Sect. 3.1. We can get the control law as follow,

$$\ddot{\theta}_a = k_a^d(\dot{\theta}_a^d - \dot{\theta}_a^r) + k_a^p(\theta_a^d - \theta_a^r) - k_a^z(p_a^d - p_a^r) \tag{10}$$

where θ_a^d, θ_a^r, $\dot{\theta}_a^d$ and $\dot{\theta}_a^r$ denote the desire and real position and velocity of the ankle joint. p_a^d And p_a^r are the desire and real ZMP of the swing leg when the foot is landing. k_a^p, k_a^d and k_a^z are the coefficients of the compliant control law.

Based on Eq. (10), we can get the change position of the ankle joint by integrating $\ddot{\theta}_a$ twice which is affected by external force and torque. When the correct position and planning position are added, we get the final desired position of the ankle joint.

$$\theta_a^e(t) = \theta_a^p(t) + \iint_0^T \ddot{\theta}_a(t)dt \tag{11}$$

where $\theta_a^e(t)$ is the final desire position of the ankle joint, $\theta_a^p(t)$ is the planning position of the ankle joint, and T is the step time.

4 Experimental Results

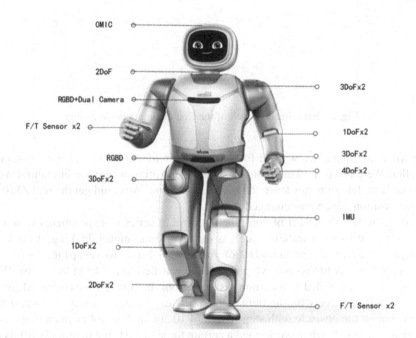

OMIC

2DoF

RGBD+Dual Camera

F/T Sensor x2

RGBD

3DoFx2

1DoFx2

2DoFx2

3DoFx2

1DoFx2

3DoFx2

4DoFx2

IMU

F/T Sensor x2

Fig. 5. Walker (UBTECH Humanoid Robot)

The proposed methods have been verified through experiments, using a humanoid robot called Walker, as shown in Fig. 5. The Walker, which is a humanoid robot developed by UBTECH, was used as the robotplatform [1]. This robot has 36 degrees of freedom, height 145 cm, and weight 77 kg. We used two F/T sensors as feedback information to achive compliant control on this full-size humanoid robot.

In five experiments, the first and second experiments are used to test the effect of single compliant controller, and the rest experiments are used to test the performance of the humanoid robot in practical applications.

In Fig. 6, we set the parameters ($k_b^p = 0.01$, $k_b^d = 10.0$ and $k_b^z = -8.0$) of the body compliant controller. In the experiment, we wanted to test the effect of the body compliant controller. We pushed the humanoid robot to the position where the humanoid would fall down if we let our hands leave the robot at this time. We could get the value of ZMP which is relative to the body coordinate and the position was moved by 0.03 m in x-axis direction. In Fig. 7, we set the parameters ($k_a^p = 100$, $k_a^d = 25$ and $k_a^z = 110$) of the ankle compliant controller, combined with the body compliant controller.

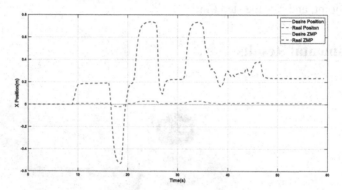

Fig. 6. Experiment Result of the Body Compliant Controller

In the experiment, we wanted to test the effect of the ankle and body compliant controller. We pushed the humanoid robot to the position where the humanoid would fall down if we let our hands leave the robot at this time. We could get the real ZMP and the joint position which was changed in Fig. 7.

In order to test the effect of compliant control, a series of experiments were done when humanoid robot is walking, such as external force impact, kicking obstacles, or pushing and releasing the humanoid robot. As shown in Fig. 8, we set up the experimental device as follows. A fitness ball weighing 10 kg was tied to a 1.45 m long rope. When the fitness ball was pulled to a certain distance from the robot, it was released, so that the fitness ball can freely hit the humanoid robot. In Fig. 9, we set up the experiment, let the robot hit the obstacle with step-length of 10 cm, and the robot can remain stable after hitting. In Fig. 9, when we applied a certain force to the robot to initially lift its foot off the ground, and then removed the force, the robot used compliant control to achieve self-stabilization (Fig. 10).

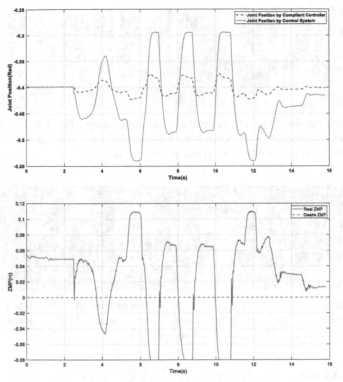

Fig. 7. Experiment Result of the Ankle Compliant Controller

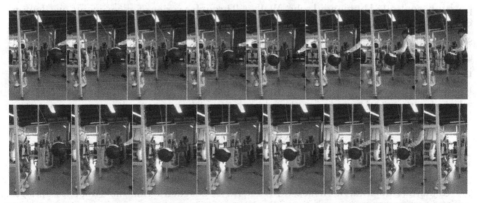

Fig. 8. Experiments for body compliant control when subjected to external object impact. A 10 kg fitness ball with a rope length of 1.45 m was released freely to impact the robot. Top: forward direction, distance between center of ball and robot is 0.7 m. Bottom: lateral direction, distance between center of ball and robot is 0.6 m.

Fig. 9. Experiments for compliant control when the swinging leg collides with an object. When walking with step-length of 10 cm per step, the robot maintained stability after colliding with an object by using its own compliant control and adjusting itself.

Fig. 10. Experiments for ankle compliant control when pushing the robot. When we applied a certain force to the robot to initially lift its foot off the ground, and then removed the force, the robot used compliant control to achieve self-stabilization.

5 Conclusions

In this paper, we propose a comprehensive approach of compliant control applied to position-controlled humanoid robot Walker. Through a series of experiments, we demonstrate that the application of compliant control on humanoid robots effectively improves stability against external disturbances and terrain variations. However, we also acknowledge that compliant control is implemented in three decoupled models, which may result in controller coupling and limit the ability to achieve whole-body compliant control in multi-rigid-body humanoid robots. In future work, we will combine gait generator and whole-body control to enhance the adaptability of humanoid robots to uneven terrain and their resistance to external disturbances.

References

1. Kajita, S., Hirukawa, H., Harada, K., Yokoi, K.: Introduction to Humanoid Robotics. Springer, Heidelberg (2014). https://doi.org/10.1007/978-3-642-54536-8
2. Huang, Q., Yokoi, K., Kajita, S., Kaneko, K., Arai, H., Koyachi, N.: Planning walking patterns for biped robot. IEEE Trans. Rob. Autom. **17**(3), 280–289 (2001)
3. Kajita, S., Morisawa, M., Miura, K., Nakaoka, S., Harada, K., Kaneko, K., et al.: Biped walking stabilization based on linear inverted pendulum tracking. In: 2010 IEEE/RSJ International Conference on Intelligent Robots and Systems, Taipei, Taiwan, pp. 4489–4496 (2010)
4. Pratt, J., Carff, J., Drakunov, S., Goswami, A.: Capture point: a step toward humanoid push recovery. In: 2006 IEEE/RAS International Conference on Humanoid Robots, Genova, Italy, pp. 200–207 (2007)

5. Koolen, T., De Boer, T., Rebula, J., Goswami, A., Pratt, J.: Capturability-based analysis and control of legged locomotion, part 1: theory and application to three simple gait models. Int. J. Rob. Res. **31**(9), 1094–1113 (2012)
6. Pratt, J., et al.: Capturability-based analysis and control of legged locomotion, part 2: application to M2V2, a lower-body humanoid. Int. J. Rob. Res. **31**(10), 1117–1133 (2012)
7. Jeong, H., Sim, O., Bae, H., Lee, K., Oh, J., Oh, J.H.: Biped walking stabilization based on foot placement control using capture point feedback. In: 2017 IEEE/RSJ International Conference on Intelligent Robots and Systems (IROS), Vancouver, BC, Canada, pp. 5263–5269 (2017)
8. Stephens, B.J., Atkeson, C.G.: Push recovery by stepping for humanoid robots with force controlled joints. In: 2010 10th IEEE-RAS International conference on humanoid robots, Nashville, TN, USA, pp. 52–59 (2010)
9. Lim, H.O., Setiawan, S.A., Takanishi, A.: Position-based impedance control of a biped humanoid robot. Adv. Robot. **18**(4), 415–435 (2004)
10. Nishiwaki, K., Kagami, S.: Frequent walking pattern generation that uses estimated actual posture for robust walking control. In: 2009 9th IEEE-RAS International Conference on Humanoid Robots, Paris, France, pp. 535–541 (2009)
11. Kim, M., Lim, D., Park, J.: Online walking pattern generation for humanoid robot with compliant motion control. In: 2019 International Conference on Robotics and Automation (ICRA), Montreal, QC, Canada, pp. 1417–1422 (2019)
12. Bae, H., Oh, J.H.: Biped robot state estimation using compliant inverted pendulum model. Robot. Auton. Syst. **108**, 38–50 (2018)
13. Jeong, H., Kim, J.H., Sim, O., Oh, J.H.: Avoiding obstacles during push recovery using real-time vision feedback. In: 2019 IEEE/RSJ International Conference on Intelligent Robots and Systems (IROS), Macau, China, pp. 483–490 (2019)
14. Kojio, Y., Ishiguro, Y., Sugai, F., Kakiuchi, Y., Okada, K., Inaba, M.: Unified balance control for biped robots including modification of footsteps with angular momentum and falling detection based on capturability. In: 2019 IEEE/RSJ International Conference on Intelligent Robots and Systems (IROS), Macau, China, pp. 497–504 (2019)

Fast Walking of Position-Controlled Biped Robot Based on Whole-Body Compliance Control

Yiting Zhu[1,2], Ye Xie[1,2], Chengzhi Gao[1,2], Dingkun Liang[1,2(✉)], Lingyu Kong[1,2], Xin Wang[1,2], Anhuan Xie[1,2,3], and Jianjun Gu[1,2,4]

[1] Research Center for Intelligent Robotics, Research Institute of Interdisciplinary Innovation, Zhejiang Laboratory, Hangzhou 311100, China
liangdk@zhejianglab.com
[2] Zhejiang Engineering Research Center for Intelligent Robotics, Hangzhou 311100, China
[3] Zhejiang University, Hangzhou 311100, Zhejiang, China
[4] Department of Electrical and Computer Engineering, Dalhousie University, Halifax, NS B3H 4R2, Canada

Abstract. When a biped robot walks at a high speed, only relying on the open-loop gait trajectory based on the linear inverted pendulum model (LIPM), the robot cannot maintain stability. Sudden contact with the ground when landing may cause the robot to be unstable. Simultaneously, when the robot walks faster, the horizontal position of the center of mass (CoM) varies greatly during a walk cycle, and the expected CoM trajectory cannot be accurately tracked, resulting in a deviation from the zero-moment point (ZMP). Aiming at the above situation that may occur in fast walking, a whole-body compliance controller with emphasis on making robot's walking more stable and faster is presented in this paper. The whole-body compliance controller consists of three parts: the CoM compliance controller, the vertical compliance controller and the foot compliance controller, which are used to improve the tracking effect of CoM, reduce the force impact of foot, and adjust the posture of the foot respectively. The simulation results show that with the whole-body compliance controller proposed in this paper, the tracking accuracy of the CoM becomes better, the posture of the robot is more stable during walking, and the landing compliance during landing are greatly improved. Finally, the walking speed of the robot can reach 1.8m/s.

Keywords: Biped robot · Motion control · Compliance control · Fast walking

1 Introduction

Biped robots are suitable for dangerous and complex application scenarios such as military, national defense, and aerospace because of their flexible movement capabilities and dexterous operating techniques [1]. High dynamic locomotion, including running, jumping and fast walking, is an important locomotion ability that can endow robots with faster movement ability and better obstacle surmounting performance. When the robot is moving at high speed, robustness and stability are key issues, not only to prevent the robot from falling, but also to ensure the safety of human on site. High-speed locomotion has challenges such as CoM trajectory tracking accuracy and impact absorbing after landing.

The generation of walking trajectory together with balance control to improve the stability of the robot has been studied. For decades, CoM trajectory generation algorithms were based on LIPM [2]. However, LIPM is oversimplified and ignores factors such as CoM momentum and leg mass, which makes the LIPM-based trajectory algorithm generation not suitable for high-speed locomotion, and lacks robustness to landing impact. Hence, the compliance control has been studied. The introduction of compliant controller provides biped robots with higher robustness and increased error tolerance when they encounter external disturbances by absorbing the effects of external disturbances, accidental contact, or model and control errors and thus makes their motion smoother and safer [3]. Particularly, compliance control is especially indispensable for position-controlled robots because of their high-stiffness joints, which make them weak in terms of impact absorption. Correspondingly, compliance control can be further divided into upper body compliance control and foot compliance control, which model and control the upper body and feet of the robot respectively to achieve different compliance characteristics.

Upper body compliance control stabilizes the posture of the upper body and tracks the reference CoM trajectory of the robot, thus imparting a converged state to the robot. Zhou et al. [4] applied the cart-table model to represent the major dynamics of the robot, assuming that a virtual spring damper is connected between the real COM position and the reference COM position, and taking the feedback of the ground reaction torque as input to generate the correction value of the COM reference. By modifying the CoM position reference, the applied torque at the joint is adjusted, resulting in a change in the contact force. Likewise, Huang et al. [5] proposed a compliance control strategy for biped robots called resistant compliance, which allows a robot to comply with the external disturbance initially and then repel the disturbance to reduce the imbalance caused by the reconciliatory motion. Caron et al. [6] used whole-body admittance control to introduce compliance for stable stair climbing at the Airbus factory.

Foot compliance control is mainly used for shock absorption when the swing leg lands on the ground suddenly. Foot compliance control was developed from impedance control of manipulators [7, 8]. Inspired by these, some researches proposed virtual spring-damper to absorb the shock at landing between the hip joint and ankle joint [9], and at ankle [10], at foot [11]. Kajita [12] developed a foot torque controller which modifies foot rotation to realize the foot reference torque calculated by the ZMP distributor, it is evaluated in the experiments of HRP-4C walking and turning on a lab floor. However, the outdoor walking speed of HRP-4C is only 0.6 km/h. Kim et al. [13] modeled the robot as a simple inverted pendulum with a compliant joint and designed the damping controllers in order to impose sufficient damping forces in ankle rolling and pitching joints without changing the steady state value to achieve dynamic stair climbing. However, if the tiptoe of the swing foot collides with the stair wall, the structural vibration of the torso is generated in the yaw direction. Therefore, foot compliance control alone cannot guarantee the elimination of vibration. Foot compliance control is also widely used in walking on uneven terrain to reduce contact impact [14, 15].

In this article, we propose a whole-body compliant control strategy for fast walking of biped robot, which mainly includes the following three aspects:

1) A *CoM Compliance Controller* is proposed to adjust the CoM trajectory according to the real-time ZMP error, to realize the accuracy tracking of the expected CoM trajectory.
2) A *Vertical Compliance Controller* based on a double spring-damper model in the vertical direction of the ankle joint is proposed to meet the impact absorbing and stability requirements of the foot.
3) A *Foot Damping Controller* is proposed to modify foot rotation to realize the foot reference torque.

The remainder of this paper is organized as follows. In Sect. 2, we introduce our gait generation method based on LIPM. In Sect. 3, we introduce the whole control frame. In Sect. 4, we present the simulation results and verify the efficiency of our control strategy. Finally, concluding remarks are in Sect. 5.

2 Related work

This paper takes the position-controlled biped robot independently developed by Zhejiang Lab (Fig. 1. Robot model) as the research object. This robot has a total of 32 degrees of freedom (DoF), and each leg has 6 DoFs, namely hip roll, hip yaw, hip pitch, knee pitch, ankle pitch and ankle roll. In order to better conform to the LIPM, the biped robot is designed to concentrate the mass on the torso as much as possible and drive the knee and ankle motors upward through the four-bar linkage mechanism to make the two legs relatively light. Two six-dimensional force/torque sensors are installed on the sole of each foot, to calculate the actual ZMP position of the robot.

Fig. 1. Robot model

We define the world coordinate system as the position between the two feet of the robot when it is standing still. The forward direction of the robot is the x-axis, the vertical upward direction is the z-axis, and the y-axis is determined by the right-hand rule, pointing from the right foot to the left foot.

The walking gait generation uses the classic algorithm based on the LIPM in [16]. For simplicity, this model ignores the angular momentum generated at the CoM and assumes a constant value Z_c for the CoM height. However, these simplifications come at the expense of balance recovery strategies: such as the variable-height strategy [17] and angular momentum balance strategy [18]. When the robot speeds up, the gait planned by the open-loop LIPM alone cannot keep it stable. Our LIPM-based stabilizer uses the contact wrench to compensate the horizontal position of the CoM, the attitude and the height of the feet, enabling the robot to walk faster.

3   Design of Controllers

The main purpose of the proposed control strategy is to absorb the landing impact, track the desired CoM trajectory and reduce the ZMP tracking error, so that the robot can walk faster and more stably. It mainly includes two aspects of compliance controllers: CoM compliance controller and ankle compliance controller. The former is to reduce the ZMP tracking error, and the latter includes two parts: the vertical compliance controller and the foot damping controller. By adjusting the compliance parameters, different compliance effects can be achieved, while ensuring that the posture of the feet is parallel to the ground.

3.1   CoM Compliance Controller Design

The CoM compliance controller uses the cart-table model to adjust the position of the CoM by calculating the position of ZMP to improve the tracking of the CoM. This controller implements the third stabilization strategy from Sect. 4.5.1 of the Introduction to Humanoid Robotics [16]. In this case we must measure the ZMP by our Force/Torque sensor to design a feedback controller. By assuming the time constant of the ZMP sensor as T, the ZMP equation is

$$p = \frac{1}{1 + sT}\left(x - \frac{z_c}{g}\ddot{x}\right) \tag{1}$$

where p represents the position of ZMP, x represents the horizontal position of the CoM.

Taking the state vector as $X = \begin{bmatrix} p & x & \dot{x} \end{bmatrix}^T$, the acceleration of the system $\ddot{x}$ as the control input u, the dynamics of LIPM can be written as:

$$\dot{X} = AX + Bu$$

$$A = \begin{bmatrix} -\frac{1}{T} & \frac{1}{T} & 0 \\ 0 & 0 & 1 \\ 0 & 0 & 0 \end{bmatrix}, B = \begin{bmatrix} -\frac{z}{gT} \\ 0 \\ 1 \end{bmatrix} \tag{2}$$

We apply the following compliance control law:

$$\Delta \ddot{x} = -k_1 \Delta p - k_2 \Delta x - k_3 \Delta \dot{x} \tag{3}$$

In the above formula, k_1, k_2 and k_3 are used to tune the acceleration of the horizontal position of CoM, which can be obtained by solving the following linear quadratic optimization problem:

$$\min J = \frac{1}{2} \int_0^{\infty} (\Delta X^T Q \Delta X + R \Delta u^2) \tag{4}$$

Then by integrating $\Delta \ddot{x}$ twice to get the adjustment value Δx of the CoM, the command CoM position x^{cmd} can be calculated by the following formula

$$x^{cmd} = x^{ref} + \Delta x \tag{5}$$

where x^{ref} is the initial CoM reference trajectory.

3.2 Ankle Compliance Controller Design

When the robot lands, there may be problems such as the landing of the foot is not parallel to the ground, the landing impact is too large, and the support is not strong enough. Therefore, we propose an ankle compliance controller to ensure the soft landing of the robot and the parallelism of the foot to the ground. The compliance controller is mainly divided into two parts, which are used to control the position and posture of the sole, called the vertical compliance controller and the foot damping controller, respectively.

A. *Vertical Compliance Controller*

The walking cycle of each leg consists of a swing period and a stance period. During the walking cycle of the robot, the swing leg is mainly affected by the impact generated by the interaction between the foot and the ground when it lands, while the support leg is mainly affected by the impact caused by the inclination of the torso during the support process, resulting in the foot not fitting the ground well. Therefore, the robot has different requirements for the support and compliance of its legs in different walking periods. In order to adjust position according to force, we introduce a Double Spring Damping (DSD) model for the ankle joint to obtain the relationship between position and the differential of force. The adopted DSD model is shown in Fig. 2, which contains four adjustable parameters, including two elements of stiffness and two elements of damping. By properly adjusting these four parameters, we can achieve different anti-impact stability effects to meet the needs of robot in different walking periods.

For those who expect to respond quickly to absorb the impact after landing, and then comply with the external force for compliant motion, we call it a compliant stability controller; it has lower requirements for resistance to impact and compliant motion and needs to maintain A certain support capability, we call it a support stability controller.

Define the state vector as $X = \begin{bmatrix} f_z & z_a & \dot{z}_a \end{bmatrix}^T$, among them, f_z is the ground reaction force(GRF) on the foot in the vertical direction measured by the force sensor, z_a and $\dot{z}_a$ are the position and velocity of the foot in the z direction respectively.

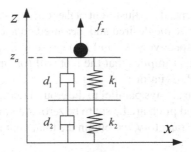

Fig. 2. The DSDS for vertical compliance controller

Define the acceleration of the foot in the vertical axis as $\Delta \ddot{z}_a$, and use it as the control quantity of the state equation, analyze the force of the model and undergo Laplace transformation, finally we obtain the state equation of the model as

$$\dot{X} = AX + Bu \qquad (6)$$

where

$$A = \begin{bmatrix} \frac{k_1+k_2}{d_1+d_2} & \frac{k_1 k_2}{d_1+d_2} & \frac{k_1 d_2+k_2 d_1}{d_1+d_2} \\ 0 & 0 & 1 \\ 0 & 0 & 0 \end{bmatrix}$$

$$B = \begin{bmatrix} \frac{d_1 d_2}{d_1+d_2} \\ 0 \\ 1 \end{bmatrix} \qquad (7)$$

Parameters k_1, k_2, d_1 and d_2 are the elastic and damping coefficients of the DSDS model respectively. In the same way, we can get the relationship between the desired force and desired foot trajectory, then we can get state equation for the error as follow:

$$\Delta \dot{X} = A \Delta X + B \Delta u \qquad (8)$$

The state feedback controller is given by

$$\Delta u = -K \Delta X \qquad (9)$$

where $K = \begin{bmatrix} k_{z1} & k_{z2} & k_{z3} \end{bmatrix}^T$, which can be determined by a standard control theory like a pole placement or the LQR optimal control.

B. *Foot Damping Controller*

The foot damping controller modifies foot rotation to track the foot reference torque. The controller is given by

$$K_d \begin{bmatrix} \Delta \dot{\theta}_r \\ \Delta \dot{\theta}_p \end{bmatrix} + K_P \begin{bmatrix} \Delta \theta_r \\ \Delta \theta_p \end{bmatrix} = \tau_d - \tau$$

$$K_d = \begin{bmatrix} k_{dr} & 0 \\ 0 & k_{dp} \end{bmatrix}, K_p = \begin{bmatrix} k_{pr} & 0 \\ 0 & k_{pp} \end{bmatrix} \qquad (10)$$

where $\Delta\theta_r$ and $\Delta\theta_p$ represents the adjustment of the foot orientation in the two directions of roll and pitch, τ_d and τ are the desired and measured contact wrench expressed at the origin of the foot frame respectively. K_p and K_d represent the gain parameters that need to be adjusted. A higher gain implies that the foot will roll and pitch faster in reaction to lateral and sagittal ZMP deviations.

We expect the feet to be always parallel to the ground during walking. Therefore, the desired torque τ_d of roll and pitch are be set to be zero. Add the calculated foot rotation adjustment to the planned trajectory, we obtain the final command foot rotation value.

4 Simulation

The simulations of walking are conducted to validate the proposed whole-body compliance control framework. Firstly, we independently verify the effectiveness of the CoM compliance controller, the vertical compliance controller and the foot damping controller. Then, we simultaneously add the CoM compliance controller and ankle compliance controller to our robot to make the robot walk as fast as possible. The vertical compliance controller parameters are listed in Table 1.

Table 1. Vertical compliance controller parameters for simulation

Controller Type	Value
compliant stability controller	$K_c = \begin{bmatrix} 0.06 & 2.001 & 500.0087 \end{bmatrix}$
stabilize stability controller	$K_s = \begin{bmatrix} 0.06 & 5000 & 201.7213 \end{bmatrix}$

Firstly, in order to verify the effectiveness of the CoM compliance controller, a 200 N thrust with a duration of 0.8 s is applied to the robot in the horizontal direction at 5 s when it stands still. The simulation comparisons are shown in Fig. 3. Where, Fig. 3(a) is the pitch angle of the robot and the ZMP position in the horizontal direction, Fig. 3(b) is the coordinates of the robot's CoM in the horizontal and vertical directions. The blue dotted line represents the open-loop trajectory curve obtained without adding any controller, and the red solid line represents the curve after adding the CoM compliance controllers. As can be seen from the figure, after adding the CoM compliance control, the oscillation period and tracking error of the CoM become smaller, and the robot stabilizes faster.

In order to verify the control effect of vertical compliance controller, the controller is added when the robot walks forward. Figure 4 shows the comparative data of the ground reaction force on the soles of the left and right foot of the open-loop and closed-loop algorithms. It can be seen from the figure that the introduction of vertical compliance control reduces the impact force by about 200 N when it just touches the ground.

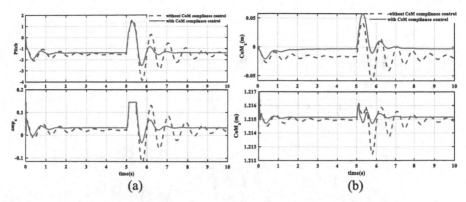

Fig. 3. The position and posture of CoM. a) is the torso pitch and ZMP position in the x direction, and b) is the CoM position in the horizontal and vertical directions.

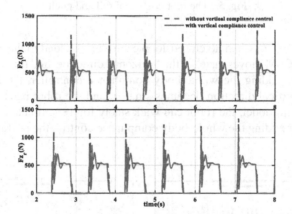

Fig. 4. The landing impacts of both feet

In order to verify the control effect of foot damping controller, the controller is added when the robot walks forward. Figure 5 shows the comparative data of the foot posture of the open-loop and closed-loop algorithms, while the upper part is roll and the lower part is pitch. It can be seen from the figure that the introduction of foot damping controller makes the posture of the foot more stable, and the robot can walker further.

Next, we introduce all the controllers mentioned above, and demonstrate the effectiveness of the controllers through the tracking effect of CoM, the torso attitude, and the maximum walking speed that the robot can reach. In the simulation, we give the robot a command to continuously accelerate forward, start from standing still, and accelerate to 1.8 m/s in 18 s. The result of the simulation is plotted in Fig. 6–Fig. 7. Figure 6a) is the position curve of the CoM in the horizontal and vertical directions, Fig. 6b) is the posture of the CoM in three directions, and Fig. 7 is the speed curve of CoM when the robot is walking. Among them, the blue dotted line represents the open-loop trajectory curve obtained without adding any controller, and the red solid line represents the curve after adding all the above-mentioned whole-body compliance controllers.

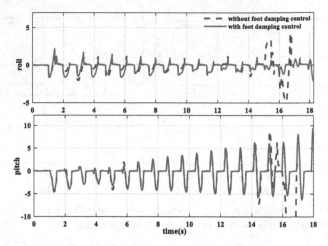

Fig. 5. The foot posture of roll and pitch

As shown in Fig. 6, when no closed-loop controller is added to the algorithm, as the speed increases, CoM moves faster in the horizontal direction, and the robot falls around 16 s. While after adding the whole-body compliance controller, the height variation of the CoM in vertical direction becomes smaller, and the robot behaves closer to the inverted pendulum model, the robot can walk stably for 18 s. It can also be seen from Fig. 6b) that after adding the whole-body compliance control, the posture at the CoM is also more stable.

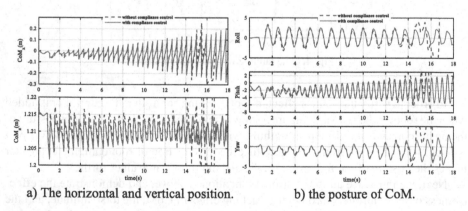

a) The horizontal and vertical position.   b) the posture of CoM.

Fig. 6. The position and posture of CoM.

Figure 7 is the speed curve, the robot will fall when it walks up to 1.3 m/s in the open loop algorithm, while after adding the whole-body compliance control, the walking speed of the robot can reach 1.8 m/s.

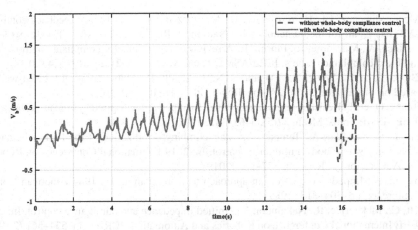

Fig. 7. The velocity of CoM

All the above simulation results show that the whole-body compliance controller can significantly improve the stability of the robot's walking process, effectively reduce the impact of the swing leg when it lands, and increase the walking speed of the robot.

5   Conclusion

For fast walking biped robots, in order to increase walking speed and reduce landing impact, we propose a whole-body compliance control framework, including CoM compliance control, vertical compliance control and foot damping control. The simulation results show that after adding the algorithm, compared with the open-loop movement, the CoM tracking accuracy is higher, the foot impact force becomes smaller, and the maximum movement speed can reach 1.8 m/s.

In the future, we will test our algorithm on our real platform. In follow-up research, we consider adding our compliant controllers to working conditions such as uneven ground and upstairs, continue to improve the balance control effect of our biped robot. In addition, when the speed increases, due to the existence of angular momentum, there will be obvious yaw problems in the walking of the robot, which is what we urgently need to solve.

Acknowledgements. This work was supported in part by Key Research Project of Zhejiang Lab under Grant No. G2021NB0AL03; and in part by the Zhejiang Provincial Natural Science Foundation of China under Grant No. LQ23F030010.

References

1. Gelin, R., Laumond, J.P.: Humanoid robot applications: introduction. In: Goswami, A., Vadakkepat, P. (eds.) Humanoid Robotics: A Reference (2016). https://doi.org/10.1007/978-94-007-7194-9_150-1

2. Alcaraz-Jiménez, J.J., Herrero-Pérez, D., Martínez-Barberá, H.: Robust feedback control of ZMP-based gait for the humanoid robot Nao. Int. J. Rob. Res. **32**(9–10), 1074–1088 (2013)
3. Calanca, A., Muradore, R., Fiorini, P.: A review of algorithms for compliant control of stiff and fixed-compliance robots. IEEE/ASME Trans. Mechatron. **21**(2), 613–624 (2016)
4. Zhou, C., Li, Z., Wang, X., Tsagarakis, N., Caldwell, D.: Stabilization of bipedal walking based on compliance control. Auton. Robot. **40**, 1041–1057 (2016)
5. Huang, Q., et al.: Resistant compliance control for biped robot inspired by humanlike behavior. IEEE/ASME Trans. Mech. **27**(5), 3463–3473 (2022)
6. Caron, S., Kheddar, A., Tempier, O.: Stair climbing stabilization of the HRP-4 humanoid robot using whole-body admittance control. In: 2019 International Conference on Robotics and Automation (ICRA), pp. 277–283 (2019)
7. Hogan, N.: Impedance control: an approach to manipulation. In: 1984 American Control Conference, pp. 304–313 (1985)
8. Ott, C., Mukherjee, R., Nakamura, Y.: Unified impedance and admittance control, In: 2010 IEEE International Conference on Robotics and Automation (ICRA), pp. 554–561 (2010)
9. Kim, J.Y., Park, I.W., Oh, J.H.: Walking control algorithm of biped humanoid robot on uneven and inclined floor. J. Intell. Rob. Syst. **48**, 457–484 (2007)
10. Yoo, S.M., Hwang, S.W., Kim, D.H., Park, J.H.: Biped robot walking on uneven terrain using impedance control and terrain recognition algorithm. In: 2018 IEEE-RAS 18th International Conference on Humanoid Robots (Humanoids), pp. 293–298 (2018)
11. Xu, W., Xiong, R., Wu, J.: Force/torque-based compliance control for humanoid robot to compensate the landing impact force. In: 2010 First International Conference on Networking and Distributed Computing, pp. 336–340 (2010)
12. Kajita, S., et al.: Biped walking stabilization based on linear inverted pendulum tracking. In: 2010 IEEE/RSJ International Conference on Intelligent Robots and Systems, pp. 4489–4496 (2010)
13. Kim, J.Y., Park, I.W., Oh, J.H.: Realization of dynamic stair climbing for biped humanoid robot using force/torque sensors. J. Intell. Rob. Syst. **56**, 389–423 (2009)
14. Dong, C., et al.: A novel hierarchical control strategy for biped robot walking on uneven terrain. In: 2019 IEEE-RAS 19th International Conference on Humanoid Robots (Humanoids), pp. 140–145 (2019)
15. Son, B.G., Kim, J.T., Park, J.H.: Impedance control for biped robot walking on uneven terrain. In: 2009 IEEE International Conference on Robotics and Biomimetics (ROBIO), pp. 239–244 (2009)
16. Kajita, S., Hirukawa, H., Harada, K., Yokoi, K.: Introduction to Humanoid Robotics. Springer, Heidelberg (2014)
17. Caron, S.: Biped stabilization by linear feedback of the variable-height inverted pendulum model. In: 2020 IEEE International Conference on Robotics and Automation (ICRA), pp. 9782–9788 (2020)
18. Lu, Y., Gao, J., Shi, X., Tian, D., Jia, Z.: Whole-body control based on landing estimation for fixed-period bipedal walking on stepping stones. In: 2020 3rd International Conference on Control and Robots (ICCR), pp. 140–149 (2020)

Whole Body Balance Control for Bipedal Robots Based on Virtual Model Control

Chengzhi Gao[1,2], Ye Xie[1,2], Yiting Zhu[1,2], Dingkun Liang[1,2(✉)], Lingyu Kong[1,2], Xin Wang[1,2], Anhuan Xie[1,2,3], and Jianjun Gu[1,2,4]

[1] Research Center for Intelligent Robotics, Research Institute of Interdisciplinary Innovation, Zhejiang Laboratory, Hangzhou 311100, China
`liangdk@zhejianglab.com`
[2] Zhejiang Engineering Research Center for Intelligent Robotics, Hangzhou 311100, China
[3] Zhejiang University, Hangzhou 311100, Zhejiang, China
[4] Department of Electrical and Computer Engineering, Dalhousie University, Halifax, NS B3H 4R2, Canada

Abstract. Due to the lack of accurate stability theoretical basis, the dynamic balance control of bipedal robots is a challenging topic. In this paper, we propose a controller that combines virtual model control and whole body control. In our framework, the whole system is simplified into a spring inverted pendulum model. Decoupling control is carried out for this model, and a virtual model is introduced to establish the relationship between the joint torque of the support leg and the state of the center of mass. The distribution of reaction force is obtained through decoupling closed-loop control. The whole body control part first uses multi task whole body control to determine the kinematics information, and then solves the joint feedforward torque through dynamical model, thus obtaining the desired force position hybrid control. Proposed algorithm improved the problem of incomplete decoupling between states and increased the stiffness of the support leg. The newly designed control framework was tested in Simscape dynamic simulation and verified the anti-interference ability and fast walking ability of Whole Body Balance Control for bipedal robots based on Virtual Model Control.

Keywords: Virtual Model Control · Whole Body Control · Null Space Project

1 Introduction

Currently, bipedal robots have high joint degrees of freedom, large overall rotational inertia, and heavy floating bases, which often limits the balance and anti-interference ability of robots. Common balance control methods include Zero Moment Point (ZMP), Hybrid Zero Dynamics (HZD), Virtual Model Control (VMC), and Model Predictive Control (MPC) and Reinforcement Learning (RL).

The ZMP method and HZD method are generally used for position control of bipedal robots. The ZMP method is one of the longest developing motion control methods for bipedal robots. The zero moment point refers to the point where the ground action torque on the contact surface between the feet of a bipedal robot and the ground is zero. The

© The Author(s), under exclusive license to Springer Nature Singapore Pte Ltd. 2023
H. Yang et al. (Eds.): ICIRA 2023, LNAI 14270, pp. 355–367, 2023.
https://doi.org/10.1007/978-981-99-6492-5_31

essence of the ZMP method is based on the ZMP stability criterion, which means that when the ZMP point falls within the support domain, it can be determined that the bipedal robot is stable. Famous robots include ASIMO [2], BHR [3], Kong II robots [4], HRP robots [5], and Lola [6], all of which use the ZMP method. However, the drawbacks of ZMP method in walking on uneven and complex terrain are obvious, as the sole of the foot does not fully contact the ground, making it impossible to calculate the position of ZMP points. The HZD method essentially adds various constraints to an accurate dynamic model and obtains the optimal trajectory through optimization. Moreover, this optimization process cannot be carried out in real time and can only generate mapping tables offline, which are then executed on physical objects through table lookup. HZD is applied to robots from Agility Robotics, including Mable, ATRIAS [7], Cassie [8], and Digit. This method can achieve good results when targeting specific problems, but cannot adapt to complex and changing environments. Overall, in terrain determined scenarios, position control methods can achieve basic uneven road walking through algorithms, but their blind walking and anti-interference capabilities are relatively poor on uneven roads.

The MPC method is gradually developed through the combination of traditional control methods and robot control. In essence, the method is to establish a linear prediction model, and then solve the future finite time domain state for each control action, and then do global optimization according to the predicted state. In 2018[9], Massachusetts Institute of Technology proposed a method of using MPC to control ground forces to achieve quadruped robot walking, and applied it to Cheetah3. They refer to this method of linearizing the model as a predictive model, and then introducing ground friction constraints to calculate ground forces as the convex model predictive control method. However, [10]there are currently few examples of applying similar CMPC methods to physical humanoid robots.

Raibert proposed a decoupling control method in 1986 [11], which achieves dynamic walking stability by controlling body posture, center of mass height, and center of mass position, rather than requiring robots to meet ZMP conditions. Pratt et al. [1]. Proposed virtual model control methods based on this, which were attempted by various laboratories in the United States. Atlas robots, Cassie robots [12], and ATRIAS robots have all applied this method. The advantage of this method is its strong robustness, and its ability to handle various complex road surfaces is generally strong. It simplifies the complex problem of humanoid control into dynamic stability control of state variables. The disadvantage is that the bipedal robot model has been simplified, resulting in poor performance for platforms that do not meet the model requirements and higher requirements for the mechanical structure of the platform itself. In order to fill the gap between the simplified model and the actual robot, a hierarchical control method based on zero space projection was adopted to provide position layer control, achieving force position hybrid control and improving the applicability of VMC in robot systems.

The paper is organized as follows: In Sect. 2, the biped robot used in this paper is briefly introduced. Section 3 introduces the proposed whole body balance control algorithm based on virtual models. Section 4 shows the simulation results conducted in the Matlab environment to confirm the effectiveness of the proposed method. Finally, the Sect. 5 pairs of papers were summarized and summarized.

2 Related Work

2.1 Biped Robot

In this paper, a self-developed biped robot with high flexibility is used as the estimation object. The core of the design of the biped robot is to focus the mass in the trunk part, so that the two legs are relatively light, in order to better conform to the inverted pendulum model, through the four-link mechanism to move the knee motor and ankle motor as upward as possible.

In this paper, we define the sagittal direction of the robot as the x-direction, and the lateral direction of the robot as the y-direction, the vertical direction is z-direction.

As shown in the Fig. 1, there are three hip motor, one knee motor and one ankle motor on each leg of the biped robot. The degree of freedom of the biped robot is $n = 6 \times 2 = 12$.

Fig. 1. Biped robot

When establishing the measurement model of state estimation, it is necessary to use the kinematics information of the robot to establish the model relative to the standing foot coordinate system.

$$P = (x, y, z) = f(\theta_1, \theta_2, \theta_3, \theta_4, \theta_5, \theta_5) \tag{1}$$

The velocity of the torso relative to the support point:

$$v = J(\theta_1, \theta_2, \theta_3, \theta_4, \theta_5)\begin{bmatrix} d\theta_1 & d\theta_2 & d\theta_3 & d\theta_4 & d\theta_5 \end{bmatrix} \tag{2}$$

where J is the Jacobian matrix relative to the support point, and $d\theta i$ is the joint angular velocity fed back by the encoder. When the kinematics model is used to estimate the state of the biped torso, the support points need to be calculated, and the support points are constantly switched during bipedal walking.

2.2 Robot Dynamics Analysis

The structure of both legs of a bipedal robot is also the same, so as long as the left leg is analyzed, the right leg can also be operated using the same method. Due to the fact that this article focuses on mobile robots, in the case of using the center of mass position as the base, a floating base dynamic equation should be used. The floating base model for the left leg is as follows.

$$A_l \begin{bmatrix} \ddot{q}_f \\ \ddot{q}_J \end{bmatrix} + b + g = \begin{bmatrix} 0_6 \\ T_l \end{bmatrix} + \begin{bmatrix} 0_6 & J_{cl} \end{bmatrix}^T f_{rl} \tag{1}$$

where, A_l is the mass matrix of the left leg, b is the Coriolis force of each link of the left leg, g is the weight moment of each link of the left leg, $\ddot{q}_f$ is the acceleration vector of the floating basis, $\ddot{q}_J$ is the acceleration of each joint of the left leg, T_l is the output torque of each joint of the left leg, J_{cl} is the Jacobian contact matrix of the left leg, and f_{rl} is the corresponding end force and ground action torque of the left leg.

Obtain the following relationship through derivation:

$$\begin{bmatrix} \tau_b \\ \tau_f \end{bmatrix} = A\ddot{q} + b + g - J_c^T f \tag{2}$$

Due to the fact that Jacobian mapping is based on the ankle joint, it can result in a higher output ankle joint torque. In reality, the ankle joint cannot have a particularly high output torque, and ankle joint auxiliary control will be used to limit it.

3 Method

3.1 Decoupling Control and Virtual Model Control

Decoupling control is the use of a certain structure to eliminate the coupling relationship between various circuits, and then independent control methods are implemented for each circuit. Using virtual model algorithm to introduce the concept of virtual force, establish the connection between the joint and center of mass force in the spring inverted pendulum model. Decouple the system into three closed loops around the centroid state, that is, attitude control, altitude control and speed control, and then obtain joint torque through the VMC algorithm. On this basis, ankle joint auxiliary control is also adopted to ensure better stability of the robot.

Attitude Controller
The attitude control of humanoid robot is the most important. In fact, as long as the robot maintains a stable posture, it can essentially be said to be a stable and non collapsing state. And according to the above, it is only necessary to establish the feedback balance of the LIP model under the support of one leg to achieve attitude control during walking. According to the classical control theory proposed by Raibert, the body attitude control method of foot robot:

$$\tau_x = k_{px}(\varphi_{dr} - \varphi_r) - k_{dx}\dot{\varphi}_r \tag{3}$$

$$\tau_y = k_{py}(\varphi_{dp} - \varphi_p) - k_{dy}\dot{\varphi}_p \qquad (4)$$

$$\tau_z = k_{pz}(\varphi_{dy} - \varphi_y) - k_{dz}\dot{\varphi}_y \qquad (5)$$

Among them, τ_x, τ_y, τ_z represent the virtual force torque values output in the rolling, pitching and yawing directions of the robot's upper body, φ_r, φ_p, φ_y are the rolling,pitching and yawing angles of the body posture, φ_{dr}, φ_{dp}, φ_{dy} are the rolling, pitching and yawing angles of the expected body posture, $\dot{\varphi}_r$, $\dot{\varphi}_p$, $\dot{\varphi}_y$ represents the rolling angular velocity, pitch angular velocity and yaw angular velocity, with k_{px}, k_{py}, k_{pz}, k_{dx}, k_{dy} and k_{dz} as the corresponding gain coefficients.

Attitude control requires a high corresponding speed. In a stable single leg standing state, the body will also have a torque due to gravity. It is necessary to introduce a feedforward torque. The torque generated by the gravity of the center of mass on the upper body will be added to the robot's attitude control as a feedforward quantity.

$$\tau_f = k_p(q_d - q) - k_d(\dot{q}_d - \dot{q}) + \tau_g \qquad (6)$$

Among them, τ_g represents torque feedforward. Adding a feedforward link can effectively accelerate the convergence speed of short attitude angles.

Height Controller
Similar to attitude control, altitude control also needs to add gravity compensation feedforward. To counteract the effect of gravity and accelerate the convergence speed of vertical position.

$$F_z = k_p(h_0 - h) - k_d(v_h - v) + F_g \qquad (7)$$

Among them, h_0 is the height of the center of mass in the set robot coordinate system, v_h is the velocity in the vertical direction of the center of mass, k_p, k_d is the PD feedback coefficient moment of the parameter to be adjusted. F_g is the vertical force exerted by gravity on the center of mass.

Ankle Joint Assist Controller
In order to avoid the impact of excessive ankle joint torque on the touchdown state, this article limits the output torque of the ankle joint. At the same time, the torque of the ankle joint is used to control the horizontal position state of the robot. Through dynamic equations, the horizontal virtual force corresponding to the ankle joint torque is derived.

$$\tau_{anklePitch} = (k_{px}(p_{xd} - p_x) - k_{dx}(\dot{p}_{xd} - \dot{p}_x))/h \qquad (8)$$

$$\tau_{ankleRoll} = (k_{py}(p_{yd} - p_y) - k_{dy}(\dot{p}_{yd} - \dot{p}_y))/h \qquad (9)$$

Among them, $\tau_{anklePitch}$, $\tau_{ankleRoll}$ is the torque of ankle motor, k_{px}, k_{dx}, k_{py}, k_{dy} are the gain coefficients, p_{xd}, p_{yd}, $\dot{p}_{xd}$, $\dot{p}_{yd}$ represent the designed motion of the centroid, and the p_x, p_y, $\dot{p}_x$, $\dot{p}_y$ represent the actual motion of the centroid. h is the height of the centroid.

On this basis, combined with the previously derived dynamic model, calculate the horizontal part of the virtual force.

$$
\begin{cases}
\tau_{anklePitch} = (A_l\ddot{q}_J + b_l + g_l)_{STanklePitch} - J_{STanklePitch}{}^T\begin{bmatrix} F_x & F_y & F_z & \tau_x & \tau_y & \tau_z \end{bmatrix} \\
\tau_{ankleRoll} = (A_l\ddot{q}_J + b_l + g_l)_{STankleRoll} - J_{STankleRoll}{}^T\begin{bmatrix} F_x & F_y & F_z & \tau_x & \tau_y & \tau_z \end{bmatrix}
\end{cases}
\tag{10}
$$

Among them, take out the row corresponding to the pitch of the ankle joint of the standing leg in the inertia term, Coriolis force term, and gravity term of the dynamic equation, which are $(A_l\ddot{q}_J + b_l + g_l)_{ST,anklePitch}$, $(A_l\ddot{q}_J + b_l + g_l)_{ST,ankleRoll}$ respectively. Solve the equation set to obtain the horizontal virtual force F_x and F_y.

Footstep Controller

In the 3D linear inverted pendulum walking mode, the swinging leg controls the motion speed by adjusting the position of the landing point. Specifically, the bipedal robot decelerates relative to the forward landing point of the support leg endpoint, and accelerates relative to the backward landing point. At the same time, the farther it is from the support leg endpoint, the greater its acceleration and deceleration.

According to the classic footstep selection model, the footstep calculation formula is as follows:

$$
x_f = \frac{\dot{x}T_s}{2} + K_x(\dot{x} - \dot{x}_d)
\tag{11}
$$

where x_f represents the landing point of the swinging leg, $\dot{x}$ represents the center of mass velocity of the bipedal robot body, $\dot{x}_d$ represents the expected center of mass velocity of the bipedal robot body, and T_s represents the walking cycle of the robot. The calculation of the foothold in the y direction is the same as x.

3.2 Whole Body Balance Control

In order to fill the gap between the simplified model and the real robot, a hierarchical control method based on null space projection is adopted to provide position layer control. By implementing hierarchical control to achieve position control goals consistent with VMC, on the one hand, the stiffness of the support legs is improved, and on the other hand, the gap between the dynamic model and the actual robot is bridged.

In this study, there are three tasks during the walking process of humanoid robots [13, 14], namely floating posture task, floating position task, and swinging leg task. These three tasks can be called Task 1, Task 2, and Task 3. The function of the floating base task is to make the robot's centroid state follow the expected centroid state. The function of the swing leg task is to swing the swing leg to the desired landing point. The first thing to be determined is the kinematics whole body controller, whose role is to determine the joint space commands from the workspace commands. Firstly, determine the relationship between the operating space and workspace without task priority, specifically the relationship between their speed:

$$
\dot{x} = J(q)\dot{q}
\tag{12}
$$

where x and q represent the workspace and joint space, respectively. Define $N\,(J)$ as the null space projection matrix of the Jacobian matrix J, then $N\,(J)$ and *Jacobian* satisfy the following relationship:

$$J \cdot N = 0 \tag{13}$$

Based on the above equation, we can obtain the derivation method of prioritized multi task Jacobian.

$$J_{i|pre} = J_i N_{i-1} \tag{14}$$

$$N_{i-1} = N_{1|0} \cdots N_{i-1|i-2} \tag{15}$$

$$N_{i-1|i-2} = I - J_{i-1|pre}^{+} J_{i-1|pre} \tag{16}$$

$$N_0 = I \tag{17}$$

Among them, J_i is the jacobian of the i-th task, N_i is the null space projection corresponding to the Jacobian of the i-th task, Matrix $N_{i|i-1}$ is a mapping matrix from the i-th null space to the i-1-th null space. With J_i^{+} being a consistent pseudo-inverse of J_i. Several pseudo-inverses have been proposed that produce different solutions[15, 16]. The simplest is the Moore-Penrose pseudo-inverse:

$$J_i^{+} = J_i^{T} (J_i J_i^{T})^{-1} \tag{18}$$

The first task has the highest priority, which means completing the first task first and then completing the others. The second task is the second highest, and after completing the first task, it will try to meet the second task as much as possible, and so on. This article sets the floating base posture task as the highest priority, which is the first task, followed by the floating base position task, which is the second task, and finally the swinging leg task, which is the third task.

Based on the relationship between workspace speed and workspace speed, the relationship between prioritized workspace changes and workspace changes can be determined.

$$\Delta q_1 = J_1^{+}(x_1^{des} - x_1) \tag{19}$$

$$\Delta q_2 = \Delta q_1 + J_{2|pre}^{+}(x_2^{des} - x_2 - J_2 \Delta q_1) \tag{20}$$

$$\Delta q_3 = \Delta q_2 + J_{3pre}^{+}(x_3^{des} - x_3 - J_3 \Delta q_2) \tag{21}$$

And the change in the operating space corresponding to the last task is directly added to the current operating space position, which is the expected operating space position.

$$q^{des} = q + \Delta q_3 \tag{22}$$

Similarly, it is possible to further determine the relationship between the expected velocity of the prioritized operating space and the expected velocity of the workspace, as well as the relationship between the expected acceleration and the expected acceleration of the workspace.

$$\dot{q}_i^{des} = \dot{q}_{i-1}^{des} + J_{i|pre}^{+}(\dot{x}_i^{des} - J_i\dot{q}_{i-1}^{des}) \tag{23}$$

$$\ddot{q}_i^{des} = \ddot{q}_{i-1}^{des} + J_{i|pre}^{+}(\ddot{x}_i^{des} - \dot{J}_i\dot{q}_i - J_i\ddot{q}_{i-1}^{des}) \tag{24}$$

In this way, all kinematics information with priority can be obtained, including the expected position, speed and acceleration of each joint and floating base. Later, when doing dynamic optimization, the acceleration command can be determined, and the position and speed in the force position hybrid control can be determined.

3.3 Hybrid Position/Force Control

Based on the virtual force and virtual torque obtained in the previous text, $f = [F_x \ F_y \ F_z \ \tau_x \ \tau_y \ \tau_z]$, they are brought into the dynamic equation to obtain the torque of each joint, which is used as the output feedforward torque. Based on the expected joint angle and angular velocity information obtained in the whole body control, the feedforward and feedback control of force position mixing can be achieved, and the output torque of each joint can be determined.

$$\tau^{cmd} = \tau_{feedforward} + k_p\left(q^{des} - q_{feedback}\right) + k_d(\dot{q}^{des} - \dot{q}_{feedback}) \tag{25}$$

This enables the virtual model control and whole body control of humanoid robots to achieve walking.

The system framework of hybrid control is as follows (Fig. 2).

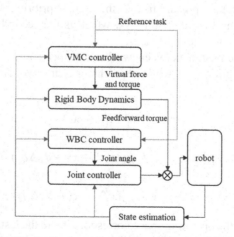

Fig. 2. System framework of hybrid control

4 Simulation

To test how the controller performs in simulation, we a multibody model of Cassie built in Simulink Multibody in MATLAB 2019b. This platform provides us with a 3D simulation that accounts for impact forces, inertia, and many other nuances present in robot's multibody dynamics. The overall model has the same number of joints, motors, and springs and similar masses, kinematics, and moments of inertia as estimated on biped robot. To reduce the simulation computation time the contact model utilizes spheres at the front and back of each toe for a total of 8 points of contact including both legs.

The proposed algorithm is verified through two simulation tasks in this paper. The first task is push-recover simulation, and the second task is fast walking simulation.

4.1 Push-recover simulation

Set the forward speed of the robot to 0 m/s, which means marking time, with a body posture angle of 0° roll and pitch, and a center of mass height of 0.87 m. Then, apply a 50 N external force to the robot's center of mass for 1 s to verify the robot's thrust balance ability. The simulation results are shown.

The roll and pitch attitude tracking effects of biped are shown in Fig. 3. Attitude tracking effects, external interference force acting at 8 s.

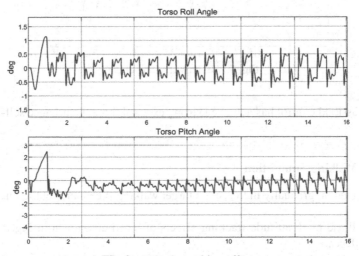

Fig. 3. Attitude tracking effects

The height tracking effect of biped is shown in Fig. 4. Height tracking effects.

The velocity tracking effects of biped are shown in Fig. 5. Velocity tracking effects.

Analysis of simulation results shows that when the robot's center of mass is disturbed by external disturbances, the speed of the robot undergoes a velocity change of 0.65 m/s, but it basically returns to stability within 2 s. At the same time, the change in attitude is also within the range of 1°. It can be seen that the biped robot based on decoupling control

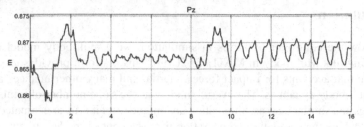

Fig. 4. Height tracking effects

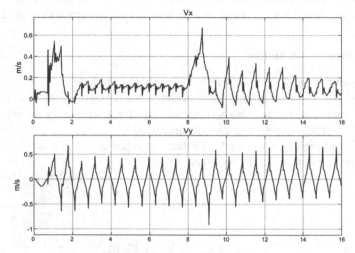

Fig. 5. Velocity tracking effects

and ankle assisted control has achieved strong external force disturbance self-balancing ability.

4.2 Fast Walking Simulation

In this simulation, gradually increase the target walking speed and set the final speed to 1 m/s.

The roll and pitch attitude tracking effects of biped are shown in Fig. 6. Attitude tracking effects.

The height tracking effect of biped is shown in Fig. 7. Height tracking effects.

The velocity tracking effects of biped are shown in Fig. 8. Velocity tracking effects.

Through the simulation results, it can be seen that the speed tracking effect of the robot is good, with an average speed of 1m/s. However, as the walking speed increases, the tracking effect of the robot's height, posture, and speed will deteriorate. This is because the swinging of the swinging legs has an increasing impact on the dynamic state of the robot's walking.

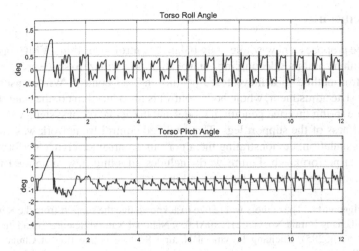

Fig. 6. Attitude tracking effects

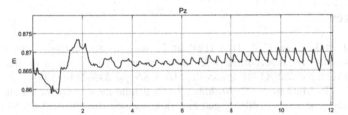

Fig. 7. Height tracking effects

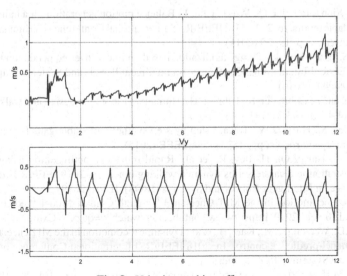

Fig. 8. Velocity tracking effects

5   Conclusion

This article proposes a new whole body balance control algorithm - VMC based WBC. This algorithm combines decoupling control algorithm with zero space projection whole body control method to achieve force position hybrid control. While ensuring high-frequency state adjustment, whole body control is introduced to compensate for the gap between the spring inverted pendulum model and the actual robot system, while improving the stiffness of the support legs. The modified control framework was validated in simscape simulation, demonstrating the algorithm's anti-interference performance and fast walking performance. Future work includes adopting new simplified models to reduce the impact of swinging legs on walking status.

Acknowledgements. The authors would like to acknowledge the support from the Key Research Project of Zhejiang (Grant No. G2021NB0AL03), National Natural Science Foundation of China (Grant No. 52105285), Zhejiang Provincial Natural Science Foundation of China (Grant No. LQ23F030010).

References

1. Hrr, J., Pratt, J., Chew, C.M., Herr, H., Pratt, G.: Adaptive virtual model control of a bipedal walking robot. In: Proceedings. IEEE International Joint Symposia on Intelligence and Systems (Cat. No. 98EX174), Rockville, MD, USA, pp. 245–251 (1998)
2. Takenaka, T., Matsumoto, T., Yoshiike, T.: Real time motion generation and control for biped robot -1st report: Walking gait pattern generation. In: 2009 IEEE/RSJ International Conference on Intelligent Robots and Systems, St. Louis, MO, USA, pp. 1084–1091 (2009)
3. Huang, Q., et al.: Historical developments of BHR humanoid robots. Adv. Hist. Stud. **8**, 79–90 (2019)
4. Sun, Y., Xiong, R., Zhu, Q., Wu, J., Chu, J.: Balance motion generation for a humanoid robot playing table tennis. In: 2011 11th IEEE-RAS International Conference on Humanoid Robots, Bled, Slovenia, pp. 19–25 (2011)
5. Kajita, S., et al.: Biped walking stabilization based on linear inverted pendulum tracking. In: 2010 IEEE/RSJ International Conference on Intelligent Robots and Systems, Taipei, Taiwan, pp. 4489–4496 (2010)
6. Nuschmann, T., Lohmeier, S., Ulbrich, H.: Humanoid robot lola: design and walking control. J. Physiol.-Paris **103**(3), 141–148 (2009)
7. Rezazadeh, S., Hurst, J.W.: Toward step-by-step synthesis of stable gaits for underactuated compliant legged robots, pp. 4532–4538. IEEE (2015)
8. Hereid, A., Harib, O., Hartley, R., et al.: Rapid trajectory optimization using C-FROST with illustrationon a cassie-series dynamic walking biped. In: 2019 IEEE/RSJ International Conference on Intelligent Robots and Systems (IROS). IEEE (2019)
9. Dynamic Locomotion in the MIT Cheetah 3 Through Convex Model Predictive Control. Accessed 10 Sept 2019. https://www.youtube.com/watch?v=q6zxCvCxhic
10. Carlo, J.D., Wensing, P.M., Katz, B., et al.: Dynamic locomotion in the MIT cheetah 3 through convexmodel-predictive control. In: 2018 IEEE/RSJ International Conference on Intelligent Robots and Systems (IROS), Madrid, pp. 1–9 (2018)
11. Raibert, M.H., Tello, E.R.: Legged robots that balance. IEEE Expert **1**(4), 89 (1986)
12. Gong, Y., Hartley, R., Da, X., et al.: Feedback control of a cassie bipedal robot: walking, standing, and riding a segway. arXiv:1809.07279 [cs, math] (2018)

13. Sentis, L., Khatib, O.: Synthesis of whole-body behaviors through hierarchical control of behavioral primitives. Int. J. Humanoid Rob. **2**(04), 505–518 (2005)
14. Gienger, M., Toussaint, M., Goerick, C.: Whole-body motion planning building blocks for intelligent systems. In: Harada, K., Yoshida, E., Yokoi, K. (eds.) Motion Planning for Humanoid Robots. Springer, Heidelberg (2010). https://doi.org/10.1007/978-1-84996-220-9_3
15. Mansard, N., Khatib, O., Kheddar, A.: A unified approach to integrate unilateral constraints in the stack of tasks. IEEE Trans. Rob. **25**(3), 670–685 (2009)
16. Kanoun, O., Lamiraux, F., Wieber, P.-B.: Kinematic control of redundant manipulators: generalizing the task priority framework to inequality tasks. IEEE Trans. Rob. **27**(4), 785–792 (2011)

Design and Implementation of Lightweight Thigh Structures for Biped Robots Based on Spatial Lattice Structure and Additive Manufacturing Technology

Hongjian Jiang[1], Lingyu Kong[1(✉)], Yu Zhang[1], Yuanjie Chen[2], Daming Nie[1], Anhuan Xie[1], Lintao Shao[1], and Shiqiang Zhu[1]

[1] Zhejiang Lab, Hangzhou 311100, China
kongly@zhejianglab.com
[2] Zhejiang Institute of Metrology, Hangzhou 310018, China

Abstract. In order to reduce the weight of the biped robot, three kinds of thigh structures based on spatial lattice structure, namely BCC, FCC, BCCZ are introduced in this paper. Finite element analysis is then carried out on these lattices, indicating that the BCCZ lattice exhibits superior compression properties. On this basis, compression experiments are conducted to confirm the accuracy of numerical simulations. In order to validate the effectiveness of the structures, the lattices are applied to construct thigh structure of the biped robot. Static analysis of the thigh structure with different types of lattices are carried out. Simulation results show that the maximum stress of the optimized thigh structure is less than the yield strength. Finally, to balance mechanical properties and lightweight effects, the BCC lattice is employed. The thigh structure is fabricated using additive manufacturing technology, and the weight compared with traditional structures is reduced by up to 30%. The optimization results are verified through experiments, demonstrating that the structure meets the design requirements.

Keywords: Biped robot · Spatial lattice structure · Finite element analysis · Compression experiment

1 Introduction

Lightweight design is a crucial objective in the fields of aerospace, automobile, and robotics [1, 2]. It encompasses design methodology, manufacturing processes, and advanced materials. Material lightweight typically involves replacing the original material with high-performance alternatives, such as aviation aluminum alloy, magnesium alloy, and composite materials. While effective, this method is limited by material technology. An alternative approach is forming process lightweight, which involves integrating multiple components to reduce the number of connectors and achieve weight reduction. However, this method is not widely used due to its high fabrication difficulty and cost [3, 4]. To overcome these limitations, researchers are turning their attention to

H. Yang et al. (Eds.): ICIRA 2023, LNAI 14270, pp. 368–379, 2023.
https://doi.org/10.1007/978-981-99-6492-5_32

lightweight design, particularly the use of spatial lattice structures [5]. These structures have been found to be lightweight and strong by studying natural biological structures like human skeleton and shellfish. Nevertheless, due to fabrication constraints, they have not been widely adopted until the recent development of additive manufacturing technology [6].

Lattice structures are multifunctional structures with porous and regular microstructures that offer advantages such as lightweight, high strength, energy absorption, heat dissipation, and sound absorption [7]. The method of lightweight design for lattice structures involves replacing solid elements with hollow units, which is essentially a topology optimization method [8]. In this paper, a method based on spatial lattice structure is proposed to reduce weight for thigh structures. The mechanical properties of the proposed design are studied using finite element analysis and experiments.

2 Design and Analysis of Spatial Lattice Structures

2.1 Introduction of Spatial Lattice Structures

Figure 1 illustrates several typical kinds of lattice structures, such as BCC, FCC, and TPMS, etc. These structures have been widely applied in aerospace and automobile industries due to their excellent mechanical properties and heat dissipation performance, etc. BCC and FCC are often used in conditions that require high strength and light weight. Due to the characteristic that the thigh structure of the biped robot is mainly subjected to compression loads, BCC and FCC, which have excellent mechanical properties, were chosen for the lattice structure. As depicted in Fig. 2, there are BCC, FCC, and BCCZ, respectively. BCC, named body-centered cubic, is consisted of eight cube body diagonal rods with excellent mechanical properties and low relative density. FCC is called face-centered cubic, who has better mechanical properties and higher relative density than BCC. To enhance the compression performance in the z-axis direction, four vertical rods was added on the basis of BCC, which is called BCCZ [9, 10].

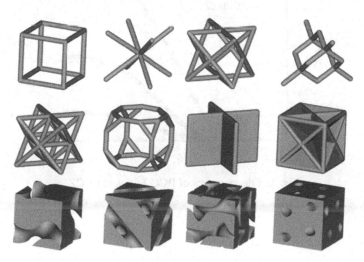

Fig. 1. Typical kinds of lattices

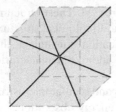
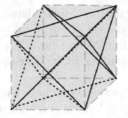
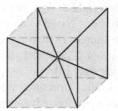

Fig. 2. BCC, FCC and BCCZ lattices

2.2 Finite Element Analysis of Spatial Lattice Structures

A quasi-static analysis model was established for the lattice structure using ABAQUS/Explicit. Beam elements were selected to build the lattice structure models, with the top and bottom planes set as discrete rigid. Under quasi-static conditions, the bottom plane was fixed while the top plane was subjected to z-axis movement [11]. To confirm that it is a quasi-static response, an energy relationship was set up for the finite element model, requiring the kinetic energy to not exceed 5%–10% of the internal energy during the procedure. The kinetic energy and internal energy are shown in Fig. 3, with the kinetic energy being less than 5% of the internal energy during the entire process, confirming it is a quasi-static response. The stress distribution and force-displacement curves of these three types of lattice structures are shown in Figs. 4 and 5, respectively. It is observed that BCCZ exhibits superior compression performance compared to BCC and FCC.

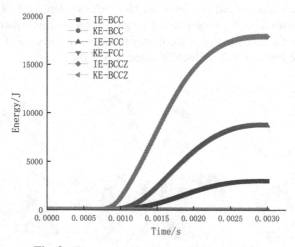

Fig. 3. Energy curves of BCC, FCC and BCCZ

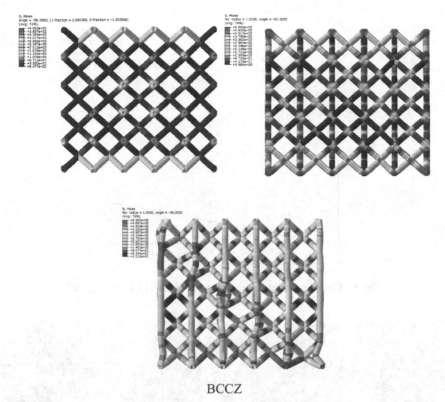

BCCZ

Fig. 4. Stress distribution of BCC, FCC and BCCZ

2.3 Compression Experiment of Spatial Lattice Structures

In this research, AlMgScZr was utilized to manufacture BCC, FCC, and BCCZ samples by employing the selective laser melting (SLM) technique, as illustrated in Fig. 6. The microstructures of all samples were found to be continuous and devoid of significant defects, as observed in Fig. 6. The samples had uniform dimensions of 25 mm × 25 mm × 25 mm, with the unit cell measuring 5 mm × 5 mm × 5 mm, and a rod diameter of 1 mm. The compression experiments were conducted on an INSTRON5982 electronic universal testing machine, with a loading rate of 2 mm/min [12–14]. The fracture regions of the samples are presented in Fig. 8, where BCC was fractured along the diagonal, and FCC was broken along the direction of the compression load. The force and displacement curves exhibited an excellent match with the simulation results in the displacement range of 0 to 1.5 mm (Figs. 5 and 9).

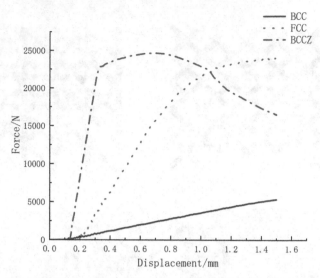

Fig. 5. Force and displacement curves of BCC, FCC and BCCZ

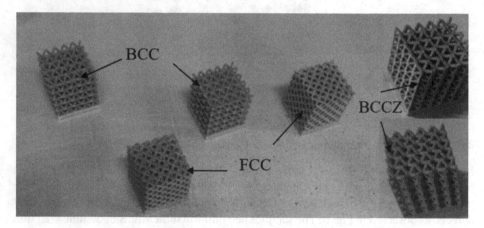

Fig. 6. Samples formed by SLM

Fig. 7. Compressive experiment by INSTRON5982 electronic universal testing machine

Fig. 8. Samples after compressive experiment

3   Design and Analysis of Thigh Structure

3.1   Design of Thigh Structure

As shown in the Fig. 10, the original version of biped robot mainly consists of waist joint, thigh structure, shank structure and foot structure. In this study, two plates of thigh structure were integrated, the optimized solid-fill model of the thigh structure is depicted in Fig. 11. To achieve the goal of weight reduction [15], the model was transformed into a thin-walled shell and sandwich structure. The lightweight design process involves the extraction of a 2mm-thick shell from the initial model, followed by boolean subtraction operation to obtain the design region. A suitable type of lattice was selected, and its parameters were determined. The design region of the solid-model was then replaced with the lattice, and the shell was merged with the lattice to obtain the lightweight structure. Additive manufacturing technology was used to fabricate the lightweight structure. The original weight of the thigh structure was 895.5g, while the

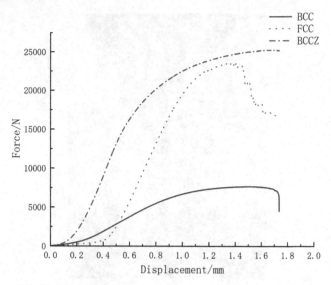

Fig. 9. Force-displacement curves for BCC, FCC and BCCZ

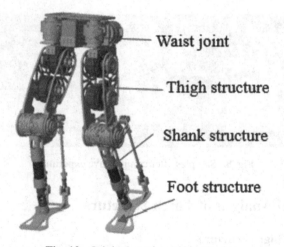

Fig. 10. Original version of biped robot

weight of the optimized structure is presented in Table 1. The approach of utilizing a thin-walled structure with sandwich features was found to be highly effective in achieving weight reduction.

3.2 Finite Element Analysis of Thigh Structure

Finite element analysis was conducted to evaluate the strength and stiffness of the optimized thigh structure. However, due to the presence of a lattice structure, static analysis presented challenges. To overcome this challenge, an equivalent model substitution

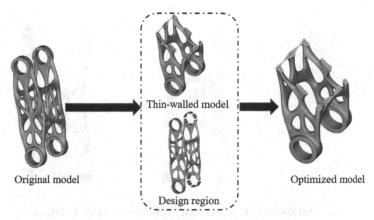

Fig. 11. Lightweight design of thigh structure

Table 1. Weight comparison between original and optimized thigh structure

Lattice type	Original weight(g)	Optimized weight(g)
BCC	895.5	627.5
FCC	895.5	645.5
BCCZ	895.5	638.0

method was adopted. Based on the quasi-static analysis, the lattice region was replaced by an equivalent material model. The stress and displacement contour plots of the thigh structure are shown in Fig. 12, which demonstrate the rationality of the lightweight design. Considering the weight reduction effect and simulation results of the optimized thigh structure, the BCC lattice type was selected to fabricate the physical sample.

4   Experiments Validation

4.1   Compression Experiment of Thigh Structure

To validate the accuracy of the simulation results, a series of experiments were carried out. Unidirectional compression experiments were conducted using an INSTRON5982 machine, as shown in Fig. 13. The compression loading rate was maintained at a constant rate of 0.05 mm/s, with the axis of the shafts coinciding with the center of the circle. The compressive force was applied to the clamp, which was fixed at the center of the shaft. From Fig. 14, the maximum compressive force was observed to be 100 kN, and the corresponding displacement was 4 mm. As illustrated in Fig. 14, the force and displacement curves were nearly linear, indicating that the process was in the elastic deformation stage and did not exhibit any plasticity fracture.

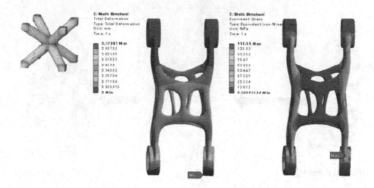

(a)   Stress and Displacement nephograms of BCC lattice

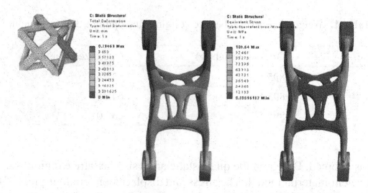

(b)   Stress and Displacement nephograms of FCC lattice

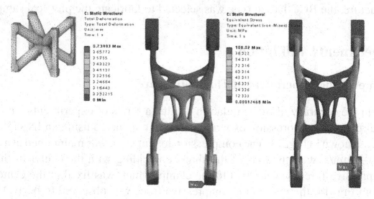

(c)   Stress and Displacement nephograms of BCCZ lattice

Fig. 12.   Stress and Displacement nephograms of BCC, FCC and BCCZ

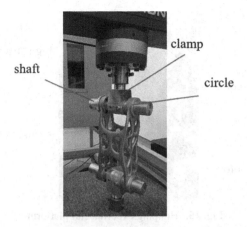

Fig. 13. Compression experiment of optimized thigh structure

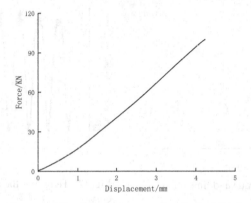

Fig. 14. Force and displacement curve of optimized thigh structure

4.2 Hopping Experiment

An experimental platform for hopping was established to evaluate the dynamic performance of the optimized thigh structure. The platform, as illustrated in Fig. 15, consists of a 3D printed thigh structure, a hip motor, a shank structure, a knee motor, and a control box. Instructions can be provided to the platform using upper computer software. During the experiment, the maximum torque reached up to 200 N.m, as shown in Fig. 16, which is twice the peak torque. The hopping height was measured using a wire sensor, as depicted in Fig. 17. The maximum hopping height was approximately 30 cm, which is obtained by subtracting 17.5 cm from 47.5 cm. The experiment results suggest that the optimized thigh structure meets the mechanical requirements for dynamic loading.

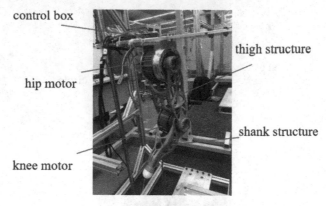

Fig. 15. Hopping experimental platform

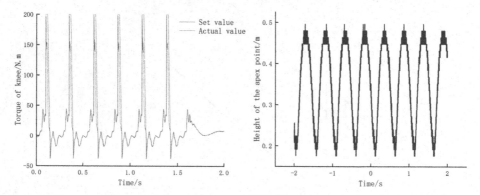

Fig. 16. Torque and time curve

Fig. 17. Height of the apex point and time curve

5 Conclusions

In this paper, a lightweight thigh structure based on spatial lattice structures is proposed, and three types of lattice structures (BCC, FCC, and BCCZ) were selected to optimize the thigh structure. Furthermore, finite element analysis and compression experiments were conducted to study the mechanical properties of these three lattice structures. The results show that BCCZ exhibits better compression performance than the other lattice structures. Next, the procedure of lightweight design is introduced, and the optimized thigh structure is obtained using these three types of lattice infill. Static analysis is then conducted on the optimized thigh structure using equivalent model substitution. Finally, to confirm the accuracy of the simulation results, a hopping experimental platform is set up, and the experimental results demonstrate the rationality of the design.

Acknowledgements. This work was supported by "Pioneer" and "Leading Goose" R&D Program of Zhejiang (No. 2023C01177), National Natural Science Foundation of China (Grants 52205034), Key Research Project of Zhejiang Lab (No. G2021NB0AL03), the National Natural Science Foundation of China (Grant No. 52205076).

References

1. Junli, L., Ziru, H., Gang, L., Qinglong, A., Ming, C., et al.: Topology optimization design and research of lightweight biomimetic three-dimensional lattice structures based on laser powder bed fusion. J. Manuf. Process. **74**, 220–232 (2022)
2. Jianrui, Z., Zhaohui, Y., Weidong, Y., Sheng, D., et al.: Lightweight design and modal analysis of calf structure of hydraulic biped robot. In: 2020 10th Institute of Electrical and Electronics Engineers International Conference on Cyber Technology in Automation, Control, and Intelligent Systems (CYBER), pp. 146–151 (2020)
3. Marre, M., Ruhstorfer, M., Tekkaya, A.E., Zaeh, M.F., et al.: Manufacturing of lightweight frame structures by innovative joining by forming processes. Int. J. Mater. Form. **2**(S1), 307–310 (2009)
4. Alan, T., Emmanuel, D.M., Alan, L., David, K.M., John, G.S., Uday, V., et al.: Materials for automotive lightweighting. Annu. Rev. Mater. Res. **49**(1), 327–359 (2019)
5. Ha, S.N., Lu, G.: A review of recent research on bio-inspired structures and materials for energy absorption applications. Composites. Part B, Eng. **181** (2020)
6. Jihong, Z., Han, Z., Chuang, W., Lu, Z., Shangqin, Y., Weihong, Z., et al.: A review of topology optimization for additive manufacturing: status and challenges. Acad. J. Second Mil. Univ. **34**(1), 91–110 (2021)
7. Sheng, W., Jun, W., Yingjie, X., Weihong, Z., Jihong, Z., et al.: Compressive behavior and energy absorption of polymeric lattice structures made by additive manufacturing. Front. Mech. Eng. **15**(2), 319–327 (2020)
8. Mengchuan, X., Ziran, X., Zhong, Z., Hongshuai, L., Yingchun, B., Daining, F., et al.: Mechanical properties and energy absorption capability of AuxHex structure under in-plane compression: theoretical and experimental studies. Int. J. Mechan. Sci. **159**, 43–57 (2019)
9. Yingang, L., et al.: Mechanical performance of a node reinforced body-centred cubic lattice structure manufactured via selective laser melting. Scripta Mater. **189**, 95–100 (2020)
10. Hairi, Z., et al.: Energy absorption diagram characteristic of metallic self-supporting 3D lattices fabricated by additive manufacturing and design method of energy absorption structure. Int. J. Solids Struct. 226–227 (2021)
11. Liming, C., et al.: Dynamic crushing behavior and energy absorption of graded lattice cylindrical structure under axial impact load. Thin-walled Struct. 127, 333–343 (2018)
12. Guo, M.F., Yang, H., Li, M.: 3D lightweight double arrow-head plate-lattice auxetic structures with enhanced stiffness and energy absorption performance. Composite Struct. **290** (2022)
13. Hao, Z., et al.: Lightweight structure of a phase-change thermal controller based on lattice cells manufactured by SLM. Chin. J. Aeronaut. **32**(7), 1727–1732 (2019)
14. Zhenyang, G., et al.: Data-driven design of biometric composite metamaterials with extremely recoverable and ultrahigh specific energy absorption. Composites Part B-eng. **251** (2023)
15. Hongyu, D., Zhaoyao, S., Yisen, H., Jingchen, L., Bo, Y., Pan, Z., et al.: Lightweight design optimization for legs of bipedal humanoid robot. Struct. Multidiscip. Optim. **64**(4), 2749–2762 (2021)

A Humanoid Robot Foot with a Lattice Structure for Absorbing Ground Impact Forces

Lan Zhang[1], Lingyu Kong[1](✉), Guanyu Huang[1], Weigang Zhou[1], Hongjian Jiang[1], Pengyu Zhao[1], Bingshan Jiang[1], Anhuan Xie[1], Shiqiang Zhu[1], and Yuanjie Chen[2]

[1] Research Center for Intelligent Robotics, Zhejiang Lab, Hangzhou 311100, China
kongly@zhejianglab.com
[2] Zhejiang Institute of Metrology, Hangzhou 310018, Zhejiang, China

Abstract. The efficient and stable walking of humanoid robots is a key and challenging issue in the study of humanoid robots. As the part that directly contacts with the outside world, the foot needs to have strong shock absorption ability to reduce the joint torque at the moment of contact with the ground, which can not only protect the mechanical structure, but also improve the motor efficiency. To improve the shock absorption performance during the locomotion of humanoid robots, this study presents a novel humanoid robot foot pad with a lattice structure. The unit cell of the lattice structure is a rhombic dodecahedron, which possesses good energy absorption capability. Quasi-static compression and impact simulations of the lattice foot pad and the robot foot were conducted in Abaqus. The simulation results indicate that compared to the solid foot pad, the foot pad designed with rhombic dodecahedral unit cells can reduce the impact force by 82%, providing better shock absorption capacity. To further verify the cushioning effect of the foot pad installed on the robot, A lattice foot pad was produced by 3D printing technology and fitted on the foot of a single-legged robot. A single-legged robot drop test was conducted, showing that when drop from a height of 24 cm above the ground, the maximum knee joint torque of the single-legged robot with the lattice foot pad decreased by about 22% compared to that without the foot pad.

Keywords: Humanoid Robot · Lattice foot pad · Shock Absorption · Single-legged Robot Drop Test

1 Introduction

Humanoid robots have structures and motion characteristics similar to humans, which can adapt to human living environments and collaborate with humans or even replace them in performing dangerous or repetitive tasks. With the development of technology, high-performance components, 3D printing and forming processes, and reinforcement learning techniques have greatly improved the performance of humanoid robots, making humanoid robots a research hotspot in the field of intelligent robots in recent years [1–4]. However, the insufficient motion performance of humanoid robots in complex environments still limits their large-scale application. Among them, the foot, as the part that

H. Yang et al. (Eds.): ICIRA 2023, LNAI 14270, pp. 380–391, 2023.
https://doi.org/10.1007/978-981-99-6492-5_33

directly contacts with the external environment, has a significant impact on the motion performance of humanoid robots. The foot not only needs to support the entire body of the robot, but also needs to have functions such as cushioning and energy absorption, maintaining body stability, and adapting to uneven terrain. Currently, the simplest method for cushioning and shock absorption is to attach shock-absorbing materials to the sole of the foot [5, 6], and there are also some designs that incorporate shock absorbers and dampers into the foot [7–9]. However, adding shock absorbers and dampers will make the foot structure more complex and heavier, and the cushioning effect of the rubber layer is limited. To solve these problems, this paper proposes a cushioning foot pad with a lattice structure.

Lattice structures are three-dimensional porous structures formed by cells with different topological geometric shapes [10]. They possess excellent mechanical properties such as light weight, high strength, high energy absorption capacity, and high damping. Lattice structures have been widely used in fields such as aerospace [11, 12], automotive [13, 14], and biomedical engineering [15, 16]. However, its application in the field of robotics is still relatively limited. The energy absorption capacity of lattice structures per unit mass is extremely high, and their energy absorption performance has become a research hotspot [17]. Wang et al. designed a novel crash box based on the human tibia as a biomimetic object, which can improve the crashworthiness and energy absorption performance [18]. Yin et al. proposed a novel automotive engine hood made by double-curvature composite sandwich hood with a pyramidal lattice core, which can not only reduce the weight of the engine hood but also reveal better pedestrian safety performance [19]. Acanfora et al. developed the lightweight shock absorbers with a novel thin additive manufactured hybrid metal/composite lattice structures and validated its effectiveness in reducing weight and energy absorption performance [20]. They also demonstrated that the configuration with lattice core produced by additive manufacturing can maximize the energy absorption capacity of hybrid aluminum/composite material dampers while maintaining reduced thickness and mass [21].

With the energy-absorbing capability of the lattice structure, this study designs a foot pad equipped with a rhombic dodecahedron lattice. Through finite element analysis and experimental testing of the lattice foot pad, it has been validated that the lattice foot pad exhibits favorable cushioning and shock absorption effects. This paper is structured as follows: the design of the lattice foot pad, the quasi-static compression simulation of the lattice foot pad and the drop impact simulation of the lattice foot pad and solid foot pad are presented in Sect. 2. The drop test of a single-legged robot with and without the lattice foot pad is demonstrated in Sect. 3. The conclusion and future work are shown in Sect. 4.

2   The Design and Simulation of the Lattice Foot Pad

2.1   The Design of the Lattice Foot Pad

Rhombic dodecahedron is a dodecahedron composed of 12 rhombuses. Due to the property of the rhombic dodecahedron that countless identical units can seamlessly fill the entire space, it is chosen as the crystal cell unit to fill the entire foot pad. The crystal cell unit of the rhombic dodecahedron is shown in Fig. 1(a). The foot pad composed of rhombic dodecahedron crystal cell units is shown in Fig. 1(b). The top shape of the lattice foot pad is identical to the bottom shape of the humanoid robot's foot structure, allowing them to fit precisely on the sole of the foot. In order to verify the cushioning and shock absorbing effects of the foot pad composed of rhombic dodecahedron crystal cells, finite element simulations of the lattice foot pad and drop tests of the single-legged robot were conducted.

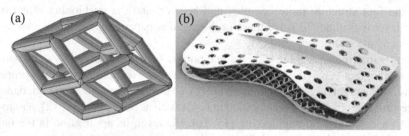

Fig. 1. The structure of the lattice foot pad. (a) The rhombic dodecahedron crystal unit cell. (b) The lattice foot pad.

2.2 Quasi-Static Compression Simulation

In order to evaluate the strength and rigidity of the proposed lattice foot pad, a quasi-static compression simulation analysis was carried out on the whole structure of the foot and the foot pad. The bottom of the foot pad was subjected to a fixed constraint and a vertical force of 1000 N (3.3 times of the single legged robot gravity) was applied at the ankle of the foot. The results show that the maximum stress of the foot pad occurs in the front area with a value of 5.8 MPa, which is lower than the yield strength of TPU material, indicating that its structural strength meets the requirements. In addition, the maximum deformation of the foot pad is located in the connection area between the foot and foot pad, with a maximum deformation of 0.585 mm, meeting the required stiffness requirements. The stress contour and deformation contour of the foot pad are shown in Fig. 2.

2.3 Drop Impact Simulation

In order to verify the cushioning performance of the lattice-structured foot pad, drop impact simulation was carried out both for the foot structure with a lattice foot pad and the foot structure with a solid foot pad. Here the solid foot pad is designed with the same geometric parameters and the same material as the lattice foot pad. A drop from a height of 64 cm above the ground was applied since it's the highest drop height in the

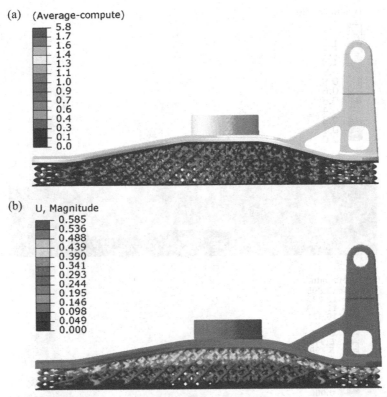

(a) (Average-compute)

(b) U, Magnitude

Fig. 2. The results of quasi-static compression analysis. (a) The stress contour of the foot pad. (b) The deformation contour of the foot pad.

experiment. A mass point with a weight of 30 kg was applied to simulate the weight of the single legged robot. The impact deformation of the lattice foot pad and the solid foot pad are shown in Fig. 3. The ground reaction force during the drop simulations are shown in Fig. 4. The red curve represents the ground reaction force of the solid foot pad, while the blue curve represents the ground reaction force of the lattice foot pad.

From Fig. 4, it can be observed that the maximum ground reaction force of the solid foot pad in the drop simulation is 302.1 kN, and the impact is completed within approximately 1.5 ms. The maximum ground reaction force of the lattice foot pad in the drop simulation is 54.5 kN, and the impact is completed in approximately 10 ms. Compared to the solid foot pad, the lattice foot pad can reduce the impact force of the drop by 82%, providing a better cushioning performance. The system kinetic energy curves of the lattice foot pad and solid foot pad during drop simulations are shown in Fig. 5. The red curve represents the system kinetic energy of the solid foot pad, while the blue

(a) U, Magnitude

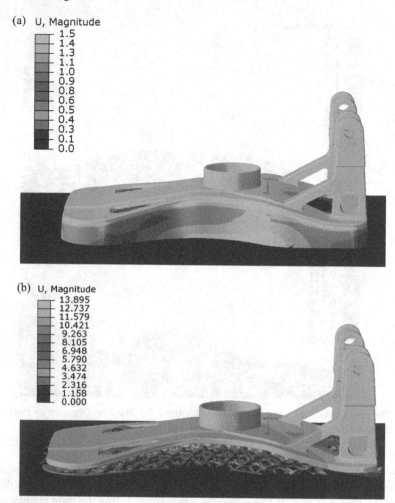

Fig. 3. The impact deformation of the lattice foot pad and solid foot pad. (a) The impact deformation of the solid foot. (b) The impact deformation of the lattice foot pad.

curve represents the system kinetic energy of the lattice foot pad. From Fig. 5, it can be seen that the lattice foot pad dissipates and absorbs more kinetic energy, demonstrating better energy absorption performance.

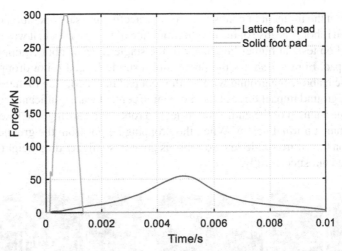

Fig. 4. The comparison of ground reaction forces in drop simulations between the lattice foot pad and the solid foot pad.

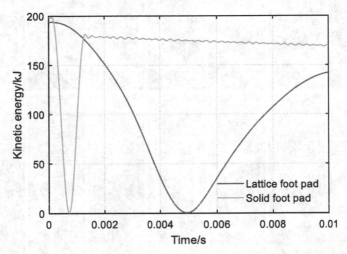

Fig. 5. The kinetic energy curves of the lattice foot pad and the solid foot pad.

3 Drop Test of a Single-Legged Robot

According to the design of the lattice foot pad, 3D printing technology was used to manufacture the lattice foot pad. To evaluate the cushioning and shock absorption performance of the foot structure with the lattice foot pad, a single-legged robot test bench with four degrees of freedom was constructed. Then, the drop tests were performed with different heights range from 24 cm to 64 cm for both single-legged robots with and without the lattice foot pad. The process of a single-legged robot dropping with a lattice foot pad from a height of 64 cm above the ground is depicted in Fig. 6. Due to the good energy absorption performance of the lattice foot pad, it can reduce the ground impact force at the moment of contact, thereby protecting the safe operation of the entire single-legged robot. Because of the height limitation of the test bench, it was not possible to conduct drop tests at higher heights with the single-legged robot equipped with the lattice foot pad. Figure 7 shows the process of a single-legged robot dropping from a height of 34cm above the ground without the foot pad installed. Due to the absence of a foot pad, the ground impact force at the moment of contact was significant, triggering the protection mechanism of the entire single-legged robot and causing it to lose power and fail to maintain a normal height. When the dropping height from the ground increases, the impact on the entire single-legged robot is greater, so higher drop height tests could not be carried out successfully.

Fig. 6. The process of a single-legged robot dropping with a lattice foot pad installed from a height of 64 cm above the ground.

The experiment shows that the single-legged robot with the lattice foot pad can maintain the integrity of the entire robot system when drop from a higher height. A direct comparison of the ground impact force between the single-legged robot with and without the lattice foot pad can validate the cushion effect of the lattice foot pad. However, due to the limitations of the experimental conditions, we were unable to obtain the ground reaction force. Nevertheless, we fully recorded the torque of each joint during the experiment, which can also verify the effect of the lattice foot pad in buffering and shock absorption by comparing the maximum joint torque of the single-legged robot with and without the lattice foot pad at the moment of contact with the ground. As the torque of the knee joint is greater than that of other joints, the torque of the knee joint was taken as an example to compare and analyze the joint torque of the single-legged robot with and without the lattice foot pad during the dropping process. Figure 8 shows the torque curves of the knee joint during three drops from a height of 64 cm for the single-legged robot equipped with the lattice foot pad. From Fig. 8, it can be observed that the torque of the knee joint sharply increases at the moment of ground contact during all three dropping processes, but the maximum torque of the knee joint is essentially the same, indicating good consistency among the three tests.

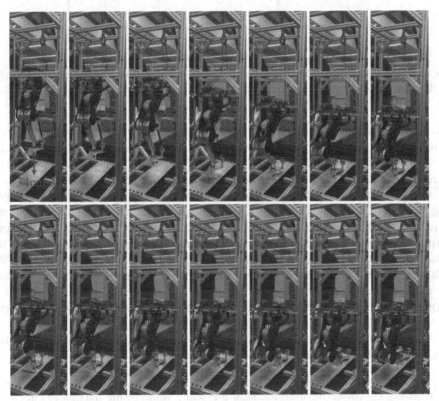

Fig. 7. The process of a single-legged robot dropping from a height of 34 cm above the ground without the foot pad installed.

Taking the average value of the maximum knee joint torque under the same experimental conditions of multiple drop tests and plotting the mean value on the same graph. Figure 9 shows the mean values of the maximum knee joint torque of the single-legged robot with the lattice foot pad installed when dropping from heights of 24 cm, 34 cm, 44 cm, 54 cm, and 64 cm, respectively. As can be seen from the figure, the higher the dropping height, the greater the maximum knee joint torque. In addition, Fig. 9 also shows the mean value of the maximum knee joint torque of the single-legged robot

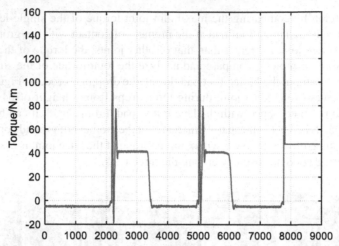

Fig. 8. The torque curves of the knee joint during three drops from a height of 64 cm for the single-legged robot equipped with the lattice foot pad.

without the foot pad when dropping from a height of 24 cm. Since the system was protected when the single-legged robot without the foot pad was dropped from a height of 34 cm, the maximum knee joint torque was not obtained. As the dropping height increases, the maximum knee joint torque also increases, so no test was conducted with the single-legged robot without foot pad at higher dropping heights. When the single-legged robot with the lattice foot pad and the single-legged robot without the foot pad were both dropped from a height of 24 cm, the mean value of the maximum knee joint torque for the single-legged robot with the lattice foot pad was 75.0 N·m, while the mean value of the maximum knee joint torque for the single-legged robot without the foot pad was 96.2 N·m. Compared with the single-legged robot without the foot pad, the single-legged robot with the lattice foot pad can reduce the maximum knee joint torque by 22% during the dropping process, demonstrating better cushioning and shock absorption effects.

By comparing the drop tests of the single-legged robot with and without the lattice foot pad, the following conclusions can be drawn:

1) When the single-legged robot with the lattice foot pad dropped from a maximum height of 64 cm above the ground, the average value of the maximum knee joint torque was 150.6 N·m, and the entire mechanical structure was intact during the test. Due to the height limitation of the test bench, no higher drop tests were conducted.
2) When the single-legged robot without foot pad dropped from a height of 34 cm above the ground, the system protection was triggered after the foot touched the ground and was unable to conduct higher drop tests.
3) When the single-legged robot with and without the lattice foot pad dropped from a height of 24 cm above the ground, the average value of the maximum knee joint torque of the single-legged robot with the lattice foot pad was reduced by about 22% compared to that without foot pad.

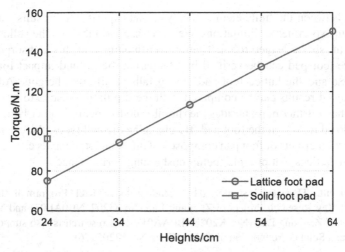

Fig. 9. The mean values of the maximum knee joint torque of the single-legged robot with the lattice foot pad installed when dropping from heights of 24 cm, 34 cm, 44 cm, 54 cm, and 64 cm, as well as the mean value of the maximum knee joint torque of the single-legged robot without the foot pad when dropping from a height of 24 cm.

The above single-legged robot drop tests demonstrate that the foot structure with the lattice foot pad can effectively absorb ground impact, greatly reducing joint torque and exhibiting a good cushioning and shock-absorbing effect.

4 Conclusion and Future Work

To mitigate the ground impact suffered by the humanoid robot during motion and protect its delicate components from damage, this study designs a foot pad with rhombic dodecahedron lattice cells. Firstly, the strength and stiffness of the lattice foot pad were validated through quasi-static compression simulation, ensuring they meet the design requirements. Subsequently, a comparative analysis of drop simulations with a height of 64 cm was conducted between the lattice foot pad and a solid foot pad of the same size. The lattice foot pad demonstrated an approximately 82% reduction in ground impact force compared to the solid foot pad, confirming its superior cushioning and shock absorption properties. To further validate the cushioning effect of the lattice foot pad, drop tests were performed on a single-legged robot. The leg with and without the lattice foot pad were dropped from the height ranging from 24 cm to 64 cm. The leg without the foot pad experienced failure at a drop height of 34 cm due to the system protection, while the leg with the lattice foot pad remained intact even at the drop height of 64 cm. When dropped from 24 cm, the leg with the lattice foot pad exhibited a 22% reduction in the maximum torque at the knee joint compared to the leg without the foot pad, further validating the cushioning and shock absorption effects of the lattice foot pad.

Although the cushioning and shock absorption effects of the lattice foot pad have been validated through finite element analysis and single-legged robot drop tests, the comparison between the finite element analysis and experimental results was not conducted due to experimental limitations. Next, we need to fabricate the solid insole and install it on the single-legged robot. Then, the cushioning and shock absorption effects of the lattice foot pad can be verified by comparing the ground impact forces of the solid foot pad and the lattice foot pad during falls at different heights. Additionally, the experimental results can be compared with the simulation results to mutually validate each other. Furthermore, besides the rhombic dodecahedron, other lattice units can also be explored to design the foot pad. By changing the cell types, the cushioning and shock absorption effects of foot pad composed of different lattice units can be evaluated, screening out lattices that provides better cushioning performance.

Acknowledgment. This work is supported by "Leading Goose" R&D Program of Zhejiang (No. 2023C01177), Key Research Project of Zhejiang Lab (No. G2021NB0AL03) and Youth Foundation Project of Zhejiang Lab (No. K2023NB0AA01). This research is also supported by the National Natural Science Foundation of China (Grant No. 52205076).

References

1. Xiaomi Official Website. https://www.mi.com/cyberone?masid=2922.0028&bd_vid=117152 73185798402331. Accessed 2 May 2023
2. YouTube. https://www.youtube.com/watch?v=ODSJsviD_SU&ab_channel=Tesla. Accessed 2 May 2023
3. YouTube. https://www.youtube.com/watch?v=tF4DML7FIWk&ab_channel=BostonDyn amics. Accessed 2 May 2023
4. Kaneko, K., et al.: Humanoid robot HRP-5P: An electrically actuated humanoid robot with high-power and wide-range joints. IEEE Robot. Autom. Let. **4**(2), 1431–1438 (2019)
5. Yamaguchi, J., Takanishi, A., Kato, I.: Experimental development of a foot mechanism with shock absorbing material for acquisition of landing surface position information and stabilization of dynamic biped walking. In: Proceedings of 1995 IEEE International Conference on Robotics and Automation, , pp. 2892–2899. Nagoya, Japan (1995)
6. Pajon, A., Caron, S., De Magistri, G., Miossec, S., Kheddar, A.: Walking on gravel with soft soles using linear inverted pendulum tracking and reaction force distribution. In: 2017 IEEE-RAS 17th International Conference on Humanoid Robotics (Humanoids), pp. 432–437. Birmingham, UK (2017)
7. Berninger, T.F., Seiwald, P., Sygulla, F., Rixen, D.J.: Evaluating the mechanical redesign of a biped walking robot using experimental modal analysis. In: Dilworth, B.J., Mains, M. (eds.) Topics in Modal Analysis & Testing, Volume 8. Conference Proceedings of the Society for Experimental Mechanics Series. Springer, Cham (2022). https://doi.org/10.1007/978-3-030-75996-4_6
8. Lohmeier, S.: Design and realization of a humanoid robot for fast and autonomous bipedal locomotion. Technische Universität München (2010)
9. Nakaoka, S.I., Hattori, S., Kanehiro, F., Kajita, S., Hirukawa, H.: Constraint-based dynamics simulator for humanoid robots with shock absorbing mechanisms. In: 2007 IEEE/RSJ International Conference on Intelligent Robots and Systems, pp. 3641–3647. San Diego, CA, USA (2007)
10. Pan, C., Han, Y., Lu, J.: Design and optimization of lattice structures: a review. Appl. Sci. **10**(18), 6374 (2020)

11. Akbay, Ö.C., Bahçe, E., Uysal, A., Gezer, I.: Production and cleaning of lattice structures used in the space and aerospace industry with metal additive manufacturing method. J. Mater. Eng. Perform. **31**(8), 6310–6321 (2022)
12. Vasiliev, V.V., Barynin, V.A., Razin, A.F.: Anisogrid composite lattice structures–development and aerospace applications. Compos. Struct. **94**(3), 1117–1127 (2012)
13. Aslan, B., Yıldız, A.R.: Optimum design of automobile components using lattice structures for additive manufacturing. Mater. Test. **62**(6), 633–639 (2020)
14. Zhang, W., Xu, J.: Advanced lightweight materials for Automobiles: a review. Mater. Des. **221**, 110994 (2022)
15. Dehghan-Manshadi, A., Venezuela, J., Demir, A.G., Ye, Q., Dargusch, M.S.: Additively manufactured Fe-35Mn-1Ag lattice structures for biomedical applications. J. Manuf. Process. **80**, 642–650 (2022)
16. Feng, J., Liu, B., Lin, Z., Fu, J.: Isotropic octet-truss lattice structure design and anisotropy control strategies for implant application. Mater. Des. **203**, 109595 (2021)
17. Yin, H., Zhang, W., Zhu, L., Meng, F., Liu, J., Wen, G.: Review on lattice structures for energy absorption properties. Compos. Struct. **304**, 116397 (2022)
18. Wang, C., Li, Y., Zhao, W., Zou, S., Zhou, G., Wang, Y.: Structure design and multi-objective optimization of a novel crash box based on biomimetic structure. Int. J. Mech. Sci. **138**, 489–501 (2018)
19. Yin, S., Chen, H., Wu, Y., Li, Y., Xu, J.: Introducing composite lattice core sandwich structure as an alternative proposal for engine hood. Compos. Struct. **201**, 131–140 (2018)
20. Acanfora, V., Saputo, S., Russo, A., Riccio, A.: A feasibility study on additive manufactured hybrid metal/composite shock absorbers. Compos. Struct. **268**, 113958 (2021)
21. Acanfora, V., Castaldo, R., Riccio, A.: On the effects of core microstructure on energy absorbing capabilities of sandwich panels intended for additive manufacturing. Materials **15**(4), 1291 (2022)

An Action Evaluation and Scaling Algorithm for Robot Motion Planning

Ruiqi Wu[1,2,3]($\boxtimes$), Chao Fan[3], Huifang Hou[3], Zihao Zhang[1,2,3], Longzhuo Wang[3], Xin Zhao[3], and Fei Chao[4]

[1] The Key Laboratory of Grain Information Processing and Control (Henan University of Technology), Ministry of Education, Zhengzhou, China
rqwu@haut.edu.cn
[2] Henan Provincial Key Laboratory of Grain Photoelectric Detection and Control, Zhengzhou, China
[3] School of Artificial Intelligence and Big Data, Henan University of Technology, Zhengzhou 450001, China
[4] The Department of Artificial Intelligence, School of Informatics, Xiamen University, Xiamen, China
fchao@xmu.edu.cn

Abstract. The evaluation and manipulation of robot motion are essential for effective motion planning. Similar to audio and video data, motion data requires transform operations and a merit function when utilizing supervised and semi-supervised algorithms. However, designing an appropriate evaluation method remains a challenge, and motion data cannot be processed with acceleration. This paper proposes a method for calculating robot posture similarity and action sequence similarity while introducing a method for scaling action sequences. First, a posture and action sequence similarity calculation method based on visual angle is proposed. Then, a method for scaling action sequences is designed, drawing on resampling techniques from the audio field. Through a series of experimental analyses, the evaluation methods demonstrated consistency with human evaluations, and the distortion rate of action sequences at different scales was less than 1%. Applying the proposed method to robot motion planning problems allows for the implementation of supervisory algorithms, resulting in intelligent robot motion planning.

Keywords: Action Evaluation · Action Retrieval · Distance Measure · Robot Movement Planning

This work was supported by the Open Project of Scientific Research Platform of Grain Information Processing Center of Henan University of Technology (KFJJ-2021-107, KFJJ-2021-108), the Key Scientific Research Projects of Higher Education Institutions in Henan Province (No. 23B520001), the Science and Technology Research Project of Henan Province under Grant 222102210108, the Science and Technology Research and Development Plan Joint fund (application research) project of Henan Province (222103810042), and the Henan Science and technology research project (222102210309).

H. Yang et al. (Eds.): ICIRA 2023, LNAI 14270, pp. 392–403, 2023.
https://doi.org/10.1007/978-981-99-6492-5_34

1   Introduction

Robot motion planning is a crucial research topic within the field of robotics. Many studies employ intelligent methods to generate and evaluate robot motion [4,5]. To assess the quality of a robot motion sequence segment, an objective and uniform evaluation standard [4,15] is vital. Without a reliable evaluation standard, various supervised and semi-supervised algorithms [2,16] cannot be used to address robot motion planning problems. Therefore, establishing an objective and uniform evaluation standard for robot motion is necessary.

Numerous scholars have investigated this problem [6,9], with some using human evaluation results as a basis for quantitative evaluation [10], while others develop relatively objective evaluation methods based on indices like motion quality and human-computer interaction [1,12]. Some researchers [13,17] combine quantitative index methods with manual evaluation to focus on different aspects. For example, Peng [14,18] evaluated the quality of motion in the form of an online questionnaire survey and designed corresponding calculation methods for the innovation of motion based on motion indicators. Despite these efforts [7,16], constructing a unified evaluation method remains a significant challenge for researchers in this field.

The proposed method offers a considerable advantage over existing methods, as it effectively avoids the subjectivity of human evaluation results while remaining consistent with human evaluations. As a result, it can serve as an objective, quantifiable evaluation standard for robot motion. This method can enhance existing motion evaluation standards, allowing for the use of various classic supervised and semi-supervised algorithms for generating and evaluating robot motion. Consequently, it promotes intelligent planning of robot motion and advances research in related fields of robot motion planning.

2   Background Knowledge

2.1   Robot Hardware

In addition to video, many studies use motion capture devices to record human motion [3,8,11]. For a robot to transition between two postures during continuous action, it must remain in a pose for a certain duration. These robot postures, which include stay time, are called key postures. Key postures often convey more information than ordinary robot postures and warrant attention. The extraction of key postures is relatively straightforward, considering only the dynamic characteristics of robot movements and a stay time exceeding a specific threshold.

The experimental platform utilizes the Alpha1P robot, produced by Chinese company UBTECH, as its foundation. Alpha1P is a humanoid robot primarily used for home entertainment, featuring a charming appearance and a high degree of freedom. Comprising 16 servo motors, the robot's range of motion spans from 0 to 180°, enabling it to mimic various human movements. The distribution of servos is shown in Fig. 1.

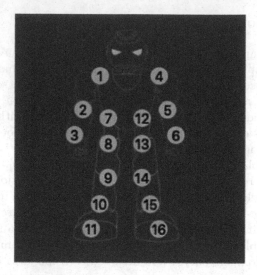

Fig. 1. Distribution diagram of robot steering gear.

2.2 Motion Representation

The robot's posture is represented by the angle values of its 16 servos. Assuming the robot posture is *pos*, and the angle values of the robot's joints are $[j_1, j_2, j_3, ..., j_16]$, the robot posture $Pos = [j_1, j_2, j_3, ..., j_16]$. To represent robot motion and robot motion sequence samples, the time factor must be considered at the posture level. Robot motion can be regarded as a set of key postures, each with independent static and running times. When representing robot motion in key posture form, the running time between each key posture and the total time the current key posture remains static must be known. Therefore, the key posture kp in robot motion can be composed of three elements and represented as $kp = [pos, r, t]$, where r denotes the running time from the current posture to the next, and t represents the sum of the current posture's static and running time. After incorporating the time factor, the robot motion Act and robot motion sequence AS can be represented using Eq. 1, with the difference between AS and Act being that AS contains more key postures.

$$\begin{cases} Act =[kp_1, \ldots, kp_n], & n \geq 2 \\ AS =[kp_1, \ldots, kp_n], & n \geq 3 \end{cases} \tag{1}$$

3 Methods

3.1 Calculation of Posture Similarity

Joint angles within the same plane coordinate system exhibit a mutual canceling effect, while those not in the same plane have a mutual strengthening

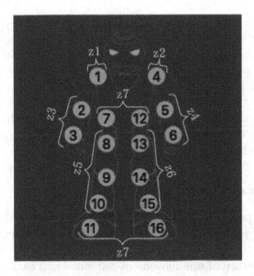

Fig. 2. Diagram of Joint Regions.

effect. Consequently, the body joints can be divided into several independent regions. The 16 joint numbers of the Alpha1P robot, as shown in
Fig. 2, can be divided into seven regions. These regions can be represented
as: $1, 4, [2, 3], [5, 6], [8, 9, 10], [13, 14, 15], [7, 11, 12, 16]$, with the difference values
of these seven regions denoted by $[z_1, z_2, z_3, ..., z_7]$. The corresponding difference
values can be calculated based on the mutual relationship between the servos in
each region.

Since the influence between regions varies, appropriate weights should be
assigned to each region based on its impact on other regions. Let the weights of
each region be $w = [w_1, w_2, ..., w_7]$. The calculation of robot posture similarity
can then be represented as:

$$s = 1 - \frac{\sum_{i=1}^{7} w_i \cdot z_i}{180}. \tag{2}$$

To eliminate the influence of invalid movements on movement distance, the
distance between robot postures must be normalized to amplify the difference
value of robot postures. First, a large number of random robot poses are sampled,
and the average distance between poses in all sampled poses is calculated as a
threshold. This threshold is then mapped to 0.5. When the similarity is greater
than the threshold, it is mapped to $[0.5, 1]$, otherwise, it is mapped to $[0, 0.5]$.
The calculation of normalization can be represented as:

$$S = \begin{cases} \dfrac{s - \tau}{2(1 - \tau)} + 0.5, & s \geq \tau \\[2mm] \dfrac{s}{2\tau}, & s < \tau \end{cases} \tag{3}$$

where s is the initial similarity value obtained, S is the similarity after secondary normalization, and τ represents the threshold used in normalization, calculated based on the average similarity between the robot posture in the database and the random robot posture. The calculation process of robot posture similarity can be summarized as follows: (1) calculate the difference values of each joint in each sub-region of the posture; (2) calculate the overall difference value based on the difference values of the sub-regions; (3) normalize the overall difference value and calculate the initial similarity; (4) normalize the initial similarity and calculate the final similarity.

3.2   Calculation of Motion Similarity

By combining the posture similarity calculation method and the dynamic time warping method, a new method for measuring robot movement similarity is proposed. First, the posture similarity algorithm calculates the similarity between each movement posture of one movement sequence and each movement posture of another movement sequence. Second, using dynamic programming, a warping path is found. Finally, the maximum similarity is calculated based on the warping path.

Assuming that the two movement sequences to be compared are $A = [pos_1, pos_2, pos_3, ..., pos_m]$ and $B = [pos_1, pos_2, pos_3, ..., pos_n]$, containing m and n postures, respectively. The similarity between A and B is calculated as follows:

First, construct a similarity matrix Sim of size $m \times n$, calculating the similarity between any two robot postures in sequences A and B. The similarity between any two robot postures can be represented in Sim as follows:

$$Sim(i,j) = S(A_i, \ B_j), i < n, j < m, \tag{4}$$

where $S(\cdot)$ represents the previously proposed robot posture similarity calculation method.

Next, a warping path $W = [w_1, w2, w_k ..., w_K]$, $max(m, n) \le K < m+n-1$, is found on the Sim matrix, where K represents the length of the warping path. The warping path must satisfy three constraints: (1) boundary condition, with the starting point and ending point of the path satisfying: $w_1 = Sim(1,1)$, $w_K = Sim(m, n)$; (2) continuity, the next point of any path point must be an adjacent point in the matrix; (3) monotonicity, when $w_k = Sim(i, j), w_{k+1} = Sim(\hat{i}, \hat{j})$, then $i \le \hat{i} \le i + 1$, $j \le \hat{j} \le j + 1$. Since the algorithm seeks the warping path with the highest similarity, w_{k+1} can be represented as:

$$w_{k+1} = max[Sim(i - 1, j), \ Sim(i, j - 1), \ Sim(i - 1, j - 1)]. \tag{5}$$

After finding the warping path, the cumulative similarity of the entire path is calculated and then normalized based on the path's length. The specific formula for calculating the normalized similarity is as follows:

$$DS(A, \ B) = \frac{\sum_{k=1}^{K} w_k}{K}. \tag{6}$$

Since the algorithm has no limit on the length of the movement sequence, it can be used for similarity calculation between movements or movement sequences and can also be employed to search for movements from motion.

3.3   Scaling Algorithm for Motion Sequences

Scientific computation requires stretching, compressing, and other operations to be performed on movement sequences. If simple scaling methods such as interpolation and uniform deletion are used to compress the posture of the movement sequence, several problems may arise. For example, stretching using interpolation will cause a sawtooth phenomenon similar to enlarging images, while deleting posture uniformly will result in the deletion of key postures. These problems resemble those encountered in audio processing, so audio processing methods can be employed to solve them. A compression algorithm for movement sequences based on downsampling techniques is established here.

A robot movement sequence is a sequence of 16-dimensional data that changes along the time axis. From the perspective of audio data, a robot movement sequence can be viewed as 16-channel audio data. Therefore, audio resampling methods can be directly used to process movement sequences. In audio resampling, a pre-trained low-pass filter is utilized. Due to the similarity of the problem, a pre-trained polyphase filter is also used here to resample the movement sequence.

4   Experimentation

4.1   Experimental Analysis of Posture Similarity Algorithm

A. Theoretical Analysis

A qualified similarity evaluation algorithm should theoretically exhibit three aspects:

(1) The evaluation function must be continuous, meaning the distance between any two robot poses obtained by proportional interpolation and the distance between the two original poses should be less than or equal to the distance between the two poses. This can also be seen as the similarity function S satisfying the Lipschitz condition. The definition of the Lipschitz condition is: for the function $f(x)$, if any x_1 and x_2 in its domain are given, there exists $L > 0$ such that $|f(x_1) - f(x_2)| \leq L|x_1 - x_2|$. When the function satisfies the Lipschitz condition, its slope must be less than the Lipschitz constant.

(2) It should reflect the different contributions of each joint in the overall similarity. Since the visual impact of changes in different body parts varies, the weights of each joint's impact on body changes are not the same. For example, changes in the legs and waist have a greater impact on the overall body than changes in the upper body.

(3) The algorithm's evaluation results should approach human visual evaluation. The ultimate goal of the algorithm is to replace human evaluation, with humans primarily evaluating the quality of actions through visual perception. Therefore, the evaluation results of the algorithm should be consistent with human intuitive visual evaluation.

Firstly, the proposed similarity algorithm only weights, sums, and normalizes the values of each joint, without nonlinear processing. Therefore, it is a continuous linear function, satisfying: $|S(x_1) - S(x_2)| \leq L|x_1 - x_2|$. In the proposed algorithm, the step size of the interpolated robot pose can be regarded as the Lipschitz constant. Secondly, the algorithm considers joint weights, assigning different weights to various joint areas within the robot's regions, which also reflects the intuitive evaluation in the visual dimension to some extent.

B. Experimental Comparison

To verify the performance of the algorithm, the proposed algorithm was compared with the cosine distance-based similarity calculation method, the similarity calculation method based on equal weights, and the similarity calculation method proposed by Wenyao in his work.

(a) Standard upright position.

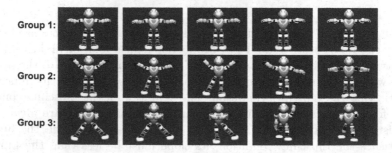

(b) Postures with different similarities.

Fig. 3. Standard posture and three groups of dancing postures.

In the experiment, three sets of robot poses were designed to test the effectiveness of the similarity method. The three sets of robot poses were designed

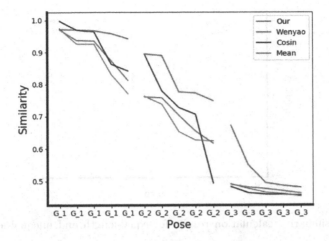

Fig. 4. Evaluation results of each algorithm on three sets of robot poses.

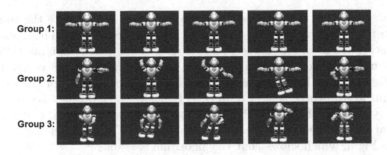

Fig. 5. Three groups of poses randomly sampled from the data set.

based on the robot's standard upright pose, divided into three groups according to the difference in similarity with the standard pose: almost the same, similar, and dissimilar, each group containing five poses. The three sets of robot poses and the standard upright pose are shown in Fig. 3. The evaluation of each algorithm on the three sets is shown in Fig. 4. To make the evaluation more intuitive, the three sets of robot poses in the four algorithms are plotted on the same graph, and sorted in descending order within each group according to the similarity value. The horizontal axis represents the group to which the robot pose belongs, and the vertical axis represents the similarity between the robot pose and the standard pose.

Compared with these comparative algorithms, the performance of the proposed algorithm is relatively better on the three sets of data, as it can correctly distinguish the three sets of data and has smaller changes in the first two sets of data than the other three algorithms, which is more in line with the visual evaluation of these two sets of data.

In addition, to test the effectiveness of the proposed algorithm in practical applications, the proposed algorithm was applied to a data set containing 2931

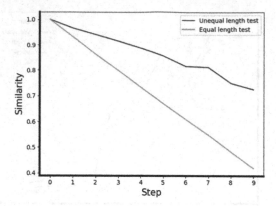

Fig. 6. The similarity calculation results for equal-length and unequal-length action sequences.

robot poses. First, the proposed algorithm was used to calculate the similarity between the standard pose and each robot pose in the data set. Then, according to the score range of the three sets in Fig. 4, robot poses that meet the corresponding range were randomly selected from the data set for visual display. From Fig. 4, it can be seen that the evaluation score interval of the proposed algorithm for the three sets of data is: [1.0, 0.94], [0.90, 0.74], [0.68, 0.48]. The randomly selected three sets of robot poses are shown in Fig. 5, and it can be seen that the differences between these three sets of robot poses are similar to those in Fig. 4, which shows that the algorithm is stable.

4.2   Experimental Analysis of Motion Similarity Algorithm

To test the effectiveness of the proposed motion similarity calculation method on equal-length and unequal-length action sequences, two sets of experiments were designed to compare a given action sequence with a set of equal-length sequences and a set of variable-length sequences, respectively. Specifically, 100 robot postures were randomly selected from the posture dataset to form a fixed frame rate representation of an action sequence, which served as the standard sequence. Then, the posture with the smallest similarity for each posture was calculated and a new action sequence was formed, which served as the maximum difference sequence. Next, ten posture sequences of varying lengths were obtained by deleting ten postures from the current sequence each time, starting from the standard sequence, with the corresponding number of postures being [100, 90, 80, ..., 10]. These ten sequences were used as unequal-length samples to calculate the action similarity with the standard sequence. This was done to show the similarity changes between the standard action sequence and its local sequences. The similarity results are shown by the blue line in Fig. 6. Next, the end of these ten posture sequences was aligned with the end of the maximum difference sequence, and the postures in the maximum difference sequence that

Table 1. Comparison of similarity after action scaling.

Scaling factor	Similarity to the original action sequence	Scaling factor	Similarity to the original action sequence
5	0.99796	0.2	0.99145
4	0.99795	0.25	0.99317
3	0.99809	0.33	0.99450
2	0.99803	0.5	0.99650

were equal in length to the standard sequence were replaced with the standard sequence to form ten equal-length action sequences, with only parts of the standard sequence overlapping. The similarity between these ten equal-length sequences and the standard sequence was then calculated, and the similarity change was shown by the orange line in Fig. 6.

From Fig. 6, it can be observed that as the variable-length sequence decreases in length, its similarity with the standard sequence gradually diminishes when the variable-length sequence is a part of the standard sequence. When the equal-length sequence comprises the minimum similarity postures of a part of the standard sequence and the rest of the sequence, its similarity with the standard sequence declines as the overlap segment decreases. The similarity of the variable-length sequence consistently surpasses that of the equal-length sequence, aligning with human intuition. This characteristic enables more precise evaluation of motion sequences with higher similarity, while the assessment of sequences with lower similarity remains relatively vague. This feature resembles the psychological mechanism of human evaluation, which focuses primarily on similar parts. However, this algorithm also has some drawbacks. As the size of the similarity matrix is related to the length of the action sequence, the size of the similarity matrix increases with the length of the action sequence. When the action sequence becomes excessively long, the computation intensifies, reducing the efficiency of the algorithm.

4.3   Motion Scaling Results Analysis

To test the effect of resampling, an action sequence was randomly selected from a dataset of 53 action sequences, and different scales of resampling were performed. The similarity between the resampled results and the original action sequence was calculated. The results are shown in Table 1, where the similarity between the different resampled actions and the original action is above 0.99, and the distortion rate of the action sequence consistently remains below 1%. The performance of the scaling algorithm can meet the application requirements in subsequent work.

5   Conclusion

This article proposes an action evaluation method and an action sequence scaling method to address the action evaluation problem and scaling operation problem in robot motion planning. First, a robot posture similarity calculation method considering visual evaluation is proposed. Through a series of experimental analyses, the evaluation of the method for humanoid robot motion essentially aligns with human evaluation results and can be used as a tool for quantifying the similarity of robot posture. Then, based on the posture similarity algorithm and dynamic time warping method, an action similarity calculation method is proposed, which can be employed to calculate the similarity between actions and to match and search for actions. Through experimental analysis, the performance of the method in calculating the similarity between different length action sequences also conforms to the psychological mechanism of human evaluation of action sequences. Finally, using the action similarity algorithm as an evaluation tool, an action sequence scaling algorithm is proposed. Through experiments, it is demonstrated that the distortion rate of the action sequence remains below 1% when different scales of action sequence scaling are performed, which essentially meets the requirements of action sequence scaling in motion planning tasks.

Although the proposed methods can address the basic processing problems of actions in motion planning, there is still room for improvement. First, the posture model is simply designed by combining the affiliation relationship between each joint in the human visual evaluation mechanism. The Riemannian manifold is more suitable for modeling the relationship between joints than the Euclidean space. In the future, Riemannian manifold theory can be employed to model the correlation rules between joints. Second, in the action similarity algorithm, as the size of the similarity matrix is related to the length of the action sequence, the size of the similarity matrix increases with the length of the action sequence. When the action sequence becomes excessively long, the computation intensifies, reducing the efficiency of the algorithm. This problem can be addressed by decreasing the accuracy of the regular path to enhance computation speed, which is also another direction for future work.

References

1. Bi, T., Fankhauser, P., Bellicoso, D., Hutter, M.: Real-time dance generation to music for a legged robot. In: IEEE International Conference on Intelligent Robots and Systems, pp. 1038–1044 (2018)
2. Chen, B., Su, J., Wang, L., Gu, Q.: Learning robot grasping from a random pile with deep Q-learning. In: Liu, X.-J., Nie, Z., Yu, J., Xie, F., Song, R. (eds.) ICIRA 2021. LNCS (LNAI), vol. 13014, pp. 142–152. Springer, Cham (2021). https://doi.org/10.1007/978-3-030-89098-8_14
3. Ehrlich, S.K., Cheng, G.: A feasibility study for validating robot actions using EEG-based error-related potentials. Int. J. Soc. Robot. **11**, 271–283 (2019)
4. Feng, C., Lan, X., Wan, L., Liang, Z., Wang, H.: A guided evaluation method for robot dynamic manipulation. In: Chan, C.S., et al. (eds.) ICIRA 2020. LNCS

(LNAI), vol. 12595, pp. 161–170. Springer, Cham (2020). https://doi.org/10.1007/978-3-030-66645-3_14

5. Fu, T., Li, F., Zheng, Y., Song, R.: Process learning of robot fabric manipulation based on composite reward functions. In: Liu, X.-J., Nie, Z., Yu, J., Xie, F., Song, R. (eds.) ICIRA 2021. LNCS (LNAI), vol. 13014, pp. 163–174. Springer, Cham (2021). https://doi.org/10.1007/978-3-030-89098-8_16

6. Johannink, T., et al.: Residual reinforcement learning for robot control. In: 2019 International Conference on Robotics and Automation (ICRA), pp. 6023–6029. IEEE (2019)

7. Kattepur, A.: Roboplanner: autonomous robotic action planning via knowledge graph queries. In: Proceedings of the 34th ACM/SIGAPP Symposium on Applied Computing, pp. 953–956 (2019)

8. Liu, N., Liu, Z., Cui, L.: A modified cartesian space DMPS model for robot motion generation. In: Yu, H., Liu, J., Liu, L., Ju, Z., Liu, Y., Zhou, D. (eds.) ICIRA 2019. LNCS (LNAI), vol. 11745, pp. 76–85. Springer, Cham (2019). https://doi.org/10.1007/978-3-030-27529-7_7

9. Losey, D.P., Srinivasan, K., Mandlekar, A., Garg, A., Sadigh, D.: Controlling assistive robots with learned latent actions. In: 2020 IEEE International Conference on Robotics and Automation (ICRA), pp. 378–384. IEEE (2020)

10. Manfrè, A., Infantino, I., Vella, F., Gaglio, S.: An automatic system for humanoid dance creation. Biol. Inspired Cogn. Archit. **15**, 1–9 (2016)

11. Menolotto, M., Komaris, D.S., Tedesco, S., O'Flynn, B., Walsh, M.: Motion capture technology in industrial applications: a systematic review. Sensors **20**(19), 5687 (2020)

12. Özen, F., Küntan, U., Tükel, D.B.: Robot-music synchronization: self-designed dance. In: IEEE EUROCON 2017-17th International Conference on Smart Technologies, pp. 582–587. IEEE (2017)

13. Peng, H., Li, J., Hu, H., Zhao, L., Feng, S., Hu, K.: Feature fusion based automatic aesthetics evaluation of robotic dance poses. Robot. Auton. Syst. **111**, 99–109 (2019)

14. Peng, W.: A robot dance generation system based on deep learning method. Master's thesis, Xiamen University (2019)

15. Phueakthong, P., Varagul, J.: A development of mobile robot based on ROS2 for navigation application. In: 2021 International Electronics Symposium (IES), pp. 517–520. IEEE (2021)

16. Ravichandar, H., Polydoros, A.S., Chernova, S., Billard, A.: Recent advances in robot learning from demonstration. Annu. Rev. Control Robot. Auton. Syst. **3**, 297–330 (2020)

17. Sunardi, M., Perkowski, M.: Music to motion: using music information to create expressive robot motion. Int. J. Soc. Robot. **10**(1), 43–63 (2018)

18. Wu, R., et al.: Towards deep learning based robot automatic choreography system. In: Yu, H., Liu, J., Liu, L., Ju, Z., Liu, Y., Zhou, D. (eds.) ICIRA 2019. LNCS (LNAI), vol. 11743, pp. 629–640. Springer, Cham (2019). https://doi.org/10.1007/978-3-030-27538-9_54

Design and Control of the Biped Robot HTY

Yun Liu[1,2], Jiawei Weng[1,2], Fan Wang[1,2], Jingge Tang[1,2], Yunchang Yao[1,2], Xingyu Chen[1,2], Lingyu Kong[1,2], Dingkun Liang[1,2], Xin Wang[1,2], Shiqiang Zhu[1,2], Yuanjie Chen[4], Anhuan Xie[1,2(✉)], and Jason Gu[3]

[1] Research Center for Intelligent Robotics, Research Institute of Interdisciplinary Innovation, Zhejiang Lab, Hangzhou, China
xieanhuan@zhejianglab.com
[2] Zhejiang Engineering Research Center for Intelligent Robotics, Hangzhou, China
[3] Department of Electrical Engineering, Dalhousie University, Halifax, NS, Canada
[4] Zhejiang Institute of Metrology, Hangzhou, China

Abstract. This paper presents the development of the bipedal robot platform, HTY, which is designed for operation in dangerous and unknown environments, with the ability to move in complex environments. The robot is equipped with a simple joint and structure layout to ensure a wide range of joint movements and has the ability to perceive the status of its foot. The modular design and scalability requirements are also met. The HTY bipedal robot has a total of 12 degrees of freedom, a height of 119 cm, and a weight of 54 kg. The developed motion planning and control framework is tested on both the Gazebo simulation platform and the physical robot, achieving stable walking. This paper mainly introduces the design concept and basic specifications of the robot.

Keywords: Dangerous scenarios · Minimalist layout · Modular design · Information perception · State feedback

1 Introduction

Compared with other mobile robots (e.g., wheeled, tracked), bipedal robots are increasingly being used in all industrial and non-industrial applications due to their ability to move in any unstructured environment [6]. Bipedal robots have always been a hot research topic in robotics. Bipedal robots take up less space in the plane direction and have high adaptability and flexibility, which enables them to adapt to more complex scenes and have a more comprehensive range of applications. The rise of the humanoid robot industry has aroused great interest among the public and treasure hunters.

"Pioneer" and "Leading Goose" R&D Program of Zhejiang (No. 2023C01177), Supported by Key Research Project of Zhejiang Lab (No. G2021NB0AL03), Zhejiang Provincial Natural Science Foundation of China under Grant No. LQ23F030010. Y. Liu is the first author.

Currently, the key core technologies for bipedal robots are body construction and stable walking anti-interference ability. The driving modes mainly include "servo motor + harmonic reducer", "high-torque servo motor + low reduction ratio", hydraulic drivers, and more. Based on biomimetics and kinematics, each leg of a bipedal robot generally has 5 to 6 degrees of freedom. Generally, fully actuated bipedal robots include hip joints, knee joints, and ankle joints, respectively, including ASIMO developed by Honda [9], HRP developed by Japanese ASIT [5], Atlas developed by Boston Dynamics [1], Optimus developed by Tesla [2], BHR developed by the Huang Qiang team at Beijing Institute of Technology [13], and WUKONG developed by the Xiong Rong team at Zhejiang University [12]. In addition, there are underactuated bipedal robots, such as Cassie bipedal robot designed by Agility Robotics in the US [7].

Motivated by the Fukushima nuclear disaster, DARPA (Defense Advanced Research Projects Agency) initiated the DRC (DARPA Robotics Challenge), a competition aimed at developing disaster response robots [10]. As a result, humanoid robots have received more attention for application in dangerous situations. In this paper, we design a fully actuated bipedal robot HTY (see Fig. 1) based on the self-developed integrated servo joint technology at ZHEJIANG LAB, which can perform large-scale joint movements and meet the needs of gait planning and motion control algorithm research.

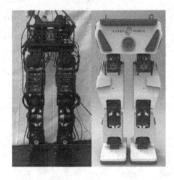

Fig. 1. The bipedal robot HTY

2　Hardware Details

2.1　Design Concept

The ultimate goal of the proposed bipedal robot is to be used for operations in dangerous and unknown scenarios, with the ability to move in complex environments such as stairs, slopes, and uneven terrain. It is hoped that this robot platform can accelerate the development of next-generation robot platforms needed for the future bipedal robot industry. The design philosophy of HTY is as follows.

Design concept:

A) Simplified joint and structural layout
B) Large joint range of motion, allowing the robot to fully squat down
C) Ability to sense information about the foot sole
D) Modular design
E) Scalability

2.2 Mechanical Structure Part

Based on the design principles A) to E), we developed the HTY bipedal robot. Its mechanical structure consists of the robot torso, thighs, shanks, and feet, as shown in Fig. 2. Table 1 shows the basic specifications of the HTY robot. The HTY robot is 1190 mm tall and weighs 54 kg, including the battery, and each leg weighs approximately 15 kg.

Table 1. HTY robot specifications

Parameter Properties	Part	Units	Value
Mass	Whole body	Kg	54
Maximum size	Height	mm	1190
	Width	mm	440
	Leg length	mm	828
Degrees	Hip	PCS	3 × 2
	Knee	PCS	1 × 2
	Ankle	PCS	2 × 2

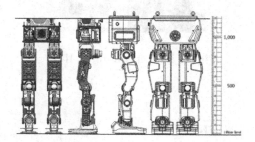

Fig. 2. Prototype of HTY

Figure 3 shows the specific details of HTY. Each leg of the robot includes three parts: the hip joint, knee joint, and ankle joint, with left and right legs symmetrically distributed. The rotation axes of the three degrees of freedom of the hip joint are perpendicular to each other and intersect at a point, which is called the hip center. The rotation axes of the two degrees of freedom of the ankle joint are perpendicular to each other and intersect at a point, which is called the ankle center. The connection between the hip center and ankle center intersects perpendicularly at the rotation axis of the knee joint. The torso contains internal components such as a computing unit, battery, attitude measurement unit, and electronic control system.

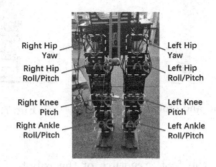

Fig. 3. The freedom configuration of HTY

Hip Joint. The hip joint of HTY has three rotational degrees of freedom, namely yaw, roll, and pitch, which rotate around the Z, X, and Y axes respectively, as shown in Fig. 4. According to the modular principle, the driving joints of the three rotational degrees of freedom are of the same type. The joint consists of a servo motor, harmonic reducer, absolute multi-turn encoder, and structural components, as shown in Fig. 5. The rated torque of the joint is 61 Nm, the peak torque is 180 Nm, the rated speed is 30 RPM, and the peak speed is 60 RPM.

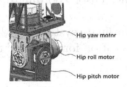

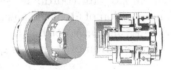

Fig. 4. Hip joint   **Fig. 5.** Driving motor

Knee Joint. The knee joint has only one Pitch degree of freedom, which is connected directly to the drive joint for a greater range of motion, as shown in Fig. 6. Rubber blocks are designed at the contact position between the robot's thigh and calf to cushion the impact during collisions.

Ankle Joint. The robot ankle joint consists of two degrees of freedom, Pitch, and Roll, as shown in Fig. 7. They are arranged in series. The Pitch direction driving joint is arranged on the lower leg through a parallel linkage transmission.

The linkage is designed to be a weak point. When the leg of the robot moves to the wrong position due to a control algorithm or software errors, this linkage can be disconnected to prevent damage to other parts.

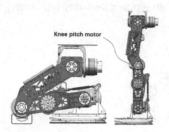

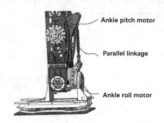

Fig. 6. Knee Joint (stand and crouch)   **Fig. 7.** Ankle joint

Foot. Figure 8 shows the foot structure of the robot. The foot of the robot is a sandwich structure consisting of an upper connection plate, two six-axis force/torque (F/T) sensors, and a lower base plate. If a single six-axis F/T sensor is used, a larger and heavier force sensor model is required to meet the requirements of allowable force and torque. However, by using the two six-axis F/T sensor solution, reduces the volume and weight of the foot.

The calculation method of the foot design in this paper is as follows.

The six-dimensional force/torque of sensor $i(i = 1, 2)$ in the sensor base coordinate system O_i is defined as:

$$f_i = [f_{x,i}, f_{y,i}, f_{z,i}, \tau_{x,i}, \tau_{y,i}, \tau_{z,i}] \tag{1}$$

The attitude transformation matrix between the sensor coordinate system and the ankle joint coordinate system is given by:

The position of O_i in the ankle joint reference coordinate system O is denoted as $p_i = (x_i, y_i, z_i)$. According to the principle of translation for force and torque, the representation of f_i in O is given by:

$$F_i = f_i + \begin{bmatrix} O_3 \times 1 \\ p_i \times [f_i] \end{bmatrix} \tag{2}$$

Therefore, the force/torque at the ankle joint is given by:

$$F = \sum_{i=1}^{2} F_i \tag{3}$$

Due to the small mass of the foot, the inertia force and Coriolis force of the foot are neglected here for ease of calculation.

Figure 9 shows the comparison between the equivalent force synthesized from the data collected by the two six-axis F/T sensors on the sole and the force collected by an external force measurement platform. The robot's two feet are placed on two force measurement platforms for stationary stepping. From Fig. 9, it can be seen that this solution can accurately measure the Z-direction force on the robot's sole. The accuracy of other dimensions requires the addition of more convenient and accurate measurement methods in the future.

Fig. 8. Foot diagram

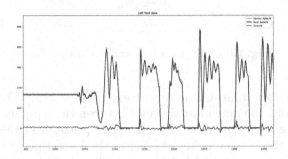

Fig. 9. Comparison of plantar force measurement and force table data

Robot Motion Range. The motion range of each driving joint of the robot cannot all reach $-180°\sim180°$. Considering the requirements of robot walking, climbing stairs, walking on uneven ground, and shell non-interference, the motion range of each joint of the robot is finally designed to meet the walking motion control range, as shown in Table 2. The table contains the motion ranges of 12 degrees of freedom, which are symmetrical between the left and right legs.

To facilitate the zero-position calibration and observation of the robot, a simple calibration method is designed in this paper. As shown in Fig. 10, there are identical circular pinholes between two parts that rotate around each other about their respective rotation axes. In addition, indicator scale lines are designed at each joint for observing whether there is a zero-position offset of the joint. This phenomenon sometimes occurs due to encoder count loss and can cause damage to the robot if it is severe.

In order to achieve bipedal locomotion, the walking of a bipedal robot is not only related to the range of motion and driving capability of each joint

Table 2. The range of motion of HTY

Joint name	Pitch(deg)	Roll(deg)	Yaw(deg)
Left hip	−80∼25	−35∼40	−30∼15
Right hip	−80∼25	−40∼35	−15∼30
Left knee	−3∼140	Null	Null
Right knee	−3∼140	Null	Null
Left ankle	−80∼3	−40∼40	Null
Right ankle	−80∼3	−40∼40	Null

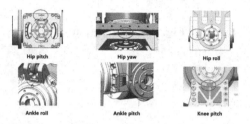

Fig. 10. Calibration hole and calibration line

but also to the structural dimensions of each component. When the HTY is standing vertically, the maximum distance between the hip joint center and the ankle joint center is 700 mm. The maximum step length in the sagittal plane is 580 mm, and the maximum step length in the lateral plane is 450 mm. The maximum foot clearance height is 520 mm, as shown in Fig. 11.

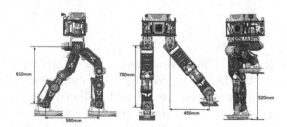

Fig. 11. HTY parameter

2.3   Electrical System Components

HTY's electrical control system includes a motion calculation unit, a drive system, a power supply system, an IMU, six-axis F/T sensors, etc. The functions of the motion calculation unit include acquiring information from the foot pressure sensors, acquiring joint position/current/speed information, acquiring IMU

(Inertial Measurement Unit) information, motion state estimation, motion control and planning, and issuing joint execution information. The drivers of the 12 driving joints use EtherCAT communication, meeting the communication rate requirements for motion control.

2.4 Software System Components

For the convenience of modularization and reuse of software, ROS is used as middleware in combination with Xenomai in this paper to improve the modularity and usability of the software system. As shown in Fig. 12, some motion control and planning programs run on the non-real-time kernel, while some low-level motion control programs run on the real-time kernel of the Xenomai system. The real-time and non-real-time kernels communicate with each other using the XDDP protocol.

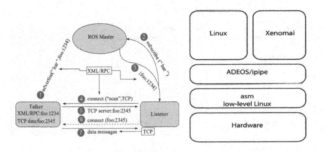

Fig. 12. the bipedal robot HTY

3 Control Architecture

The stability of robot walking is an important index for evaluating the walking gait of a biped robot, and it is also the first index to be satisfied in designing the walking gait in this paper. There are many stability criteria for biped robot walking control, among which the most commonly used one is the Zero Moment Point (ZMP) stability criterion proposed by Yugoslav scholar Vukobratovic in 1969 [4]. Kjita proposed the Linear Inverted Pendulum Model (LIPM) and extended it from two dimensions to three dimensions [3], keeping the vertical height of the robot's center of mass, and simplifying the dynamic system of the robot into a linear system, greatly simplifying the problem of gait planning and walking control.

On the premise of satisfying the ZMP stability criterion, this paper combines the linear inverted pendulum model to simplify robot kinematic calculations, inputs the robot's motion target state, and adjusts the foothold point and foothold time based on the observed foothold and body state information to achieve robot walking. This scheme is simple and easy to use, is convenient for quickly verifying and iterating robot systems, and can also be used for anti-disturbance feedback control testing.

3.1   Robot Walking Planning Method

Figure 13 shows the gait planning and control diagram based on the LIPM and ZMP stability criteria. Firstly, the center of mass (CoM) and the footstep are planned separately based on the input commands, which are typically forward velocity, lateral velocity, and yaw rate. The CoM reference trajectory is generated by the motion planner and the ZMP generator. The footstep trajectory is generated by the footstep planner. Based on the CoM trajectory and the footstep trajectory, the inverse kinematics solver for the legs can calculate the joint trajectories of the legs.

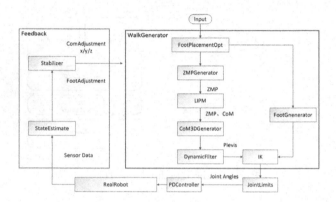

Fig. 13. Gait planning and control

By employing a three-dimensional LIPM, the forward and lateral movements are decoupled into two planar LIPMs for motion planning. To enable the robot to turn, the Yaw rotation degree of freedom of the two hip joints is used to map the turning speed to the corresponding hip joint of the swing leg in the Yaw direction.

In order to deal with environmental conditions such as stairs and uneven terrain, adjustments to the robot's centroid planning and foothold planning are necessary. When climbing stairs, the planning of the centroid and foothold needs to be adjusted accordingly, while maintaining the height of the torso relative to the ground.

3.2   Robot Dynamic Walking Control Method

During actual bipedal walking, the terrain conditions are typically uneven and far from ideal, and the robot's structural parameters can also contain errors, in addition to external disturbances that can cause deviations from ideal motion trajectories. Therefore, in addition to the motion planning and control framework presented in Sect. 3.1, a gait feedback regulator must be designed to achieve dynamic walking control of the robot.

The gait dynamic walking feedback control regulator mainly consists of two parts.

The first part is the state observation and estimation module, which mainly includes foot six-dimensional F/T perception, joint information perception, and trunk state estimation. The foot six-dimensional F/T perception part obtains the equivalent combined force of the ankle joint through two six-dimensional F/T sensors. The joint information perception part obtains the real-time position/current/speed of 12 joints through a communication protocol. The trunk state estimation obtains real-time information by installing an inertial measurement unit (IMU) on the trunk and combines an extended Kalman filter (EKF) to estimate the trunk posture trajectory and other information.

The second part is the feedback adjustment part, which mainly includes landing detection, joint closed-loop adjustment, and COM and foothold adjustment. The real-time equivalent combined force obtained by the foot six-dimensional F/T perception part can accurately judge the state of each foot of the robot through threshold judgment. According to the real-time position of 12 joints, the joint closed-loop adjustment part can use a PID controller for closed-loop feedback tracking. The COM and foothold adjustment part uses the real-time landing status of each foot, the real-time state of the trunk, and the feedback adjustment of the robot's reference COM and foothold planning, and gives the adjusted optimized COM and foothold planning to be executed in the next walking cycle [8,11]. This part is not the focus of this paper, and detailed feedback adjustment control strategies will be provided by other researchers in the future.

4   Experimental Results

Based on the gait planning and control framework designed in Sect. 3.1, this paper implements walking experiments of the HTY robot in both simulation and real environments. Figure 14, Fig. 15, and Fig. 16 show snapshots of the robot's forward, lateral, and turning.

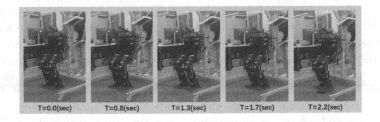

Fig. 14. Video snapshots genius (walk forward)

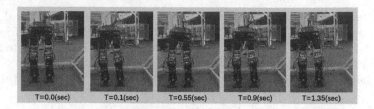

Fig. 15. Video snapshots genius (walk lateral)

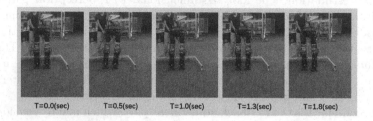

Fig. 16. Video snapshots genius (turning)

These walking patterns are generated based on the gait planning and control framework proposed in this paper, which enables rapid validation of the walking ability of the biped robot and has feedback adjustment and disturbance rejection capabilities. The walking step length of the HTY biped robot is 150 mm/step, and the walking cycle is 0.9 sec/step. Figure 14 shows the stable forward walking of the HTY biped robot, and Fig. 15 shows the stable lateral walking. Figure 16 shows its stable turning ability (5°/step). The success of the experiments demonstrates the effectiveness of the design and development of the HTY biped robot.

5   Conclusions

This paper presents the design details and motion control planning strategy of a bipedal robot system named HTY. It pays special attention to the use of concise joint and structural layout to ensure a large range of joint motion, enables foot state information perception, and meets the requirements of modular design and scalability. HTY can successfully achieve abilities such as forward, lateral, turning, and composite walking in both simulation and actual environments, with a walking cycle of 0.9 s, forward step length of 15 cm, lateral step length of 5 cm, and walking angle of 5°. The robot platform is a user-friendly human-sized bipedal robot platform, which can accelerate the development of the next generation of bipedal robot platforms required by the future bipedal robot industry.

Future work includes further improving HTY and developing a full-size humanoid robot system with an upper body, as well as developing a whole-body coordinated motion planning and controller. The paper will also increase the modularity level and reduce the number of robot parts. It is hoped that this system will continue to be iteratively developed and enter several dangerous and unknown scenarios to assist or replace human workers in corresponding tasks.

References

1. Ackerman, E.: For better or worse: tesla bot is exactly what we expected. IEEE Spectr. **1** (2022)
2. Gong, Y., et al.: Feedback control of a cassie bipedal robot: walking, standing, and riding a segway. In: 2019 American Control Conference (ACC), pp. 4559–4566. IEEE (2019)
3. Kajita, S., Kanehiro, F., Kaneko, K., Yokoi, K., Hirukawa, H.: The 3D linear inverted pendulum mode: a simple modeling for a biped walking pattern generation. In: Proceedings 2001 IEEE/RSJ International Conference on Intelligent Robots and Systems. Expanding the Societal Role of Robotics in the the Next Millennium (Cat. No. 01CH37180), vol. 1, pp. 239–246. IEEE (2001)
4. Kajita, S., Tani, K.: Study of dynamic biped locomotion on rugged terrain-derivation and application of the linear inverted pendulum mode. In: Proceedings. 1991 IEEE International Conference on Robotics and Automation, pp. 1405–1406. IEEE Computer Society (1991)
5. Kaneko, K., et al.: Humanoid robot HRP-4-humanoid robotics platform with lightweight and slim body. In: 2011 IEEE/RSJ International Conference on Intelligent Robots and Systems, pp. 4400–4407. IEEE (2011)
6. Khan, M.S., Mandava, R.K.: A review on gait generation of the biped robot on various terrains. Robotica 1–43 (2023)
7. Krotkov, E., et al.: The DARPA robotics challenge finals: results and perspectives. In: The DARPA Robotics Challenge Finals: Humanoid Robots to the Rescue, pp. 1–26 (2018)
8. Shi, Y., et al.: Bio-inspired equilibrium point control scheme for quadrupedal locomotion. IEEE Trans. Cogn. Dev. Syst. **11**(2), 200–209 (2018)
9. Shigemi, S., Goswami, A., Vadakkepat, P.: ASIMO and humanoid robot research at honda. In: Humanoid Robotics: A Reference, pp. 55–90 (2018)
10. Vukobratović, M., Borovac, B.: Zero-moment point-thirty five years of its life. Int. J. Humanoid Rob. **1**(01), 157–173 (2004)
11. Wang, X., Li, M., Guo, W., Wang, P., Sun, L.: Velocity control of a bounding quadruped via energy control and vestibular reflexes. J. Bionic Eng. **11**(4), 556–571 (2014)
12. Wang, Z., Wei, W., Xie, A., Zhang, Y., Wu, J., Zhu, Q.: Hybrid bipedal locomotion based on reinforcement learning and heuristics. Micromachines **13**, 1688 (2022)
13. Yu, Z., et al.: Design and development of the humanoid robot BHR-5. Adv. Mech. Eng. **6**, 852937 (2014)

SPSOC: Staged Pseudo-Spectral Optimal Control Optimization Model for Robotic Chinese Calligraphy

Dongmei Guo[1,2] , Huasong Min[1(✉)] , and Guang Yan[1]

[1] Wuhan University of Science and Technology, Wuhan 430081, China
dmguo@aust.edu.cn, mhuasong@wust.edu.cn
[2] Anhui University of Science and Technology, Huainan 232001, China

Abstract. As the executive module of writing tasks, writing control models play a crucial role in robotic Chinese calligraphy. In this study, in contrast to most of the current models that only consider the optimization of writing trajectory, according to the writing characteristics of Chinese calligraphy, a writing control model based on the pseudo-spectral optimal control method is proposed to optimize the writing trajectory and control parameters of the robotic arm. In the proposed model, we describe the robot writing problem as a trajectory optimization problem. The optimal trajectory fitting curves of the skeletons of basic strokes are designed by the least square fitting method. Moreover, the staged pseudo-spectral optimal control optimization model of qibi, xingbi and shoubi is incorporated into the SPSOC. In addition to optimizing the writing trajectory, we also analysis the trajectory control parameters to ensure that the parameters of the control model at each stage are conformed by writing characteristics and rules. Compared with the existing control methods, the results of several experiments prove that the proposed model SPSOC can simulate the writing rules of calligraphy well based on the writing control characteristics.

Keywords: Trajectory Optimization · Optimal Control · Robotic Chinese Calligraphy

1 Introduction

Chinese calligraphy is a charming and ancient form of artistic expression based on writing Chinese characters. It is highly valued as an artistic practice with a long history and an important part of Chinese traditional culture and art [1]. As a tool for traditional Chinese calligraphy, the brush has occupied a cherished position in the culture of traditional Chinese calligraphy since its invention [2]. With the development of robots, robotic arms have been used to simulate human calligraphy behavior and calligraphy creation in recent years [3, 4].

The works written by robotic calligraphy should be considered not only the simulation of the stroke model, but also the stroke skeleton and the optimization control of the actual writing trajectory. Wang Y et al. [5] proposed a trajectory optimization

© The Author(s), under exclusive license to Springer Nature Singapore Pte Ltd. 2023
H. Yang et al. (Eds.): ICIRA 2023, LNAI 14270, pp. 416–428, 2023.
https://doi.org/10.1007/978-981-99-6492-5_36

method based on cubic B-spline interpolation. Inspired by Wang Y, Yan G [3] and Li J et al. [6] proposed to control the writing trajectory by using Non-Uniform Rational B-Spline (NURBS). However, only the discrete waypoint interpolation method cannot fully reflect the trajectory state and a large error is existed between the optimized trajectory and the real trajectory of strokes. Xie Z et al. [7] studied brush character of writing models and minimized the input energy of writing trajectory by an optimal function approximation. Wang S et al. [8] described the calligraphy writing problem as a trajectory optimization problem, and applied pseudo-spectral optimal control (PSOC) method to update the writing process dynamically. Huebel N [9] calculated the error between the reference character and the drawing character according to the projection position. Garrido J et al. [10] applied Lloyd algorithm and improved hidden Markov model to train the expected trajectory of joint space. A trajectory control algorithm was proposed by Wen Y et al. [11] for robotic manipulator. Berio D et al. [12] proposed the generation method of interactive curves and motion paths. There were also spline based methods proposed by Berio D [13] to control polygon shape by synthesizing a continuous virtual trajectory [14]. Zhao S et al. [15] proposed to generate and complete writing animation. The skeletons of calligraphy strokes were extracted to calculate a trajectory point.

To address the existing problems, this paper studies trajectory optimization model for robotic calligraphy considering both the writing rules and parameters of the end-effector. As the pseudo-spectral method is usually used to optimize the model and control of the continuous trajectory. We propose a staged trajectory optimization model based on the pseudo-spectral optimal control principle. To fit the discrete skeleton points, the least square optimization method is used to generate the fitting curve. The phased Legendre pseudo-spectral and Legendre-Gauss-Lobatto (LGL) interpolation are defined to optimize the writing trajectory state, which not only satisfies the smooth and continuous writing operation of the end-effector, but also ensures the writing rules of Chinese calligraphy. As the pseudo-spectral method can be differentiated at high order interpolation points, the smooth writing trajectory, velocity and acceleration can be guaranteed.

The main contributions of this study are summarized as follows:

- Compared with the existing trajectory optimization model, we propose a staged pseudo-spectral method for optimal writing trajectories based on writing rules with better performance for robotic Chinese calligraphy.
- In the proposed model, the optimal curve function of basic strokes is designed, and the staged Legendre pseudo-spectral method is used to optimize the trajectory state of each stroke in different writing stages.
- Several experiments show that our proposed model outperforms some existing models in Chinese Calligraphy trajectory optimization.

2   Proposed Method

In this study, we only focus on the end position and discuss how the end-effector of the robotic arm can perform the writing task with an optimal trajectory in Cartesian space. The stroke skeleton is extracted as the writing trajectory. By fitting the writing trajectory, the discrete trajectory points can be generated the optimal smooth curve. The unconstrained least square curve fitting is used to fit the discrete skeleton points to generate the fitting curve. With the trajectory state simulation, we can map the writing trajectory into the state function of continuous time t, to achieve the stroke trajectory optimization. The whole writing control process is divided into two parts: state simulation and state optimization of stroke writing trajectory.

2.1 Stroke Trajectory Points Representation

We initialize coordinates (x_i, y_i, z_i) to determine the three-dimension position of writing trajectory, and denote as $T_i = (x_i, y_i, z_i)$, (x_i, y_i) represents the two-dimensional coordinates of the trajectory, z_i represents the pressing height of the brush pen. Then trajectory can be defined as

$$tra = \{(x_0, y_0, z_0), (x_1, y_1, z_1) \ldots (x_{m-1}, y_{m-1}, z_{m-1})\} \tag{1}$$

$$z_0 = z_1 = \ldots z_{m-1} = c \tag{2}$$

where m is the number of skeleton points. As the track is extracted by single pixel skeleton points, all the values of z are the same fixed value c.

2.2 Stroke Trajectory Curve Fitting

The stroke trajectory curve fitting model is approximated by superposition of polynomial functions of different order, as y can be represented by x, it can be give as

$$(x, y, z) = f(x, z) = \sum_{i=0}^{n} a_i(x, z)^i = a_0 + a_1(x, z) + \ldots + a_n(x, z)^n \tag{3}$$

where n is order of Polynomial.

2.3 Stroke Trajectory State Simulation

The calligraphy robot follows the fitting writing track from the beginning of the writing (starting point) to the end of the writing (ending point) in the time domain $[t_0, t_f]$. We define the state function of the stroke trajectory and use the state curve represented by a quintic polynomial. The constraints of trajectory state equation are as follows: at the initial moment, $t = t_0$, $Tra = 0$; at the termination time, $t = t_f$, $Tra = 1$. The velocity and acceleration at the starting point and the ending point are zero.

The trajectory generated by the three-dimensional position of the stroke is regarded as the open-loop control trajectory. For arbitrary time t_i, the dynamic update model of the state trajectory is denoted as

$$tra(t_{i+1}) = f(tra(t_i), u(t_i)) \tag{4}$$

$$u(t_i) = \frac{dtra(t_i)}{dt} \tag{5}$$

where $u(t_i)$, $t_i \in [t_0, t_f]$ is open-loop trajectory control parameter.

2.4 Stroke Trajectory Planning Based on Staged Legendre Pseudo-Spectral Method

To ensure the continuity and smoothness of the writing trajectory of robotic end effector, it is also necessary to optimize the stroke trajectory state in Cartesian space. Lagrange interpolation polynomial is taken as the base function in trajectory optimization. As a kind of pseudo-spectral control method, compared with other interpolation methods, LGL interpolation has obvious advantages. Most of the traditional interpolation points are discrete points with equal spacing, but this interpolation method has a large error at the endpoints, which is easy to produce "Runge" phenomenon. The root of the first-order derivative of legendre orthogonal polynomial are chosen as the LGL coordination points to realize discretization of the continuous region. As LGL coordination points show non-uniform distribution, the accuracy and precision can be ensured at the endpoints, while the endpoints approximation error can be effectively reduced.

Stroke Trajectory State Based On LGL Interpolation Points. By given the stroke trajectory fitting curve, the relationship of three-dimensional trajectory state variable can be obtained as

$$tra(t_i) = f(x(t_i), y(t_i), z(t_i)) = f(x(t_i), f(x(t_i)), z(t_i)) \tag{6}$$

where $t_i \in [t_0, t_f]$.

Then the trajectory point (x_i, y_i, z_i) can be denoted as the stroke trajectory state based on LGL in the defined time domain $\tau_i \in [\tau_0, \tau_N]$ as the following equation.

$$Tra(\tau_i) = f(x(\tau_i), y(\tau_i), z(\tau_i)) = f(x(\tau_i), f(x(\tau_i)), z(\tau_i)) \tag{7}$$

where $\tau_i \in [\tau_0, \tau_N]$ and $(N + 1)$ is the number of LGL interpolation points.

Lagrange Interpolation. In the Legendre pseudo-spectral method, the Lagrange interpolation polynomial is used to approximate the state $tra(t)$ at $\tau, \tau \in [\tau_0, \tau_N]$. As the roots of the first-order derivative of the Legendre orthogonal polynomial are located in the interval $[-1,1]$, it needs to be transformed into the time domain $[t_0, t_f]$. When the discrete trajectory state variables are obtained in the $(N + 1)$ LGL points i ($i = 0, 1,...,$ N), then the three-dimensional trajectory at time τ, is shown in the following equation.

$$tra(\tau) \approx Tra(\tau) = \sum_{i=0}^{N} L_i(\tau)Tra(\tau_i) \tag{8}$$

$$Tra(\tau_i) = \{(X_0, X_1, \ldots X_N), (Y_0, Y_1, \ldots Y_N), (Z_0, Z_1, \ldots Z_N)\} \tag{9}$$

where $Tra(\tau)$ is the approximate polynomial of order N of $tra(\tau)$, $Tra(\tau_i)$ represents the function value of the polynomial curve at the LGL coordination point, $L_i(\tau)$ is the Lagrange interpolation basis function.

$$L_i(\tau) = \prod_{j=0, j \neq i}^{N} \frac{\tau - \tau_j}{\tau_i - \tau_j} \tag{10}$$

where the Lagrange polynomial satisfies the property.

$$L_i(\tau_j) = \begin{cases} 1, & i = j \\ 0, & i \neq j \end{cases} \tag{11}$$

2.5 Velocity Optimization

With time variable, the robotic arm moves from the start point to the end point along the stroke fitting trajectory. By time domain transformation, the definition time domain $[t_0, t_f]$ can be translated into the definition interval of Legendre orthogonal polynomial. According to the rules of calligraphy writing, the writing process is divided into three stages: starting, moving and ending. Each stage is connected by smooth tracks based on the optimal approximation strategy of piecewise Legendre pseudo-spectral method, and the trajectory state between each two stages is continuous and derivable. All of three-stage velocity optimization curves are connected to form an optimal writing control trajectory.

In order to ensure smooth and continuous writing trajectories, the velocity curves of different three stages should be satisfied the following relationship.

$$\begin{cases} v_{qstart} = 0 \\ v_{qend} = v_{xstart} \\ v_{xend} = v_{sstart} \\ v_{send} = 0 \end{cases} \tag{12}$$

where $v_{qstart}, v_{qend}, v_{xstart}, v_{xend}, v_{sstart}, v_{send}$ represents the initial velocity of qibi, the termination velocity of qibi, the initial velocity of xingbi, the termination velocity of xingbi, the initial velocity of shoubi and the termination velocity of shoubi respectively. $v_{qend}, v_{xstart}, v_{xend}, v_{sstart}$ correspond to time parameter value $\tau_{qend}, \tau_{xstart}, \tau_{xend}, \tau_{sstart}$.

According to conditions the velocity curve should be satisfied, that is, the derivatives at the termination state of qibi and the initial velocity of xingbi are the same; while the state derivatives are the same at the termination velocity of xingbi and the initial velocity of shoubi. Then, the derivatives of the trajectory point states $P_{qend}, P_{xstart}, P_{xend}, P_{sstart}$ at $\tau_{qend}, \tau_{xstart}, \tau_{xend}, \tau_{sstart}$ hold the piecewise function as

$$\begin{cases} Tra(\tau_{qend})\prime = Tra(\tau_{xstart})\prime \\ Tra(\tau_{xend})\prime = Tra(\tau_{sstart})\prime \end{cases} \tag{13}$$

where $Tra(\tau_{qend})\prime, Tra(\tau_{xstart})\prime, Tra(\tau_{xend})\prime, Tra(\tau_{sstart})\prime$ represents the derivative of the trajectory state at the termination velocity of qibi, the initial velocity of xingbi, the termination velocity of xingbi and the initial velocity of shoubi respectively, then $Tra(\tau_{qend})\prime$, $Tra(\tau_{xstart})\prime, Tra(\tau_{xend})\prime, Tra(\tau_{sstart})\prime$ can be obtained by the following equation.

$$ira(\tau_k) \approx \dot{T}ra(\tau_k) = \sum_{i=0}^{N} \dot{L}_i(\tau_k) Tra(\tau_i) \tag{14}$$

where

$$k = [01, \ldots, P_{qend}, \ldots, P_{xstart}, \ldots, P_{xend}, \ldots, P_{sstart}, \ldots, N] \tag{15}$$

$$\dot{L}_i(\tau_k) = \sum_{l=0}^{N} \frac{\prod_{j=0, j \neq i, l}^{N} (\tau_k - \tau_j)}{\prod_{j=0, j \neq i}^{N} (\tau_i - \tau_j)} \tag{16}$$

We set $D_{ki} = \dot{L}_i(\tau_k)$ as pseudo-spectral differential matrix of $(N + 1) \times (N + 1)$ order.

$$D_{ki} = \begin{cases} \dfrac{P_N(\tau_k)}{P_N(\tau_i)(\tau_k - \tau_i)}, & i \neq k; \\ -N(N+1)/4, & i = k = 0; \\ N(N+1)/4, & i = k = N; \\ 0, & \textit{otherwise.} \end{cases} \tag{17}$$

2.6 Acceleration Optimization

Similar to the velocity optimization, the derivatives of velocity at discrete points τ_{qend}, τ_{xstart}, τ_{xend}, τ_{sstart} can be derived. The acceleration at each discrete point is obtained, which corresponds to the acceleration control of the robot's writing trajectory, respectively meeting the writing requirements in different stages, as shown in the following Equation.

$$\begin{cases} a_{qstart} = 0 \\ a_{qend} = a_{xstart} \\ a_{xend} = a_{sstart} \\ a_{send} = 0 \end{cases} \tag{18}$$

The acceleration of different stages can be calculated as

$$\ddot{tra}(\tau_k) \approx \ddot{T}ra(\tau_k) = \sum_{i=0}^{N} \dot{L}_i(\tau_k)\dot{T}ra(\tau_i) \tag{19}$$

where $k = [0, \ldots, P_{qend}, \ldots, P_{xstart}, \ldots, P_{xend}, \ldots, P_{sstart}, \ldots, N], \dot{L}_i(\tau_k)$ is defined as Eq. (17).

2.7 Staged Pseudo-Spectral Optimal Control

In our defined trajectory, (x_i, y_i) coordinates determine the position of the writing trajectory. The staged pseudo-spectral optimal control writing model of robotic arm is depicted in Algorithm 1.

Algorithm 1: **Stroke Writing trajectory optimization**

Require: the trajectory of skeletonize stroke by BSGAN and the maximum number n+1 of points on the stroke;

Ensure: the optimized trajectory parameters of robotic arm;

1: Initialize the number of LGL nodes;

2: Input the number of LGL nodes n+1

3: Input time interval t

4:    for i in 0: n do

5:        Calculate the value of LGL nodes

6:        calculate trajectory writing states at LGL nodes by Equation (7).

7:        Lagrange interpolation

8:        Output trajectory optimization curve of position

9:        Output optimization curve of velocity

10:        Output optimization curve of acceleration

11:    end for

3   Experiments and Analysis

3.1   Determination of Model Functions

In the nonlinear optimization, there are usually many choices to determine the degree of optimization polynomial. In the experiment, each stroke was sampled densely to simulate continuous strokes. We tried all fitting polynomials between 3 and 8 degrees for each stroke, and calculated the root mean square error RMSE between the predicted value and the observed sample. Among them the least error was selected to ensure strokes of different length and complexity. Table 1. Least square fitting root mean square error RMSE for stroke "horizontal". By comparative analysis, the quintic polynomial was selected as the optimal control curve model. Different strokes just correspond to different coefficients, and the form of the fitting curve is a quintic polynomial.

Table 1.   Least square fitting root mean square error RMSE for stroke "horizontal".

Fit polynomial degree n	RMSE
3	0.0120
4	0.0303
5	0.0082
6	1.9060
7	2.7751
8	1.9593

3.2 Trajectory Optimization Model

Figure 1 Quintic polynomial fitting curves. Shows the quintic polynomial fitting curves. It can be seen that the position curves fit the discrete sample points well with better performance. On the basis of local characteristics, the overall optimized curve is more smooth.

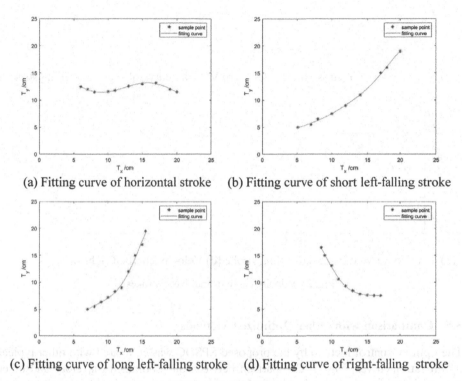

(a) Fitting curve of horizontal stroke   (b) Fitting curve of short left-falling stroke

(c) Fitting curve of long left-falling stroke   (d) Fitting curve of right-falling stroke

Fig. 1. Quintic polynomial fitting curves.

3.3 Velocity Curve

According to equal (12)–(17), the velocity control curve of robotic end effector was obtained with the differentiable trajectory position curve at different stages, the velocity curves are continuous and present the trapezoidal curves, which conforms to the three-stage characteristics of the writing rule in a whole, as shown in Fig. 2. Velocity curve of four basic strokes.

3.4 Acceleration Curve

The acceleration control curve of robotic end effector was obtained with the differentiable velocity curve at different stages, as shown in Fig. 3. Acceleration curve of four basic strokes. The acceleration curves are continuous and present the S-shaped curves, which conforms to the three-stage characteristics of the writing rule in a whole.

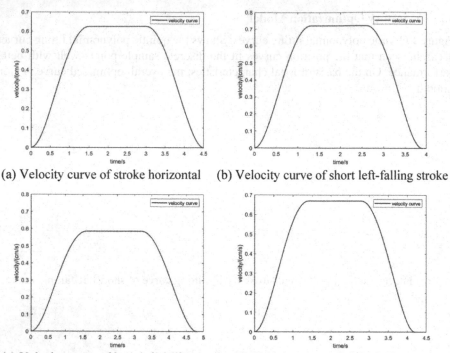

(a) Velocity curve of stroke horizontal   (b) Velocity curve of short left-falling stroke

(c) Velocity curve of long left-falling stroke (d) Velocity curve of right-falling stroke

Fig. 2. Velocity curve of four basic strokes.

3.5   Comparison with Other Optimized Methods

The optimal control method by the proposed SPSOC was compared with other typical optimization curves. Fig. 4. Comparison between our optimized trajectory and other trajectory optimization models. Shows the comparison between our optimized trajectory and other trajectory optimizations. It can be seen from the Figure that both B-spline curve and NURBS curve pay more attention to local features and ignore the overall smoothness of the writing trajectory, thus leading to poor performance of the optimized trajectory.

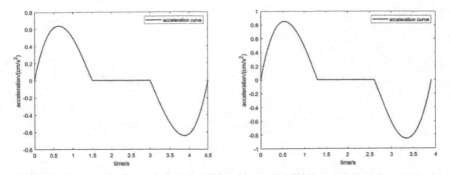

(a) Acceleration curve of horizontal stroke (b) Acceleration curve of short left-falling stroke

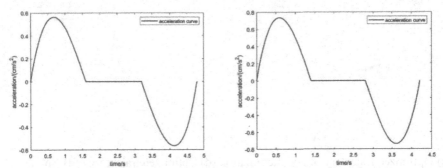

(c) Acceleration curve of long left-falling stroke (d) Acceleration curve of right-falling stroke

Fig. 3. Acceleration curve of four basic strokes.

3.6 Characters and Painting Generation

Chinese characters can be formed by the robotic end-effector along the optimized trajectory. On the basis of basic stroke writing, the application of our calligraphy robot platform was extended to draw a simple Chinese painting-plum blossom, as shown in Fig. 5. The Robotic Calligraphy System, the reference images and the actual written results, the Chinese painting. Figure 6 Comparative results in Chinese calligraphy. Shows comparative results of different methods in Chinese calligraphy.

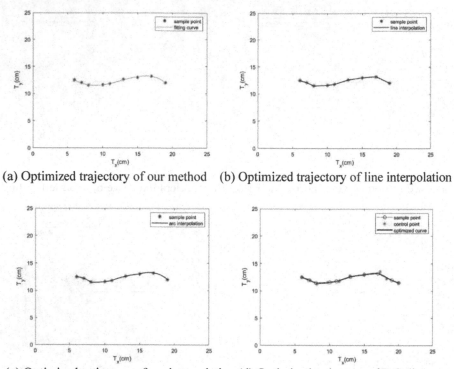

(a) Optimized trajectory of our method   (b) Optimized trajectory of line interpolation

(c) Optimized trajectory of arc interpolation (d) Optimized trajectory of B-Spline

Fig. 4. Comparison between our optimized trajectory and other trajectory optimization models.

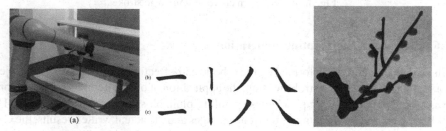

Fig. 5. The Robotic Calligraphy System, the reference images and the actual written results, the Chinese painting.

(a) reference stroke   (b) stroke written by other method   (b) stroke written by our method

Fig. 6. Comparative results in Chinese calligraphy.

4 Conclusions and Future Works

Based on the Legendre pseudo-spectral method, the staged Legendre pseudo-spectral LGL interpolation has been used to optimize the writing trajectory. It can satisfy the writing rules of Chinese calligraphy and continuous writing operation of robotic end-effector. Since the pseudo-spectral method is differentiated at high order interpolation points, the smooth writing trajectory, velocity and acceleration can be generated with better performance by the optimized trajectory. In addition to Chinese calligraphy, the proposed method can also be applied to other fields, such as robotic Chinese painting, robot welding, robot marking and so on.

Acknowledgments. This work is supported by the National Natural Science Foundation of China (Grant No.62073249).

References

1. Guo, D., Min, H.: Survey of calligraphy robot. Control Dec. **37**(7), 1665–1674 (2022)
2. Huang, L., Hou, Z., Zhao, Y., Zhang, D.: Research progress on and prospects for virtual brush modeling in digital calligraphy and painting. Front. Inform. Technol. Electron. Eng. **20**(10), 1307–1321 (2019)
3. Yan, G., Guo, D., Min, H.: Robot calligraphy based on footprint model and brush trajectory extraction. In: Cognitive Systems and Information Processing: 7th International Conference. ICCSIP, Revised Selected Papers, pp. 437–451. Springer, Cham (2023)
4. Lin, H.-I., Chen, X., Lin, T.-T.: Calligraphy brush trajectory control of by a robotic arm. Appl. Sci. **10**(23), 8694 (2020)
5. Wang, Y., Min, H.: Robot calligraphy system based on brush modeling. CAAI Trans. Intell. Syst. **16**(4), 707–716 (2021)
6. Li, J., Min, H., Zhou, H., et al.: Robot brush-writing system of Chinese calligraphy character. In: Yu, H., Liu, J., Liu, L., Ju, Z., Liu, Y., Zhou, D. (eds.) Intelligent Robotics and Applications. ICIRA 2019. LNCS, vol. 11745. Springer, Cham (2019). https://doi.org/10.1007/978-3-030-27529-7_8
7. Xie, Z., Hiroyuki, F., Akinori, H., Hiroyuki, K.: Modeling and manipulating dynamic font-based hairy brush characters using control-theoretic b-spline approach. IFAC-PapersOnLine **53**(2), 4731–4736 (2020)
8. Wang, S., Chen, J., Deng, X., Hutchinson, S., Dellaert, F.: Robot calligraphy using pseudospectral optimal control in conjunction with a novel dynamic brush model. In: 2020 IEEE/RSJ International Conference on Intelligent Robots and Systems (IROS), pp. 6696–6703. IEEE (2020)
9. Huebel, N., Mueggler, E., Waibel, M., et al.: Towards robotic calligraphy. In: 2012 IEEE/RSJ International Conference on Intelligent Robots and Systems, pp. 5165–5166. IEEE (2012)
10. Garrido, J., Yu, W., Soria, A.: Human behavior learning for robot in joint space. Neurocomputing **155**, 22–31 (2015)
11. Wen, Y., Pagilla, P.: A 3D path following control scheme for robot manipulators. IFAC-PapersOnLine **53**(2), 9968–9973 (2020)
12. Berio, D., Calinon, S., Leymarie, F.: Dynamic graffiti stylisation with stochastic optimal control. In: Proceedings of the 4th international conference on movement computing, pp. 1–8 (2017)

13. Berio, D., Calinon, S., Leymarie, F.: Generating calligraphic trajectories with model predictive control. Graphics Interface, pp. 55–59 (2017)
14. Mohan, V., Morasso, P., Zenzeri, J., et al.: Teaching a humanoid robot to draw 'Shapes.' Auton. Robot. **31**(1), 21–53 (2011)
15. Zhao, S., Zhang, X., Chen, L.: Trajectory generation for calligraphy writing animation. In: Proceedings of the 2022 2nd International Conference on Control and Intelligent Robotics, pp. 455–459 (2022)

Obstacle Avoidance Path Planning Method Based on DQN-HER

Kailong Li⬤, Fusheng Zha⬤, Pengfei Wang, Wei Guo, Yajing Zang$^{(\boxtimes)}$ ⬤,
and Lining Sun⬤

Harbin Institute of Technology, Harbin 150006, China
{22b308001,19b908057}@stu.hit.edu.cn, {zhafusheng,wangpengfei,
wguo01,lnsun}@hit.edu.cn

Abstract. In recent years, mobile robots have been widely applied in different areas, such as medicine, rescue and home service. Obstacle avoidance path planning is one of the most important issues for mobile robots. Researchers have paid attention to the methods integrated with reinforcement learning (RL). Even though the sparse reward problem of RL is proven to be solvable by Hindsight Experience Replay (HER), obstacle avoidance is still a thorny problem. Therefore, we proposed a DQN (Deep Q-learning Network)-HER RL method with proactive obstacle avoidance skill to learn the obstacle avoidance path planning task. We built simulations in Webots and designed an ablation experiment. The results showed our method improved learning stability and efficiency. In addition, we are planning to apply our method to the heterogeneous multi-robot system for multi-robot path planning in future work.

Keywords: Hindsight Experience Replay · Deep Q-learning Network · Path Planning · Proactive Obstacle Avoidance Skill

1 Introduction

Researches on mobile robots are significant in robotics. One of the most important issues for mobile robots is path planning. Path planning is the capacity of a mobile robot to move from the initial position to the destination without any collision. Nowadays, mobile robots are not only employed in industrial fields but also utilized in medicine, rescuing, home service and many other fields. Therefore, the accuracy and efficiency of path planning are critical for mobile robots.

The path planning strategies can be classified into two categories, traditional and intelligent approaches [1]. Traditional approaches such as artificial potential field (APF), A* algorithm, Dijkstra algorithm and Rapidly-exploring Random Tree (RRT), cannot

Supported in part by the National Natural Science Foundation of China (U2013602, 52075115, 51521003, 61911530250), National Key R\&D Program of China (2020YFB13134), Self-Planned Task (SKLRS202001B, SKLRS202110B) of State Key Laboratory of Robotics and System (HIT), Shenzhen Science and Technology Research and Development Foundation (JCYJ20190813171009236), and Basic Scientific Research of Technology (JCKY2020603C009).

H. Yang et al. (Eds.): ICIRA 2023, LNAI 14270, pp. 429–438, 2023.
https://doi.org/10.1007/978-981-99-6492-5_37

handle the uncertain objects in the environment except artificial potential field. Also, they require high computational costs, which is not suitable for real-time path planning. Intelligent approaches, including genetic algorithms, fuzzy logic, neural networks, firefly algorithm, particle swarm optimization, ant colony optimization, bacterial foraging optimization, artificial bee colony and many others, have recently been accepted as the most popular tool for path planning. They do a fantastic job of managing the environment's uncertainty. In recent years, reinforcement learning (RL) has risen because of its remarkable ability to apply in the unknown environment [2]. Reinforcement learning allows the agent (or robot) to interact with the environment to acquire feedback rewards which promote the agent to take better action. In addition, RL does not require a data set for training, which is different from machine learning. At present, researchers have paid a lot of attention to applying RL in robotics path planning and made great progress. Chen L, et al. proposed a Conditional Deep Q-network integrated with the fuzzy logic algorithm for autonomous driving [3]. Gao H, et al. used RL to optimize the key parameters in MPC in order to make a wheeled robot move better in slipping conditions [4]. Although RL performs well in some fields, it has limitations. For instance, the sparse reward is one of the most important problems in RL, which could influence training efficiency. As a result, we proposed an RL-based path planning strategy combined with Hindsight Experience Replay (HER) [5] in this paper, which can improve the training progress.

The rest of this paper is presented as follows. Related work is presented in Sect. 2. The path planning approach based on deep reinforcement learning and Hindsight Experience Replay is described in Sect. 3. In Sect. 4, the simulation experiment and results are explained. Section 5 is the conclusions.

2 Related Work

2.1 Path Planning Based on Deep Reinforcement Learning

The foundation of reinforcement learning is Markov Decision Process (MDP), whose objective is to find out the optimal policy [6]. MDP is defined as a tuple $(\mathcal{S}, \mathcal{A}, \mathcal{P}, \mathcal{R}, \gamma)$, where $\mathcal{S}$ is the set of states, $\mathcal{A}$ is a set of actions, $\mathcal{P} = p(s_{t+1}|s_t, a_t)$ is the transition probability, $\mathcal{R}$ is the reward function, $p(s_0)$ is the initial state distribution, and $\gamma \in [0, 1]$ is the discount factor [7]. When the agent in state s_t takes an action a_t based on policy π, it will acquire a reward $r_t = (s_t, a_t)$ and update its state to s_{t+1}. The transition probability $\mathcal{P} = p(s_{t+1}|s_t, a_t)$ is the distribution of states. A discount sum of future rewards called *return* [7] is defined as:

$$\mathcal{R}_t = \sum_{i=t}^{\infty} \gamma^{i-t} r \tag{1}$$

The action-value function is defined as [7]:

$$\mathcal{Q}^{\pi}(s_t, a_t) = \mathbb{E}[\mathcal{R}_t|s_t, a_t] \tag{2}$$

where π is policy, leading the agent take actions. For each $(s, a) \in (\mathcal{S}, \mathcal{A})$, there is an optimal policy π^*. The action-value function of all optimal policies is called optimal action-value function Q^*, which satisfies the Bellman equation [7]:

$$Q^*(s, a) = \mathbb{E}_{s' \sim p(\cdot | s, a)} \left[r(s, a) + \gamma \max_{a' \in A} Q^*(s', a') \right] \tag{3}$$

In path planning, S includes the location and velocity of the agent, coordinates of the destination and data from sensors. Actions usually include going forward, going back, turning left, turning right and stopping. For some legged robots, jumping could also be an action.

However, RL is not appropriate for high dimensional data which could decrease the training efficiency. Therefore, Deep reinforcement learning (DRL) is proposed. DRL is the combination of deep neural networks (DNN) and reinforcement learning (RL) [2]. Deep Q-Networks (DQN) is the representative of DRL. DQN is developed from Q-learning, which is a value-based algorithm. In Q-learning, a Q-table is used for recording the values of the action-value function for all actions at state s_t. Then the agent selects the largest value and takes the corresponding action. While in DQN, a neural network is used for approximating Q^*. The transition tuples (s_t, a_t, r_t, s_{t+1}) are saved in an experience replay buffer. The tuples stored in the experience replay buffer can be sampled for training.

DQN can deal with high-dimensional input data. Nevertheless, it takes a large time to train the model, especially training in large-scale maps. One important reason is reward sparsity. To solve this problem, we integrate HER with DQN.

2.2 Hindsight Experience Replay

HER can be applied in an off-policy RL method, such as DQN and DDPG. The thinking of HER is quite simple. Set a state g as the goal for the agent to achieve. We can acquire a state sequence $s_0, s_1, \cdots, s_T$ after experiencing some episodes. Then save every transition $s_t \rightarrow s_{t+1}$ to the experience replay buffer and set a subset for other goals. The new goals could influence the actions of the agent instead of the environment dynamics [5]. By replaying the trajectory to other goals, the agent can learn how to achieve the original goal g. This process is called HER, which can improve the learning efficiency of RL under sparse rewards.

The HER-RL algorithms were mostly applied in robot arms and manipulators. Wang S, et al. proposed a Hierarchical Decoupling Optimization (HDO) method to generate a collision-free trajectory for a 6-DoF free-floating space robot [8]. Zuo G combined HER with DDPG to solve the motion planning problem for the manipulator [9]. Kuang Y, et al. developed a Goal Density-based HER method, which is used for completing multi-goal tasks of manipulator [10]. HER improves the training process in these examples, so we decide to introduce HER to our path planning method.

3 Method

When conducting path planning tasks using RL in complex environments, the initial policy of the reinforcement learning agents is often randomized, which would make the players get stuck in local traps and lead to lower learning efficiency for RL. To solve this issue, we are trying to propose a DQN-HER RL path planning method with a proactive obstacle avoidance skill. We give a reward function with obstacle punishment term to DQN RL and then use HER to get more learning samples in order to make the RL process more stable. Finally, the proactive obstacle avoidance skill is used to overcome the influences of friction on the players when moving in complex environments. The details of the proposed method are explained as follows.

3.1 DQN Reinforcement Learning

The DQN reinforcement learning method is based on the traditional Q-learning reinforcement learning method and uses neural networks to approximate Q-values for task learning. In this paper, we combined the simple DQN reinforcement learning method with the HER algorithm. The state and action settings for the DQN method are defined by formulas (4) and (5).

$$s = \{x, y, \theta\} \tag{4}$$

$$a \in \{a_1, a_2, a_3, a_4\} \tag{5}$$

where s is a 3D continuous variable obtained directly from the simulation environment. While a is discrete movement command for the car players running in the complex environment. As shown in (5), there are four different command options a_1, a_2, a_3 and a_4, which present *"forward"*, *"backwards"*, *"left turn"*, and *"turn right"*, respectively.

To enable the agent to learn path planning in obstacle-filled environments, we define a reward function that is dense and dependent on the distance to the target position and the distance to obstacles. We obtain the distance to the target position from the feedback provided by the simulation environment and measure the distance to obstacles using laser sensors.

Assuming that the distances between the obstacles and the three laser sensors are d_{ob}^i, and $i \in \{1, 2, 3\}$. We set a distance threshold D_{thres} for d_{ob}^i to consider where the obstacle has an influence on the car's movement. That is to say, we only take the obstacle into consideration when $d_{ob}^i < D_{thres}$. Finally, we define the overall impact of the surrounding obstacles on the car's movement by formula (6).

$$p_{ob}^i = \begin{cases} D_{thres} - d_{ob}^i & \text{if } d_{ob}^i \leq D_{thres} \\ 0 & else \end{cases} \tag{6}$$

The overall impact of the surrounding obstacles detected by the three laser sensors is defined as P_{ob}, and can be computed as formula (7).

$$P_{ob} = \sum_{i=1}^{n} p_{ob}^{i} \tag{7}$$

Finally, the reward function for the DQN algorithm is set as formula (8).

$$r = \begin{cases} K_{\text{target}} \Delta d_{\text{target}} + K_{ob} P_{ob} \\ K_{\text{target}} \Delta d_{\text{target}} \end{cases} \tag{8}$$

Here, Δd_{target} represents the variation of the distance between the car and the target position d_{target} after executing action a in state s. K_{target} and K_{ob} are manually set constants that adjust the weight relationship between the reinforcement learning agent learning the path planning to reach the target location and obstacle avoidance. In this paper, we set them to $K_{\text{target}} = 200$ and $K_{ob} = -5$.

3.2 DQN-HER Reinforcement Learning

The HER method is commonly used to improve off-policy reinforcement learning algorithms with sparse rewards. Although we have set a dense reward function for DQN, the addition of rewards for obstacles causes some irregular fluctuations in the reward during the reinforcement learning process when encountering obstacles, making the learning process of the naive DQN reinforcement learning method unstable, which makes it similar to the condition of DQN RL with sparse reward in some degree. Therefore, we will use HER to improve the performance of naive DQN RL.

Unlike the naive DQN RL, DQN-HER takes into account the environment state s as well as the current goal g as the input information of the RL network. In this way, the state of DQN-HER can be represented as formula (9).

$$s^{HER} = \{s, g\} \tag{9}$$

g represents the current target position, denoted as $g = \{x_t, y_t\}$. For the path planning task, we set the task target position as $G_T = (x_T, y_T)$. During the RL process, the agent samples the existing state transition data from the experience replay buffer, sets the target position as the previously reached position, and recalculates the reward, thus obtaining more learning samples.

The pseudocode for the DQN-HER reinforcement learning algorithm is depicted in Algorithm. 1.

Algorithm. 1. DQN-HER path planning method

Initialize DQN network N.

Initialize replay buffer R.

for episode = 1, M do

    for t=0, T-1 do

        Sample an action a_t at s_t^{HER} using $\varepsilon - greedy$

        Execute a_t and get the next state s_{t+1}^{HER}

        Compute the reward $r(s_t^{HER}, a_t)$

        Store transition $(s_t^{HER}, a_t, r_t, s_{t+1}^{HER})$ in replay buffer R

        Store the achieved goal s_{t+1}^{HER}

        if achieve the

            G_T stop the episode

    end for

    Change the goal of $\hat{s}_t^{HER}, \hat{s}_{t+1}^{HER}$ in transitions

    Sample more transitions $(\hat{s}_t^{HER}, a_t, r_t, \hat{s}_{t+1}^{HER})$ for DQN

    for t=1, N do

    Sample a minibatch B from the replay buffer R

    Optimizing the weights of DQN network using B

    end for

end for

3.3 Proactive Obstacle Avoidance Skill

It is notable that during the path planning RL process in complex environments, the friction between the car and the obstacle affects the steering action of the car upon contact. Therefore, we set the car's turning action to first reverse, then turn as shown in Fig. 1 in order to overcome this issue. And we call the skill proactive obstacle avoidance skill. In subsequent experiments, we compared the RL process with and without the proactive obstacle avoidance skill.

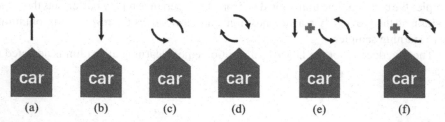

Fig. 1. The action of DQN. (a) Forward. (b) Backwards. (c) Turn left. (d) Turn right. (e) Turn left with the proactive obstacle avoidance skill. (f) Turn left with the proactive obstacle avoidance skill.

4 Experiment and Evaluation

4.1 Experiment

To verify the performance of the proposed DQN-HER reinforcement learning algorithm with the proactive obstacle avoidance skill, we established an experimental platform in Webots [11] simulation software and conducted simulation experiments of the DQN-HER path planning task.

The reinforcement learning was carried out under the environment of Ubuntu + Pytorch. And the OpenAI Gym was employed to establish the interface between the Webots environment and the reinforcement learning agent, enabling simulation experiments for RL. The interaction process between RL and the simulation environment is illustrated in Fig. 2.

As shown in Fig. 2, in the Webots environment, several sensors are equipped on the robot. To be specific, three distance sensors are equipped leftwards, rightwards and forwards, respectively. What's more, a GPS and a gyro are set on the top of the robot, which can provide the velocity and yaw angle of the robot.

We illustrated the overall process of the DQN-HER path planning process as Fig. 3. Since action a consists of four kinds of discrete movement commands, we use the regularized 5D output to represent the Q values of these actions and select the action corresponding to the maximum Q value as the output action. Notably, we use two output dimensions to represent the forward action command to increase the probability of the forward command being selected because the car mainly moves forward in the real world.

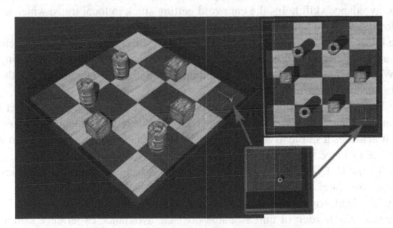

Fig. 2. The Simulation Environment and Robot

We conducted the ablation experiments with four kinds of experiment configurations as follows in the simulation environment.

1. DQN RL with proactive obstacle avoidance skill.
2. DQN-HER RL with proactive obstacle avoidance skill.
3. DQN RL without proactive obstacle avoidance skill.
4. DQN-HER RL without proactive obstacle avoidance skill.

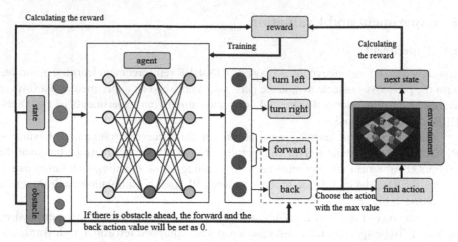

Fig. 3. The Overall Process of the DQN-HER Path Planning Process

4.2 Evaluation

The results of the ablation experiments are shown in Fig. 4. We can see that the DQN-HER RL process with proactive obstacle avoidance skill is the most stable one and achieves the most reward. This is because the HER algorithm provides more transition samples for DQN, reduces the impact of unstable obstacle penalties on the RL process, and makes the reinforcement learning process more stable. In addition, the proactive obstacle avoidance skill helps the car avoid getting stuck in local traps, which makes it easier for the agent to learn path planning strategies.

The DQN RL with proactive obstacle avoidance skill experienced some fluctuations in the early stages and still had problems in the later stages even after acquiring some skills. We think it is because the sparse and uncertain obstacle penalties make the DQN unstable during the learning process.

The DQN RL without proactive obstacle avoidance skill experiences larger fluctuations in the early stages due to the absence of obstacle avoidance techniques. Even though it achieves a stable average return value in the later stages, its average reward is low and the variance was large, resulting in unsatisfactory results.

Finally, the DQN-HER RL without proactive obstacle avoidance skill achieved the worst learning effect. We believe that it is due to the lack of obstacle avoidance movements, which leads to more collisions with the environment for the car in the early stages and increases the burden of unreasonable obstacle avoidance experience sampling for DQN.

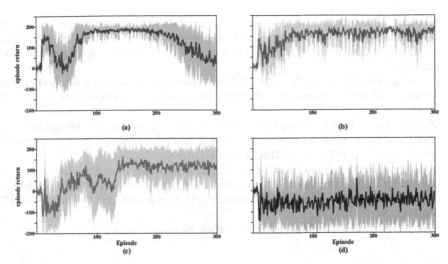

Fig. 4. The results of ablation experiments: (a) is DQN RL with proactive obstacle avoidance skill; (b) is DQN-HER RL with proactive obstacle avoidance skill; (c) is DQN RL without proactive obstacle avoidance skill; (d) is DQN-HER RL without proactive obstacle avoidance skill.

5 Conclusion

To conclude, we proposed a DQN-HER reinforcement learning algorithm to figure out sparse rewards and used our method for path planning. In addition, a proactive obstacle avoidance skill is applied to avoid the local dilemma. Then we designed some simulation experiments to compare our method with other methods. The results of simulation experiments showed that our method displayed the best learning stability and efficiency among all four methods we tested. As for future work, we are planning to apply our method to the heterogeneous multi-robot system for multi-robot path planning.

References

1. Patle, B.K., Pandey, A., Parhi, D.R.K., et al.: A review: on path planning strategies for navigation of mobile robot. Defence Technol. **15**(4), 582–606 (2019)
2. Sadr, A.S., Khojasteh, M.S., Malek, H., et al.: an efficient planning method for autonomous navigation of a wheeled-robot based on deep reinforcement learning. In: 2022 12th International Conference on Computer and Knowledge Engineering (ICCKE), pp. 136–141. IEEE (2022)
3. Chen, L., Hu, X., Tang, B., et al.: Conditional DQN-based motion planning with fuzzy logic for autonomous driving. IEEE Trans. Intell. Transp. Syst. **23**(4), 2966–2977 (2020)
4. Gao, H., Zhou, R., Tomizuka, M., et al.: Reinforcement learning based online parameter adaptation for model predictive tracking control under slippery condition. In: 2022 American Control Conference (ACC), pp. 2675–2682. IEEE (2022)
5. Andrychowicz, M., Wolski, F., Ray, A., et al.: Hindsight experience replay. Adv. Neural Inform. Process. Syst. **30** (2017)
6. Demir, A., Sezer, V.: Motion planning and control with randomized payloads using deep reinforcement learning. In: 2019 Third IEEE International Conference on Robotic Computing (IRC), pp. 32–37. IEEE (2019)

7. Chen, X., Ghadirzadeh, A., Folkesson, J., et al.: Deep reinforcement learning to acquire navigation skills for wheel-legged robots in complex environments. In: 2018 IEEE/RSJ International Conference on Intelligent Robots and Systems (IROS), pp. 3110–3116. IEEE (2018)

8. Wang, S., Cao, Y., Zheng, X., et al.: Collision-free trajectory planning for a 6-DoF free-floating space robot via hierarchical decoupling optimization. IEEE Robot. Autom. Let. **7**(2), 4953–4960 (2022)

9. Zuo, G., Lu, J., Pan, T.: Sparse reward based manipulator motion planning by using high speed learning from demonstrations. In: 2018 IEEE International Conference on Robotics and Biomimetics (ROBIO), pp. 518–523. IEEE (2018)

10. Kuang, Y., Weinberg, A.I., Vogiatzis, G., et al.: Goal density-based hindsight experience prioritization for multi-goal robot manipulation reinforcement learning. In: 2020 29th IEEE International Conference on Robot and Human Interactive Communication (RO-MAN), pp. 432–437. IEEE (2020)

11. Webots Homepage. http://www.cyberbotics.com. Accessed 21 May 2023

Realizing Human-like Walking and Running with Feedforward Enhanced Reinforcement Learning

Linqi Ye[1]([envelope]), Xueqian Wang[2], and Bin Liang[3]

[1] Institute of Artificial Intelligence, Collaborative Innovation Center for the Marine Artificial Intelligence, Shanghai University, Shanghai 200444, China
yelinqi@shu.edu.cn
[2] Center of Intelligent Control and Telescience, Tsinghua Shenzhen International Graduate School, Tsinghua University, Shenzhen 518055, China
[3] Navigation and Control Research Center, Department of Automation, Tsinghua University, Beijing, China

Abstract. Locomotion control of legged robots is a challenging problem. Recently, reinforcement learning has been applied to legged locomotion and made a great success. However, the reward signal design remains a challenging problem to produce a humanlike motion such as walking and running. Although imitation learning provides a way to mimic the behavior of humans or animals, the obtained motion may be restricted due to the over-constrained property of this method. Here we propose a novel and simple way to generate humanlike behavior by using feedforward enhanced reinforcement learning (FERL). In FERL, the control action is composed of a feedforward part and a feedback part, where the feedforward part is a periodic time-dependent signal generated by a state machine and the feedback part is a state-dependent signal obtained by a neural network. By using FERL with a simple feedforward of two feet stepping up and down alternately, we achieve humanlike walking and running for a simulated biped robot, Ranger Max. Comparison results show that the feedforward is key to generating humanlike behavior, while the policy trained with no feedforward only results in some strange gaits. FERL may also be extended to other legged robots to generate various locomotion styles, which provides a competitive alternative for imitation learning.

Keywords: Reinforcement Learning · Biped Robot · Locomotion Control

1 Introduction

Biped robots have long been a hot research field, especially when Tesla showcased their humanoid robot, the prototype of Optimus on September 30, at AI Day 2022. It is reported that the aim of Optimus is to perform "repetitive or boring" tasks in homes or factories for people. However, although the hardware of Optimus is super powerful, which can even lift a piano with the linear actuator used in Optimus, the locomotion performance of the robot is still far behind human beings as can be seen from their video demos. The fundamental reason is that a biped robot is unstable and has many degrees of freedom, which makes it difficult to control.

© The Author(s), under exclusive license to Springer Nature Singapore Pte Ltd. 2023
H. Yang et al. (Eds.): ICIRA 2023, LNAI 14270, pp. 439–451, 2023.
https://doi.org/10.1007/978-981-99-6492-5_38

Reinforcement learning has shown its feasibility to control legged robots recently. Reinforcement learning control is usually model-free, which learns the optimal behavior to maximize a given reward. In 2017, Deepmind applies reinforcement learning to train several simulated legged robots on a diverse set of challenging terrains and obstacles, using a simple reward function based on forward velocity [1]. They obtained some simulated agents that are good at traversing obstacles. However, the behavior of the agents looks strange. In 2019, ETH achieved a breakthrough by using reinforcement learning to control a real quadruped robot ANYmal [2]. The robot has gained locomotion skills like high-speed running and recovering from any falling states, which goes beyond what had been achieved with traditional control methods. Since then, reinforcement learning has received more and more attention in the field of legged locomotion.

To generate natural-looking locomotion behaviors, many researchers have focused on reward design. An intuitive way is to set an imitation-related reward to encourage the robot to mimic a given reference motion. In [3, 4], some reference joint angles are designed and incorporated into the reward signal to train the robot Cassie. In [5], motion capture data from a real dog is used as reference trajectories in the reward to train the robot Laikago. In [6], by imitating some reference trajectories with different foot sequences, a quadruped robot learns to walk, trot, pacing, bounding, and transit among them. In [7], simple sine waves are applied to the robot's foot to implement imitation learning. Besides, it is also possible to use a reference-free reward. In [8], a time-varying reward is designed, which can generate all common bipedal gaits and can achieve blind bipedal stair traversal by using stair-like terrain randomization [9]. Using a similar method with a foot-swing reward, robust high-speed running for quadruped robots is achieved [10]. Recently, a method called adversarial motion priors has been proposed [11, 12], which trains a discriminator to predict whether a motion produced by the agent is good or not. In this way, natural gait can be learned efficiently.

Another way to realize natural motion by reinforcement learning is to use a hierarchical control structure. In [13], a structured neural network controller is proposed for the robot ATRIAS, where reinforcement learning takes care of the high-level policy and the low-level policy is a feedback-based reactive stepping controller. In [14], a hierarchical learning framework was proposed for quadruped robots, which uses reinforcement learning as the high-level policy to adjust the low-level trajectory generator. In [15], a cascade-structure controller was proposed for the robot Digit, which combines reinforcement learning with intuitive feedback in a cascade structure. In [16], a hybrid locomotion policy was proposed for a biped robot, which uses a model-free learning-based control for the stance phase and a heuristics control for the swing phase.

In this paper, we propose FERL, which has a feedforward-feedback control structure and is different from the aforementioned work. FERL removes the need for tedious reward design. It is similar to the hierarchical control structure, which uses reinforcement learning to learn only a part of the controller. But FERL uses a parallel control structure rather than a hierarchical one. We apply FERL to a simulated biped robot, Ranger Max, and compare it with the pure reinforcement learning method, which shows that FERL can learn much more natural locomotion behavior under the same reward setting.

2 Methods

2.1 The FERL Control Framework

The proposed FERL control framework has a feedforward-feedback structure, as shown in Fig. 1. Compared to traditional reinforcement learning, which uses a controller purely based on a neural network, FERL adds an additional feedforward control action, which works parallelly with the neural network to generate the control action. In this framework, the control action is a summation of the output of the neural network and the time-based feedforward signal. Considering that walking and running are periodic motions that can be well characterized by a state machine, we decide to adopt a state machine to generate the feedforward signal. Using other methods such as central pattern generator (CPG) are also suitable for generating the feedforward signal.

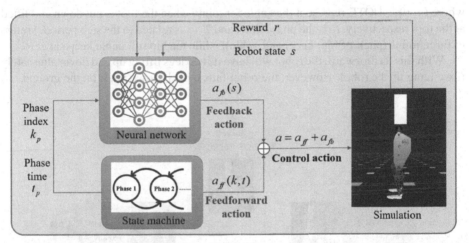

Fig. 1. The control framework of FERL. The control action is composed of a feedforward part and a feedback part, where the feedforward part is a periodic time-dependent signal generated by a state machine and the feedback part is a state-dependent signal obtained by a neural network.

In this controller, if we remove the neural network, then it becomes open-loop control. If we hang the robot in the air, its legs can move in a given motion sequence with the feedforward signal. However, since a biped robot has a floating base, it will likely fall if we put it on the ground. Although the robot may walk stably, say if the open-loop control satisfies static stability criteria, it is not robust to even a small disturbance. Therefore, we need necessary stabilization to make a feedback action, while this is exactly what the reinforcement learning part is doing. Therefore, the proposed controller combines the advantages of both reinforcement learning and open-loop control, where open-loop control provides a simple way to generate a periodic motion and reinforcement learning searches the optimal solution to stabilize that motion. As a result, the combination of feedforward and feedback can result in natural and robust bipedal locomotion behavior.

2.2 Feedforward Signal Design

The feedforward we applied is a simple stepping motion that actuates the two feet to go up and down alternately. To achieve this, a state machine is used as shown in Fig. 2. We insert two double stance phases to make the motion smoother. During the foot lifting phase, each joint angle follows a sinusoidal command as follows

$$\theta^i = \theta^i_1 + \left(\theta^i_{21} - \theta^i_1\right)\frac{1 - cos\left(2\pi * t_p/T_{step}\right)}{2} \tag{1}$$

where θ^i_1, θ^i_2, QUOTE represent the angle for joint i when the foot is put down and lifted at the top, respectively. t_p is the phase time, and T_{step} is related to the step period. i refers to three joints (pitch of hip, knee, and ankle), while the hip roll angle keeps at zero.

With this feedforward, the robot will have its two legs lifting up and down alternately if we hang up the robot. However, the robot falls quickly if we put it on the ground.

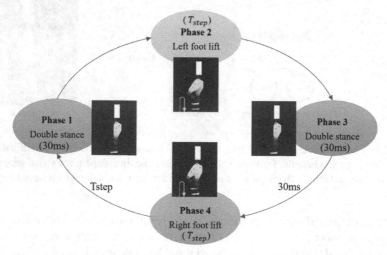

Fig. 2. The state machine for the feedforward action.

2.3 Reinforcement Learning

We explore three different control methods in order to make a comparison.

Case 1. RL
In this case, the feedforward is turned off and the control action is obtained only by the neural network.

Case 2. FERL (Fixed Period)
In this case, we enable the feedforward and use a fixed step period T_{step} for the state machine. Using a fixed step period may constrain the style of gaits.

Case 3. FERL (Varied Period)
In this case, we enable the feedforward and use a varied step period T_{step} for the feedforward. T_{step} is also assigned as a control action and is adjusted by the neural network. This gives more flexibility for the resulting gait style.

In all cases, the observations are the same, $(q, \omega, v, \theta_i, \dot{\theta}_i, k_p, t_p)$, which consists of 28 variables in total, explained as follows

q is the orientation of the body expressed by a quaternion, containing 4 variables.

ω is the angular velocity of the body, containing 3 variables.

v is the velocity of the body, containing 3 variables.

θ_i is the angle of each joint, containing 8 variables.

$\dot{\theta}_i$ is the angular velocity of each joint, containing 8 variables.

k_p, t_p are phase variables, containing 2 variables.

For RL and FERL (fixed period), we use the desired angle for each joint θ_i^{cmd} as the action, which contains 8 variables in total. While for FERL (varied period), T_{step} is added as an additional action, which has 9 actions in total. In all cases, the joints are set to position control mode with a spring factor of 200 and a damper factor of 10.

2.4 Reward Design

Due to the incorporation of the feedforward signal, there is no need for a tedious reward design. Indeed, we found a simple reward is enough to generate a natural motion with FERL. While the feedforward signal gives a good initial reference motion for the robot, the main function of reinforcement learning is to serve as a stabilizer and regulator. On one hand, to stabilize the robot, we should keep the robot not falling (body height not too low) and keep the body upright. On the other hand, to avoid ending up stepping in place, we should use a reward to encourage forward walking. To this end, we design the reward as a combination of three components

$$r = r_a + r_u + r_v \tag{2}$$

Each component is explained as follows

r_a to stay alive, $r_a = 1$, the robot receives this reward per time step for not falling.

r_u to keep the body upright, $r_u = -0.05\theta_{pitch} - 0.05\theta_{roll} - 0.05\theta_{yaw}$.

r_v to encourage forward velocity, $r_v = v_x$, where v_x is the forward walking velocity.

Besides, we end the episode if the robot falls (body height is 0.4 m lower than its initial height) or if the time step reaches 1000.

3 Simulation Results

3.1 Simulation Settings

The robot model used in the simulation is the Ranger Max biped robot, which is an upgraded version of the Cornell Ranger [17] robot. The model specifications including dimension and mass distribution are shown in Fig. 3. The robot uses a three-stage chain drive for all joints, which can provide a peak torque of about 200 Nm and a peak angular velocity of about 10 rad/s for each joint. Although each leg only has four degrees of freedom, it is capable of exhibiting excellent dynamic walking as shown later.

We use the ML-Agents package in Unity software for the simulation and reinforcement training. The PhysX physics engine is used and a fixed timestep of 0.01 s is adopted for simulation. For reinforcement learning, we use the PPO algorithm for training and the parameters are shown in Table 1.

With the three methods introduced in the previous section, we trained 8 million steps for each of them. The reward setting is the same and no curriculum is applied. As a result, the cumulative reward curves of the three methods are shown in Fig. 4. It can be seen that the trends of the three curves are similar, which all have a significant rise after 1 million training steps and finally achieved a large cumulative reward. Specifically, the maximum cumulative rewards achieved by the three methods in the order from large to small are: FERL (varied period) 11429, RL 11114, and FERL (fixed period) 9079, respectively. However, although RL without any feedforward can achieve a large cumulative reward close to FERL (varied period), the obtained policy will possibly lead to strange behavior, which will be shown later.

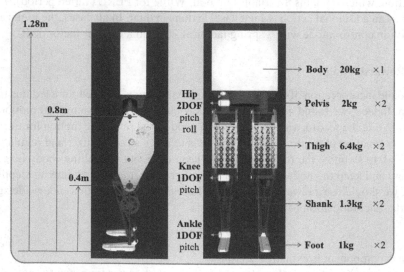

Fig. 3. Specifications of the Ranger Max biped simulation model.

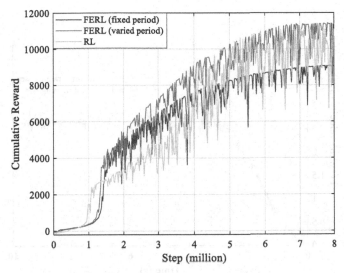

Fig. 4. Cumulative reward with respect to the training step.

Table 1. Training parameters of PPO.

Hyperparameters	Network_settings
batch_size: 2048	normalize: true
buffer_size: 20480	hidden_units: 512
learning_rate: 0.0003	num_layers: 3
beta: 0.005	vis_encode_type: simple
epsilon: 0.2	memory: null
lambd: 0.95	goal_conditioning_type: hyper
num_epoch: 3	deterministic: false

3.2 Simulation Results of RL

We select two policies trained by RL to apply to the robot, one at 3.6 million training steps, and one at 8 million training steps. The forward velocities of the robot's body for the two policies are shown in Fig. 5. It can be seen that for the 3.6 M policy, the robot achieves a forward velocity of about 2.7 m/s, and for the 8 M policy, the robot achieves a forward velocity of about 4.3 m/s.

The gait sequences resulting from the two policies are shown in Figs. 6 and 7, respectively. It can be observed that no leg alternation occurs in both gait sequences, where the left leg always keeps in the front. The joint angles seem to vary slightly and the robot hops frequently to move forward. Although the robot achieves a high speed in this way, it is obviously not humanlike. From the video, we can see that the leg is shaking with a high frequency, which looks strange and is not feasible for a real robot.

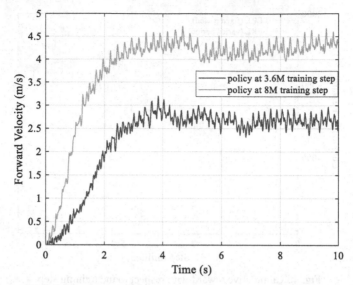

Fig. 5. Forward walking velocity for policies trained with RL.

Fig. 6. Gait sequence resulting from policy trained with RL at 3.6 million training steps. This results in a non-human-like hopping gait without leg alternation.

Fig. 7. Gait sequence resulting from policy trained with RL at 8 million training steps. This still results in a non-humanlike hopping gait without leg alternation.

3.3 Simulation Results of FERL with Fixed Step Period

We select two policies trained by FERL with a fixed step period to apply to the robot, one at 2.4 million training steps, and one at 8 million training steps. The forward velocities of the robot's body for the two policies are shown in Fig. 8. It can be seen that for the 2.4 M policy, the robot achieves a forward velocity of about 1.7 m/s, and for the 8 M policy, the robot achieves a forward velocity of about 3 m/s.

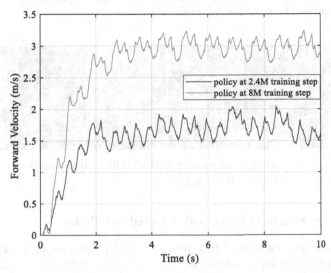

Fig. 8. Forward walking velocity of policy trained with FERL (fixed period).

The gait sequences resulting from the two policies are shown in Figs. 9 and 10, respectively. It can be observed that the gaits look much more natural now, where leg alternation occurs normally in both gait sequences. Specifically, the 2.4 M policy leads to a humanlike walking gait, where the stance leg keeps relatively straight and a significant foot push-off is observed. Interestingly, the 8 M policy leads to a humanlike skipping gait, where one leg hops for a small distance during the other leg swing. Why does running gait not occur? We speculate this might be because the step period ($T_{step} = 400$ ms) we selected is too big for running, and skipping happens to be the optimal gait for the selected step period.

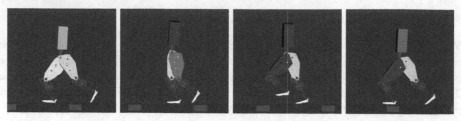

Fig. 9. Gait sequence resulting from policy trained with FERL (fixed period) at 2.4 million training steps. This results in a humanlike walking gait.

Fig. 10. Gait sequence resulting from policy trained with FERL (fixed period) at 8 million training steps. This results in a humanlike skipping gait.

3.4   Simulation Results of FERL with a Varied Step Period

We select two policies trained by FERL with a varied step period to apply to the robot, one at 2.4 million training steps, and one at 8 million training steps. The forward velocities of the robot's body for the two policies are shown in Fig. 11. It can be seen that for the 2.4 M policy, the robot achieves a forward velocity of about 2.2 m/s, and for the 8 M policy, the robot achieves a forward velocity of about 4.3 m/s.

The gait sequences resulting from the two policies are shown in Figs. 12 and 13, respectively. It can be observed that the gait of the 2.4 M policy is similar to that obtained by the previous method, which is a humanlike walking gait. But the 8M gait is a little different from the previous one, which is a humanlike running gait now.

Running can occur mainly because of the application of a varied step period T_{step}. To verify this, we show the histograms of T_{step} for the 2.4 M and 8 M policy in Fig. 14. It can be seen that distributions of QUOTE T_{step} are quite different for the two policies. For the 2.4 M policy, T_{step} mostly distributes in the middle around 300–450, while for the 8 M policy, T_{step} has the highest frequency at the shortest period 200. Therefore, during the training process, in order to go fast to get more rewards, the robot decreases T_{step} and transits to a running gait, which is similar to what we humans do when we need to go faster.

Simulation video link: https://www.bilibili.com/video/BV1Rc411G7xd/

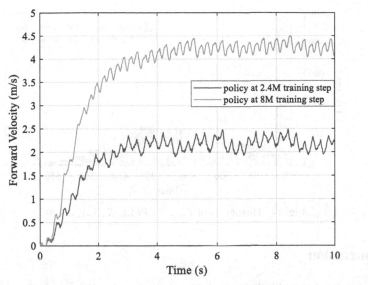

Fig. 11. Forward walking velocity of policy trained with FERL (varied period).

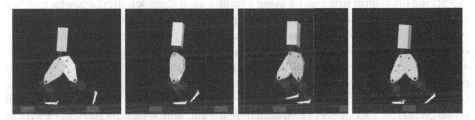

Fig. 12. Gait sequence resulting from policy trained with FERL (varied period) at 2.4 million training steps. This results in a humanlike walking gait.

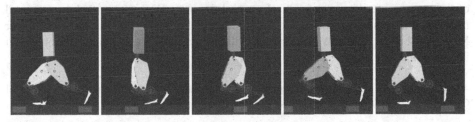

Fig. 13. Gait sequence resulting from policy trained with FERL (varied period) at 8 million training steps. This results in a human-like running gait.

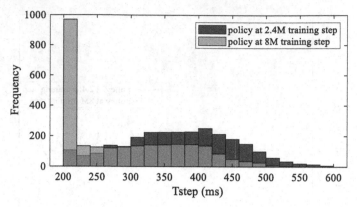

Fig. 14. Histogram of T_{step} for FERL (varied period).

4 Conclusion

How to generate humanlike behavior by reinforcement learning is a challenging problem. While traditional methods usually focus on the reward design, we instead consider modifying the control structure by using a feedforward-feedback structure, which allows for generating humanlike motion with a simple reward and no need for a curriculum. The proposed FERL method combines the advantages of both reinforcement learning and open-loop control, leading to robust and natural walking and running gaits in a simple and fast manner. We compare three different control methods in this paper, which are pure RL, FERL with a fixed step period, and FERL with a varied step period. With the same reward design and training setup, the three methods finally result in different gait styles. While pure RL leads to a strange hopping gait with no leg alternation, FERL can lead to natural human-like gaits. Specifically, FERL with a fixed step period leads to walking and skipping, and FERL with a varied step period leads to walking and running. It verifies the importance of the control structure and demonstrates the effectiveness of the proposed feedforward-feedback control structure. We have verified the proposed method on a simulated biped robot Ranger Max in this paper. The real robot of Ranger Max is still under assembly now and we will test our methods on the real robot once it is completed.

Acknowledgment. This work was supported by the National Natural Science Foundation of China No. 62003188 and No.92248304.

References

1. Heess, N., et al.: Emergence of locomotion behaviours in rich environments. arXiv preprint arXiv:1707.02286 (2017)
2. Hwangbo, J., et al.: Learning agile and dynamic motor skills for legged robots. Sci. Robot. **4**(26), eaau5872 (2019)

3. Xie, Z., Berseth, G., Clary, P., Hurst, J., van de Panne, M.: Feedback control for cassie with deep reinforcement learning. In: 2018 IEEE/RSJ International Conference on Intelligent Robots and Systems (IROS), pp. 1241–1246. IEEE (2018)

4. Li, Z., et al.: Reinforcement learning for robust parameterized locomotion control of bipedal robots. In: 2021 IEEE International Conference on Robotics and Automation (ICRA), pp. 2811–2817. IEEE (2021)

5. Peng, X.B., Coumans, E., Zhang, T., Lee, T.W., Tan, J., Levine, S.: Learning agile robotic locomotion skills by imitating animals. arXiv preprint arXiv:2004.00784 (2020)

6. Shao, Y., Jin, Y., Liu, X., He, W., Wang, H., Yang, W.: Learning free gait transition for quadruped robots via phase-guided controller. IEEE Robot. Autom. Let. 7(2), 1230–1237 (2021)

7. Wu, Q., Zhang, C., Liu, Y.: Custom sine waves are enough for imitation learning of bipedal gaits with different styles. In: 2022 IEEE International Conference on Mechatronics and Automation (ICMA), pp. 499–505. IEEE (2022)

8. Siekmann, J., Godse, Y., Fern, A., Hurst, J.: Sim-to-real learning of all common bipedal gaits via periodic reward composition. In: 2021 IEEE International Conference on Robotics and Automation (ICRA), pp. 7309–7315. IEEE (2021)

9. Siekmann, J., Green, K., Warila, J., Fern, A., Hurst, J.: Blind bipedal stair traversal via sim-to-real reinforcement learning. arXiv preprint arXiv:2105.08328 (2021)

10. Bellegarda, G., Chen, Y., Liu, Z., Nguyen, Q.: Robust high-speed running for quadruped robots via deep reinforcement learning. In: 2022 IEEE/RSJ International Conference on Intelligent Robots and Systems (IROS), pp. 10364–10370. IEEE (2022)

11. Vollenweider, E., Bjelonic, M., Klemm, V., Rudin, N., Lee, J., Hutter, M.: Advanced skills through multiple adversarial motion priors in reinforcement learning. arXiv preprint arXiv: 2203.14912 (2022)

12. Escontrela, A., et al.: Adversarial motion priors make good substitutes for complex reward functions. In: 2022 IEEE/RSJ International Conference on Intelligent Robots and Systems (IROS), pp. 25–32. IEEE (2022)

13. Li, T., Geyer, H., Atkeson, C.G., Rai, A.: Using deep reinforcement learning to learn high-level policies on the atrias biped. In: 2019 International Conference on Robotics and Automation (ICRA), pp. 263–269. IEEE (2019)

14. Tan, W., et al.: A hierarchical framework for quadruped locomotion based on reinforcement learning. In: 2021 IEEE/RSJ International Conference on Intelligent Robots and Systems (IROS), pp. 8462–8468. IEEE (2021)

15. Castillo, G. A., Weng, B., Zhang, W., Hereid, A.: Robust feedback motion policy design using reinforcement learning on a 3d digit bipedal robot. In: 2021 IEEE/RSJ International Conference on Intelligent Robots and Systems (IROS), pp. 5136–5143. IEEE (2021)

16. Wang, Z., Wei, W., Xie, A., Zhang, Y., Wu, J., Zhu, Q.: Hybrid bipedal locomotion based on reinforcement learning and heuristics. Micromachines 13(10), 1688 (2022)

17. Bhounsule, P.A., et al.: Low-bandwidth reflex-based control for lower power walking: 65 km on a single battery charge. Int. J. Robot. Res. 33(10), 1305–1321 (2014)

Research on Target Trajectory Planning Method of Humanoid Manipulators Based on Reinforcement Learning

Keyao Liang[1] , Fusheng Zha[1] , Wentao Sheng[2], Wei Guo[1],
Pengfei Wang[1(✉)], and Lining Sun[1]

[1] Harbin Institute of Technology, Harbin 150006, China
hitliangky@163.com, {zhafusheng,wguo01,wangpengfei,lnsun}@hit.edu.cn
[2] School of Intelligent Manufacturing, Nanjing University of Science and Technology
(NJUST), Nanjing 210094, China
shengwt@njust.edu.cn

Abstract. The goal of most asymmetrically coordinated manipulative tasks of humanoid manipulators is multilevel. For example, a bottle cap screwing task is composed of several sub-objectives, such as reaching, grasping, aligning, and screwing. In addition, the flexible interaction requirements of dual-arm robots challenge the trajectory planning methods of manipulator with high dimensional and strong coupling characteristics. However, the traditional reinforcement learning algorithms cannot quickly learn and generate the required trajectories above. Based on the idea of multi-agent control, a dual-agent deep deterministic policy gradient algorithm is proposed in this paper, which uses two agents to simultaneously plan the coordinated trajectory of the left arm and the right arm online. This algorithm solves the problem of online trajectory planning for multi-objective tasks of humanoid manipulators. The design of observations and actions in the dual-agent structure can reduce the dimension and decouple the humanoid manipulators' trajectory planning problem to a certain extent, thus speeding up the learning speed. Moreover, a reward function is constructed to realize the coordinated control between the two agents, to promote dual-agent to generate continuous trajectories for multi-objective tasks. Finally, the effectiveness of the proposed algorithm is verified in Baxter multi-objective task simulation environment under the Gym. The results show that this algorithm can quickly learn and online plan the coordinated trajectory of humanoid manipulators for multi-objective tasks.

Keywords: Multi-objective trajectory planning · Bimanual coordination · Deep deterministic policy gradient

Supported in part by the National Natural Science Foundation of China (U2013602, 52075115, 51521003, 61911530250), National Key R&D Program of China (2020YFB13134), Self-Planned Task (SKLRS202001B, SKLRS202110B) of State Key Laboratory of Robotics and System (HIT), Shenzhen Science and Technology Research and Development Foundation (JCYJ20190813171009236), and Basic Scientific Research of Technology (JCKY2020603C009).

1   Introduction

In recent years, dual-arm robot has been widely used in manufacture and life. It has unique advantages in high coordination precision assembly field and complex multi-task field. The characteristics of dual-arm robots and the need for flexible interaction challenge the trajectory planning methods of manipulator with high dimensional and strong coupling characteristics.

Firstly, the dual-arm robot is a complex nonlinear system with high order and strong coupling, which is difficult to be studied by conventional models and methods. Secondly, most operational tasks of dual-arm robots are multi-objective, and the trajectory required by the robots is a continuous trajectory to reach each sub-objective in turn, which increases the dimension of the trajectory planning problem in the task space. In addition, the redundant dual-arm robot has 14 degrees of freedom and high coordination between its arms. The dual-arm robot needs a more accurate and fast trajectory planning algorithm, which can not only realize the cooperative work of both arms but also avoid self-collision. Therefore, it is necessary to study the coordinated trajectory planning method of dual-arm robots.

At present, the research on online motion planning of manipulator mainly focuses on constraint models and nonlinear solving problems. Vahrenkamp et al. proposed a dual-arm obstacle avoidance algorithm [1] based on rapidly exploring random tree(RRT). This method is based on strategy search, which satisfies the self-collision constraint and ensures the grasping feasibility of both arms. Fang et al. dealt with the self-collision avoidance problem for humanoid robots in an efficient way [2]. Self-collision avoidance was introduced as a constraint for each task in a hierarchical Inverse Kinematic (IK) problem. H. Andy Park et al. proposed a general whole-body control framework [3] based on Gauss' principle of least constraint, which can uniformly deal with all constraints imposed on human-like systems. Markus et al. proposed whole-body trajectories and time-varying kinematic feedback controllers [4] by solving a Constrained Sequential Linear Quadratic Optimal Control problem. They addressed the problem of kinematic trajectory planning for mobile manipulators with non-holonomic constraints, and holonomic operational-space tracking constraints. However, the above methods can not effectively solve the motion planning problem of multi-objective cooperative tasks in a small space, which severely limits the application range of dual-arm robots.

In multi-objective dual-arm coordination tasks, most methods realize task planning based on imitation learning. Andrea et al. proposed an innovative approach [5] for human activity prediction, exploiting both priori information and knowledge revealed during the operation. The approach can achieve good performance through both off-line simulated sequences and in a realistic co-assembly involving a human operator and a dual arm collaborative robot. Gianluca et al. combined off-the-shelf soft-articulated robotic components with the framework of Dynamic Movement Primitives, to generalize human trajectories and impedance regulation skills [6]. Dennis et al. present a demonstration programming approach [7], based on the Dirichlet Process Gaussian Mixture Model (DPGMM) and Gaussian Mixture Regression (GMR), which could automatically derive task constraints for a constraint-based robot controller from data and adapt them with respect to previously unseen situations (contexts). Kazuhiro et al. proposed a body role division approach [8] that combines both types of knowledge using a single human demonstration, which could teach a complex task sequence to a robot. Heecheol et al. proposed applying a Transformer [9], a variant of self-attention architecture, to deep imitation learning to solve dual-arm manipulation tasks in the real world. However, these planning methods based on imitation learning can only reproduce the demonstration trajectory, and it is difficult to optimize or learn the new trajectory independently.

Reinforcement learning methods search for optimal strategies in action space through interactive means, and have made significant progress in game operation [10], automatic driving [11], robot operation [12], dialogue system [13] and other fields. At present, reinforcement learning algorithm based on actor-critic(AC) framework is widely used in robot field. According to whether the action network outputs action distribution or specific action values, reinforcement learning algorithms based on the AC framework can be divided into deterministic policy methods (DDPG [14]) and stochastic policy methods (PPO [15], A3C [16], SAC [17]). Among them, DDPG algorithm has achieved very good results in the continuous control problem. However, the characteristics of dual-arm robots and the high-dimensional problem of trajectory planning brought by multi-objective tasks will increase the search space of reinforcement learning, and the training process is easy to fall into local optimization, so the training results are difficult to converge. In addition, the traditional reinforcement learning method cannot control the cooperative operation of both arms.

In this paper, based on the idea of multi-agent control, a dual-agent deep deterministic policy gradient algorithm is proposed to quickly learn and online generate the dual-arm coordination trajectory for multi-objective tasks. The main contributions are as follows:

(1) Based on DDPG algorithm, a dual-agent structure is constructed which can simultaneously plan the coordinated trajectories of the left and right arms online. The reasonable allocation of input and output can reduce the dimension and decouple the humanoid manipulators' trajectory planning problem to a certain extent, thus speeding up the learning speed.
(2) A reward function is constructed to realize the coordination control between two agents, and to promote dual-agent to learn a continuous coordination trajectory for multi-objective tasks.
(3) The effectiveness of this algorithm has been verified in experiments. The results show that this algorithm can quickly learn and online plan the coordination trajectory of dual-arm for multi-objective tasks.

2   Preliminary Knowledge

2.1   Reinforcement Learning

Reinforcement learning consists of agent and the environment that can interact with agent, and its basic model is markov decision process (MDP). MDP is a theoretical framework for achieving goals through interactive learning.

MDP defines the learning process as a quad (S, A, P, R): s_t is a complete description of environment state at a certain time t, S is a set of state sequences; a_t is the agent's action at a certain time t, A is a set of action sequences; P is the state transition function; r is the reward signal obtained after interacting with the environment, and R is an artificial reward function.

In reinforcement learning, a episode, also named as a trajectory, consists of state and action sequences, $\tau = (s_0, a_0, s_1, a_1, \cdots)$. The objective of the agent is to maximize the cumulative reward of a trajectory, $R(\tau)$, which can be defined as:

$$R(\tau) = \sum_{t=0}^{\infty} \gamma^t r_t \tag{1}$$

where γ is the discount factor, $\gamma \in (0, 1)$. The goal of reinforcement learning is to learn an optimal strategy π to maximize the expected goal $J(\pi)$, which can be defined as:

$$J(\pi) = \underset{\tau \sim \pi}{E}[R(\tau)] \tag{2}$$

2.2   Deep Deterministic Policy Gradient

Deep deterministic policy gradient(DDPG) is an online deep reinforcement learning algorithm under AC framework. DDPG combines the advantages of the deterministic policy gradient algorithm and the DQN algorithm.

In this algorithm, the empirical data $(s_t, a_t, r_t, s_{t+1}, done)$ obtained from the interaction between the agent and the environment are stored in an experience pool, which is sampled in batches when the parameters of networks are updated. Noise is added to the action output of the actor network in the training stage to enhance the exploration ability of the agent. DDPG algorithm consists of four networks, which are Actor $\mu(\cdot|\theta^\mu)$, Critic $Q(\cdot|\theta^Q)$, Target Actor $\mu'(\cdot|\theta^{\mu'})$ and Target Critic $Q'(\cdot|\theta^{Q'})$.

The parameters of the Critic network are updated by minimizing MSBE losses Lc by the gradient descent method:

$$L_c = (y - q)^2 = (Q(s_i, a_i|\theta^Q) - (r_i + \gamma(1 - done)Q'(s_{i+1}, a'|\theta^{Q'})))^2 \tag{3}$$

where $a' = \mu'(s_{i+1}|\theta^{\mu'})$. The parameters of the Actor network are updated by maximizing the cumulative expected return J by the gradient ascent method:

$$\nabla_{\theta^\mu} J = \underset{s \sim \mu}{E}\left[\nabla_a Q(s, a|\theta^Q)|_{s=s_i, a=\mu(s_i)} \nabla_{\theta^\mu} \mu(s|\theta^\mu)|_{s_i}\right] \tag{4}$$

The parameters of the target networks are updated by way of soft update:

$$\begin{cases} \theta^{Q'} \leftarrow \tau\theta^Q + (1-\tau)\theta^{Q'} \\ \theta^{\mu'} \leftarrow \tau\theta^\mu + (1-\tau)\theta^{\mu'} \end{cases} \tag{5}$$

where τ is the soft update rate.

3   Method

This paper proposes a dual-agent deep deterministic policy gradient (DADDPG) algorithm, which can quickly learn and generate dual-arm coordination trajectories for multi-objective tasks. The algorithm will be introduced in detail from three aspects: structure, update process, and reward function design. The structure of DADDPG algorithm is shown in the Fig. 1.

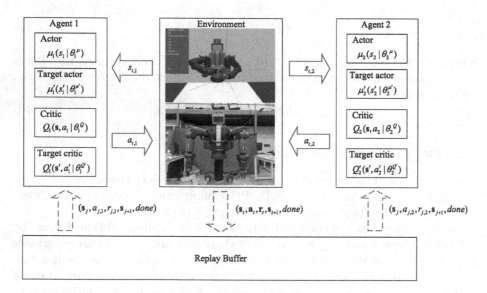

Fig. 1. Block diagram of DADDPG algorithm. Replay Buffer stores the interaction transitions $(\mathbf{s}_t, \mathbf{a}_t, \mathbf{r}_t, \mathbf{s}_{t+1}, done)$ between the agent and the environment. Sample the interaction transitions in batches $(\mathbf{s}_j, \mathbf{a}_j, \mathbf{r}_j, \mathbf{s}_{j+1}, done)$ from the Replay Buffer as network parameters are updated.

3.1   Structure of DADDPG

DADDPG algorithm contains two agents, and each agent contains four networks. There are eight networks in total, which are Actor $\mu_1(\cdot|\theta_1^\mu)$, $\mu_2(\cdot|\theta_2^\mu)$, Critic $Q_1(\cdot|\theta_1^Q)$, $Q_2(\cdot|\theta_2^Q)$, Target Actor $\mu_1'(\cdot|\theta_1^{\mu'})$, $\mu_2'(\cdot|\theta_2^{\mu'})$, and Target Critic $Q_1'(\cdot|\theta_1^{Q'})$, $Q_2'(\cdot|\theta_2^{Q'})$.

Observation $s_t = (s_{t,1}, s_{t,2})$, action $a_t = (a_{t,1}, a_{t,2})$, reward $r_t = (r_{t,1}, r_{t,2})$. The state of the environment s_t observed by the agent. Agent1 inputs the observation $s_{t,1}$ and outputs the action $r_{t,1}$. Agent2 inputs the observation $s_{t,2}$ and outputs the action $r_{t,2}$. The environment executes the action a_t and returns the environment state s_{t+1} and reward r_t. The pseudo-code for DADDPG algorithm is as follows:

Algorithm 1. DADDPG algorithm

For agent $i = 1$ to 2:

i. Randomly initialize critic network $Q_i(s, a_i|\theta_i^Q)$ and actor network $\mu_i(s_i|\theta_i^\mu)$ with weights θ_i^Q and θ_i^μ

ii. Initialize target network Q_i' and μ_i' with $\theta_i^{Q'} \leftarrow \theta_i^Q$, $\theta_i^{\mu'} \leftarrow \theta_i^\mu$

Initialize replay buffer R

for episode $= 1$, **M do**

    Initialize a random process $\mathcal{N}$ for action exploration

    Receive initial observation state $s_1 = (s_{1,1}, s_{1,2})$

    for $t = 1$, **T do**

        for agent $i = 1$ to 2 **do**

            select action $a_{t,i} = \mu(s_{t,i}|\theta^\mu) + \mathcal{N}_t$ according to the current policy and exploration noise

        end for

        Execute action $a_t = (a_{t,1}, a_{t,2})$ and observe reword $r_t = (r_{t,1}, r_{t,2})$ and observe new state $s_{t+1} = (s_{t+1,1}, s_{t+1,2})$ and observe signal *done*

        Store transition $(s_t, a_t, r_t, s_{t+1}, done)$ in R

        Sample a random minibatch of N transitions $(s_j, a_j, r_j, s_{j+1}, done)$ from R

        for agent $i = 1$ to 2 **do**

            Set $y_j = r_{j,i} + \gamma(1 - done)Q_i'(s_{j+1}, \mu_i'(s_{j+1,i}|\theta_i^{\mu'})|\theta_i^{Q'})$

            Update critic by minimizing the loss: $L = \frac{1}{N}\sum_j (y_j - Q_i(s_j, a_{j,i}|\theta_i^Q))^2$

            Update the actor policy using the samples policy gradient:

$$\nabla_{\theta_i^\mu} J \approx \frac{1}{N}\sum_j \nabla_{a_i} Q_i(s, a_i|\theta^Q)|_{s=s_j, a_i=\mu_i(s_{j,i})} \nabla_{\theta_i^\mu} \mu_i(s_i|\theta_i^\mu)|_{s_{j,i}}$$

            Update the target networks:

$$\theta_i^{Q'} \leftarrow \tau\theta_i^Q + (1 - \tau)\theta_i^{Q'}$$

$$\theta_i^{\mu'} \leftarrow \tau\theta_i^\mu + (1 - \tau)\theta_i^{\mu'}$$

        end for

    end for

end for

3.2　Update Process

The update process of parameters for both agents is similar.

For the agent$i$, the parameters of the Critic network are updated by minimizing MSBE loss Lc by the gradient descent method:

$$L_c = (y_i - q_i)^2 = (Q_i(\mathbf{s}_j, a_{j,i}|\theta_i^Q) - r_{j,i} + \gamma(1 - done)Q_i'(\mathbf{s}_{j+1}, \mu_i'(s_{j+1,i}|\theta_i^{\mu'})|\theta_i^{Q'}))^2 \tag{6}$$

The parameters of the Actor network are updated by maximizing the cumulative expected return J of agent$i$ by the gradient ascent method:

$$\nabla_{\theta_i^\mu} J = \underset{\mathbf{s} \sim \mu_1, \mu_2}{E} \left[\nabla_{a_i} Q_i(\mathbf{s}, a_i|\theta^Q)|_{\mathbf{s}=\mathbf{s}_j, a_i=\mu_i(s_{j,i})} \nabla_{\theta_i^\mu} \mu_i(s_i|\theta_i^\mu)|s_{j,i} \right] \tag{7}$$

The parameters of the target networks are updated by way of soft update:

$$\begin{cases} \theta_i^{Q'} \leftarrow \tau\theta_i^Q + (1 - \tau)\theta_i^{Q'} \\ \theta_i^{\mu'} \leftarrow \tau\theta_i^\mu + (1 - \tau)\theta_i^{\mu'} \end{cases} \tag{8}$$

where τ is the soft update rate.

3.3   The Design of Reward Function

For multi-objective tasks and dual-arm coordination needs, three reward items are designed: r_{step}, r_{goal} and $r_{coordinate}$

$$r_{step} = -distance(pos\_gripper_i, pos\_finalgoal_i) \tag{9}$$

where $i = 1, 2$.

$$r_{goal} = \begin{cases} \sum_j rg_j \ , \ if \ goal_j = True \\ 0 \quad , \ if \ goal_j = False \end{cases} \tag{10}$$

where j is the number of sub-objective. rg is constant.

$$r_{coordinate} = \begin{cases} rc \ , \ if \ all \ goal = True \\ 0 \ , \ else \end{cases} \tag{11}$$

where rc is constant. For each agent, the reward can be calculated by the reward function. The reward function is the sum of three terms:

$$R = r_{step} + r_{goal} + r_{coordinate} \tag{12}$$

4   Experiments

The effectiveness of DADDPG algorithm has been verified in a Gym simulation environment of Baxter robot multi-objective task. This task has three sub-goals: reaching, grasping, and aligning. The details and results of the experiment are as follows.

4.1   Experiments Setup

A multi-objective task simulation environment for the Baxter robot was created in Gym, as shown in the Fig. 2. The black block is the object block for the left arm. The yellow block is the object block for the right arm. The red sphere is the target position for the left arm. The blue sphere is the target position for the right arm.The settings of DADDPG algorithm are shown in the Table 1.

Table 1. DADDPG Settings

item		description
soft update rate τ		0.005
range of action values		$[-1, 1]$
action **a**	action of left arm a_l	4
	action of right arm a_r	4
observation **s**	observation of left arm s_l	28
	observation of left arm s_r	28
actor network	number of layers	3
	input and output of hidden layer	400, 300
critic network	number of layers	3
	input and output of hidden layer	400, 300

Observation. In Baxter's multi-objective task simulation environment, the state of the environment is represented by the observation $\mathbf{s} = (s_l, s_r)$. s_l is the state of the robot's left arm and its target, including the position of the left gripper, the position of the left object block, the relative position of the object block and the left gripper, the state of the two fingers of the left gripper, the orientation of the left object block, the linear velocity of the left object block, the angular velocity of the left object block, the linear velocity of the left gripper, the speed of the two fingers of the left gripper, the position of the left target. s_r is the state of the robot's right arm and its target, including the above variables corresponding to the right arm.

Action. Action $\mathbf{a} = (a_l, a_r)$ controls each arm of the robot respectively. a_l controls the left arm of the robot, including the position of the left gripper and the state of the fingers of the left gripper. a_r controls the right arm of the robot, including the position of the right gripper and the state of the fingers of the right gripper.

Goal. The multi-objective task has three sub-goals: reaching, grasping, and aligning. Reaching: The arms of the robot should reach their respective object blocks from the initial position. Grasping: The arms of the robot should grasp their respective object blocks. Aligning: The robot's arms should align the position of the blocks from top to bottom. Completing these three sub-goals in turn, the dual-arm robot accomplishes this multi-objective task.

Reward. The reward function is shown in Sect. 3.3. Set the reward of subgoal reaching $rg_1 = 1$, the reward of subgoal grasping $rg_2 = 20$, the reward of coordinate $rc = 3500$.

4.2   Results

After training, DADDPG algorithm can generate the trajectory of completing a multi-objective task online, as shown in Fig. 2. Different from traditional trajectory planning, the trajectory planned online by DADDPG algorithm includes not only the gripper position, but also the fingers' state.

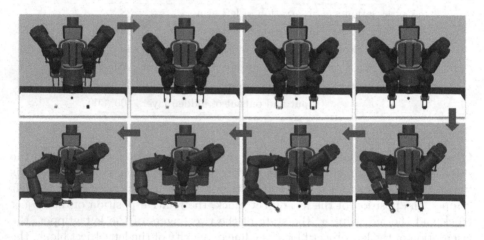

Fig. 2. Multi-objective task completion process. Baxter's arms reach the position of their respective object blocks, then grasp their respective object blocks, and finally align the two object blocks.

For Baxter's multi-objective task, under the same setting of the reward function proposed in this paper, the training curves of DADDPG algorithm, Multi-Agent Deep Deterministic Policy Gradient(MADDPG) algorithm, and single DDPG algorithm were compared(see Fig. 3). In the figure, the horizontal axis is the number of training iterations, and the vertical axis is the average return. The average return of DADDPG converges around 6500 epochs. The average return of MADDPG converges around 8700 epochs. The average return of DDPG falls into local optimality around 2000 epochs and begins to rise around 6000 epochs, and the agent cannot successfully learn the multi-objective task. The convergence time for DADDPG is 74% of MADDPG's convergence time The results

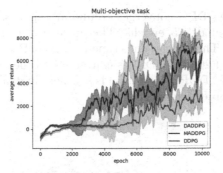

Fig. 3. Average return on Baxter's multi-objective task.

show that the training convergence speed of DDPG algorithm is significantly faster than the other two algorithms.

To verify the effectiveness of the reward function designed in this paper, the training curves of DADDPG algorithm under different reward function Settings were compared(see Fig. 4). In Fig. 4a, the average return of DADDPG without r_{goal} falls into local optimal at about 500 epochs. In Fig. 4b, the average return curve of DADDPG with sparse r_{step} falls into local optimal at about 6000 epochs. The results show that the proposed reward function can improve the performance and convergence rate of DADDPG algorithm. It realizes the coordination control between the two agents and prompts the agents to learn a continuous trajectory for multi-objective tasks.

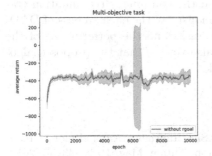 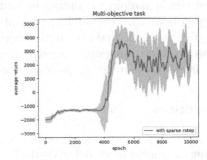

(a) DADDPG algorithm without r_{goal} (b) DADDPG algorithm with sparse r_{step}

Fig. 4. Average return of DADDPG algorithm with different reward functions on Baxter's multi-objective tasks

In addition, the performance of DADDPG algorithm was also verified on dual-arm single-objective task (see Fig. 5). A simulation environment for Baxter's dual-arm reach task was created and the agent was trained in it. Set the reward of subgoal reaching $rg_1 = 1$, and the reward of coordinate $rc = 100$. The average return of DADDPG converges around 375 epochs. MADDPG's average return converges around 575 epochs. The average return of DDPG converges around 1950 epochs. The convergence time for DADDPG is 65% of MADDPG's convergence time and 20% of DDPG's convergence time. The results show that the performance of DADDPG algorithm is excellent in dual-arm single-objective tasks besides multi-objective tasks.

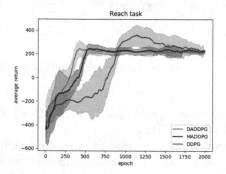

Fig. 5. Average return on Baxter's dual-arm reach task.

5   Conclusion

DADDPG algorithm proposed in this paper can quickly learn the multi-objective task of the humanoid manipulators and plan the continuous coordination trajectory of both arms online. Experiments demonstrate the effectiveness of DADDPG algorithm in dual-arm multi-objective tasks and the performance of the proposed reward function. The experiment also verifies that the proposed algorithm is effective on the single-objective task.

References

1. Vahrenkamp, N., Asfour, T., Dillmann, R.: Simultaneous grasp and motion planning: humanoid robot ARMAR-III. IEEE Rob. Autom. Mag. **19**(2), 43–57 (2012)
2. Fang, C., Rocchi, A., Hoffman, E.M., Tsagarakis, N.G., Caldwell, D.G: Efficient self-collision avoidance based on focus of interest for humanoid robots. In: 2015 IEEE-RAS 15th International Conference on Humanoid Robots (Humanoids), pp. 1060–1066. IEEE, Seoul, Korea (South) (2015)
3. Park, H.A., Lee, C.S. George: extended cooperative task space for manipulation tasks of humanoid robots. In: 2015 IEEE International Conference on Robotics and Automation (ICRA), pp. 6088–6093. IEEE, Seattle, WA, USA (South) (2015)
4. Giftthaler, M., Farshidian, F., Sandy, T., Stadelmann, L., Buchli, J.: Efficient kinematic planning for mobile manipulators with non-holonomic constraints using optimal control. In: 2017 IEEE International Conference on Robotics and Automation (ICRA), pp. 3411–3417. IEEE, Singapore (2017)

5. Casalino, A., Massarenti, N., Zanchettin, A.M., Rocco, P.: Predicting the human behaviour in human-robot co-assemblies: an approach based on suffix trees. In: 2020 IEEE/RSJ International Conference on Intelligent Robots and Systems (IROS), pp. 11108–11114. IEEE, Las Vegas, NV, USA (2020)
6. Lentini, G., Grioli, G., Catalano, M.G. Bicchi, A.: Robot programming without coding. In: 2020 IEEE International Conference on Robotics and Automation (ICRA), pp. 7576–7582. IEEE, Paris, France (2020)
7. Mronga, D., Kirchner, F.: Learning context-adaptive task constraints for robotic manipulation. Rob. Auton. Syst. **141**, 103779 (2021)
8. Sasabuchi, K., Wake, N., Ikeuchi, K.: Task-oriented motion mapping on robots of various configuration using body role division. IEEE Rob. Autom. Lett. **6**(2), 413–420 (2021)
9. Kim, H., Ohmura, Y., Kuniyoshi, Y.: Transformer-based deep imitation learning for dual-arm robot manipulation. In: 2021 IEEE/RSJ International Conference on Intelligent Robots and Systems (IROS), pp. 8965–8972. IEEE, Prague, Czech Republic (2021)
10. Ye, D., Liu, Z., Sun, M., Shi, B., Zhao, P.: Mastering complex control in moba games with deep reinforcement learning. In: Proceedings of the AAAI Conference on Artificial Intelligence, pp. 6672–6679 (2020)
11. Sallab, A.E.L., Abdou, M., Perot, E., Yogamani, S.: Deep reinforcement learning framework for autonomous driving. Elect. Imaging **29**(19), 70–76 (2017)
12. Duan, Y., Chen, X., Houthooft, R., Schulman, J., Abbeel, P.: Benchmarking deep reinforcement learning for continuous control. In: International Conference on machine learning, pp. 1329–1338. PMLR, New York, USA (2016)
13. Cuayáhuitl, H., Yu, S., Williamson, A., Carse, J.: Scaling up deep reinforcement learning for multi-domain dialogue systems. In: 2017 International Joint Conference on Neural Networks (IJCNN), pp. 3339–3346. IEEE, Anchorage, AK, USA (2017)
14. Lillicrap, T.P: Continuous control with deep reinforcement learning. arXiv preprint arXiv:1509.02971 (2015)
15. Schulman, J., Wolski, F., Dhariwal, P., Radford, A., Klimov, O.: Proximal policy optimization algorithms. arXiv preprint arXiv:1707.06347 (2017)
16. Mnih, V., et al: Asynchronous methods for deep reinforcement learning. In: International Conference on Machine Learning, pp. 1928–1937. PMLR, New York, USA (2016)
17. Haarnoja, T., Zhou, A., Abbeel, P., Levine, S.: Soft actor-critic: off-policy maximum entropy eep reinforcement learning with a stochastic actor. In: International Conference on Machine Learning, pp. 1861–1870. PMLR, New York, USA (2018)

Study on the Impact Performance of the Joint Cycloid Reducer for Legged Robots

Shuting Ji[✉], Tengyue Wei, and Jialin Li

Faculty of Materials and Manufacturing, Beijing University of Technology, Beijing 100124,
China
jishuting@bjut.edu.cn

Abstract. To enhance the running and jumping abilities of legged robots in
unstructured environments, joint actuators must have high impact resistance for
high torque transmission. A cycloid-pin gear transmission is applied in joint actuators to resist the instantaneous impact of the legged robots. In order to study
the impact performance of the transmission, the impact force model of the gear
meshing pair was proposed based on H-C contact collision model. The transient
dynamics module in Ansys Workbench was used to verify the correctness of the
meshing impact model. Then the influence of eccentricity and equidistance modification on meshing impact forces were studied. It is shown that eccentricity is
the main parameter affecting the impact performance of gear meshing. The result
provides a design method to enhance the impact resistance of cycloidal reducer,
and is of great significance for improving the fast motion ability of legged robots.

Keywords: Legged Robots · Cycloid-pin Gear Transmission · Impact Force ·
Transient Dynamics

1 Introduction

Legged robots can be widely applied in various environments such as outer space exploration, military reconnaissance, war conflicts, and disaster rescue. The joint actuator,
core module of legged robot, directly determines the robot's motion balance, stability,
and anti-interference ability. When Cheetah runs [1], the joint actuator needs to withstand an impact torque several times the rated torque in a very short period of time, as
shown in Fig. 1. The improvement of impact resistance of joint actuators can significantly enhance the adaptability and dynamic response ability of legged mobile robots in
unstructured environments [2, 3].

Harmonic transmission, cycloid transmission and involute planetary transmission are
three commonly used transmissions for legged robots' joint. Involute planetary transmission has the advantages of high transmission efficiency, strong backdrivability, and
easy manufacture. However, this type of reducer has a large transmission backlash and is
prone to vibration during high-speed running of legged robots. Harmonic transmission
has the advantages of smooth transmission, compact structure and high transmission
accuracy, but with high transmission ratio and low backdrivability. This type of reducer

H. Yang et al. (Eds.): ICIRA 2023, LNAI 14270, pp. 464–475, 2023.
https://doi.org/10.1007/978-981-99-6492-5_40

has insufficient impact resistance and is prone to damage during the running and jumping of legged robots. The cycloid transmission has a compact structure, high load-bearing capacity, high stiffness, and strong impact resistance, making it more suitable for legged robots operating in unstructured environments. In recent years, it has gradually been applied to legged robots, such as the hip and knee joints of Cassie robots.

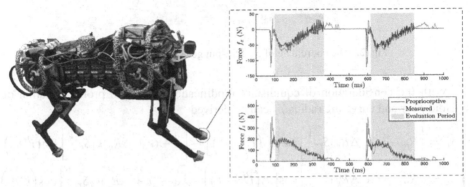

Fig. 1. Wave force on legs and feet under impact [1].

Some scholars have conducted research on the overall impact resistance of legged robots, such as MIT Cheetah's impact tests and the Impact Mitigation Factor (IMF) study [1, 4]. Some scholars have designed structures to resist impact force. Lee [5] proposed a subcarrier structure to improve the impact resistance of cycloid reducer during the motion of legged robots. Some scholars have studied the meshing impact forces of gear reducer. He [6] used a new calculation method based on the slice method to determine the meshing impact of helical gears; Ding [7] used the semi-finite element method to predict dynamic loading meshing impact and developed a new sensitive misalignment-based optimization to improve dynamic meshing impact.

From the above literature, researches on the impact characteristics of legged robots and involute gears have made certain progress. However, further research is needed on the impact resistance of cycloidal reducer. Based on H-C contact collision model, a meshing impact force model of cycloid-pin gear transmission is proposed. Then, the effects of eccentricity and equidistant modification are studied. It provides a theoretical method for studying meshing impact force of cycloid reducer, and improving the impact resistance capacity of the legged robot joints.

2 The Transmission Principle of Cycloid-pin Gear

The cycloid-pin gear transmission system is shown in Fig. 2. The pin teeth are numbered in clockwise from Pin 1. The systems $X_p O_p Y_p$ and $X_c O_c Y_c$ are fixed with the distribution circle of the pin teeth and cycloid gear, respectively. In the working process, the cycloid gear rotates around O_p with the angle θ_p, and rotates around O_c with the angle θ_c, simultaneously. The relationship, $\theta_c = \theta_p / z_c$, needs to be satisfied. Therefore, the gear transmission ratio is $i^H = z_p / z_c$.

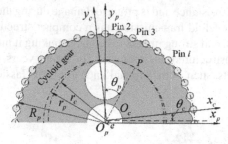

Fig. 2. The coordinate of cycloid-pin gear transmission system.

With the consideration of equidistant modification, the tooth profile equation of cycloid gear and curvature radius ρ_c can be derived:

$$\begin{cases} x_c = \left[R_p - (r + \Delta R_g)S_r^{-\frac{1}{2}}\right]\sin\left[\theta_p\left(i^H - 1\right)\right] - \left[e - (r + \Delta R_g)k_1 S_r^{-\frac{1}{2}}\right]\sin\left(i^H\theta_p\right) \\ y_c = \left[R_p - (r + \Delta R_g)S_r^{-\frac{1}{2}}\right]\cos\left[\theta_p\left(i^H - 1\right)\right] - \left[e - (r + \Delta R_g)k_1 S_r^{-\frac{1}{2}}\right]\cos\left(i^H\theta_p\right) \end{cases}$$

(1)

$$\rho_c = \frac{R_p(S_r)^{3/2}}{k_1(z_p + 1)\cos\theta_p - (1 + z_p k_1^2)} + (r + \Delta R_g) \tag{2}$$

where ΔR_g is equidistant modification; e is eccentricity; r_p is pitch circle radius of the pin tooth; r_c is the pitch circle radius of the cycloid gear; P is pitch point; r is the radius of pin gear; R_p is the distribution circle radius of pin gear; $k_1 = ez_p/R_p$, which is short-range coefficient; $S_r = k_1^2 + 1 - 2k_1\cos\theta_p$.

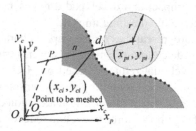

Fig. 3. The modified tooth profile clearance of cycloid-pin gear.

Due to the tooth side clearance caused by tooth profile modification and loading deformation of gear meshing pairs, meshing point of cycloid gear deviates from the theoretical one, and the relative meshing velocity is generated along the meshing normal line. When the modified cycloid gear overcomes the tooth side clearance, contact collision happens, causing the instantaneous meshing impact. Figure 3 shows the tooth side clearance d_i, which can be expressed as:

$$d_i = \sqrt{(x_{pi} - x_{ci})^2 + (y_{pi} - y_{ci})^2} - r \tag{3}$$

where (x_{ci}, y_{ci}) is the coordinates of meshing point on cycloid gear, and (x_{pi}, y_{pi}) is the geometric center coordinates of the ith pin tooth.

3   Meshing Impact Force

According to the collision theory of classical mechanics, the elastic collision process is divided into two phases, compression phase and restitution phase. The compression displacement is the main part of the total collision displacement, thus other deformation can be ignored. The meshing impact of cycloid-pin gear is equivalent to the nonlinear contact collision of two cylinders along the common normal line. The maximum force of contact collision is the maximum meshing impact force.

Based on H-C contact collision model [8], a mechanical model for the meshing impact of cycloid-pin gear transmission can be expressed as:

$$F = F_N + \chi \delta^n \dot{\delta} \tag{4}$$

where χ is the hysteresis damping factor; δ is the collision deformation; $\dot{\delta}$ is the relative collision velocity.

3.1   Contact Force

After impact of meshing gears, small contact deformation occurs between cycloid gear and pin tooth. As shown in Fig. 4, the width of the contact area is $2b$, and the length is L. It is assumed that the elastic modulus and Poisson's ratio of cycloid gear and pin gear are the same ($E_1 = E_2 = E$, $\mu_1 = \mu_2 = \mu$). According to the Hertz formula and the radius of curvature formula of the cycloid gear, it can be simplified as:

$$b = \sqrt{\frac{8F_N \rho^*(1 - \mu^2)}{\pi L E}} \tag{5}$$

where ρ^* is comprehensive radius of curvature; F_N is contact collision force between the cycloid gear and pin gear.

According to the geometric relationship of Fig. 4, the cycloid deformation δ_c can be obtained:

$$\delta_c = |\rho_c| \left(1 - \sqrt{1 - \left(\frac{b}{\rho_c}\right)^2} \right) \tag{6}$$

It is assumed that $x = (b/\rho_c)^2$, δ_c can be expressed as:

$$\delta_c = f(x) = f(0) + f'(0)x + \frac{f^2(0)}{2}x^2 \ldots + \frac{f^n(0)}{n!}x^n + Rn(x) \approx \frac{b^2}{2|\rho_c|} \tag{7}$$

Combined with Eqs. (5)–(7), the contact collision force F_N can be written as:

$$F_N = \frac{\pi L E \rho_c \delta_c}{4\rho^*(1 - \mu^2)} \tag{8}$$

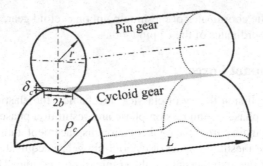

Fig. 4. The equivalent contact model of cycloid-pin gear.

3.2 Damping Force

The impact collision phases between the cycloid gear and the pin gear are shown in Fig. 5. $V_1^{(-)}$, $V_1^{(+)}$ are the velocities of cycloid gear at the initial and separation time, respectively; $V_2^{(-)}$, $V_2^{(+)}$ are the velocities of pin gear at the initial and separation time, respectively. At the end of compression phase, cycloid gear and pin gear move together at the common instantaneous velocity $V_{12}^{\max}$.

According to the conservation of momentum and energy and Newton's coefficient of restitution c_r in the process of collision, the dissipated energy ΔE_c [9] caused by the damping force during compression phase can be expressed as:

$$\Delta E_c = \int_0^{\delta_{c\,\max}} \chi \delta_c^n \dot{\delta}^{(-)} \sqrt{1 - (\frac{\delta_c}{\delta_{c\,\max}})^2} d\delta_c \approx \frac{2}{n+2} \chi \dot{\delta}_c^{(-)} \delta_{c\,\max}^{n+1} \tag{9}$$

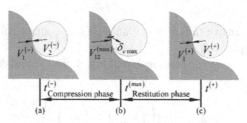

Fig. 5. The impact between the cycloid gear and pin gear: (a) Beginning of the compression phase; (b) Maximum compression deformation; (c) Ending of the restitution phase.

The initial kinetic energy $T^{(-)}$ of meshing gear pair is transformed into the kinetic energy T^s, elastic strain energy $U^{\max}$, and the dissipated energy ΔE_c. Thus, the energy conservation between the start and end of the compression phase can be expressed as follows:

$$T^{(-)} = T^s + U^{\max} + \Delta E_c \tag{10}$$

In order to analyze the influence factors of contact force, the contact force between cycloid gear and pin gear can be expressed as:

$$F_N = \frac{\pi LE}{4(1 - \mu^2)} S \tag{11}$$

where S is the nonlinear deformation coefficient:

$$S = \frac{\rho_c \delta_c}{\rho^*(1 - \mu^2)} \tag{12}$$

According to the Eqs. (2) and (12), the contact force of cycloid-pin gear is related to the cycloid deformation δ_c, eccentricity e and equidistance modification ΔR_g. The multivariate nonlinear fitting of S can be derived as:

$$S = f(e, \Delta R_g) \delta_c^{g(e, \Delta R_g)} \tag{13}$$

where $n = g(e, \Delta R_g)$, which is deformation contribution coefficient n of the damping force.

The maximum potential energy U^{max} can be expressed as:

$$U^{max} = \int_0^{\delta_{max}} F_N d\delta = \frac{\pi LEf(e, \Delta R_g)\delta_{c\,max}^{n+1}}{8(1 - \mu^2)(g(e, \Delta R_g) + 1)} \tag{14}$$

The momentum balance from instants $t^{(-)}$ to $t^{(max)}$ is:

$$m_1 v_1^{(-)} + m_2 v_2^{(-)} = (m_1 + m_2) v_{12}^{max} \tag{15}$$

When the dissipated energy ΔE_c is taken into account, the Eq. (10) can be rewritten as:

$$\frac{1}{2} m_1 [V_1^{(-)}]^2 + \frac{1}{2} m_2 [V_2^{(-)}]^2 = U^{max} + \Delta E_c + \frac{1}{2}(m_1 + m_2)[V_{12}^{(max)}] \tag{16}$$

Combined with the Eqs. (9), (14), (15), and (16), χ can be expressed as:

$$\chi = \frac{\pi LE(g(e, \Delta R_g) + 2)(1 - c_r)f(e, \Delta R_g)}{8(1 - \mu^2)(g(e, \Delta R_g) + 1)\dot{\delta}_c^{(-)}} \tag{17}$$

Combined Eqs. (4) and (17), the impact force model can be written as:

$$F = F_N + \frac{\pi LE(g(e, \Delta R_g) + 2)(1 - c_r)f(e, \Delta R_g)}{8(1 - \mu^2)(g(e, \Delta R_g) + 1)\dot{\delta}_c^{(-)}} \delta_c^{g(a, \Delta R_g)} \dot{\delta}_c \tag{18}$$

According to Hertz collision dynamics theory, the loss of kinetic energy of the elastic body is consumed by the impact force. The relationship among kinetic energy loss, deformation and impact force can be written as:

$$\frac{1}{2} \frac{m_1 m_2}{m_1 + m_2} (\dot{\delta}_{ct}^2 - \dot{\delta}_{c(t+1)}^2) = \frac{1}{2}(F_t + F_{t+1})(\delta_{ct} - \delta_{c(t+1)}) \tag{19}$$

where δ_{ct} is the deformation of cycloid gear, $\dot{\delta}_{ct}$ is the relative meshing velocity of cycloid-pin transmission and F_t is the impact force of cycloid gear at time t.

The Eq. (19) can be represented as the monodic quadratic equation about $\dot{\delta}_{c(t+1)}$, hence:

$$A\dot{\delta}^2_{c(t+1)} + B\dot{\delta}_{c(t+1)} + C = 0 \tag{20}$$

$$\dot{\delta}_{c(t+1)} = \frac{-B - \sqrt{B^2 - 4AC}}{2A} \tag{21}$$

where $A = m;;$

$B = \frac{(n+2)(1-c_r)f(e,\Delta R_g)\pi LE}{3(1-\mu^2)(g(e,\Delta R_g)+1)c_r\dot{\delta}_c^{(-)}}\delta_c^{g(e,\Delta R_g)}(\delta_{c(t+1)} - \delta_{ct});$

$C = -m\dot{\delta}_{c(t+1)}+$

$(\delta_{c(t+1)} - \delta_{ct})\Big[F_t + F_{t+1}+ \frac{(g(e,\Delta R_g)+2)(1-c_r)f(e,\Delta R_g)\pi LE}{3(1-\mu^2)(g(e,\Delta R_g)+1)c_r\dot{\delta}_c^{(-)}}\delta_{ct}^{g(e,\Delta R_g)}\dot{\delta}_{c(t+1)}\Big].$

The calculation progress started from the initial point of the impact, and the iterative step size is $\delta_{c(t+1)} - \delta_{ct} = 0.001$ mm. Substituted the initial impact velocity $\dot{\delta}_{c0}$ [10] and initial compression deformation δ_{c0} into Eq. (21), the maximum deformation of the cycloid gear δ_{cmax} and the maximum impact force F_{max} can be obtained from Eq. (20).

3.3 Impact Force

Taking a typical cycloid-pin gear transmission as an example, the variation of initial clearance and contact deformation of cycloid-pin pair with the pin tooth number is shown in Fig. 6. The meshing pair corresponding to the 6th pin gear is the initial meshing pair as is shown in Fig. 6(a), After revolution of 1×10^{-3} s in no-load condition, meshing pair corresponding to the 7th pin tooth start to mesh as shown in Fig. 6(b).

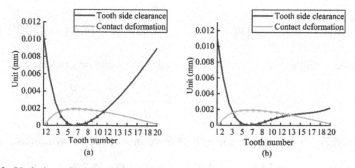

Fig. 6. Variation of initial clearance and contact deformation with pin tooth number.

It is assumed that the design range of eccentricity e is 0.99–1.01 mm, and the range of equidistant modification is 0.01–0.1 mm. The contact deformation δ_c varies from 0 to 0.002 mm. After substituting parameters into the Eq. (13), the fitting formula of S can be obtained as follows:

$$S = (4.8055e + 16.0641\Delta R_g)\delta_c^{(0.9356e+0.2911\Delta R_g)} \tag{22}$$

The fitting accuracy parameters is shown in Table 1, indicating that the fitting function has a good fitting effect.

Table 1. The relevant data of fitting.

	SSE	R-square	RMSE
Value	3.54×10^{-4}	0.9959	0.08

By substituting the obtained fitting coefficient into Eq. (18), the formula of the meshing impact force of the 7th meshing pairs is obtained, the variation of the meshing impact force is shown in Fig. 7. After 6.95×10^{-6} s, the tooth side clearance of gear pair becomes 0, and the impact force rapidly increases to 128.6 N.

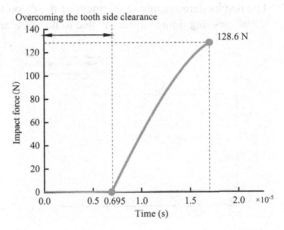

Fig. 7. Variation of the meshing impact force with time.

4 Simulation of Meshing Impact Force

4.1 Finite Element Analysis of Cycloid-Pin Gear Transmission

3D model of cycloid-pin gear is generated in Creo and imported into the transient structural module in Ansys Workbench. The pin gear is fixed, and the cycloid gear rotates around its central axis for 1 ms. The conditions set are shown in Fig. 8.

4.2 Analysis of Simulation Results

The simulation and theoretical results of the meshing impact force corresponding to 7th pin gear are shown in Fig. 9. Due to the limitations of simulation iteration steps, in order to visually observe the changes in cycloidal gear impact force and obtain the maximum

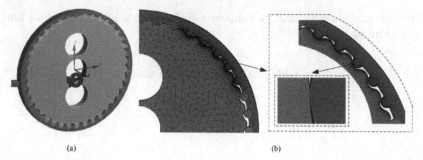

(a)   (b)

Fig. 8. Analysis of simulation model: (a) The boundary condition; (b) Triangular mesh of cycloidal-pin.

accuracy of the simulation curve, Gaussian fitting method is used for the simulation data. The meshing impact force of simulation is smaller than the theoretical results, and the difference is 4.8%. The results demonstrate correctness of the theoretical impact force model. The time of initial meshing time is different, due to the different initial position.

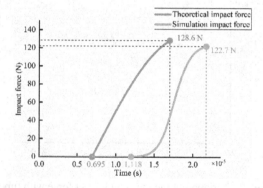

Fig. 9. The simulation and theoretical results of impact force varying with time.

5 Influence of Design Parameters on Impact Force

5.1 Influence of Eccentricity e on Meshing Impact Force

As shown in Fig. 10, the design range of eccentricity e is 0.99–1.01 mm. It shows that, the smaller the e is, the greater the meshing impact force is. The tooth side clearance d_i increases with the increase of e, thus the initial meshing time will be slightly longer.

5.2 Influence of Equidistance Modification ΔR_g on Meshing Impact Force

As shown in Fig. 11, the design range of ΔR_g is 0.01–0.1 mm. It shows that, the smaller the ΔR_g is, the greater the impact force is. The tooth side clearance d_i increases with the increase of ΔR_g, thus the initial meshing time will be increased.

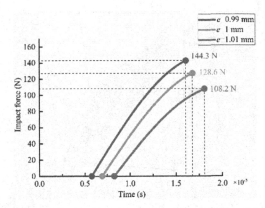

Fig. 10. The influence of e on the meshing impact force.

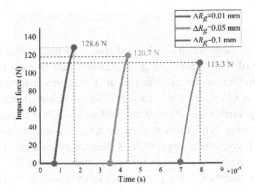

Fig. 11. The influence of ΔR_g on the meshing impact force.

5.3 Influence of Multivariable

The combined influence of eccentricity e and equidistance modification ΔR_g on the impact force is shown in Fig. 12. By changing the eccentricity and equidistance modification of the same unit, the meshing impact force changes more with the change of eccentricity. The influence of e on the meshing impact force is greater than that of ΔR_g. The influence of ΔR_g on the initial meshing is greater than that of e.

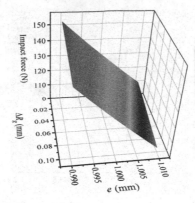

Fig. 12. The influence of ΔR_g and e on the meshing impact force.

6 Conclusions

To improve the fast running ability of legged robots in unstructured environments, the impact performance of the cycloid-pin gear meshing pair in joint reducer was studied. A meshing impact model of the cycloid-pin gear transmission mechanism was established based on the H-C impact force model. The variation of impact force with time was revealed through numerical algorithms, and was verified through Ansys finite element transient dynamics. The influence of eccentricity and tooth profile parameters on meshing impact force was analyzed. It is demonstrated that meshing impact force decrease with the increase of eccentricity and equidistant modification. The result is important for improvement of impact resistance of cycloid-pin transmission. It also has great significance to improving the fast running ability of legged robots.

Acknowledgment. This research is supported by the National Natural Science Foundation of China (Grant No. 51905009) and Key R&D Projects in Hebei Province of China (Grant No. 20311802D).

References

1. Wensing, P.M., Wang, A., Seok, S., Otten, D., Lang, J., Kim, S.: Proprioceptive actuator design in the MIT cheetah: impact mitigation and high-bandwidth physical interaction for dynamic legged robots. IEEE Trans. Robot. **33**(3), 509–522 (2017)
2. Hwangbo, J., Lee, J., Dosovitskiy, A.: Learning agile and dynamic motor skills for legged robots. Sci. Robot. **4**(26) (2019)
3. Castelli, K., Gavioli, M., Dmytriyev, Y., et al.: Mechanical design and development of a continuous rotational variable stiffness actuator. In: 2021 3rd International Congress on Human-Computer Interaction, Optimization and Robotic Applications (HORA), pp. 1–6 (2021)
4. Seok, S., Wang, A., Otten, D.: Actuator design for high force proprioceptive control in fast legged locomotion. In: Proceedings of the. IEEE/RSJ International Conference on Intelligent Robots and Systems. Pp. 1970–1975 (2012)

5. Lee, K., Hong, S., Oh, J.-H.: Development of a lightweight and high-efficiency compact cycloidal reducer for legged robots. Int. J. Precis. Eng. Manuf. **21**(3), 415–425 (2019). https://doi.org/10.1007/s12541-019-00215-9
6. He, Z., Zhang, T., Lin, T.: Novel mathematical modelling method for meshing impact of helical gear. Mech. Mach. Theory **152**, 103949 (2020)
7. Ding, H., Rong, S., Rong, K.: Sensitive misalignment-based dynamic loaded meshing impact diagnosis mechanism for aviation spiral bevel gear transmission. Expert Syst. Appl. **200**, 116969 (2022)
8. Lankarani, H.M., Nikravesh, P.E.: A contact force model with hysteresis damping for impact analysis of multibody systems. J. Mech. Des. **112**(3), 369–376 (1990)
9. Flores, P., Machado, M., Silva, M.T.: On the continuous contact force models for soft materials in multibody dynamics. Multibody Syst. Dyn. **25**(3), 357–375 (2011)
10. Ji, S.T., Li, J.L., Zhang, Y.M.: Study on off-line meshing-in impact characteristics of cycloid-pin gear drive mechanism of RV reducer. J. Xi'an Jiaotong Univ. **09**, 1–11 (2023)

An Optimal Configuration Solution of 8-DOF Redundant Manipulator for Flying Ball

Ziwu Ren[✉][iD], Zhongyuan Wang, Zibo Guo, and Licheng Fan[iD]

School of Mechanical and Electrical Engineering, Soochow University,
Suzhou 215131, China
zwren@suda.edu.cn

Abstract. A method that can obtain an optimal hitting configuration of the 8-DOF manipulator for flying ball is proposed. In this method, the position and orientation of the end-effector are firstly determined, and an analytic inverse kinematic solution of the manipulator is derived. Then, an 'away limitation level' of the manipulator constituted the objective function, and a teaching-learning-based optimization (TLBO) algorithm is used to optimize the redundant parameters. This method can solve the hitting configuration optimum problem of the humanoid manipulator according to the center position and its Cartesian velocity direction of the end-effector. Simulation results demonstrate the effectiveness of this method.

Keywords: 8-DOF Humanoid Manipulator · Inverse kinematics · Geometrical Method · Teaching-learning-based Optimization

1 Introduction

The joint structure of the 7-DOF humanoid manipulator is in accord with the physiological characteristics of human arm, so it can move flexibly [1,2]. However, if the waist joint of the humanoid robot can work with auxiliary actions to constitute an 8-DOF redundant manipulator during the operation process, it will not only expand the work space of the robotic system, but also alleviate the performance requirement of the 7-DOF manipulator.

When executing the motion for a flying ball, there are innumerable configurations to meet the requirement of the same target for the 8-DOF manipulator. Due to the connecting link structure and figuration design, each joint has its own physical constraint. Thus, people expect that each joint position can be away from its physical limitation as far as possible, which can not only make the manipulator place in a natural configuration posture, but also leave as much joint space as possible to avoid the physical constraints for the trajectory planning.

This work was supported by Jiangsu (Industry Foresight and Key Core Technology) Key Research and Development Project under grant No. BE2022137.

The hitting configuration optimum problem of the redundant manipulator for flying ball can be transformed into an equivalent minimization problem, which can be solved through the numerical optimization method. Currently there are many various methods to solve the inverse kinematics problem of the manipulator, including: (1) algebraic numerical methods, such as Jacobian pseudo-inverse method [3], gradient projection method [4], and weighted least-norm method [5]. The algebraic numerical methods usually have cumulate errors, which lead to the inaccurate control of the manipulator. (2) numerical iteration methods, such as Newton-Raphson method [6], neural networks [7], and genetic algorithms [8]. For the numerical iterative methods, the optimal result is obtained in the solution space by iteration, however, it takes a long time to solve this problem and the obtained solution is just an approximate solution. (3) geometrical methods [9, 10]. For the geometrical methods, the obtained solution has high accuracy with little time-consuming, but they heavily rely on the particular geometric features and are lack of universality [11, 12]. Generally speaking, for the inverse kinematics problem of the redundant manipulator, it is necessary to define a certain constraint criterion to select an appropriate inverse solution while satisfying the desired end-effector pose [13, 14].

In order to make the joint positions of the hitting configuration of manipulator away from the limitation as much as possible, a novel method is developed to solve the optimal hitting configuration problem of an 8-DOF humanoid manipulator for flying ball in this paper. According to the center position and the Cartesian velocity direction of the end-effector tool, an analytic inverse kinematic solution of the 8-DOF manipulator is derived by the geometrical method. Then teaching-learning-based optimization algorithm is adopted to determine the redundant parameters therein, where an 'away limitation level' of the redundant manipulator is used as the fitness function. Simulation results demonstrates that this method is more efficient because of the fewer optimization parameters.

2   Mechanical Joint Model and Forward Kinematics Analysis of the 8-DOF Manipulator

Consider the actual physical model (left) and the joint structure model (right) of the 8-DOF manipulator shown in Fig. 1, where the end-effector tool is a racket, a_0 is the rotation direction of waist joint, and $a_1 \sim a_7$ are respectively the rotation directions of the shoulder, elbow, and wrist joint, $\sum_W$ is the world coordinate frame, D is the shoulder breadth, L_1 is the length from the shoulder center to the elbow center, L_2 is the length from the elbow center to the wrist center, and L_3 is the length from the wrist center to the racket center. According to the Fig. 1, the unit vectors of eight joint axes directions $a_0 \sim a_7$ are respectively described as follows:

$$\begin{cases} a_0 = (0,0,1) & a_1 = (0,1,0) \\ a_2 = (1,0,0) & a_3 = (0,0,1) \\ a_4 = (1,0,0) & a_5 = (0,0,1) \\ a_6 = (1,0,0) & a_7 = (0,1,0) \end{cases} \tag{1}$$

 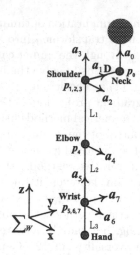

Fig. 1. Actual physical model(left) and joint structure model (right) of the 8-DOF manipulator

Table 1. Joint position range of the 8-DOF manipulator (°)

Range	q_0	q_1	q_2	q_3	q_4	q_5	q_6	q_7
Upper	−30	−126	−133	-180	0	−180	−80	−42
Lower	30	90	15	90	120	180	80	85

According to the designed physical model, Table 1 shows the position range of each joint of the 8-DOF manipulator. Define the joint variables of the 8-DOF manipulator as an 8×1 vector, i.e., $q = (q_0, q_1, q_2, q_3, q_4, q_5, q_6, q_7)^T$. Then the position and orientation (p_j, R_j) of each connecting rod can be obtained by [6]:

$$\begin{cases} p_j = p_i + R_i b_j \\ R_j = R_i R_{a_j}(q_j) \end{cases} \tag{2}$$

where p_i and R_i are respectively the absolute position and orientation of the mother connecting rod in world coordinate frame, a_j and b_j are respectively the unit vectors of axis directions and the origin coordinate in the coordinate frame of mother connecting rod, $R_{a_j}(q_j)$ is the rotation matrix when the axis vector a_j turns around q_j radians, in which the rotation matrix can be computed by the Rodrigues formula [6], and the origin coordinate b_j $(j = 1, 2, \cdots, 8)$ in the coordinate frame of mother connecting rod are given by:

$$\begin{cases} b_1 = (0, -D, 0)^T & b_2 = (0, 0, 0)^T \\ b_3 = (0, 0, 0)^T & b_4 = (0, 0, -L_1)^T \\ b_5 = (0, 0, -L_2)^T & b_6 = (0, 0, 0)^T \\ b_7 = (0, 0, 0)^T & b_8 = (0, 0, -L_3)^T \end{cases} \tag{3}$$

3   Analytic Inverse Kinematic Solution of 8-DOF Redundant Manipulator

To obtain an optimal hitting configuration of this 8-DOF manipulator for flying ball, the position and orientation of the end-effector(racket) should be firstly determined according to the end-effector's center and its Cartesian velocity.

3.1   Position and Orientation Determination of the End-Effector

Suppose that the direction of the Cartesian velocity $V = [V_x, V_y, V_z]^T$ is perpendicular to the racket back at the hitting moment. As shown in Fig. 2, for the Cartesian velocity V of the racket, the orientation R_8 of the racket can be obtained according to its transformation relationship between the local coordinate frame $\sum_R$ and the world coordinate $\sum_W$.

$$\begin{bmatrix} V_x/\|V\| \\ V_y/\|V\| \\ V_z/\|V\| \end{bmatrix} = R_z(\varphi)R_y(\gamma)R_x(\phi) \cdot \begin{bmatrix} 0 \\ -1 \\ 0 \end{bmatrix} \tag{4}$$

where V is the norm of the Cartesian velocity, ϕ, γ and φ are the roll, pitch and yaw angle of the racket's rotation around the x, y and z axis respectively, $s_\phi = \sin(\phi)$ and $c_\phi = \cos(\phi)$ are respectively the brief descriptions of the roll angle ϕ, and other angle abbreviations have the similar meaning. Let the yaw angle φ around the z axis be the redundant attitude angle of the racket orientation R_8, then from (4) the other two attitude angles can be derived by [15]:

$$\begin{cases} \phi = \cos^{-1}\left(\cos\left(\varphi\right) \cdot \left(-V_y/\|V\|\right) - \sin\left(\varphi\right) \cdot \left(-V_x/\|V\|\right)\right) \\ \gamma = \mathrm{atan2}\left(\cos\left(\varphi\right) \cdot \left(\frac{-V_x}{\|V\|}\right) + \sin\left(\varphi\right) \cdot \left(\frac{-V_y}{\|V\|}\right), \left(\frac{-V_z}{\|V\|}\right)\right) \end{cases} \tag{5}$$

Similarly, when the direction of the Cartesian velocity V is perpendicular to the racket front, the orientation R_8 of the racket can be determined by:

$$\begin{bmatrix} V_x/\|V\| \\ V_y/\|V\| \\ V_z/\|V\| \end{bmatrix} = R_z(\varphi)R_y(\gamma)R_x(\phi) \cdot \begin{bmatrix} 0 \\ 1 \\ 0 \end{bmatrix} \tag{6}$$

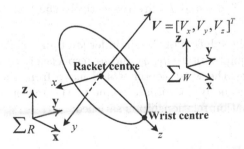

Fig. 2. Diagram of the racket velocity in different coordinate

Based on the redundant angle φ, the two attitude angles ϕ and γ of the racket orientation R_8 can also be calculated by [15]:

$$
\begin{cases}
\phi = \cos^{-1} \left(\cos(\varphi) \cdot (V_y/\|V\|) - \sin(\varphi) \cdot (V_x/\|V\|) \right) \\
\gamma = \mathrm{atan2} \left(\cos(\varphi) \cdot \left(\frac{V_z}{\|V\|} \right) + \sin(\varphi) \cdot \left(\frac{V_y}{\|V\|} \right), \left(\frac{V_z}{\|V\|} \right) \right)
\end{cases}
\tag{7}
$$

From the above, it can be concluded that the racket orientation R_8 can be calculated according to the Cartesian velocity when given the yaw angle φ. As such, when the racket position and orientation (P_8, R_8) are known, the position and orientation (p_7, R_7) of the end-effector can be determined by:

$$
\begin{aligned}
R_7 &= R_8 \\
p_7 &= P_8 - R_7 \cdot (0 \quad 0 \quad -L_3)^T
\end{aligned}
\tag{8}
$$

where L_3 is the length from the wrist center to the racket center.

3.2   Geometric Expression of Inverse Kinematic Solution

Consider the joint structure model of the 8-DOF manipulator shown in Fig. 1, if the waist joint angle q_0 is assumed to be known, we can calculate the elbow joint angle firstly. If the desired position and orientation of the end-effector is given by (p_7, R_7), and the position and orientation of the body (the neck) is (p_0, R_0), then according to (2) the shoulder position can be given by

$$
p_1 = p_0 + R_0 \begin{pmatrix} 0 \\ -D \\ 0 \end{pmatrix}
\tag{9}
$$

where D is the shoulder width, and the orientation of the neck is $R_0 = R_z(q_0)$.

As such, the vector from the should center to the wrist center $\overrightarrow{p_1 p_7}$ in the body coordinate frame can be given by $r = R_0^T(p_7 - p_1) = (r_x, r_y, r_z)^T$. Then according to the triangle which is defined by the three points, that is, shoulder, elbow and wrist, the elbow joint angle q_4 can be determined by

$$
q_4 = \pi - \arccos \left(\frac{L_1^2 + L_2^2 - C^2}{2L_1 \cdot L_2} \right)
\tag{10}
$$

where the distance between the shoulder center and the wrist center is $C = \|r\| = \sqrt{r_x^2 + r_y^2 + r_z^2}$, L_1 and L_2 are respectively the length of the upper arm and the lower arm.

Next, consider the solution of the shoulder joint angles. As is shown in Fig. 3, when the shoulder joints rotate q_1, q_2 and q_3 respectively around the axis directions a_1, a_2 and a_3, the wrist center would move from the initial point J in the yoz plane of the body coordinate frame to the target point G. Thus, the following transformation relationship is satisfied:

$$
R_{a_1}(q_1) R_{a_2}(q_2) R_{a_3}(q_3) \begin{pmatrix} 0 \\ y_1 \\ z_1 \end{pmatrix} = \begin{pmatrix} r_x \\ r_y \\ r_z \end{pmatrix}
\tag{11}
$$

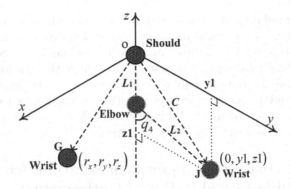

Fig. 3. Calculation diagram of the should joint angles

where $y_1 = L_2 \cdot \sin q_4$ and $z_1 = -\sqrt{C^2 - (L_2 \cdot \sin q_4)^2}$ are the components of the vector r on the yoz plane of the body coordinate frame. Suppose the joint q_3 is used to describe the redundancy of the manipulator, then the results of the joints q_1 and q_2 can be given by

$$q_1 = \text{atan2}\,(-r_z, r_x) \pm \text{atan2}\left(\sqrt{r_x^2 + r_z^2 - (y_1 s_3)^2}, -y_1 s_3\right) \tag{12}$$

$$q_2 = \text{atan2}\,(-z_1, y_1 c_3) \pm \text{atan2}\left(\sqrt{(y_1 c_3)^2 + z_1^2 - r_y^2}, r_y\right) \tag{13}$$

where the angle abbreviations $s_3 = \sin(q_3)$, $c_3 = \cos(q_3)$.

Finally, determine the solution of the wrist joints. According to the rotation matrix relation between the connecting links, the following constraint is satisfied:

$$\boldsymbol{R}_{a_5}(q_5)\boldsymbol{R}_{a_6}(q_6)\boldsymbol{R}_{a_7}(q_7) = \boldsymbol{R}_{a_4}^{-1}(q_4)\boldsymbol{R}_{a_3}^{-1}(q_3)\boldsymbol{R}_{a_2}^{-1}(q_2)\boldsymbol{R}_{a_1}^{-1}(q_1)\boldsymbol{R}_{a_0}^{-1}(q_0)\boldsymbol{R}_7 \tag{14}$$

substituting the formula (10), (12) and (13) into (14), then the constraint (14) become

$$\begin{pmatrix} c_5 c_7 - s_5 s_6 s_7 & -s_5 c_6 & c_5 s_7 + s_5 s_6 c_7 \\ s_5 c_7 + c_5 s_6 s_7 & c_5 c_6 & s_5 s_7 - c_5 s_6 c_7 \\ -c_6 s_7 & s_6 & c_6 c_7 \end{pmatrix} = \begin{pmatrix} R_{11} & R_{12} & R_{13} \\ R_{21} & R_{22} & R_{23} \\ R_{31} & R_{32} & R_{33} \end{pmatrix} \tag{15}$$

where the abbreviations $s_i = \sin(q_i)$, $c_i = \cos(q_i)(i = 5, 6, 7)$. Comparing the left and right matrix elements of the equal sign in (15), the solutions for q_5, q_6 and q_7 can be derived as follows:

$$q_5 = \text{atan2}\,(-R_{12}, R_{22}) \tag{16}$$

$$q_6 = \text{atan2}\,(R_{32}, -R_{12} s_5 + R_{22} c_5) \tag{17}$$

$$q_7 = \text{atan2}\,(-R_{31}, R_{33}) \tag{18}$$

Hence, it can be seen from the above calculation process that the attitude angle φ, the joint angles q_0 and q_3 are set as the redundant parameters to describe the redundancy of the manipulator. In short, the decision vector of the 8-DOF manipulator for optimal hitting configuration can be represented as $\lambda = (\varphi, q_0, q_3)$. For this 8-DOF manipulator, each joint has its physical constraint due to the mechanical design, thus not all the kinematic solutions are feasible. In order to make the obtained solution far away from the joint limitation, it is necessary to adopt an efficient optimization method to select the optimal redundant parameters to make the manipulator leave as much joint space as possible for the subsequent trajectory planning.

4   Optimal Hitting Configuration Solution Scheme Based on Teaching-Learning-Based Optimization

Teaching-learning-based optimization method(TLBO) [16,17] is a population-based algorithm inspired from the philosophy of teaching and learning. In TLBO, the population is considered as a group of learners, and different design variables are analogous to different subjects offered to learners [18]. The learners' result is analogous to the fitness, and the best solution obtained so far is considered as the teacher. TLBO algorithm achieves performance enhancement through two modes of learning, i.e. teacher phase and learner phase. The mechanism, basic definition and detailed implementation of the TLBO, can be referred to specific literature [16,17].

4.1   Hitting Configuration Optimization Scheme Based on TLBO Algorithm

While searching the optimal hitting configuration of the 8-DOF redundant manipulator for the flying ball, it is necessary to select an optimal combination of the redundant parameters, that is φ, q_0 and q_3, to make the solution far away from its joint limitation as far as possible.

In order to select an optimal hitting configuration of the 8-DOF manipulator, it is necessary to define a fitness function for the TLBO algorithm. Consider the actual physical range of each joint shown in Table 1, the following 'away limitation level' of the manipulator is defined as the minimization fitness function, which represents the extent of the solution away from the joint position limitation.

$$\mu = \max \left[\left| \frac{q_0 - q_0^{\mathrm{mid}}}{(q_0^{\mathrm{max}} - q_0^{\mathrm{min}})/2} \right|, \cdots \left| \frac{q_i - q_i^{\mathrm{mid}}}{(q_i^{\mathrm{max}} - q_i^{\mathrm{min}})/2} \right|, \cdots, \left| \frac{q_7 - q_7^{\mathrm{mid}}}{(q_7^{\mathrm{max}} - q_7^{\mathrm{min}})/2} \right| \right] \quad (19)$$
$$(i = 0, 1, \cdots, 7)$$

where q_i^{min}, q_i^{mid}, and q_i^{max} denote respectively the lower bound, middle value, and the upper bound of the ith joint, μ is the 'away limitation level' index. $\mu > 1$ means that the obtained solution is beyond the joint physical limitation.

According to the above mentioned, the fitness function of the TLBO algorithm can be formulated as following:

$$\min f(\lambda) = \mu \quad (20)$$

where $\boldsymbol{\lambda} = (\varphi, q_0, q_3)$ represents the individual in TLBO. The fitness function value can represent the margin away from the joint position limitation. The smaller the fitness function value, the further away from the joint physical limitation of the manipulator.

5   Simulation and Experiment

For the joint structure model shown in Fig. 1, assuming the shoulder width $D = 0.14$ m, the length from the shoulder to elbow center $L_1 = 0.26$ m, the length from the elbow to wrist center $L_2 = 0.25$ m, and the length from the wrist to racket center $L_3 = 0.14$ m. Suppose the shoulder center is the origin of the world coordinate frame $\sum_W$, the position of the neck is $\boldsymbol{p}_0 = [0.00 \quad 0.14 \quad 0.00]^T$ m. For this 8-DOF redundant manipulator, if the desired position and Cartesian velocity of the racket center are respectively given by:

$$\boldsymbol{p}_8 = [0.25 \quad 0.40 \quad -0.35]^T \text{m} \tag{21}$$

$$\boldsymbol{V} = [V_x, V_y, V_z]^T = [2 \quad 0 \quad 0]^T \text{m/s} \tag{22}$$

Suppose that the Cartesian velocity direction of the racket is perpendicular to its racket back, then the orientation $\boldsymbol{R}_8$ of the racket can be derived, and the analytic inverse solution can be achieved according to the position and orientation of the end-effector.

To select an appropriate hitting configuration of the 8-DOF manipulator, the TLBO algorithm is adopted to determine the decision vector $\boldsymbol{\lambda} = (\varphi, q_0, q_3)$, where the yaw angle is $\varphi \in [-\pi, \pi]$, and the joint variables are $q_0 \in [-\pi/6, \pi/6]$ and $q_3 \in [-\pi, \pi/2]$ respectively according to Table 1. As to the other parameters setting in TLBO, the maximum evolutionary iteration is set as $T=15$, the population size N is set as 30, and the fitness function is shown in (19) and (20). Then after iterative evolution with TLBO algorithm, the optimal result obtained is $\boldsymbol{\lambda}_{\text{opt}} = (\varphi, q_0, q_3)_{\text{opt}} = (0.1871, 0.4203, -0.6279)$ rad. The corresponding fitness function value, i.e., the value of 'away limitation level', is $\mu = 0.8028$, which indicates that each joint angle of the obtained optimal hitting configuration are all within its physical limitation.

Substituting the obtained optimal parameters $(\varphi, q_0, q_3)_{\text{opt}}$ into the geometric expression of each joint, the optimal solution can be calculated as follows:

$$\boldsymbol{q} = [0.4203 \ -0.4328 \ 0.0071 \ -0.6279 \ 0.7953 \ 1.3938 \ 0.3858 \ -0.5145] \text{ rad} \tag{23}$$

Figure 4(a) shows the link configuration diagram of the practical 8-DOF manipulator. The result demonstrates that the position and orientation of the racket center satisfy the requirements of the formulae (21) and (22). In Fig. 4(a) the racket is facing straight ahead, that is, the direction of the racket velocity $\boldsymbol{V}$ is perpendicular to the racket back.

Similarly, if the desired position and Cartesian velocity of the racket center are respectively given by:

$$\boldsymbol{p}_8 = [0.25 \quad -0.40 \quad -0.35]^T \text{m} \tag{24}$$

$$\boldsymbol{V} = [V_x, V_y, V_z]^T = [2 \quad 0 \quad 0]^T \text{m/s} \tag{25}$$

(a) perpendicular to the racket back

(b) perpendicular to the racket front

Fig. 4. Diagram of the link configuration of the 8-DOF manipulator

In this case, the velocity direction of the racket is assumed to be perpendicular to its racket front. Through the same process, the optimal variables $(\varphi, q_0, q_3)_{opt} = (1.8537, 0.3715, -2.8219)$ rad can be obtained. The optimal solution can also be computed by

$$q = \begin{bmatrix} 0.3715 & -0.1163 & -0.4392 & -2.8219 & 0.6341 & 1.2066 & -0.5638 & -0.5827 \end{bmatrix} \text{rad} \tag{26}$$

Figure 4(b) shows the link configuration diagram of the 8-DOF manipulator for this solution (26), which verifies that the position of the racket center and the orientation of the racket. In Fig. 4(b), the direction of the racket velocity V is perpendicular to the racket front.

In order to validate the effectiveness of the proposed method for the optimal hitting configuration of the 8-DOF manipulator, the gradient projection method (GPM) [4,19] is adopted to solve this problem. Thereinto, gradient projection method (GPM) [19] has been widely used in the literature for the manipulator kinematic control. For this 8-DOF manipulator, the GPM can compute the joint velocity vectors as:

$$\dot{q} = J^+ \dot{x} + k \left(I - J^+ J \right) \nabla H \left(q \right) \tag{27}$$

where $\dot{x}$ is a 6×1 vector consisting of three linear and three rotational velocity components, $\dot{q}$ is an 8×1 vector consisting of joint velocities, J is a 6×8 vector Jacobian matrix, J^+ is the Moore-Penrose inverse of the Jacobian, and $\nabla H \left(q \right)$ is the gradient vector of the optimized objective function $H \left(q \right)$. In order to avoid joint limits, the following minimization function is defined by:

$$H \left(q \right) = \sum_{i=1}^{8} \frac{1}{4} \frac{\left(q_{i\,max} - q_{i\,min} \right)^2}{\left(q_{i\,max} - q_i \right) \left(q_i - q_{i\,min} \right)} \tag{28}$$

where q_i is the ith joint angle, and $q_{i\,max}$ and $q_{i\,min}$ are the upper and lower limits of the joint angle q_i respectively.

Based on the above, the GPM is used to solve this configuration optimization problem, and compared with the results of the proposed method in this paper on the running time, solution accuracy and 'away limitation level'. The attitude angle φ of the end-effector cannot be determined by the GPM. As such, we suppose the yaw angle φ of the racked as $\varphi=0$ in GPM, namely the optimization variable dimension is $n=8$, and the limitation of the other joints is shown in Table 1. With respect to the rest of the parameters, the initial joint angles are defined as $q = (0, 0, 0.01, 0, 0.01, 0, 0, 0)$, the scalar coefficient k is set as 0.86 and the maximum evolutionary iteration of the GPM is $T = 2500$. Once the error, which is $err(\Delta p, \Delta R)$, is less than 10^{-6}, the whole procedure will stop immediately.

Table 2. Comparison results of different methods for solving the optimal hitting configuration of the 8-DOF manipulator

Methods	n	$err(\Delta p, \Delta R)$	μ	t/s
Gradient-Projection Method [1]	8	9.9305E-7	1.4052	0.0917
Proposed method (TLBO-based analytic solution)	3	0	0.8028	0.0245

[1] In the GPM, the optimization variable dimension is 8, in which the yaw angle of the racket is fixed to zero, that is, $\varphi=0$.

As is shown in Table 2, compared with the results of the GPM, the proposed method in this paper has great advantages in terms of the solution accuracy. Besides, the 'away limitation level' μ and running time t are also smaller than the corresponding value of the GPM. By analyzing the causes, it can be attributed to the facts as follows.

1). The proposed method performs the iterative optimization procedure based on the obtained analytic inverse kinematic solution of the 8-DOF manipulator. Therefore, the dimension of the optimization variables is reduced greatly, and it has no end-effector error (position and orientation) in theory.

2). With respect to the GPM, although consuming-time of the GPM is very little, the 'away limitation level' μ is greater than 1, which means the obtained solution of the GPM is invalid. In addition, the obtained joint angles are just approximate solution. Simultaneously, the GPM is short of the characteristic of redundancy of the racket attitude due to fixing the yaw angle φ.

6   Conclusion

A solution for optimal configuration method of an 8-DOF redundant manipulator for flying ball is presented. This method can obtain the optimal hitting configuration of the manipulator based on the position of the racket center and its Cartesian velocity direction. On the basis of the obtained analytic inverse kinematics solution of the manipulator, the TLBO algorithm is adopted to search for the three redundant parameters, which can obtain a result that is away from the joint angle limitation as far as possible. This method has advantages of fewer optimization parameters, faster solving speed, and so on. Simulation results demonstrate the effectiveness of this method.

In the future, the idea of this method will be applied to solve the kinematic optimum problem of other types of manipulators with different joint model.

References

1. Tian, Y., Chen, X., Jia, D., Meng, F., Huang, Q.: Design and kinematic analysis of a light weight and high stiffness manipulator for humanoid robots. Robot **33**(3), 332–339 (2011)
2. Ren, Z., Zhu, Q., Xiong, R.: A joint physical constraints avoidance method for inverse kinematics problem of redundant humanoid manipulator. J. Mech. Eng. **50**(19), 58–65 (2015)
3. Tevatia, G., Schaal, S.: Inverse kinematics for humanoid robots. In IEEE International Conference on Robotics and Automation(ICRA), pp. 294–299. IEEE Press, San Francisco, USA (2000)
4. Dubey, R.V., Euler, J.A., Babcock, S.M.: Real-time implementation of an optimization scheme for seven-degree-of-freedom redundant manipulators. IEEE Trans. Robot. Autom. **7**(2), 579–588 (1991)
5. Chan, T.F., Dubey, R.V.: A weighted least-norm solution based scheme for avoiding joint limits for redundant joint manipulators. IEEE Trans. Robot. Autom. **11**(2), 286–292 (1995)
6. Kajita, S.J.: Humanoid Robots. Tsinghua University Press, Tsinghua, Beijing (2007)
7. Koker, R., Oz, C., Cakar, T., Ekiz, H.: A study of neural network based inverse kinematics solution for a three-joint robot. Robot. Auton. Syst. **49**(3), 227–234 (2004)
8. Nearchou, A.C.: Solving the inverse kinematics problem of redundant robots operating in complex environments via a modified genetic algorithm. Mech. Mach. Theory **33**(3), 273–292 (1998)
9. Fang, C., Ding, X.: Anthropomorphic arm kinematics oriented to movement primitive of human arm triangle. Robot **34**(3), 257–264 (2012)
10. Xu, W., Yan, L., Mu, Z., Wang, Z.: Dual arm-angle parameterisation and its applications for analytical inverse kinematics of redundant manipulators. Robotica **34**(12), 2669–2688 (2016)
11. Yin, F., Wang, Y., Wei, S.: Inverse kinematic solution for robot manipulator based on electromagnetism-like and modified DFP algorithms. Acta Automatica Sinica **37**(1), 74–82 (2011)
12. Zhao, J., Wang, W., Cai, H.: Generation of closed-form inverse kinematics for reconfigurable robots. J. Mech. Eng. **42**(8), 210–214 (2006)
13. Shimizu, M., Kakuya, H., Yoon, W., Kitagaki, K., Kosuge, K.: Analytical inverse kinematic computation for 7-DOF redundant manipulators with joint limits and its application to redundancy resolution. IEEE Trans. Rob. **24**(5), 1131–1142 (2008)
14. Wang, Y., Sun, L., Yan, W., Liu, J.: An analytic and optimal inverse kinematic solution for a 7-DOF space manipulator. Robot **36**(5), 592–599 (2014)
15. Ren, Z., Hu, B., Wang, Z., Sun, L., Zhu, Q.: Knowledge database-based multi-objective trajectory planning of 7-DOF manipulator with rapid and continuous response to uncertain fast-flying objects. IEEE Trans. Rob. **39**(2), 1012–1028 (2023)

16. Rao, R.V., Savsani, V.J., Vakharia, D.P.: Teaching-learning-based optimization: a novel method for constrained mechanical design optimization problems. Comput. Aided Des. **43**(3), 303–315 (2011)
17. Rao, R.V., Savsani, V.J., Vakharia, D.P.: Teaching-learning- based optimization: An optimization method for continuous non-linear large scale problems. Inf. Sci. **183**(1), 1–15 (2012)
18. Rao, R.V., Patel, V.: An improved teaching-learning-based optimization algorithm for solving unconstrained optimization problems. Scientia Iranica **20**(3), 710–720 (2013)
19. Liegeois, A.: Automatic supervisory control of the configuration and behavior of multibody mechanisms. IEEE Trans. Syst. Man Cybern. SMC **7**(12), 868–871 (1977)

Smooth Composite-Space RRT: An Improved Motion Planner for Manipulators Under Incomplete Orientation Constraint

Jiangping Wang[⊠], Nan Li, Wei Song, Wenjuan Du, and Wenxuan Chen

Intelligent Robotic Research Center, Zhejiang Lab, Hangzhou, China
wangjiangping@zhejianglab.com

Abstract. The incomplete orientation constraint (IOC), which is not necessary to require an end-effector motion constrained by all three spatial directions, exists widely in practical manipulation tasks. For example, when moving a container of liquid from one place to another, we can rotate the container horizontally or tilt it slightly if it is not full. In our previous work [1], a Composite-space RRT algorithm is presented to solve such a problem for spherical wrist manipulators that plans collision-free paths in the composite space. However, the planned path exhibits shaking or ripple like fluctuations, which will lead to shaking at the robot's end-effector tool and bad performance of the task. In this paper, we propose a Smooth Composite-space RRT algorithm that combines the Composite-space RRT algorithm with B-spline interpolation method to improve the smoothness of the orientation path. And we demonstrate the effectiveness of our approach on the Willow Garage's PR2 simulation platform in Robot Operating System (ROS) with two IOC cases.

Keywords: Path and motion planning · Manipulation · Incomplete orientation constraint (IOC)

1 Introduction

Many practical manipulation tasks, such as moving a plate of food or a cup full of water, require complete or partial constraints on the orientation of the robot's end-effector in three spatial directions. If not all the orientation angles (such as Roll, Pitch, Yaw) are fixed in these tasks, it is called an incomplete orientation constraint (IOC [2,3]) problem. Actually, the IOC has many practical applications in our daily life. For instance, when moving a container of liquid from one place to another in a narrow environments, sometimes we need to rotate the container horizontally or tilt it slightly to avoid obstacles.

This Research Supported by China Postdoctoral Project (No. 2021M692960); Center-initiated Research Project of Zhejiang Lab (No.2021NB0AL01); Science and Technology on Space Intelligent Control Laboratory (No. K2022EA2KE01).

In this paper, we discuss the motion planning for robotic manipulation under the IOC problems, where the robot is required to find a collision-free joint space path from an initial configuration to a goal configuration while subjecting the IOC imposed on its end-effector all along the motion. In our previous work [1], a Composite-space RRT algorithm is presented to solve such a problem for spherical wrist manipulators that searches collision-free paths in the composite space formed by the variables of the robot's main-arm joints and its end-effector orientation angles. However, the path planned by the Composite-space RRT algorithm exhibits shaking or ripple like fluctuations, which will lead to shaking at the robot's end-effector and bad performance of the task.

To avoid shaking in the planned orientation paths, we improve our planning framework by combing the Composite-space RRT algorithm with B-spline interpolation in this paper. Specifically, a Smooth Composite-space RRT algorithm is proposed that uses the Composite-space RRT algorithm to calculate a composite-space path meeting the IOC requirements. Then, the B-spline interpolation method is used to smooth the planned composite-space path. Finally, a joint space path can be obtained by transforming the composite-space path with the orientation inverse kinematics.

2 Related Work

In this section, we give a brief overview of prior research work in incomplete orientation constraint (IOC) and motion planning with such constraints.

The IOC problem was firstly named in [2], which was used for task space trajectory tracking problem in the view of robot control. Because of the unused DOF of the task, the robot is functional redundancy. Lots of control methods have been developed to address this functional redundancy in the IOC problem. For example, Huo and Baron et al. [4,5] used a twist-decomposition algorithm to decompose end-effector position and orientation at the robot wrist in the IOC problem. In order to control robots with functional redundancy, Sekimoto [6] proposed to add a virtual joint to the robot and calculate the redundant resolution with extended Jacobian. Zlajpah [7] proposed a modified orientation control algorithm based on the task space rotation, where a time-variant task frame was used to represent the functional redundancy as one or more rows of Jacobian matrix.

The IOC problem can also be addressed by the constrained motion planning approaches. Constrained motion planning [8,9] is an extension to the basic motion planning [10], which is to generate collision-free paths that satisfy the pose constraint imposed on the robot's end-effector. For example, Stilman [11] designed two projection strategies Tangent Space Sampling (TS) and First-Order Retraction (FR) for task constrained motion planning to handle tasks like rotating doors about fixed axes, sliding drawers along fixed trajectories or holding objects level during transport. He [12] also presented a sampling-based motion planner that enforces soft rotation constraints. Our previous work [1] also addressed such IOC problem with the Composite-space RRT algorithm. Bonilla

[13] presented a constrained motion planning method for dual-arm robots with constraint of closed kinematic chains, which combines constraint relaxation with random sampling sub-optimal planner. Cohen et al. [14] proposed a search-based motion planning algorithm for the task of dual-arm object manipulation with an upright orientation constraint, where the object's global yaw angle is redundant. However, there are few papers to discuss the smoothness of orientation paths, which is the main focus of this paper.

3   Problem Description

In this section, we start with the mathematical description of the IOC. Then the problem of motion planning under IOC is introduced referring to the basic motion planning problem.

3.1   Incomplete Orientation Constraint (IOC)

IOC refers to that changing the orientation of the manipulator's end-effector has no effect on the task performance. It is well-known that the orientation can be represented by rotation matrices, Euler angles or unit quaternion. Euler angles have an intuitive physical meaning and allow bounds on rotation to be intuitively specified, thus we use them to mathematically describe IOC problem in this work.

IOC imposed on the manipulator's end-effector is relative to the world frame and the 3-dimensional Roll-Pitch-Yaw (RPY) Euler angles $\phi = [\alpha, \beta, \gamma]^T$ about fixed axes introduced indicates this rotation. Thus, the rotation of the manipulator's end-effector relative to the world frame $\boldsymbol{R}_{end}^{world} \in SO(3)$ is defined as:

$$\boldsymbol{R}_{end}^{world} = \boldsymbol{R}(\gamma, \beta, \alpha) = Rot(z, \alpha)Rot(y, \beta)Rot(x, \gamma). \tag{1}$$

Hence, we can define the mathematical formula of IOC by limiting Roll-Pitch-Yaw (RPY) angles as follows:

$$\phi_{IOC} = \begin{bmatrix} \alpha \\ \beta \\ \gamma \end{bmatrix}, \; where \begin{cases} \alpha \in (\alpha_{min}, \alpha_{max}); \\ \beta \in (\beta_{min}, \beta_{max}); \\ \gamma \in (\gamma_{min}, \gamma_{max}). \end{cases} \tag{2}$$

where, α, β and γ are random values within the task constraints. α is a fixed value if $\alpha_{min} = \alpha_{max}$, and it is the same with others. Therefore, α, β and γ can not be all fixed values in the IOC problem.

3.2   Motion Planning Under IOC

The basic motion planning is to find the motion that enables the robot to perform the assigned task without collision with obstacles. An effective way to solve the motion planning problem is to represent the robot as a moving point in configuration space or C-space (denoted as $\mathcal{C}$). The region that causes a collision between the robot and obstacles or itself, is called the C-space obstacle region $\mathcal{C}_{obs} \subseteq \mathcal{C}$. The region in C-space, excluding $\mathcal{C}_{obs}$, is called the free C-space $\mathcal{C}_{free} = \mathcal{C} \setminus \mathcal{C}_{obs}$. Given an initial configuration $q_{init} \in \mathcal{C}_{free}$ and a goal configuration $q_{goal} \in \mathcal{C}_{free}$, the motion planning problem can be defined as finding a continuous path τ such that

$$\tau : [0,1] \to \mathcal{C}_{free},$$
$$\tau(0) = q_{init}; \ \tau(1) = q_{goal}. \tag{3}$$

Motion planning under IOC problem addressed in this paper can be characterized mathematically as follows. Consider a robotic manipulator with n degrees of freedoms (DOFs) and its end-effector motion is limited by IOC. Such constraints imposed on the robot's motion can be represented by a kinematic function $F(q) : \mathcal{C}_n \to SO(3)$. It means that the robot's configuration parameters $q = (q_1, q_2, \ldots, q_n)$ need to satisfy the kinematic constraint $F(q) \in \phi_{IOC}$ all along the motion. From the perspective of C-space, this kinematic constraint reduces the feasible region in $\mathcal{C}_{free}$ and even the dimensions of $\mathcal{C}_n$. The sub-manifold embedded in the ambient $\mathcal{C}_n$ is also known as the constraint manifold $\mathcal{M}$, where all the configurations must satisfy the kinematic constraint:

$$\mathcal{M} = \{q = (q_1, q_2, \ldots, q_n) \in \mathcal{C}_n \mid F(q) \in \phi_{IOC}\}. \tag{4}$$

Similar to the mathematical notations and description of the basic motion planning, the set of all collision-free configurations in $\mathcal{M}$ forms the free constraint manifold $\mathcal{M}_{free} = \mathcal{M} \cap \mathcal{C}_{free}$. Thus, motion planning under IOC can be defined as finding a continuous path τ in $\mathcal{M}_{free}$ from an initial configuration $q_{init} \in \mathcal{M}_{free}$ to a goal configuration $q_{goal} \in \mathcal{M}_{free}$, such that

$$\tau : [0,1] \to \mathcal{M}_{free},$$
$$\tau(0) = q_{init}; \ \tau(1) = q_{goal}. \tag{5}$$

For motion planning under IOC, $\mathcal{M}_{free}$ often occupies a small volume in $\mathcal{C}_{free}$ because of the IOC imposed on the manipulator's end-effector. Furthermore, the joint-space trajectory generated within $\mathcal{C}_{free}$ may exhibit shaking or ripple like fluctuations, which will lead to shaking at the robot's end-effector and bad performance of the task.

4   Soft Composite-Space RRT Algorithm

In this section, we provide an overview of the Composite-space RRT algorithm in our previous work. On this basis, we propose the Soft Composite-space RRT algorithm and provide the details of the algorithm.

4.1   Overview of the Composite-Space RRT Algorithm

Our previously proposed Composite-space RRT Algorithm is designed to find collision-free paths by the Rapidly-exploring Random Trees (RRT) algorithm

---

Algorithm 1. Composite-space RRT Algorithm

Input: $V_q = \{q_{init}\}; E_q = \emptyset; T_c = (V_c, E_c) = \emptyset$
Output: $T_q = (V_q, E_q);$
  1: $x_{init} \leftarrow Fmap(q_{init});$
  2: $V_c \leftarrow V_c \bigcup \{x_{init}\};$
  3: **for** $i = 1 \ldots n$ **do**
  4:     $x_{rand} \leftarrow SampleConfig(i);$
  5:     $x_{near} \leftarrow Nearest(V_c, x_{rand});$
  6:     $x_{new}, \delta(x_{near}, x_{new}) \leftarrow Steer(x_{near}, x_{rand});$
  7:     $q_{new}, \delta(q_{near}, q_{new}) \leftarrow Map(x_{new}, \delta(x_{near}, x_{new}));$
  8:     **if** $ValidationChecking(\delta(q_{nearest}, q_{new}))$ **then**
  9:         $V_q \leftarrow V_q \bigcup \{q_{new}\}; E_q \leftarrow E_q \bigcup \delta(q_{near}, q_{new});$
 10:         $V_c \leftarrow V_c \bigcup \{x_{new}\}; E_c \leftarrow E_c \bigcup \delta(x_{near}, x_{new});$
 11:     **end if**
 12: **end for**
 13: **return** $T_q \leftarrow (V_q, E_q); T_c \leftarrow (V_c, E_c);$

---

in the composite space, where the composite-space configuration x is consist of the robot's main-arm joints $q^{arm} = (q_1, q_2, \ldots, q_{n-3})$ and the end-effector orientation angles $\phi = (\alpha, \beta, \gamma)$.

$$x = [\underbrace{q_1, q_2, \ldots, q_{n-3}}_{q^{arm}}, \underbrace{\alpha, \beta, \gamma}_{\phi}] \tag{6}$$

As shown in Algorithm 1, The Composite-space RRT algorithm begins with an empty composite-space filling tree $T_c = (V_c, E_c)$ and a joint-space filling tree $T_q = (V_q, E_q)$ rooted at the initial joint configuration $q_{init} \in V_q$. Then it continuously expands unexplored areas of the composite space X with T_c by the RRT algorithm (Line 3-12), where the root of the T_c is the initial composite-space configuration $x_{init} \in V_c$ calculated by the manipulator forward kinematics function $Fmap()$ (Line 1-2). The Composite-space RRT algorithm typically consists of the following functional components:

- **SampleConfig():** The uniformly random samples of composite space can be obtained by sampling the main-arm joint and the orientation angles with constraints. The uniformly random samples of the main-arm joint can be straightforward by random and uniform sampling of the joint positions. To deal with Euler angles with additional lower bounds $\phi_{min} = (\alpha_{min}, \beta_{min}, \gamma_{min})$ and upper bounds $\phi_{max} = (\alpha_{max}, \beta_{max}, \gamma_{max})$, the Composite-space RRT algorithm used a linear interpolation method with uniform spherical sampling to obtain uniformly-distributed random Euler angles satisfying the constraints.
- **Nearest():** The nearest node q_{near} is selected by measuring the distance between nearby nodes of the tree. In the Composite-space RRT algorithm, a *scaled* distance metric $\rho(x_a, x_b)$ between x_a and x_b is used to balance the relative importance of the main-arm joints component $\|q_a^{arm} - q_b^{arm}\|$ and the end-effector orientation component $\rho(\phi_a, \phi_b)$ by a scale parameter s $(0 < s < 1)$:

$$\rho(x_a, x_b) = s \cdot \|q_a^{arm} - q_b^{arm}\| + (1-s) \cdot \rho(\phi_a, \phi_b), \ 0 < s < 1 \tag{7}$$

$\|q_a^{arm} - q_b^{arm}\|$ is the standard Euclidean distance between vectors q_a^{arm} and q_b^{arm}. And $\rho(\phi_a, \phi_b) = arccos(\|(Q_a \cdot Q_b)\|)$ is the distance metric between ϕ_a and ϕ_b, which is defined as the shortest arc length between unit quaternion Q_a (converted by ϕ_a) and Q_b (converted by ϕ_b).

- **Steer():** The steer function is to generate a new node x_{new} by moving a step size ϵ from the nearest node x_{near} to the random node x_{rand}. The Composite-space RRT algorithm performs the linear interpolation for main-arm joints q_{arm} and adopts the Slerp (Spherical Linear Interpolation [15]) method to achieve orientation interpolation. The geometric formula of slerp between unit quaternion Q_a and Q_b is defined as:

$$slerp(Q_a, Q_b, t) = \frac{sin((1-t)\omega)}{sin\omega} Q_a + \frac{sin(t\omega)}{sin\omega} Q_b, \tag{8}$$

where $t \in [0, 1]$ is the discrete vector of rotation and ω is the angle of rotation. Q_a and Q_b are converted by Euler angles ϕ_a and ϕ_b respectively.

- **Map():** In order to obtain the joint-space motion and detect its effectiveness, the Composite-space RRT algorithm uses the $Map()$ function to convert the new node x_{new} and the new branch $\delta(x_{near}, x_{new})$ into a new joint-space node q_{new} and a new joint-space branch $\delta(q_{near}, q_{new})$ by the analytical inverse kinematics (IK) of spherical wrist.

- **ValidationChecking():** In the Composite-space RRT algorithm, it is not only necessary to perform collision detection on $\delta(q_{near}, q_{new})$, but also to check its effectiveness. $\delta(q_{near}, q_{new})$ is collision-free only when all the segments are collision-free, and it is valid only when all the intermediate nodes satisfy the given orientation constraints.

4.2   Soft Composite-Space RRT Algorithm

For the actual robot physical system, robot motion planning often requires not only a collision-free motion path, but also the smoothness of the planned path. This is because non-smooth motion paths may cause the velocity and acceleration generated by the trajectory planner to exceed its limit range, making it difficult for the robot controller to effectively track the planned path. In addition, jumping, shaking, or ripple like fluctuations in the planned path may cause shaking at the robot end or even the robot body, affecting its motion performance and tracking accuracy. And a smooth planning path can make the robot's motion more stable, reduce the stress and wear of each joint of the robot, and reduce the energy consumption of each joint driver.

For the motion planning under IOC problem, although the non-smooth orientation path generated by the Composite-space RRT algorithm does not lead to planning failure, it can cause the manipulator's end-effector to "sway back and

Algorithm 2. Soft Composite-space RRT Algorithm

Input: q_{init}; q_{goal};
Output: T_q;
 1: T_q; $T_c \leftarrow CompositeSpaceRRT(q_{init}, q_{goal})$;
 2: $x_{points} \leftarrow Knot(T_c)$;
 3: $T_c^{new} \leftarrow Bspline(x_{points})$;
 4: $T_q^{new} \leftarrow Map(T_c^{new})$;
 5: **return** T_q^{new};

---

forth" or "shake up and down", affecting the execution of the task. For example, when moving a cup full filled with water, one does not want the end-effector to shake and cause water splashing during the movement. The main reason for the non-smooth orientation path is the use of random sampling with IOC in the rotation group $SO(3)$. Therefore, we propose the Smooth Composite-space RRT algorithm in this paper that combines the Composite-space RRT algorithm with B-spline interpolation method. The pseudo-code of the Smooth Composite-space RRT algorithm proposed in this paper is shown in Algorithm 2. The algorithm process is as follows:

- **Step 1:** A collision-free joint space path T_q connecting q_{init} and q_{goal}, and its corresponding composite-space path T_c connecting x_{init} and x_{goal} can be calculated by the Composite Space RRT algorithm. According to our preliminary work, the planned joint-space T_q can meet collision free and IOC constraints, but the motion of the manipulator's end-effector exhibits shaking or ripple like fluctuations.
- **Step 2:** To obtain smooth orientation paths, the Smooth Composite-space RRT algorithm combines the Composite-space RRT algorithm with B-spline interpolation method. The input of the B-spline interpolation is denoted as several control nodes x_{points}, which are calculated by the $Knot$ function based on the nodes in T_c.
- **Step 3:** A smooth Composite-space path T_c^{new} can be generated by the B-spline interpolation function $Bspline$. It's obvious that T_c^{new} is a fitting and smoothing curve of T_c generated by the Composite-space RRT algorithm.
- **Step 4:** Similar to the $Map()$ function in the Composite-space RRT algorithm, the proposed Smooth Composite-space RRT algorithm converts T_c^{new} into a new joint-space path T_q^{new} by the analytical Inverse Kinematics (IK) of spherical wrist.

5 Simulation Experiments and Results

In this section, we compare the performance of our planning algorithm with the Composite-space RRT algorithm by two simulation experiments. The experiment requires the PR2 manipulator to move a cup of water from one side of the table (shown as green) to the other. Both the two algorithms are coded in the Open Motion Planning Library (OMPL) [16] of Robot Operating System (ROS) with the same software and hardware configuration parameters.

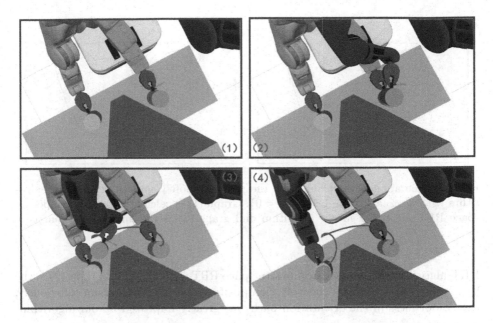

Fig. 1. Snapshots of moving a cup from start pose (green arm with cup) to goal pose (yellow arm with cup) while avoiding the obstacles (green baffle). In order to cross the narrow passage, the roll angle keeps on changing and adjusting during the motion. (Color figure online)

5.1   Evaluation Index

We use the variance of orientation variation $Var(\Delta\phi)$ to evaluate the smoothness of the orientation paths, which is defined as

$$Var(\Delta\phi) = \frac{1}{n}\sum_{k=1}^{n}(\Delta\phi_k - \overline{\Delta\phi})^2, \tag{9}$$

where n is the number of sampling nodes; $\Delta\alpha, \Delta\beta, \Delta\gamma$ are the difference of Euler angles between the adjacent nodes. $\Delta\phi = \sqrt{((\Delta\alpha)^2 + (\Delta\beta)^2 + (\Delta\gamma)^2))/3}$ is the variation of orientation between nodes and $\overline{\Delta\phi} = \frac{1}{n}\sum_{k=1}^{n}\Delta\phi_k$ is the average value.

5.2   Simulation Results

Figure 1 showed a series of snapshots that the simulated PR2 robot moves a cup vertically in a narrow passage environment, which was implemented by our Soft Composite-space RRT algorithm with $\phi_{IOC} = \{\alpha \in (-1, 1); \beta = \gamma = 0\}$. In order to cross the narrow passage while avoiding the obstacles, the roll angle keeps on changing and adjusting during the motion.

Figure 2 presented the orientation paths by our Soft Composite-space RRT algorithm, where graph (1) is the orientation path obtained by Composite-space

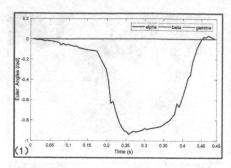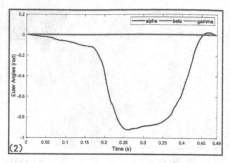

Fig. 2. Orientation paths planned by the proposed Soft Composite-space RRT algorithm with $\phi_{IOC} = \{\alpha \in (-1, 1); \beta = \gamma = 0\}$. Graph (1) is calculated by the Composite-space RRT algorithm in our algorithm and graph (1) is the final orientation path.

RRT algorithm in our Soft Composite-space RRT algorithm and graph (2) is the final orientation path by the Soft Composite-space RRT algorithm. Obviously, the smoothness of the orientation path was greatly improved by our algorithm.

5.3   Discussion

To highlight the performance of our method, two IOC cases as our previous work was implemented in our algorithm. As our Soft Composite-space RRT algorithm belongs to the randomized algorithm, we carried out 20 times repetitive experiments for each cases. The comparative result of simulation experiment is given in Table 1.

According to statistical data of $Var(\Delta\phi)$, both the Composite-space RRT algorithm and the Soft Composite-space RRT algorithm can successfully solve the motion planning under IOC problem, but our Soft Composite-space RRT algorithm has significant improvement in smoothing of the orientation path than the Composite-space RRT algorithm.

Table 1. Simulation results using the Soft Composite-space RRT algorithm and the Composite-space RRT algorithm.

Cases	$\phi_{IOC} = \{\alpha \in (-1, 1); \beta = \gamma = 0\}$		$\phi_{IOC} = \{\alpha, \beta, \gamma \in (-1, 1)\}$	
Planner	**Soft Composite-space RRT**	Composite-space RRT	**Soft Composite-space RRT**	Composite-space RRT
$Var(\Delta\phi)$	$5.42\text{x}10^{-6}\ rad$	$1.065\text{x}10^{-5}\ rad$	$3.71\text{x}10^{-5}\ rad$	$2.147\text{x}10^{-4}\ rad$
Success Rate	100%	100%	100%	100%

6   Conclusions

The Composite-space RRT algorithm we proposed earlier has been verified to be able to efficiently solve the problem of motion planning under IOC. In order to further improve the smoothness of the end-effector orientation path, the Smooth

Composite-space RRT algorithm is proposed in this article, which combines the Composite-space RRT algorithm with B-spline interpolation method to eliminate shaking or ripple in the path.

Our Smooth Composite-space RRT algorithm considers the IOC problem from the perspective of path and motion planning. It uses the Composite-space RRT algorithm to generated the composite-space and joint-space paths that meet the constraints of collision free and IOC, and smooth the planned paths through B-spline interpolation method. The simulation results in two different cases have demonstrated that the Smooth Composite-space RRT algorithm can help to improve the smoothness of the orientation path. We will also try to integrate the Smooth Composite-space RRT algorithm into more IOC problem in future work.

References

1. Wang, J., Liu, S., Zhang, B., Yu, C.: Manipulation planning with soft constraints by randomized exploration of the composite configuration space. Int. J. Control Autom. Syst. **19**(3), 1340–1351 (2021). https://doi.org/10.1007/s12555-019-0727-8
2. Li, G., Song, D., Xu, S., et al.: On perpendicular curve-based model-less control considering incomplete orientation constraint. IEEE/ASME Trans. Mechatron. **26**(3), 1479–1489 (2021)
3. Li, G., Xu, S., Song, D., et al.: On perpendicular curve-based task space trajectory tracking control with incomplete orientation constraint. IEEE Trans. Autom. Sci. Eng. **20**(2), 1244–1261 (2023)
4. Huo, L., Baron, L.: The joint-limits and singularity avoidance in robotic welding. Indus. Rob. Inter. J. **35**(5), 456–464 (2008)
5. Huo, L., Baron, L.: The self-adaptation of weights for joint-limits and singularity avoidances of functionally redundant robotic-task. Rob. Comput.-Integ. Manuf. **27**(2), 367–376 (2011)
6. Sekimoto, M., Arimoto, S.: Experimental study on reaching movements of robot arms with redundant dofs based upon virtual spring-damper hypothesis. In: IEEE/RSJ International Conference on Intelligent Robots and Systems, Beijing, China, pp. 562–567 (2006)
7. Zlajpah, L.: On orientation control of functional redundant robots. In: IEEE International Conference on Robotics and Automation (ICRA), Singapore, pp. 2475–2482 (2017)
8. Milton, C., Jennings, D.: Path planning for a manipulator with constraints on orientation. J. Intell. Rob. Syst. **11**(1–2), 67–77 (1994)
9. Kingston, Z., Moll, M., Kavraki, L.E.: Sampling-based methods for motion planning with constraints. Annual Rev. Control Rob. Auton. Syst. **1**, 159–185 (2018)
10. Lavalle, S.M.: Planning Algorithms. Cambridge University Press, England (2006)
11. Stilman, M.: Task constrained motion planning in robot joint space. In: IEEE/RSJ International Conference on Intelligent Robots and Systems, San Diego, CA, USA, pp. 3074–3081 (2007)
12. Kunz, T., Stilman, M.: Manipulation planning with soft task constraints. In: IEEE/RSJ International Conference on Intelligent Robots and Systems, Vilamoura-Algarve, Portugal, pp. 1937–1942 (2012)

13. Bonilla, M., Farnioli, E., Pallottino L., Bicchi, A.: Sample-based motion planning for robot manipulators with closed kinematic chains. In: IEEE International Conference on Robotics and Automation (ICRA), Seattle, WA, USA, pp. 2522–2527 (2015)
14. Cohen, B., Chitta, S., Likhachev, M.: Search-based planning for dual-arm manipulation with upright orientation constraints. In: IEEE International Conference on Robotics and Automation (ICRA), Saint Paul, MN, USA, pp. 3784–3790 (2012)
15. Shoemake, K.: Animating rotation with quaternion curves. In: Proceedings of the 12th Annual Conference on Computer Graphics and Interactive Techniques, San Francisco, California, USA, pp. 245–254 (1985)
16. Sucan, I.A., Moll, M., Kavraki, L.E.: The open motion planning library. IEEE Robot. Autom. Mag. 19(4), 72–82 (2012)

Cooperative Control of Dual-Arm Robot of Adaptive Impedance Controller Based on RBF Neural Network

Tongyan Zhang[1,2,3,4], Ting Wang[2,3,4(✉)], Shiliang Shao[2,3,4(✉)], Zonghan Cao[1,2,3,4], Xinke Dou[2,3,4], and Hongwei Qin[2,3,4,5]

[1] School of Artificial Intelligence, Shenyang University of Technology, Shenyang, China
[2] State Key Laboratory of Robotics, Shenyang Institute of Automation, Chinese Academy of Sciences, Shenyang, China
{wangting,shaoshiliang}@sia.cn
[3] Institutes for Robotics and Intelligent Manufacturing, Chinese Academy of Sciences, Shenyang, China
[4] School of Software, Shenyang University of Technology, Shenyang, China
[5] School of Information Engineering, Shenyang University of Chemical Technology, Shenyang, China

Abstract. Traditional impedance control methods often fail to accurately track force signals in unknown or changing environments, resulting in failure or instability in tasks such as coordinated handling. To solve the above problems, this paper adds the RBF neural network strategy, based on the traditional impedance control. First a model for the contact force between the dual redundant robotic arms and the environment is constructed, and the RBF neural network is used to estimate the stiffness of the changing environment online. Then, a dynamic adaptive force control co-simulation model is established. The change in the contact force is adapted to adjust the parameters of the two-arm impedance model to compensate for unknown environmental changes. Simulation experiments showed that the enhanced impedance control strategy is appropriate for the force-interaction circumstances of the robotic arm within the positional environment, has a stronger durability, enhances the sturdiness of the two-armed working together robot in an environment that shifts, and has a more effective force control effect.

Keywords: Impedance control · Radial basis function neural networks · Dual-arm coordination · Force signal tracking

1 Introduction

Due to their great accuracy and efficiency, dual-arm robots that collaborate have come to be widely used in many different industries and service sectors [1]. Robot functioning in tasks like collaborative handling requires force contact. To ensure effectiveness and stability while carrying out the mission, the robot must correctly track and react to signals from outside forces. Hogan's 1984 proposal of the impedance control approach, a traditional force control strategy, is still frequently employed today. Although it

© The Author(s), under exclusive license to Springer Nature Singapore Pte Ltd. 2023
H. Yang et al. (Eds.): ICIRA 2023, LNAI 14270, pp. 499–512, 2023.
https://doi.org/10.1007/978-981-99-6492-5_43

doesn't directly control the robot's mobility, it more effectively displays the robotic arm cannot be directly controlled by the impedance control model, which instead reflects changes in the connection among the rotary motion of the machine's arm and external interaction forces [2, 3]. The impedance properties of the robotic arm can be modified to regulate the forces that interact with the outside environment by altering the three matrix components of inertia, damping that is present and rigidity in the impedance control method [4]. However, dealing with ambiguous or shifting external settings presents difficulties for conventional impedance-control techniques. They frequently mistrack force signals, which results in unstable operations and task failures. Researchers have studied impedance control in dual-arm cooperation in depth.

Reference [5] in order to increase the redundant robotic arm's ability to track the target, a multi-priority control approach is developed for impedance control of dual redundant robotic arms. This method dynamically changes the motion error between the two arms. Reference [6] offered a methodology for fostering the development of human-like dynamic impedance skills, which allows robots to effectively learn motion and stiffness control strategies from humans. For this purpose, the muscle activity of human limbs was monitored to estimate the variable stiffness. Reference [7] proposed a scheme for dual arm collaborative compliance control has been proposed, the proposed collaborative compliance scheme can achieve control of mechanical arm force, and through simulation testing, it has been found that the proposed method can achieve object handling with minimal force. Reference [8] focuses on the problem of position and force tracking in the motion control process of dual robotic arms. On the basis of traditional admittance control, an adaptive rate mechanism is added, and the force applied to the object between the two arms is decomposed. In order to better account for unknown errors in the robotic arm trajectory, the decomposed internal and external forces are distributed to the object's tip and the control model's parameters are updated using online tracking error. In [9], the learning ability of fuzzy neural network structures was used to approximate the uncertain dynamics of robots with unknown dynamics and constraint conditions online. In simulations, the proposed control method performed well in handling interactions between robots and the environment. Reference [10] enabling collaborative human operations, an unbalanced two-handed coordinate control approach for dual-arm exoskeletons was presented. The variable stiffness was estimated using the impedance factor approximation approach, the experimental results showed that the suggested dual-arm coordinated controller was effective. Reference [11] to enable smooth dual-arm collaborative functioning in master-slave systems, an auxiliary control mechanism based on detectors and auxiliary controllers was developed, the effectiveness of this method was demonstrated through an experiment. Reference [12] proposes two control schemes, the feasibility of these two schemes was tested through simulation.

The RBF neural network impedance controller proposed in this article can achieve precise force/torque tracking and control, enabling the robotic arm to quickly adapt and respond to changes in external forces when in contact with the environment. In the application of a dual robotic arm system, high-precision collaborative operation can be achieved, enabling two robotic arms to cooperate with each other and complete complex tasks together, improving production efficiency and operational flexibility. The remainder of this essay is divided into the following sections: The kinematic models of the objects and the dual arms, as well as the motion constraints of the dual arms, are built in Sect. 2. In Sect. 3, the concepts of impedance control and RBF neural networks are explained, and the proposed improved controller is designed. The simulation environment for this paper's simulation is built in Sect. 4, and several tests are employed to show the advantages of the control scheme. The results of the investigation and suggestions for further work are offered in Sect. 5.

2 Dual Arm Robot Model

2.1 Motion Constraint Relationships of Double Arm Robots

In the collaborative handling process of dual-arm robots, imitating human behavior is often simpler [13]. The collaborative motion of dual-arm robots is generally classified into two categories: absolute and relative motion. The subordinate arm follows the motion of the main arm, achieving complete kinematic constraints on the dual-arm motion chain [14].

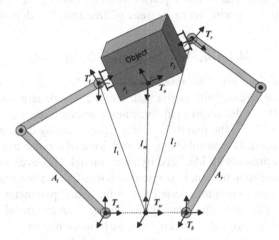

Fig. 1. Closed-loop system diagram of a dual-arm robot.

In Fig. 1, l_1, l_2, and l_m denote, respectively, the position vectors of the dual arms' end effectors in relation to the world coordinate system and the center of mass of the item being manipulated in relation to the world coordinate system. The position vectors of the left- and right-arm end-effector coordinate systems, in relation to the object's center of mass, are represented by the symbols r_1 and r_2, respectively. The basic coordinate systems for T_a and T_b, respectively, are A_l and A_r. The coordinate systems for the left and right arms' end-effectors are T_l and T_r, respectively. A geometrically closed kinematic chain is formed by the arms and the item when a dual-arm collaborative robot manipulates them, in the form shown in Eq. (1):

$$l_k = l_m + {}^oT_w^T r_k \tag{1}$$

where l_k ($k = 1, 2$) stands for the position vector from the world coordinate system to the manipulator's end effector, $^oT_w^T$ for the pose transformation matrix of the object coordinate system in the world coordinate system, and r_k ($k = 1, 2$) for the position vector from the object's center of mass to the manipulator's end effector.

The following constraint relationship holds if the velocity of the robotic arm's end effector and the contact point with the manipulated object is designated as $\dot{P}_k = [\dot{p}_k^T \; w_k^T]^T$ and the desired motion trajectory of the object being manipulated is represented by $(x, \dot{x}, \ddot{x})$, where $\dot{x} = [\dot{y}^T \; w^T]^T$:

$$\begin{cases} \dot{P}_k = \dot{y} + \omega \times r_k \\ \omega_k = \omega \\ \ddot{P}_k = \ddot{y} + \omega \times r_k + \omega \times (\omega \times r_k) \\ \dot{\omega}_k = \dot{\omega} \end{cases} \tag{2}$$

2.2 Dynamic Analysis of Dual Robotic Arms

In this study, the Lagrangian–Euler equation is used to model the dynamics of the two arms. For a robotic arm with seven degrees of freedom, the dynamic model can be expressed as:

$$M_k(q_k)\ddot{q}_k + C_k(q_k, \dot{q}_k)\dot{q}_k + G_k(q_k) = \tau_k \tag{3}$$

where the left and right arms are represented by the letters $k = l, r$, q_k, $\dot{q}_k$, and $\ddot{q}_k$, respectively; the positive-definite inertia matrix of the robotic arm is represented by the letters $M_k(q_k) \in R^{7\times7}$; the centrifugal force and Coriolis force are represented by the letters $C_k(q_k, \dot{q}_k) \in R^{7\times7}$; the gravity vector is represented by the letters $G_k(q_k) \in R^7$; and $\tau_k \in R^7$ represents the control torque of each joint of robotic arm.

Equation (3) represents an idealized dynamic model. However, in practice, robotic arms are subject to problems, such as uncontrollable friction between joints, external disturbances, and parameters that do not match the actual parameters. Therefore, with full consideration of the above influencing factors, the dynamic model of the robotic arm can be designed using $f_k(\dot{q}_k) \in R^7$ to represent the joint friction force that the robotic arm k experiences during collaborative handling. External disturbances are represented by $\tau_d \in R^7$, and the error between the marked and actual values of the physical parameters of the robotic arm is represented in increments of $M_k = M_{b_k} + \Delta M_k$, $C_k = C_{b_k} + \Delta C_k$, $G_k = G_{b_k} + \Delta G_k$, $M_{b_k}, C_{b_k}, G_{b_k}, \Delta M_k, \Delta C_k$ and $\Delta G_k \in R^{7\times7}$. Thus, the dual-arm dynamics model can be expressed as

$$M_{b_k}(q_k)\ddot{q}_k + C_{b_k}(q_k, \dot{q}_k)\dot{q}_k + G_{b_k}(q_k) + \tau_\Delta + f_k(\dot{q}_k) + \tau_d = \tau_k, \tag{4}$$

where $\tau_\Delta = \Delta M_k(q_k)q_k + \Delta C_k(q_k, q_k)q_k + \Delta G_k(q_k)$. If the joint angle position and angular velocity of the robotic arm are designed as $x_1 = q$ and $x_2 = \dot{q}$, the state-space equation of Eq. (7) can be expressed as

$$\begin{cases} \dot{x}_1 = x_2 \\ \dot{x}_2 = M_0^{-1}[\tau_k - (\tau_\Delta + \tau_d + C_{b_k}x_2 + G_{b_k} + f_k)] \end{cases} \tag{5}$$

3   Design of RBF Neural Network-Based Adaptive Impedance Controller

Impedance control is a robot control method aimed at achieving flexible interactions between a robot system and the external environment. By emulating human motion control strategies, the control adjusts the force and stiffness of the robot to adapt to different interactive tasks [15, 16]. The core idea of impedance control is to consider the robot as a combination of a virtual spring and damper, as shown in Fig. 2.

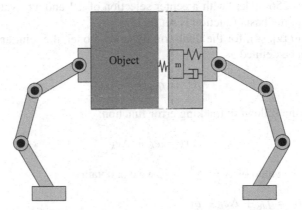

Fig. 2. Impedance control model of the dual-arm robot.

RBF neural networks use a weighted combination of a collection of RBFs depending on the distance that lies between the network input and the focal point of each basis function in order to approximate a target function or pattern. An input layer, a hidden layer, and an output layer make up the network structure. As seen in Fig. 3:

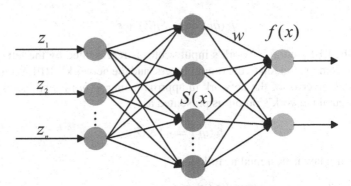

Fig. 3. Topology of the RBF neural network.

In Fig. 3 above, the input of RBF neural network is $Z \in \Omega \subset R^n$, w represents the weight vector of RBF neural network output layer, and $S(x)$ represents the Radial basis function vector. In this paper, Gaussian function is selected as the basis function of the neural network. The Gaussian function is as follows:

$$S_i(Z) = \exp\left[-\frac{\|Z - \mu_i\|^2}{\sigma_i^2}\right] = \exp\left[-\frac{(Z - \mu_i)^T (Z - \mu_i)}{\sigma_i^2}\right], \ i = 1, 2, \ldots, l \quad (6)$$

In the above formula, $\mu_i = [\mu_1, \mu_2, \ldots, \mu_n]^T$ represents the center point of the Gaussian function, and σ_i represents the width of the Gaussian function. The RBF network structure used in this article is three inputs and two outputs. Each $S(x)$ in the hidden layer has 256 nodes, with a center selection of ± 1 and a σ_i value of 0.01. The variance value of the basis function is set to 25.

According to Eq. (4), for the dual-arm dynamic model, the joint angle error of the robotic arm can be defined as:

$$e_k(t) = q_{d_k}(t) - q_k(t) \quad (7)$$

We assume the following tracking error function:

$$r_k = \dot{e}_k + \Lambda e_k \quad (8)$$

With the given value of $\Lambda = \Lambda^T > 0$, we can obtain

$$\begin{aligned} r_k &= \dot{q}_{d_k} + \Lambda e_k - \dot{q}_k \\ M_{b_k} \dot{r}_k = M_{b_k}(q_k)\left(\ddot{q}_{d_k} + \Lambda \dot{e}_k - \ddot{q}_k\right) &= M_{b_k}\left(\ddot{q}_{d_k} + \Lambda \dot{e}_k\right) - M_{b_k} \ddot{q}_k \\ &= -C_{b_k}(q_k, \dot{q}_k) r_k - \tau_k + \tau_d + f_k(\dot{q}_k) + \tau_\Delta \end{aligned} \quad (9)$$

Given that $f_k(\dot{q}_k)$ is unknown in the actual collaborative operation of the robotic arm, it is important to approximatively represent the function of $f_k(\dot{q}_k)$ using the RBF neural network when the value of $Z = [q_k \ \dot{q}_k \ q_{d_k} \ \dot{q}_{d_k}]$ is utilized as the input. Produces the following outcome:

$$f_k(\dot{q}_k) = w^T S_i(Z) + \varepsilon \quad (10)$$

When the RBF neural network's input vector is represented by the letters Z, w for the weights from the hidden to the output layers, and the network's RBF vector is shown by $S_i(Z)$, and the error of the network in approximating $f_k(\dot{q}_k)$ is expressed by ε. As a result, the neural network's output is presented as:

$$\hat{f}_k(\dot{q}_k) = \hat{w}^T S_i(Z) \quad (11)$$

The control law is designed as follows:

$$\tau = \hat{w}^T S_i(Z) + K_v r_k + \tau_\Delta \quad (12)$$

Furthermore, we obtain the following equation:

$$M_{b_k} \dot{r}_k = -\left(k_v + C_{b_k}(q_k, \dot{q}_k)\right) r_k + \varepsilon \quad (13)$$

$$\varepsilon = \tau_d + w^T S_i(Z) + \xi(x) \tag{14}$$

Here, $\xi(x)$ represents the minimum reconstruction error vector of the neural network. By designing the Lyapunov function as $V = \frac{1}{2} r^T M_{b_k}(q_k) r_k$, we can substitute the function into Eqs. (12) and (13) to obtain

$$\dot{V} = r_k^T \varepsilon - r_k^T K_v r \tag{15}$$

which indicates that the stability of the control system depends on ε.

According to the derived equations, the impedance control rate of the neural network can be determined as follows:

$$\tau = K_v r_k + \hat{w}^T S_i(Z) + \tau_\Delta - v(t) \tag{16}$$

where $v(t)$ is a robust term primarily used to stabilize modeling errors and external disturbances.

To prove the stability of the control model, we designed the following Lyapunov function:

$$V = \frac{1}{2} r_k^T M_{b_k}(q_k) r_k + \frac{1}{2} tr(w^T \Gamma_\theta^{-1} w) \tag{17}$$

By taking the derivative with respect to time, we obtain.

$$\dot{V} = r_k^T \left(M_{b_k}(q_k) \dot{r}_k + C_k(q_k, \dot{q}_k) r_k \right) + tr(w^T \Gamma_\theta^{-1} \dot{w}) \tag{18}$$

Substituting $v(t) = 0$ yields.

$$\dot{V} = -r_k^T K_v r_k + r_k^T (\varepsilon + \tau_d) + tr(w^T \Gamma^{-1} \dot{w}) - r_k^T w^T S_i(Z) \tag{19}$$

Assuming that under the conditions of $v(t) = 0$, τ_d, and $\varepsilon \neq 0$, the adaptive update rate of the weight w of the RBFNN network is designed as $\dot{w} = \Gamma_\theta S_i(Z) r_k^T$ and $\|r\| \geq \frac{(\varepsilon_N + b_d)}{k_{v\,min}}$, substituting Eq. (19) into the adaptive update rate yields.

$$\dot{V} \leq k_{v\,min} \|r\|^2 + (\varepsilon_N + b_d) \|r\| \tag{20}$$

When the conditions are met,

$$\|r\| > \frac{(\varepsilon_N + b_d)}{k_{v\,min}} \tag{21}$$

Knowing $V > 0$ and $\dot{V} \leq 0$, it can be concluded that the controller is stable. The overall control block diagram of the system is shown in Fig. 4 below.

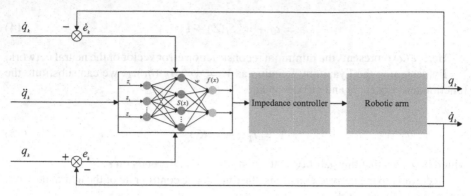

Fig. 4. System control block diagram

4   Simulation Design

4.1   Simulation Environment

The adaptive impedance control technique founded on the RBF neural network model suggested in this paper for the simultaneous working of two arms has to be tested for feasibility, MATLAB 2021b was used as the simulation experimental platform to construct two robotic arms, each having seven degrees of freedom, through the improved Denavit-Hartenberg(DH) method and robot toolbox and perform simulation verification. The seven coordinate systems of the improved Modified Denavit Hartenberg(MDH) parameter method are represented by the numbers 0–7, as shown in Fig. 5, and the parameter values are presented in Table 1:

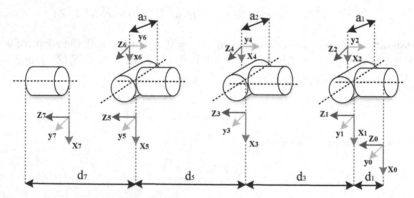

Fig. 5. MDH Diagram of the Robotic Arm

A target object was constructed in the simulation model, with a length, width, and height of 0.4 m, 0.36 m, and 0.2 m, respectively. The two robotic arms were 0.4 m apart, and their ends were placed at both ends of the object in the initial state. A diagram of the simulation model is shown in Fig. 6.

Table 1. MDH Parameter Table

Number	Wheelbase	Axial offset	Twisted corners	Rotation angle
1	0	145.5	0	θ_1
2	187.5	0	−90	θ_2
3	0	243.5	90	θ_3
4	153.5	0	−90	θ_4
5	0	248.5	90	θ_5
6	145.5	0	−90	θ_6
7	0	225.5	90	θ_7

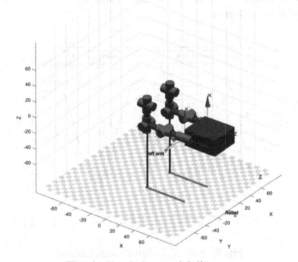

Fig. 6. Simulation model diagram

4.2 Simulation Results

(1) Simulation testing of different force-tracking signal types.

A 50-N step force signal was input. Step-signal tracking was accomplished using impedance control and adaptive impedance control, as shown in Fig. 7. The RBF adaptive impedance control, however, reacted more quickly.

Next, enter a slope force signal between 0 and 100 N. Figure 8 shows that compared to conventional impedance control, enhanced RBF neural network adaptive impedance control offers less overshoot and steady-state errors. Figure 8 shows a significant overshoot event at the start of a conventional impedance control.

As shown in Fig. 9 below, the input sinusoidal force signal for tracking test can find that the traditional impedance control model has obvious phase lag phenomenon when tracking the sinusoidal force signal, and the amplitude is smaller than expected,

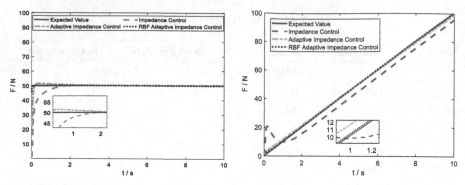

Fig. 7. Step force signal tracking   **Fig. 8.** Slope force signal tracking

additionally, the enhanced RBF adaptive impedance control model performs well in tracking sinusoidal force signals.

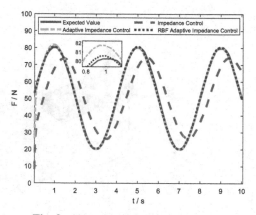

Fig. 9. Sinusoidal force signal tracking

(2) (2) Test simulation with abrupt change in contact force.

A simulation test was run with a sudden shift in the contact force. The initial contact force was 50 N, the anticipated contact force, of 50 N was reached in <2 s. At 3 s, the contact force changed to 80 N, and the expected value changed to 20 N. As shown in Fig. 10, the control system achieved a rapid response and reached a stable state under sudden force changes.

(3) Stiffness testing in various environments.

Control model testing was conducted in different stiffness environments of 300 and 500, and the contact force was designed to be 50 N. The contact force response curves are shown in Fig. 11 for the environmental stiffnesses of 300 and 500, respectively. As the environmental stiffness increased, the contact force response speed increased, indicating that the algorithm had good adaptability in different stiffness environments.

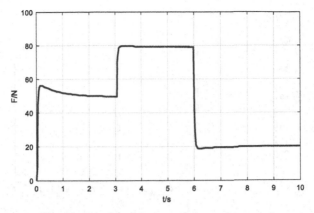

Fig. 10. Results of the contact force change test

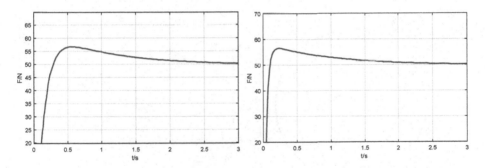

Fig. 11. 300 and 500 environmental stiffness test results

(4) Environmental stiffness mutation test.

As shown in Fig. 12 below, the initial contact force expectation of the design is 50N, the contact force reaches the expected 50N in about 2s, and then increases the environmental stiffness at the 3s, when the contact force becomes larger, under the improved control model, it can be quickly adjusted, and at the 6s, the environmental stiffness decreases, and the contact force can quickly return to the contact force expectation after a sharp decrease, reflecting that the control model can face the sudden change in environmental stiffness well.

(5) Circular trajectory tracking test.

Using the RBF neural network adaptive impedance controller, the trajectory of the manipulated object and the spatial movement of the ends of the arms is traced in the XOZ plane, as shown in Fig. 13. Under the driving force of the two-arm dynamic model, the clamped rigid body completes the circular trajectory movement and achieves good trajectory tracking.

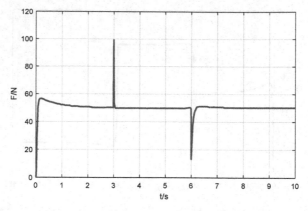

Fig. 12. Force response curve for sudden changes in environmental stiffness

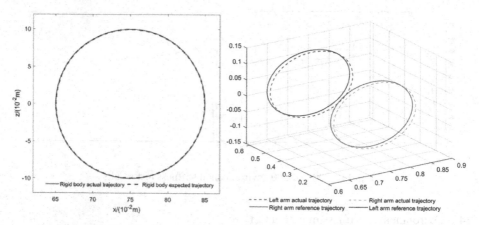

Fig. 13. Circular tracking rendering of robotic arms and objects

5 Conclusion

In order to lessen the effects of unmanageable friction, outside disturbances, and parameter mismatches across joints driving the movement of a robotic arm, this research suggests an adaptive impedance management technique founded on an RBF neural network. We built a dual seven-degree of freedom robotic arm model and ran simulation tests using the simulation software MATLAB platform in order to assess the algorithm's performance. Through simulation tests that included different force monitoring signals, contact force changes, variations in environmental stiffness, environmental rigidity changes, and circular trajectory tracking, the standard impedance control technique and another adaptive impedance management approach were compared to the suggested adaptive impedance control solution built on the RBF neural network. The RBF neural network-based adaptive impedance control technique outperformed expectations in terms of tracking performance. The findings showed that this dynamic impedance control method is appropriate for force-interaction situations involving the mobility of robotic arms in uncharted environments due to its quick response, high control precision, and good steady-state performance. At present, verification is only conducted in a simulation environment. In the future, the designed controller will be further verified through physical platforms, and system experiments will be conducted in more collaborative operation scenarios. The impact of external disturbances on the operation of the dual arm system will also be further considered.

Acknowledgements. This research is supported by the joint fund project of the National Natural Science Foundation of China (Grant number U20A20201), Autonomous Project of State Key Laboratory of Robotics (Grant number 2022-Z02,2022-Z19), Liaoning Province Applied Basic Research Program Project (Grant number 2023JH2/101300141) and the Natural Science Foundation of Liaoning Province (Grant number 2021-MS-032).

References

1. Qin, H., Shao, S., Wang, T., Yu, X., Jiang, Y., Cao, Z.: Review of autonomous path planning algorithms for mobile robots. Drones **7**(3), 211 (2023)
2. Véronneau, C., et al.: Modular magnetorheological actuator with high torque density and transparency for the collaborative robot industry. IEEE Robot. Autom. Let. **8**(2), 896–903. IEEE Press (2023)
3. Farrens, A.J., Schmidt, K., Cohen, H., Sergi, F.: Concurrent contribution of co-contraction to error reduction during dynamic adaptation of the wrist. IEEE Trans. Neural Syst. Rehabil. Eng. **31**, 1287–1296. IEEE Press (2023)
4. Ozdamar, I., Laghi, M., Grioli, G., Ajoudani, A., Catalano, M.G., Bicchi, A.: A Shared autonomy reconfigurable control framework for telemanipulation of multi-arm systems. IEEE Robot. Autom. Let. **7**(4), 9937–9944. IEEE Press (2022).
5. Zhang, F., Qu, J., Liu, H., et al.: A multi-priority control of asymmetric coordination for redundant dual-arm robot. Int. J. Humanoid Rob. **16**(1), 49–60 (2019)
6. Yang, C., Zeng, C., Fang, C., et al.: A DMPs-based framework for robot learning and generalization of humanlike variable impedance skills. IEEE/ASME Trans. Mechatron. **2**(1), 1–12 (2018)
7. Lei, Y., Yang, Y., Xu, W., et al.: Dual-arm coordinated motion planning and compliance control for capturing moving objects with large momentum. In: IEEE/RSJ International Conference on Intelligent Robots & Systems. IEEE (2018)
8. Duan, J., Gan, Y., Chen, M., et al.: Symmetrical adaptive variable admittance control for position/force tracking of dual-arm cooperative manipulators with unknown trajectory deviations. Robot. Comput. Integrat. Manufac. **57**, 357–369 (2019)
9. Wei, H., Yiting, et al.: Adaptive fuzzy neural network control for a constrained robot using impedance learning. IEEE Trans. Neural Networks Learn. Syst. **5**(4), 32–43 (2017)
10. Li, Z., Bo, H., Ajoudani, A., et al.: Asymmetric bimanual control of dual-arm exoskeletons for human-cooperative manipulations. IEEE Trans. Robot. PP(99), 1–8 (2017)
11. Shirato, T., Liu, Y., Matsuzaka, A., et al.: Assist control for dual arm cooperative manipulation by remote controlled robot. In: 2018 IEEE International Conference on Robotics and Biomimetics (ROBIO). IEEE (2018)
12. Lei, Y., Mu, Z., Xu, W., et al.: Coordinated compliance control of dual-arm robot for payload manipulation: Master-slave and shared force control. In: IEEE/RSJ International Conference on Intelligent Robots & Systems. IEEE (2016)

13. Li, J., Zhang, B., Yao, J., Zhao, M., Xu, Z., Zhao, X.: Vitality interface system and neuroid collaborative control for intelligent prosthetic arms. Robotics **44**(05), 546–563 (2022)
14. Liang, X., et al.: Active compliance adaptive interactive control of lower limb rehabilitation robots. Robotics **43**(05), 547–556 (2021)
15. Duan, J., Gan, Y., Dai, X.: Hybrid position/force control based on variable impedance model during double arm coordinated handling. Robotics **41**(06), 795–802+812 (2019)
16. Jiao, C., Yu, L., Su, X., et al.: Adaptive hybrid impedance control for dual-arm cooperative manipulation with object uncertainties. Automatica **5**(4), 140–153 (2022)

Trajectory Tracking Control for Robot Manipulator Under Dynamic Environment

Yushi Wang[1], Yanbo Pang[1], Qingkai Li[1], Wenhan Cai[1],
and Mingguo Zhao[1,2]([✉])

[1] Department of Automation, Tsinghua University, Beijing, China
mgzhao@mail.tsinghua.edu.cn
[2] Beijing Innovation Center for Future Chips, Tsinghua University, Beijing, China

Abstract. During the operation process of the manipulator, it is important to be aware of the environmental changes or external disturbances that may occur. These can impact the manipulator's effectiveness and should be considered for optimal performance. We conducted research that combined model predictive control (MPC) and whole-body control (WBC) to present a controller for this scenario. Our MPC predicted the end-effector motion using the linearized robot dynamics equation in operational space and provided feasible trajectories while considering obstacles represented by linear inequality constraints. In WBC, we set the end-effector task as the highest priority and adopted hierarchical quadratic programming (HQP) to prevent disturbances from affecting the end-effector. To verify the expected performance of our controller, we conducted simulations and experiments on the Flexiv Rizon 4s. The results showed that our controller performed well and met the desired criteria.

Keywords: Model predictive control · Whole-body control · Robot manipulator

1 Introduction

Humans can work in complex and variable environments. We also hope that robots deal with changes or disturbances in the working environment during operation. Therefore, how to make robots have human-like dexterity and robustness is an important research topic in robotics.

Robot manipulators usually have redundant degrees of freedom for higher flexibility and a greater range of motion. Configuring redundant manipulators in various ways without altering the end-effector's position or orientation is possible. The controller can be designed to take advantage of the redundancy of manipulators to respond to environmental disturbances.

Supported by STI 2030-Major Projects 2021ZD0201402.

© The Author(s), under exclusive license to Springer Nature Singapore Pte Ltd. 2023
H. Yang et al. (Eds.): ICIRA 2023, LNAI 14270, pp. 513–524, 2023.
https://doi.org/10.1007/978-981-99-6492-5_44

Whole-body control (WBC) has been widely applied to redundant manipulators to solve multi-task control problems [6,9]. As early as 1987, there were WBC methods based on null space projection [8,11], using pseudo-inverse to establish different priority hierarchies for multiple tasks. The lower priority task is solved in the null space of the higher priority task, and thus the priority hierarchy is guaranteed [3]. WBC methods based on quadratic programmings, such as weighted quadratic programming (WQP) [1] and hierarchical quadratic programming (HQP) [5,7], have become popular because they can explicitly consider inequality constraints. Compared with WQP, which sets task priorities by different weights, HQP ensures a strict priority hierarchy by solving multiple optimization problems sequentially.

To deal with sudden environmental changes, such as obstacles on the trajectory of the manipulator, model predictive control (MPC) is considered to predict the robot's movement in the short term and optimize the control law in advance to avoid sudden impact on obstacles.

MPC is a finite-time optimal control method widely used in quadrupedal robots [4,12]. There are also some examples of MPC for robot manipulators. For example, Carron et al. [2] improve the accuracy of the manipulator model through data-driven methods to achieve high-precision trajectory tracking. Pankert et al. [13] applied MPC to mobile manipulators to make the end effector track the trajectory while maintaining stability constraints. Since MPC needs to repeatedly calculate the optimal control problem in the future, it requires many computing resources, which poses a challenge to real-time performance. Therefore, MPC often runs at a lower control frequency, and simplified linear models are used as system models in MPC problems. In this case, MPC problems can be expressed by quadratic programming problems. WBC added after MPC compensates for the error caused by model simplification to ensure that the manipulator tracks the optimization results given by MPC.

This paper presents a manipulator controller based on MPC and WBC. The block diagram of our controller is shown in Fig. 1. This controller can use the manipulator's redundancy to eliminate disturbances on the end-effector task from the environment. Furthermore, when the end-effector task has to be adjusted in response to the environmental changes, the controller can respond in advance by predicting the trajectory of the manipulator, showing robustness under changing environments. The effectiveness of this method is verified both by simulations and experiments.

The rest of this paper is organized as follows: In Sect. 2, we derive the mathematical formulation of the MPC problem. Section 3 constructs the WBC problem and briefly describes the algorithm we use. Section 4 provides simulations and experiments based on a 7-DOF manipulator. Finally, Sect. 5 concludes this paper.

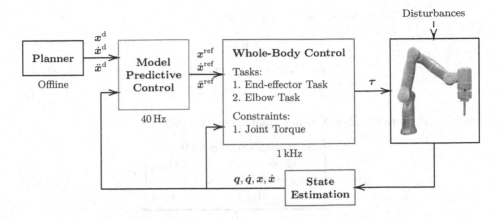

Fig. 1. Block diagram of the robot controller

2   Model Predictive Control Avoiding Dynamic Obstacles

For a fixed-based robot, its multi-body dynamics can be formulated as

$$M(q)\ddot{q} + b(q, \dot{q}) + g(q) = \tau, \tag{1}$$

where $q, \dot{q}, \ddot{q} \in \mathbb{R}^n$ are respectively the generalized position, velocity and acceleration vector, $M(q) \in \mathbb{R}^{n \times n}$ is the generalized inertia matrix, $b(q, \dot{q}) \in \mathbb{R}^n$ is the Coriolis and centrifugal term, $g(q) \in \mathbb{R}^n$ is the gravitational term and $\tau \in \mathbb{R}^n$ are the generalized force.

We define the net generalized force $\tau_{\mathrm{net}} \in \mathbb{R}^n$ as

$$\tau = \tau_{\mathrm{net}} + b(q, \dot{q}) + g(q). \tag{2}$$

We compensate for the Coriolis and centrifugal term as well as the gravitational term directly in the generalized force, so we use the net generalized force for calculations.

The transformation from the generalized coordinates to the Cartesian coordinates is given by

$$\ddot{x} = J(q)\ddot{q} + \dot{J}(q)\dot{q}, \tag{3}$$

$$\tau_{\mathrm{net}} = J(q)^\top F_{\mathrm{net}}, \tag{4}$$

where $\ddot{x} \in \mathbb{R}^6$ is the Cartesian acceleration vector, $J(q) \in \mathbb{R}^{6 \times n}$ is the Jacobian matrix and $F_{\mathrm{net}} \in \mathbb{R}^6$ is the net Cartesian wrench. The dynamic equation in Cartesian coordinates can be expressed as

$$\ddot{x} = J(q)M(q)^{-1}J(q)^\top F_{\mathrm{net}} + \dot{J}(q)\dot{q}. \tag{5}$$

We define the state values $\boldsymbol{x}, \dot{\boldsymbol{x}}$ and $\ddot{\boldsymbol{x}}$ as

$$\boldsymbol{x} = \begin{bmatrix} \psi\ \theta\ \phi\ x\ y\ z \end{bmatrix}^{\top}, \tag{6}$$

$$\dot{\boldsymbol{x}} = \begin{bmatrix} \omega_x\ \omega_y\ \omega_z\ v_x\ v_y\ v_z \end{bmatrix}^{\top}, \tag{7}$$

$$\ddot{\boldsymbol{x}} = \begin{bmatrix} \alpha_x\ \alpha_y\ \alpha_z\ a_x\ a_y\ a_z \end{bmatrix}^{\top}, \tag{8}$$

where ψ, θ, ϕ are the Z-Y-X Euler angles, then we have

$$\frac{\mathrm{d}}{\mathrm{d}t}\boldsymbol{x} = \underbrace{\begin{bmatrix} \cos\phi/\cos\theta\ \sin\phi/\cos\theta\ 0 \\ -\sin\phi\quad\quad \cos\phi\quad\quad 0\ \boldsymbol{0}_{3\times3} \\ \cos\phi\tan\theta\ \sin\phi\tan\theta\ 1 \\ \boldsymbol{0}_{3\times3}\quad\quad\quad\quad \boldsymbol{I}_{3\times3} \end{bmatrix}}_{\boldsymbol{I}'}\dot{\boldsymbol{x}}, \tag{9}$$

$$\frac{\mathrm{d}}{\mathrm{d}t}\dot{\boldsymbol{x}} = \ddot{\boldsymbol{x}}. \tag{10}$$

The discrete state space equations can be approximated as

$$\boldsymbol{x}_{k+1} = \boldsymbol{x}_k + \frac{\mathrm{d}}{\mathrm{d}t}\boldsymbol{x}_k\Delta t = \boldsymbol{x}_k + \boldsymbol{I}'\dot{\boldsymbol{x}}_k\Delta t, \tag{11}$$

$$\dot{\boldsymbol{x}}_{k+1} = \dot{\boldsymbol{x}}_k + \frac{\mathrm{d}}{\mathrm{d}t}\dot{\boldsymbol{x}}_k\Delta t = \dot{\boldsymbol{x}}_k + \ddot{\boldsymbol{x}}_k\Delta t. \tag{12}$$

By combining (5), (11), (12) and taking $\boldsymbol{F}_{\mathrm{net}}$ as the control actions $\boldsymbol{u}$, the discrete state space equations of the system can be expressed as

$$\underbrace{\begin{bmatrix} \boldsymbol{x}_{k+1} \\ \dot{\boldsymbol{x}}_{k+1} \\ 1 \end{bmatrix}}_{\bar{\boldsymbol{x}}_{k+1}} = \underbrace{\begin{bmatrix} \boldsymbol{I}_{6\times6}\ \Delta t\boldsymbol{I}'\quad \boldsymbol{0}_{6\times1} \\ \boldsymbol{0}_{6\times6}\ \boldsymbol{I}_{6\times6}\ \Delta t\dot{\boldsymbol{J}}(\boldsymbol{q})\dot{\boldsymbol{q}} \\ \boldsymbol{0}_{1\times6}\ \boldsymbol{0}_{1\times6}\quad 1 \end{bmatrix}}_{\boldsymbol{A}} \underbrace{\begin{bmatrix} \boldsymbol{x}_k \\ \dot{\boldsymbol{x}}_k \\ 1 \end{bmatrix}}_{\bar{\boldsymbol{x}}_k} + \underbrace{\begin{bmatrix} \boldsymbol{0}_{6\times6} \\ \Delta t\boldsymbol{J}(\boldsymbol{q})\boldsymbol{M}(\boldsymbol{q})^{-1}\boldsymbol{J}(\boldsymbol{q})^{\top} \\ \boldsymbol{0}_{1\times6} \end{bmatrix}}_{\boldsymbol{B}} \boldsymbol{u}_k. \tag{13}$$

We can represent obstacles in the working environment of the robot as a combination of several linear inequality constraints as

$$\boldsymbol{b}_{\mathrm{lC}} \preceq \boldsymbol{C}\bar{\boldsymbol{x}}_k \preceq \boldsymbol{b}_{\mathrm{uC}}, \tag{14}$$

where $\bar{\boldsymbol{x}}_k \in \mathbb{R}^{13}$ is the state values at time k, $\boldsymbol{C} \in \mathbb{R}^{n_c \times 13}$ is the constraint matrix, $\boldsymbol{b}_{\mathrm{lC}} \in \mathbb{R}^{n_c}, \boldsymbol{b}_{\mathrm{uC}} \in \mathbb{R}^{n_c}$ are respectively the upper and lower bound vectors of the constraint, n_c is the number of constraints. The environment may change over time, and the constraints will change accordingly.

The MPC problem is defined as

$$\begin{aligned} \underset{\bar{\boldsymbol{x}}_k, \boldsymbol{u}_k}{\mathrm{minimize}}\quad & \sum_{k=1}^{n}\left\|\bar{\boldsymbol{x}}_k - \bar{\boldsymbol{x}}_k^{\mathrm{d}}\right\|_Q^2 + \sum_{k=0}^{n-1}\|\boldsymbol{u}_k\|_K^2 \\ \mathrm{subject\ to}\quad & \bar{\boldsymbol{x}}_{k+1} = \boldsymbol{A}\bar{\boldsymbol{x}}_k + \boldsymbol{B}\boldsymbol{u}_k \\ & \boldsymbol{b}_{\mathrm{lC}} \preceq \boldsymbol{C}\bar{\boldsymbol{x}}_k \preceq \boldsymbol{b}_{\mathrm{uC}}, \end{aligned} \tag{15}$$

where $\boldsymbol{Q} \in \mathbb{R}^{13\times13}, \boldsymbol{K} \in \mathbb{R}^{6\times6}$ are the weight matrix.

In order to eliminate equality constraints and reduce the dimension of optimization variables, $\bar{x}_k$ is represented by u_k:

$$
\begin{bmatrix} \bar{x}_1 \\ \bar{x}_2 \\ \vdots \\ \bar{x}_n \end{bmatrix} = \underbrace{\begin{bmatrix} A \\ A^2 \\ \vdots \\ A^n \end{bmatrix}}_{\hat{A}} \bar{x}_0 + \underbrace{\begin{bmatrix} B & 0_{13\times6} & \cdots & 0_{13\times6} \\ AB & B & \cdots & 0_{13\times6} \\ \vdots & \vdots & \ddots & \vdots \\ A^{n-1}B & A^{n-2}B & \cdots & B \end{bmatrix}}_{\hat{B}} \underbrace{\begin{bmatrix} u_0 \\ u_1 \\ \vdots \\ u_{n-1} \end{bmatrix}}_{\hat{u}}. \tag{16}
$$

Substituting (16) into (15), the MPC problem can be expressed as

$$
\begin{aligned}
\underset{\hat{u}}{\text{minimize}} \quad & \hat{u}^\top \left(\hat{B}^\top \hat{Q} \hat{B} + \hat{K} \right) \hat{u} + 2\hat{u}^\top \hat{B}^\top \hat{Q} \left(\hat{A}\bar{x}_0 - \hat{x}^{\mathrm{d}} \right) \\
\text{subject to} \quad & \hat{b}_{\mathrm{lC}} - \hat{C}\hat{A}\bar{x}_0 \preceq \hat{C}\hat{B}\hat{u} \preceq \hat{b}_{\mathrm{uC}} - \hat{C}\hat{A}\bar{x}_0,
\end{aligned} \tag{17}
$$

where $\hat{u}, \hat{x}^{\mathrm{d}}, \hat{b}_{\mathrm{lC}}, \hat{b}_{\mathrm{uC}}$ are respectively the augmented vectors of $u_k, \bar{x}_k^{\mathrm{d}}, b_{\mathrm{lC}}, b_{\mathrm{uC}}$ and $\hat{Q}, \hat{K}, \hat{C}$ are respectively the diagonal matrices of Q, K, C. (17) is a standard form of quadratic programming problem.

Solving this optimization problem, the optimal solution $\hat{u}^*$ is obtained. According to (5), (11) and (12), we can get a reference trajectory that satisfies constraints in the working environment:

$$
\ddot{x}^{\mathrm{ref}} = \dot{J}(q)\dot{q} + J(q)M(q)^{-1}J(q)^\top u_0^*, \tag{18}
$$

$$
\dot{x}^{\mathrm{ref}} = \dot{x}_0 + \ddot{x}^{\mathrm{ref}}\Delta t, \tag{19}
$$

$$
x^{\mathrm{ref}} = x_0 + I'\dot{x}_0\Delta t. \tag{20}
$$

The linear inequality constraints in the MPC problem change simultaneously with the working environment so that the manipulator can adjust the trajectory online according to the actual situation during operation to avoid collision with obstacles. $x^{\mathrm{ref}}, \dot{x}^{\mathrm{ref}}, \ddot{x}^{\mathrm{ref}}$ can be used as a reference trajectory for subsequent modules to track.

3   Whole-Body Control Resisting Environmental Disturbances

In order to achieve the goal that the end-effector of the manipulator tracks the reference trajectory under environmental disturbances, the WBC problem in this paper consists of the following two tasks, whose priorities decrease successively:

- Task 1: The end-effector of the manipulator tracks the reference trajectory through PD feedback
- Task 2: Set motion damping at the elbow of the manipulator

The control problem can be expressed as

$$\ddot{x}_1 = \ddot{x}_1^{\text{ref}} + K_d(\dot{x}_1^{\text{ref}} - \dot{x}_1) + K_p \begin{bmatrix} e_{1,\text{ori}} \\ x_{1,\text{pos}}^{\text{ref}} - x_{1,\text{pos}} \end{bmatrix}, \tag{21}$$

$$\ddot{x}_{2,\text{pos}} = -K_f \dot{x}_{2,\text{pos}}, \tag{22}$$

where $\ddot{x}_1 \in \mathbb{R}^6, \ddot{x}_{2,\text{pos}} \in \mathbb{R}^3$ are respectively the acceleration of the end-effector and elbow of the manipulator, $\dot{x}_1^{\text{ref}}, \ddot{x}_1^{\text{ref}} \in \mathbb{R}^6$ are respectively the reference velocity and acceleration of the end-effector of the manipulator, $\dot{x}_1 \in \mathbb{R}^6, \dot{x}_{2,\text{pos}} \in \mathbb{R}^3$ are respectively the actual velocity of the end-effector and elbow, $e_{1,\text{ori}} \in \mathbb{R}^3$ is the angle-axis representation of the error between the reference and actual orientation of the end-effector, $x_{1,\text{pos}}^{\text{ref}}, x_{1,\text{pos}} \in \mathbb{R}^3$ are respectively the reference and actual position of the end-effector, $K_d, K_p \in \mathbb{R}^{6\times6}, K_f \in \mathbb{R}^{3\times3}$ are the feedback parameters in the form of diagonal matrices.

In order to ensure strict priority hierarchies, HQP is used to solve the optimization problems of each priority level in turn, while higher priority tasks are taken as constraints.

The two tasks can be expressed as

$$\ddot{x}_1 - \dot{J}_1(q)\dot{q} = J_1(q)\ddot{q}, \tag{23}$$

$$\ddot{x}_{2,\text{pos}} - \dot{J}_2(q)\dot{q} = J_2(q)\ddot{q}, \tag{24}$$

where $J_1(q) \in \mathbb{R}^{6\times n}, J_2(q) \in \mathbb{R}^{3\times n}$ are respectively the Jacobian matrix of the end-effector and elbow of the manipulator with respect to the generalized coordinate vector. $\ddot{q}$ is the optimization variable of the WBC problem.

Firstly, we consider the optimization problem for the first task, which can be derived as

$$\underset{\ddot{q}}{\text{minimize}} \quad \left\| J_1(q)\ddot{q} - \left(\ddot{x}_1 - \dot{J}_1(q)\dot{q}\right) \right\|_{Q_1}^2 + \|\ddot{q}\|_{K_1}^2 \tag{25}$$
$$\text{subject to} \quad \tau_{\min} \preceq M(q)\ddot{q} + b(q,\dot{q}) + g(q) \preceq \tau_{\max},$$

where $Q_1 \in \mathbb{R}^{6\times6}, K_1 \in \mathbb{R}^{n\times n}$ are the weight matrix and $\tau_{\min}, \tau_{\max} \in \mathbb{R}^n$ are the torque limits for joint motors.

Note that inequality constraints need to be considered in the optimization problem of each priority level. If constraints are not considered initially, there may be a conflict between constraints of high-priority tasks and inequality constraints, resulting in no solution for low-priority problems.

By solving the first optimization problem, the optimal solution $\ddot{q}_1^*$ is obtained. On this basis, the optimization problem of the second task can be derived as

$$\underset{\ddot{q}}{\text{minimize}} \quad \left\| J_2(q)\ddot{q} - \left(\ddot{x}_{2,\text{pos}} - \dot{J}_2(q)\dot{q}\right) \right\|_{Q_2}^2 + \|\ddot{q}\|_{K_2}^2$$
$$\text{subject to} \quad J_1(q)\ddot{q} = J_1(q)\ddot{q}_1^* \tag{26}$$
$$\tau_{\min} \preceq M(q)\ddot{q} + b(q,\dot{q}) + g(q) \preceq \tau_{\max}.$$

The additional equality constraint ensures that the first task, which has higher priority, will not be affected when solving this optimization problem. The equality constraint can also be equivalently expressed as

$$\ddot{q} = N_1 u + \ddot{q}_1^*, \tag{27}$$

where $N_1 \in \mathbb{R}^{n \times (n-6)}$ is a matrix consisting of the basis of the null space of $J_1(q)$ and $u \in \mathbb{R}^{n-6}$ is the new optimization variable. N_1 can be obtained by Gaussian elimination or singular value decomposition of $J_1(q)$.

Since $J_1(q)N_1 = 0$, the equality constraint in (26) is always satisfied, Therefore, (26) can be simplified as

$$\underset{u}{\text{minimize}} \quad \left\| J_2(q)\left(N_1 u + \ddot{q}_1^*\right) - \left(\ddot{x}_{2,\text{pos}} - \dot{J}_2(q)\dot{q}\right) \right\|_{Q_2}^2 + \|N_1 u + \ddot{q}_1^*\|_{K_2}^2$$

$$\text{subject to} \quad \tau_{\min} \preceq M(q)\left(N_1 u + \ddot{q}_1^*\right) + b(q,\dot{q}) + g(q) \preceq \tau_{\max}. \tag{28}$$

Substituting the optimal solution u^* of (28) into (27), the optimal solution of the WBC problem can be obtained:

$$\ddot{q}^* = N_1 u^* + \ddot{q}_1^*. \tag{29}$$

The optimal generalized force can be obtained according to the multi-rigid body dynamics equation of the robot:

$$\tau^* = M(q)\ddot{q}^* + b(q,\dot{q}) + g(q), \tag{30}$$

which can be used as the torque instruction for joint motors assigned to each joint.

WBC maps the trajectory in task-space to joint-space and resists environmental disturbances in the null space of the mapping. The redundancy of the manipulator is utilized to minimize the impact on the end-effector.

4   Simulations and Experiments

We conduct simulations in the open-source robot simulator Webots [10] to verify the performance of MPC and WBC. Then, experiments are carried out on a real robot demonstrating the capabilities of our controller in the real world. The robot we used is the Flexiv Rizon 4s, a 7-DOF manipulator.

4.1   Simulations for Avoiding Dynamic Obstacles

The simulation process for avoiding dynamic obstacles is shown in Fig. 2. The end-effector of the manipulator moves cyclically along a circular trajectory in the horizontal plane, while an obstacle suddenly appears on the trajectory of the end-effector. The period of the circular movement is 10 s. The obstacle is applied in the second round.

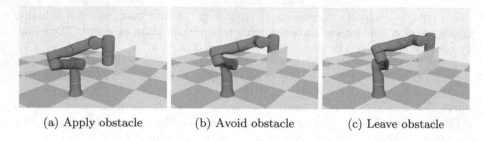

(a) Apply obstacle   (b) Avoid obstacle   (c) Leave obstacle

Fig. 2. Simulation process for avoiding dynamic obstacles

The movement of the end-effector in x direction is shown in Fig. 3, where the dashed blue line and shadow respectively represent the occurrence time and position of the obstacle. The end-effector tracks the reference trajectory well when no obstacle is applied. After the obstacle appears in x direction, the end-effector deviates from the reference trajectory in advance to avoid collision with the obstacle.

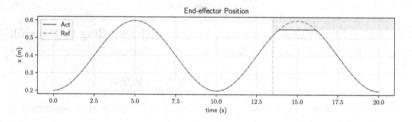

Fig. 3. End-effector motion in x direction. (Color figure online)

Figure 4 illustrates how MPC responds to the suddenly imposed obstacle, where the green line is the optimal trajectory given by MPC. Before the obstacles are applied, the trajectory optimized by MPC coincides with the reference trajectory so that the end-effector tracks the reference trajectory. When the obstacle appears, the corresponding inequality constraint is added to the MPC problem at the same time. MPC takes into account the constraint and adjusts the trajectory to steer clear of the obstacle.

The simulation results show that MPC can adjust the trajectory of the manipulator online to deal with dynamic obstacles in the working environment.

4.2   Simulations for Resisting Environmental Disturbance

In order to verify the effectiveness of WBC, a fixed external force is applied to the elbow of the manipulator for 10 s in simulations. The simulation process is shown in Fig. 5. The external force applied is fixed as 10 N and its direction is perpendicular to the elbow.

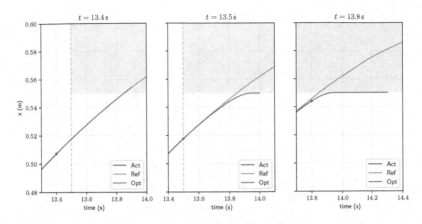

Fig. 4. Optimization results of model predictive control. (Color figure online)

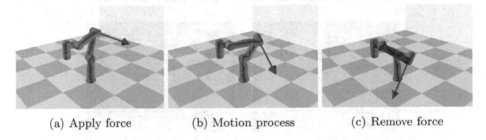

(a) Apply force   (b) Motion process   (c) Remove force

Fig. 5. Simulation process for resisting environmental disturbance

The motion trajectory of the end-effector and the elbow of the manipulator under external force is shown in Fig. 6. Due to the disturbance of external force, the elbow of the manipulator produces a large movement of 50.02 cm, while the maximum error of the position of the end-effector is only 1.62 cm. WBC takes advantage of the redundancy of the manipulator to resist external force from the environment, thus keeping the position of the end-effector almost stationary.

4.3   Experiments

We validate our controller on the real Flexiv Rizon 4s robot, and the experimental process is shown in Fig. 7. A laser pointer is placed on the end-effector of the manipulator so that the motion of the end-effector can be reflected by the laser onto the paper. According to the preset task, the end-effector repeatedly moves along a circular trajectory, and the laser tracks the circle on the paper when there is no disturbance.

During the circular motion of the manipulator, we successively apply two disturbances, the time of which is shown as the shaded area in Fig. 8. We record the motion of the manipulator for three rounds. The second round can be regarded as a control group without disturbance to form a comparison.

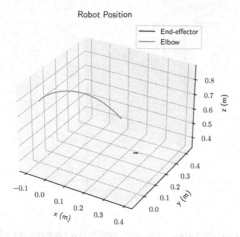

Fig. 6. End-effector and elbow motion under disturbance

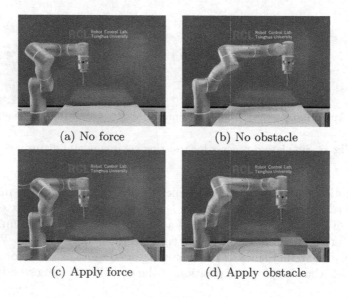

(a) No force   (b) No obstacle

(c) Apply force   (d) Apply obstacle

Fig. 7. Snapshots of the experiment on the real robot

The first disturbance is an external force applied to the elbow of the manipulator. Since the end-effector task is at the highest priority hierarchy in WBC, the movement of the elbow is affected by the external force to some extent compared with the control group, while the end-effector still tracks the reference trajectory well. The second one is an obstacle on the reference trajectory of the end-effector. A new constraint is added to MPC after the obstacle appears. In order to avoid collisions with the obstacle, the movements of both the end-effector and the elbow are changed in advance.

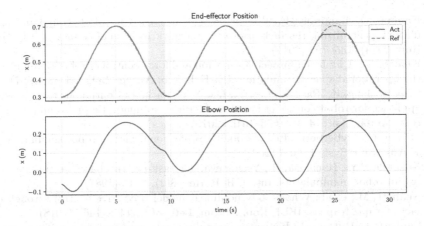

Fig. 8. End-effector and elbow motion in x direction

5   Conclusion

We present a manipulator controller specifically designed to perform in dynamic environments. Our controller employs a combination of WBC and MPC to guarantee that environmental disturbances do not impact the end-effector. Additionally, MPC proactively modifies the end-effector trajectory to respond to environmental changes. We have confirmed the controller's robustness under dynamic conditions through rigorous simulations and experiments, yielding promising results. We plan to incorporate perception modules into the manipulator in our future work. By utilizing these modules, the controller will automatically adapt to changes in the environment.

References

1. Abe, Y., Da Silva, M., Popović, J.: Multiobjective control with frictional contacts. In: Proceedings of the 2007 ACM SIGGRAPH/Eurographics Symposium on Computer Animation, pp. 249–258 (2007)
2. Carron, A., Arcari, E., Wermelinger, M., Hewing, L., Hutter, M., Zeilinger, M.N.: Data-driven model predictive control for trajectory tracking with a robotic arm. IEEE Rob. Autom. Lett. **4**(4), 3758–3765 (2019)
3. Dietrich, A., Ott, C., Albu-Schäffer, A.: An overview of null space projections for redundant, torque-controlled robots. Int. J. Rob. Res. **34**(11), 1385–1400 (2015)
4. Ding, Y., Pandala, A., Park, H.W.: Real-time model predictive control for versatile dynamic motions in quadrupedal robots. In: 2019 International Conference on Robotics and Automation (ICRA), pp. 8484–8490. IEEE (2019)
5. Escande, A., Mansard, N., Wieber, P.B.: Hierarchical quadratic programming: fast online humanoid-robot motion generation. Int. J. Rob. Res. **33**(7), 1006–1028 (2014)
6. Faroni, M., Beschi, M., Pedrocchi, N.: Inverse kinematics of redundant manipulators with dynamic bounds on joint movements. IEEE Rob. Autom. Lett. **5**(4), 6435–6442 (2020)

7. Kanoun, O., Lamiraux, F., Wieber, P.B.: Kinematic control of redundant manipulators: generalizing the task-priority framework to inequality task. IEEE Trans. Rob. **27**(4), 785–792 (2011)

8. Khatib, O.: A unified approach for motion and force control of robot manipulators: the operational space formulation. IEEE J. Rob. Autom. **3**(1), 43–53 (1987)

9. Kim, S., Jang, K., Park, S., Lee, Y., Lee, S.Y., Park, J.: Continuous task transition approach for robot controller based on hierarchical quadratic programming. IEEE Rob. Autom. Lett. **4**(2), 1603–1610 (2019)

10. Michel, O.: Cyberbotics ltd. webots^{TM}: professional mobile robot simulation. Int. J. Adv. Rob. Syst. **1**(1), 5 (2004)

11. Nakamura, Y., Hanafusa, H., Yoshikawa, T.: Task-priority based redundancy control of robot manipulators. Int. J. Rob. Res. **6**(2), 3–15 (1987)

12. Neunert, M., et al.: Whole-body nonlinear model predictive control through contacts for quadrupeds. IEEE Rob. Autom. Lett. **3**(3), 1458–1465 (2018)

13. Pankert, J., Hutter, M.: Perceptive model predictive control for continuous mobile manipulation. IEEE Rob. Autom. Lett. **5**(4), 6177–6184 (2020)

Pattern Recognition and Machine Learning for Smart Robots

A High-Temperature Resistant Robot for Fixed-Point Firefighting

Fang Li[1,2]([✉]), Yujie Huang[1], Jiaqi Sun[1], Xiaodong Zhao[1], and Yingchao He[1]

[1] Shenzhen Futian Hongling Science Middle School, Futian District, Shenzhen, China
lifang061@163.com
[2] Shenzhen Futian Academy of Educational Sciences,
Futian District, Shenzhen, China

Abstract. In order to reduce fire hazards and ensure the safety of firefighters, this paper proposes a high-temperature resistant robot for fixed-point firefighting. We first design a thermal protection structure to wrap the main body of the robot, which can effectively protect the normal operation of internal components. At the same time, with a high-temperature-resistant metal crawler chassis, the robot can be applied to various complex terrains. Besides, this robot respectively has automatic mode and cooperative mode to choose from. In the automatic working mode, the robot automatically identifies the fire point location based on flame detection and puts out the fire, realizing real-time monitoring of the working environment. In the cooperative working mode, firefighters can remotely control it. The cameras located at the front and rear ends of the robot allow the operator to observe the foreground and background of the robot in real-time. Meanwhile, it is equipped with laser ranging sensors to avoid hitting any obstacles and surrounding objects. It does not require firefighters to be exposed to unnecessary dangerous environments, and can autonomously find the fire point before the fire gets out of control, and use fire extinguishing bombs to extinguish the fire the first time.

Keywords: Fixed-point firefighting · Firefighting robot · Flame detection

1 Introduction

According to statistics from the National Fire and Rescue Administration, from January to October 2022, a total of 703,000 fires were reported across the country, with 1,557 deaths, 1,769 injuries, and direct property losses of 5.85 billion yuan [7]. Firefighters are high-risk occupations. They are often faced with huge life-threatening and personal safety threats at the fire scene, especially in nuclear power plants, oil refineries, liquefied petroleum gas storage tanks and other environments. In contrast, the use of robots that can operate autonomously and be

H. Yang et al. (Eds.): ICIRA 2023, LNAI 14270, pp. 527–536, 2023.
https://doi.org/10.1007/978-981-99-6492-5_45

controlled remotely to replace or assist firefighters in rescue activities will significantly reduce the need for firefighters to enter dangerous environments, improve firefighters' work efficiency, and reduce the risk of accidents.

At present, many researches on fire-fighting robots have been done at home and abroad. For example, in 2002, Japan proposed an unmanned monitor nozzle vehicle, which can deal with large-scale fires [6]. In 2011, Tan et al. in Malaysia proposed a ground vehicle for firefighting, which can be controlled remotely to fight fires [10]. However, these robots are only suitable for outdoors due to their large size. The Fire Searcher invented in South Korea can be used indoors, but the robot only has a reconnaissance function to help firefighters understand the fire environment [5]. In 2014, the U.S. NAVY designed the first bi-pedal firefighting robot SAFFIR, which can move autonomously on the entire cabin ship and interact with people to handle dangerous firefighting tasks usually performed by humans [1]. In 2019, the QRob designed by Mohd Aliff et al. has a smaller size and is also suitable for indoor fire fighting [2], but neither of the above two robots has perfect high-temperature resistance, and it is difficult to fight fires at the fire scene for a long time.

Compared with foreign countries, the development and production of fire-fighting robots in China started relatively late. In 2002, Zheng [13] designed a remote control firefighting robot ZXPJ01 that integrates multiple functions. The robot uses an articulated crawler chassis to keep the robot balanced when facing rough terrain, so as to replace firefighters to enter the complicated environment for on-site fire fighting and rescue. At present, the JMX-LT50 [8,11] fire-fighting robot designed and manufactured by Shanghai Qiangshi Equipment Company is the most widely used in the country. This fire-fighting robot uses a six-wheeled travel method, which can overcome obstacles and move on different terrains. However, this robot is only suitable for long-distance fire fighting around the fire scene [12]. All of the above robots can effectively extinguish fires, but they are only non-autonomous robots, requiring operators to remotely control them to determine their movement and search positions.

In a word, the current firefighting robots have some limitations [2,9], such as single function, weak heat resistance, and lack of autonomy. Hence, this paper designs a high-temperature resistant robot for fixed-point firefighting (as shown in Fig. 1). The robot itself has excellent high-temperature resistance performance. Based on this, there are two working modes: automatic mode and cooperative mode. It can independently find the fire point before the fire gets out of control, and use the fire extinguishing bomb to extinguish the fire the first time. At the same time, firefighters can also use the cooperative mode to remotely control the robot to assist in firefighting.

2   Methodology

The realization of this robot can be mainly divided into four parts. To begin with, we design the mechanical structure of the robot. Then, the function implementation of this robot. Next, we design the control programming. Lastly, all

Fig. 1. A High-Temperature Resistant Robot for Fixed-Point Firefighting.

the above parts are assembled together, and the experimental test is carried out to determine the effect of the robot on fire extinguishing.

2.1 Mechanical Structure

We used SolidWorks software to design a 3D diagram of the overall structure of the robot, as shown in Fig. 2. Two laser ranging sensors and a flame sensor are installed on the front end of the robot. The laser ranging sensors are used to avoid hitting obstacles during work, and the flame sensor is used to identify flames. The positioning throwing structure, the mechanical arm and other components are installed on the upper part of the crawler chassis. In addition, micro-cameras for observing the foreground and background are installed on the front and rear of the robot, respectively.

2.2 Function Implementation

Electronics are key components in robot development. It mainly includes several types, such as microcontrollers, DC motors with wheels, transmitters, remote controls, etc. Figure 3 shows the main working block diagram of this robot. The red line represents the automatic working mode. When a flame is detected, the detection result is transmitted to the microcontroller (Arduino Mega 2560). With the assistance of the automatic obstacle avoidance function, the motor drives (IBT-2) the robot to move, and at the same time drives the fire extinguishing bomb throwing device to extinguish the fire. The blue line represents the cooperative working mode. At this point, the firefighters' operating instructions are used as the input of the system. The operator can monitor and control the movement of the robot in real-time through the camera (700-line wide-angle camera) connected to the smartphone, and carry out fire fighting.

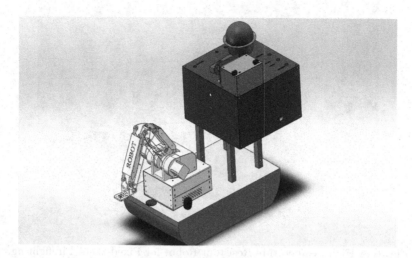

Fig. 2. 3D Structure of the High-Temperature Resistant Robot for Fixed-Point Fire-fighting.

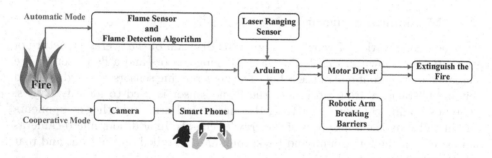

Fig. 3. The Main Working Block Diagram of the High-Temperature Resistant Robot for Fixed-Point Firefighting. The red line is the automatic working mode, and the blue line is the cooperative working mode. (Color figure online)

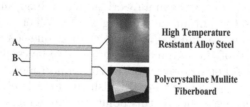

Fig. 4. Thermal Protection Structure Illustration.

Thermal Protection Structure Design. In order to ensure that the robot can work normally in a high-temperature environment for a long time, a thermal protection structure is designed in this paper(as shown in Fig. 4), which can be divided into three layers, which are "A", "B", and "A". Where "A" is high-temperature resistant alloy steel (high-temperature resistance 800 °C), and "B" is polycrystalline mullite fiberboard (high-temperature resistance 1600 °C). "A" is used to ensure the mechanical strength of the robot, while "B" provides the excellent heat insulation effect. Through practical experiments, the thickness of polycrystalline mullite fiberboard is selected as 40 mm.

According to investigations, the actual maximum temperature at the fire scene of petrochemical production, and storage of hydrocarbon materials and products is about 1100 °C to 1200 °C [3,4]. The flamethrower is selected as the fire source in the experiment, and the maximum temperature of the fire source is about 1200 °C to 1300 °C. The outdoor temperature of the day is about 11 °C. We choose 10 mm, 20 mm, 30 mm to 60 mm thickness, and polycrystalline mullite fiberboard with a size of 150 mm*150 mm for the experiment. In the experiment. First, we use a flamethrower to continuously burn the thermal protection structure for 30 s. Then, we choose the infrared thermometer to measure the temperature on the back of the thermal protection structure. The results are shown in Table 1. After this experiment, it can be found that as the thickness of the Polycrystalline Mullite fiberboard increases, the heat insulation rate also increases and tends to be stable at 40 mm. The heat insulation rate does not change significantly from 10 mm to 60 mm, mainly because the thermal protection structure itself has a high heat-resistant temperature. The Table 2 keeps the thickness of the polycrystalline mullite fiberboard at 40 mm constant and takes the monitoring time as a variable to observe the change of the internal temperature with time. It can be seen from the results that with the increase of time, the internal temperature also rises slowly and then tends to be stable. In conclusion, the above information proves the effectiveness of the thermal protection structure.

Table 1. Experimental Test Results of Heat Insulation Layer Thickness

Polycrystalline Mullite Fiberboard Thickness (mm)	10	20	30	40	50	60
Temperature (°C)		20.7	17.6	16.4	14.9	15.7	15.8
Heat Insulation Rate (%)		93.1	94.1	94.5	95.0	94.8	94.7

Table 2. Test results of Heat Insulation Layer with thickness of 40 mm

Time(s)	30	60	90	120
Temperature (°C)	16.4	18.7	18.6	20.4

Barrier-Breaking Function Design. Since it is inevitable that obstacles will hinder the work at the fire scene, we have added a barrier-breaking function to this robot. To realize this function, we use a programmable and switchable robotic arm. This robotic arm is a three-axis robotic arm, and it is fixed on the front half of the robot body. The front end of the robotic arm can be equipped with a mechanical gripper. During remote control, firefighters can use the control interface to control the robotic arm to remove obstacles. The mechanical gripper tool at the front end can be replaced with a chainsaw to cut obstacles according to actual needs.

Travelling Mechanism Design. The application scenarios of this robot are mainly concentrated in flammable and explosive places such as petrochemical plants, large warehouses, and industrial and mining factories. The terrain of these places is complex, and other walking structures cannot be well applied in fire scenes. Hence, we choose the caterpillar locomotion mechanism to solve the above problems. Considering that the robot needs to be used in fire scenes for a long time, the material of the caterpillar locomotion mechanism must be high temperature resistant.

Self-cooling Structure Design. The shell of the robot can already achieve fire resistance and high-temperature resistance to ensure its normal working. In order to further ensure the normal operation of the internal components of the body, we designed a self-cooling structure, as shown in Fig. 5. This cooling system is installed in the robot body, and it is mainly composed of a water pump, a reservoir, a water cooling radiator, and a water block. The main function of the water block is to take away the heat of the body, and then the radiator dissipates heat. After completing the installation, the control board is placed on the water block. Among them, the water-cooled pipeline adopts the high-temperature resistant silicone tube, which can withstand 300 °C.

Flame Detection. The main working scene of this firefighting robot is set in a high-risk environment, such as in nuclear power plants, oil refineries, liquefied petroleum, gas storage tanks, and etc. After the robot is started, it will patrol the entire working environment and monitor whether there is a flame in real-time. In order to ensure the accuracy and sensitivity of flame detection, this work chooses the combination of sensor detection and flame detection algorithm. As long as the flame information is detected, the automatic fire extinguishing mode will be activated and an alarm will be issued. We choose the five-way flame sensor, which has a wide detection range (greater than 120°) and high sensitivity to flames compared to other sensors. Its basic principle is to use a special infrared receiving tube to detect the infrared rays generated by the flame, and then convert the brightness of the flame into a level signal with high and low changes and input it to the central processing unit, and finally the central processing unit makes corresponding judgments according to the signal changes.

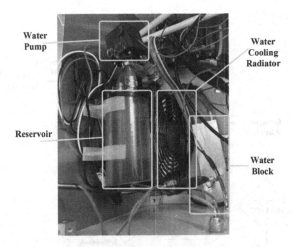

Fig. 5. Self-cooling Structure Illustration.

The flame detection algorithm builds a real-time flame detection model based on a lightweight YOLOv5 neural network. This method can not only effectively reduce the false alarm rate, but also can improve the efficiency of flame detection.

Fire Extinguishing Function Design. This work uses the method of throwing fire-extinguishing balls to extinguish the fire. Therefore, we designed a throwing structure. Its basic principle is that the main control board controls the rotation of the steering gear, thereby driving the upper pole to rotate, and then throws the fire extinguishing balls out. When the surface of the fire extinguishing ball encounters fire, it will automatically explode to extinguish the fire.

Automatic Obstacle Avoidance Function Design. In order to ensure the safety and efficiency of this robot in the automatic working mode, we have added an automatic obstacle avoidance function to the machine. Laser ranging sensors are installed on both sides of the machine. If the distance detected by the left sensor is less than the threshold and the distance detected by the right sensor is greater than the set threshold, the robot turns to the right; on the contrary, the robot turns to the left; otherwise, it continues to move along the search path.

2.3 Control Programming

Remote Control Design. The remote control of this firefighting robot is mainly divided into two parts. One is to control the machine's travel and throwing structure, and the other is to control the mechanical arm. The detailed principles are as follows:

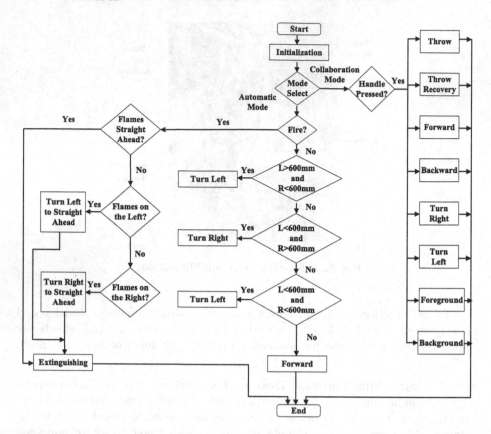

Fig. 6. Basic Working Flow Chart of the High-Temperature Resistant Robot for Fixed-Point Firefighting.

Control Firefighting Robots to Move and Throwing Structures. In the cooperative working mode, the walking of the robot and the throwing of fire-extinguishing bombs are controlled by the ps2 wireless handle. It is mainly composed of two parts, the controller and the receiver. The controller is mainly responsible for sending button information. The receiver is connected to the main control board, and it is used to receive the information sent by the controller and transmit it to the main control board. The main control board can also send commands to the controller through the receiver.

Control the Robotic Arm of Firefighting Robot. In the collaborative working mode, firefighters can remotely control the robotic arm to carry out obstacle-breaking work. The realization principle is to use the WiFi module to communicate wirelessly with the controller of the robotic arm. The specific implementation method is that the robotic arm first connects to the router through the WiFi module, and obtains the assigned fixed IP address. Then set the assigned

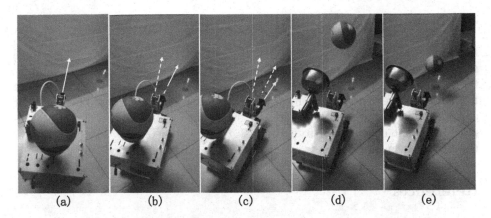

(a)   (b)   (c)   (d)   (e)

Fig. 7. Automatic Mode Fire Extinguishing Experiment. (a) and (b) show that the firefighting robot successfully realizes the automatic obstacle avoidance function after encountering an obstacle in the automatic working mode. (b) and (c) are the firefighting robots successfully locating the direction of the fire source after identifying the fire source. (d) and (e) show that the firefighting robot successfully and automatically throws the firefighting bomb to locate and extinguish the fire.

IP address on the corresponding control software, and then connect to the same router.

All data from the sensors are monitored and processed by the Arduino Mega. The main flowchart of the whole program is shown in Fig. 6. This firefighting robot has two working modes, automatic mode and collaborative mode. The cooperative mode is mainly to control the movement and the throwing of fire-extinguishing bombs to extinguish the fire under the real-time monitoring of the operator. The automatic mode includes real-time detection of the flame, alarm and control of the robot to move to a suitable location for fixed-point fire extinguishing.

2.4 Result

Figure 7 shows that this high-temperature resistant robot for fixed-point fire-fighting automatically recognizes the flame and puts it out in the automatic working mode. In this experiment, we chose a burning candle as the fire source and a basketball instead of a fire extinguisher bomb. This robot performs real-time search in the working scene. First, (a) and (b) in Fig. 7 is to avoid obstacles after detecting obstacles during the search process. Then, (b) and (c) are the fire source detected by the robot in the process of continuing the search to locate the fire source. After accurately locating the fire source, (d) and (e) show the robot throwing fire-extinguishing bombs to extinguish the fire. It can be seen from the picture that the fire extinguishing bomb thrown by the robot can accurately locate the fire source.

3   Conclusion

In order to reduce fire hazards, ensure the safety of firefighters, and solve the shortcomings of current firefighting robots, this paper proposes a high-temperature resistant robot for fixed-point firefighting, which does not require firefighters to be exposed to unnecessary dangerous environments. The fire point can be found independently before the fire is out of control, and the fire extinguishing bomb can be used to extinguish the fire immediately, so as to improve the fire extinguishing efficiency and ensure the safety of life and property.

References

1. Alhaza, T., Alsadoon, A., Alhusinan, Z., Jarwali, M., Alsaif, K.: New concept for indoor fire fighting robot. Procedia Social Behav. Sci. **195**, 2343–2352 (2015)
2. Aliff, M., Sani, N.S., Yusof, M., Zainal, A.: Development of fire fighting robot (qrob). Int. J. Adv. Comput. Sci. Appl. **10**(1), 142–147 (2019)
3. Beneberu, E., Yazdani, N.: Performance of cfrp-strengthened concrete bridge girders under combined live load and hydrocarbon fire. J. Bridge Eng. **23**(7), 04018042 (2018)
4. Carmel Group: Passive fire proofing (2012). http://carmel-group.co.il/en/passive-fire-proofing/. Accessed 5 May 2023
5. Chang, P.H., Kang, Y.H., Cho, G.R., Kim, J.H., Kim, Y.B.: Control architecture design for a fire searching robot using task oriented design methodology. In: International Joint International on Sice-icase (2007)
6. Miyazawa, K.: Fire robots developed by the Tokyo fire department. Adv. Rob. **16**(6), 553–556 (2002)
7. National Fire and Rescue Administration: National fire situation report released from january to october this year (2022). https://www.119.gov.cn/qmxfxw/mtbd/spbd/2022/33316.shtml. Accessed 1 May 2023
8. Nikitin, V., Golubin, S., Belov, R., Gusev, V., Andrianov, N.: Development of a robotic vehicle complex for wildfire-fighting by means of fire-protection roll screens. In: IOP Conference Series: Earth and Environmental Science, vol. 226, p. 012003. IOP Publishing (2019)
9. Suresh, J.: Fire-fighting robot. In: 2017 International Conference on Computational Intelligence in Data Science (ICCIDS), pp. 1–4. IEEE (2017)
10. Tan, C.F., Alkahari, M.R., Rahman, M.A.: Development of ground vehicle for fire fighting purpose (2011)
11. Tan, C.F., Malingam, S.D.: Fire fighting mobile robot: state of the art and recent development. Aust. J. Basic Appl. Sci. **7**(10), 220–230 (2013)
12. Tanyıldızı, A.K.: Design, control and stabilization of a transformable wheeled fire fighting robot with a fire-extinguishing, ball-shooting turret. Machines **11**(4), 492 (2023)
13. Xu, Z., Xu, C., Dun, X.: Development of zxpj01 fire-fighting robot. Robot **2**, 159–164 (2002)

Multiscale Dual-Channel Attention Network for Point Cloud Analysis

Wentao Li[1,2,3], Jian Cui[1,2,3], Haiqing Cao[4], Huixuan Zhu[1,2,3], Sen Lin[5(✉)], and Yandong Tang[1,2]

[1] State Key Laboratory of Robotics, Shenyang Institute of Automation, Chinese Academy of Sciences, Shenyang 110016, China
[2] Institutes for Robotics and Intelligent Manufacturing, Chinese Academy of Sciences, Shenyang 110169, China
[3] University of Chinese Academy of Sciences, Beijing 100049, China
[4] Unit 32681, PLA, Tieling 112609, China
[5] School of Automation and Electrical Engineering, Shenyang Ligong University, Shenyang 110159, China
lin_sen6@126.com

Abstract. Point clouds are the most popular representation of 3D vision tasks and have a wide range of applications in the field of smart robots today. The disordered and unstructured nature of 3D points makes it more difficult for researchers to extract information from point clouds. When extracting information from point clouds, most methods ignore the geometric structure of local regions, making information extraction insufficient and thus affecting the model effect; or over-construct complex feature extractors to obtain more adequate information in local regions, which leads to extremely complex network models and dilutes the importance of points in the global structure. To this end, our approach proposes a multiscale dual-channel attention convolutional neural network model that considers both the extraction of information in the local structure and ensures the effectiveness of global information aggregation. The model effectively balances the fusion of local and global features and considers the effective combination of local and global features of point clouds in a more comprehensive way. It shows good performance on the classical datasets ModelNet40 and ShapeNet Part.

Keywords: Point cloud analysis · Multiscale feature extraction · Dual-channel Attention Learning

1 Introduction

Point cloud classification and segmentation tasks play an important role in 3D visual processing as the basis for 3D scene understanding and analysis. With the rapid development of sensor technology in recent years, 3D sensors such as 3D scanners, LIDAR and RGB-D cameras are becoming more and more accessible to the public, and the 3D data collected by these sensors contain rich geometric information and can be widely used in different fields such as robotics [1, 2], computer vision [3, 4] and remote sensing [5].

© The Author(s), under exclusive license to Springer Nature Singapore Pte Ltd. 2023
H. Yang et al. (Eds.): ICIRA 2023, LNAI 14270, pp. 537–548, 2023.
https://doi.org/10.1007/978-981-99-6492-5_46

Convolutional neural networks (CNNs) were first used to the field of picture classification by AlexNet [6], demonstrating their promise and power in data processing as deep learning technology advances. Since then, more and more researchers have improved on top of the CNN infrastructure to continuously enhance its performance.

However, point cloud data cannot be directly processed by earlier convolutional neural networks, so it needs to be voxelized into a 3D grid. However, this method requires a large amount of computation, occupies more memory and consumes more time when extracting features. For this reason, Wang et al. [7] proposed an Octree based approach to improve feature processing and reduce some computational overhead by dynamically adjusting the size of the resolution. Then PointGrid [8] samples a fixed number of points within each grid cell to enhance the fineness of local features while minimizing computational overhead.

Due to the complexity of the voxelization process and the tendency to lose point cloud feature information during the conversion process, more and more studies focus on the direct processing of the original point cloud data. PointNet [9] is a pioneer in the direct application of deep learning to raw point cloud data, although it evaluates each point's attributes separately and ignores local features. PointNet++ [10] improves it by proposing a hierarchical structure, using a ball query to process local area features, and improving the recognition power of local features by continuously stacking multi-scale features, and its recognition accuracy is greatly improved compared with PointNet. PointNet++, to a certain extent, sacrifices a certain amount of computational efficiency and resource consumption in exchange for the improvement of final accuracy by increasing the amount of information. Nevertheless, its hierarchical architectural idea has been continuously borrowed by networks such as PointWeb [11]. Since then, more and more research has been conducted to construct graph convolution and design various point convolution operators from local features, and the model structure has become more and more complex.

This research develops a point cloud classification and segmentation network based on multiscale feature extraction and dual-channel attention learning. First, the multiscale feature extraction structure can extract local feature information with larger receptive fields, more information and tighter connections. Then, the spatial attention module and the channel attention module are made to improve the ability of feature information from the spatial domain and channel domain, respectively, to be represented in a way that is discriminative. Finally, the output features are combined and passed through multiple multi-layer perceptron for deeper feature extraction. Through experimental tests, the network can effectively improve the classification and segmentation accuracy of point clouds. The following is a summary of the main contributions of the proposed work:

- To collect geometric features in a learning and end-to-end way, the proposed architecture combines sampling, grouping, and pooling cascades.
- The spatial attention module and the channel attention module are proposed to improve the ability to learn feature information in the spatial and channel domains.
- Extensive experiments show that our proposed architecture delivers equivalent performance to current state-of-the-art methods on benchmark datasets, such as the ModelNet40 [12] and ShapeNet-Part [13] datasets, in addition to having a simpler modular design.

2 Related Work

2.1 Point Based Methods

After PointNet and PointNet++ were proposed in point-based methods, there is redundancy in the features learned at different scales due to the overlap of point clouds at different scales. A-CNN [14] alleviates this problem by introducing toroidal convolution, which ensures that there is no duplication in the point clouds after grouping by imposing a toroidal local region. Similarly, By using an adaptive convolution kernel and point cloud reordering, PointCNN [15] enhances the capacity for generalization by adapting the input point clouds.

2.2 Graph Convolutional Networks (GCNs)

The graph-based approach focuses on constructing directed graphs in a local region, thus considering the topology between discrete points in the local region, and using graph convolution for information aggregation, which, as a local operation, allows easy sharing of kernel weights at different locations. By dynamically constructing graph convolution in each layer of the network, DGCNN [16] continuously calculates the neighborhood of each point in each layer of the feature space, thereby improving the construction of a static overall graph. Other GCN-based methods use spectral graph convolution [17, 18], which is characterized as a spectral filter between the graph signal and the eigen-vector of the Laplacian matrix.

2.3 Attention Based Methods

In previous approaches, there are also some works that learn local features by using attention mechanisms and thus obtain global contextual information. For example, Randla-Net [19] uses randomly sampled points instead of a complex sampling scheme when sampling point clouds, and despite its efficiency, it loses key points that are easily lost, so a novel local feature aggregation module is used to gradually increase the point cloud receptive field to achieve efficient retention of aggregated information. A-SCN [20] describes the spatial relationships between points in terms of shape context and obtains rotation and scale invariance through operations such as subsampling, rotation and scaling, but introduces many hyperparameters into the model, which may make the model behave unstably across different datasets and tasks. PointASNL [21] introduces an adaptive sampling method to reduce the error problem in point cloud sampling and improve the accuracy and stability of point cloud processing, but it may also cause a certain computational burden. Similarly, Point Transformer uses a self-attentive mechanism to establish the connection between points, but it may over-focus on dense regions and ignore sparse regions when the point cloud density varies greatly, leading to a decrease in prediction accuracy. Similarly, Xu et al. proposed GDANet [22] combines graph convolution and self-attentiveness mechanisms to improve the characterization of information.

All the above methods, although effective, lack better utilization of adjacency relationships within local regions, which may lead to ineffective capture of local changes in geometry and orientation.

3 Methodology

We propose a new end-to-end network architecture named multiscale dual-channel attention network, which uses a multiscale feature extraction module to obtain point cloud features in different neighborhoods and expand the receptive field. Based on the multiscale feature extraction, the dual-channel attention module is used to obtain more detailed local features, and finally these features are stitched together to extract more adequate local features. Spatial attention and channel attention are both parts of the dual-channel attention module. We introduce the specifics of each module in this section (see Fig. 1).

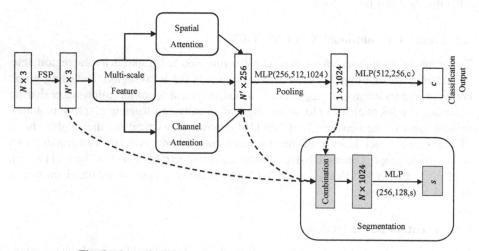

Fig. 1. Overall point cloud classification and segmentation network

3.1 Multiscale Feature Extraction Module

First, the input point cloud data with N points and feature dimension D of 3 is represented in the form of a set: $X = \{x_1, x_2, x_3, \ldots, x_N\}$ with $x_i \in \mathbb{R}^D$, where the three dimensions of each point x_i represent the location information of the point, and other dimensional feature information is not considered for the time being.

Multiscale feature extraction can effectively expand the receptive field in point cloud information extraction by encoding information on point clouds of different scales, and then combining the information obtained by encoding to make the aggregated information more effective and lessen the interference of noise points. It effectively avoids the disadvantage that the information extraction is more easily affected by noise when there are few points in the point cloud of a sparse area produced by a ball query when the distribution of the point cloud is uneven.

Since point cloud data is a set of unordered point cloud collection, if convolution of points is performed directly, we can get the global information of points, but the structure of the point in the local area is ignored, and the effective neighborhood information cannot be extracted. If a small neighborhood is delineated for each point for information extraction, a large number of neighborhood overlaps will be generated, resulting in information redundancy, and at the same time, a large number of computations will be added. Therefore, it is necessary to select effective sampling points for the information extraction of point clouds.

We choose the Farthest Point Sampling (FPS) method to select a number of m sampling points, denoted as $P = \{p_i\}_{i=1}^{m}$, and then use the sampling point as the center point to divide the local area by using the ball query method, so as to divide the point cloud into a spherical area centered on the sampling point. For the same sampling points, we set different query radii for regional division, and then the point clouds in the regions are aggregated by convolution. Due to the different query radii, when convolution is performed, the feature dimensionality aggregated in the regions with smaller query radius is low, and the feature dimensionality aggregated in the regions with larger query radius is high, and finally the extracted features at different scales are stitched to obtain multiscale features: $F\prime \in R^{C \times H \times W}$.

3.2 Spatial Attention Module

The multiscale feature extraction module is realized by grouping the point clouds in multiple scales and then performing information extraction. Although certain neighborhood information is obtained, the information is still aggregated in a smaller area, and the structural characteristics of the point clouds are still not considered in the local area, which is not essentially different from the direct acquisition of global information in the PointNet, but only operates at a different scale. We propose a dual-channel attention module that is combined with a multiscale information extraction module in order to force the network to pay greater attention to the effective information while ignoring the acquisition of secondary information.

As illustrated in Fig. 2, to further improve the effect of point cloud in local useful region, we design a spatial attention module, which pools the maximum value and average value of multiscale feature information respectively, and then merges the pooled features. Stitching features uses SoftMax function to calculate the score, called spatial attention coefficient, recorded as H_s. The multiscale features are reencoded by using spatial attention coefficient, calculated by the following equation:

$$F_s = H_s(F^{'}) \otimes F^{'}, \tag{1}$$

where $\otimes$ denotes multiplication. Through this process, we can distinguish the importance of multiscale features in different regions in the space, to give higher weights to the important regional features in the space, and the spatial attention coefficients are calculated as follows:

$$H_s(F\prime) = \gamma\left(Conv(Concat[mp(F\prime), ap(F\prime)])\right), \tag{2}$$

where γ represents the softmax normalization function; $Conv$ denotes the convolution operation; $Concat$ denotes the splicing operation; $mp(\cdot)$ denotes the maximum pooling function; $ap(\cdot)$ denotes the average pooling function.

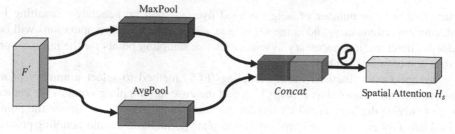

Fig. 2. Spatial Attention Module

3.3 Channel Attention Module

The spatial attention module enhances the discrimination of local features by propagating long-distance contextual relationships along the spatial domain. However, the role of channel information cannot be ignored, and to further enhance the capability of local information, inspired by Wei et al. [23], we enhance the multi-scale feature information from the perspective of the channel domain and design the channel attention module as shown in Fig. 3 to make the neural network more focused on useful feature information by exploring the interdependence between channel information. Finally, different modules are combined and used in a multiscale approach to increase the perceptual field and increase the information extraction ability, while the dual attention module is used to enhance feature information from two different perspectives so that different modules function in turn to improve the discriminative representation of effective feature information.

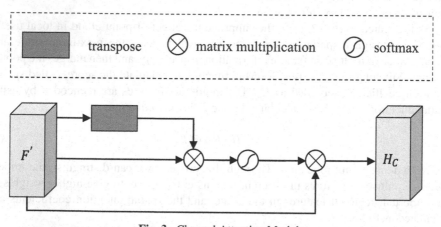

Fig. 3. Channel Attention Module

We use the channel attention module to convert the multiscale feature information into channel attention coefficients, to enhance the weight of useful channel information for the purpose of enhancing multiscale features from the channel domain, and the calculation process is shown as follows:

$$F_c = H_C(F') \otimes F', \tag{3}$$

where F_c denotes the characteristics of the attention of the output channel; H_c denotes the channel attention coefficient matrix generation process. we can compute the coefficient as:

$$H_C(F\prime) = \gamma \, (trp(F\prime) \otimes F\prime), \tag{4}$$

where $trp(\cdot)$ denotes the transpose; γ denotes the softmax normalization function.

4 Experimental Results and Analysis

4.1 Datasets

We evaluate our model on various tasks such as point cloud classification and part segmentation. The classification experiments use the ModelNet40 dataset, in which 1024 points are uniformly sampled for each model as the initial data points for the experiments. The segmentation experiments use the ShapeNet Part dataset, in which 2048 points are sampled uniformly for each model as the initial data points of the experiments. In the subsections that follow, we provide greater information on each task.

ModelNet40 is a largescale 3D CAD model dataset, which includes 40 different classes with 9843 objects for training and 2468 objects for testing.

ShapeNet Part is a large-scale dataset for fine-grained part-level analysis of 3D models. More than 16,000 3D models from 16 different object categories are included, including things like seats, tables, and airplanes. Each 3D model has part-level segmentation annotations, where each portion is given a distinct category.

4.2 Point Cloud Classification

All experiments are performed on the NVIDIA TITAN XP GPU, Linux Ubuntu operating system and Python3.6 and Tensorflow1.14 deep learning framework for experiments. For both classification and part segmentation, we employed the Adam optimizer with a learning rate of 0.001. We trained the classification and segmentation networks for 250 iterations each. Both the classification and portion segmentation batch sizes remain at 16.

In Table 1, We evaluate the shape classification results on ModelNet40 datasets using our method in comparison to a number of advanced approaches. Compared to point cloud-based approaches (with 1024 points), including PointNet, PointNet++, Kd-Net [24], Pointwise [25]. Our model is more accurate. On ModelNet40, our model performs marginally better than the other four models in terms of average category accuracy and overall classification accuracy.

To further validate the performance of the network model, in Table 2, we measure the performance of the model in terms of model size, memory consumption, and accuracy. The ability to achieve a high accuracy rate with a low model complexity reflects

Table 1. Classification results on ModelNet40 dataset. AAC is accuracy average class, OA is overall accuracy.

Model	AAC(%)	OA(%)
PointNet	86.2	89.2
PointNet++	89.4	91.9
KD-Net	88.5	91.8
Pointwise	89.1	91.6
Ours	**89.7**	**92.3**

Table 2. Model performance comparison

Model	Size(MB)	Consume(MiB)	OA(%)
PointNet	41.8	2678	89.2
PointNet++	19.9	11393	91.9
DGCNN	22.1	4870	92.2
Point2Sequence	21.8	11865	**92.3**
Ours	**16.9**	**4516**	**92.3**

excellent model performance. By comparing with PointNet, PointNet++, DGCNN and Point2Sequence [26], our model achieves lower space complexity and time complexity with the highest possible accuracy.

To find the best number of sampling points named as "nsample". The "nsample" refers to the number of points sampled using a ball query within a local receptive field. To optimize network parameters and seek the best model, we conducted experiments with different nsample values. The size of the local receptive field affects the extraction of local features. If the receptive field is too small, local feature information may not be fully extracted, whereas if it is too large, it may increase the complexity of the model. Since ball query involves radius size, if the nsample value is greater than the number of points in the sphere, the points in the sphere will be reused, affecting the extraction of local features. Therefore, based on literature and experiments, we fixed the first receptive field radius to $r_1 = 0.1$ and $nsample = 20$, and tested the impact of different numbers of neighbors on the results at the second receptive field $r_2 = 0.3$, thus finding the optimal nsample value. As shown in Table 3, when nsample is 65, the classification accuracy is the highest. When increasing the nsample value further, the accuracy begins to decrease slightly. Experimental results demonstrate that the best classification effect is achieved with 65 sampled points within the sphere at the second receptive field $r_2 = 0.3$.

Table 3. Analysis of the best nsample value

nsample	AAC(%)	OA(%)
55	89.0	91.6
60	89.1	92.1
65	**89.7**	**92.3**
70	89.4	92.2
75	88.6	92.0

4.3 Point Cloud Segmentation

Table 4 displays the experimental findings for the segmentation of point cloud parts. The mean IoU metric is used to quantitatively evaluate the segmentation performance. As can be shown in Table 4, our model outperforms PointNet and SRINet [27] in terms of segmentation outcomes. Our model, however, performs somewhat worse than PointNet++. Our model performs the best in each of the seven of these categories when measured against particular criteria. Since pointnet++ aggregates scale information for all points locally using PointNet for each level of scale after grouping through multiple scales, this causes a large amount of computation. Our model extracts scale information through dual channels, which saves more computation and memory space, although may have the problem of insufficient information extraction.

We also visualize the segmentation ground truths and predictions in Fig. 4. It shows the visualization results of a table and a chair after part segmentation experiment, and in Fig. 5 shows the visualization results of a lamp and a car after a seg-mentation experiment. Intuitively, the predictions of our method are close to the truth.

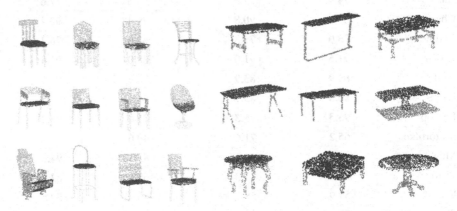

Fig. 4. Visualization results of a table and a chair after part segmentation

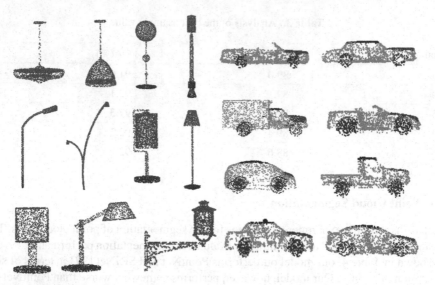

Fig. 5. Visualization results of a lamp and a car after part segmentation

Table 4. Part segmentation results

Method	PointNet	PointNet++	SRINet	Our
IoU	83.7	**85.1**	73.5	84.7
Airplane	**83.4**	82.4	72.6	82.3
Bag	78.7	79.0	74.0	**80.3**
Cap	82.5	**87.7**	68.0	85.8
Car	74.9	77.3	48.6	**77.6**
Chair	89.6	**90.8**	79.4	90.4
Earphone	73.0	71.8	61.0	**76.2**
Guitar	**91.5**	91.0	88.0	91.4
Knife	**85.9**	**85.9**	78.5	80.9
Lamp	80.8	**83.7**	75.4	83.5
Laptop	**95.3**	**95.3**	75.0	95.2
Motorbike	65.2	**71.6**	49.6	69.1
Mug	93.0	94.1	82.3	**94.5**
Pistol	81.2	81.3	65.4	**82.2**
Rocket	57.9	58.7	46.7	**59.5**
Skateboard	72.8	76.4	53.1	**76.9**
Table	80.6	**82.6**	72.4	82.2

5 Conclusion

We propose a point cloud classification and segmentation network based on multiscale feature extraction and dual-channel attention, which extracts multiscale features by different radius size and number of samplings points and uses spatial attention module and channel attention module for feature enhancement. Experimental comparisons on ModelNet40 and ShapeNet Part datasets demonstrate that this method can effectively improve point cloud classification and segmentation accuracy while reducing model complexity and is more efficient than other algorithms.

References

1. Maturana, D., Scherer, S.: Voxnet: a 3d convolutional neural network for real-time object recognition. In: 2015 IEEE/RSJ International Conference on Intelligent Robots and Systems (IROS), pp. 922–928. IEEE (2015)
2. Yurong, Y., et al.: Pseudo-LiDAR++: Accurate Depth for 3D Object Detection in Autonomous Driving. arXiv - CS - Computer Vision and Pattern Recognition (2019)
3. Yilun, C., Shu, L., Xiaoyong, S., Jiaya, J.: DSGN: Deep Stereo Geometry Network for 3D Object Detection. arXiv - CS - Computer Vision and Pattern Recognition (2020)
4. Hang, S., Subhransu, M., Evangelos, K., Erik, L.-M.: Multi-view Convolutional Neural Networks for 3D Shape Recognition. arXiv - CS – Graphics (2015)
5. Shahzad, M., Schmitt, M., Zhu, X.X.: Segmentation and crown parameter extraction of individual trees in an airborne TomoSAR point cloud. Int. Arch. Photogramm. Remote. Sens. Spat. Inf. Sci. **40**, 205–209 (2015)
6. Iandola, F.N., Han, S., Moskewicz, M.W., Ashraf, K., Dally, W.J., Keutzer, K.: SqueezeNet: AlexNet-level accuracy with 50x fewer parameters and< 0.5 MB model size. arXiv preprint arXiv:1602.07360 (2016)
7. Wang, P.-S., Liu, Y., Guo, Y.-X., Sun, C.-Y., Tong, X.: O-cnn: octree-based convolutional neural networks for 3d shape analysis. ACM Trans. Graph. **36**, 1–11 (2017)
8. Le, T., Duan, Y.: Pointgrid: a deep network for 3d shape understanding. In: Proceedings of the IEEE Conference on Computer Vision and Pattern Recognition, pp. 9204–9214 (2018)
9. Qi, C.R., Su, H., Mo, K., Guibas, L.J.: Pointnet: deep learning on point sets for 3d classification and segmentation. In: Proceedings of the IEEE Conference on Computer Vision and Pattern Recognition, pp. 652–660 (2017)
10. Qi, C.R., Yi, L., Su, H., Guibas, L.J.: Pointnet++: deep hierarchical feature learning on point sets in a metric space. Adv. Neural Inform. Process. Syst. **30** (2017)
11. Zhao, H., Jiang, L., Fu, C.-W., Jia, J.: Pointweb: enhancing local neighborhood features for point cloud processing. In: Proceedings of the IEEE/CVF Conference on Computer Vision and Pattern Recognition, pp. 5565–5573 (2019)
12. Zhirong, W., et al.: 3D ShapeNets: A Deep Representation for Volumetric Shapes. arXiv - CS - Computer Vision and Pattern Recognition (2014)
13. Yi, L., et al.: A scalable active framework for region annotation in 3D shape collections. ACM Trans. Graph. (2016)
14. Artem, K., Zichun, Z., Jing, H.: A-CNN: Annularly Convolutional Neural Networks on Point Clouds. arXiv - CS - Computer Vision and Pattern Recognition (2019)
15. Yangyan, L., Rui, B., Mingchao, S., Wei, W., Xinhan, D., Baoquan, C.: PointCNN: Convolution On $\mathcal{X}$-Transformed Points. arXiv - CS – Graphics (2018)
16. Wang, Y., Sun, Y., Liu, Z., Sarma, S.E., Bronstein, M. M., Solomon, J.M.: Dynamic graph CNN for learning on point clouds. ACM Trans. Graph. (2019)

17. Liu, J., Ni, B., Li, C., Yang, J., Tian, Q.: Dynamic points agglomeration for hierarchical point sets learning. In: Proceedings of the IEEE/CVF International Conference on Computer Vision, pp. 7546–7555 (2019)

18. Yiru, S., Chen, F., Yaoqing, Y., Dong, T.: Mining Point Cloud Local Structures by Kernel Correlation and Graph Pooling. arXiv - CS - Computer Vision and Pattern Recognition (2017)

19. Hu, Q., et al.: Randla-net: Efficient semantic segmentation of large-scale point clouds. In: Proceedings of the IEEE/CVF Conference on Computer Vision and Pattern Recognition, pp. 11108–11117 (2020)

20. Xie, S., Liu, S., Chen, Z., Tu, Z.: Attentional shapecontextnet for point cloud recognition. In: Proceedings of the IEEE Conference on Computer Vision and Pattern Recognition, pp. 4606–4615 (2018)

21. Xu, Y., Chaoda, Z., Zhen, L., Sheng, W., Shuguang, C.: PointASNL: Robust Point Clouds Processing using Nonlocal Neural Networks with Adaptive Sampling. arXiv - CS - Computer Vision and Pattern Recognition (2020)

22. Mutian, X., Junhao, Z., Zhipeng, Z., Mingye, X., Xiaojuan, Q., Yu, Q.: Learning Geometry-Disentangled Representation for Complementary Understanding of 3D Object Point Cloud. arXiv - CS - Computer Vision and Pattern Recognition (2020)

23. Jiacheng, W., Guosheng, L., Kim-Hui, Y., Tzu-Yi, H., Lihua, X.: Multi-Path Region Mining For Weakly Supervised 3D Semantic Segmentation on Point Clouds. arXiv - CS - Computer Vision and Pattern Recognition (2020)

24. Roman, K., Victor, L.: Escape from Cells: Deep Kd-Networks for the Recognition of 3D Point Cloud Models. arXiv - CS - Computer Vision and Pattern Recognition (2017)

25. Binh-Son, H., Minh-Khoi, T., Sai-Kit, Y.: Pointwise Convolutional Neural Networks. arXiv - CS - Machine Learning (2017)

26. Xinhai, L., Zhizhong, H., Yu-Shen, L., Matthias, Z.: Point2Sequence: Learning the Shape Representation of 3D Point Clouds with an Attention-based Sequence to Sequence Network. arXiv - CS - Computer Vision and Pattern Recognition (2018)

27. Xiao, S., Zhouhui, L., Jianguo, X.: SRINet: Learning Strictly Rotation-Invariant Representations for Point Cloud Classification and Segmentation. arXiv - CS - Computer Vision and Pattern Recognition (2019)

Study on Quantitative Precipitation Estimation and Model's Transfer Performance by Incorporating Dual Polarization Radar Variables

Yanqin Wen, Jun Zhang, Zhe Liang, Di Wang$^{(\boxtimes)}$, and Ping Wang

Tianjin University, Tianjin 300072, China
wangdi2015@tju.edu.cn

Abstract. Short-time heavy precipitation belongs to a sudden and catastrophic convective weather. Accurate quantitative precipitation estimation is of great significance for preventing heavy precipitation disaster caused by convective systems. At present, quantitative precipitation estimation mostly relies on radar reflectivity (Ref) maps provided by the conventional Doppler radar, but the physical information that reflectivity can provide is quite limited. Dual-polarization radar can provide additional polarization variables, these variables have additional storm microphysical state and dynamic structure information, which helps to improve the accuracy of quantitative precipitation estimation. To this end, a neural network model incorporating multiple radar polarization variables is designed in this paper. We also introduce an attention mechanism module based on the reflectivity to combine the differential reflectivity (Zdr) and differential phase shift rate (Kdp) for inference constraints and result correction. The experimental results show that the model in this paper reduced the prediction RMSE by 11.49%–27.23% compared with the traditional Z-R relationship and by 7.51%–18.27% compared with the deep learning model QPENet. Meanwhile, this paper tested the transfer performance of the model, using data from Central China and South China respectively after training with data from the Central USA. The results show that the model performs better in Central China at the same latitude, which fully illustrates the obvious difference of convective system evolution mechanism in different latitudes.

Keywords: Quantitative Precipitation Estimation · Dual Polarization Radar · Deep Learning

1 Introduction

Short-time heavy precipitation refers to convective precipitation with rainfall greater than 20 mm in one hour [1], which is a typical kind of strong convective weather and it is the main cause of natural disasters such as floods and mudslides. Due to the characteristics of rapid development, localized and short duration of short-time heavy precipitation, it becomes a challenging task to accurately predict short-time heavy precipitation within a short period of time.

H. Yang et al. (Eds.): ICIRA 2023, LNAI 14270, pp. 549–563, 2023.
https://doi.org/10.1007/978-981-99-6492-5_47

Meteorological radar observations are an important basis for quantitative precipitation estimation. Radar can observe the distribution of water vapor in the atmosphere and thus estimate the intensity of precipitation in the corresponding area. This is reflected by an approximate exponential relationship between the reflectivity of the echoes, Z, and the value of the rain gauge, R: $Z = aR^b$, also known as the Z-R relationship [2]. However, the traditional Z-R relationship is difficult to apply to daily weather forecast because the formation mechanisms of convective and laminar precipitation are different [3]. Laminar precipitation has uniform and stable airflow motion, which is suitable for point-to-point direct mapping like traditional Z-R relations; convective precipitation has complex vertical motion and higher radar reflectivity than laminar precipitation, which requires more complex Z-R relations to describe the convective system.

There are some machine learning methods for quantitative precipitation estimation. Kuang et al. [4] used random forests with linear chains of conditional random fields, while considering the spatial and temporal correlation of precipitation processes; Zhang et al. [5] built a learning model using wavelet transform and support vector machine to make the estimation results more consistent with specific meteorological environments. However, these models only extend the generality of precipitation models, and the forecast accuracy for specific strong convective precipitation needs to be improved.

Currently, dual-polarization radar is one of the advanced devices for detecting and studying precipitation microphysical processes. In 1976, Seliga and Bringi [6] proposed to use the differential reflectivity provided by dual-polarization radar to improve the precipitation estimation accuracy. After that, studies on the involvement of dual-polarization radar in precipitation estimation were carried out: Ruzanski et al. [7] used differential phase shift for precipitation estimation; Ryzhkov et al. [8] jointly used differential reflectivity and differential phase shift for precipitation estimation; and Bringi et al. [9] used three variables, namely reflectivity, differential reflectivity, and differential phase shift, to predict precipitation together. These methods effectively improve the accuracy of quantitative precipitation estimation compared to the conventional Z-R.

Deep learning is a major branch of machine learning. With the rapid improvement of hardware computing power, deep learning has achieved remarkable results in various fields. Quantitative dual-polarization radar precipitation estimation models based on deep learning have emerged one after another. Tan et al. [10] constructed a neural network model to estimate precipitation based on dual-polarization radar data with rainfall station data in Dallas-Fort Worth metropolitan area and Florida; Chen et al. [11] designed a neural network model based on fusion mechanism to improve the accuracy of CMORPH satellite precipitation estimation products using dual-polarization radar observation data; Wang et al. [12] proposed a water condensate identification method based on deep learning and fuzzy logic algorithm, which effectively improves the model's ability to identify various water condensates using dual-polarization radar observation data.

Deep learning, with its powerful modeling capabilities, can learn complex nonlinear weather evolution patterns from historical information. Most of the existing deep learning models only modify the network model somewhat by feeding various dual-polarization radar variables into the network as a whole. However, the physical mechanisms of each dual-polarization radar variable to improve precipitation estimation are different from each other. If they directly input to the network without differentiation, the learning pressure of the neural network will increase and the precipitation estimation accuracy will be affected to a certain extent. Therefore, the structure of the neural network model needs to be reasonably designed according to the characteristics of dual-polarization radar variables. This paper designed a convolution-based multi-input neural network based on the characteristics of three physical variables provided by dual-polarization radar: reflectivity (Ref), differential reflectivity (Zdr), and differential phase shift (Kdp). Reflectivity and differential phase shift rate are used to jointly estimate precipitation intensity. Differential reflectivity is used to distinguish strong convective precipitation from hail weather. An attention mechanism is also used to guide the network model to autonomously focus on the region that needs the most attention.

This paper is organized as follows: Section 2 introduces the data used in this study; Sect. 3 gives the methodology proposed in this paper; Sect. 4 shows the test results with the analysis of a case, and Sect. 5 is the analysis of the model migration performance test. Section 6 provides the conclusion.

2 Data

The dual-polarization radar data used in this paper were obtained from the National Centers for Environmental Information (NCEI) ACHIVE Type II data. The selected 11 radar stations cover Kansas and Oklahoma, with the site numbers KTWX, KICT, KEAX, KVNX, KUEX, KOAX, KDDC, KSGF, KINX, and KLNX, whose locations are shown in Fig. 1. Meanwhile, the frequent hailstorm weather in the area provides sufficient negative samples for the estimation of precipitation particles by dual-polarization radar.

The live precipitation data are from the NCEI Cooperative Observer Program (COOP), which provides meteorological observations of minimum temperatures, snowfall, hour-by-hour precipitation, and 24-h precipitation totals across the United States.

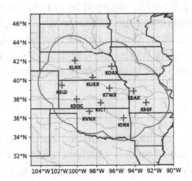

Fig. 1. Radar coverage area diagram.

We chose to build the dataset using observations between January 2013 and June 2019, and used interpolation methods to convert the observations from multi-cone polar data to 3D grid point data in Cartesian coordinates. Select the CAPPI image of the

2 km height layer and downsampled to a size of 128 × 128 with a resolution of 4 km. Precipitation data were also interpolated from irregular points to a precipitation grid of the same size. The three types of radar data (Ref, Kdp, Zdr) for 10 consecutive time points between two adjacent hours are selected as a sample, and the COOP hour-by-hour precipitation corresponding to the first moment in the sample is chosen as the corresponding precipitation data for spatio-temporal matching. A total of 2023 samples were collected after screening, and randomly divided into training set, validation set and test set according to the ratio of 6:2:2.

3　Methods and Model

3.1　Characterization of Dual-Polarization Radar Variables

The reflectivity (Ref) reflects the scale and density of precipitation particles within the observation area, and is the most direct observed quantity reflecting the intensity of precipitation. The differential phase shift rate (Kdp) is the derivative of the phase difference between the horizontally and vertically polarized waves with respect to the radar distance. It reflects the distribution of liquid water content in the storm area, and it is closer to a linear relationship with precipitation intensity, and is less affected by electromagnetic wave attenuation, so the combination of the two variables can enhance the model's ability to predict precipitation intensity [13].

However, the observation of high reflectivity cells does not mean that only strong convective precipitation is likely to occur in the region. Mason [14] showed that convective cells with reflectivity intensity greater than 55 dBZ are more likely to produce hail. Therefore, we also need the model to correctly distinguish the heavy convective precipitation and hail weather. The differential reflectivity Zdr is the logarithm of the ratio of the horizontal reflectivity factor to the vertical reflectivity factor, which can reflect the morphological information of water vapor particles in the atmosphere to some extent. If the particle is precipitation, it will be dragged by gravity traction. So the corresponding Zdr value will be larger than 0, and the Zdr value is positively correlated with the particle size. If the particle is hail, its shape is close to spherical, so the ratio of horizontal reflectivity to vertical reflectivity is close to 1, and the Zdr value is close to 0. Therefore, we can effectively distinguish precipitation from hail according to the Zdr value.

3.2　Model Design

Based on the characteristics of the Ref, Kdp and Zdr for precipitation estimation, we designed a two-stage constrained model, which we referred to the network structure used by Wang et al. [15]. Firstly, Ref and Kdp are sent to "Model I" to obtain an improved preliminary precipitation estimate. Then Zdr is sent to "Model II". "Model II will output a weight matrix of the same size as the radar image. Each point in the matrix represents the probability that convective precipitation will actually occur at that point. The high reflectivity area in Model I will be corrected by Model II to remove the part that is actually hail. The structure is shown in Fig. 2.

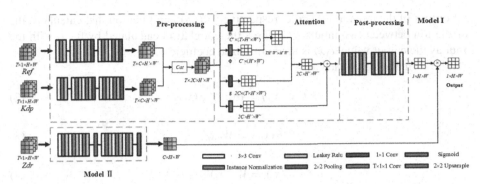

Fig. 2. Schematic diagram of the model structure.

Pre-processing Module

The preprocessing module consists of five convolutional blocks and two pooling layers. Each convolution block consists of a 2D convolution operation, an Instance Normalization (IN) layer and an activation function Leakey Relu. Ref and Kdp are processed by the preprocessing module and then stacked in the channel dimension. Then they are send into the subsequent attention module. The module's parameters are shown in Table 1.

Table 1. Pre-processing module parameters.

Layer	Kernel Size	Kernel Number	Output Size
Conv-1 × 3	3 × 3	(64, 128, 128)	128 × 128 × 128
Pooling	2 × 2	–	128 × 64 × 64
Conv-2 × 2	3 × 3	(256, 128)	128 × 64 × 64
Pooling	2 × 2	–	128 × 32 × 32

Attention Module

In 2017, the attention mechanism was born [16]. It was inspired by the human attention mechanism, which means that people tend to selectively focus on the most important part of information when they take in information and block out the rest of useless information. The attention mechanism is also applicable to the processing of radar echo images: for a single radar echo image, the areas of high reflectivity tend to trigger strong convective weather, and these areas of high reflectivity are the areas that the model needs to pay most attention to. To address this issue, we introduce an attention module that enables the model to adaptively find the most valuable regions of the image for analysis.

The mathematical representation of the attentional mechanism is:

$$y_i = \frac{1}{C(x)} \sum_{\forall j,t} f(x_i, x_{jt}) g(x_{jt}), \tag{1}$$

where i denotes the index of an output point in the graph, j and t denote the location of points associated with region i (spatial and temporal dimensions). x, y are the input and output of the attention module, respectively. $f(\cdot, \cdot)$ is a function that calculates the correlation between two inputs. $g(x)$ fuses the correlation calculated by $f(\cdot, \cdot)$ with the input as the output value. $c(x)$ is the normalized coefficient.

The formula f is defined as:

$$f(x_i, x_{jt}) = \theta(x_{jt})^T \varphi(x_i), \tag{2}$$

$$\theta(x_{jt}) = W_\theta x_{jt}, \tag{3}$$

$$\varphi(x_i) = W_{\varphi 1} x_i W_{\varphi 2}. \tag{4}$$

In Eq. (2)–(4), $W_{\varphi 1}, W_\theta \in R^{C' \times C}$, $W_{\varphi 2} \in R^T$, $x_{jt} \in R^C$, $x_i \in R^{C \times T}$, C and C' denote the number of feature channels before and after the calculation, and T denotes the spatial dimension of the data. Correlation is defined using inner product. Before calculating correlation using f, $\theta(\cdot)$ and $\varphi(\cdot)$ will transform the input x to features required to calculate the correlation, while achieving the goal of improving the computational efficiency and satisfying the data form. W_θ and W_φ are calculated by 1×1 and $T \times 1 \times 1$ convolution operation.

The correlation between the point at position i in the output data and the point at j in the input data at time t is denoted as β_{ijt}. It is necessary to normalize β_{ijt}, thus use it as an attention factor, and the normalization of β_{ijt} is defined by the Softmax function as follows:

$$\beta_{ijt} = f(x_i, x_{jt}) = \theta(x_{jt})^T \varphi(x_i), \tag{5}$$

$$\frac{1}{C}\beta_{ijt} = softmax(\beta_{ijt}) = \frac{1}{\sum_{jt} e^{\beta_{ijt}}}\beta_{ijt}. \tag{6}$$

Ultimately, the output of point i is expressed as:

$$y_i = \frac{1}{\sum_{jt} e^{\theta(x_{jt})^T \varphi(x_i)}} \sum_{jt} e^{\theta(x_{jt})^T \varphi(x_i)} g(x_{jt}). \tag{7}$$

Post-processing Module

The post-processing module has the opposite structure to the pre-processing module, and its task is to convert the feature maps processed by the attention module to the complete precipitation field at a set resolution. It consists of five convolution blocks and two upsampling operations. The structure of the convolution blocks is the same as that of the pre-processing module, but the last convolution block only contains a 1×1 convolution operation to merge the feature maps of all channels. Its parameters are shown in Table 2:

Table 2. Post-processing module parameters.

Layer	Kernel Size	Kernel Number	Output Size
Upsample	2×2	–	$256 \times 64 \times 64$
Conv-1 $\times$ 2	3×3	$(256, 256)$	$256 \times 64 \times 64$
Upsample	2×2	–	$256 \times 128 \times 128$
Conv-2 $\times$ 2	3×3	$(128, 128)$	$128 \times 128 \times 128$
Conv-3 $\times$ 1	3×3	(1)	$1 \times 128 \times 128$

Zdr-processing Module (Model II)

The input of the Zdr correction model are ten consecutive Zdr images, and the output is a precipitation weather probability prediction lattice point map. Therefore, we need fuse the ten images. The correction model is divided into two parts; the first part consists of three stacked 2D convolution blocks, which aim to extract the local features in the original images. Then a 3D convolution operation is performed to fuse the 10 images. The second part consists of three stacked 2D convolution blocks to obtain more advanced semantic information and fine-tune it. Finally a sigmoid function constrain the value of each point to (0, 1). The model parameters are shown in Table 3.

Table 3. Zdr-processing module parameters.

Layer	Kernel Size	Kernel Number	Output Size
Conv-1 $\times$ 3	3×3	$(64, 128, 128)$	$128 \times 128 \times 128$
Conv3d	$10 \times 1 \times 1$	–	$128 \times 128 \times 128$
Conv-2 $\times$ 3	3×3	$(128, 64, 1)$	$1 \times 128 \times 128$
Sigmoid	-	–	$1 \times 128 \times 128$

3.3 Loss Function

The existing deep learning methods of quantitative precipitation estimation usually use mean square error (MSE) as the loss function. In reality, the frequency of weak precipitation is much higher than strong precipitation. Using MSE as the loss function will lead the model to pay more attention on the weak precipitation, resulting in the underestimation of strong precipitation. In this regard, the model training in this paper uses

the precipitation intensity-based weighted MSE (WMSE) [17], which directs the model
to focus more on strong precipitation by setting different weights for different precipitation thresholds. Thus it can improve the accuracy of estimating strong precipitation.
The WMSE is calculated as follows:

$$Loss_{WMSE}(y, \hat{y}) = \sum_{h,w} weight_{h,w} \times (y_{h,w} - \hat{y}_{h,w})^2. \tag{8}$$

When the hourly precipitation threshold is 0, 1, 5, 10, 20, 30 mm, the corresponding
$weight_{h,w}$ is 1, 2, 5, 10, 20, 30. $y_{h,w}$ represents the real rainfall at point (h,w), and $\hat{y}_{h,w}$
represents the rainfall estimate at point (h,w).

4 Experiments and Analysis

4.1 Evaluation Indicators

We use the root mean square error (RMSE), the mean absolute error (MAE), and the
correlation coefficient (CC) as indicators to evaluate the accuracy of model estimation.
The formulas for RMSE, MAE, and CC are as follows:

$$RMSE = \sqrt{\frac{1}{N} \sum_{i=1}^{N} (y - \hat{y})^2}, \tag{9}$$

$$MAE = \sqrt{\frac{1}{N} \sum_{i=1}^{N} |y - \hat{y}|}, \tag{10}$$

$$CC = \frac{Cov(y, \hat{y})}{\sigma_y \sigma_{\hat{y}}}, \tag{11}$$

where σ represents the variance and $Conv$ represents the covariance in Eq. (11).

4.2 Testing with Different Variables

This experiment uses the reflectivity (Ref) jointly with the differential phase shift rate
(Kdp) to estimate the precipitation intensity, and then the differential reflectivity (Zdr)
to revise the precipitation intensity. To demonstrate the contribution of Kdp and Zdr
on the precipitation estimation, six sets of experiments are designed in this section for
comparison:

(1) Precipitation estimation using reflectivity only, the model is noted as Ref-attention.
(2) Precipitation estimation using differential phase shift rate only, the model is denoted
     as Kdp-attention.
(3) Precipitation estimation using reflectivity and differential phase shift rate, the model
     is denoted as Ref-Kdp-attention.
(4) Precipitation estimation using reflectivity and differential reflectivity, the model is
     denoted as Ref-Zdr-attention.
(5) Precipitation estimation using differential phase shift rate and differential reflectivity,
     the model is denoted as Kdp-Zdr-attention.

(6) Precipitation estimation using reflectivity, differential reflectivity and differential phase shift rate, the model is denoted as Ref-Kdp-Zdr-attention.

The test results are shown in Table 4. As can be seen from Table 4, the model performance is somewhat improved with the introduction of differential reflectivity and differential phase shift rate. But Kdp cannot replace the role of Ref in the task of precipitation estimation, it only helps Ref to predict precipitation. With the introduction of Zdr, the model prediction performance is further improved to achieve the best results. It indicates that all three radar variables have an irreplaceable role in predicting precipitation.

Table 4. RMSE, MAE and CC of different models under different precipitation thresholds

Models	0 mm	0.1 mm	1 mm	5 mm	10 mm	20 mm	30 mm
RMSE(mm)							
Ref-attention	2.250	4.677	5.912	8.601	12.405	19.196	25.244
Kdp-attention	2.503	4.897	6.007	8.969	12.952	20.165	27.041
Ref-Kdp-attention	**2.228**	4.570	**5.691**	8.240	11.589	17.535	23.485
Ref-Zdr-attention	2.297	4.628	5.795	8.268	11.714	17.904	24.015
Kdp-Zdr-attention	2.419	4.820	5.964	9.004	12.882	19.393	25.456
Ref-Kdp-Zdr-attention	2.230	**4.567**	5.701	**8.073**	**11.368**	**17.115**	**22.743**
MAE(mm)							
Ref-attention	**0.864**	2.606	3.673	6.065	9.880	17.200	23.734
Kdp-attention	1.044	2.915	3.777	6.160	9.991	17.665	24.923
Ref-Kdp-attention	0.913	2.625	3.628	5.949	9.033	14.877	21.719
Ref-Zdr-attention	0.909	2.676	3.702	5.806	9.047	15.202	21.673
Kdp-Zdr-attention	1.019	2.772	3.755	6.336	10.239	16.935	23.155
Ref-Kdp-Zdr-attention	0.868	**2.566**	**3.539**	**5.690**	**8.713**	14.211	**20.021**
CC							
Ref-attention	0.639	0.583	0.514	0.465	0.420	**0.403**	**0.281**
Kdp-attention	0.580	0.539	0.482	0.380	0.283	0.146	0.045
Ref-Kdp-attention	0.662	0.616	0.564	0.507	0.466	0.353	0.367
Ref-Zdr-attention	0.652	0.610	0.549	0.496	0.445	0.337	0.232
Kdp-Zdr-attention	0.599	0.555	0.505	0.421	0.367	0.269	0.011
Ref-Kdp-Zdr-attention	**0.672**	**0.628**	**0.578**	**0.534**	**0.489**	0.355	0.270

4.3 Testing with Different Variables

Three comparative algorithms have been chosen to demonstrate the advantages of the model proposed in this paper:

(1) Traditional Z-R relationship: the Z-R relationship directly shows the association between radar reflectivity Z and precipitation estimates R. The calculation formula is:

$$Z = 300R^{1.4}. \tag{12}$$

(2) Convolutional model without attention mechanism: The attention mechanism is excluded from the model proposed in this paper to verify the enhancement of the precipitation estimation by the attention mechanism.

(3) QPENet [18], a deep learning model based on dual polarization radar variables: This algorithm was proposed by Yonghua Zhang in 2021 and focuses on quantitative precipitation estimation for typhoon landfall.

The test results are shown in Table 5:

Table 5. RMSE, MAE and CC of different algorithms under different precipitation thresholds

Algorithms	0 mm	0.1 mm	1 mm	5 mm	10 mm	20 mm	30 mm
RMSE(mm)							
Z-R	2.884	5.861	7.435	11.094	15.312	21.996	25.696
Ref-Kdp-Zdr	2.278	4.624	5.818	8.343	11.785	17.996	24.420
QPENet	2.313	4.923	6.350	9.878	13.890	19.847	24.589
Ref-Kdp-Zdr-attention	**2.230**	**4.567**	**5.701**	**8.073**	**11.368**	**17.115**	**22.743**
MAE(mm)							
Z-R	0.869	2.896	4.379	8.026	12.251	19.403	23.386
Ref-Kdp-Zdr	0.900	2.647	3.697	5.906	9.133	15.530	22.709
QPENet	0.842	2..548	3.745	7.269	11.513	17.423	21.287
Ref-Kdp-Zdr-attention	**0.868**	**2.566**	**3.539**	**5.690**	**8.713**	**14.211**	**20.021**
CC							
Z-R	0.507	0.470	0.422	0.343	0.283	0.230	0.231
Ref-Kdp-Zdr	0.648	0.604	0.536	0.467	0.439	0.310	**0.320**
QPENet	0.622	0.583	0.525	0.480	0.374	0.300	0.011
Ref-Kdp-Zdr-attention	**0.672**	**0.628**	**0.578**	**0.534**	**0.489**	**0.355**	0.270

It can be seen that the QPENet and our model perform better than the traditional Z-R relationship for the task of quantitative precipitation estimation. Our model further improves the precipitation estimation accuracy with the help of attention mechanism compared to QPENet.

4.4 Case Study

We select an example of precipitation estimation to demonstrate the improvement by the dual-polarization radar variables more visually. The case is selected from the radar observation sequence of KEAX radar at 04:00–05:00 on May 7, 2019. Figure 3(a) shows the reflectivity, differential reflectivity and differential phase shift rate respectively. Figure 3 (b) embeds the rainfall reality in the pseudo-color map of differential phase shift rate.

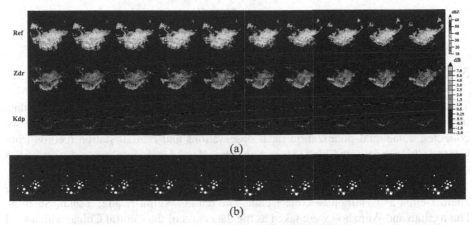

Fig. 3. Case visualization: (a) reflectivity image sequence; differential reflectivity image sequence and differential phase shift rate image sequence; (b) actual precipitation(white dot's radius) at the observation site.

It can be seen that most of the recording points with heavy precipitation are concentrated in the regions with reflectivity greater than 40 dBZ. The differential reflectivity and differential phase shift rate in these regions are both high, indicating that these regions are very likely to have heavy precipitation weather.

The precipitation estimation errors for this paper's model and the comparison model Z-R relationship and QPENet in case are given in Fig. 4, where the horizontal coordinate is the actual precipitation and the vertical coordinate is the difference between the precipitation estimate of each model and the actual precipitation.

It can be seen that:

(1) Among all precipitation records (0.762 mm/h−19.812 mm/h) in this case, the precipitation estimation deviation given by our model is controlled within 2 mm/h. The error fluctuation of the comparison model QPENet is large, and the Z-R relationship performs the worst, especially at the actual point of 3.302 mm/h, which gives a precipitation estimation error close to 14 mm/h. an error rate of more than 300%;

(2) When observing the three real points with stronger precipitation over 10 mm/h, all three models underestimated, among which our model underestimated by 2–3 mm/h and the QPENet model underestimated by 5.6–7 mm/h, which is more than 1 times higher than our model.

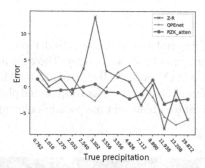

Fig. 4. Error curves of precipitation estimation for different models in the case.

5   Model Transferring Performance Testing

The model in Sect. 4 of this paper was trained by the dual-polarimetric radar data in the USA. To test the generalization ability of the model to different regions, we collected some dual-polarization radar observations and rainfall station records from Central China and South China to investigate the effect of regional climate characteristics on the quantitative dual-polarization radar precipitation estimates.

We select Shijiazhuang, Yantai, Suizhou, Huangshan, Wenzhou, Guangzhou, Shenzhen, Beihai and Haikou to collect data. The data of Shijiazhuang, Yantai, Suizhou, Huangshan and Wenzhou were taken as the data class of the Central China, with a total of 302 samples. The data from Guangzhou, Shenzhen, Beihai and Haikou were taken as the data class of South China, with 799 samples.

Our model is denoted as QPEatten-RKZ, where the subscript s indicates that the model is trained with USA data only, and the subscript s-t indicates that the model is trained with U.S. data and then corrected with Chinese data. The subscript t indicates that the model is trained with Chinese data only. The method proposed in the literature [15] is noted as QPEatten-R. The test results under the data of radar stations in China are shown in Table 6:

Table 6. RMSE of test results between original model and transfer learning model.

Model	Epoch	Data	0 mm	1 mm	5 mm	10 mm	20 mm	30 mm
QPEatten-RKZ$_s$	–	USA	2.23	5.70	8.07	11.37	17.12	22.74
QPEatten-RKZ$_t$	30	China	2.35	5.65	7.91	9.81	13.38	17.25
QPEatten-RKZ$_{s-t}$	16	China	2.34	5.65	7.81	9.51	12.94	16.85
		South China	2.19	6.21	8.63	10.29	13.60	17.19
		Central China	2.77	4.89	6.70	8.36	11.81	**16.10**
QPEatten-R	–	China	**1.36**	**3.23**	**5.12**	**7.15**	**11.72**	17.03

From Table 6, it can be seen that:

1) The precipitation estimation accuracy of the model is improved regardless of whether the model is trained directly using Chinese data or using Chinese data for transfer learning of the original model. The reason for this should be the greater density of precipitation observation stations in China, which results in more accurate precipitation labels obtained from radar data, as illustrated by the precipitation model evaluation results obtained based on single-polarization radar data in the last row of Table 6.

2) Comparing the data in rows 2 to 5 of the Table 6, two advantages of transfer learning are demonstrated:

Advantage 1: the training time is almost halved, which is more beneficial to the training and tuning of larger scale deep models.

Advantage 2: transfer learning is more effective due to the overall reduction of precipitation estimation error with high efficiency.

3) Comparing the data in the 2–3 and last rows of the table, the advantage of the precipitation estimation model based on dual-polarization radar data is not seen, except for the review results under the 30 mm/h precipitation threshold indicating that QPEatten-RKZs-t is better than QPEatten-R. Preliminary analysis of the possible reasons are two:

Reason 1: the amount of data is not sufficient. The sample size of the single-polarization precipitation estimation model built by our team is 21,027 cases, and the sample size used for training the model and selecting the parameters is 12,616 cases and 4,205 cases, while the sample size of dual-polarization radar in USA in this paper is 1,213 cases and 405 cases, which is one order of magnitude less, and the sample used for transfer learning is even less.

Reason 2: the Chinese data used for transfer learning are geographically scattered, among which the precipitation distribution in the detection area of five radars in the Central China is obviously different from that in the detection area of four radars in South China (Fig. 5).

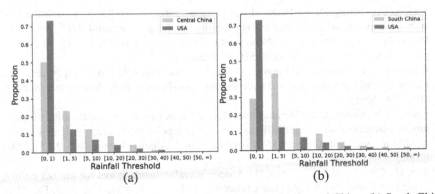

Fig. 5. Histogram of rainfall statistics in different regions:(a) Central China; (b) South China

6 Conclusion

According to the physical mechanism of reflectivity, differential reflectivity and differential phase shift rate, we designed a precipitation estimation neural network. It uses radar reflectivity and differential phase shift rate to estimate precipitation intensity, and then uses differential reflectivity data to correct precipitation intensity. Through systematic tests, it was verified that using the three radar data at the same time had the best performance. Compared with the traditional Z-R relationship, the precipitation estimation error is reduced by 11%−27%, and compared with the deep learning model QPENet, the precipitation estimation error is reduced by 7%−18%. It shows that our model has a better capability to learn the internal association between dual-polarization radar variables and precipitation. Meanwhile, this paper tested the transfer performance of the model, using data from Central China and South China respectively after training with data from the Central USA. The results show that the model performs better in Central China at the same latitude, which fully illustrates the obvious difference of convective system evolution mechanism in different latitudes.

In the future, we hope to introduce environmental field data like slope and elevation to further improve the accuracy of quantitative precipitation estimation.

References

1. Yu, X.: Nowcasting thinking and method of flash heavy rain. Torrential Rain Disaster **32**(3), 202–209 (2013)
2. Wilson, J.W., Brandes, E.A.: Radar measurement of rainfall-a summary. Bull. Am. Meteor. Soc. **60**(9), 1048–1060 (1979)
3. Song, L., Chen, M., Cheng, C., et al.: Characteristics of summer QPE error and a climatological correction method over Beijing-Tianjin-Hebei region. Acta Meteorol. Sin. **77**, 497–515 (2019)
4. Kuang, Q., Yang, X., Zhang, W., et al.: Spatiotemporal modeling and implementation for radar-based rainfall estimation. IEEE Geosci. Remote Sens. Lett. **13**(11), 1601–1605 (2016)
5. Zhang, C., Wang, H., Zeng, J., et al.: Short-Term dynamic radar quantitative precipitation estimation based on wavelet transform and support vector machine. J. Meteorol. Res. **34**(2), 413–426 (2020)
6. Seliga, T.A., Bringi, V.N.: Potential use of radar differential reflectivity measurements at orthogonal polarizations for measuring precipitation. J. Appl. Meteorol. **15**(1), 69–76 (1976)
7. Ruzanski, E., Chandrasekar, V.: Nowcasting rainfall fields derived from specific differential phase. J. Appl. Meteorol. Climatol. **51**(11), 1950–1959 (2012)
8. Ryzhkov, A.V., Schuur, T.J., Burgess, D.W., et al.: The joint polarization experiment: polarimetric rainfall measurements and hydrometeor classification. Bull. Am. Meteor. Soc. **86**(6), 809–824 (2005)
9. Bringi, V.N., Huang, G.J., Chandrasekar, V., et al.: A methodology for estimating the parameters of a gamma raindrop size distribution model from polarimetric radar data: application to a squall-line event from the TRMM/Brazil campaign. J. Atmos. Oceanic Tech. **19**(5), 633–645 (2002)
10. Tan, H., Chandrasekar, V., Chen, H.: A deep neural network model for rainfall estimation using polarimetric WSR-88DP radar observations. In: Agu Fall Meeting, AGU Fall Meeting Abstracts 2016, pp. IN11B-1622 (2016)

11. Chen, H., Chandrasekar, V., Tan, H., et al: Development of deep learning based data fusion approach for accurate rainfall estimation using ground radar and satellite precipitation products. In: Agu Fall Meeting, AGU Fall Meeting Abstracts 2016, pp. H12D–03 (2016)
12. Wang, H., Ran, Y., Deng, Y., et al.: Study on deep-learning based identification of hydrometeors observed by dual polarization Doppler weather radars. EURASIP J. Wirel. Commun. Netw. **2017**(1), 173 (2017)
13. Mahale, V.N., Zhang, G., Xue, M.: Fuzzy logic classification of S-band polarimetric radar echoes to identify three-body scattering and improve data quality. J. Appl. Meteorol. Climatol. **53**(8), 2017–2033 (2014)
14. Mason, B.J.: The Physics of Clouds. Clarendon Press, Oxford (2010)
15. Wang, C., Wang, P., Wang, P., et al.: A spatiotemporal attention model for severe precipitation estimation. IEEE Geosci. Remote Sens. Lett. **19**, 1–5 (2022)
16. Vaswani, A., Shazeer, N., Parmar, N., et al: Attention is all you need. In: 30th International Proceedings of Neural Information Processing Systems, Long Beach, USA (2017)
17. Shi, X., Gao, Z., Lausen, L., et al: Deep learning for precipitation nowcasting: a benchmark and a new model. In: 30th International Proceedings of Neural Information Processing Systems, vol. 30. Long Beach, USA (2017)
18. Zhang, Y., Bi, S., Liu, L., et al.: Deep learning for polarimetric radar quantitative precipitation estimation during landfalling typhoons in South China. Remote Sens. **13**(16), 3157 (2021)

Research on Object Detection Methods in Low-Light Conditions

Feifan Wang[1,2,3], Xi'ai Chen[2,3(✉)], Xudong Wang[2,3,4], Weihong Ren[5], and Yandong Tang[2,3]

[1] School of Automation and Electrical Engineering, Shenyang Ligong University, Shenyang 110159, China

[2] State Key Laboratory of Robotics, Shenyang Institute of Automation, Chinese Academy of Sciences, Shenyang 110016, China
chenxiai@sia.cn

[3] Institutes for Robotics and Intelligent Manufacturing, Chinese Academy of Sciences, Shenyang 110169, China

[4] University of Chinese Academy of Sciences, Beijing 100049, China

[5] School of Mechanical Engineering and Automation, Harbin Institute of Technology (Shenzhen), Shenzhen 518055, China

Abstract. Low-light images are images taken in poorly illuminated environments. Such images suffer from colour distortion, loss of detail and blurriness, which seriously affects the detection accuracy of object detection tasks. In order to improve the accuracy of object detection in low-light images, we propose a low-light image object detection algorithm based on image enhancement. The algorithm is jointly trained on the input side of the YOLOv5 network in combination with an unsupervised low-light enhancement model. The training phase optimises the overall network with the loss of object detection so that the image enhancement results are more favourable for improving the object detection accuracy. In the feature extraction phase, we design a feature enhancement model based on an attention mechanism. Our algorithm is tested on the publicly available ExDark dataset and achieves a mean average precision (mAP) of 79.15%, which is a 4.25% improvement over the baseline.

Keywords: Deep learning · Low-light enhancement · Object detection · Attention mechanisms

1 Introduction

Object detection is an important downstream task in the field of computer vision, which has made great progress in recent years and is widely used in many areas, such as pedestrian detection [1], video surveillance [2], and unmanned driving [3]. Existing object detection algorithms are generally designed for natural light scenes, and under normal lighting conditions, as shown in Fig. 1(a)(b). It is very beneficial for the detection network to extract the target features shown in natural light scenes. However, under low light conditions, such as night scenes, as shown in Fig. 1(c)(d). This lead to degradation of the captured images, such as reduced contrast and background noise, which is not conducive to the extraction of target features, thus leading to a reduction in the detection accuracy of object detection, which is a major challenge for the object detection task.

Fig. 1. Comparison of images under different lighting conditions.

While early low-light object detection methods [4,5] generally used infrared cameras to acquire data for detection based on infrared target datasets, the imaging principle of infrared cameras results in low sensitivity to objects with small outdoor temperature differences for effective discrimination. In addition, some researchers have proposed enhancement methods for low-light images and have attempted to enhance the low-light images before inputting them into the object detection network to improve the accuracy of detection. Some algorithms based on histogram equalisation [6] use additional prior summation constraints in an attempt to amplify the greyscale difference between neighbouring pixels, thereby extending dynamic range of image. The MBLLEN [7] method extracts rich image features in different light components based on retinex theory [8], uses multiple sub-networks for image enhancement and then fuses the output images of each sub-network. Image quality is enhanced from multiple directions, but the algorithm requires training using paired bright and dark datasets.

The above enhancement methods are all based on human vision for enhancement, which provides a high improvement in image quality in terms of visual sensation, but may not be conducive to object detection accuracy for computer vision object detection tasks. To solve the above problems, we developed an object detection method for low-light images. In this method, we design a low-light enhancement model based on convolutional neural network, and combine it with a YOLOv5 [9] object detection network. Finally, we optimize the entire network using the object detection loss, so that the results of low-light enhancement are more favourable to object detection than to the human vision effects. In the feature extraction phase of the object detection module, we design a feature enhancement module on the basis of attention mechanism to boost the detection accuracy of smaller object.

The contribution of this work can be summarised in the following three points. Firstly, we design a low-light enhancement model that enhances the low-light image by learning the global information of the low-light image, thus improving the object detection accuracy. Secondly, We propose an object detection network for the detection of low-light images. The network combines a low-light enhancement model with an object detection model end-to-end, allowing for direct detection of the input low-light image. Finally, based on the attention mechanism, we design a feature enhancement model. The model is embedded in an object detection network to improve the accuracy of object detection.

2   Method

The proposed low-light object detection network consists of two main components: a low-light enhancement network and a YOLOv5 object detection network. The two are trained together by cascading, overall model structure is shown in Fig. 2.

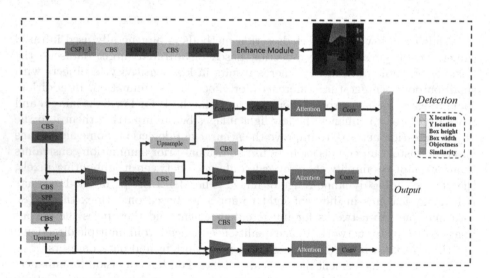

Fig. 2. Algorithmic framework: In this model, the low-light enhancement network is cascaded with the object detection and trained jointly end-to-end. Low-light images are enhanced by the enhancement model and enter the object detection network for detection.

2.1   Low-Light Image Enhancement Network

This section consists of two parts: a parameter generation network and an image correction network, as shown in Fig. 3.

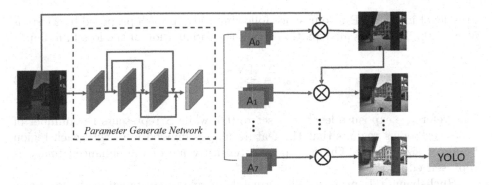

Fig. 3. Low-light image enhancement network: In this network, the Parameter Generation Network produces a 24-channel mapping matrix from input images. This matrix is then divided into 8 parameter matrices, denoted as A. The channels and sizes of the 8 matrices are the same with the input image. Image correction network takes the input image and multiplies it with the first parameter matrix, A_0. The resulting output is then multiplied with the next parameter matrix, A_1, and the process is repeated iteratively to get the final image.

After obtaining the image to be enhanced, the image is first scaled and normalised to a fixed size and is then used as input to the parametric generation network. The network is composed of 7 convolution layers. Each layer of the convolutional kernel has 24 output channels of size 3×3 with a step size of 1. The ReLU activation function is applied to the first six convolution layers, while the last convolution layer is activated using Tanh. The final output is a mapping matrix A with 24 channels and the same size as the input image. The matrix A obtained by the parametric generation network and the low-light image to be detected are used as input to the image correction network. The matrix A is first divided into N three-dimensional matrices with the same structure as the input image, where N is 8. The input image is operated with the corresponding values on these N feature maps to obtain a preliminary enhanced feature map, which can be expressed by Eq. (1):

$$P^o_{x,y} = P^i_{x,y} + \lambda(P^i_{x,y} - (P^i_{x,y})^2) \tag{1}$$

In this equation, x, y are the pixel coordinates and λ is a trainable enhancement factor with a size in the range$(0, 1)$. The output image P^o is enhanced by several iterations of the enhancement calculation to a range of intervals more conducive to detection.

To guide the network to a reasonable enhancement mapping relationship, two loss functions, exposure loss and colour consistency loss, are designed for enhancement network.

The Exposure Loss serves to constrain the dynamic range of the enhanced image by penalizing underexposed and overexposed regions. Specifically, this loss function computes the error between the average intensity value of a local region in the enhanced image and a reference exposure level E, which is defined as the grey level in the RGB colour space following the approach proposed by Mertens et al. [10]. The following equation shows the formulation of the loss function:

$$L_{\exp ose} = \frac{1}{S} \sum_{k=1}^{S} |Y_k - E| \tag{2}$$

The reference exposure level E is set to 0.6, while S represents the number of non-overlapping regions that the feature map is divided into, with each region being of size 16×16. The flat mean intensity value of the enhanced image is represented by Y.

Buchsbaum [11] proposed the principle of colour constancy in the greyscale world, which means that the true colour of an object remains stable when the external light changes. Based on this theory, a colour constancy loss is designed in this paper to correct the colour deviation of the enhanced image. The loss function is as follows:

$$L_{color} = \sum_{(p,q\in\varepsilon)} G(J^p - J^q)^2, \varepsilon = \{(R,B),(B,G),(G,R)\} \tag{3}$$

In this equation, p and q refer to a pair of color channels, while J^p and J^q denote the average intensity values of channel p and channel q, respectively, in the enhanced image. The variable ε represents a list of channel combinations.

The overall loss of the image enhancement module is obtained by combining the two loss functions above with the following equation:

$$L_{total} = L_{\exp ose} + L_{colar} \tag{4}$$

We use two loss functions to pre-train the low-light enhancement network and obtain its corresponding parameters. The trained enhancement network is then combined with YOLOv5 object detection network, and then optimised the end to end network with object detection loss to further improve its performance.

2.2   Object Detection Network

YOLO partitions the input image into a grid of cells with a size of $S1 \times S2$ (7×7), and detects the centre of the object falling into all cells. The model predicts M bounding boxes for all objects, along with a confidence score associated with each bounding box, as given by the following equation:

$$C_b = P(O) \cdot L \tag{5}$$

In this equation, C_b represents the confidence level of the prediction result. $P(O)$ denotes the probability of an object being present in the bounding box, while O indicates the existence of an object. The variable L represents the intersection over union (IoU) score between predicted bounding box and ground truth bounding box. Each bounding box comprises five prediction values, including the coordinates (x, y) that correspond to the center of box, as well as its width (w), height (h), and confidence score.

Each cell also predicts a set of conditional category probabilities for each bounding box: $P(s|O)$ represents the probability that an object belongs to each category, given that the predicted bounding box contains the object, where s represents the category. Combining Eq. (5), the conditional category probabilities are multiplied by the corresponding bounding box confidence rates to obtain a specific category confidence rate for each bounding box, as shown in Eq. (6):

$$C_{s_i} = P(s_i|O) \cdot P(O) \cdot L = P(s_i) \cdot L \tag{6}$$

The category confidence rate encodes both the probability that the object in the bounding box belongs to the category and the accuracy of the bounding box location, as shown in Eq. (6).

The YOLO algorithm uses the mean squared sum error as loss function to optimise the module parameters. Overall error consists of three components and is calculated as shown in Eq. (7).

$$l = L_r + L_o + L_c \tag{7}$$

L_r, L_o and L_c are the bounding box position loss, bounding box confidence loss and category loss, respectively. The specific equations are as follows:

$$L_r = \lambda_r \sum_{i=0}^{s^2} \sum_{j=0}^{M} \Pi_{ij}^{obj} [(\hat{b}_x^{ij} - b_x^{ij})^2 + (\hat{b}_y^{ij} - b_y^{ij})^2]$$

$$+ \lambda_r \sum_{i=0}^{s^2} \sum_{j=0}^{M} \Pi_{ij}^{obj} [(\sqrt{\hat{b}_\omega^{ij}} - \sqrt{b_\omega^{ij}})^2 + (\sqrt{\hat{b}_h^{ij}} - \sqrt{b_h^{ij}})^2] \tag{8}$$

$$L_o = \sum_{i=0}^{s^2} \sum_{j=0}^{M} \Pi_{ij}^{obj} (\hat{c}_x^{ij} - c_x^{ij})^2 + \lambda_n \sum_{i=0}^{s^2} \sum_{j=0}^{M} \Pi_{ij}^{n} (\hat{c}_x^{ij} - c_x^{ij})^2 \tag{9}$$

$$L_c = \sum_{i=0}^{s^2} \sum_{j=0}^{M} \Pi_{ij}^{obj} \sum_{c \in classes} (\hat{p}_c^{ij} - p_c^{ij})^2 \tag{10}$$

where Π_{ij}^{obj} indicates whether the $j-th$ bounding box of the $i-th$ grid contains a target, and takes the value 1 if it contains a target, and 0 otherwise. Π_{ij}^{n} is the opposite of Π_{ij}^{obj}, and takes the value 0 if it contains a target, and the value 1 if it does not; $\hat{c}_x^{ij}$ and c_x^{ij} represent the confidence levels of the predicted and true bounding boxes, respectively. The variable $\hat{p}_c^{ij}$ represents the probability that an object in the predicted bounding box belongs to category c, λ_r, λ_n denote the weighting parameters of the loss function.

2.3 Feature Enhanced Network

In feature-enhanced networks, channel weights are learned using a channel attention network. This involves first performing global average pooling on the feature map to obtain a set of feature vectors, where each value represents the relevance of the corresponding channel. These vectors are then fed through two fully connected layers with different activation functions to obtain the weights for each channel. The first layer compresses the C channels into C/r to reduce computational complexity and uses the $ReLU$ activation function, while the second layer restores the number of channels back to C and uses the $Sigmoid$ activation function to output the final channel weights. Attention is then weighted according to the importance of each channel, highlighting the important channels and suppressing the less important ones. The network is deconstructed as shown in Fig. 4.

The feature enhancement network makes the target region of feature map more visible. The module can be flexibly ported to other network architectures and is able to bring improvements in detection accuracy with a slight loss of computational performance.

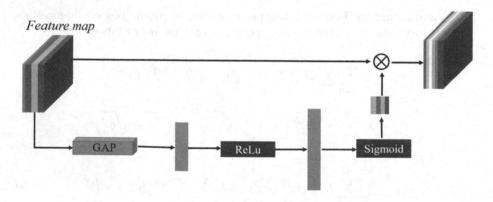

Fig. 4. Feature Enhanced Network

3 Experimental Results and Analyses

3.1 Datasets

In this paper, we use the ExDark dataset [12], a collection of low-light images including 12 object classes, with a total of 7363 images. The dataset is randomly divided into a training set, a validation set, and a test set, with the split ratio being 7:1:2.

3.2   Comparison Tests

Through experimental validation, the proposed algorithm achieves 79.10% mAP on the test set, which is an improvement in detection accuracy mAP compared to the current state-of-the-art object detection algorithms such as YOLOv3 [13], YOLOv5 and YOLOX [14]. In addition, this paper combines the Kind [15] and Zero-DCE [16] image luminance enhancement algorithms with a object detection network for experimentation. The low-light images are first enhanced, and then the enhanced images are detected and compared with the low-light object detection algorithm proposed in this paper. Table 1 shows the test results of other object detection methods on the ExDark dataset.

Table 1. Experimental comparison of different object detection algorithms.

Methods	YOLOv3	YOLOv5	YOLOX	Kind+	Zero-DCE+	Ours
mAP/%	69.34	74.90	75.26	63.21	71.42	79.15
Times/ms	9.2	7.9	11.2	42.1	67.3	20.3

Figure 5 gives a comparison of our proposed low-light object detection algorithm with other mainstream detection algorithms. Our algorithm reduces the rate of missed detection of small targets to a certain extent compared with other previous algorithms. The recognition accuracy of the algorithm proposed in this paper is also higher when the objects are jointly detected.

Experimental results show that our low-light image object detection algorithm still has advantages in terms of detection result. Although the contrast low-light enhancement methods have a certain effect of improving the human vision, it is not conducive to improve the detection accuracy for the object detection task of computer vision. In addition, the enhancement process consumes a large amount of computing resources, which is detrimental to high-performance real-time detection.

3.3   Ablation Experiments

To further explore the effectiveness of the proposed algorithm, we conducted ablation experiments on the low-light enhancement module and the feature enhancement module, and analysed the effect of the sub-module on the detection results and verified them by deleting the sub-module. The experimental results of the ablation experiment are shown in Table 2, where LEM stands for low-light enhancement model and FEM stands for feature enhancement model.

Low-Light Enhancement Network. This section adds an enhancement module, which improves mAP by 2.22% on the Exdark dataset compared to the baseline, effectively improving the object detection accuracy of low-light images.

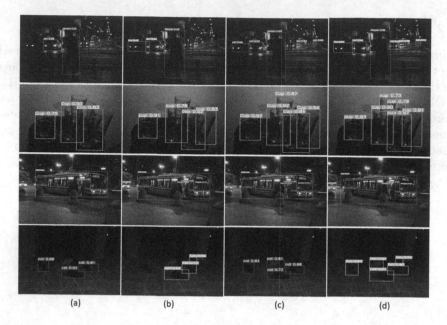

(a)   (b)   (c)   (d)

Fig. 5. Detection effects of different algorithms: (a) YOLOv3, (b) YOLOv5, (c) YOLOX and (d) Ours.

Table 2. Ablation experiments

Methods	YOLOv5	YOLOv5+LEM	YOLOv5+FEM	YOLOv5+LEM+FEM
$mAP/\%$	74.90	77.12	76.24	79.15

After enhancement, the variability of its target features from normal illumination is reduced, allowing the detection network to obtain more features for subsequent object detection tasks during feature extraction.

Feature Enhancement Network. The feature enhancement module has been added in this section. The detection accuracy of the model on the Exdark dataset is improved by 1.34% compared to the baseline. In this module, we use an attention mechanism that suppresses background noise and effectively enhances the detection network's attention to the semantic and positional information of the object, thus improving the detection results.

4   Conclusion

In this paper, we propose a method for object detection tasks in low illumination conditions. In this method, we design an enhancement module that enhances the brightness of image by learning global information about the input image. The low-light enhancement module is also cascaded with the object detection network to achieve end-to-end joint optimization, thereby making the enhancement effect of the enhancement module more beneficial to the object detection task. We also design a feature enhancement module to improve object detection accuracy by weighting different channels to enhance target features and suppress background noise. The proposed method is more robust and has higher detection accuracy than other object detection methods in low light conditions. However, our algorithm can only be used for low light scenes, we will try to investigate object detection tasks under complex lighting scenes in subsequent studies.

Acknowledgements. This work was supported by the Youth Innovation Promotion Association of the Chinese Academy of Sciences under Grant 2022196 and Y202051, in part by the National Natural Science Foundation of China under Grant 61821005, in part by the Natural Science Foundation of Liaoning Province under Grant 2021-BS-023.

References

1. Xu, Z., Li, B., Yuan, Y., Dang, A.: Beta r-cnn: looking into pedestrian detection from another perspective. arXiv:2210.12758 (2022)
2. Nawaratne, R., Alahakoon, D., De Silva, D., Yu, X.: Spatiotemporal anomaly detection using deep learning for real-time video surveillance. IEEE Trans. Ind. Inf. **16**(1), 393–402 (2019)
3. Wen, L.H., Jo, K.H.: Deep learning-based perception systems for autonomous driving: a comprehensive survey. Neurocomputing **489**, 255–270 (2022)
4. Yang, S., Liu, W., Deng, C., Zhang, X.: Color fusion method for low-light-level and infrared images in night vision. In: 2012 5th International Congress on Image and Signal Processing, pp. 534–537. IEEE (2012)
5. Wei, Y., You, X., Li, H.: Multiscale patch-based contrast measure for small infrared target detection. Pattern Recogn. **58**, 216–226 (2016)
6. Rong, Z., Li, Z., Dong-Nan, L.: Study of color heritage image enhancement algorithms based on histogram equalization. Optik **126**(24), 5665–5667 (2015)
7. Lv, F., Lu, F., Wu, J., Lim, C.: Mbllen: low-light image/video enhancement using cnns. In: BMVC, vol. 220, p. 4 (2018)
8. Pan, X., Li, C., Pan, Z., Yan, J., Tang, S., Yin, X.: Low-light image enhancement method based on retinex theory by improving illumination map. Appl. Sci. **12**(10), 5257 (2022)
9. Jocher, G., et al.: ultralytics/yolov5: v5. 0-yolov5-p6 1280 models, aws, supervise. ly and youtube integrations. Zenodo (2021)
10. Mertens, T., Kautz, J., Van Reeth, F.: Exposure fusion: a simple and practical alternative to high dynamic range photography. In: Computer Graphics Forum, vol. 28, pp. 161–171. Wiley Online Library (2009)
11. Buchsbaum, G.: A spatial processor model for object colour perception. J. Franklin Inst. **310**(1), 1–26 (1980)
12. Loh, Y.P., Chan, C.S.: Getting to know low-light images with the exclusively dark dataset. Comput. Vision Image Underst. **178**, 30–42 (2019)
13. Redmon, J., Farhadi, A.: Yolov3: an incremental improvement. arXiv preprint arXiv:1804.02767 (2018)
14. Ge, Z., Liu, S., Wang, F., Li, Z., Sun, J.: Yolox: exceeding yolo series in 2021. arXiv preprint arXiv:2107.08430 (2021)

15. Zhang, Y., Zhang, J., Guo, X.: Kindling the darkness: a practical low-light image enhancer. In: Proceedings of the 27th ACM International Conference on Multimedia, pp. 1632–1640 (2019)
16. Guo, C., et al.: Zero-reference deep curve estimation for low-light image enhancement. In: Proceedings of the IEEE/CVF Conference on Computer Vision and Pattern Recognition, pp. 1780–1789 (2020)

Image Recovery and Object Detection Integrated Algorithms for Robots in Harsh Battlefield Environments

Xudong Wang[1,2,3], Xi'ai Chen[1,2(✉)], Feifan Wang[1,2,4], Chonglong Xu[5], and Yandong Tang[1,2]

[1] State Key Laboratory of Robotics, Shenyang Institute of Automation, Chinese Academy of Sciences, Shenyang 110016, China
chenxiai@sia.cn
[2] Institutes for Robotics and Intelligent Manufacturing, Chinese Academy of Sciences, Shenyang 110169, China
[3] University of Chinese Academy of Sciences, Beijing 100049, China
[4] School of Automation and Electrical Engineering, Shenyang Ligong University, Shenyang 110159, China
[5] Chi Technology(Shenyang) Limited, Shenyang 110170, China

Abstract. Battlefield environments are harsher than normal environments, and the images captured by imaging equipment are more prone to degradation. Degraded images seriously affect the analysis of military intelligence and the deployment of intelligent weapons. To address this issue, we propose an image recovery algorithm, which recovers degraded battlefield images based on a physical imaging model and uses a lightweight network to estimate the parameters of physical model. In addition, we propose a strategy to joint training of the image recovery module and the object detection module. Specifically, we integrate the recovery module to the front of YOLO detector to jointly optimize the two modules with detection loss. The image recovery module is light-weight without significant adverse impact on the real-time running of object detection, which can be easily deployed to intelligent unmanned devices such as battlefield robots. The experimental results show that the proposed algorithm achieves better recovery performance in battlefield environments, and the joint training strategy effectively improve the accuracy of object detection.

Keywords: Battlefield Robots · Intelligence Weapons · Environment Perception · Image Recovery · Object Detection

1 Introduction

Modern warfare is accelerating from the era of information to the era of intelligence. Intelligent unmanned systems such as military robots play an important role in the development of modern warfare [1,2]. However, in general, the intelligence images acquired through military reconnaissance methods are subject to

H. Yang et al. (Eds.): ICIRA 2023, LNAI 14270, pp. 575–585, 2023.
https://doi.org/10.1007/978-981-99-6492-5_49

varying degrees of degradation, as shown in Fig. 1. It not only affects access to military information, but also causes serious interference to upper-level intelligent steps such as object identification, localization and precision guidance of intelligent weapons [3,4]. In this work, we focus our attention on improving the image recovery and object detection ability of robot in harsh battlefield environments.

Fig. 1. Degraded quality images are inevitable in the battlefield environment. This has caused the loss of military intelligence, as well as affecting the proper functioning of intelligent weapons.

Although there are different tiny particles in the atmosphere, the physical mechanisms leading to degradation phenomena in the imaging process are similar. There are three classes methods for the recovery of images degraded by the presence of tiny particles in the atmosphere. Image enhancement based algorithms are used to enhance the details of the image, which use image enhancement techniques to further improve the contrast of the image and make appear clearer, for example histogram equalization [5], wavelet transform algorithm [6] and differential equation algorithm [7–9]. The physical model-based recovery algorithm is mainly based on the model of atmospheric scattering proposed by McCartney [10,11], and the inverse operation is performed to obtain a clear image based on the imaging principle of particle degradation images. The most classical algorithm is the dark channel a priori dehazing algorithm proposed by He [12], on the basis of which a large number of improved algorithms have appeared [13,14]. Deep learning-based image recovery algorithms use convolutional neural networks to form an end-to-end recovery model, such as DehazeNet [15], MSBDN [16] and D4 [17].

However, these image recovery algorithms are designed for normal environments. In contrast, the battlefield environment is harsher and more challenging for recovery algorithms. In addition, the above algorithms all aim to enhance human vision for image recovery while do not guarantee an effective enhancement for object detection task. To solve these problems, we propose an image recovery and object detection algorithm applied for battlefield robots. The image recovery module is based on a physical imaging model with a light-weight network structure that does not significantly degrade the real-time performance of the detection algorithm. We use YOLOv5 as the base object detector and propose a joint training strategy for integrating image recovery and object detection module. The experimental results show that the proposed algorithm effectively improves the capability of robots for object detection in complex battlefield environments.

2   Method

In this section, we introduce the proposed method. We model the degradation imaging process of the battlefield environment and propose an image recovery network, then finish with a joint optimization strategy.

2.1   Degradation Imaging Process and Recovery Model

Firstly, we model the imaging process of degraded images in battlefield environment. The degraded imaging process by the presence of particles in the atmosphere follows the atmospheric scattering model proposed by [10,11], which can be shown as the Fig. 2.

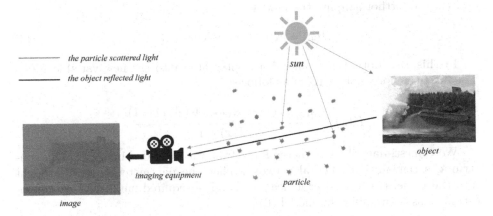

Fig. 2. The process of degraded imaging due to the presence of particles in atmosphere.

The atmospheric scattering model has been the classical description of the degraded imaging process:

$$I(x) = J(x)t(x) + A(1 - t(x)) \tag{1}$$

where the $I(x)$ is degraded image captured by robots, the $J(x)$ is radiation intensity of object. The A is global atmospheric light, which is a constant when in a natural parallel light environment. The $t(x)$ is mediaum transmission map, the definition as follows:

$$t(x) = e^{-\beta d(x)} \tag{2}$$

where the $d(x)$ is scene depth and the β is particle density scattering coefficient. Model (2) and (1) show that the particle density in degraded images $I(x)$ is directly related to scene depth $d(x)$ and particle density β.

The model (1) is adjusted to obtain the expression of the recovery image $J(x)$ as the output:

$$J(x) = \frac{1}{t(x)}I(x) - A\frac{1}{t(x)} + A \tag{3}$$

Using model (3) allows a clear image to be recovered. The classic image recovery strategy has followed the similar three steps:

step1. Using a network model or other methods to estimate the transmission matrix $t(x)$ from the degraded image $I(x)$;

step2. Using some empirical methods to estimate A, such as taking the maximum value of pixels in the degraded image.

step3. The clear image $J(x)$ is calculated by model (3).

In fact, due to the more complex and harsher battlefield environment, the parameter A is no longer globally consistent, i.e., it should be expressed as $A(x)$. This greatly increases the difficulty of parameters estimation in the atmospheric scattering model. Inspired by the literature [18], we combine the parameters A and $t(x)$ to further simplify the model:

$$J(x) = K(x)I(x) - K(x) + 1 \tag{4}$$

In this way, both $1/t(x)$ and A are integrated into the new variable $K(x)$. The specific expression of $K(x)$ as follows:

$$K(x) = \frac{\frac{1}{t(x)}\left(I(x) - A(x)\right) + (A(x) - 1)}{I(x) - 1} \tag{5}$$

We can estimate the parameter $K(x)$ from the degraded image $I(x)$ by construing a convolutional neural network. Then the parameter $K(x)$ is brought into the model (4) to recover a clear image. The required number of parameter estimations is simplified by model (6).

2.2 Algorithm Structure

The image restoration module contains an imaging model based restorer, and with a *Gamma* corrector. We use YOLOv5 as the object detection model to implement joint training. The algorithm structure is showed in Fig. 3.

To further reduce the computational complexity, the degraded images are first down-sampled. The size of the image after the down-sampling operation is one-fourth of the original size. After the convolution operation is performed on the down-sampled image, it is up-sampled for the size recovery.

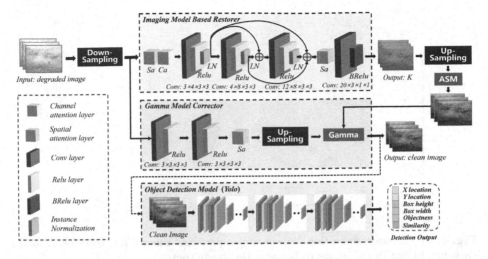

Fig. 3. Algorithm structure. The degraded image is recovered by the image recovery module and then fed into the detector to constitute the integrated recovery and detection algorithm.

The down-sampled image is convoluted in four layers to extract features and form the parameter matrix $K(x)$ in the physical imaging model. Specifically, in imaging model based restorer, the feature maps extracted by each 3×3 convolution kernel are fixed at the same size as the down-sampled image, which will facilitate the fusion of features from different layers. The number of output channels for the first three layers of convolution is 4, 8 and 8 respectively. Before being fed into the final convolution layer, the 20 sets of feature maps are stitched together. After the final layer of convolution, the feature set is adjusted to parameter matrix $K(x)$ with a channel number of 3. The parameter matrix $K(x)$ is up-sampled to obtain the same size as the original image. Finally, the improved atmospheric scattering model (ASM) is used to calculate the recovery of clear image.

Meanwhile, the down-sampled image is convolved in two layers to constitute the *Gamma* correction parameter $\gamma_{1,2,3}$. The *Gamma* parameter matrix is up-sampled to obtain the same size as the original image to perform *Gamma* corrector. The process of *Gamma* corrector as follows:

$$P_o = P_i = (r_i^{\gamma_{ri}}, g_i^{\gamma_{gi}}, b_i^{\gamma_{bi}}) \tag{6}$$

where the $\gamma_{r,g,b}$ is correction parameter. The correction parameter is applied to each pixel value by the number of channels.

The *Gamma* correction is shown in Fig. 4. Specifically, when $\gamma < 1$, the curve is up-convex and the output value is larger than the input value. When $\gamma = 1$, the curve is a straight line, the input value is equal with the output value, without correction. When $\gamma > 1$, the curve is down-convex and the output value is smaller than the input value. The contrast of the recovered image is further enhanced by the *Gamma* transformation of the pixel values.

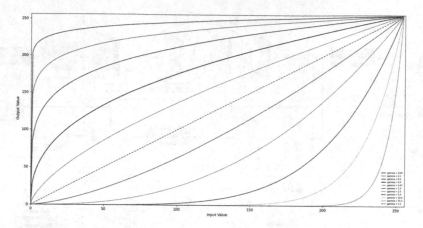

Fig. 4. The *Gamma* correction. The corrector performs a non-linear transformation of each pixel point in the image to improve the image contrast.

In addition, we use the spatial attention mechanism and the channel attention mechanism from literature [19] to improve the accuracy of parameter estimation. The network is more robust during training by instance normalization layer [20], and the BRelu [15] activation function limits the output range of the parameters.

Finally, the recovered images are fed into the YOLO object detection network to improve the accuracy of object recognition and localization for battlefield robots in harsh environments.

2.3 Integrated Method of Image Recovery and Detection

In this section, we introduce the training methods of the algorithm, including the image recovery module based on perceptual loss [21] training method, and the integrated recovery and detection optimization training method.

We perform end-to-end supervised training for the image recovery module, and use the perceptual loss function:

$$Loss = \frac{1}{C_j H_j W_j} \left\| F_j\left(\hat{y}\right) - F_j(y) \right\|_2^2 \tag{7}$$

where the F denotes the VGG 16 network [22]; j denotes different layer of VGG network and C, H, W is the size of the feature map. Taking the recovered image and clear reference image into VGG network, and using MSE on the paired feature maps extracted from the VGG network. The use of perceptual loss allows the recovery module to learn information about higher-level semantics.

We use a trained image recovery module which had the ability to recover clear images from degraded military images. In addition, we propose an integrated method of image recovery and detection, to make the recovered images not only improve human vision but also enhance the accuracy of subsequent object detection tasks. The whole training process is shown in Algorithm 1.

Algorithm 1. Integrated Method of Image Recovery and Detection

---

Input: Image Recovery Model; Object Detection Model.
Output: Image Recovery and Detection Integrated Model.
1: End-to-end supervised training for image Recovery Model.
2: Loading the pre-trained image Recovery Model to Detection Model.
3: **while** Conducting joint training **do**
4:    Calculating YOLO bounding box position regression loss: $Loss_{reg}$
5:    Calculating YOLO bounding box confidence loss: $Loss_{conf}$
6:    Calculating YOLO class loss: $Loss_{class}$
7:    Calculating the sum loss: $Loss_{sum} = \alpha \times Loss_{class} + \beta \times Loss_{conf} + \gamma \times Loss_{reg}$
8:    Using the sum loss to jointly train Recovery Model and Object Detection Model.
9: **end while**
10: **return** Image Recovery and Detection Integrated Model.

In this algorithm, class loss calculates the correctness of the objects classification in the anchor frame; bounding box confidence loss calculates the confidence degree for the predicted object; bounding box position regression loss calculates the regression error between the prediction box and the label box.

With the above joint training strategy, an integrated network of recovery and detection can be obtained. The clear image provided by the recovery module not only improves human vision, but also facilitates subsequent object detection tasks, enhancing the capabilities of intelligent robots in battle.

3   Experiments

In this section, we perform experimental tests for the proposed algorithm. Image recovery tests are performed on a degraded image dataset from a simulated battlefield environment, and object detection experiments are also performed on the degraded image dataset.

3.1   Experimental Settings

We train the proposed algorithm on AMD 78500H and NVIDIA RTX 3060 Laptop by Pytorch 1.8.1 with CUDA 11.1.

The dataset RESIDE OTS [23] is used to train the image recovery model with Adam optimizer and 0.001 initial learning rate. We train the network for 50 epochs in total. The dataset HAZY PASCAL VOC is used to train the integrated image recovery and detection model (pre-trained on the COCO dataset).

3.2   Image Recovery Experiments

We collected 1000 images of the battlefield environment from the Internet and constructed a degraded image dataset using the degraded synthesis method of the literature [24]. The test results of the proposed algorithm are compared with the state-of-the-art algorithm DPC [12], AOD-Net [18], GCANet [25], FFANet [26], MSBDN-DFF [16], and Zheng Z [27].

The test results in the whole test dataset are shown in Table 1, and some of the test results are shown in Fig. 5. Our proposed algorithm has impressive recovery results and the space occupation size of the algorithm is significantly less than other algorithms. Specifically, the proposed algorithm achieves the highest SSIM of 0.863, PSNR of 18.02, space occupancy of 20 kb and inference time of only 23.39 ms.

Table 1. The quantified results of the recovery test on the battlefield environment dataset.

Methods/Evaluation	DCP	AOD-Net	GCANet	FFANet	MSBDN	Zheng Z	Ours
SSIM↑	0.720	0.615	**0.809**	0.574	0.677	0.620	**0.863**
PSNR(dB)↑	12.04	11.99	**17.14**	10.03	12.19	11.64	**18.02**
Inference time(ms)↓	47.80	**3.43**	56.01	55.09	83.64	64.88	**23.39**
Params(M)↓	-	**18×10⁻³**	0.70	4.46	28.71	34.55	**22×10⁻³**

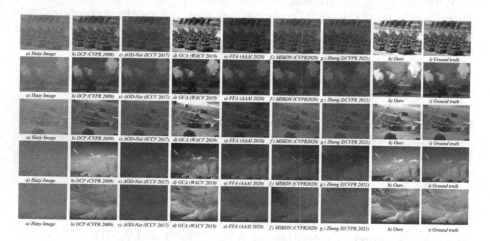

Fig. 5. Some of the recovery results on the battlefield environment dataset.

3.3   Object Detection Experiments

The YOLOv5 is an object detection algorithms with excellent detection accuracy and real-time performance, which has excellent detection performance in normal environments. To improve the performance of object detection in harsh environments, we integrate the image recovery module into YOLOv5.

We performed object detection training on the PASCAL VOC 2012 and testing on the RTTS [23] dataset. The RTTS dataset is an object detection dataset for haze environment to simulate the battlefield environment. Specifically, we used the degraded synthesis method of the literature [24] to construct the simulated battlefield environment PASCAL VOC dataset, and used this dataset to train the proposed integrated model with $\alpha = \beta = \gamma = 1$. We use Algorithm 1 for integrate training. The test results in the whole dataset are shown in Table 2.

In Table 2, the baseline is to use only the YOLOv5 to perform object detection, the others are to use integrated model with connection of different recovery networks. The proposed algorithm achieves the best object detection performance with 0.614 mAP, improving the mAP by 0.024 compared to the baseline detection network. Some of the test results are shown in Fig. 6. The proposed algorithm achieves more accurate object detection.

Table 2. The quantified results of the object detection test on the RTTS dataset.

Methods/Evaluation	Base	A-YOLO	G-YOLO	F-YOLO	M-YOLO	Z-YOLO	Ours
mAP-All ↑	0.590	0.588	0.595	0.594	0.533	**0.600**	**0.614**
mAP-Car ↑	0.721	0.718	**0.731**	0.725	0.687	**0.729**	0.702
mAP-Motorbike ↑	0.450	0.419	0.453	0.457	0.380	**0.462**	**0.528**
mAP-Person ↑	**0.809**	0.811	0.807	**0.809**	0.760	**0.813**	0.787
mAP-Bus ↑	0.396	0.392	**0.425**	0.408	0.323	0.421	**0.443**
mAP-Bicycle ↑	0.573	0.571	0.557	0.571	0.515	**0.574**	**0.608**
time(ms) ↓	**27.04**	**30.57**	83.05	52.48	103.57	91.78	49.57

Fig. 6. Some of the detection results on battlefield environment and RTTS dataset.

The proposed integrated recovery and object detection algorithm can be embedded into a military robot system to enhance its battlefield environment perception and combat capabilities.

4 Conclusion

We propose an integrated algorithm for image recovery and object detection for harsh battlefield environments. The algorithm has a light-weight structure, which can be easily deployed in battlefield robots. The proposed image recovery module is based on a physical imaging model while using the Gamama correction technique. Further, we integrate the trained image recovery model into YOLOv5 for end-to-end joint optimization. The joint optimization makes the recovered images not only enhance the human vision, but also improve the accuracy of object detection for subsequent high-level computer vision tasks. The experimental results show that the proposed algorithm has impressive recovery and object detection performance compared to other SOTA algorithms, and also has a light-weight structure. In the future, we will aim to deploy the proposed algorithm in actual battlefield robots to take its advantage of application.

Acknowledgements. This work was supported by the Youth Innovation Promotion Association of the Chinese Academy of Sciences under Grant 2022196 and Y202051, in part by the National Natural Science Foundation of China under Grant 61821005, in part by the Natural Science Foundation of Liaoning Province under Grant 2021-BS-023.

References

1. Swett, B.A., Hahn, E.N., Llorens, A.J.: Designing robots for the battlefield: State of the art. In: Robotics, AI, and Humanity (2021)
2. Wang, N., Li, Z., Liang, X., Hou, Y., Yang, A.: A review of deep reinforcement learning methods and military application research. Math. Probl. Eng. (2023)
3. Boulanin, V., Verbruggen, M.: Mapping the development of autonomy in weapon systems (2016)
4. Sparrow, R.: Robotic weapons and the future of war (2011)
5. Thanh, L.T., Thanh, D.N.H., Hue, N.M., Prasath, V.B.S.: Single image dehazing based on adaptive histogram equalization and linearization of gamma correction. In: 2019 25th Asia-Pacific Conference on Communications, pp. 36–40 (2019)
6. Khan, H.: Localization of radiance transformation for image dehazing in wavelet domain. Neurocomputing **381**, 141–151 (2020)
7. Singh, D., Kumar, V.: Dehazing of remote sensing images using fourth-order partial differential equations based trilateral filter. IET Comput. Vis. **12**, 208–219 (2017)
8. Qin, X., Liu, X., Mu, C., Mei, K.: A summary of research progress of single image to remove rain and fog based on deep learning. In: Symposium on Novel Photoelectronic Detection Technology and Application (2021)
9. Thiruvikraman, P.K., kumar, D.T.A., Rajmohan, R., Pavithra, M.: A survey on haze removal techniques in satellite images (2021)
10. Narasimhan, S.G., Nayar, S.K.: Chromatic framework for vision in bad weather. In: IEEE Conference on Computer Vision and Pattern Recognition, vol. 1, 598–605 vol 1 (2000)
11. Narasimhan, S.G., Nayar, S.K.: Vision and the atmosphere. Int. J. Comput. Vis. **48**, 233–254 (2002)
12. He, K., Sun, J., Tang, X.: Single image haze removal using dark channel prior. In: IEEE Conference on Computer Vision and Pattern Recognition, pp. 1956–1963 (2009)
13. Tarel, J.P., Hautière, N., Caraffa, L., Cord, A., Halmaoui, H., Gruyer, D.: Vision enhancement in homogeneous and heterogeneous fog. IEEE Intell. Transp. Syst. Mag. **4**, 6–20 (2012)

14. Chen, C., Do, M.N., Wang, J.: Robust image and video dehazing with visual arti-fact suppression via gradient residual minimization. In: Leibe, B., Matas, J., Sebe, N., Welling, M. (eds.) ECCV 2016. LNCS, vol. 9906, pp. 576–591. Springer, Cham (2016). https://doi.org/10.1007/978-3-319-46475-6_36

15. Cai, B., Xu, X., Jia, K., Qing, C., Tao, D.: Dehazenet: an end-to-end system for single image haze removal. IEEE Trans. Image Process. **25**, 5187–5198 (2016)

16. Dong, H., et al.: Multi-scale boosted dehazing network with dense feature fusion. In: IEEE Conference on Computer Vision and Pattern Recognition, pp. 2154–2164 (2020)

17. Yang, Y., Wang, C., Liu, R., Zhang, L., Guo, X., Tao, D.: Self-augmented unpaired image dehazing via density and depth decomposition. In: IEEE Conference on Computer Vision and Pattern Recognition, pp. 2027–2036 (2022)

18. Li, B., Peng, X., Wang, Z., Xu, J., Feng, D.: Aod-net: all-in-one dehazing network. In: IEEE International Conference on Computer Vision, pp. 4780–4788 (2017)

19. Woo, S., Park, J., Lee, J.-Y., Kweon, I.S.: CBAM: convolutional block attention module. In: Ferrari, V., Hebert, M., Sminchisescu, C., Weiss, Y. (eds.) ECCV 2018. LNCS, vol. 11211, pp. 3–19. Springer, Cham (2018). https://doi.org/10.1007/978-3-030-01234-2_1

20. Huang, X., Belongie, S.J.: Arbitrary style transfer in real-time with adaptive instance normalization. In: IEEE International Conference on Computer Vision, pp. 1510–1519 (2017)

21. Johnson, J., Alahi, A., Fei-Fei, L.: Perceptual losses for real-time style transfer and super-resolution. In: Leibe, B., Matas, J., Sebe, N., Welling, M. (eds.) ECCV 2016. LNCS, vol. 9906, pp. 694–711. Springer, Cham (2016). https://doi.org/10.1007/978-3-319-46475-6_43

22. Simonyan, K., Zisserman, A.: Very deep convolutional networks for large-scale image recognition. Clin. Orthop. Relat. R. (2014)

23. Li, B., et al.: Benchmarking single-image dehazing and beyond. IEEE Trans. Image Process. **28**, 492–505 (2017)

24. Huang, S.C., Le, T.H., Jaw, D.W.: Dsnet: joint semantic learning for object detec-tion in inclement weather conditions. IEEE Trans. Pattern Anal. Mach. Intell. **43**, 2623–2633 (2020)

25. Chen, D., et al.: Gated context aggregation network for image dehazing and derain-ing. In: IEEE Winter Conference on Applications of Computer Vision, pp. 1375–1383 (2018)

26. Qin, X., Wang, Z., Bai, Y., Xie, X., Jia, H.: Ffa-net: feature fusion attention net-work for single image dehazing. In: AAAI Conference on Artificial Intelligence (2020)

27. Zheng, Z., et al.: Ultra-high-definition image dehazing via multi-guided bilateral learning. In: IEEE Conference on Computer Vision and Pattern Recognition, pp. 16180–16189 (2021)

A Fuzzy-Based Improved Dynamic Window Approach for Path Planning of Mobile Robot

Yue Zhu and Tongli Lu[✉]

School of Mechanical Engineering, Shanghai Jiao Tong University, Shanghai, China
tllu@sjtu.edu.cn

Abstract. Robot path planning algorithms can plan a safe path from one point to another, and Dynamic Window Approach (DWA) is a commonly used planning algorithm. However, such method usually does not consider the direction of the robot, so that the robot at the planning end point has a large deviation from the desired direction. At the same time, the robot is not sensitive enough to dynamic obstacles during planning. In this paper, a fuzzy-based improved DWA is proposed for path planning of mobile robot. In the local path planning, the cost functions of the traditional DWA are optimized to regulate the robot direction. The fuzzy controller is introduced to dynamically tune the planning tendency of the robot in each stage. Compared with the traditional DWA algorithm, the improved DWA algorithm can enable the robot to complete the planning with end-direction constraints in unknown environments. Simulations of two static scenes and two dynamic scenes show that robot can move to the destination in high direction accuracy and effectively avoid obstacle with fuzzy-based DWA.

Keywords: Path planning · improved DWA algorithm · fuzzy logic

1 Introduction

The path planning of mobile robot is one of the hot topics recently [1]. Robot motion planning can ensure that the robot reaches the destination safely and quickly. The existing researches mainly focus on how to plan the path successfully, but not much consideration is given to the kinematic constraints of the robot. For the path planning of loading, parking and other scenarios, the robot with the kinematic constraints not only needs to effectively plan the path to the end point, but also needs to satisfy that the robot can move in the desired direction at the end point. In addition, in some small scenes, there may also be dynamic obstacles that interfere with the path planning of the robot besides static obstacles.

The commonly used path planning algorithms include A*, D*, RRT* [2–4]. These planning algorithms focus on seeking a nearest path from the starting point to the end point. The curvature obtained by these planning algorithms is not continuous and the path may not satisfy the robot kinematic constraints. Dmitri Dolgov et al. of Stanford AI proposed Hybrid A* algorithm in 2010, which improves the A* algorithm to make the searched path conform to the vehicle kinematic constraints [5]. However, the above methods have map dependence and cannot avoid dynamic obstacles [6].

Dynamic window approach (DWA) algorithm was firstly proposed by Dieter Fox et al. [7]. Considering that this algorithm can be applied in the unknown environment, DWA is widely used in the path planning of robots. Masato et al. improve the DWA with virtual manipulators (VM) [8]. The algorithm corrects the candidate paths of the DWA based on the VM and the predicted positions of static and dynamic obstacles. Therefore, in dynamic obstacles environment, DWA can generate non-straight path and non-arc path that can avoid obstacles. Zizhao Wang et al. design an Adaptive Planner Parameter Learning from Interventions (APPLI) [9]. The robot can dynamic the parameters learned from a full human demonstration, and achieves better performance compared to the planner with static default parameters [10]. Zenan Lin et al. propose a two-layer path-planning method which include PSO-based APF and fuzzy-based DWA [11]. This method can plan a shorter and smoother path with the aid of PSO-based APF, meanwhile quickly react to the moving obstacles and avoid them by fuzzy-based DWA.

In this paper, we propose an improved DWA algorithm based on fuzzy logic for robots with kinematic constraints. Based on the requirements of path planning, the cost functions of DWA are optimized, and the avoidance strategy for dynamic obstacles is added. In order to ensure that the robot can satisfy the desired direction of the end point when it reaches the end point, this paper designs fuzzy rules to tune the weight in different stages.

This paper is organized as follows. Section 2 introduces the design of the cost functions of the improved DWA based on the robot kinematic constraints. Section 3 describes the composition of fuzzy controller, including membership functions and fuzzy rules. Section 4 shows the performance of the method in different scenarios in simulation. Section 5 summarizes and concludes the paper.

2 Improved Dynamic Window Approach

2.1 Design of Dynamic Window

The DWA algorithm is usually applied to mobile robots that can rotate in all directions. The object of this paper is a mobile robot with a guide wheel. This type of robot has the constraint of minimum turning radius, and it cannot achieve in-place steering. Therefore, the traditional DWA is not suitable for this kind of robot. In the case of low speed, the robot will not drift, so that the robot kinematic model can be regarded as a two-wheeled bicycle model. Therefore, the improved DWA algorithm will use the two-wheeled bicycle model as the robot kinematic model to predict the trajectory.

As shown in the Fig. 1, the state variables of the bicycle model are the front wheel angle δ, speed v and heading φ. Based on the robot's own parameters, the following kinematic model can be established.

$$\begin{cases} \dot{v} = a \\ \dot{\delta} = \omega \\ \dot{\varphi} = \frac{v \cdot \tan(\delta)}{L_w} \end{cases}, \tag{1}$$

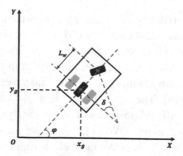

Fig. 1. Two-wheeled Bike Model.

Where a is the longitudinal acceleration of the robot, ω is the rotation angular velocity of the robot guide wheel, and L_w is the wheelbase of the robot.

When the robot moving, the longitudinal acceleration and the front wheel angle velocity cannot be infinite. The longitudinal acceleration range and the angular acceleration range are set artificially according to the appropriate robot motion conditions. According to these two soft constraints, the window S_1 is generated as follows.

$$S_1 = \left\{ (\delta, v) \middle| \frac{\delta - \delta_0}{dt} \in [\omega_{min}, \omega_{max}], \frac{v - v_0}{dt} \in [a_{min}, a_{max}] \right\} \tag{2}$$

The front wheel rotation Angle has a physical hard constraint, and the speed is limited by the soft constraint of the motion demand. Then we generate the window S_2.

$$S_2 = \{ (\delta, v) | \delta \in [\delta_{min}, \delta_{max}], v \in [0, v_{max}] \}, \tag{3}$$

The union of the two sets is the feasible space of the robot, resulting in the following final window S.

$$S = S_1 \cap S_2, \tag{4}$$

Based on the kinematic model and dynamic window, the states in the window are discretized with a fixed resolution to obtain the sampled state. According to all the sampled states, the future trajectory within the prediction time t_p can be calculated.

2.2 Cost Functions Optimization

The traditional DWA does not have a cost function for the destination direction, and that will lead a large deviation between the planning destination direction and the goal direction. Therefore, it is necessary to consider adding the final direction error to the cost functions to achieve·the accuracy requirements in the final direction. In order to adjust the direction of the robot to meet the direction requirements of the end point, the new final direction cost function and its normalization are as follows.

$$\Delta yaw_f(\delta, v) = \frac{\Delta yaw(\delta, v) - \min_{(\delta_i, v_j) \in S} \left(\Delta yaw(\delta_i, v_j) \right)}{\max_{(\delta_i, v_j) \in S} \left(\Delta yaw(\delta_i, v_j) \right) - \min_{(\delta_i, v_j) \in S} \left(\Delta yaw(\delta_i, v_j) \right)}, \tag{5}$$

Where $\Delta yaw(\delta, v)$ is the difference between the direction of the robot and the desired direction when the predicted time t_p passes under control volume (δ, v).

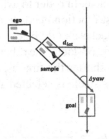

Fig. 2. The physical meaning of lateral error and final direction error.

If only the final direction deviation of the end point is added, it will happen that the robot moves parallel to the end point direction and cannot approach the end point. Ideally, the robot should be able to approach the end point straight up in the final stage. Therefore, the new cost function is considered. The robot first approaches the target line which the final direction lies. And then robot adjusts its direction to move straight into the end point. According to the states in the dynamic window, the distance from the predict position to the target line is regarded as the lateral distance from the robot to the destination. The physical meaning of lateral error and final direction error is shown in Fig. 2. The lateral distance cost function and its normalization are designed as follows.

$$dist_{lat}(\delta, v) = \frac{d_{lat}(\delta, v) - \min_{(\delta_i, v_j) \in S} \left(d_{lat}(\delta_i, v_j)\right)}{\max_{(\delta_i, v_j) \in S} \left(d_{lat}(\delta_i, v_j)\right) - \min_{(\delta_i, v_j) \in S} \left(d_{lat}(\delta_i, v_j)\right)}, \tag{6}$$

Where $d_{lat}(\delta, v)$ is the lateral distance from the robot to the destination when the predicted time t_p passes under control volume (δ, v).

Combining the two optimized cost functions, the robot is able to approach the expected pose of the goal as close as possible at the planning end point.

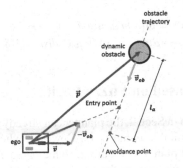

Fig. 3. Dynamic obstacle scene.

When avoiding obstacles, the traditional DWA filters the path according to the observation of the current frame, and does not analyze the motion characteristics of dynamic obstacles. Therefore, when an obstacle approaches from the side or rear, the robot will be forced into a corner by the obstacle. In order to avoid the dynamic obstacle as shown in Fig. 3, the original obstacle cost function needs to be modified.

The risk rank of dynamic obstacles should be evaluated. If the robot moves towards the motion trajectory of the dynamic obstacle, the robot will break into the trajectory after a certain time at entry point. The shorter the time is, the more dangerous the dynamic obstacle is. The most dangerous obstacle is selected as the avoidance object. The entry time t_{in} is calculated as follows.

$$t_{in} = \frac{\|\vec{p}\|^2}{(\vec{v} - \vec{v_{ob}}) \cdot \vec{p}}, \tag{7}$$

According to the entry point, it can calculate whether the robot has the conditions to surpass the dynamic obstacle. If the entry point is in front of the obstacle, the obstacle is considered to have the conditions to surpass. According to whether the obstacle can be surpassed, an avoidance point is selected on the trajectory of the obstacle. The distance l_a between the avoidance point and obstacle is calculated as follows.

$$l_a = \begin{cases} t_p \vec{v_{ob}} + d_o, \text{if can surpass} \\ t_p \vec{v_{ob}} - d_o, \text{if can't surpass} \end{cases}, \tag{8}$$

Where t_p is the predict time, d_o is the distance to avoid.

A new cost function for dynamic obstacle is designed as follows.

$$dist_{avoid}(\delta, v) = \frac{d_{avoid}(\delta, v) - \min\limits_{(\delta_i, v_j) \in S} (d_{avoid}(\delta_i, v_j))}{\max\limits_{(\delta_i, v_j) \in S} (d_{avoid}(\delta_i, v_j)) - \min\limits_{(\delta_i, v_j) \in S} (d_{avoid}(\delta_i, v_j))}, \tag{9}$$

Where $d_{avoid}(\delta_i, v_j)$ is the distance from the robot to the avoidance point when the predicted time t passes under control volume (δ, v).

Combined with cost functions, the sum of cost functions is obtained, and the planner will traverse the paths in the window and select the one with the minimum cost as the plan at the next moment.

$$\begin{aligned} Cost(\delta, v) = {} &\omega_1 \cdot heading(\delta, v) + \omega_2 \cdot \Delta yaw_f(\delta, v) \\ &+ \omega_3 \cdot dist_{lat}(\delta, v) + \omega_4 \cdot dist_{avoid}(\delta, v), \end{aligned} \tag{10}$$

3 Tuned Weights Based on Fuzzy Logic

With the total cost function in Sect. 2, the planner can already find the path from the robot to the destination under suitable parameters. However, when the robot is far from the end point, the planner will plan a long detour, so the parameters of the DWA algorithm need to be tuned in real time to meet the needs of each planning stage. Fuzzy logic is one of the methods that are often used to tune parameters dynamically [12].

3.1 Membership Functions

The parking process is divided into three parts: approaching the end point, lateral adjustment and direction adjustment. When the distance from the end point is far, the robot needs to approach the end point quickly. When the robot is in the vicinity of the end point, it needs to approach lateral position first, and then adjust the direction to the end point. When the parameters are tuned, the final direction weight ω_2 is kept unchanged, and the above process is realized by adjusting the heading weight ω_1 and the lateral distance weight ω_3.

According to the above three stages, the fuzzy controller is designed as a system with three inputs and two outputs, where the inputs are the final direction error, lateral distance error and Euclidean distance between the end point and the robot, and the outputs are the heading weight and lateral distance weight. The domain of Euclidean distance is $[0, 12\,\text{m}]$, and its fuzzy subsets are $\{S, M, B\}$. When the distance between the robot and the end point gradually decreases from 12 m, the membership degree of the Euclidean distance will first slowly trend from B to M, so as to ensure that the robot can get ready for parking while approaching the end point. Below 6 m, this membership will then rapidly tend to S, making the robot fully enter the parking stage. The domain of the lateral distance error is $[0, 6\,\text{m}]$, and the universe of the final direction error is $[0, 90°]$, and both fuzzy subsets are $\{S, M, B\}$. The membership function of the lateral distance error is uniformly distributed to ensure the function changes smoothly. The membership function of the final direction error is more inclined to B when the error is large, so as to ensure that the robot can adjust its direction in a large range at the final stage. The input membership functions are shown in Fig. 4.

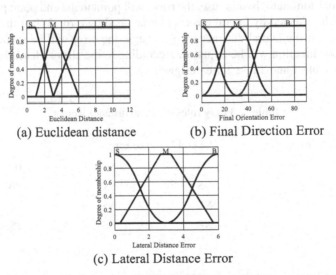

(a) Euclidean distance   (b) Final Direction Error

(c) Lateral Distance Error

Fig. 4. The membership functions of inputs.

3.2 Fuzzy Rules

"IF-THEN" logic is used to calculate fuzzy membership values in controller design. The output membership functions are shown in Fig. 5. The domain of heading weight is [0, 2], and its fuzzy subsets are $\{N, ZO, P\}$. When the scene is large, the robot is similar to the traditional DWA in the beginning stage, which gives priority to moving toward the goal. In this case, the membership function of the heading weight will be more inclined to P. The domain of the lateral distance weight is [0, 5], and its fuzzy subsets are $\{PS, NS, NB, PB\}$.

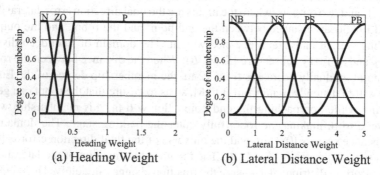

(a) Heading Weight   (b) Lateral Distance Weight

Fig. 5. The membership functions of outputs.

When the Euclidean distance between the end point and the robot is large, the heading weight is more dominant. In this case, the robot will point to the end point preferentially, and will not be affected by lateral error and final heading error. When the robot enters the final stage, if the lateral distance error is large, the error will be reduced first, and then the robot direction will be adjusted. According to the above ideas, the fuzzy rules as shown in Table 1 and Table 2 are designed.

Table 1. Fuzzy rules of lateral distance weight.

Final Direction Error	Lateral Distance Error		
	S	M	B
S	NS	PS	PB
M	NB	NS	PS
B	NB	NS	PS

Table 2. Fuzzy rules of heading weight.

Final Direction Error	Euclidean distance		
	S	M	B
S	N	ZO	ZO
M	N	ZO	P
B	ZO	P	P

4 Simulation

The improved DWA algorithm is verified by simulation in MATLAB. Table 3 shows the parameters of improved DWA algorithm. Because there are obstacles around the scene, the desired speed of the robot is set at 1.2 m/s for safety. The simulated model does not consider the case of drift.

Table 3. Improved DWA parameters.

parament	value
max guide wheel angle	36°
max speed	1.5 m/s
max acceleration	0.5 m/s^2
max guide wheel angular speed	18°/s
Wheel base	1.0 m
robot width	1.2 m
robot length	1.6 m
default heading weight	0.1
default direction weight	0.8
default lateral distance weight	1.8
default avoidance weight	3.0

Considering that the outputs of the fuzzy controller, the final direction weight is a fixed value of 0.8. When the dynamic obstacle is far away, the avoidance weight w_4 needs to be appropriately small. Here, the cosine curve is used to tune w_4, and the specific function is shown below.

$$w_4 = \begin{cases} 3(1 - \cos(\frac{\pi x}{8})), & 0 < x < 8\,m \\ 6, & 8\,m \leq x \end{cases}, \tag{11}$$

Where x is the distance between the robot and the obstacle.

The path planned by traditional DWA [7] is difficult to meet the desired direction requirements of the end point. Figure 6 shows different scenarios to verify the effect of the algorithm when it reaches the end point.

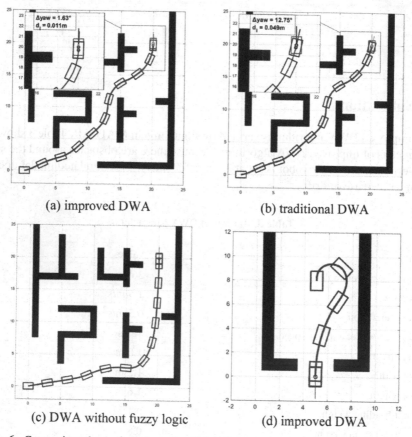

(a) improved DWA

(b) traditional DWA

(c) DWA without fuzzy logic

(d) improved DWA

Fig. 6. Comparison the performance of traditional and improved DWA in static scenarios.

In Fig. 6, The blue box represents the robot, the red box represents the target pose, and the black box represents the obstacle. The planning results of the improved DWA algorithm and the traditional DWA algorithm are shown in Fig. 6 (a) and (b) respectively. Although the traditional DWA can also plan the path to the end point, the final direction error reaches 12.75°, which is unacceptable. With the improved DWA algorithm, the robot can approach the end point first and adjust its pose in the last stage to achieve the desired direction of the end point. The final direction error of the planned path is 1.63° and the lateral error is 0.011 m, which has good performance. The planning results of DWA algorithm without fuzzy logic are shown in Fig. 6 (c). Although it had good pose at the end point, the lateral distance was shortened too early in the planning process, resulting in a long detour. As a result, the overall planning path length is long and the planning efficiency is reduced. Figure 6 (d) shows the planning results for another special scenario. When the heading of the robot is completely opposite to the destination direction, the robot can turn around to complete the planning.

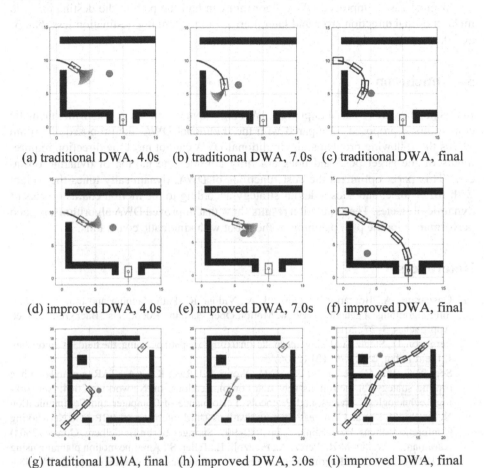

(a) traditional DWA, 4.0s (b) traditional DWA, 7.0s (c) traditional DWA, final

(d) improved DWA, 4.0s (e) improved DWA, 7.0s (f) improved DWA, final

(g) traditional DWA, final (h) improved DWA, 3.0s (i) improved DWA, final

Fig. 7. Comparison the performance of traditional and improved DWA in dynamic scenarios. (Color figure online)

In addition, the traditional DWA is difficult to avoid dynamic obstacles. Figure 7 shows two dynamic scenarios to observe the obstacle avoidance strategy of the algorithms.

The pink circular obstacle in Fig. 7 is a dynamic obstacle. Figure 7 (a), (b), (c) show the planning result of traditional DWA. As the obstacle approaches from one side of the robot, the robot is forced to turn to the corner to avoid the obstacle. Finally get stuck in the corner leading to the failure of the plan. In Fig. 7 (d), (e), (f), after the robot observes the obstacle, the improved DWA judges that the obstacle is fast, so it needs to go around the rear and turn early to complete the avoidance behavior. Figure 7 (g) shows another failure scenario with traditional DWA. The moving obstacle in this scenario is not fast, but it still interferes with the robot. In the improved DWA algorithm, the entry point of the robot is in the front of the obstacle, which has the conditions for surpassing. The improved DWA planned the overtaking path and reached the end in Fig. 7 (h), (i).

In most cases, improved DWA algorithm can find the path to the destination, and make the final direction error and lateral error of the planning destination less than 3° and 0.1m respectively.

5 Conclusion

In this paper, a fuzzy-based improved DWA algorithm for mobile robots with kinematic constraints is proposed. Compared with the traditional DWA, the proposed algorithm solves the following problems: the traditional DWA cannot meet the direction requirements of the target pose and does not fully consider the motion of dynamic obstacles. This paper optimizes the cost functions of DWA, dynamically tunes the weight with fuzzy logic, and adds a detour strategy according to the motion characteristics of dynamic obstacles. The simulation results show that improved DWA algorithm has good performance for the path planning of the robot with kinematic constraints.

References

1. Gasparetto, A., Boscariol, P., Lanzutti, A., Vidoni, R.: Path planning and trajectory planning algorithms: a general overview. Motion Oper. Planning Robot. Syst. Background Pract. Approaches, 3–27 (2015)
2. Ferguson, D., Stentz, A.: Using interpolation to improve path planning: the field D* algorithm. J. Field Robot. **23**(2), 79–101 (2006)
3. Seet, B.C., Liu, G., Lee, B.S., Foh, C.H., Wong, K.J., Lee, K.K.: A-STAR: a mobile ad hoc routing strategy for metropolis vehicular communications. In: Networking 2004: Networking Technologies, Services, and Protocols; Performance of Computer and Communication Networks; Mobile and Wireless Communications Third International IFIP-TC6 Networking Conference Athens, Proceedings 3, pp. 989–999. Springer Berlin Heidelberg, Greece (2004)
4. Karaman, S., Walter, M.R., Perez, A., Frazzoli, E., Teller, S.: Anytime motion planning using the RRT. In 2011 IEEE International Conference on Robotics and Automation, pp. 1478–1483. IEEE (2011)
5. Dolgov, D., Thrun, S., Montemerlo, M., Diebel, J.: Path planning for autonomous vehicles in unknown semi-structured environments. Int. J. Robot. Res. **29**(5), 485–501 (2010)
6. Sedighi, S., Nguyen, D.V., Kuhnert, K.D.: Guided hybrid A-star path planning algorithm for valet parking applications. In 2019 5th International Conference on Control, Automation and Robotics (ICCAR), pp. 570–575. IEEE (2019)
7. Fox, D., Burgard, W., Thrun, S.: The dynamic window approach to collision avoidance. IEEE Robot. Autom. Mag. **4**(1), 23–33 (1997)
8. Kobayashi, M., Motoi, N.: Local path planning: dynamic window approach with virtual manipulators considering dynamic obstacles. IEEE Access **10**, 17018–17029 (2022)
9. Wang, Z., Xiao, X., Liu, B., Warnell, G., Stone, P.: APPLI: Adaptive planner parameter learning from interventions. In 2021 IEEE International Conference on Robotics and Automation (ICRA), pp. 6079–6085 (May 2021). IEEE (2022)
10. Xu, Z., Xiao, X., Warnell, G., Nair, A., Stone, P.: Machine learning methods for local motion planning: a study of end-to-end vs. parameter learning. In 2021 IEEE International Symposium on Safety, Security, and Rescue Robotics (SSRR), pp. 217–222. IEEE (2021)

11. Lin, Z., Yue, M., Chen, G., Sun, J.: Path planning of mobile robot with PSO-based APF and fuzzy-based DWA subject to moving obstacles. Trans. Inst. Meas. Control. **44**(1), 121–132 (2022)
12. Herrera, F., Lozano, M., Verdegay, J.L.: Tuning fuzzy logic controllers by genetic algorithms. Int. J. Approximate Reasoning **12**(3–4), 299–315 (1995)

Is the Encoder Necessary in DETR-Type Models?-Analysis of Encoder Redundancy

Liu Huan[1,2], Lin Sen[1(✉)], and Han Zhi[2,3]

[1] School of Automation and Electrical Engineering, Shenyang Ligong University,
Shenyang 110159, China
lin_sen6@126.com
[2] State Key Laboratory of Robotics, Shenyang Institute of Automation, Chinese
Academy of Sciences, Shenyang 110016, China
[3] Institutes for Robotics and Intelligent Manufacturing, Chinese Academy of
Sciences, Shenyang 110016, China

Abstract. Object detection model DETR (Detection Transformer) based on the Transformer architecture has demonstrated outstanding performance in various benchmark tests. However, these models often have a large number of parameters, which can make them slow and computationally intensive. Therefore, it is crucial to optimize the performance of these models by identifying any redundancy in the recognition model. This paper analyzes the internal mechanism of DETR detection and reveals that the backbone network and the transformer decoder already serve the intended purpose of the encoder module. The analysis results are validate through experimental design. It is find that the encoder module does not fulfill its initial intended role in the network but instead increases the parameter count and computational complexity of the entire network. For example, the performance of a single-layer encoder is equivalent to that of six layers. When using a Transformer backbone network, the encoder does not provide performance improvement to the overall architecture. Therefore, it is possible to optimize DETR-like architectures by using suitable module components without employing the encoder structure.

Keywords: Network Lightweight Design · Detection Transformer · Attention

1 Introduction

Object detection is an important task in the field of computer vision, aimed at locating and classifying objects in images. In recent years, the development of deep learning technology has significantly advanced object detection and greatly

Supported by organization National Natural Science Foundation of China under Grant 61991413, National Natural Science Foundation of China under Grant 61821005, Natural Science Foundation of Liaoning Province under Grant 2021-BS-023.

promoted the development of other visual tasks, such as object tracking, instance segmentation, and pose estimation. Modern object detection networks aim to pursue performance while maintaining simplicity and modularity. CNN-based methods [1–5] have dominated the object detection task for many years. Such methods view the design of object detection networks as a modular combination process, usually composed of three modules: backbone [6–10], neck [11], and detection head [1,2], each playing a different role in the entire detection network. Carion et al. proposed a new type of detection network called DETR [12]. DETR has made significant progress in the field of object detection. The network architecture of DETR [12] is simpler than previous object detection networks and has competitive performance. Like CNN-based detection methods, DETR's network architecture also adopts a modular design, composed of a backbone network, Transformer encoder, Transformer decoder, and prediction head.

The DETR [12] network architecture consists of a backbone network that extracts image features to generate semantic feature maps, while the module used for object localization is the Transformer decoder. In DETR [12], the role of the Transformer encoder is to fuse global information and refine features to promote the detection performance of the decoder. Due to the inability of CNN structures to globally model features, DETR [12] uses a CNN [7] structure for the backbone network and designs the encoder to compensate for this deficiency. However, in DETR [12], the decoder design is inefficient and converges slowly, so the encoder also plays a role in detection to some extent, helping to improve the model's performance. Therefore, using a design with multiple stacked encoding modules is a reasonable choice in DETR [12].

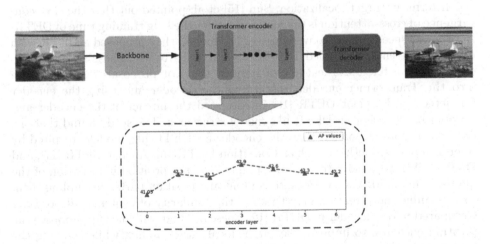

Fig. 1. The number of layers in an encoder has little impact on performance.

The modular design of detection networks aims to enable the free replacement of different components to cope with different application scenarios. For detection networks, the backbone network module is a common replaceable component, and the performance of the detector largely depends on the backbone network. In the two years since the emergence of DETR [12], ViT [13] has shown that visual Transformer models using Transformer encoders can achieve performance comparable to that of traditional convolutional neural networks under large-scale pretraining. In this context, new network architectures have emerged, such as networks using convolutional networks and multi-head self-attention mechanisms [6,9,14]. These networks can better capture global feature relationships. However, this also raises a natural question: when using these updated backbone networks, is there still a need for the encoder to fuse global information throughout the network? After all, these new backbone networks already have the ability to globally model features.

Indeed, modular design of detection networks allows for flexible component replacement to adapt to different application scenarios. Among these components, the backbone network module is a common replaceable component, and the performance of the detector largely depends on the backbone network. In the two years since the emergence of DETR [12], ViT [13], a visual transformer model using a transformer encoder, has achieved performance comparable to traditional convolutional neural networks with large-scale pretraining. This has led to the emergence of new network architectures such as networks that use convolutional networks and multi-head self-attention mechanisms [6,9,14]. These networks can better capture global feature relationships. However, this also raises a natural question: is it still necessary for the encoder to integrate global information throughout the network when using these updated backbone networks? After all, these new backbone networks already have the ability to model global features.

In terms of target localization, Sun [15] et al. pointed out that the slow convergence of cross-attention is the main reason for the long training time of DETR. In order to speed up the convergence of the model, they proposed a DETR with a prior representation, called TSP-FCOS and TSP-RCNN. These methods generate a set of fixed-size features of interest (FoI) or proposals and feed them into the Transformer encoder, discarding the decoder and using the encoder for detection. Efficient DETR [16] investigated the impact of the encoder and decoder on detection in DETR-like model structures. The study found that the decoder is more important than the encoder for DETR-like models. Inspired by reference points, methods such as Condition DETR[15], Anchor DETR [17], and DAB-DETR [20] associate reference points with the position information of the queries, and divide the queries into content and position parts, decoupling them to determine the attention map through the similarity of content and position. Compared to the decoder in DETR [12], these methods only need to improve the position encoding to improve the target localization ability, while avoiding the problem of slow convergence of cross-attention in the decoder. It is worth noting that the spatial computational complexity of the encoder is proportional to the square of the input sequence length, which limits the network's ability to detect small targets to some extent. However, existing network design, [17–20] still follows the original design of using a 6-layer encoder in DETR. Therefore, further research and discussion are needed to determine whether the encoder module can play a role when using more advanced decoder network architectures.

This article conducted an in-depth study on the role of the encoder module in detection networks and arrived at the following conclusions: First, in DETR-type models, the encoder module design is redundant, and the performance using one-layer encoder is even better than that using six-layer encoder; Second, the ability to globally model features can improve the detection performance of large objects, and not using an encoder and using a module that can globally model the backbone network can also improve the detection performance of large objects; Finally, the main role of the encoder is to use the attention mechanism to utilize the correlation between features, thereby making the output features conducive to detection. These conclusions provide valuable references for designing more efficient and accurate detection networks.

2   DETR Network Analysis

2.1   Analysis of Module Role in DETR

Backbone Network. The role of the backbone network is to extract the original image $x_{img} \in \mathbb{R}^{3 \times H_0 \times W_0}$ through a series of convolution and pooling structures to a low-resolution feature map $F \in \mathbb{R}^{C \times H \times W}$ with semantic information of the image.

Transformer Encoder. The Transformer encoder consists of a multi-headed self-attentive and feed-forward pre-connected network. The main role is played by the self-idea mechanism, and the low-resolution feature maps $F \in \mathbb{R}^{C \times H \times W}$ output by the backbone network. Transformer expects the feature map to be in the form of a sequence as input, and the line compresses the spatial dimension of the low-resolution feature map into one dimension to $F_E \in \mathbb{R}^{d \times n}, n = H \times W$. The core component in the transformer encoder is the self-attentive module. The calculation in the attention mechanism is as follows:

$$F_d = attention(Q, K, V) = softmax\left(\frac{Q \cdot K^T}{\sqrt{d}}\right) \bullet V$$
$$Q_n = W_Q F_E = [q_1, q_2, \dots, q_n]^T, q_j \in \mathbb{R}^{1 \times n}, j = 1, 2, \dots, n \quad (1)$$
$$K_n = W_K F_E = [k_1, k_2, \dots, k_n]^T, k_j \in \mathbb{R}^{1 \times n}, j = 1, 2, \dots, n$$
$$V_n = W_V F_E = [v_1, v_2, \dots, v_n]^T, v_j \in \mathbb{R}^{1 \times n}, j = 1, 2, \dots, n$$

In Eq. 1 of self-attention Q, K, V are obtained by projecting F_E onto three different linear projections. it can be considered as a weighted summation of the linear projections V_e of F_e. where the i-th spatial feature vector in f_i, is generated by

$$f_i = \sum_{i=1}^{n} w_j \cdot v_j, j = 1, 2, \dots$$
$$w_j = \frac{e^{q_i \cdot k_j^T}}{\sum_{j=1}^{n} e^{q_i \cdot k_j^T}} \quad (2)$$

When generating the i-th feature f_i in self-attention, all v_i are weighted, so that the self-attention mechanism of the decoder is able to fuse global information and use weights that are similar to q_i with respect to all k_i. Therefore, when generating f_i, a relatively large weight is given to the i-th feature vector with similar location and semantic similarity. Thus self-attentiveness has two features in extracting features, global modeling, and effective use of correlations between data.

Transformer Decoder. Plays a key role in the detection network, and this study considers that the decoder module will also play the role of the corresponding encoder in detection, and the main core components of the decoder in the Detection transformer are the self-attention mechanism and the interactive attention mechanism. In Fig. 2, our decoder is compared with the general transformer decoder in which the positions of the self-awareness mechanism and the interactive attention mechanism are swapped, and it is found in the experiments that the swapping of the positions of the interactive attention and the self-awareness does not affect the final performance. In order to facilitate the decoder interpretability, the decoder structure shown in Fig. 2 is adopted in this paper

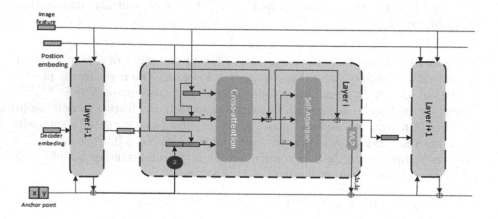

Fig. 2. The sketch of the transformer decoder structure.

The input part of the decoder at the time of detection randomly initializes a series of anchor points $A \in \mathbb{R}^{m \times 2}, a_i = x_i, y_i, i = 1, 2, \ldots$. The anchor point will encode the bit value information for the coordinate point by Eq. 3 .

$$PE(pos, 2i) = \sin\left(\frac{pos}{T^{2i/d}}\right)$$
$$PE(pos, 2i+1) = \sin\left(\frac{pos}{T^{2i/d}}\right)$$

(3)

The features near the anchor point will be extracted by the interactive attention mechanism .

$$Q_D = cat\,(W_Q F'_M, P_A)$$
$$K_D = cat\,(W_K F_D, P_F) \tag{4}$$
$$V_D = W_V F_D$$

In Eq. 4, F_D is the feature map of the image, F'_M is the output of the previous layer of the decoder, the 0 vector at the first layer of the coder, P_A is the position encoding of the anchor point, and P_F is the position encoding of the image features. where $cat()$ is the concat function, which stitches the projection of the image features with the position information. Unlike self-attention, the query Q_D is a linear projection of F'_M, stitched together with the location code.

When extracting features, A needs to be weighted and summed, so the features extracted by the interactive attention in the decoder also contain global information.

$$Q_D \cdot K_D{}^T = (W_Q F'_M) \bullet (W_K F_D)^T + P_A \bullet P_F^T \tag{5}$$

The weight is composed of two parts, namely, the similarity of semantic features $(W_Q F'_M) \bullet (W_K F_D)^T$ and the similarity of position $P_A \bullet P_F^T$. The feature map V_D with similar semantic and positional attributes to the query Q_D will have a larger weight, thus enabling the interactive attention mechanism to extract semantic features near the anchor point.In the self-attention module, similar to the decoder, the features extracted by the interactive attention are further fused with global information, and a new feature map $F_M \in \mathbb{R}^{m \times 2}$ is output by utilizing the correlation between the features. The feature map F_M is fed into two separate feedforward fully connected networks to generate the class information $Z_{class} \in \mathbb{R}^{m \times 100}$ for auxiliary loss, and the offset values $\Delta A \in \mathbb{R}^{N \times 2}$ for updating the coordinates of anchor boxes $A = A + \Delta A$ in the next layer.

2.2 Redundancy Analysis of Encoder Module

Redundancy in Detection Function. The interactive attention in the decoder generates queries based on the coordinate information of the input anchor points and the feature information output by the previous decoder layer. It then calculates the dot product between all features in the image feature map and assigns a larger weight to the features closer to the center point of the anchor box, which is used to fuse information on the feature map. The extracted image features are then encoded with global information using the self-attention mechanism, which utilizes the internal correlation of the information to generate the features for direct prediction. The newly generated features serve two purposes: one is to generate the offset values of the bounding boxes, correcting the information of the bounding boxes so that the center point of the anchor box is closer to the center point of the detected feature region in the next layer. The other is to use the fused features directly for classification.

The difference in feature extraction between the encoder and decoder for object detection lies in the difference in the queries used in the attention mechanism. The core of the encoder is self-attention mechanism, while the decoder uses the interaction attention mechanism to extract features. The queries for self-attention in the encoder are learned directly from the image features, thus the number of queries is consistent with the length of the feature sequence. From the perspective of object detection, a more dense query can be considered as extracting features from more dense anchor points in the feature map. For example, for an input image size of 800*1333 and after a typical backbone network with 32x downsampling, the length of the flattened feature map exceeds 1k. The number of queries in the encoder is consistent with this length, which means that there is an anchor point at each pixel position, and each anchor point is extracting features. This obviously brings huge computational costs. In contrast, in more efficient decoders, typically 300 anchor points are randomly initialized and transformed into queries, and their coordinates are updated layer by layer to make them more flexible for object localization. In DETR, there are only 100 queries and a low-efficiency design, so it may need the help of the encoder in feature extraction. However, the current design of the decoder has more dense and efficient queries compared to DETR, and their inherent mechanisms in object detection are consistent. Therefore, we believe that the encoder no longer plays an expected role in object detection.

Structural Redundancy. In the analysis of the role of the encoder, it is attributed to its internal attention mechanism, which is different from the two characteristics of CNN networks. One is the ability to model global information, and the other is the use of feature similarity in the attention mechanism when fusing features.

Currently, combining self-attention mechanisms with convolutional networks or using stacked attention modules to form deep neural networks is a hot research topic in backbone network studies. Many backbone networks have the ability to model global features and fuse features like the encoder, especially networks based on Transformer [6,9,13,14], which are directly stacked from various encoder variants.

For a detection network, the backbone network module is a common replacement component. When replacing the existing backbone network of the DETR architecture with a Transformer-based backbone network, the Transformer-based backbone network already has the ability to globally model feature fusion like the encoder in DETR. Therefore, the design of the encoder in this case is a redundant structure.

3   Experimental Results

To validate our thoughts on the role of the encoder in the model, we conducted experiments using the COCO 2017 dataset for evaluation. The dataset contains 117,000 images in the training set and 5,000 images in the test set. We used the same data augmentation techniques as DETR-like models during training, with a maximum short edge of 800 and a maximum long edge of 1333 for randomly cropped images. The learning rate for the encoder and decoder modules was set to 1e-4, and the batch size was set to 8 for training. We trained the model for 50 epochs and set the learning rate to 1e-5 at the 40th epoch. We conducted experiments in three aspects to verify our thoughts on the role of the encoder in the model.

3.1 The Number of Encoder Layers Has Little Effect on Detection Performance

The decoder has already fulfilled the role of the encoder in the entire detection network. We re-evaluated the impact of different encoder layer numbers on performance using the DAB-DETR [20] model, which only changed the decoder's structure for the DETR architecture. We evaluated the impact of different encoder layer numbers on performance under the existing decoder. The results in Fig. 3 were trained on the complete coco2017 training set and tested on the coco2017 validation set. It can be observed that from 1 layer to 6 layers, the number of encoder layers is not positively correlated with performance. Therefore, the number of encoder layers in the entire modular network does not have a significant impact on the network's performance.

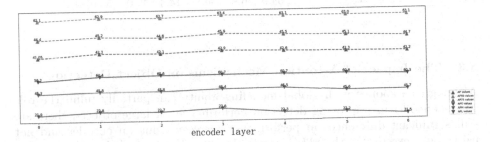

Fig. 3. Impact of the number of encoder layers on network performance.

3.2 Impact of Global Modeling Capability on Performance

From observing Fig. 3, it can be seen that there is not a significant difference in performance between the 1-layer encoder and the 6-layer encoder. However, there is a significant difference in performance between having no encoder (0-layer encoder) and having a 1-layer encoder. This experiment investigates the impact of global modeling ability on performance, as mentioned in DETR [12] that the global modeling ability of the encoder can improve the performance of detecting large objects. The experiment uses the CSwin-tiny [6] with global modeling ability, the Resnet-50 [7] without global modeling ability, and the Swin-transformer [9]to verify the impact of global modeling ability on performance. The metrics are used to compare the performance of these different backbone networks with and without the encoder. The experiment is trained using one-eighth of the

COCO training set to verify the results. Firstly, when using Resnet-50 with and without the encoder, the AP_L differs by 4.6, while using Swin-tiny, the AP_L differs by 3.5. Secondly, when using CSwin-tiny with and without the encoder, the AP_L differs by 0.2. The performance comparison of these two different backbone networks with and without the encoder is compared. As mentioned in DETR, global modeling ability can improve the performance of detecting large objects. A backbone with global modeling ability can also improve the performance of detecting large objects (Table 1).

Table 1. The influence of the number of Transformer encoder layers on network performance.

backbone	encoder layer	AP	AP_{50}	AP_{75}	AP_S	AP_M	AP_L
Resnet-50	0	29.2	50.3	30.7	12.2	32.9	43.0
	1	30.3	51.1	31.3	12.1	35.5	47.6(+4.3)
Swin-tiny	0	30.1	52.3	31.0	12.0	36.5	44.8
	1	31.2	53.3	32.4	14.2	36.5	48.3(+3.5)
Cswin-tiny	0	33.9	55.9	35.2	13.9	35.7	52.1
	1	34.9	56.6	36.8	14.4	40.0	51.9(-0.2)

3.3   The Impact of Attention Mechanisms on Object Detection

Although backbones with global modeling ability can partially fulfill the role of the encoder in improving detection performance for large objects, there are still significant differences in performance between using an encoder and not using one, except for the AP_L metric. When using an encoder, it acts as a learnable module that directly maps the feature output of the backbone network to features that are better suited for the decoder to use for detection. Without an encoder, the decoder uses the feature map output directly from the backbone for detection. To eliminate the impact of this layer, the study fine-tuned the weights of the top layer of the backbone network when not using an encoder, in order to make the feature map output by the backbone network more favorable for the decoder to detect. This was done to investigate whether the encoder module can still play a role in detection.

In the experiment, Resnet-50 [7], Swin-tiny [9], and CSwin-tiny [6] were used to study the impact of the encoder-decoder architecture on detection performance. Swin-tiny [9] is a network stacked with Transformer encoders and uses local window attention mechanism, which lacks global modeling capability. [6] has global modeling capability based on Swin-tiny. These three backbone networks were used to verify the impact of attention mechanism on feature extraction for detection performance. From the table, it can be seen that when using CSwin-tiny and Swin-tiny, adding an encoder has almost no impact on detection performance, while for Resnet-50, adding an encoder still has a significant impact on detection performance. Therefore, the feature extraction method of attention mechanism has a significant impact on detection performance (Table 2).

Table 2. The impact of global modeling capability on the overall network performance.

backbone	encoder layer	AP	AP_{50}	AP_{75}	AP_S	AP_M	AP_L
Resnet-50	0	29.1	49.1	30.0	11.2	35.2	45.7
	1	30.3	51.1	31.3	12.1	35.5	47.6
Swin-tiny	0	32.0	53.1	32.7	13.4	37.2	48.5
	1	31.2	53.3	32.4	14.2	36.5	48.3
Cswin-tiny	0	35.2	55.9	37.1	14.6	39.8	52.4
	1	34.9	56.6	36.8	14.4	40.0	51.9

4   Conclusion

Starting from the role of modules in the entire network, this paper analyzes the impact of the encoder in the DETR-like model on the detection architecture and verifies it through experiments. The study find that increasing the number of encoder layers does not have an impact on performance, and even using a 1-layer encoder performs better than using a 6-layer encoder. This is because the decoder already has the role of the encoder in detection, and adding an encoder only brings structural redundancy. Global modeling of features can improve the detection ability of large objects, even without using an encoder. The main role of the encoder in detection is due to its unique feature extraction method. The attention mechanism can effectively utilize the important information of feature correlation in feature extraction, so when using a network modeled by the attention mechanism as the backbone network, the encoder can be omitted. In short, the encoder module is not a necessary module in the DETR-like architecture, and in some cases, not using the encoder module does not affect performance.

References

1. Girshick, R.: Fast r-cnn. In: Proceedings of the IEEE International Conference on Computer Vision, pp. 1440–1448 (2015)
2. He, K., Gkioxari, G., Dollár, P., Girshick, R.: Mask r-cnn. In: Proceedings of the IEEE International Conference on Computer Vision, pp. 2961–2969 (2017)
3. Liu, W., et al.: SSD: single shot multibox detector. In: Leibe, B., Matas, J., Sebe, N., Welling, M. (eds.) ECCV 2016. LNCS, vol. 9905, pp. 21–37. Springer, Cham (2016). https://doi.org/10.1007/978-3-319-46448-0_2

4. Redmon, J., Divvala, S., Girshick, R., Farhadi, A.: You only look once: unified, real-time object detection. In: Proceedings of the IEEE Conference on Computer Vision and Pattern Recognition, pp. 779–788 (2016)

5. Yang, Z., Liu, S., Hu, H., Wang, L., Lin, S.: Reppoints: point set representation for object detection. In: Proceedings of the IEEE/CVF International Conference on Computer Vision, pp. 9657–9666 (2019)

6. Dong, X., et al.: Cswin transformer: a general vision transformer backbone with cross-shaped windows. In: Proceedings of the IEEE/CVF Conference on Computer Vision and Pattern Recognition, pp. 12124–12134 (2022)

7. He, K., Zhang, X., Ren, S., Sun, J.: Deep residual learning for image recognition. In: Proceedings of the IEEE Conference on Computer Vision and Pattern Recognition, pp. 770–778 (2016)

8. Howard, A.G., et al.: Mobilenets: efficient convolutional neural networks for mobile vision applications. arXiv preprint arXiv:1704.04861 (2017)

9. Liu, Z., et al.: Swin transformer: hierarchical vision transformer using shifted windows. In: Proceedings of the IEEE/CVF International Conference on Computer Vision, pp. 10012–10022 (2021)

10. Yang, J., et al.: Focal self-attention for local-global interactions in vision transformers. arXiv preprint arXiv:2107.00641 (2021)

11. Lin, T.Y., Dollár, P., Girshick, R., He, K., Hariharan, B., Belongie, S.: Feature pyramid networks for object detection. In: Proceedings of the IEEE Conference on Computer Vision and Pattern Recognition, pp. 2117–2125 (2017)

12. Carion, N., Massa, F., Synnaeve, G., Usunier, N., Kirillov, A., Zagoruyko, S.: End-to-end object detection with transformers. In: Vedaldi, A., Bischof, H., Brox, T., Frahm, J.-M. (eds.) ECCV 2020. LNCS, vol. 12346, pp. 213–229. Springer, Cham (2020). https://doi.org/10.1007/978-3-030-58452-8_13

13. Dosovitskiy, A., et al.: An image is worth 16x16 words: transformers for image recognition at scale. arXiv preprint arXiv:2010.11929 (2020)

14. Lin, T.Y., Goyal, P., Girshick, R., He, K., Dollár, P.: Focal loss for dense object detection. In: Proceedings of the IEEE International Conference on Computer Vision, pp. 2980–2988 (2017)

15. Sun, Z., Cao, S., Yang, Y., Kitani, K.M.: Rethinking transformer-based set prediction for object detection. In: Proceedings of the IEEE/CVF International Conference on Computer Vision, pp. 3611–3620 (2021)

16. Yao, Z., Ai, J., Li, B., Zhang, C.: Efficient detr: improving end-to-end object detector with dense prior. arXiv preprint arXiv:2104.01318 (2021)

17. Wang, Y., Zhang, X., Yang, T., Sun, J.: Anchor detr: query design for transformer-based detector. In: Proceedings of the AAAI Conference on Artificial Intelligence, vol. 36, pp. 2567–2575 (2022)

18. Li, F., Zhang, H., Liu, S., Guo, J., Ni, L.M., Zhang, L.: Dn-detr: accelerate detr training by introducing query denoising. In: Proceedings of the IEEE/CVF Conference on Computer Vision and Pattern Recognition, pp. 13619–13627 (2022)

19. Meng, D., et al.: Conditional detr for fast training convergence. In: Proceedings of the IEEE/CVF International Conference on Computer Vision, pp. 3651–3660 (2021)

20. Liu, S., et al.: Dab-detr: dynamic anchor boxes are better queries for detr. In: International Conference on Learning Representations

21. Vaswani, A., et al.: Attention is all you need. In: Advances in Neural Information Processing Systems 30 (2017)

22. Zhu, X., Su, W., Lu, L., Li, B., Wang, X., Dai, J.: Deformable detr: deformable transformers for end-to-end object detection. arXiv preprint arXiv:2010.04159 (2020)
23. Dai, X., Chen, Y., Yang, J., Zhang, P., Yuan, L., Zhang, L.: Dynamic detr: end-to-end object detection with dynamic attention. In: Proceedings of the IEEE/CVF International Conference on Computer Vision, pp. 2988–2997 (2021)
24. Roh, B., Shin, J., Shin, W., Kim, S.: Sparse detr: efficient end-to-end object detection with learnable sparsity. arXiv preprint arXiv:2111.14330 (2021)

Image Enhancement Algorithm Based on Multi-scale Convolution Neural Network

Hu Luo[1], Jianye Liu[1], Xu Zhang[1,2], and Dawei Tu[1(✉)]

[1] School of Mechatronic Engineering and Automation, Shanghai University, Shanghai, China
tdw@shu.edu.cn
[2] Huazhong University of Science and Technology Wuxi Research Institute, Jiangsu, China

Abstract. Underwater image acquisition is susceptible to color distortion, insufficient exposure, and blurry details caused by the characteristics of underwater scenes. To address the above issues, this paper proposes an underwater image enhancement algorithm based on multi-scale underwater convolutional neural networks, combining convolutional neural networks with underwater scene physical imaging models. Firstly, improve the underwater imaging model to make the imaging process of underwater objects more natural and reasonable; Then design encoder, multi-scale convolution, and decoder network modules for estimating background scattered light, direct transmission component, and backward transmission component, respectively. At the same time, the overall network design combined with the residual network model introduced skip connections to reduce the complexity of network computation. Finally, the underwater image is reconstructed based on the improved underwater imaging model. The enhancement results of underwater images show that compared to a single scale network, the method proposed in this paper can effectively eliminate the impact of underwater environmental factors. While restoring image color, it also enhances texture details, and achieves better results in quantitative evaluation, providing a new approach to underwater image enhancement.

Keywords: Underwater image · Image enhancement · Imaging model · Convolutional neural network · Skip connection

1 Introduction

Underwater imaging plays an important role in deep-sea resource exploration, underwater aquaculture, and underwater robot applications. Due to the underwater environment such as light scattering and absorption, underwater images have serious problems such as color distortion and blurred details [1], which not only affects people's visual experience, but also poses severe challenges for computer vision processing such as image segmentation, image classification, and image recognition [2].

In recent years, various image enhancement algorithms have emerged. Existing image enhancement algorithms can be divided into two categories: traditional image enhancement algorithms and deep learning-based image enhancement algorithms. In traditional image enhancement algorithms, contrast limited adaptive histogram equalization (CLAHE) [3] algorithm improves the contrast of images by local histogram equalization, thus improving the visual effects of images. However, due to the special properties of underwater light propagation, this algorithm is difficult to achieve a good enhancement effect. Two improvement methods are proposed by Dong Lili et al. [4] to improve the deficiency of histogram equalization algorithm, but the enhanced results cannot guarantee the contrast and texture details of the image at the same time. Drews et al. [5] believed that underwater red channel information. Iqbal et al. [6] proposed an unsupervised underwater image enhancement method based on color balance and contrast correction, but this method presupposes that the color cast is one of the attributes of the image, so when the blue color cast of the image is not obvious, the enhancement effect of the method is not obvious. Chiang et al. [7] combined DCP with wavelength-dependent compensation methods and applied them to the problem of shadow removal in underwater images. Peng et al. [8] proposed an underwater scene depth estimation method based on image blur and light absorption, and used the image imaging model to enhance the underwater image, which solved the problem of difficult image restoration due to poor underwater lighting conditions. However, the traditional underwater image enhancement algorithm is affected by various specific physical factors of the water body due to the lack of training with a large amount of data, and the robustness of the algorithm is poor.

Deep learning-based image enhancement algorithms are new technologies developed in recent years. Convolutional Neural Network (CNN) model has good performance in perception and enhancement of image quality through a large number of paired data in the dataset [9]. Especially for underwater images, many CNN-based residual models [10] have made significant progress in color enhancement, contrast enhancement, and shadow removal. Xu Yan et al. [11] mapped underwater images to clear images by using CNN to automatically extract features, whose visual effects were more realistic than those of traditional algorithms, but there was still room for improvement in local deblurring and detail enhancement of images. Li et al. [12] propose a CNN model based on a priori underwater scene, which provides a robust data-driven solution for underwater image and video enhancement, but does not take into account the difference in attenuation coefficient of different types of water light [13].

This paper presents a multi-scale convolutional neural network based underwater image enhancement algorithm. Firstly, the underwater imaging model is improved to make it more consistent with the actual situation of underwater object imaging. A multi-scale convolutional neural network architecture is proposed, which uses the encoding network, multi-scale convolution and decoding network modules, respectively, to estimate the background scattered light, direct transmission components, backward transmission components, and finally reconstruct the obtained underwater image with high image quality.

2 The Improved Underwater Imaging Model

The atmospheric scattering model proposed by Jaffe-McGlamery [14] describes the process of foggy image and is widely used in underwater imaging. Therefore, the underwater image degradation model can be expressed as:

$$I_c(x) = J_c(x)t(x) + A_c(1 - t(x)) \, c \in \{r, g, b\} \tag{1}$$

where, x represents the coordinates of a pixel, $I_c(x)$ is the actual underwater image taken, $J_c(x)$ is the original colorless clear underwater scene, $J_c(x)t_c(x)$ represents the direct component of imaging, A_c is the global background light intensity, $t(x)$ is the medium transmittance map, c represents the red, green, and blue channels.

However, the direct-path attenuation coefficient and the backscatter attenuation coefficient are not the same [15], and this paper introduces a dual transmittance underwater imaging model [16]:

$$I_c(x) = J_c(x)t_c^D(x) + A_c(1 - t_c^B(x)) \tag{2}$$

where, $t_c^D(x)$ represents the direct-path transmittance rate, while $t_c^B(x)$ denotes the backscatter transmittance rate.

According to the Beer-Lambert law, the underwater light energy exponentially decreases as the transmission distance increases, and the transmittance rate can be expressed as:

$$t(x) = e^{-\beta_c d(x)} \tag{3}$$

where, β represents the wavelength-dependent medium attenuation coefficient, $d(x)$ denotes the distance between the scene point x and the camera.

In traditional underwater image generation models, it is usually assumed that the global environment light A_c is uniformly distributed over the entire scene, but in real-world underwater scenes, a completely uniform background light is almost impossible. Therefore, by introducing an uneven background light $B(x)$ and a weight η to simulate the background light under natural scenes. η is randomly generated in the interval of [0,1] that is uniformly distributed. The improved underwater image formation model is:

$$I_c(x) = J_c(x)t_c^D(x) + A_c(1 - t_c^B(x)) + \eta B(x) \, c \in \{r, g, b\} \tag{4}$$

Combining Eq. (3) with Eq. (4), the improved underwater imaging model can be derived as follows:

$$J_c(x) = (I_c(x) - A_c - \eta B(x))e^{\beta_c^D d(x)} + A_c e^{(\beta_c^D - \beta_c^B)d(x)} \tag{5}$$

3 Multi-scale Underwater Convolution Neural Network

According to Eq. (5), global environmental light A_c and transmission transmittance parameters $e^{\beta_c^D d(x)}$, $e^{\beta_c^B d(x)}$ are unknown parameters. In this paper, a multi-scale underwater convolutional neural network is proposed, as shown in Fig. 1. When constructing the convolutional neural network, a encoder module is first constructed to directly estimate A_c from the input image. Then a multi-scale convolutional module is constructed to obtain direct transmission mapping parameters $e^{\beta_c^D d(x)}$ and backward transmission mapping parameter $e^{\beta_c^B d(x)}$ respectively using the estimated A_c and the input image. Finally, the underwater image can be reconstructed according to Eq. (5). Further design and elaboration of the encoder module, multi-scale convolution block, decoder module, jump connection, network loss function robustness and other modules of the multi-scale convolutional neural network structure are as follows.

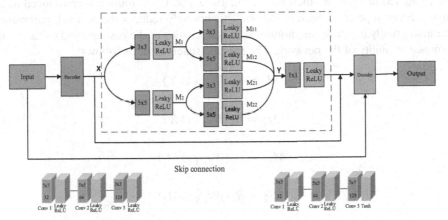

Fig. 1. Multiscale Convolutional Neural Network Structure

3.1 The Encoder Module

In order to recover the details of low-quality underwater images in convolutional neural networks, this paper introduces encoder and decoder modules into the network structure. The encoder consists of 3 convolution layers of different sizes, with the convolution kernel size of 7×7, the number of feature maps of 32, the convolution kernel size of 5×5, the number of feature maps of 64, and the convolution kernel size of 3×3, with the number of feature maps of 128, as shown in Fig. 1. In order to avoid gradient explosion and accelerate model convergence, a nonlinear activation function Leak ReLU is connected to each convolution layer in the network. This function has a very small gradient in the negative half interval, so it can avoid the problem of weight parameters not being updated due to input being less than zero. As shown in Eq. (6):

$$f(x) = \begin{cases} x, x \geq 0 \\ \alpha x, x < 0 \end{cases} \tag{6}$$

where, α is the value at a certain position on the feature map; typically taking a value of 0.01.

3.2 The Multiscale Convolutional Blocks

When image features are extracted using convolutional neural networks (CNNs), connections are usually made between layers. However, continuous convolution alone is not enough to restore details in low-quality underwater images. To enhance image feature representation, in this study, we refer to the DenseNet network [17] and introduce a separation and fusion operation strategy for feature maps in multiscale convolutional blocks to fully extract deep features from images. Two paths are established with 3×3 and 5×5 convolution kernels, respectively, to extract features at different scales, and the extracted features are then fused. Finally, a 1×1 convolution is introduced as the fusion layer to promote feature fusion. This not only reduces the network parameters, but also greatly increases the nonlinear characteristics of the network and enhances the expression ability of the network. The specific statement is as follows:

$$M_1 = R_L(W^1_{3\times3} \otimes X) \tag{7}$$

$$M_2 = R_L(W^2_{5\times5} \otimes X) \tag{8}$$

$$M_{11} = R_L(W^1_{3\times3} \otimes M_1) \tag{9}$$

$$M_{12} = R_L(W^1_{5\times5} \otimes M_1) \tag{10}$$

$$M_{21} = R_L(W^2_{5\times5} \otimes M_2) \tag{11}$$

$$M_{22} = R_L(W^2_{3\times3} \otimes M_2) \tag{12}$$

$$Y = M_{11} \oplus M_{12} \oplus M_{21} \oplus M_{22} \tag{13}$$

where, X is the input feature map, Y is the output feature map, A_c represents the convolution kernel of the feature extraction layer, A_c represents the convolution operation, $\oplus$ represents the summation operation, and R_L represents the activation function.

3.3 The Decoder Module

The decoder module connects the multi-scale convolution module and the encoder module through a connection operation. The convolution kernels of this module are symmetrical with those of the encoder module, and the introduction of symmetrical inverse convolution layers can refine the extracted texture features. The trained inverse convolution layer can also reconstruct the original image in the received feature map, restoring more image details. Similarly, the non-linear activation function Leak ReLU is connected after each convolution layer in this module. However, the output layer of this module should be connected to the tanh activation function to correct the pixel value range.

3.4 The Skip Connection

Due to the multiple convolution filtering operations that underwater images and their feature maps undergo, gradient explosions may occur, and information from some local regions of the image may be lost during feature extraction. In order to avoid such problems during training, this paper combines the residual network model and introduces skip connections [18] in the overall network design. A 7×7 convolution layer is added to the final output layer to extract features from the input image, and then the extracted information is fused with the decoder module to ensure that the original information of the input image is not lost during the deep information extraction process.

3.5 The Loss Function

In order to restore underwater images, we chose to use the sum of Manhattan distance loss (L1 loss) and structural similarity loss (SSIM loss) as the overall loss function in this paper. This is because we found through comparison that it can effectively preserve image edges and details, thus reducing the error. L1 loss measures the absolute difference in pixel values between a batch of images output by the network and their corresponding labeled images in the training set:

$$L_1 = \frac{1}{n}(\sum_{i=1}^{n} |f(x_i, \theta) - y_i|) \tag{14}$$

where, x_i represents the image in training samples, y_i is the label image corresponding to x_i, θ is the network parameter.

The structural similarity loss is a metric for measuring the perceived difference between two images, and its expression is as follows:

$$SSIM(x) = \frac{2\mu_x(p)\mu_y(p) + c_1}{\mu_x^2(p) + \mu_y^2(p) + c_1} * \frac{2\sigma_{xy}(p) + c_2}{\sigma_x^2(p) + \sigma_y^2(p) + c_2} \tag{15}$$

$$L_{SSIM}(x) = \frac{1}{n}\sum_{i=1}^{n} SSIM(x_i) \tag{16}$$

where, $\mu_x(p)$ and $\mu_y(p)$ represent the mean values of training X sample and its labeled image Y in the image block near pixel p, $\sigma_x(p)$ and $\sigma_y(p)$ represent the standard deviation of the image block, $\sigma_{xy}(p)$ is the covariance of the two. The final loss function is the sum of L_1 loss and $SSIM$ loss:

$$L = 1 - \alpha)L_1 + \alpha L_{SSIM} \tag{17}$$

where, α represents the weight of the current loss function, which is set to 0.2.

4 Experiment Verification and Analysis

4.1 Experimental Environment and Dataset

The experiments were conducted on a desktop computer with 12 GB Nvidia Geforce 3060 graphics card, an Intel Core i5-12600KF CPU, and 32 GB RAM. The design and training of the multi-scale convolutional neural network were implemented using the PyTorch deep learning framework in Python. The U45 and UIEB public datasets were used for training and testing. U45 is a non-paired dataset, while UIEB is a paired dataset composed of real-world underwater images and their corresponding high-quality reference images obtained from various traditional methods. It consists of three subsets: 890 raw underwater images, their corresponding high-quality reference images, and 60 underwater test images.

4.2 Experimental Result

The algorithm in this paper outputs the final enhanced image. During the training process, each training image corresponds to a ground truth image as the training target, making it a supervised model. The data was divided into batches of size 32 during the training process, including both the training images and the ground truth images. The learning rate was set to 0.0001, and the Adam gradient descent method was used to optimize the network parameters. The training was conducted for 300 epochs.

The experiment compared the proposed method with several existing underwater image enhancement methods, including the underwater dark channel prior method (UDCP) proposed by Drews et al., the unsupervised underwater image enhancement algorithm (UCM) proposed by Iqbal et al., the underwater scene depth estimation method based on image blur and light absorption (IBLA) proposed by Peng et al., and the underwater image enhancement algorithm based on underwater scene prior convolutional neural networks (UWCNN) proposed by Li et al.. Six typical underwater images from the UIEB and U45 datasets were selected for testing, and the effects of different methods on the raw images were observed. The results are shown in Fig. 2.

From Fig. 2, it can be seen that all algorithms have a certain degree of defogging effect on the image, but the UDCP and IBLA algorithms are generally dark, and the saturation of the image is enhanced, but the restoration effect on the image color is not significant. The UCM algorithm enhances the brightness and contrast of images, but the restoration of image colors is not accurate. The UWCNN algorithm improves the clarity of the image, but the restored image is bluish and shows excessive enhancement in local image regions. Compared with the raw image, the algorithm proposed in this article is visually more realistic, with obvious image details. It restores the color of the underwater image while maintaining appropriate brightness and contrast, and the overall effect is also better.

4.3 Objective Evaluation and Analysis

This paper uses objective evaluation methods to compare the performance of different enhancement methods from a quantitative perspective. Underwater image quality

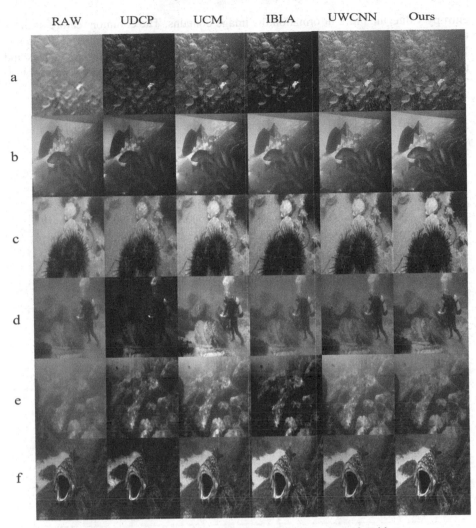

Fig. 2. Enhancement effects of raw images and various algorithms

evaluation indicators can be divided into two types: full-reference indicators and no-reference indicators, depending on whether there is a reference image. Since the processed images lack real reference images, this paper chooses to use no-reference indicators. No-reference indicators calculate the quality score of the current image only based on the distorted image. The commonly used no-reference indicators are UCIQE [19], UIQM [20], and entropy evaluation criteria (Entropy) [21]. UCIQE evaluates different attributes of underwater images, including chromaticity, contrast, and saturation, in the CIELab space, and the weighted sum of the three is used as the standard value of this evaluation indicator. UIQM is a linear combination of underwater chromaticity, sharpness, and contrast, which is in line with human visual perception of image quality. Entropy refers to the average information content of the image, and the larger the entropy value, the more information the image contains. The common feature of these three evaluation indicators is that the larger the value, the better the quality of the image. UCIQE, UIQM, and entropy evaluation criteria are compared for the raw images and the enhanced images in Fig. 2, and the values of various indicators are shown in Table 1, Table 2, and Table 3 (Table 4).

Table 1. The UCIQE value of raw images and various algorithm enhanced images

	RAW	UDCP	UCM	IBLA	UWCNN	Ours
a	0.2788	0.5086	0.3893	0.5213	0.5420	**0.5464**
b	0.4254	0.5124	0.4095	0.4367	**0.5488**	0.5204
c	0.4095	0.4848	0.4653	0.5009	0.5396	**0.6101**
d	0.2774	0.5608	0.5641	0.4524	0.5648	**0.5879**
e	0.4556	0.4948	0.3735	**0.5839**	0.5294	0.5642
f	0.4517	0.5531	0.5007	0.5559	**0.6114**	0.6006
avg	0.3831	0.5191	0.4504	0.5085	0.5560	**0.5716**

Table 2. The UIQM value of raw images and various algorithm enhanced images

	RAW	UDCP	UCM	IBLA	UWCNN	Ours
a	2.0147	4.2179	3.8169	4.7899	5.2930	**5.5899**
b	1.2935	**4.7954**	3.8970	4.3540	4.5672	4.2922
c	1.8010	4.6133	4.0719	5.0502	4.9958	**5.2743**
d	2.2040	**4.6517**	1.9510	4.4310	4.6142	4.2096
e	1.9397	4.2254	4.0825	3.9029	4.7842	**4.8818**
f	2.8506	4.1584	4.3489	5.2545	6.4997	**7.1216**
avg	2.0173	4.4437	3.6947	4.6304	5.1257	**5.2282**

From Table 1, after raw images in Fig. 1 is enhanced by the algorithm and five other comparison algorithms, the UCIQE values of the three images processed by the algorithm a, c, and d are higher than those of other enhancement algorithms, and the average UCIQE values of the six images are the highest among all algorithms. As can be seen from Table 2, the UIQM values of the three images processed by the algorithm a, e, and f are higher than those used by other enhancement algorithms. Similarly, Table 3 shows that the Entropy values of the four images processed by the algorithm a, e, d, and f are higher than those using other augmentation algorithms, and the average Entropy values of the six images are the highest among all algorithms. The larger the values of UCIQE, UIQM and Entropy, the better the image enhancement effect, so from the objective indicators, the overall performance of the algorithm proposed in this paper is better than the existing image enhancement algorithm.

Table 3. The Entropy value of raw images and various algorithm enhanced images

	RAW	UDCP	UCM	IBLA	UWCNN	Ours
a	6.5045	6.9424	6.5520	6.2494	7.3604	**7.5883**
b	7.5918	7.4468	7.3349	**7.7400**	7.6453	7.6942
c	7.4519	7.5378	7.4022	**7.7008**	7.5244	7.4308
d	6.5823	6.8624	6.3539	6.7392	6.8553	**7.1233**
e	7.2386	7.5211	6.7554	6.4329	**7.5248**	7.3239
f	7.3858	6.8038	7.1672	7.5158	7.4415	**7.6691**
avg	7.1258	7.1857	6.9276	7.0630	7.3920	**7.4716**

Table 4. The UCIQE, UIQM, and Entropy averages of raw images and various algorithm enhanced images

	RAW	UDCP	UCM	IBLA	UWCNN	Ours
UCIQE	0.3213	0.4821	0.4418	0.4725	0.5312	**0.5428**
UIQM	1.8350	4.3862	3.3269	4.5108	**5.2183**	5.0945
Entropy	6.7495	6.8347	6.6086	6.8058	7.1044	**7.2308**

5 Conclusion

This paper combines an improved underwater imaging model with deep learning methods to propose a multi-scale convolutional neural network underwater image enhancement method. By designing encoder, multi-scale convolution, and decoder network modules, they are used to estimate background scattered light, directly transmit components, backward transmit components, and finally reconstruct clear underwater images. The comparative experiment adopts subjective visual and objective evaluation indicators, and the results show that the proposed method has significant advantages over existing image enhancement algorithms. It can qualitatively and quantitatively improve the image quality in different underwater scenes and has good robustness. This opens up new ideas for the research of underwater image enhancement methods.

Acknowledgements. This research is partially supported by the National Natural Science Foundation of China (Grant No. 62176149 and Grant No. 61673252).

References

1. Ji, Y., Li, C., Tu, D., et al.: Study on sharpness enhancement of underwater light field imaging. J. Electron. Measurement Instrum. **35**(4), 7 (2021)
2. Jiang, Z., Qin, L.: A Low-illumination image enhancement method based on U-Net generative adversarial network. Acta Electron. Sin. **48**(2), 7 (2020)

3. Zuiderveld, K.: Contrast limited adaptive histogram equalization. Graph. Gems, 474–485 (1994)
4. Dong, L., Ding, C., Xu, W.: Two improved methods for image enhancement based on histogram equalization. Acta Electron. Sin. **46**(10), 2367 (2018)
5. Drews, P., Nascimento, E.R., Botelho, S., et al.: UDCP MATLAB code of the paper underwater depth estimation and image restoration based on single images. IEEE Comput. Graph. Appl. **36**(2), 24–35 2016
6. Iqbal, K., Odetayo, M.O., James, A.E., et al.: Enhancing the low quality images using unsupervised colour correction method IEEE. In: 2010 IEEE International Conference on Systems, Man and Cybernetics, pp. 1703–1709. IEEE (2010)
7. Chiang, J.Y., Chen, Y.C.: Underwater image enhancement by wavelength compensation and Dehazing. IEEE Trans. Image Process. **21**(4), 1756–1769 (2012)
8. Peng, Y.-T., Cosman, P.C.: Underwater image restoration based on image blurriness and light absorption. IEEE Trans. Image Process. **26**(4), 1579–1594 (2017)
9. Ignatov, A., Kobyshev, N., Timofte, R., et al.: DSLR-quality photos on mobile devices with deep convolutional networks. In: Proceedings of the IEEE International Conference on Computer Vision, pp. 3277–3285 (2017)
10. Liu, P., Wang, G., Qi, H., et al.: Underwater image enhancement with a deep residual framework. IEEE Access **7**, 94614–94629 (2019)
11. Yan, X., Meishuang, S.: Underwater image enhancement method based on convolutional neural network. J. Jilin Univ. Eng. Sci. **48**(6), 9 (2018)
12. Li, C., Anwar, S., Porikli, F.: Underwater scene prior inspired deep underwater image and video enhancement. Pattern Recogn. **98**, 107038 (2020)
13. Berman, D., Treibitz, T., Avidan, S.: Diving into haze-lines: color restoration of underwater images. In: Proceedings of British Machine Vision Conference (BMVC), **1**(2), 2 (2017)
14. Mcglamery B L . A computer model for underwater camera systems. In: Proceedings of Spie, vol. 208 (1980)
15. Galdran, A., Pardo, D., Picón, A., et al.: Automatic red-channel underwater image restoration. J. Vis. Commun. Image Representation, **26**, 132–145 (2015)
16. Wang, G., Tian, J., Li, P.: Image color correction based on double transmission underwater imaging model. Acta Optica Sin. **39**(9), 0901002 (2019)
17. Huang, G., Liu, Z., Van Der Maaten, L., et al.: Densely connected convolutional networks. In: Proceedings of the IEEE Conference on Computer Vision and Pattern Recognition, pp. 4700–4708 (2017)
18. He, K., Zhang, X., Ren, S., et al.: Deep residual learning for image recognition. In: 2016 IEEE Conference on Computer Vision and Pattern Recognition (CVPR), pp. 770–778. IEEE (2016)
19. Yang, M., Sowmya, A.: An underwater color image quality evaluation metric. IEEE Trans. Image Process. **24**(12), 6062–6071 (2015)
20. Panetta, K., Gao, C., Agaian, S.: Human-visual-system-inspired underwater image quality measures. IEEE J. Oceanic Eng. **41**(3), 541–551 (2016)
21. Tan, S., Wang, S., Zhang, X., et al.: Visual information evaluation with entropy of primitive. IEEE Access, 1 (2018)

Author Index

A

An, Yongfeng 162

B

Bao, Qin 32

C

Cai, Wenhan 513
Cao, Chongjing 113
Cao, Haiqing 537
Cao, Zonghan 499
Chao, Fei 392
Che, Honglei 186
Chen, Chin-Yin 162
Chen, Chunyu 333
Chen, Feifei 138
Chen, Han 162
Chen, Huangyu 63
Chen, Kun 150
Chen, Renliang 85
Chen, Siyuan 235
Chen, Wenxuan 488
Chen, Xi'ai 564, 575
Chen, Xingyu 247, 404
Chen, Yeheng 270
Chen, Yuanjie 368, 380, 404
Cheng, Chao 247
Cui, Jian 537

D

Dai, Junjie 162
Ding, Menglong 235
Dong, Yangyang 206
Dou, Xinke 499
Du, Wenjuan 270, 488

F

Fan, Chao 392
Fan, Licheng 476

Fan, Xiru 45
Feng, Kai 32
Feng, Ruiqi 12
Fu, Yang 197

G

Gan, Jianfeng 150
Gao, Chengzhi 344, 355
Gao, Xing 113
Ge, Ligang 333
Ge, Qi 53
Gong, Weizhuang 32
Gu, Guoying 174
Gu, Jason 294, 404
Gu, Jianjun 247, 258, 344, 355
Gu, Liang 3
Guo, Dongmei 416
Guo, Wei 429, 452
Guo, Yonghua 22
Guo, Zibo 476

H

Han, Renwu 12
Han, Yu 22
He, Xiangnan 53
He, Yingchao 527
Hou, Huifang 392
Hu, Quan 322
Hu, Xiazi 138
Hu, Zechen 322
Hua, Qiang 247
Huan, Liu 598
Huang, Bing 162
Huang, Feng 197
Huang, Guanyu 380
Huang, Yayu 309
Huang, Yongshan 294
Huang, Yujie 527

H. Yang et al. (Eds.): ICIRA 2023, LNAI 14270, pp. 621–623, 2023.
https://doi.org/10.1007/978-981-99-6492-5

J
Ji, Huangwei   138
Ji, Shuting   464
Jia, Jingchao   186
Jiang, Bingshan   235, 380
Jiang, Hongjian   368, 380

K
Kang, Xi   150
Kong, Lingyu   235, 247, 344, 355, 368, 380,
    404

L
Li, Fang   527
Li, Jialin   464
Li, Jinjian   322
Li, Kailong   429
Li, Nan   270, 488
Li, Qingkai   513
Li, Qipeng   197
Li, Weihao   22
Li, Wentao   537
Liang, Bin   439
Liang, Chao   258
Liang, Dingkun   258, 294, 344, 355, 404
Liang, Huwei   220
Liang, Keyao   452
Liang, Zhe   549
Lin, Sen   537
Liu, Jianye   610
Liu, Qian   309
Liu, Xiao   247
Liu, Yun   258, 404
Lu, Biao   282
Lu, Tongli   586
Luo, Hu   610
Luo, Kai   138

M
Mao, Dun   125
Min, Huasong   416
Mu, Yukang   235

N
Nie, Daming   368

P
Pang, Yanbo   513
Peng, Jianqing   22
Piao, Minnan   282

Q
Qin, Hongwei   499
Qiu, Siqi   63
Qiu, Wanglin   53

R
Ren, Weihong   564
Ren, Ziwu   476

S
Sen, Lin   598
Shao, Lintao   368
Shao, Shiliang   499
Shen, Xiaofei   309
Sheng, Wentao   452
Song, Wei   488
Sun, Jiaqi   527
Sun, Lining   429, 452
Sun, Wenjie   220

T
Tang, Jingge   258, 404
Tang, Yandong   537, 564, 575
Tu, Baining   282
Tu, Dawei   610

W
Wang, Chenxi   197
Wang, Chenyang   220
Wang, Di   549
Wang, Dong   45, 71
Wang, Fan   258, 404
Wang, Feifan   564, 575
Wang, Fuguang   97
Wang, Gang   186
Wang, Jiangping   270, 488
Wang, Jinqiang   71
Wang, Lijun   197
Wang, Longzhuo   392
Wang, Peng   258, 309
Wang, Pengfei   429, 452
Wang, Ping   549
Wang, Ting   499

Wang, Xin 258, 294, 344, 355, 404
Wang, Xudong 564, 575
Wang, Xueqian 439
Wang, Yaohui 53
Wang, Yawu 125
Wang, Yongbin 206
Wang, Yushi 513
Wang, Zhenghan 309
Wang, Zhongyuan 476
Wei, Tengyue 464
Wen, Jifu 186
Wen, Yanqin 549
Weng, Jiawei 258, 404
Wu, Chuang 113
Wu, Jaining 138
Wu, Jundong 125
Wu, Ruiqi 392

X
Xia, Zequn 206
Xie, Anhuan 85, 235, 247, 258, 294, 344,
    355, 368, 380, 404
Xie, Ye 344, 355
Xiong, Jiaming 294
Xiong, Yi 53
Xu, Chonglong 575
Xu, Peng 150
Xu, Zhidong 97

Y
Yan, Guang 416
Yan, Jihong 97
Yan, Peinan 138, 174
Yan, Xufei 85
Yao, Yunchang 404

Ye, Linqi 439
Yu, Qinghua 45

Z
Zang, Yajing 429
Zha, Fusheng 429, 452
Zhang, Biao 12
Zhang, Fei 220
Zhang, Jun 549
Zhang, Lan 235, 380
Zhang, Tongyan 499
Zhang, Xu 610
Zhang, Youchao 63
Zhang, Yu 368
Zhang, Yuan-Fang 63
Zhang, Yue 125
Zhang, Zihao 392
Zhang, Zijian 206
Zhao, Mingguo 513
Zhao, Pengyu 235, 380
Zhao, Weipeng 3
Zhao, Xiaodong 527
Zhao, Xin 392
Zhi, Han 598
Zhou, Chunyang 322
Zhou, Jiangchen 333
Zhou, Weigang 247, 380
Zhu, Huixuan 537
Zhu, Shiqiang 247, 368, 380, 404
Zhu, Xiaoyang 63
Zhu, Yinlong 32
Zhu, Yiting 344, 355
Zhu, Yue 586
Zhu, Zixiao 45
Zou, Jiang 174

Printed in the United States
by Baker & Taylor Publisher Services